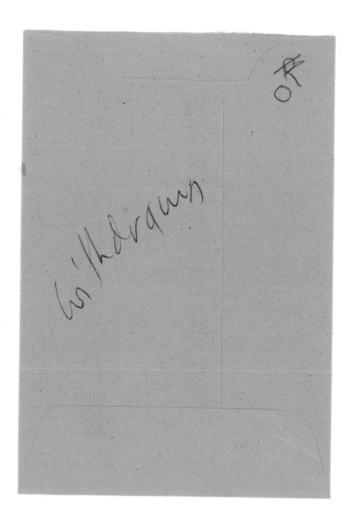

The Problems of
PHILOSOPHY

Introductory
Readings

The Problems of
PHILOSOPHY

Introductory
Readings

edited by

William P. Alston *and* Richard B. Brandt
The University of Michigan

ALLYN AND BACON, INC., BOSTON

Library of Congress Catalog Card Number: 67-16882

Printed in the United States of America

Fourth Printing . . . . . August, 1970

PREFACE 🦎

    This book is designed to bring together under one cover a wide variety of significant readings on those parts of philosophy with which an educated person today should be familiar. We agree with the ancients that a knowledge of philosophy is important for living a good life, and in line with this we have focused on those problems an understanding of which must illuminate the thinking and experience of everyone, whether or not he is a professional philosopher. Unfortunately, we have not been able to include all the problems that satisfy this description. We have had to omit, for example, problems in aesthetics and social philosophy, and many problems in the philosophy of science and the philosophy of mind. Those we have included are the ones that seem to us to combine crucial importance with suitability as a doorway into the subject.

    In choosing the readings our primary aim has been to select clear and lively material that represents the major points of view on the problems covered in the book. In some instances there is an embarrassment of riches, and our selection from many fine presentations of a given position could not be justified by clear marks of superiority. Readings from relatively recent philosophers are more numerous, although there are selections from the classical figures, including Aristotle, Aquinas, Anselm, Descartes, Locke, Berkeley, Hume, Kant, and Mill. This distribution of the readings is not a result of any deliberate attempt to provide a balance one way or the other; in each case we have simply striven to include the selection that best presents the point of view in question, whether the selection was written yesterday or 2000 years ago, although in case of doubt we have given preference to a selection from a classical figure.

    The introduction to each part is intended to explain what the problems are and to provide a wider context within which the student can see the point of each of the selections, as well as their interconnections. Where an important position or argument could not be represented in the readings, we have made some reference to it in our introduction, so that the student can hope to gain a reasonably adequate view of the problem from the part as a whole.

The bibliographies at the end of each chapter are not intended to be exhaustive. For more comprehensive bibliographies we refer the reader to the admirable work of Paul Edwards and Arthur Pap in *A Modern Introduction to Philosophy*. Our aim has been to provide lists of readings that the beginning student will find helpful in the preparation of papers. Often a student finds that writing papers is his most valuable educational experience in philosophy. The bibliographies are organized around topics which seem to us suitable for student papers; presumably every student will be interested in at least some one of them, and every student will find a few topics of a level of difficulty suitable to his tastes and abilities. We have had particularly in mind the problems of students in large classes at institutions with limited library facilities. We have, therefore, as far as possible listed readings that are available in anthologies, especially paperbacks, with the thought that the instructor can order an adequate quantity of these for the library, thereby making provision for papers by a large number of students on a variety of topics without undue expense.

It seems clear that not all the readings in this book can be covered in a one-semester course. We have deliberately provided a surplus, so as to make possible a variety of different groups of selections, in accordance with the predilections of different instructors. There is also considerable room for choice in the order in which the parts are covered; each part has been prepared as an independent unit, though there are cross-references in the introduction. The order of presentation in the book is one that will commend itself to many instructors, but we feel that an equally sound course could be constructed beginning with the free-will problem, with ethics, or with epistemology. Whatever order an instructor uses, he may wish to have students read the introduction to Part V at the outset, since certain crucial distinctions (analytic-synthetic, a priori-a posteriori) are introduced there which recur throughout the book.

This work is in every sense a joint product. The choice of selections represents joint decisions, and all the introductions have been read and discussed in several drafts. However, William Alston had the primary responsibility for Parts I, III, and IV, Richard Brandt for Parts II, V, and VI.

We wish to express gratitude to our undergraduate students at the University of Michigan and Swarthmore College for helping us to see over the years what is possible and what is desirable in an introductory course. Acknowledgment is due to our daughters, Kathleen and Karen, for Herculean labors with the tedious mechanical details of the preparation of the manuscript.

William P. Alston
Richard B. Brandt

CONTENTS 🦎

PART III: FREE WILL AND DETERMINISM

PART IV: MIND AND BODY

PART V: THE FOUNDATIONS OF KNOWLEDGE

Contents

PART VI: PERCEIVING THE MATERIAL WORLD

ANTHOLOGIES*

1. ABERNATHY-LANGFORD (Abernathy, G. L. and Langford, T. A., eds.). *Philosophy of Religion.* New York: The Macmillan Company, 1962.

2. ALSTON (Alston, W. P., ed.). *Religious Belief and Philosophical Thought.* New York: Harcourt, Brace, & World, 1963.

3. BRANDT (Brandt, R. B., ed.) *Value and Obligation.* New York: Harcourt, Brace, & World, 1961.

4. BRONSTEIN-KRIKORIAN-WIENER (Bronstein, D. J., Krikorian, Y. H., and Wiener, P. P., eds.). *Basic Problems of Philosophy (3rd ed.).* Englewood Cliffs, New Jersey: Prentice-Hall, Inc., 1964.

5. BRONSTEIN-SCHULWEIS (Bronstein, D. J. and Schulweis, H. M., eds.). *Approaches to the Philosophy of Religion.* Englewood Cliffs, New Jersey: Prentice-Hall, Inc., 1954.

6. CANFIELD AND DONNELL (Canfield, J. V. and Donnell, F. H., eds.). *Readings in the Theory of Knowledge.* New York: Appleton-Century-Crofts, 1964.

7. DEWEY (Dewey, R. E., Gramlich, F. W., and Loftsgordon, D., eds.). *Problems of Ethics.* New York: The Macmillan Company, 1961.

8. EDWARDS-PAP (Edwards, Paul and Pap, Arthur, eds.). *A Modern Introduction to Philosophy* (rev. ed.). New York: The Free Press, 1965.

9. EKMAN (Ekman, Rosalind, ed.). *Readings in the Problems of Ethics.* New York: Charles Scribner's Sons, 1965.

*Referred to in lists of suggested readings.

10. Hick (Hick, J., ed.). *Historical Selections in the Philosophy of Religion*. Englewood Cliffs, New Jersey: Prentice-Hall, Inc., 1964.

11. Hirst (Hirst, R. J., ed.). *Perception and the External World*. New York: The Macmillan Company, 1965.

12. Jarrett-McMurrin (Jarrett, J. L. and McMurrin, S. M., eds.). *Contemporary Philosophy*. New York: Holt, Rinehart and Winston, 1954.

13. Johnson (Johnson, Oliver, ed.). *Ethics*. New York: The Dryden Press, 1958.

14. Johnson (Johnson, Oliver, ed.). *Ethics: Selections from Classical and Contemporary Writers*. New York: Holt, Rinehart and Winston, 1965.

15. Mandelbaum-Gramlich-Anderson (Mandelbaum, Maurice, Gramlich, F. W., and Anderson, A. R., eds.). *Philosophic Problems*. New York: The Macmillan Company, 1957.

16. Melden (Medlen, A. I., ed.). *Ethical Theories*. Englewood Cliffs, New Jersey: Prentice-Hall, Inc., 1955.

17. Nagel and Brandt (Nagel, E., and Brandt, R. B., eds.). *Meaning and Knowledge*. (New York: Harcourt, Brace & World, 1965.)

18. Randall-Buchler-Shirk (Randall, J. H., Buchler, Justus, and Shirk, Evelyn, eds.). *Readings in Philosophy*. New York: Barnes and Noble, 1956.

19. Sellars and Hospers (Sellars, W., and Hospers, J., eds.). *Readings in Ethical Theory*. New York: Appleton-Century-Crofts, 1952.

20. Singer-Ammerman (Singer, M. G., and Ammerman, R. R., eds.). *Introductory Readings in Philosophy*. New York: Scribner's, 1962.

21. Smart (Smart, Ninian, ed.). *Historical Selections in the Philosophy of Religion*. New York: Harper & Row, 1962.

22. Sprague-Taylor (Sprague, Elmer, and Taylor, P. W., eds.). *Knowledge and Value*. New York: Harcourt, Brace & World, 1959.

23. Swartz (Swartz, R. J., ed.). *Perceiving, Sensing, and Knowing*. Garden City, New York: Doubleday & Company, 1965.

INTRODUCTION ❧

This volume is designed to introduce the reader to philosophy by presenting some of the best discussions of some of its major problems. When the reader has completed his examination of this book, he will have a reasonably accurate conception of what philosophy is. It may be helpful, however, if he can begin with at least an approximate idea of the subject-matter of philosophy; the present introductory remarks are intended to make this possible. It is not a simple matter to draw even rough outlines, since, in the twenty-five centuries during which persons called "philosophers" have been reflecting, the interests of these persons have led in all directions, and there is something arbitrary in specifying a point at which they stopped their "philosophy" and were talking of something else instead. Nevertheless, what we shall say represents the consensus of most living philosophers on this matter.

One cannot demarcate philosophy in terms of the kinds of objects it studies in the way one can define sociology as the study of society or institutions, and zoology as the study of animals. In one way or another, philosophy is concerned with practically everything. What is distinctive of philosophy is rather the *kind* of questions with which it deals. If we survey the questions which by common consent are accounted "philosophical," their common features lead us to the following definition of the subject: *Philosophy is an attempt to arrive at reasoned answers to important questions which, by reason of their ultimacy and/or generality, are not treated by any of the more special disciplines.* Exactly what is meant by this, and especially what is meant by saying that a question is "ultimate" or "general," requires an explanation. In order to provide this, we shall first set down some of the questions discussed by the readings in this book; then we shall explain in what sense they are ultimate or general questions and why they are not treated by the sciences.

Some of the questions considered in the parts that follow are these:

1

I. *Religious Belief*

1. Is there a God?

2. What is meant by the word "God"?

3. Can religious statements be claimed to have meaning and to be verifiable in roughly the same way as the statements of the sciences?

II. *Value and Obligation*

4. What kinds of things (events, experiences) are worthwhile or desirable in themselves?

5. What kinds of actions are morally right or wrong?

6. Why should one take morality seriously?

7. What is it for something to be desirable or right; in other words, what do "desirable" and "right" mean, or what should they mean?

8. Are ethical judgments subjective or objective?

III. *Free Will and Determinism*

9. Do human beings ever have a "free" choice among alternative actions? In what sense of "free"?

10. Are all human actions causally determined?

11. Can human beings be held responsible for their actions?

IV. *Mind and Body*

12. What is consciousness, and what is its relation to the body?

13. Do persons survive the death of their bodies?

14. Is it *self-contradictory* to say that a person has survived the death of his body, given what it is for a person to be the *same* person at different times? What is it for a person at one time to be the *same* as a person at a different time?

V. *The Foundations of Knowledge*

15. What is it to "know" something?

16. Can we justify believing things about the future on the basis of observation of what has happened in the past (the "problem of induction")?

17. Is it possible, or how is it possible, to know things (e.g., in logic or mathematics) independently of observation (the "problem of a priori knowledge")?

VI. *Perceiving the Material World*

18. What is it to perceive (see or hear or feel) something?

19. In what way, if at all, is perception a basis of knowledge?

20. In what sense of "material world" do we have reason for thinking that there is a material world? What kind of reason do we have?

We have said that philosophy is an attempt to arrive at reasoned answers to *important* questions. It seems scarcely worthwhile to debate the issue of whether the above questions are humanly important. Most of them obviously are; and in the case of any one that is not plainly so at first glance, the more clearly we see what the question is and what its connections with other questions are, the more we shall be convinced that it *is* important.

Is it equally clear that the above questions are not treated by any of the existing sciences? Does not the psychological theory of perception concern itself with question 18, the psychology of motivation with question 10, and the theory of criminal law with question 11? Even a cursory examination of the textbooks in these fields will indicate that the answers to these questions are negative. The psychology of perception is concerned with discovering correlations or explanations of correlations; for instance, it tries to find out when objects look three-dimensional and what makes them do so, or when normal persons are subject to a certain kind of illusion and why. Doubless many or most psychologists have some sort of conception of how perceiving is to be analyzed; but this is not part of their job as psychologists. Much the same may be said for the theory of motivation. This branch of psychology aims to find appropriate types of "law" in human behavior — for instance, whether it is true, and if so why, that the returning commuter's steps tend to quicken when he espies his home in the distance. But to find cases of regular behavior and to seek genetic or other explanations for it is one thing; to consider whether there is reason to think that in every detail human conduct is an instance of causal law is another. The problem of what is being done by the theory of the criminal law is less straightforward, but insofar as this discipline does not merge into the philosophy of law — insofar as it remains a descriptive or explanatory discipline — it does not concern itself with question 11.

The questions of the sciences and those of philosophy seem to be different, then. But what is there about philosophical questions, and about the sciences, which makes them so?

We have suggested that one reason lies in the "ultimacy" of at least many philosophical questions. But what is meant by saying that a question is "ultimate"? There are several related senses of the word "ultimate," and we shall now explain the ones of interest in the present context. First, in speaking of questions as "ultimate," sometimes we mean that *some answer to them is taken for granted by anyone who uses the methods of the sciences*, and hence the questions can hardly be treated by the sciences. Obvious examples of questions that are ultimate in this sense are 16 and 17. The methods of the physical and social sciences involve beginning with observations, and forming universal laws and making predictions about the future on the basis of these observations. For instance, the chemist feels free to predict how unobserved samples of copper will behave on the basis of his information about how observed samples have behaved; the biologist feels free to predict how certain features of plants or organisms will reappear in later generations on the basis of a theory summarizing the regularities observed thus far. When the philosopher, by contrast, asks how we can *justify* making inferences about unobserved events on the basis of relevant observed events, he is asking about the justification of the fundamental forms of scientific inference. The scientist *uses* these forms of inference to arrive at conclusions; if he tried to inquire into their justification by the same methods he would be moving in a circle. How could one reasonably *use* a form of inference to show that that form of inference is justified? Parallel things could be said of question 17 and the methods of logic and mathematics as well as for questions 19 and 20. The scientist *assumes* that there is in some sense a material world and that he can find out about it by observation. His method of answering questions about the supposed material world is that of relying on observations. How then could he *use* observation to answer the question as to whether observation is a reliable source of premises for scientific inference? And the same for the questions about in what sense there is a material world and in what sense we can observe it. These cannot be answered by observation in the way in which observation can tell what kinds of leaves mark the varieties of elm tree that are attacked by the Dutch elm disease. Much the same can be said about question 12.

Certain other questions of philosophy are "ultimate" in a slightly different but closely related sense. These are questions about the nature of basic concepts. They are "ultimate" in that the concepts they concern are used by all or almost all the sciences and are the special province of none; hence it is not the business of one particular science to analyze or clarify them. (It is true that scientists, especially physicists, sometimes write on such matters; but when they do their colleagues do not think of them as solving problems of physics, but rather as indulging in philosophy.) For example, there are concepts of knowledge, of proof, of hypothesis, of theory, of law, and of causal connection. These are all used freely in the sciences generally and, of course, in physics. However, it is not the job of the physicist to clarify the conceptions of knowledge and hypothesis. It is his business to produce knowledge and useful hypotheses, but not to explain what it is to have knowledge or to entertain an hypothesis. How would he use a cyclotron to do *this* job? These conceptions are used by the scientists, and, in many contexts, to avoid error it is highly important to be clear exactly what they are. The task of making them clear is by tradition a philosophical one.

So far we have been concentrating on ways in which philosophical problems are "ultimate" relative to the sciences, because we have wanted to make clear the difference between the problems of philosophy and the problems of the sciences. One might infer from this that philosophy is concerned only with the sciences and is important only for the thinking of the scientist. Such an inference would be totally mistaken, however, for the problems of philosophy stand in much the same relation to ordinary common-sense thinking. The question of what it is to perceive something (18), and the question of how, if at all, perception is a basis for knowledge underlie our ordinary unsystematic perceptual knowledge (or supposed knowledge) as much as they underlie scientific knowledge. Again, in the everyday conduct of life we assume that inductive inferences are justifiable, just as much as the sciences do. Philosophical thinking is not relevant *only* to disciplined scientific thinking.

The "ultimacy" of philosophical problems in relation to ordinary thinking is perhaps most obvious in the case of the problems of values, of moral philosophy. We all consider it important to determine reasonable answers to such questions as: "How good was the performance?" "Which is more important for me now, to finish my education or to get married?" or "Do I have an obligation to concern myself with the personal problems of my students?" The philosophical problems dealing with values (4 to 8) underlie these queries in both of the ways already mentioned. First, in giving reasons in support of a particular answer to such questions, we are assuming that we know what considerations are relevant in deciding a particular value issue. We have to *assume* this in tackling a particular value problem. Again, we are using fundamental concepts like "right" and "desirable" in our evaluative thinking, but using these concepts is an enterprise different from that of getting clear what their nature is — which is the philosophical problem. Thus our ordinary ethical thinking presupposes answers to questions like 4 to 8; the philosophical problems underlie our thinking about particular ethical questions, just as questions 16 and 17 underlie particular scientific inquiries. Whether thinking about particular ethical problems is, or should be, a kind of scientific inquiry is itself one of the problems of ethics. If our answer to 7 is such as to render ethical statements subject to an empirical test, the answer is affirmative; if not, it is negative. But whatever position is taken on the relation between scientific inquiry and the resolution of ethical problems, it is clear that answers to philosophical problems like 4 to 8 are presupposed in our ethical thinking.

We mentioned above a second feature of some philosophical questions as a reason why they cannot well be treated by the special disciplines: their generality, or scope. Questions with this feature usually belong under the heading "metaphysics." Examples are: "Is the physical universe self-subsistent, or does it owe its existence to a supernatural creator?" "Is man simply a very complicated kind of machine, or does his nature contain something spiritual which distinguishes him from all purely physical things?" "Is everything that happens, including human actions, determined to happen just as it does by the operation of causes?" These questions are substantially equivalent to our questions 1, 12, and 10. They have great "generality" or "scope" in several senses. In the first place, the evidence relevant to their answer is not confined to any one science. Whether the physical universe is self-subsistent raises issues in the theory of evolution, in astrophysics, and in physics (e.g., the status of the principle of entropy). Second, science does not furnish the only considerations relevant to a reasonable answer to these questions. Physics and the other sciences are concerned with regularities *in* the universe and their explanation; but the question as to whether the facts should receive a theistic interpretation is a question as to whether the universe *as a whole* has a certain relation to another kind of being. Again, the answer to the third question just listed obviously does not depend solely on the results of scientific investigation. Suppose we have a great many causal laws; does this show that events not covered by these causal laws are also caused? Evidently not. But neither does the fact that certain types of events have up to now resisted any causal explanation (e.g., some types of quantum phenomena, which physics regards as subject only to statistical law) prove that they are not subject to causal law. The content of many different sciences, then, bears on these questions; and considerations are relevant which are not the province of the sciences at all. In this sense some questions of philosophy are of great generality or scope and necessarily fall outside the territory of any of the particular disciplines.

The reader may agree that, for the reasons given, many or all of our questions do necessarily fall outside the subject matter of the sciences. But he may say: "Very well, so much the worse for philosophy. These questions cannot be answered, for scientific method is our only source of knowledge." It may be worth while for us to comment briefly on this reaction and on some related views of the philosophic enterprise.

Some twentieth-century philosophers (particularly those called "logical positivists") would underwrite this scepticism about many parts of traditional philosophy. One part of philosophy, however, escapes their criticisms — the part often called "critical philosophy" or "the analysis of concepts." This part of philosophy is the enterprise of getting clear about the nature of fundamental concepts (like "knowledge" or "right") and of suggesting how these concepts might be modified or made precise in a helpful way; it also involves getting clear what standards of evidence are used in the sciences and to what extent these standards can be shown to be useful ones. The logical positivists, however, despair of the other questions of philosophy, and advocate that philosophers cease wasting their time reflecting on them.

The present is not the place to debate this issue. (See readings 9 and 10.) Suffice it to say that we are not prepared to abjure the traditional philosophical aim of providing a reasoned comprehensive view of nature, man, and the norms of human life. Our choice of readings corresponds with this decision. But, in order that our readings may be representative of contemporary thought, "conceptual analysis" bulks larger than would have been the case had we drawn more heavily on older works.

A similar objection sometimes raised against philosophical thinking by persons who rightly see that it is different from the sciences is that it is mere "armchair thinking." This characterization is correct — if it is dissociated from pejorative connotations and given a proper interpretation. Of course it would be a mistake to think that the philosopher makes no use of empirical information. Any such conception would be quickly dispelled by a glance, say, at discussions of the mind-body problem, where findings of physiology are appealed to, or at discussions of perception, where facts about illusions play a large role. The proper interpretation is this: For the reasons given above, it is unwarranted to confine our thinking about fundamental questions to any particular method or to some particular set of premises — say, observational ones. To accept any such limitation would amount to having already answered certain philosophical questions in one way rather than another. The distinctive activity of philosophy lies in the post-fact-gathering phase: the retirement to one's "armchair" in order to ponder all considerations that seem relevant, decide which of these are to be given most weight, follow cogent reasoning wherever it may lead, and arrive at an answer that seems to do justice to all these relevant considerations.

A final reproach often brought against philosophy is the failure of philosophers to agree, even after centuries of discussion. Philosophy, it is said, does not make progress in the way physics or biology does; ethical and metaphysical positions that were opposing each other over 2000 years ago in the time of Plato and Aristotle are still live alternatives. This claim cannot be denied, although one should not overlook the reality of a great deal of progress. The nature and implications of various philosophical positions have become clearer through the centuries, and particular views have become more developed through having to take account of a wider range of facts and meet a wider range of objections. For instance, the materialism of today is undoubtedly a more elaborate and subtle position than the materialism of ancient Greece. The same can be said for most other recurrent philosophical positions. Nevertheless, it is a striking fact that the history of philosophy does not exhibit the progressive elimination of rival alternatives to nearly the same degree as the history of science does.

It is a mistake, however, to regard this fact as a reason for abstaining from reflection on philosophical problems. It simply reflects a point already made above, that there is not a simple method (such as observation and generalization from observation) for answering the questions of philosophy. We have to follow any cogent arguments that are put forward, and we cannot limit them in advance to any particular type. If all philosophers were to agree that the empirical study of overt human behavior is the only way to reach acceptable theories about the mind, there would presumably be convergence toward a common philosophy of mind; but such agreement would involve ignoring certain considerations to which philosophers are properly sensitive. Then, too, there is another difficulty: the problems of philosophy are very much interconnected. Philosophical reflection is rather like a game of chess, in that a move early on may make a great difference to the disposition of various pieces at a later stage. It is impossible, sometimes, to foresee the effects of one change in a theory on related theories; years or even centuries of exposure to criticisms may be necessary to show that one thesis has implications that compel its retraction. Such difficulties, however, will be less a reproach than a challenge to many minds; they make philosophical reflection interesting.

Part I

RELIGIOUS BELIEF

INTRODUCTION

In the sphere of religion, as elsewhere, philosophy is concerned with the clarification and reasoned assessment of fundamental beliefs. Of course, a religion is much more than a set of beliefs. It is a complex organization of individual and social activities, involving ritual, prayer, and moral effort, as well as distinctive beliefs and their organization into systems of theology. Philosophers, in attempting to understand religion and to see its relation to other areas of human experience, have paid some attention to all aspects of religion. Nevertheless, in line with the aim of rational assessment, they have concentrated on religious beliefs, since it is only if these are justified that there can be any justification for the rest of the religion. One is rationally justified in praying to the Virgin only if one is rationally justified in believing that the Virgin exists and might be moved by one's prayers.

The religious beliefs on which a philosopher concentrates will be determined by the character of the religious tradition out of which the philosophizing emerges. If this book of readings had been compiled in the context of (East) Indian religion, our selections would be much concerned with the beliefs that the spatiotemporal world is illusory and that the only reality is an ineffable featureless One. However, in our religious tradition, the Judaeo-Christian, the fundamental beliefs are the existence of an omnipotent, supremely good personal creator of the world (God)[1] and the immortality of man. The other distinctive beliefs can be seen to rest on these two, for they all have to do with the nature, plans, and activities of God, especially as directed to men, and with the conditions of one rather than another sort of life after death. Some consideration of the question of immortality will be

---

[1] According to orthodox Christian theology the creator is *three* persons in one substance, rather than strictly a single person, but we shall have to ignore that refinement.

found in Part IV. This section is focused on the belief in the existence of God, hereinafter termed "theism."

Most prominent European philosophers from Plato onwards have attempted to provide a rational justification for theism, and the bulk of these attempts have involved using some form of one of the classic triad of arguments — the Ontological Argument, the Cosmological Argument, and the Teleological Argument. The latter two have the form of hypothetical arguments. (See Reading 53.) They start with some pervasive fact about the world and argue that God is required for an adequate explanation of this fact. The Ontological Argument, by contrast, is purely a priori; it employs no factual premise. Its contention is that just by reflecting on the concept of God one can see that God exists.

Let us first consider the Ontological Argument. As presented by St. Anselm it has the form of a *reductio ad absurdum*. Try to deny the proposition to be proved (the existence of God) and one falls into a contradiction. For the concept of God is the concept of an absolutely perfect being ("that than which nothing greater can be conceived"). Now, among the things that make one being more perfect than another is existence; i.e., it is better to exist than not to exist. Hence if we were to deny that God exists, we would be asserting that the most perfect being lacks a perfection (i.e., we would be asserting that one can conceive something greater than *that than which nothing greater can be conceived*). And this is a contradiction. Hence there is no consistent alternative to admitting that God exists.

The late Alfred North Whitehead once said that the greatest accomplishment in philosophy is to be refuted afresh in each century. By this standard St. Anselm deserves highest honors. Most of his successors are convinced that the argument is invalid; surely proving the existence of God could not be that easy. Many philosophers, beginning with St. Thomas Aquinas, have had a shot at specifying what is wrong with it. But no one is quite satisfied with the refutations of others, and so the issue remains a live one. In the process, philosophers have been stimulated to dig deeply into the logic of existential statements. The most common critical line, first made prominent by Immanuel Kant, is that it is a mistake to regard existence as a property, and hence a mistake to think of it as one of the properties that something must have if it is to be perfect. This criticism is set forth in Reading 7.

The first three arguments in Reading 2 are variant forms of the Cosmological Argument. In each of them Aquinas begins by taking an obvious, nonspecific fact about the world — that something is in motion (first argument) ("is changing" would better represent the scope of Aquinas' intent); that there are things the existence of which is not necessary (third argument); or that some things are caused by other things (second argument). He then argues in each case that facts of the sort with which we start can be adequately explained only if we carry the explanation back to a being that is *self-sufficient*, that contains within itself its own explanation (a "necessary being"). In each case, the reasoning depends on the claim that an infinite regress of explanation is impossible. The basic structure of all the arguments can best be seen in Aquinas' "second way," which may be reformulated as follows:

1. There are things in the world about us that are brought into existence by other things. Let us consider one of these, A, which is brought into existence by B.

2. Either B is brought into existence by something else, C, or it needs no cause because it is itself a necessary being.

3. On the first alternative, the same problem arises for C; and if C is caused by something else, D, the same problem arises for D, . . .

4. An infinite regress of causes is impossible.

5. Hence at some point we must get back to a *necessary* being that functions as the ultimate source of the entire chain, without itself deriving its existence from anything more ultimate.

This argument is often interpreted as requiring that the world must have had a beginning in time. On this reading the argument is incompatible with the view that the universe is of infinite extent temporally (no beginning and no end). But this cannot be Aquinas' intent, for elsewhere in the *Summa Theologica* he argues that one cannot show by rational argument (apart from reliance on the divine revelation contained in the Bible) that the world had a beginning. Hence, contrary to what one might suppose from reading this presentation of the argument, the series of causes envisaged by Aquinas is not a temporally ordered series, each member of which temporally precedes that of which it is the cause. This means that we are not concerned here with *producing* causes, for what brings A into existence must exist and exercise its causality before A exists. Aquinas is concerned rather with sustaining causes. This kind of causality can be roughly exemplified by a case of writing. When I am writing, at a given moment the pen is kept in motion by my hand, which in turn is kept in motion by the activity of certain muscles, which in turn are kept going by neural excitations, which in turn . . . . This sort of causality does not figure in modern ways of thinking about the physical world, and if Aquinas' argument were essentially dependent on that concept, it would have to be abandoned as outmoded. However, there is a reformulation which will free it from entanglement with the details of medieval physics. If we take as our starting point the physical universe as a whole (in its entire extent both in space and in time), we can avoid making any assumptions about the ways in which its parts are interrelated, as well as about whether it is finite or infinite. So transformed, the argument will run as follows:

1. The physical universe is temporally either finite or infinite.

2. If it is finite, the beginning of its existence must have been due to some cause.

3. Even if it is temporally infinite, there must be some cause the action of which is responsible for the fact that this universe exists rather than some other, and rather than none at all.

4. Even if this cause owes its existence to some other cause in a similar manner, an infinite regress of such causes is impossible.

5. Therefore, the entire system ultimately owes its existence to an uncaused first cause.

This formulation clearly brings out the essential claim of the Cosmological Argument, that the physical universe is not self-sufficient but ultimately depends for its existence on a being that is self-sufficient. Moreover, it brings out that claim without resting it on any particular conception of the internal structure of the universe.

Nagel, in his critique of the Cosmological Argument in Reading 7, is obviously thinking in terms of a temporal series of causes, but the criticisms he makes are relevant to St. Thomas' arguments and even to our modified version of them. First, Nagel says that even if an infinite regress of causes is impossible "why cannot the world itself be self-caused?" Why not halt the regress at that point? This is to reject step 3 in our reformulation. The Thomistic answer is that by reflection one can see that there is no intrinsic necessity to the existence of the physical universe. If we had a complete description of the universe — perhaps in terms of a list of particles and an account of the position of each particle at each moment — one could not tell just by reading the description whether it is a description of the real world or a description of an imaginary world. The nature of the universe does not require its existence. In Aquinas' words, it is "possible for it to be and not to be."

Nagel's second criticism is that there is no reason to suppose an infinite regress of causes to be impossible. He quite rightly points out that there is no contradiction in the general notion of an infinite series, but this is of doubtful relevance to the Cosmological Argument, for Aquinas and other proponents of the argument do not maintain the impossibility of any kind of infinite series. Aquinas' specific point about an infinite regress of causes is this: If there is no first member, there is no source for the causal efficacy transmitted from one member of the series to another, and hence we cannot understand how any members of the series possess such efficacy. A coin can be passed from person to person indefinitely, but a presupposition of all this activity is that somewhere back along the line the coin was minted. A more up-to-date version of the claim would be in terms of causal explanation. If asked to explain the existence of an oak tree, I may reply by showing how it developed from an acorn. But, says the Thomist, as long as the existence of the acorn requires explanation in terms of something else I have not completed the job; and if the factors I bring in to explain the existence of the acorn are themselves in need of explanation by reference to something else,

I still have work to do. I haven't really explained the existence of the oak tree until I have traced it back to an agent that doesn't need to be explained by reference to something else; only then will I have completed the job. In these terms the claim that an infinite regress of causes is impossible is a claim that the world must be such that it is in principle (not necessarily in practice) possible to give a final complete explanation for any given fact.

It will be noted that Aquinas ends each of his arguments with such phrases as "this everyone understands to be God," and "this all men speak of as God." Isn't he trying to pull a rabbit out of a hat here? Even if the Cosmological Argument establishes the existence of a necessary being, it does not follow that this necessary being is an omnipotent supremely good personal being. (Anselm is in a better position in this respect since he starts with the concept of perfection and, as he makes explicit in Chapter V of Reading 1, he can infer that God has any attribute it is better to have than not to have.) To do justice to Aquinas, we must note that in these phrases he is anticipating the subsequent course of his argument, in which he attempts to show that necessary existence implies the possession of the other divine attributes.

The Teleological Argument begins from more specific facts about the world, and thereby aims directly at a more concrete conception of the creator. The facts in question are those of "design" or "adaptation." A case of design is a situation in which things are so disposed as to bring about results that are beneficial to the beings involved, even though those beings themselves did not exercise any foresight in bringing them about. For example, the ears of rabbits are formed so as to focus sounds from the rear, the quarter of greatest danger. The claim of the Teleological Argument is that such facts can be explained only by supposing that some conscious agent "behind the scenes" deliberately arranged things so that these fortunate results would ensue. "Design" presupposes a designer. This formulation is that of A. E. Taylor in Reading 4. Sometimes, as in Reading 3, the form is that of an argument from analogy. Artifacts like ships and houses are produced by a designing intelligence. Since the universe is similar to an artifact in embodying "design" and "adaptation," it is probably produced by a similar cause. The two forms are closely connected. Taylor's basic reason for maintaining that design can be explained only by a designer is that the only instance in which we have an insight into the cause of design is in the case of the creations of human intelligence, and that therefore we are justified in supposing that this is the ultimate source in every case. Thus Taylor's argument rests on just the sort of analogy brought out in Hume's *Dialogues* (Reading 3).

In its earlier formulation in Aquinas (the "fifth way") the argument reflects a teleological physics, in which one thinks of all physical processes as directed to ends. With the development of a mechanistic physics in the sixteenth and seventeenth centuries, the argument shifts its center of emphasis to the biological realm, finding its examples in the ways in which organic structures and instinctive activities are suited to the survival of the organism.

The elaborate critique of the argument by Philo in Hume's *Dialogues* makes three fundamental points:

1. The analogy between the physical universe and a house or ship is not strong enough to bear the weight of the argument.

2. There are equally plausible alternative explanations for the presence of design, e.g., the idea, based on the analogy between the universe and an organism, that it was generated from parent universes.

3. Even if the argument is valid, the most it proves is that each case of design is due to some intelligent being. It does not show that all the design in the universe is due to one being, or, if it is, that this one being is omnipotent or perfectly good. This objection is analogous to the question raised above, as to whether the Cosmological Argument can establish the existence of God, even if it does succeed in establishing the existence of a necessary being.

The selection from A. E. Taylor represents an attempt by a twentieth-century philosopher to restate and defend the argument. Although he does not explicitly discuss Hume, we can extract from his presentation some reactions to the above criticisms. Point 1 is answered, in effect, by the insistence that the crucial point of similarity is simply the presence of design and that other dissimilarities (size, complexity, etc.) are irrelevant. Unfortunately, Taylor does not take sufficient account of the difference between (a) the presence of various cases of adaptation of one thing to another *within* the universe and (b) the universe as a whole being adapted to the realization of some desirable end. Taylor concentrates on (a), but it is only on the assumption of (b) that we can carry through the analogy of the universe as a whole to an artifact and hence infer that the universe as a whole was designed by an intelligent being. Taylor considers objection 2 at some length, in the currently more relevant form of the claim that the Darwinian theory of evolution provides an explanation of organic adaptation in terms of natural mechanisms, thereby obviating the necessity of an appeal to supernatural causes. Here Taylor points out that the Darwinian theory simply has the function of explaining the emergence of more complex from less complex organisms, and hence does not provide a complete explanation of organic adaptation. The question still remains, however, as to whether other scientific theories might not take the ball from there and provide a chemical explanation of the emergence of the simplest organisms from inorganic matter. As for point 3, Taylor admits that the Teleological Argument will not do the whole job and needs supplementation if we are to have an adequate rational basis for belief in God.

All the arguments we have been considering set out to provide *indirect* evidence for the existence of God; they are designed to show that we must *suppose* God to exist if we are to set our intellectual house in order. Many believers have felt no need of such indirect evidence because they have supposed themselves to have a direct experience of the presence of God, at least as direct and unmistakable as our normal sensory experience of physical objects. Let us call such persons "mystics." One might take footprints in the snow as an indication that someone had been prowling around one's house the night before, but if one had *seen* the prowler one would not need to rely on such indirect indications. The mystic supposes himself to be in the second kind of position with respect to his belief in the existence of God. In Reading 5, James presents a wealth of concrete detail, illustrating the variety of experiences that have been taken to involve a direct experience of the divine, and he raises, in a sympathetic manner, questions about the trustworthiness of such experiences but fails to arrive at a clear-cut answer. In Reading 6 Russell defends a negative answer to the question.

If one tries to find rational grounds for deciding whether mystical experiences do involve a direct awareness of an objectively existing deity, there are two directions he may take. On the one hand, he can look to the testimony of others for confirmation or disconfirmation. On the other hand, he can look at facts about the state of the experiencer which might throw light on the trustworthiness of his experience. Both kinds of considerations have their analogues in the critical examination of sense-perception. Thus if a man claims to have seen a Russian plane flying over Detroit, we could determine whether anyone else in the vicinity at that time had seen it, or we could determine whether the man is sane, whether he is emotionally disturbed, or whether he had generally been a trustworthy reporter.

Both James and Russell make use of both approaches. As for the first, both writers allude to what James calls a "pretty distinct theoretic drift" in the reports mystics make on the basis of their experiences. At widely separated times and places men have claimed to have experienced an all-encompassing, blissful, unified reality. However, James admits that he can find this unanimity only by restricting himself to mysticism of the "classical" type, and that when we admit other varieties the mutual confirmation becomes weaker. Thus some mystics think themselves to be in contact with a personal deity, others with an impersonal absolute unity.

The most common argument along the second line is the negative argument, presented by Russell, that since mystical experiences spring from abnormal conditions we cannot expect them to be in correspondence with objective reality. It has been maintained that a person will have mystical experiences only if he is suffering from some psychotic or neurotic condition, but there is not sufficient evidence for such an extreme position. A more plausible claim would be that the mystical experience involves a temporary abnormal state of consciousness and/or the nervous system. But whatever the abnormality alleged, the argument is subject to the retort made by James elsewhere in the *Varieties of Religious Experience* that "If there were such a thing as inspiration from a higher realm, it might well be that the neurotic temperament would furnish the chief condition of the requisite receptivity" (p. 37). In other words, the standards of normality and abnormality that we frame on the basis of what is conducive to success in dealing with the physical environment may not be applicable to the problem of dealing with a "supernatural environment." Where the environment is radically different, the conditions of effective and veridical contact with it may be quite different. Sunglasses aid accurate observation in the Arizona desert, but not in the fogbound Aleutians.

A less specialized negative argument along the second line would be that since the occurrence of mystical experiences can be explained in terms of purely natural psychological and sociological factors, without having to bring any supernatural deity into the explanation, the experience can provide no basis for asserting the existence of a deity. This argument raises subtle and complex issues into which we cannot go here. It is worthy of note that whereas James thinks that mystical experience can be psychologically explained in terms of the operations of the subconscious mind, yet he takes seriously the possibility that the experience still might be putting us in touch with the supernatural *through* the subconscious.

Thus far we have been considering possible reasons for believing in God. Now it is time to give the atheist his innings and examine possible grounds for disbelief. Although atheists and agnostics have been in the minority in the history of philosophy, they have provided some bases for disbelief, in addition to criticizing arguments on the other side. By far the strongest and most often cited of these bases is the problem of evil. Since human beings and other sentient creatures undergo suffering, deprivation, and frustration, how can we suppose that the world is the work of an omnipotent, perfectly good deity? For such a being would not wish to create a world with undesirable features, and, being omnipotent, nothing could force Him to do anything other than what He chose to do. This problem has plagued theistic thought throughout its history, the Book of Job in the Old Testament being one of the earliest explicit presentations, and various solutions have been proposed. In Reading 8, an attempt by a contemporary Christian thinker to grapple with the problem, we have a lucid review of some of these solutions.

In recent times antitheistic philosophers have tended to brand theism as meaningless, rather than false.[2] There have always been problems about the intelligibility of theism. In Chapters VI — VIII of Reading 1, St. Anselm struggles to reconcile some apparently discrepant divine attributes, such as being omnipotent *and* incapable of lying, and being compassionate *and* not subject to passion. In Hume's *Dialogues* Demea maintains that terms like "thought," "love," and "pity" when applied to God cannot mean what they mean in application to man. Hence, since we get whatever understanding we have of these terms from our experience of the human qualities so denominated, their meaning as applied to God is "totally incomprehensible, and the

---

[2] Hence the use in the preceding sentence of the more general term "antitheistic," rather than "atheist." If an atheist is one who holds that it is *false* that God exists, then one who holds the theistic position to be meaningless is not an atheist; for a proposition must be intelligible in order to be either true or false. "The slithy toves did gyre and gimble in the wabe" is neither true nor false. It has not gotten so far as to be capable of falsity.

infirmities of our nature do not permit us to reach any ideas which in the least correspond to the ineffable sublimity of the Divine attributes." (Demea does not explain how, in this case, he can claim not to be speaking gibberish when he affirms belief in a loving God.)

This problem becomes more intractable as one's concept of God removes Him more from any similarity to man. In less sophisticated religions, where the gods are thought of (at least half-seriously) as existing in a bodily form, what can be meant by speaking of them as commanding, expressing anger, and forgiving is not so problematic. But in classical Christian theology God is unmistakably understood to be not only immaterial and so not existing in space, but as not existing in time either. There is no succession of moments in the divine existence. He exists in an "eternal now." All this poses severe difficulties for the interpretation of terms that, in their ordinary sense, imply bodily movements, such as "command" or "punish," or that imply temporal succession, even apart from bodily movements, such as "think" or "decide." Some theologians, including Aquinas, make things even worse for themselves by insisting that God is absolutely simple and without parts or aspects, so that such activities as deciding and forgiving cannot be really distinct in God. In the face of such difficulties, theists have tried to show that there is enough of the ordinary meaning of the term left to enable us to give some sense to theological statements, while their opponents have argued that there is nothing left, or at least not enough to yield statements with any religious significance. Even if it is not complete nonsense to say that God will forgive those who truly turn unto Him, the opponents have claimed there is not enough content left in the notion of forgiveness to warrant our using this as a reason for making the turn.

Today the charge of meaninglessness is most often leveled in the name of the Verifiability Principle, as in Reading 9. This principle, brought to the fore in the work of the "Vienna Circle" (see Reading 46), holds that one is making a genuine assertion only if what he says is capable of empirical confirmation or disconfirmation, i.e., only if the truth of what one is saying would make a difference to the future course of our sense experience. This is the point of the parable of the gardener, presented in Reading 9. To take another example, if I assert that my oak tree is getting larger, there are empirical tests for this; I can measure it at various times and compare the measurements. But if I assert that everything in the universe is expanding at a constant rate, there is no posssibility of any test. Successive measurements will not detect this phenomenon, for *if* it is going on, all my measuring instruments are expanding just in the same proportion as the things measured. The future course of our experience would be just the same whether what I say is true or false. Hence it may be doubted that I am making a serious assertion in saying, "Everything is expanding at the same rate." It would seem that I am just playing with words.

There is no doubt that religious beliefs, as held by unreflective believers, have the kind of implications for experience that make empirical test possible. Thus the theology of a given tribe may be taken to imply that if the rain dance is gone through properly rain will ensue; and many Christians hold beliefs about God which imply that if one addresses requests to the saints or to the Virgin in certain ways, these requests will be granted. Believers may be slow to take to heart empirical disconfirmations arrived at by following out these implications, but that is another matter. However, as theology becomes more sophisticated it becomes increasingly remote from the possibility of such tests. One no longer professes to know what God will do under any given conditions, the final consummation is pushed off into the indefinite future, and it looks as if God's love is taken to be compatible with any observable state of affairs whatever. Hence the suggestion by Flew that "God loves His creatures" has been emptied of any assertive force.

One may respond to this challenge by attacking the Verifiability Principle and arguing that empirical testability is not necessary for one's utterance to constitute a genuine assertion. In Reading 10, Hick takes the other alternative of arguing that Christian theology is susceptible of an empirical test — not in the present life but after death. Of course, this consideration can show the meaningfulness of theology only if it makes sense to talk about a person carrying on such a verification after death. Hick's attempt to demonstrate the meaningfulness of this supposition leads him into problems concerning the conditions under which we have the *same* person at different times, problems we shall encounter again in Part IV.

1

THE INCONCEIVABILITY
OF GOD'S
NONEXISTENCE

St. Anselm

St. Anselm (1033-1109) was Archbishop of Canterbury and the most important phi-losopher of the eleventh century.

CHAPTER II.

Truly there is a God, although the fool hath said in his heart,
There is no God.

And so, Lord, do thou, who dost give understanding to faith, give me, so far as thou knowest it to be profitable, to understand that thou art as we believe; and that thou art that which we believe. And, indeed, we believe that thou art a being than which nothing greater can be conceived. Or is there no such nature, since the fool hath said in his heart, there is no God? (Psalms xiv, 1). But, at any rate, this very fool, when he hears of this being of which I speak — a being than which nothing greater can be conceived — understands what he hears, and what he understands is in his understanding; although he does not understand it to exist.

For, it is one thing for an object to be in the understanding, and another to understand that the object exists. When a painter first conceives of what he will afterwards perform, he has it in his understanding, but he does not yet understand it to be, because he has not yet performed it. But after he has made the painting, he both has it in his understanding, and he understands that it exists, because he has made it.

Hence, even the fool is convinced that something exists in the understanding, at least, than which nothing greater can be conceived. For, when he hears of this, he understands it. And whatever is understood, exists in the understanding. And assuredly that, than which nothing greater can be conceived, cannot exist in the understanding alone. For, suppose it exists in

Chapters II through VIII of *Proslogium,* tr. by S. N. Deane, Open Court Publishing Company, 1903.

the understanding alone: then it can be conceived to exist in reality; which is greater.

Therefore, if that, than which nothing greater can be conceived, exists in the understanding alone, the very being, than which nothing greater can be conceived, is one, than which a greater can be conceived. But obviously this is impossible. Hence, there is no doubt that there exists a being, than which nothing greater can be conceived, and it exists both in the understanding and in reality.

CHAPTER III.

God cannot be conceived not to exist. — God is that, than which nothing greater can be conceived. — That which can be conceived not to exist is not God.

And it assuredly exists so truly, that it cannot be conceived not to exist. For, it is possible to conceive of a being which cannot be conceived not to exist; and this is greater than one which can be conceived not to exist. Hence, if that, than which nothing greater can be conceived, can be conceived not to exist, it is not that, than which nothing greater can be conceived. But this is an irreconcilable contradiction. There is, then, so truly a being than which nothing greater can be conceived to exist, that it cannot even be conceived not to exist; and this being thou art, O Lord, our God.

So truly, therefore, dost thou exist, O Lord, my God, that thou canst not be conceived not to exist; and rightly. For, if a mind could conceive of a being better than thee, the creature would rise above the Creator; and this is most absurd. And, indeed, whatever else there is, except thee alone, can be conceived not to exist. To thee alone, therefore, it belongs to exist more truly than all other beings, and hence in a higher degree than all others. For, whatever else exists does not exist so truly, and hence in a less degree it belongs to it to exist. Why, then, has the fool said in his heart, there is no God (Psalms xiv. 1), since it is so evident, to a rational mind, that thou dost exist in the highest degree of all? Why, except that he is dull and a fool?

CHAPTER IV.

How the fool has said in his heart what cannot be conceived. — A thing may be conceived in two ways: (1) when the word signifying it is conceived; (2) when the thing itself is understood. As far as the word goes, God can be conceived not to exist; in reality he cannot.

But how has the fool said in his heart what he could not conceive; or how is it that he could not conceive what he said in his heart? since it is the same to say in the heart, and to conceive.

But, if really, nay, since really, he both conceived, because he said in his heart; and did not say in his heart, because he could not conceive; there is more than one way in which a thing is said in the heart or conceived. For, in one sense, an object is conceived, when the word signifying it is conceived; and in another, when the very entity, which the object is, is understood.

In the former sense, then, God can be conceived not to exist; but in the latter, not at all. For no one who understands what fire and water are can conceive fire to be water, in accordance with the nature of the facts themselves, although this is possible according to the words. So, then, no one who understands what God is can conceive that God does not exist; although he says these words in his heart, either without any, or with some foreign signification. For, God is that than which a greater cannot be conceived. And he who thoroughly understands this, assuredly understands that this being so truly exists, that not even in concept can it be non-existent. Therefore, he who understands that God so exists, cannot conceive that he does not exist.

I thank thee, gracious Lord, I thank thee; because what I formerly believed by thy bounty, I now so understand by thine illumination, that if I were unwilling to believe that thou dost exist, I should not be able not to understand this to be true.

CHAPTER V.

God is whatever it is better to be than not to be; and he, as the only self-existent being, creates all things from nothing.

What art thou, then, Lord God, than whom nothing greater can be conceived? But what art thou, except that which, as the highest of all beings, alone exists through itself, and creates all other things from nothing? For, whatever is not this is less than a thing which can be conceived of. But this cannot be conceived of thee. What good, therefore, does the supreme Good lack, through which every good is? Therefore, thou art just, truthful, blessed, and whatever it is better to be than not to be. For it is better to be just than not just; better to be blessed than not blessed.

CHAPTER VI.

How God is sensible (sensibilis) although he is not a body. — God is sensible, omnipotent, compassionate, passionless; for it is better to be these than not be. He who in any way knows, is not improperly said in some sort to feel.

But, although it is better for thee to be sensible, omnipotent, compassionate, passionless, than not to be these things; how art thou sensible, if thou art not a body; or omnipotent, if thou hast not all powers; or at once compassionate and passionless? For, if only corporeal things are sensible, since the senses encompass a body and are in a body, how art thou sensible, although thou art not a body, but a supreme Spirit, who is superior to body? But, if feeling is only cognition, or for the sake of cognition, — for he who feels obtains knowledge in accordance with the proper functions of his senses; as through sight, of colors; through taste, of flavors, — whatever in any way cognises is not inappropriately said, in some sort, to feel.

Therefore, O Lord, although thou art not a body, yet thou art truly sensible in the highest degree in respect of this, that thou dost cognise all things in the highest degree; and not as an animal cognises, through a corporeal sense.

Chapter VII.

How he is omnipotent, although there are many things of which he is not capable — To be capable of being corrupted, or of lying, is not power, but impotence. God can do nothing by virtue of impotence, and nothing has power against him.

But how art thou omnipotent, if thou art not capable of all things? Or, if thou canst not be corrupted, and canst not lie, nor make what is true, false — as, for example, if thou shouldst make what has been done not to have been done, and the like — how art thou capable of all things? Or else to be capable of these things is not power, but impotence. For, he who is capable of these things is capable of what is not for his good, and of what he ought not to do; and the more capable of them he is, the more power have adversity and perversity against him; and the less has he himself against these.

He, then, who is thus capable is so not by power, but by impotence. For, he is not said to be able because he is able of himself, but because his impotence gives something else power over him. Or, by a figure of speech, just as many words are improperly applied, as when we use "to be" for "not to be," and "to do" for what is really "not to do," or "to do nothing." For, often we say to a man who denies the existence of something: "It is as you say it to be," though it might seem more proper to say, "It is not, as you say it is not." In the same way, we say: "This man sits just as that man does," or, "This man rests just as that man does"; although to sit is not to do anything, and to rest is to do nothing.

So, then, when one is said to have the power of doing or experiencing what is not for his good, or what he ought not to do, impotence is understood in the word power. For, the more he possesses this power, the more powerful are adversity and perversity against him, and the more powerless is he against them.

Therefore, O Lord, our God, the more truly art thou omnipotent, since thou art capable of nothing through impotence, and nothing has power against thee.

Chapter VIII.

How he is compassionate and passionless. God is compassionate, in terms of our experience, because we experience the effect of compassion. God is not compassionate, in terms of his own being, because he does not experience the feeling (affectus) *of compassion.*

But how art thou compassionate, and, at the same time, passionless? For, if thou art passionless, thou dost not feel sympathy; and if thou dost not feel sympathy, thy heart is not wretched from sympathy for the wretched; but this is to be compassionate. But if thou art not compassionate, whence cometh so great consolation to the wretched? How, then, art thou compassionate and not compassionate, O Lord, unless because thou art compassionate in terms of our experience, and not compassionate in terms of thy being.

Truly, thou art so in terms of our experience, but thou art not so in terms of thine own. For, when thou beholdest us in our wretchedness, we experience the effect of compassion, but thou dost not experience the feeling. Therefore, thou art both compassionate, because thou dost save the wretched, and spare those who sin against thee; and not compassionate, because thou art affected by no sympathy for wretchedness.

2

FROM NATURE
TO GOD

St. Thomas Aquinas

St. Thomas Aquinas is the most famous of the medieval Christian philosophers and has become something like the official philosopher of the Roman Catholic Church.

The existence of God can be proved in five ways.

The first and more manifest way is the argument from motion. It is certain, and evident to our senses, that in the world some things are in motion. Now whatever is moved is moved by another, for nothing can be moved except it is in potentiality to that towards which it is moved; whereas a thing moves inasmuch as it is in act. For motion is nothing else than the reduction of something from potentiality to actuality. But nothing can be reduced from potentiality to actuality, except by something in a state of actuality. Thus that which is actually hot, as fire, makes wood, which is potentially hot, to be actually hot, and thereby moves and changes it. Now it is not possible that the same thing should be at once in actuality and potentiality in the same respect, but only in different respects. For what is actually hot cannot simultaneously be potentially hot; but it is simultaneously potentially cold. It is therefore impossible that in the same respect and in the same way a thing should be both mover and moved, *i.e.*, that it should move itself. Therefore, whatever is moved must be moved by another. If that by which it is moved be itself moved, then this also must needs be moved by another, and that by another again. But this cannot go on to infinity, because then there would be no first mover, and, consequently, no other mover, seeing that subsequent movers move only inasmuch as they are moved by the first mover; as the staff moves only because it is moved by the hand. Therefore it is necessary to arrive at a first mover, moved by no other; and this everyone understands to be God.

The second way is from the nature of efficient cause. In the world of

This selection comprises the "Reply" of Part I, Question 2, Article 3, of the *Summa Theologica*. It is reprinted from *The Basic Writings of St. Thomas Aquinas*, ed. A. C. Pegis, by permission of the publishers, Random House, Inc.

sensible things we find there is an order of efficient causes. There is no case known (neither is it, indeed, possible) in which a thing is found to be the efficient cause of itself; for so it would be prior to itself, which is impossible. Now in efficient causes it is not possible to go on to infinity, because in all efficient causes following in order, the first is the cause of the intermediate cause, and the intermediate is the cause of the ultimate cause, whether the intermediate cause be several, or one only. Now to take away the cause is to take away the effect. Therefore, if there be no first cause among efficient causes, there will be no ultimate, nor any intermediate, cause. But if in efficient causes it is possible to go on to infinity, there will be no first efficient cause, neither will there be an ultimate effect, nor any intermediate efficient causes; all of which is plainly false. Therefore it is necessary to admit a first efficient cause, to which everyone gives the name of God.

The third way is taken from possibility and necessity, and runs thus. We find in nature things that are possible to be and not to be, since they are found to be generated, and to be corrupted, and consequently, it is possible for them to be and not to be. But it is impossible for these always to exist, for that which can not-be at some time is not. Therefore, if everything can not-be, then at one time there was nothing in existence. Now if this were true, even now there would be nothing in existence, because that which does not exist begins to exist only through something already existing. Therefore, if at one time nothing was in existence, it would have been impossible for anything to have begun to exist; and thus even now nothing would be in existence — which is absurd. Therefore, not all beings are merely possible, but there must exist something the existence of which is necessary. But every necessary thing either has its necessity caused by another, or not. Now it is impossible to go on to infinity in necessary things which have their necessity caused by another, as has been already proved in regard to efficient causes. Therefore we cannot but admit the existence of some being having of itself its own necessity, and not receiving it from another, but rather causing in others their necessity. This all men speak of as God.

The fourth way is taken from the gradation to be found in things. Among beings there are some more and some less good, true, noble, and the like. But *more* and *less* are predicated of different things according as they resemble in their different ways something which is the maximum, as a thing is said to be hotter according as it more nearly resembles that which is hottest; so that there is something which is truest, something best, something noblest, and, consequently, something which is most being, for those things that are greatest in truth are greatest in being, as it is written in *Metaph*.ii. Now the maximum in any genus is the cause of all in that genus, as fire, which is the maximum of heat, is the cause of all hot things, as is said in the same book. Therefore there must also be something which is to all beings the cause of their being, goodness, and every other perfection; and this we call God.

The fifth way is taken from the governance of the world. We see that things which lack knowledge, such as natural bodies, act for an end, and this is evident from their acting always, or nearly always, in the same way, so as to obtain the best result. Hence it is plain that they achieve their end, not fortuitously, but designedly. Now whatever lacks knowledge cannot move towards an end, unless it be directed by some being endowed with knowledge and intelligence; as the arrow is directed by the archer. Therefore some intelligent being exists by whom all natural things are directed to their end; and this being we call God.

3

A CRITIQUE
OF THE ARGUMENT
FROM DESIGN

David Hume

*David Hume (1711-1776) was perhaps the greatest of the British empiricist philos-
ophers of the seventeenth and eighteenth centuries.*

Not to lose any time in circumlocutions, said CLEANTHES, addressing himself to Demea, much less in replying to the pious declamations of Philo, I
shall briefly explain how I conceive this matter. Look around the world,
contemplate the whole and every part of it: you will find it to be nothing but
one great machine, subdivided into an infinite number of lesser machines,
which again admit of subdivisions to a degree beyond what human senses and
faculties can trace and explain. All these various machines, and even their
most minute parts, are adjusted to each other with an accuracy which ravishes
into admiration all men who have ever contemplated them. The curious
adapting of means to ends throughout all nature resembles exactly, though
it much exceeds, the productions of human contrivance, of human design,
thought, wisdom, and intelligence. Since therefore the effects resemble each
other, we are led to infer, by all the rules of analogy, that the causes also
resemble, and that the Author of Nature is somewhat similar to the mind of
man, though possessed of much larger faculties, proportioned to the grandeur
of the work which he has executed. By this argument *a posteriori*, and by
this argument alone, do we prove at once the existence of a Deity and his
similarity to human mind and intelligence.

. . .

How Strong Is the Analogy?

PHILO, after a short pause, proceeded in the following manner.

That all inferences, Cleanthes, concerning fact are founded on experience, and that all experimental reasonings are founded on the supposition

From Parts II—IX of the *Dialogues Concerning Natural Religion*, a work published
posthumously. Subheadings added by the editors. It is a matter of controversy as to
the extent to which the various participants in the *Dialogues* represent Hume's own
views, but he is usually identified with Philo.

that similar causes prove similar effects, and similar effects similar causes, I shall not at present much dispute with you. But observe, I entreat you, with what extreme caution all just reasoners proceed in the transferring of experiments to similar cases. Unless the cases be exactly similar, they repose no perfect confidence in applying their past observation to any particular phenomenon. Every alteration of circumstances occasions a doubt concerning the event, and it requires new experiments to prove certainly that the new circumstances are of no moment or importance. A change in bulk, situation, arrangement, age, disposition of the air, or surrounding bodies, any of these particulars may be attended with the most unexpected consequences. And unless the objects be quite familiar to us, it is the highest temerity to expect with assurance, after any of these changes, an event similar to that which before fell under our observation. The slow and deliberate steps of philosophers here, if anywhere, are distinguished from the precipitate march of the vulgar, who, hurried on by the smallest similitude, are incapable of all discernment or consideration.

But can you think, Cleanthes, that your usual phlegm and philosophy have been preserved in so wide a step as you have taken when you compared to the universe, houses, ships, furniture, machines, and from their similarity in some circumstances inferred a similarity in their causes? Thought, design, intelligence, such as we discover in men and other animals, is no more than one of the springs and principles of the universe, as well as heat or cold, attraction or repulsion, and a hundred others which fall under daily observation. It is an active cause by which some particular parts of nature, we find, produce alterations on other parts. But can a conclusion, with any propriety, be transferred from parts to the whole? Does not the great disproportion bar all comparison and inference? From observing the growth of a hair, can we learn anything concerning the generation of a man? Would the manner of a leaf's blowing, even though perfectly known, afford us any instruction concerning the vegetation of a tree?

But allowing that we were to take the *operations* of one part of nature upon another for the foundation of our judgment concerning the *origin* of the whole (which never can be admitted), yet why select so minute, so weak, so bounded a principle as the reason and design of animals is found to be upon this planet? What peculiar privilege has this little agitation of the brain which we call *thought,* that we must thus make it the model of the whole universe? Our partiality in our own favor does indeed present it on all occasions, but sound philosophy ought carefully to guard against so natural an illusion.

So far from admitting, continued PHILO, that the operations of a part can afford us any just conclusion concerning the origin of the whole, I will not allow any one part to form a rule for another part if the latter be very remote from the former. Is there any reasonable ground to conclude that the inhabitants of other planets possess thought, intelligence, reason, or anything similar to these faculties in men? When nature has so extremely diversified her manner of operation in this small globe, can we imagine that she incessantly copies herself throughout so immense a universe? And if thought, as we may well suppose, be confined merely to this narrow corner and has even there so limited a sphere of action, with what propriety can we assign it for the original cause of all things? The narrow views of a peasant who makes this domestic economy the rule for the government of kingdoms is in comparison a pardonable sophism.

But were we ever so much assured that a thought and reason resembling the human were to be found throughout the whole universe, and were its activity elsewhere vastly greater and more commanding than it appears in this globe, yet I cannot see why the operations of a world constituted, arranged, adjusted, can with any propriety be extended to a world which is in its embryo state, and is advancing toward that constitution and arrangement. By observation we know somewhat of the economy, action, and nourishment of a finished animal, but we must transfer with great caution that observation to the growth of a fetus in the womb, and still more to the formation of an animalcule in the loins of its male parent. Nature, we find, even from our limited experience, possesses an infinite number of springs and principles which incessantly discover themselves on every change of her position and situation. And what new and unknown principles would actuate her in so new and unknown a situation as that of the formation of a universe, we cannot, without the utmost temerity, pretend to determine.

A very small part of this great system, during a very short time, is very imperfectly discovered to us; and do we thence pronounce decisively concerning the origin of the whole?

Admirable conclusion! Stone, wood, brick, iron, brass, have not, at this time, in this minute globe of earth, an order or arrangement without human art and contrivance; therefore, the universe could not originally attain its order and arrangement without something similar to human art. But is a part of nature a rule for another part very wide of the former? Is it a rule for the whole? Is a very small part a rule for the universe? Is nature in one situation a certain rule for nature in another situation vastly different from the former?

.   .   .

How the most absurd argument, replied CLEANTHES, in the hands of a man of ingenuity and invention, may acquire an air of probability! Are you not aware, Philo, that it became necessary for Copernicus and his first disciples to prove the similarity of the terrestrial and celestial matter because several philosophers, blinded by old systems and supported by some sensible appearances, had denied this similarity? But that it is by no means necessary that theists should prove the similarity of the works of nature to those of art because this similarity is self-evident and undeniable? The same matter, a like form; what more is requisite to show an analogy between their causes and to ascertain the origin of all things from a divine purpose and intention? Your objections, I must freely tell you, are no better than the abstruse cavils of those philosophers who denied motion, and ought to be refuted in the same manner, by illustrations, examples, and instances rather than by serious argument and philosophy.

Suppose, therefore, that an articulate voice were heard in the clouds, much louder and more melodious than any which human art could ever reach; suppose that this voice were extended in the same instant over all nations and spoke to each nation in its own language and dialect; suppose that the words delivered not only contain a just sense and meaning, but convey some instruction altogether worthy of a benevolent Being superior to mankind. Could you possibly hesitate a moment concerning the cause of this voice, and must you not instantly ascribe it to some design or purpose? Yet I cannot see but all the same objections (if they merit that appellation) which lie against the system of theism may also be produced against this inference.

Might you not say that all conclusions concerning fact were founded on experience; that when we hear an articulate voice in the dark and thence infer a man, it is only the resemblance of the effect which leads us to conclude that there is a like resemblance in the cause; but that this extraordinary voice, by its loudness, extent, and flexibility to all languages, bears so little analogy to any human voice that we have no reason to suppose any analogy in their causes; and consequently that a rational, wise, coherent speech proceeded, you knew not whence, from some accidental whistling of the winds, not from any divine reason or intelligence? You see clearly your own objections in these cavils, and I hope too you see clearly that they cannot possibly have more force in the one case than in the other.

But to bring the case still nearer the present one of the universe, I shall make two suppositions which imply not any absurdity, or impossibility. Suppose that there is a natural, universal, invariable language, common to every individual of human race, and that books are natural productions which perpetuate themselves in the same manner with animals and vegetables, by descent and propagation. Several expressions of our passions contain a universal language: all brute animals have a natural speech, which, however limited, is very intelligible to their own species. And as there are infinitely fewer parts and less contrivance in the finest composition of eloquence than in the coarsest organized body, the propagation of an *Iliad* or *Aeneid* is an easier supposition than that of any plant or animal.

Suppose, therefore, that you enter into your library thus peopled by natural volumes containing the most refined reason and most exquisite beauty; could you possibly open one of them and doubt that its original cause bore the strongest analogy to mind and intelligence? When it reasons and discourses; when it expostulates, argues, and enforces its views and topics; when it applies sometimes to the pure intellect, sometimes to the affections; when it collects, disposes, and adorns every consideration suited to the subject; could you persist in asserting that all this, at the bottom, had really no meaning, and that the first formation of this volume in the loins of its original parent proceeded not from thought and design? Your obstinacy, I know, reaches not that degree of firmness; even your skeptical play and wantonness would be abashed at so glaring an absurdity.

But if there be any difference, Philo, between this supposed case and the real one of the universe, it is all to the advantage of the latter. The anatomy of an animal affords many stronger instances of design than the perusal of Livy or Tacitus; and any objection which you start in the former case, by carrying me back to so unusual and extraordinary a scene as the first formation of worlds, the same objection has place on the supposition of our vegetating library. Choose then your party, Philo, without ambiguity or evasion; assert either that a rational volume is no proof of a rational cause or admit of a similar cause to all the works of nature.

.   .   .

It sometimes happens, I own, that the religious arguments have not their due influence on an ignorant savage and barbarian, not because they are obscure and difficult, but because he never asks himself any question with regard to them. Whence arises the curious structure of an animal? From the copulation of its parents. And these whence? From *their* parents? A few removes set the objects at such a distance that to him they are lost in darkness and confusion; nor is he actuated by any curiosity to trace them further. But this is neither dogmatism nor skepticism, but stupidity, a state of mind very different from your sifting, inquisitive disposition, my ingenious friend. You can trace causes from effects; you can compare the most distant and remote objects; and your greatest errors proceed not from barrenness of thought and invention but from too luxuriant a fertility, which suppresses your natural good sense by a profusion of unnecessary scruples and objections.

Is the Divine Nature Intelligible to Man?

Here I could observe, Hermippus, that Philo was a little embarrassed and confounded; but while he hesitated in delivering an answer, luckily for him, DEMEA broke in upon the discourse and saved his countenance.

Your instance, Cleanthes, said he, drawn from books and language, being familiar, has, I confess, so much more force on that account; but is there not some danger too in this very circumstance, and may it not render us presumptuous by making us imagine we comprehend the Deity and have some adequate idea of his nature and attributes? When I read a volume, I enter into the mind and intention of the author; I become him, in a manner, for the instant, and have an immediate feeling and conception of those ideas which revolved in his imagination while employed in that composition. But so near an approach we never surely can make to the Deity. His ways are not our ways. His attributes are perfect but incomprehensible. And this volume of nature contains a great and inexplicable riddle, more than any intelligible discourse or reasoning.

The ancient Platonists, you know, were the most religious and devout of all the pagan philosophers, yet many of them, particularly Plotinus, expressly declare that intellect or understanding is not to be ascribed to the Deity, and that our most perfect worship of him consists, not in acts of veneration, reverence, gratitude, or love, but in a certain mysterious self-annihilation of all our faculties. These ideas are, perhaps, too far stretched, but still it must be acknowledged that, by representing the Deity as so intelligible and comprehensible and so similar to a human mind, we are guilty of the grossest and most narrow partiality, and make ourselves the model of the whole universe.

All the *sentiments* of the human mind — gratitude, resentment, love, friendship, approbation, blame, pity, emulation, envy — have a plain reference to the state and situation of man, and are calculated for preserving the existence and promoting the activity of such a being in such circumstances. It seems therefore unreasonable to transfer such sentiments to a supreme existence or to suppose him actuated by them; and the phenomena, besides, of the universe will not support us in such a theory. All our *ideas* derived from the senses are confessedly false and illusive, and cannot therefore be supposed to have place in a supreme intelligence. And as the ideas of internal sentiment, added to those of the external senses, compose the whole furniture of human understanding, we may conclude that none of the *materials* of thought are in any respect similar in the human and in the divine intelligence. Now as to the *manner* of thinking, how can we make any comparison between them or suppose them anywise resembling? Our thought is fluctuating, uncertain, fleeting, successive, and compounded; and were we to remove these circumstances we absolutely annihilate its essence, and it would in such a case be an abuse of terms to apply to it the name of thought or reason. At least, if it appear more pious and respectful (as it really is) still to retain these terms when we mention the Supreme Being, we ought to acknowledge that their meaning, in that case, is totally incomprehensible, and that the infirmities of our nature do not permit us to reach any ideas which in the least correspond to the ineffable sublimity of the divine attributes.

. . .

It seems strange to me, said CLEANTHES, that you, Demea, who are so sincere in the cause of religion, should still maintain the mysterious, incomprehensible nature of the Deity, and should insist so strenuously that he has no manner of likeness or resemblance to human creatures. The Deity, I can readily allow, possesses many powers and attributes of which we can have no comprehension. But if our ideas, so far as they go, be not just and adequate and correspondent to his real nature, I know not what there is in this subject worth insisting on. Is the name, without any meaning, of such mighty importance? Or how do you mystics, who maintain the absolute incomprehensibility of the Deity, differ from skeptics or atheists, who assert that the first cause of all is unknown and unintelligible? Their temerity must be very great if, after rejecting the production by a mind — I mean a mind resembling the human (for I know of no other) — they pretend to assign, with certainty,

any other specific intelligible cause; and their conscience must be very scrupulous indeed if they refuse to call the universal unknown cause a God or
Deity, and to bestow on him as many sublime eulogies and unmeaning epithets as you shall please to require of them.

Who could imagine, replied DEMEA, that Cleanthes, the calm, philosophical Cleanthes, would attempt to refute his antagonists by affixing a nickname
to them, and, like the common bigots and inquisitors of the age, have recourse
to invective and declamation instead of reasoning? Or does he not perceive
that these topics are easily retorted, and that *anthropomorphite* is an appellation as invidious and implies as dangerous consequences as the epithet of
mystic with which he has honored us? In reality, Cleanthes, consider what
it is you assert when you represent the Deity as similar to a human mind and
understanding. What is the soul of man? A composition of various faculties,
passions, sentiments, ideas, united, indeed, into one self or person, but still
distinct from each other. When it reasons, the ideas which are the parts of its
discourse arrange themselves in a certain form or order which is not preserved
entire for a moment, but immediately gives place to another arrangement.
New opinions, new passions, new affections, new feelings arise which continually diversify the mental scene and produce in it the greatest variety and
most rapid succession imaginable. How is this compatible with that perfect
immutability and simplicity which all true theists ascribe to the Deity? By
the same act, say they, he sees past, present, and future; his love and hatred,
his mercy and justice, are one individual operation; he is entire in every point
of space and complete in every instant of duration. No succession, no change,
no acquisition, no diminution. What he is implies not in it any shadow of
distinction or diversity. And what he is this moment he ever has been and
ever will be, without any new judgment, sentiment, or operation. He stands
fixed in one simple, perfect state; nor can you ever say, with any propriety,
that this act of his is different from that other, or that this judgment or idea
has been lately formed and will give place, by succession, to any different
judgment or idea.

I can readily allow, said CLEANTHES, that those who maintain the perfect
simplicity of the Supreme Being, to the extent in which you have explained
it, are complete mystics, and chargeable with all the consequences which I
have drawn from their opinion. They are, in a word, atheists, without knowing it. For though it be allowed that the Deity possesses attributes of which we
have no comprehension, yet ought we never to ascribe to him any attributes
which are absolutely incompatible with that intelligent nature essential to
him. A mind whose acts and sentiments and ideas are not distinct and successive, one that is wholly simple and totally immutable, is a mind which
has no thought, no reason, no will, no sentiment, no love, no hatred, or, in a
word, is no mind at all. It is an abuse of terms to give it that appellation,
and we may as well speak of limited extension without figure, or of number
without composition.

Pray consider, said PHILO, whom you are at present inveighing against.

You are honoring with the appellation of *atheist* all the sound, orthodox divines, almost, who have treated of this subject; and you will at last be yourself found, according to your reckoning, the only sound theist in the world. But if idolaters be atheists, as I think may justly be asserted, and Christian theologians the same, what becomes of the argument, so much celebrated, derived from the universal consent of mankind?

DOES THE WORLD-DESIGNER HAVE TO BE EXPLAINED?

But because I know you are not much swayed by names and authorities, I shall endeavor to show you a little more distinctly the inconveniences of that anthropomorphism which you have embraced, and shall prove that there is no ground to suppose a plan of the world to be formed in the divine mind, consisting of distinct ideas differently arranged, in the same manner as an architect forms in his head the plan of a house which he intends to execute.

It is not easy, I own, to see what is gained by this supposition, whether we judge of the matter by *reason* or by *experience*. We are still obliged to mount higher in order to find the cause of this cause which you have assigned as satisfactory and conclusive.

If *reason* (I mean abstract reason, derived from inquiries *a priori*) be not alike mute with regard to all questions concerning cause and effect, this sentence at least it will venture to pronounce: that a mental world or universe of ideas requires a cause as much as does a material world or universe of objects, and, if similar in its arrangement, must require a similar cause. For what is there in this subject which should occasion a different conclusion or inference? In an abstract view they are entirely alike, and no difficulty attends the one supposition which is not common to both of them.

Again, when we will needs force *experience* to pronounce some sentence, even on these subjects which lie beyond her sphere, neither can she perceive any material difference in this particular between these two kinds of worlds, but finds them to be governed by similar principles, and to depend upon an equal variety of causes in their operations. We have specimens in miniature of both of them. Our own mind resembles the one, a vegetable or animal body the other. Let experience, therefore, judge from these samples. Nothing seems more delicate, with regard to its causes, than thought; and as these causes never operate in two persons after the same manner, so we never find two persons who think exactly alike. Nor indeed does the same person think exactly alike at any two different periods of time. A difference of age, of the disposition of his body, of weather, of food, of company, of books, of passions, any of these particulars, or others more minute, are sufficient to alter the curious machinery of thought and communicate to it very different movements and operations. As far as we can judge, vegetables and animal bodies are not more delicate in their motions, nor depend upon a greater variety or more curious adjustment of springs and principles.

How therefore shall we satisfy ourselves concerning the cause of that Being whom you suppose the Author of Nature, or, according to your system of anthropomorphism, the ideal world into which you trace the material? Have we not the same reason to trace that ideal world into another ideal world or new intelligent principle? But if we stop and go no further, why go so far? Why not stop at the material world? How can we satisfy ourselves without going on *in infinitum?* And after all, what satisfaction is there in that infinite progression? Let us remember the story of the Indian philosopher and his elephant. It was never more applicable than to the present subject. If the material world rests upon a similar ideal world, this ideal world must rest upon some other, and so on without end. It were better, therefore, never to look beyond the present material world. By supposing it to contain the principle of its order within itself, we really assert it to be God, and the sooner we arrive at that divine Being, so much the better. When you go one step beyond the mundane system, you only excite an inquisitive humor which it is impossible ever to satisfy.

. . .

You have displayed this argument with great emphasis, replied CLEANTHES. You seem not sensible how easy it is to answer it. Even in common life, if I assign a cause for any event, is it any objection, Philo, that I cannot assign the cause of that cause, and answer every new question which may incessantly be started? And what philosophers could possibly submit to so rigid a rule, philosophers who confess ultimate causes to be totally unknown, and are sensible that the most refined principles into which they trace the phenomena are still to them as inexplicable as these phenomena themselves are to the vulgar? The order and arrangement of nature, the curious adjustment of final causes, the plain use and intention of every part and organ, all these bespeak in the clearest language an intelligent cause or author. The heavens and the earth join in the same testimony; the whole chorus of nature raises one hymn to the praises of its Creator. You alone, or almost alone, disturb this general harmony. You start abstruse doubts, cavils, and objections; you ask me what is the cause of this cause? I know not, I care not, that concerns not me. I have found a Deity, and here I stop my inquiry. Let those go further who are wiser or more enterprising.

I pretend to be neither, replied PHILO; and for that very reason I should never, perhaps, have attempted to go so far, especially when I am sensible that I must at last be contented to sit down with the same answer which, without further trouble, might have satisfied me from the beginning. If I am still to remain in utter ignorance of causes and can absolutely give an explication of nothing, I shall never esteem it any advantage to shove off for a moment a difficulty which you acknowledge must immediately, in its full force, recur upon me. Naturalists indeed very justly explain particular effects by more general causes though these general causes themselves should remain in the end totally inexplicable, but they never surely thought it satisfactory to explain a particular effect by a particular cause which was no more to be accounted for than the effect itself. An ideal system, arranged of itself, without a precedent design, is not a whit more explicable than a material one which attains its order in a like manner; nor is there any more difficulty in the latter supposition than in the former.

THE ARGUMENT DOES NOT ESTABLISH THE EXISTENCE OF AN INFINITE DEITY

But to show you still more inconveniences, continued PHILO, in your anthropomorphism, please to take a new survey of your principles. *Like effects prove like causes.* This is the experimental argument; and this, you say too, is the sole theological argument. Now it is certain that the liker the effects are which are seen and the liker the causes which are inferred, the stronger is the argument. Every departure on either side diminishes the probability and renders the experiment less conclusive. You cannot doubt of the principle; neither ought you to reject its consequences.

Now, Cleanthes, said PHILO, with an air of alacrity and triumph, mark the consequences. *First,* by this method of reasoning you renounce all claim to infinity in any of the attributes of the Deity. For as the cause ought only to be proportioned to the effect, and the effect, so far as it falls under our cognizance, is not infinite, what pretensions have we, upon your suppositions, to ascribe that attribute to the divine Being? You will still insist that, by removing him so much from all similarity to human creatures, we give in to the most arbitrary hypothesis, and at the same time weaken all proofs of his existence.

Secondly, you have no reason, on your theory, for ascribing perfection to the Deity, even in his finite capacity, or for supposing him free from every error, mistake, or incoherence in his undertakings. There are many inexplicable difficulties in the works of nature which, if we allow a perfect author to be proved *a priori,* are easily solved, and become only seeming difficulties from the narrow capacity of man, who cannot trace infinite relations. But according to your method of reasoning, these difficulties become all real, and perhaps will be insisted on as new instances of likeness to human art and contrivance. At least you must acknowledge that it is impossible for us to tell, from our limited views, whether this system contains any great faults or deserves any considerable praise if compared to other possible and even real systems. Could a peasant, if the *Aeneid* were read to him, pronounce that poem to be absolutely faultless, or even assign to it its proper rank among the productions of human wit, he who had never seen any other production?

But were this world ever so perfect a production, it must still remain uncertain whether all the excellences of the work can justly be ascribed to the workman. If we survey a ship, what an exalted idea must we form of the ingenuity of the carpenter who framed so complicated, useful, and beautiful a machine? And what surprise must we feel when we find him a stupid mechanic who imitated others, and copied an art which, through a long succession of ages, after multiplied trials, mistakes, corrections, deliberations, and controversies, had been gradually improving? Many worlds might have been botched and bungled, throughout an eternity, ere this system was struck out; much labor lost, many fruitless trials made, and a slow but continued improvement carried on during infinite ages in the art of world-making. In such subjects, who can determine where the truth, nay, who can conjecture where the probability lies, amidst a great number of hypotheses which may be proposed, and a still greater which may be imagined?

And what shadow of an argument, continued PHILO, can you produce from your hypothesis to prove the unity of the Deity? A great number of men join in building a house or ship, in rearing a city, in framing a commonwealth; why may not several deities combine in contriving and framing a world? This is only so much greater similarity to human affairs. By sharing the work among several, we may so much further limit the attributes of each, and get rid of that extensive power and knowledge which must be supposed in one deity and which, according to you, can only serve to weaken the proof of his existence. And if such foolish, such vicious creatures as man can yet often unite in framing and executing one plan, how much more those deities or demons, whom we may suppose several degrees more perfect?

To multiply causes without necessity is indeed contrary to true philosophy, but this principle applies not to the present case. Were one deity antecedently proved by your theory, who were possessed of every attribute requisite to the production of the universe, it would be needless, I own (though not absurd), to suppose any other deity existent. But while it is still a question whether all these attributes are united in one subject or dispersed among several independent beings, by what phenomena in nature can we pretend to decide the controversy? Where we see a body raised in a scale, we are sure that there is in the opposite scale, however concealed from sight, some counterpoising weight equal to it; but it is still allowed to doubt whether that weight be an aggregate of several distinct bodies or one uniform united mass. And if the weight requisite very much exceeds anything which we have ever seen conjoined in any single body, the former supposition becomes still more probable and natural. An intelligent being of such vast power and capacity as is necessary to produce the universe, or, to speak in the language of ancient philosophy, so prodigious an animal, exceeds all analogy and even comprehension.

But further, Cleanthes, men are mortal, and renew their species by generation, and this is common to all living creatures. The two great sexes of male and female, says Milton, animate the world. Why must this circumstance, so universal, so essential, be excluded from those numerous and limited deities? Behold, then, the theogeny of ancient times brought back upon us.

And why not become a perfect anthropomorphite? Why not assert the deity or deities to be corporeal, and to have eyes, a nose, mouth, ears, etc.? Epicurus maintained that no man had ever seen reason but in a human figure, therefore the gods must have a human figure. And this argument, which is deservedly so much ridiculed by Cicero, becomes, according to you, solid and philosophical.

In a word, Cleanthes, a man who follows your hypothesis is able, perhaps, to assert or conjecture that the universe sometime arose from something like design, but beyond that position he cannot ascertain one single circumstance, and is left afterwards to fix every point of his theology by the utmost license of fancy and hypothesis. This world, for aught he knows, is very faulty and imperfect, compared to a superior standard, and was only the first rude essay of some infant deity who afterwards abandoned it, ashamed of his lame performance. It is the work only of some dependent, inferior deity, and is the object of derision to his superiors. It is the production of old age and dotage in some superannuated deity, and ever since his death has run on at adventures, from the first impulse and active force which it received from him. You justly give signs of horror, Demea, at these strange suppositions, but these, and a thousand more of the same kind, are Cleanthes' suppositions, not mine. From the moment the attributes of the Deity are supposed finite, all these have place. And I cannot, for my part, think that so wild and unsettled a system of theology is, in any respect, preferable to none at all.

These suppositions I absolutely disown, cried CLEANTHES; they strike me, however, with no horror, especially when proposed in that rambling way in which they drop from you. On the contrary, they give me pleasure when I see that, by the utmost indulgence of your imagination, you never get rid of the hypothesis of design in the universe, but are obliged at every turn to have recourse to it. To this concession I adhere steadily, and this I regard as a sufficient foundation for religion.

.   .   .

It must be a slight fabric indeed, said DEMEA, which can be erected on so tottering a foundation. While we are uncertain whether there is one deity or many, whether the deity or deities to whom we owe our existence be perfect or imperfect, subordinate or supreme, dead or alive, what trust or confidence can we repose in them? What devotion or worship address to them? What veneration or obedience pay them? To all the purposes of life the theory of religion becomes altogether useless, and even with regard to speculative consequences its uncertainty, according to you, must render it totally precarious and unsatisfactory.

OTHER EXPLANATIONS OF THE EXISTENCE OF THE UNIVERSE

To render it still more unsatisfactory, said PHILO, there occurs to me another hypothesis which must acquire an air of probability from the method of reasoning so much insisted on by Cleanthes. That like effects arise from like causes: this principle he supposes the foundation of all religion. But there is another principle of the same kind, no less certain and derived from the same source of experience, that where several known circumstances are observed to be similar, the unknown will also be found similar. Thus, if we see the limbs of a human body, we conclude that it is also attended with a human head, though hid from us. Thus, if we see, through a chink in a wall, a small part of the sun, we conclude that were the wall removed we should see the whole body. In short, this method of reasoning is so obvious and familiar that no scruple can ever be made with regard to its solidity.

Now if we survey the universe, so far as it falls under our knowledge, it bears a great resemblance to an animal or organized body, and seems actuated with a like principle of life and motion. A continual circulation of matter in it produces no disorder, a continual waste in every part is incessantly repaired, the closest sympathy is perceived throughout the entire system, and each part or member, in performing its proper offices, operates both to its own preservation and to that of the whole. The world therefore, I infer, is an animal, and the Deity is the *soul* of the world, actuating it, and actuated by it.

You have too much learning, Cleanthes, to be at all surprised at this opinion, which, you know, was maintained by almost all the theists of antiquity, and chiefly prevails in their discourses and reasonings. For though sometimes the ancient philosophers reason from final causes, as if they thought the world the workmanship of God, yet it appears rather their favorite notion to consider it as his body, whose organization renders it subservient to him. And it must be confessed that, as the universe resembles more a human body than it does the works of human art and contrivance, if our limited analogy could ever, with any propriety, be extended to the whole of nature, the inference seems juster in favor of the ancient than the modern theory.

There are many other advantages, too, in the former theory which recommended it to the ancient theologians. Nothing more repugnant to all their notions, because nothing more repugnant to common experience, than mind without body, a mere spiritual substance which fell not under their senses nor comprehension, and of which they had not observed one single instance throughout all nature. Mind and body they knew because they felt both; an order, arrangement, organization, or internal machinery in both they likewise knew, after the same manner, and it could not but seem reasonable to transfer this experience to the universe, and to suppose the divine mind and body to be also coeval and to have, both of them, order and arrangement naturally inherent in them and inseparable from them.

. . .

But here, continued PHILO, in examining the ancient system of the soul of the world, there strikes me, all of a sudden, a new idea which, if just, must go near to subvert all your reasoning, and destroy even your first inferences on which you repose such confidence. If the universe bears a greater likeness to animal bodies and to vegetables than to the works of human art, it is more probable that its cause resembles the cause of the former than that of the latter, and its origin ought rather to be ascribed to generation or vegetation than to reason or design. Your conclusion, even according to your own principles, is therefore lame and defective.

Pray open up this argument a little further, said DEMEA, for I do not rightly apprehend it in that concise manner in which you have expressed it.

Our friend Cleanthes, replied PHILO, as you have heard, asserts that since no question of fact can be proved otherwise than by experience, the existence of a Deity admits not of proof from any other medium. The world, says he, resembles the works of human contrivance; therefore its cause must also resemble that of the other. Here we may remark that the operation of one very small part of nature, to wit, man, upon another very small part, to wit, that inanimate matter lying within his reach, is the rule by which Cleanthes judges of the origin of the whole; and he measures objects, so widely disproportioned by the same individual standard. But to waive all objections drawn from this topic, I affirm that there are other parts of the universe (besides the machines of human invention) which bear still a greater resemblance to the fabric of the world, and which therefore afford a better conjecture concerning the universal origin of this system. These parts are animals and vegetables. The world plainly resembles more an animal or a vegetable than it does a watch or a knitting-loom. Its cause, therefore, it is more probable, resembles the cause of the former. The cause of the former is generation or vegetation. The cause, therefore, of the world we may infer to be something similar or analogous to generation or vegetation.

But how is it conceivable, said DEMEA, that the world can arise from anything similar to vegetation or generation?

Very easily, replied PHILO. In like manner as a tree sheds its seed into the neighboring fields and produces other trees, so the great vegetable, the world, or this planetary system, produces within itself certain seeds which, being scattered into the surrounding chaos, vegetate into new worlds. A comet, for instance, is the seed of a world, and after it has been fully ripened by passing from sun to sun and star to star, it is at last tossed into the unformed elements which everywhere surround this universe, and immediately sprouts up into a new system.

Or if, for the sake of variety (for I see no other advantage), we should suppose this world to be an animal, a comet is the egg of this animal, and in like manner as an ostrich lays its egg in the sand, which, without further care, hatches the egg and produces a new animal, so . . . I understand you, says DEMEA. But what wild, arbitrary suppositions are these? What *data* have you for such extraordinary conclusions? And is the slight, imaginary resemblance of the world to a vegetable or an animal sufficient to establish the same inference with regard to both? Objects which are in general so widely different — ought they to be a standard for each other?

Right, cries PHILO. This is the topic on which I have all along insisted.

I have still asserted that we have no *data* to establish any system of cosmogony. Our experience, so imperfect in itself and so limited both in extent and duration, can afford us no probable conjecture concerning the whole of things. But if we must needs fix on some hypothesis, by what rule, pray, ought we to determine our choice? Is there any other rule that the greater similarity of the objects compared? And does not a plant or an animal, which springs from vegetation or generation, bear a stronger resemblance to the world than does any artificial machine, which arises from reason and design?

. . .

THE FIRST-CAUSE ARGUMENT

But if so many difficulties attend the argument *a posteriori,* said Demea, had we not better adhere to that simple and sublime argument *a priori* which, by offering to us infallible demonstration, cuts off at once all doubt and difficulty? By this argument, too, we may prove the *infinity* of the divine attributes, which, I am afraid, can never be ascertained with certainty from any other topic. For how can an effect which either is finite or, for aught we know, may be so, how can such an effect, I say, prove an infinite cause? The unity too of the Divine Nature it is very difficult if not absolutely impossible to deduce merely from contemplating the works of nature; nor will the uniformity alone of the plan, even were it allowed, give us any assurance of that attribute. Whereas the argument *a priori* . . .

You seem to reason, Demea, interposed CLEANTHES, as if those advantages and conveniences in the abstract argument were full proofs of its solidity. But it is first proper, in my opinion, to determine what argument of this nature you choose to insist on; and we shall afterwards, from itself better than from its *useful* consequences, endeavor to determine what value we ought to put upon it.

The argument, replied DEMEA, which I would insist on is the common one. Whatever exists must have a cause or reason of its existence, it being absolutely impossible for anything to produce itself or be the cause of its own existence. In mounting up, therefore, from effects to causes, we must either go on in tracing an infinite succession without any ultimate cause at all, or must at last have recourse to some ultimate cause that is *necessarily* existent. Now that the first supposition is absurd may be thus proved. In the infinite chain or succession of causes and effects, each single effect is determined to exist by the power and efficacy of that cause which immediately preceded; but the whole eternal chain or succession, taken together, is not determined or caused by anything; and yet it is evident that it requires a cause or reason, as much as any particular object which begins to exist in time. The question is still reasonable, why this particular succession of causes existed from eternity, and not any other succession or no succession at all. If there be no necessarily existent being, any supposition which can be formed is equally possible; nor is there any more absurdity in nothing's having existed from eternity than there is in that succession of causes which constitutes the universe. What was it, then, which determined something to exist rather than nothing, and bestowed being on a particular possibility, exclusive of the rest? *External causes* there are supposed to be none. *Chance* is a word without a meaning. Was it *nothing*? But that can never produce anything. We must, therefore, have recourse to a necessarily existent Being, who carries the *reason* of his existence in himself, and who cannot be supposed not to exist without an express contradiction. There is consequently such a Being; that is, there is a Deity.

I shall not leave it to Philo, said CLEANTHES (though I know that starting objections is his chief delight), to point out the weakness of this metaphysical reasoning. It seems to me so obviously ill-grounded, and at the same time of so little consequence to the cause of true piety and religion, that I shall myself venture to show the fallacy of it.

I shall begin with observing that there is an evident absurdity in pretending to demonstrate a matter of fact, or to prove it by any arguments *a priori*. Nothing is demonstrable unless the contrary implies a contradiction. Nothing that is distinctly conceivable implies a contradiction. Whatever we conceive as existent, we can also conceive as nonexistent. There is no being, therefore, whose nonexistence implies a contradiction. Consequently there is no being whose existence is demonstrable. I propose this argument as entirely decisive, and am willing to rest the whole controversy upon it.

It is pretended that the Deity is a necessarily existent being; and this necessity of his existence is attempted to be explained by asserting that if we knew his whole essence or nature we should perceive it to be as impossible for him not to exist as for twice two not to be four. But it is evident that this can never happen, while our faculties remain the same as at present. It will still be possible for us, at any time, to conceive the nonexistence of what we formerly conceived to exist; nor can the mind ever lie under a necessity of supposing any object to remain always in being, in the same manner as we lie under a necessity of always conceiving twice two to be four. The words, therefore, *necessary existence,* have no meaning, or, which is the same thing, none that is consistent.

But further, why may not the material universe be the necessarily existent Being, according to this pretended explication of necessity? We dare not affirm that we know all the qualities of matter; and for aught we can determine, it may contain some qualities which, were they known, would make its nonexistence appear as great a contradiction as that twice two is five. I find only one argument employed to prove that the material world is not the necessarily existent Being; and this argument is derived from the contingency both of the matter and the form of the world. "Any particle of matter," it is said,[1] "may be *conceived* to be annihilated, and any form may be *conceived* to be altered. Such an annihilation or alteration, therefore, is not

---

[1] Dr. Clarke.

impossible." But it seems a great partiality not to perceive that the same argument extends equally to the Deity, so far as we have any conception of him, and that the mind can at least imagine him to be nonexistent or his attributes to be altered. It must be some unknown, inconceivable qualities which can make his nonexistence appear impossible or his attributes unalterable; and no reason can be assigned why these qualities may not belong to matter. As they are altogether unknown and inconceivable, they can never be proved incompatible with it.

Add to this that in tracing an eternal succession of objects it seems absurd to inquire for a general cause or first author. How can anything that exists from eternity have a cause, since that relation implies a priority in time and a beginning of existence?

In such a chain too, or succession of objects, each part is caused by that which preceded it, and causes that which succeeds it. Where then is the difficulty? But the *whole,* you say, wants a cause. I answer that the uniting of these parts into a whole, like the uniting of several distinct counties into one kingdom, or several distinct members into one body, is performed merely by an arbitrary act of the mind, and has no influence on the nature of things. Did I show you the particular causes of each individual in a collection of twenty particles of matter, I should think it very unreasonable should you afterwards ask me what was the cause of the whole twenty. This is sufficiently explained in explaining the cause of the parts.

Though the reasonings which you have urged, Cleanthes, may well excuse me, said PHILO, from starting any further difficulties, yet I cannot forbear insisting still upon another topic. It is observed by arithmeticians that the products of 9 compose always either 9 or some lesser product of 9 if you add together all the characters of which any of the former products is composed. Thus, of 18, 27, 36, which are products of 9, you make 9 by adding 1 to 8, 2 to 7, 3 to 6. Thus, 369 is a product also of 9; and if you add 3, 6, and 9, you make 18, a lesser product of 9.[2] To a superficial observer so wonderful a regularity may be admired as the effect either of chance or design; but a skillful algebraist immediately concludes it to be the work of necessity, and demonstrates that it must forever result from the nature of these numbers. Is it not probable, I ask, that the whole economy of the universe is conducted by a like necessity, though no human algebra can furnish a key which solves the difficulty? And instead of admiring the order of natural beings, may it not happen that, could we penetrate into the intimate nature of bodies, we should clearly see why it was absolutely impossible they could ever admit of any other disposition? So dangerous is it to introduce this idea of necessity into the present question! And so naturally does it afford an inference directly opposite to the religious hypothesis!

But dropping all these abstractions, continued PHILO, and confining ourselves to more familiar topics, I shall venture to add an observation, that the

[2] *Republique des Lettres,* Aug. 1685.

argument *a priori* has seldom been found very convincing, except to people of a metaphysical head who have accustomed themselves to abstract reasoning, and who, finding from mathematics that the understanding frequently leads to truth through obscurity and contrary to first appearances, have transferred the same habit of thinking to subjects where it ought not to have place. Other people, even of good sense and the best inclined to religion, feel always some deficiency in such arguments, though they are not perhaps able to explain distinctly where it lies. A certain proof that men ever did and ever will derive their religion from other sources than from this species of reasoning.

4

A MODERN
RESTATEMENT
OF THE ARGUMENT
FROM DESIGN

A. E. Taylor

A. E. Taylor (1869-1945) was Professor of Moral Philosophy at the University of Edinburgh, and was known both as an interpreter of Plato and as an original philosopher.

THE PHYSICAL REALM DOES NOT ESTABLISH
THE EXISTENCE OF GOD

Confining ourselves, then, to that aspect of real "fact" (though carefully remembering that this aspect is not the whole of any real concrete fact) of which natural science can take account, we have to ask whether it is true that, considered exclusively in this aspect, the facts either give definite reasons for denying God's existence, or at any rate afford no reason for asserting it. We may take it, I think, as unquestioned for the purpose of our argument that whatever else the existence of God means, it means *at least* that the facts which make up the history of the natural world are connected by an underlying purpose, and that purpose one which a clear and upright intelligence, fully informed of its nature, would recognize and welcome as morally good. No one can worship and trust a mere blind tendency or trend with no directing purpose, and no one can worship a being whose purposes, however ingenious, he has to condemn as morally evil or frivolous; and where there is no trust and worship, it is mere abuse of language to talk of belief in God. Do the facts of the world-order, then, so far as the sciences take them into account, disclose, or even suggest, the presence of a directing purpose, and that purpose a morally good one throughout the course of nature? Does nature exhibit recognizable traces of what Paley called "prospective contrivance"?

If we are to answer the question satisfactorily, we need to be quite clear as to what we mean to include in the word "science." Are we thinking ex-

From Section IV of *Does God Exist?* (1947), reprinted by permission of the publishers, Macmillan & Co., Ltd. and Macmillan Co. of Canada, Ltd. Subheadings added by the editors.

clusively of the sciences which extend to the inorganic as well as to the organic "world," or are we taking the study of "*animated* nature" also into account? When we say "science" do we mean exclusively physics and chemistry, or perhaps physics only, or are we including biology and psychology? This is not exactly the same as the question which it so closely resembles, whether the laws of biology and psychology are or are not simply applications of more general chemical and physical laws to an exceptionally complex set of facts. Even if we hold that this is so, and that, in the last resort, there are no "laws of nature" except those of chemistry and physics, or perhaps those of physics alone, it might still be the case that if there is in nature an underlying purpose and a good one, the evidence of its presence only becomes visible to *us* when we consider the course of "animated" nature; in inanimate nature the purpose might be there and yet we might be unable to detect it, just as a series of markings on a stone may really be an inscription in some unfamiliar language, and yet we may be unable to distinguish the scratches from mere weather-markings, if they are very few and simple. It is important, therefore, to remember that when we speak of the facts of nature as bearing witness, or failing to bear witness, to the existence of nature's God, we *ought* to mean the facts of nature as a whole, and that the facts of nature as a whole include not only those disclosed to us in physics and chemistry, but all that biology has to tell us of the facts about the life-history of plant and animal species, and psychology about those of conscious knowing, willing and feeling. The question is what sort of order in nature is presupposed by *all* these facts taken together.

When we try in this way to take a synoptic view of all the facts, we are forced, I think, to admit that, taken by themselves, those which can be detected in the inorganic realm do not go very far to provide the theist with any confirmation of his belief. Taken by themselves, the laws of physics and chemistry reveal only one type of order in the natural world, a *causal* order. The sciences would become impossible if we could not presume that nature is a *causal* order, that is, that there are definite laws of sequence pervading it, such that a determinate set of conditions in the present demand a determinate continuation in the future, "natural agents" *tend* to behave in definite and ascertainable ways. If we could be spectators of a system of "natural agents" in which there was no trace of life or sentience, as far as I can see, this *causal* order is the only kind of order the appearances would suggest, and all that we could aspire to as an "explanation" of them. In our account of such a system we should have to accept it as an ultimate fact, behind which we could not go, that a given process *tends* to continue itself in a definite way, but why this should be so would be a question to which the apparent facts would suggest no answer; we could not produce even a faint presumption that the continuation to which a process tends is *intended* by anyone or anything. For all that we could say, such an insentient and lifeless world might have *no* purpose behind it: or if it did occur to us, as it very probably would, that the purposelessness was only apparent, the source of the suggestion would not be anything in the appearances presented by such a "world" itself; it would be in our own familiarity with purposes and intentions as an important feature of the very different "world" in which we live and move and have *our* being. A world without sentience and life *might* quite well be a world where there was no directing intelligence or controlling purposes. And if all we knew about the actual world were only what we can learn in the physical or chemical laboratory, so far as I can see, atheism might conceivably be true.

. . .

The Adaptation in the Organic Realm Presupposes a Designer

When we turn to the facts about living organisms which are the subject-matter of the biological sciences, we find ourselves at once confronted with what, on the face of it, looks to be a further type of order in nature, *teleological* order. The way in which a process shall take place appears to be determined not simply by reference to the earlier stages of natural process of which it is the continuation, but even more by reference to the later and still future results which are to come out of the present. (Hence the name *teleological* order, from the Greek *telos, end,* last phase.)

It is not that the processes taking place in living organisms appear in any way to violate the causal laws of physics. On the contrary, it seems that, so far as can be ascertained, the behaviour of the components of the living organism conforms throughout to these laws. Thus transformations of energy taking place within the organism, like similar transformations in the realm of the inorganic, appear to conform strictly to the principle of Conservation of Energy; there is an increase or decrease of energy of a specific kind only at the cost of a proportional decrease or increase somewhere of energy of another kind. But the important point is this. There are indefinitely numerous ways in which a natural process can be continued in strict conformity with the principle of Conservation, just as there is a great (though not an indefinite) variety of ways in which a move may be made at chess without violating any of the rules of the game. But the healthy organism in normal conditions continues the process by responding to the present situation with just that continuation which is valuable as preserving the individual organism or making for the continuance of the species, just as the good chess-player meets his opponent's move by making just that reply out of the many open to him which is best adapted to achieve a result which still lies in the future, the winning of the game. Examples of this thorough-going adaptation of the behaviour of the living organism to a state of things which is still future are so common and obvious that it may be enough to mention only one or two. "Wherever there is need for an extra supply of oxygen, as, for instance, during muscular exertion, the membrane assumes an active rôle, and pushes oxygen inwards without regard to the mechanical laws of diffusion."[1] Here it is a

---

[1] J. S. Haldane quoted in Stout, *Mind and Matter,* p. 107.

need which the individual organism will experience in the immediate future which appears to determine just which of many mechanically equally possible responses shall be adopted. Numerous insects "instinctively" deposit their eggs on a particular kind of leaf which will supply suitable nourishment for the coming generation of grubs, though the insects themselves will die before the eggs are hatched. The principles of physics would be equally respected if any other kind of leaf evoked the same expenditure of energy in egg-depositing, but in fact it is evoked only by the special kind of leaf which will form the appropriate nourishment of creatures whom the egg-depositing insect will never live to see. Hence the adaptation is to a remoter future and the advantage secured is to the benefit of the still unborn offspring, not of the egg-depositing insect. The life of organic nature is pervaded throughout by "prospective adaptations" of this kind, and the problem is how to account for this patent fact.

It is the same, of course, with the familiar everyday life of human beings. But here we know, or think we know, the explanation of the fact. So far as the mechanical laws involved in its working are concerned, it is all one to my gramophone whether it plays Palestrina or plays ragtime. If it plays Palestrina, that is because *I* have selected the record, and I have selected that record *prospectively* because I, or someone else whom I am wishing to entertain, would rather have that form of entertainment. If we would rather have ragtime, I should have put on a different record, and the mechanism of the instrument would equally readily have responded. The reason why it actually gives a Palestrina response is that this was the one I looked for and wanted. The machine does not give me Palestrina because it is so built that it can only do that one thing, as Lewis Carroll's baker could only bake bride-cake. Similarly, when I find that the egg-laying of a particular moth only happens on the leaves of the white poplar, I may properly ask, is this because something or someone wants the eggs laid on the particular kind of leaf which will be suitable food for the future grubs, or because the creature's egg-laying machinery happens to be so built that it can only work in that way? Is it just a coincidence that it is also the one way by which the grubs will be ensured of nourishment?

Or we may take a different illustration which sets our point in fuller relief. Consider the behaviour of a cat watching a mouse-hole, or stalking a small bird. Here we have an elaborate and highly complicated series of movements of the animal's whole body connected by the way in which the whole succession is adapted to a particular future event, the capture of the prey. It is this event yet to come which gives the whole series its distinctive character. As far as the working of the machinery which I call the cat's body is concerned, there might as well have been any one of a hundred other series of movements and arrests of movement which would have been in equal conformity with all the laws of physics, only none of these would have been equally successful in leading up to the capture. What has determined the selection of this particular series as against all the other possibilities is that all through the cat's movements have been adapted to the movements of the mouse or the bird, and not only to those which the mouse or bird has already made, but to those which it will make next, exactly as a good chess-player's moves are determined not only by the moves his opponent has made, but to those which he will yet have to make. Can we completely account for the prospective attention which guides the whole course of the animal's behaviour by reference to the physical laws which are exemplified by every event in nature, organic and inorganic alike? This is the question which it is, I think, safe to say that all the most eminent psychologists — and the question is one for an expert in psychology, not for a chemist or a physicist, or even a biologist as such — are agreed to answer with, NO.

The laws of physics and chemistry — let me repeat again — as they can be discovered alike in the processes of the inorganic and of the organic realm do not provide any complete account of the characteristic behaviour of living creatures. It is not that anyone suggests that the processes going on in the living organism fail to conform to the various laws of physics, that of the Conservation of Energy and the rest: for all we know, these laws may be exactly exemplified in all these processes. The point is that there is a great outstanding characteristic of vital processes which the completest statement of the laws of physics leaves unaccounted for. As Whitehead has said, the electrons within the living organism, no doubt, run as "blindly" as the electrons in a lump of inorganic matter, but they do not run in the same way.[2] There are countless ways in which they might run, all of them in accord with the known laws of physics, but the actual way in which they do tend to run is always one which is "prospectively" adapted to the preservation of the individual organism or the species to which it belongs. While the organism is in normal health the tendency is actually successful; even in disease it persists; the organism reacts against the disorder by efforts to "right itself," or if they fail, it dies. But so far as the laws of physics alone are concerned, processes of "prospective" *misadaptation* stand on the same footing with, and should be just as probable as, those of prospective adaptation. This is inevitably so, for the simple reason that in the very formulation of a law of physics it is always assumed that the course of events in the future, which while it is still future is, of course, inaccessible to our observation and measurement, is determined entirely by reference to what has already occurred, been observed and measured. To introduce any reference to the still unborn future as playing a part in determining the present would be to introduce reference to a "factor" which, in the nature of the case, has not been, and could not have been, subjected to measurement. And this would be fatal to the whole purpose of a physical enquiry, the discovery of formulae which will permit us to calculate the as yet unobserved from measurements already made. For

2 *Science and the Modern World*, p. 112 ff.

the purpose of such an enquiry we both necessarily and legitimately ignore the possibility of the prospective adaptation of the present event to an "end" still in the future.

Yet such prospective adaptation is the most palpable and obvious character of the processes of organic life, and it has to be accounted for somehow. To put the point quite crudely: For one way in which the electrons which make up the organism can "blindly run" so as to secure this prospective adaptation, there are thousands of alternative ways, all alike conforming to the known laws of physics, in which they might run so as not to secure it. Hence if the laws of physics were a complete account of the conditions determining the course of natural processes, it would be antecedently immensely improbable that organisms should come into existence, or that, if by any accident they arose, they should persist. But it is the actual fact that they have arisen and display a remarkable power of persisting by adjusting themselves to their "environment." Unless we are to take refuge in a paradox like Tertullian's *certum est quia absurdum,* we can only draw the inference that the conditions taken into account in physics are not the only conditions which determine the course of processes within the living organism; there must be some further condition which removes what would otherwise be the indefinitely high improbability of the occurrence of that prospective adaptation which we see to be the fact in the realm of the organic.

Now there is just one known condition which, if we suppose it to be present, would remove this improbability, and that is the presence of *mind* as somehow determining the course of events. The one case in which the existence of mind as a fact is directly and immediately disclosed to us is our own, and nothing is clearer than that, in our own case, the distinctive character of mind is that, by its very nature, it is forward-reaching and shows its presence by the devising of adaptations to situations not yet present, but anticipated. It would, for example, be conclusive evidence that a man of advanced years had not sunk into a condition of complete dementia to show that he performs acts which are not merely responses to actual stimulus, and so adaptations to the present, but presuppose anticipation of situations which have not yet arisen and are preparatory adaptations to these anticipated situations. However enfeebled an old man's intellectual powers might be, no judge and jury would decide that his mind was completely "in abeyance," if it were proved that he had anticipated his own death and so expressed the wish to make a prospective disposition of his property. Similarly in a criminal case, if the defence set up were that the perpetrator of some deed were imbecile and incapable of understanding the "character of his action," the worth of the plea would depend on the court's judgment on the question whether the accused could anticipate what would come out of what he was doing. A man who places an obstacle on the road is "capable of understanding" the character of his action if he can *foresee* what may happen to a car driving along the road, "incapable" if he cannot. And speaking generally, we all in everyday life judge of a man's intelligence by the extent to which what he does and avoids doing is determined by purpose and intention, prospective adaptation to future situations before they arise. The more completely a man is emancipated from this determination by reference to the future, the more he lives simply in the present, the more "sub-human" and merely "animal" do we pronounce his way of living.

·   ·   ·

THE DARWINIAN THEORY OF EVOLUTION AS AN ALTERNATE EXPLANATION

Let us consider for a moment the general character of the counter-argument which might be produced in favour of what I have called the theory of coincidence. And to avoid underrating its strength, let us take the supposition which is most favourable to it that of the correctness of a rigidly "Darwinian" doctrine of the "origin of species," as though it were unquestionable, though, in point of fact, Darwin was not himself a thorough-going "Darwinian," and, so far as a layman can gather, the biologists of the present day are still less so. That is, we will assume for the purpose of discussion that "natural selection" is a complete account of the "origin of species." We are to think of organisms as perpetuating themselves by the repeated reproduction of the same pattern, subject only to minute individual variations due to conditions too intricate and complex for specification. These variations we are to think of as taking place in all sorts of directions, some of them being favourable to the organism's chance of maintaining itself in being and reproducing its life, some unfavourable, some neutral, and the "laws of nature" are to be impartial as between these three types of variation. But variations in any of these directions, once introduced, are to perpetuate themselves, so that there is the possibility that in the course of a great number of generations there may be an accumulation of many minute variations in the direction of better adaptation to the environment sufficient to constitute a recognizably distinct species. So much being assumed, we shall then reason thus.

Every individual variation which happens to be in the direction of better adaptation to its environment, will, of course, have an improved, if only a minutely improved, chance of keeping itself alive and leaving behind it descendants which inherit its advantages. An accumulation of such favourable variations sufficient to constitute a new species will thus have a very great advantage in the competition for survival, with the result that less well-adapted competitors will, in the end, fail to maintain themselves in being, and will vanish from the world. In the end, then, we shall be left with a number of distinct surviving species which happen to be specially well fitted to their particular environment. It will look as though this adaptation were the result of intelligent design, but the appearance will be delusive. What has really occurred is only that the slow pressure of a relatively stable environment has eliminated all types but those which happen to be specially well suited to itself. (The process was called by Darwin natural *selection*, but we must, of course, carefully remember that word *selection*, though convenient, is clogged with misleading associations. There has been no *selecting*, no picking out of any individuals or types to survive, but only the gradual dying-off of those least able to adjust themselves to their situation, and this process of dying-off requires no directing intelligence for its explanation; the habitat makes its inhabitants by the simple process of killing off anyone who does not "fit in." We may call this the "survival of the fittest," but if we do so we must be careful to remember that the "fittest" do not mean the most highly gifted, the most intelligent, the most virtuous, or those who, by whatever standard of valuation we please to assume, are in some way "better" than their neighbours and rivals, but simply those who "fit in" to the habitat in question. The fittest in some environments may be the most versatile, or intelligent, or morally deserving, but in others they may equally well be the most hide-bound, the stupidest or the most knavish. "It is the fittest to survive who survive" amounts in fact to little more than the tautology that in the long run those who have the best chances of hanging-on in a specified environment are those who do hang on.)

It is obvious that when a theory of this kind is put forward as explaining away all appearance of "design" in nature some large assumptions are being made about the actual facts and that these assumptions might conceivably be called in question. Is it a fact that individual variations from type occur impartially in every direction, or does variation exhibit a preponderant trend in some definite direction (in which case we should have at least a *prima facie* suggestion of purposive determination by an end)? And again, if the first view is the true one, is it by slow accumulation of such "random" minute variations that new species originate, or do they, as has been held more recently by some, come into being by sudden and considerable large-scale "mutations"? These are questions of fact which must be settled before the "Darwinian" theory can be regarded as established, and the facts are of a kind on which it is for the biological expert and for no one else to pronounce. It would be presumptuous for a layman in biology to assert an opinion of his own about them. But without going into any disputable questions of fact, we can see, even though we may not be biological experts at all, that the whole theory is strictly what it originally professed to be, a theory about the way in which new species of organisms come into being. It is not a theory of the *origin* of organisms or of life; it takes organisms as known to be already in existence and professes only to explain how they are modified by the action of their environment upon them. It presupposes as already existing the antithesis between the living organism and the environment upon which and against which it maintains, or fails to maintain, itself. And, as we have already contended, purposiveness, determination of the present by reference to an end which is still in the future, is there wherever there is a living organism. The strictest "neo-Darwinism" thus offers us no explanation of the appearance of "prospective contrivance" in nature; on the contrary, it consciously or unconsciously assumes its reality, and therefore leaves our preceding argument unaffected. The suggestion so powerfully borne in upon the unsophisticated mind by a general survey of nature, that the rise and persistence of living organisms implies intelligent pre-adaptation of the lifeless background to be an "environment" for them is at least not weakened, it may be is strengthened, by increasing knowledge of the details of the adaptation.

. . .

Misunderstandings of the Argument from Design

. . . Thus the thought which is at the basis of the familiar "argument from design" will be thoroughly justified, and we shall see that Kant was right when he said in his *Critique of Pure Reason,* just before proceeding to a devastating attack upon the misuse of the argument in popular theology, that it "deserves never to be spoken of without reverence," and that it would be "utterly in vain to attempt to lessen its prestige."

What has told against this "prestige" in the judgment of more hasty thinkers than Kant has, in fact, been confusion between the substance of the "argument" and certain unjustifiable assumptions which are really unessential to it but have often been conjoined with it by well-meaning but inconsiderate divines and philosophers in a hurry to make out the case for Theism. It has too often been assumed that if the course of events is really directed by a purposive intelligence, the purpose of that intelligence must lie in some single result to be attained at the end of the world's history and to which all that precedes is a mere "means," as the scaffolding is a mere means to the erection of a house. There must be some one "far-off divine event" to which "the whole creation moves." To make this assumption is to take it for granted that the one typical example of the working of intelligence is to be seen in the crafts and industries, where it is true that the whole elaborate process of construction has no worth or interest except as a means to the existence of the manufactured article. But the making of houses, or ships, or (to take Paley's famous example) watches is not the only, and I think we may say not the supreme, example of constructive intelligence. Intelligence is also shown, and as most of us would perhaps say, is more triumphantly shown, in the fashioning of a great poem or drama or symphony. But it would be ridiculous to say that in *Paradise Lost* or *Hamlet* or the *Eroica* symphony the whole work is a mere means to the final paragraph or scene or chord. All three are intensely purposive, but the purpose of Milton or Shakespeare or Beethoven is to make a work which shall be throughout a thing of high beauty, with the inherent worth which belongs to a beautiful thing. The beauty is not concentrated in the closing lines or notes, it is, except where the artist's performance falls short of his intentions, diffused over the whole. If we are to talk about "means" at all, the last book of the poem, the last scene of the tragedy, the last movement of the symphony are as much "means" to all that has preceded them, as it is to them. For its own full effect the close must be led up to by *this* beginning and *this* middle and no other; equally *this* beginning and middle, as we say, "call for" this ending; it also is a "means" to them, since they would not be beautiful as they are if they had led up to a different close. A work of art is defective if the beauties of any of its parts are only "incidental," irrelevant to their places as parts in this particular whole. It is true that all deep and vital religion does hold that the world's history leads up to a final result which lies outside and beyond that history, but it is not essential to the "argument from design" that this should be so. Even if the meaning and value of that history could be shown to lie entirely in itself, this would leave the general argument for the presence of purpose throughout that history unaffected.

Again, it is not implied in the argument that we human beings must have the key to all the designs of the intelligence controlling the course of the world's history, and it would be strange if we had. Each of us knows well enough that he is often in the dark as to the precise purposes which direct the conduct of his neighbours; he may be quite sure that they are acting with a purpose, though quite unable to say what that purpose is. And I think any one of us who is himself neither a Milton nor a Shakespeare nor a Beethoven must feel that it would be intolerable presumption in him to profess that he knows what is *the* purpose dominating their great works. In a general way, we can no doubt say that the purpose of a Milton in giving the best years of his life to composing *Paradise Lost* is to make a thing of high beauty. But things of high beauty are many and different, and we may be sure that Milton had some more definite purpose than this in making just this poem and no other; what that more definite purpose was, we shall, if we are modest men, admit that we can only know so far as the poet himself has been pleased to tell us; the rest is his secret. It would be still more presumptuous to assume that if there is a divine purpose in the history of the universe we can say, apart from any appeal to something which we take to be an actual "revelation" emanating from God Himself, precisely what that purpose is. At most we can say that such a purpose, whatever it is, must be a wise and a good one. We have no right to assume further that it could only be the widest diffusion of the maximum pleasure over the creation. God may have some purpose with His creatures different from that of giving them all as much enjoyment as possible; indeed, on reflection, we might see reason to hold that to "make everyone jolly" at all costs would be a purpose worthy neither of divine wisdom nor of divine goodness. Hence it is no proof of the absence of intellect and moral purpose from the universe at large to dwell, as has so often been done, on the presence of so much suffering which we cannot see to fulfil any good purpose, or on the frequent prosperity of the vicious and ill-fortune of the virtuous. These familiar facts are at most no more than "difficulties"; they make it hard for us to recognize wise and beneficent purpose in the course of events. But if our general argument for the presence and operation of intelligence throughout the universe is sound, and if we can further give equally sound reasons for holding that the world-directing intelligence must be morally good as well as intelligent, these difficulties are no solid ground for "doubt," just as the mysterious conduct of a friend in some matter may perplex me, if I have not the clue to it, but does not disturb my confidence in his honour and integrity, if I have sufficient independent grounds to be assured of them.

It is, of course, a still more obvious perversion of the thought of the "argument from design" to assume, as was done in antiquity by some of the Stoic philosophers and in later days by too many divines, that if there is a purpose in things, that purpose can only be the promotion of *human* convenience. We have no right to take it for granted not merely that God is just and benevolent in His dealings with us, but that we are the sole objects of His care. Known to the Lord are all His ways, but they are not all known to us; He may have a more intimate concern for us than for any other of His creatures, but we do not *know* that this is so. We do not know that He made the stars merely that they might twinkle in our sky, or the roses merely that we might enjoy their fragrance. That some of the creatures, as far as we can see, serve no human purpose is no proof that they are there for no purpose at all, nor even a proof that they do not serve our own advantage in ways which we do not as yet suspect. To accept the principle of the "argument from design" commits us neither to holding that man is the one end of all the purposes of God, nor to imagining that we know fully what God's purposes for man are. We need to keep these cautions in mind if we are not to prejudice the "design argument" by confusing it with an infantile caricature of itself. If we are duly careful not to forget them, I think we shall find on reflection that the time-honoured argument really deserves the respect with which Kant spoke of it. To say with Butler that our eyes were "given us to see with," if we leave the matter there, may be to assimilate the universe too closely to a gigantic factory, but it is nearer the truth than to say that we see because we somehow happen to have eyes. Nature is not exactly like a large establishment for the mass-production of Ingersoll watches, but when all is said, is it not more like that than it is like an unending harlequinade with no point in particular?

5 ❧

ARE MEN
EVER DIRECTLY
AWARE OF GOD?

William James

William James (1842-1910), a member of a distinguished family that included Henry James, the novelist, was equally renowned as a psychologist and as a philosopher.

THE NATURE OF MYSTICAL EXPERIENCE

Over and over again in these lectures I have raised points and left them open and unfinished until we should have come to the subject of Mysticism. Some of you, I fear, may have smiled as you noted my reiterated postponements. But now the hour has come when mysticism must be faced in good earnest, and those broken threads wound up together. One may say truly, I think, that personal religious experience has its root and centre in mystical states of consciousness; so for us, who in these lectures are treating personal experience as the exclusive subject of our study, such states of consciousness ought to form the vital chapter from which the other chapters get their light. Whether my treatment of mystical states will shed more light or darkness, I do not know, for my own constitution shuts me out from their enjoyment almost entirely, and I can speak of them only at second hand. But though forced to look upon the subject so externally, I will be as objective and receptive as I can; and I think I shall at least succeed in convincing you of the reality of the states in question, and of the paramount importance of their function.

First of all, then, I ask, What does the expression "mystical states of consciousness" mean? How do we part off mystical states from other states?

The words "mysticism" and "mystical" are often used as terms of mere reproach, to throw at any opinion which we regard as vague and vast and sentimental, and without a base in either facts or logic. For some writers a "mystic" is any person who believes in thought-transference, or spirit-return. Employed in this way the word has little value: there are too many less

From Lectures XVI & XVII, "Mysticism," of *The Varieties of Religious Experience* (1902). Subheadings added by the editors.

58

ambiguous synonyms. So, to keep it useful by restricting it, I will do what I did in the case of the word "religion," and simply propose to you four marks which, when an experience has them, may justify us in calling it mystical for the purpose of the present lectures. In this way we shall save verbal disputation, and the recriminations that generally go therewith.

1. *Ineffability.* — The handiest of the marks by which I classify a state of mind as mystical is negative. The subject of it immediately says that it defies expression, that no adequate report of its contents can be given in words. It follows from this that its quality must be directly experienced; it cannot be imparted or transferred to others. In this peculiarity mystical states are more like states of feeling than like states of intellect. No one can make clear to another who has never had a certain feeling, in what the quality or worth of it consists. One must have musical ears to know the value of a symphony; one must have been in love one's self to understand a lover's state of mind. Lacking the heart or ear, we cannot interpret the musician or the lover justly, and are even likely to consider him weak-minded or absurd. The mystic finds that most of us accord to his experiences an equally incompetent treatment.

2. *Noetic quality.* — Although so similar to states of feeling, mystical states seem to those who experience them to be also states of knowledge. They are states of insight into depths of truth unplumbed by the discursive intellect. They are illuminations, revelations, full of significance and importance, all inarticulate though they remain; and as a rule they carry with them a curious sense of authority for aftertime.

These two characters will entitle any state to be called mystical, in the sense in which I use the word. Two other qualities are less sharply marked, but are usually found. These are: —

3. *Transiency.* — Mystical states cannot be sustained for long. Except in rare instances, half an hour, or at most an hour or two, seems to be the limit beyond which they fade into the light of common day. Often, when faded, their quality can but imperfectly be reproduced in memory; but when they recur it is recognized; and from one recurrence to another it is susceptible of continuous development in what is felt as inner richness and importance.

4. *Passivity.* — Although the oncoming of mystical states may be facilitated by preliminary voluntary operations, as by fixing the attention, or going through certain bodily performances, or in other ways which manuals of mysticism prescribe; yet when the characteristic sort of consciousness once has set in, the mystic feels as if his own will were in abeyance, and indeed sometimes as if he were grasped and held by a superior power. This latter peculiarity connects mystical states with certain definite phenomena of secondary or alternative personality, such as prophetic speech, automatic writing, or the mediumistic trance. When these latter conditions are well pronounced, however, there may be no recollection whatever of the phenomenon, and it may have no significance for the subject's usual inner life, to which, as it were, it makes a mere interruption. Mystical states, strictly so-

called, are never merely interruptive. Some memory of their content always remains, and a profound sense of their importance. They modify the inner life of the subject between the times of their recurrence. Sharp divisions in this region are, however, difficult to make, and we find all sorts of gradations and mixtures.

These four characteristics are sufficient to mark out a group of states of consciousness peculiar enough to deserve a special name and to call for careful study. Let it then be called the mystical group.

ANALOGUES OF MYSTICAL EXPERIENCE

Our next step should be to gain acquaintance with some typical examples. Professional mystics at the height of their development have often elaborately organized experiences and a philosophy based thereupon. But you remember what I said in my first lecture: phenomena are best understood when placed within their series, studied in their germ and in their overripe decay, and compared with their exaggerated and degenerated kindred. The range of mystical experience is very wide, much too wide for us to cover in the time at our disposal. Yet the method of serial study is so essential for interpretation that if we really wish to reach conclusions we must use it. I will begin, therefore, with phenomena which claim no special religious significance, and end with those of which the religious pretensions are extreme.

The simplest rudiment of mystical experience would seem to be that deepened sense of the significance of a maxim or formula which occasionally sweeps over one. "I've heard that said all my life," we exclaim, "but I never realized its full meaning until now." "When a fellow monk," said Luther, "one day repeated the words of the Creed: 'I believe in the forgiveness of sins,' I saw the Scripture in an entirely new light; and straightway I felt as if I were born anew. It was as if I had found the door of paradise thrown wide open." This sense of deeper significance is not confined to rational propositions. Single words, and conjunctions of words, effects of light on land and sea, odors and musical sounds, all bring it when the mind is tuned aright. Most of us can remember the strangely moving power of passages in certain poems read when we were young, irrational doorways as they were through which the mystery of fact, the wildness and the pang of life, stole into our hearts and thrilled them. The words have now perhaps become mere polished surfaces for us; but lyric poetry and music are alive and significant only in proportion as they fetch these vague vistas of a life continuous with our own, beckoning and inviting, yet ever eluding our pursuit. We are alive or dead to the eternal inner message of the arts according as we have kept or lost this mystical susceptibility.

A more pronounced step forward on the mystical ladder is found in an extremely frequent phenomenon, that sudden feeling, namely, which sometimes sweeps over us, of having "been here before," as if at some indefinite past time, in just this place, with just these people, we were already saying just these things. As Tennyson writes:

"Moreover, something is or seems
 That touches me with mystic gleams,
 Like glimpses of forgotten dreams —

"Of something felt, like something here;
 Of something done, I know not where;
 Such as no language may declare."

. 　 . 　 .

Somewhat deeper plunges into mystical consciousness are met with in yet other dreamy states. Such feelings as these which Charles Kingsley describes are surely far from being uncommon, especially in youth : —

"When I walk the fields, I am oppressed now and then with an innate feeling that everything I see has a meaning, if I could but understand it. And this feeling of being surrounded with truths which I cannot grasp amounts to indescribable awe sometimes. . . . Have you not felt that your real soul was imperceptible to your mental vision, except in a few hallowed moments?"

. 　 . 　 .

The next step into mystical states carries us into a realm that public opinion and ethical philosophy have long since branded as pathological, though private practice and certain lyric strains of poetry seem still to bear witness to its ideality. I refer to the consciousness produced by intoxicants and anaesthetics, especially by alcohol. The sway of alcohol over mankind is unquestionably due to its power to stimulate the mystical faculties of human nature, usually crushed to earth by the cold facts and dry criticisms of the sober hour. Sobriety diminishes, discriminates, and says no; drunkenness expands, unites, and says yes. It is in fact the great exciter of the *Yes* function in man. It brings its votary from the chill periphery of things to the radiant core. It makes him for the moment one with truth. Not through mere perversity do men run after it. To the poor and the unlettered it stands in the place of symphony concerts and of literature; and it is part of the deeper mystery and tragedy of life that whiffs and gleams of something that we immediately recognize as excellent should be vouchsafed to so many of us only in the fleeting earlier phases of what in its totality is so degrading a poisoning. The drunken consciousness is one bit of the mystic consciousness, and our total opinion of it must find its place in our opinion of that larger whole.

Nitrous oxide and ether, especially nitrous oxide, when sufficiently diluted with air, stimulate the mystical consciousness in an extraordinary degree. Depth beyond depth of truth seems revealed to the inhaler. This truth fades out, however, or escapes, at the moment of coming to; and if any words remain over in which it seemed to clothe itself, they prove to be the veriest nonsense. Nevertheless, the sense of a profound meaning having been there persists; and I know more than one person who is persuaded that in the nitrous oxide trance we have a genuine metaphysical revelation.

Some years ago I myself made some observations on this aspect of nitrous oxide intoxication, and reported them in print. One conclusion was forced upon my mind at that time, and my impression of its truth has ever since remained unshaken. It is that our normal waking consciousness, rational consciousness as we call it, is but one special type of consciousness, whilst all about it, parted from it by the filmiest of screens, there lie potential forms of consciousness entirely different. We may go through life without suspecting their existence; but apply the requisite stimulus, and at a touch they are there in all their completeness, definite types of mentality which probably somewhere have their field of application and adaptation. No account of the universe in its totality can be final which leaves these other forms of consciousness quite disregarded. How to regard them is the question — for they are so discontinuous with ordinary consciousness. Yet they may determine attitudes though they cannot furnish formulas, and open a region though they fail to give a map. At any rate, they forbid a premature closing of our accounts with reality. Looking back on my own experiences, they all converge towards a kind of insight to which I cannot help ascribing some metaphysical significance. The keynote of it is invariably a reconciliation. It is as if the opposites of the world, whose contradictoriness and conflict make all our difficulties and troubles, were melted into unity. Not only do they, as contrasted species, belong to one and the same genus, but *one of the species,* the nobler and better one, *is itself the genus, and so soaks up and absorbs its opposite into itself.* This is a dark saying, I know, when thus expressed in terms of common logic, but I cannot wholly escape from its authority. I feel as if it must mean something, something like what the hegelian philosophy means, if one could only lay hold of it more clearly. Those who have ears to hear, let them hear; to me the living sense of its reality only comes in the artificial mystic state of mind.

I just now spoke of friends who believe in the anæsthetic revelation. For them too it is a monistic insight, in which the *other* in its various forms appears absorbed into the One.

> "Into this pervading genius," writes one of them, "we pass, forgetting and forgotten, and thenceforth each is all, in God. There is no higher, no deeper, no other, than the life in which we are founded. 'The One remains, the many change and pass;' and each and every one of us *is* the One that remains. . . . This is the ultimatum. . . . As sure as being — whence is all our care — so sure is content, beyond duplexity, antithesis, or trouble, where I have triumphed in a solitude that God is not above."

.   .   .

Certain aspects of nature seem to have a peculiar power of awakening such mystical moods.

.   .   .

Here is a record from the memoirs of that interesting German idealist, Malwida von Meysenburg: —

> "I was alone upon the seashore as all these thoughts flowed over me, liberating and reconciling; and now again, as once before in distant days in the Alps of Dauphiné, I was impelled to kneel down, this time before the illimitable ocean, symbol of the Infinite. I felt that I prayed as I had never prayed before, and knew now what prayer really is: to return from the solitude of individuation into the consciousness of unity with all that is, to kneel down as one that passes away, and to rise up as one imperishable. Earth, heaven, and sea resounded as in one vast world-encircling harmony. It was as if the chorus of all the great who had ever lived were about me. I felt myself one with them, and it appeared as if I heard their greeting: 'Thou too belongest to the company of those who overcome.' "

.   .   .

MYSTICAL EXPERIENCE IN RELIGION

We have now seen enough of this cosmic or mystic consciousness, as it comes sporadically. We must next pass to its methodical cultivation as an element of the religious life. Hindus, Buddhists, Mohammedans, and Christians all have cultivated it methodically.

In India, training in mystical insight has been known from time immemorial under the name of yoga. Yoga means the experimental union of the individual with the divine. It is based on persevering exercise; and the diet, posture, breathing, intellectual concentration, and moral discipline vary slightly in the different systems which teach it. The yogi, or disciple, who has by these means overcome the obscurations of his lower nature sufficiently, enters into the condition termed *samâdhi,* "and comes face to face with facts which no instinct or reason can ever know." He learns —

> "That the mind itself has a higher state of existence, beyond reason, a superconscious state, and that when the mind gets to that higher state, then this knowledge beyond reasoning comes. . . . All the different steps in yoga are intended to bring us scientifically to the superconscious state or Samâdhi. . . . Just as unconscious work is beneath consciousness, so there is another work which is above consciousness, and which, also, is not accompanied with the feeling of egoism. . . . There is no feeling of *I,* and yet the mind works, desireless, free from restlessness, objectless, bodiless. Then the Truth shines in its full effulgence, and we know ourselves — for Samâdhi lies potential in us all — for what we truly are, free, immortal, omnipotent, loosed from the finite, and its contrasts of good and evil together, and identical with the Atman or Universal Soul."

The Vedantists say that one may stumble into superconsciousness sporadically, without the previous discipline, but it is then impure. Their test of its purity, like our test of religion's value, is empirical: its fruits must be good for life. When a man comes out of Samâdhi, they assure us that he remains "enlightened, a sage, a prophet, a saint, his whole character changed, his life changed, illumined."

The Buddhists used the word "samâdhi" as well as the Hindus; but "dhyâna" is their special word for higher states of contemplation. There seem to be four stages recognized in dhyâna. The first stage comes through concentration of the mind upon one point. It excludes desire, but not discernment or judgment: it is still intellectual. In the second stage the intellectual functions drop off, and the satisfied sense of unity remains. In the third stage the satisfaction departs, and indifference begins, along with memory and self-consciousness. In the fourth stage the indifference, memory, and self-consciousness are perfected. [Just what "memory" and "self-consciousness" mean in this connection is doubtful. They cannot be the faculties familiar to us in the lower life.] Higher stages still of contemplation are mentioned — a region where there exists nothing, and where the mediator says: "There exists absolutely nothing," and stops. Then he reaches another region where he says: "There are neither ideas nor absence of ideas," and stops again. Then another region where, "having reached the end of both idea and perception, he stops finally." This would seem to be, not yet Nirvâna, but as close an approach to it as this life affords.

.   .   .

In the Christian church there have always been mystics. Although many of them have been viewed with suspicion, some have gained favor in the eyes of the authorities. The experiences of these have been treated as precedents, and a codified system of mystical theology has been based upon them, in which everything legitimate finds its place. The basis of the system is "orison" or meditation, the methodical elevation of the soul towards God. Through the practice of orison the higher levels of mystical experience may be attained. It is odd that Protestantism, especially evangelical Protestantism, should seemingly have abandoned everything methodical in this line. Apart from what prayer may lead to, Protestant mystical experience appears to have been almost exclusively sporadic. It has been left to our mind-curers to reintroduce methodical meditation into our religious life.

The first thing to be aimed at in orison is the mind's detachment from outer sensations, for these interfere with its concentration upon ideal things. Such manuals as Saint Ignatius's Spiritual Exercises recommend the disciple to expel sensation by a graduated series of efforts to imagine holy scenes. The acme of this kind of discipline would be a semi-hallucinatory mono-ideism — an imaginary figure of Christ, for example, coming fully to occupy the mind. Sensorial images of this sort, whether literal or symbolic, play an enormous part in mysticism. But in certain cases imagery may fall away entirely, and in the very highest raptures it tends to do so. The state of consciousness becomes then insusceptible of any verbal description. Mystical teachers are unanimous as to this. Saint John of the Cross, for instance, one of the best of them, thus describes the condition called the "union of love," which, he says, is reached by "dark contemplation." In this the Deity compenetrates the soul, but in such a hidden way that the soul —

finds no terms, no means, no comparison whereby to render the sublimity of the wisdom and the delicacy of the spiritual feeling with which she is filled. . . . We receive this mystical knowledge of God clothed in none of the kinds of images, in none of the sensible representations, which our mind makes use of in other circumstances. Accordingly in this knowledge, since the senses and the imagination are not employed, we get neither form nor impression, nor can we give any account or furnish any likeness, although the mysterious and sweet-tasting wisdom comes home so clearly to the inmost parts of our soul. Fancy a man seeing a certain kind of thing for the first time in his life. He can understand it, use and enjoy it, but he cannot apply a name to it, nor communicate any idea of it, even though all the while it be a mere thing of sense. How much greater will be his powerlessness when it goes beyond the senses! This is the peculiarity of the divine language. The more infused, intimate, spiritual, and supersensible it is, the more does it exceed the senses, both inner and outer, and impose silence upon them. . . . The soul then feels as if placed in a vast and profound solitude, to which no created thing has access, in an immense and boundless desert, desert the more delicious the more solitary it is. There, in this abyss of wisdom, the soul grows by what it drinks in from the well-springs of the comprehension of love, . . . and recognizes, however sublime and learned may be the terms we employ, how utterly vile, insignificant, and improper they are, when we seek to discourse of divine things by their means."

I cannot pretend to detail to you the sundry stages of the Christian mystical life. Our time would not suffice, for one thing; and moreover, I confess that the subdivisions and names which we find in the Catholic books seem to me to represent nothing objectively distinct. So many men, so many minds: I imagine that these experiences can be as infinitely varied as are the idiosyncrasies of individuals.

The cognitive aspects of them, their value in the way of revelation, is what we are directly concerned with, and it is easy to show by citation how strong an impression they leave of being revelations of new depths of truth. Saint Teresa is the expert of experts in describing such conditions, so I will turn immediately to what she says of one of the highest of them, the "orison of union."

"In the orison of union," says Saint Teresa, "the soul is fully awake as regards God, but wholly asleep as regards things of this world and in respect of herself. During the short time the union lasts, she is as it were deprived of every feeling, and even if she would, she could not think of any single thing. Thus she needs to employ no artifice in order to arrest the use of her understanding: it remains so stricken with inactivity that she neither knows what she loves, nor in what manner she loves, nor what she wills. In short, she is utterly dead to the things of the world and lives solely in God. . . . I do not even know whether in this state she has enough life left to breathe. It seems to me she has not; or at least that if she does breathe, she is unaware of it. Her intellect would fain understand something of what is going on within her, but it has so little force now that it can act in no way whatsoever. So a person who falls into a deep faint appears as if dead. . . .

"Thus does God, when he raises a soul to union with himself, suspend the natural action of all her faculties. She neither sees, hears, nor understands, so long as she is united with God. But this time is always short, and it seems even shorter than it is. God establishes himself in the interior of this soul in such a way, that when she returns to herself, it is wholly impossible for her to doubt that she has been in God, and God in her. This truth remains so strongly impressed on her that, even though many years should pass without the condition returning, she can neither forget the favor she received, nor doubt of its reality. If you, nevertheless, ask how it is possible that the soul can see and understand that she has been in God, since during the union she has neither sight nor understanding, I reply that she does not see it then, but that she sees it clearly later, after she has returned to herself, not by any vision, but by a certitude which abides with her and which God alone can give her. I knew a person who was ignorant of the truth that God's mode of being in everything must be either by presence, by power, or by essence, but who, after having received the grace of which I am speaking, believed this truth in the most unshakable manner. So much so that, having consulted a half-learned man who was as ignorant on this point as she had been before she was enlightened, when he replied that God is in us only by 'grace,' she disbelieved his reply, so sure she was of the true answer; and when she came to ask wiser doctors, they confirmed her in her belief, which much consoled her. . . .

"But how, you will repeat, *can* one have such certainty in respect to what one does not see? This question, I am powerless to answer. These are secrets of God's omnipotence which it does not appertain to me to penetrate. All that I know is that I tell the truth; and I shall never believe that any soul who does not possess the certainty has ever been really united to God."

. . .

The deliciousness of some of these states seem to be beyond anything known in ordinary consciousness. It evidently involves organic sensibilities, for it is spoken of as something too extreme to be borne, and as verging on bodily pain. But it is too subtle and piercing a delight for ordinary words to denote. God's touches, the wounds of his spear, references to ebriety and to nuptial union have to figure in the phraseology by which it is shadowed forth. Intellect and senses both swoon away in these highest states of ecstasy. "If our understanding comprehends," says Saint Teresa, "it is in a mode which remains unknown to it, and it can understand nothing of what it comprehends. For my own part, I do not believe that it does comprehend, because, as I said, it does not understand itself to do so. I confess that it is all a mystery in which I am lost." In the condition called *raptus* or ravishment by theologians, breathing and circulation are so depressed that it is a question among the doctors whether the soul be or be not temporarily dissevered from the body. One must read Saint Teresa's descriptions and the very exact distinctions which she makes, to persuade one's self that one is dealing, not with imaginary experiences, but with phenomena which, however rare, follow perfectly definite psychological types.

To the medical mind these ecstasies signify nothing but suggested and imitated hypnoid states, on an intellectual basis of superstition, and a corporeal one of degeneration and hysteria. Undoubtedly these pathological conditions have existed in many and possibly in all the cases, but that fact tells us nothing about the value for knowledge of the consciousness which they induce. To pass a spiritual judgment upon these states, we must not content ourselves with superficial medical talk, but inquire into their fruits for life.

Their fruits appear to have been various. Stupefaction, for one thing, seems not to have been altogether absent as a result. You may remember the helplessness in the kitchen and schoolroom of poor Margaret Mary Alacoque. Many other ecstatics would have perished but for the care taken of them by admiring followers. The "other-worldliness" encouraged by the mystical consciousness makes this over-abstraction from practical life peculiarly liable to befall mystics in whom the character is naturally passive and the intellect feeble; but in natively strong minds and characters we find quite opposite results. The great Spanish mystics, who carried the habit of ecstasy as far as it has often been carried, appear for the most part to have shown indomitable spirit and energy, and all the more so for the trances in which they indulged.

Saint Ignatius was a mystic, but his mysticism made him assuredly one of the most powerfully practical human engines that ever lived. Saint John of the Cross, writing of the intuitions and "touches" by which God reaches the substance of the soul, tells us that —

> "They enrich it marvelously. A single one of them may be sufficient to abolish at a stroke certain imperfections of which the soul during its whole life had vainly tried to rid itself, and to leave it adorned with virtues and loaded with supernatural gifts. A single one of these intoxicating consolations may reward it for all the labors undergone in its life — even were they numberless. Invested with an invincible courage, filled with an impassioned desire to suffer for its God, the soul then is seized with a strange torment — that of not being allowed to suffer enough."

.   .   .

The Intellectual Content of Mysticism

Mystical conditions may, therefore, render the soul more energetic in the lines which their inspiration favors. But this could be reckoned an advantage only in case the inspiration were a true one. If the inspiration were erroneous, the energy would be all the more mistaken and misbegotten. So we stand once more before that problem of truth which confronted us at the end of the lectures on saintliness. You will remember that we turned to mysticism precisely to get some light on truth. Do mystical states establish the truth of those theological affections in which the saintly life has its root?

In spite of their repudiation of articulate self-description, mystical states in general assert a pretty distinct theoretic drift. It is possible to give the outcome of the majority of them in terms that point in definite philosophical directions. One of these directions is optimism, and the other is monism. We pass into mystical states from out of ordinary consciousness as from a less into a more, as from a smallness into a vastness, and at the same time as from an unrest to a rest. We feel them as reconciling, unifying states. They appeal to the yes-function more than to the no-function in us. In them the unlimited absorbs the limits and peacefully closes the account. Their very denial of every adjective you may propose as applicable to the ultimate truth — He, the Self, the Atman, is to be described by "No! no!" only, say the Upanishads — though it seems on the surface to be a no-function, is a denial made on behalf of a deeper yes. Whoso calls the Absolute anything in particular, or says that it is *this,* seems implicitly to shut it off from being *that* — it is as if he lessened it. So we deny the "this," negating the negation which it seems to us to imply, in the interests of the higher affirmative attitude by which we are possessed. The fountain-head of Christian mysticism is Dionysius the Areopagite. He describes the absolute truth by negatives exclusively.

> "The cause of all things is neither soul nor intellect; nor has it imagination, opinion, or reason, or intelligence; nor is it reason or intelligence; nor is it spoken or thought. It is neither number, nor order, nor magnitude, nor littleness, nor equality, nor inequality, nor similarity, nor dissimilarity. It neither stands, nor moves, nor rests. . . . It is neither essence, nor eternity, nor time. Even intellectual contact does not belong to it. It is neither science nor truth. It is not even royalty or wisdom; not one; not unity; not divinity or goodness; nor even spirit as we know it," etc., *ad libitum.*

But these qualifications are denied by Dionysius, not because the truth falls short of them, but because it so infinitely excels them. It is above them. It is *super*-lucent, *super*-splendent, *super*-essential, *super*-sublime, *super everything* that can be named.

·   ·   ·

Thus come the paradoxical expressions that so abound in mystical writings. As when Eckhart tells of the still desert of the Godhead, "where never was seen difference, neither Father, Son, nor Holy Ghost, where there is no one at home, yet where the spark of the soul is more at peace than in itself."

To this dialectical use, by the intellect, of negation as a mode of passage towards a higher kind of affirmation, there is correlated the subtlest of moral counterparts in the sphere of the personal will. Since denial of the finite self and its wants, since asceticism of some sort, is found in religious experience to be the only doorway to the larger and more blessed life, this moral mystery intertwines and combines with the intellectual mystery in all mystical writings.

> "Love," continues Behmen, is Nothing, for "when thou art gone forth wholly from the Creature and from that which is visible, and art become Nothing to all that is Nature and Creature, then thou art in that eternal One, which is God himself, and then thou shalt feel within thee the highest virtue of Love. . . . The treasure of treasures for the soul is where she goeth out of the Somewhat into that Nothing out of which all things may be made. The soul here saith, *I have nothing,* for I am utterly stripped and naked; *I can do nothing,* for I have no manner of power, but am as water poured out; *I am nothing,* for all that I am is no more than an image of Being, and only God is to me I AM; and so, sitting down in my own Nothingness, I give glory to the eternal Being, and *will nothing* of myself, that so God may will all in me, being unto me my God and all things."

In Paul's language, I live, yet not I, but Christ liveth in me. Only when I become as nothing can God enter in and no difference between his life and mine remain outstanding.

.   .   .

I have now sketched with extreme brevity and insufficiency, but as fairly as I am able in the time allowed, the general traits of the mystic range of consciousness. *It is on the whole pantheistic and optimistic, or at least the opposite of pessimistic. It is anti-naturalistic, and harmonizes best with twice-bornness and so-called other-worldly states of mind.*

Is Mystical Experience Veridical?

My next task is to inquire whether we can invoke it as authoritative. Does it furnish any *warrant for the truth* of the twice-bornness and super-naturality and pantheism which it favors? I must give my answer to this question as concisely as I can.

In brief my answer is this — and I will divide it into three parts: —

(1) Mystical states, when well developed, usually are, and have the right to be, absolutely authoritative over the individuals to whom they come.

(2) No authority emanates from them which should make it a duty for those who stand outside of them to accept their revelations uncritically.

(3) They break down the authority of the non-mystical or rationalistic consciousness, based upon the understanding and the senses alone. They show it to be only one kind of consciousness. They open out the possibility of other orders of truth, in which, so far as anything in us vitally responds to them, we may freely continue to have faith.

I will take up these points one by one.

1.

As a matter of psychological fact, mystical states of a well-pronounced and emphatic sort *are* usually authoritative over those who have them. They have been "there," and know. It is vain for rationalism to grumble about this. If the mystical truth that comes to a man proves to be a force that he can live by, what mandate have we of the majority to order him to live in another way? We can throw him into a prison or a madhouse, but we cannot change his mind — we commonly attach it only the more stubbornly to its beliefs. It mocks our utmost efforts, as a matter of fact, and in point of logic it absolutely escapes our jurisdiction. Our own more "rational" beliefs are based on evidence exactly similar in nature to that which mystics quote for theirs. Our senses, namely, have assured us of certain states of fact; but mystical experiences are as direct perceptions of fact for those who have them as any sensations ever were for us. The records show that even though the five senses be in abeyance in them, they are absolutely sensational in their epistemological quality, if I may be pardoned the barbarous expression — that is, they are face to face presentations of what seems immediately to exist.

The mystic is, in short, *invulnerable,* and must be left whether we relish it or not, in undisturbed enjoyment of his creed. Faith, says Tolstoy, is that by which men live. And faith-state and mystic state are practically convertible terms.

2.

But I now proceed to add that mystics have no right to claim that we ought to accept the deliverance of their peculiar experiences, if we are ourselves outsiders and feel no private call thereto. The utmost they can ever ask of us in this life is to admit that they establish a presumption. They form a consensus and have an unequivocal outcome; and it would be odd, mystics might say, if such a unanimous type of experience should prove to be altogether wrong. At bottom, however, this would only be an appeal to numbers, like the appeal of rationalism the other way; and the appeal to numbers has no logical force. If we acknowledge it, it is for "suggestive," not for logical reasons: we follow the majority because to do so suits our life.

But even this presumption from the unanimity of mystics is far from being strong. In characterizing mystic states as pantheistic, optimistic, etc., I am afraid I over-simplified the truth. I did so for expository reasons, and to keep the closer to the classic mystical tradition. The classic religious mysticism, it now must be confessed, is only a "privileged case." It is an *extract,* kept true to type by the selection of the fittest specimens and their preservation in "schools." It is carved out from a much larger mass; and if we take the larger mass as seriously as religious mysticism has historically taken itself, we find that the supposed unanimity largely disappears. To begin with, even religious mysticism itself, the kind that accumulates traditions and makes schools, is much less unanimous than I have allowed. It has been both ascetic and antinomianly self-indulgent within the Christian church. It is dualistic in Sankhya, and monistic in Vedanta philosophy. I called it pantheistic; but the great Spanish mystics are anything but pantheists. They are with few exceptions non-metaphysical minds, for whom "the category of personality" is absolute. The "union" of man with God is for them much more like an occasional miracle than like an original identity. How different again, apart from the happiness common to all, is the mysticism of Walt Whitman, Edward Carpenter, Richard Jeffries, and other naturalistic pantheists, from the more distinctively Christian sort. The fact is that the mystical feeling of enlargement, union, and emancipation has no specific intellectual content whatever of its own. It is capable of forming matrimonial alliances with material furnished by the most diverse philosophies and theologies, provided only they can find a place in their framework for its peculiar emotional mood. We have no right, therefore, to invoke its prestige as distinctively in favor of any special belief, such as that in the absolute idealism, or in the absolute monistic identity, or in the absolute goodness, of the world. It is only relatively in favor of all these things — it passes out of common human consciousness in the direction in which they lie.

So much for religious mysticism proper. But more remains to be told, for religious mysticism is only one half of mysticism. The other half has no accumulated traditions except those which the text-books on insanity supply. Open any one of these, and you will find abundant cases in which mystical ideas are cited as characteristic symptoms of enfeebled or deluded states of mind. In delusional insanity, paranoia, as they sometimes call it, we may have a *diabolical* mysticism, a sort of religious mysticism turned upside down. The same sense of ineffable importance in the smallest events, the same texts and words coming with new meanings, the same voices and visions and leadings and missions, the same controlling by extraneous powers; only this time the emotion is pessimistic: instead of consolations we have desolations; the meanings are dreadful; and the powers are enemies to life. It is evident that from the point of view of their psychological mechanism, the classic mysticism and these lower mysticisms spring from the same mental level, from that great subliminal or transmarginal region of which science is beginning to admit the existence, but of which so little is really known. That region contains every kind of matter: "seraph and snake" abide there side by side. To come from thence is no infallible credential. What comes must be sifted and tested, and run the gauntlet of confrontation with the total context of experience, just like what comes from the outer world of sense. Its value must be ascertained by empirical methods, so long as we are not mystics ourselves.

Once more, then, I repeat that non-mystics are under no obligation to acknowledge in mystical states a superior authority conferred on them by their intrinsic nature.

3.

Yet, I repeat once more, the existence of mystical states absolutely overthrows the pretension of non-mystical states to be the sole and ultimate dictators of what we may believe. As a rule, mystical states merely add a supersensuous meaning to the ordinary outward data of consciousness. They are excitements like the emotions of love or ambition, gifts to our spirit by means of which facts already objectively before us fall into a new expressiveness and make a new connection with our active life. They do not contradict these facts as such, or deny anything that our senses have immediately seized. It is the rationalistic critic rather who plays the part of denier in the controversy, and his denials have no strength, for there never can be a state of facts to which new meaning may not truthfully be added, provided the mind ascend to a more enveloping point of view. It must always remain an open question whether mystical states may not possibly be such superior points of view, windows through which the mind looks out upon a more extensive and inclusive world. The difference of the views seen from the different mystical windows need not prevent us from entertaining this supposition. The wider world would in that case prove to have a mixed constitution like that of this world, that is all. It would have its celestial and its infernal regions, its tempting and its saving moments, its valid experiences and its counterfeit ones, just as our world has them; and it would be a wider world all the same. We should have to use its experiences by selecting and subordinating and substituting just as is our custom in this ordinary naturalistic world; we should be liable to error just as we are now; yet the counting in of that wider world of meanings, and the serious dealing with it, might, in spite of all the perplexity, be indispensable stages in our approach to the final fullness of the truth.

In this shape, I think, we have to leave the subject. Mystical states indeed wield no authority due simply to their being mystical states. But the higher ones among them point in directions to which the religious sentiments even of nonmystical men incline. They tell of the supremacy of the ideal, of vastness, of union, of safety, and of rest. They offer us *hypotheses,* hypotheses which we may voluntarily ignore, but which as thinkers we cannot possibly upset. The supernaturalism and optimism to which they would persuade us may, interpreted in one way or another, be after all the truest of insights into the meaning of this life.

· · · ·

6

A SKEPTICAL VIEW
OF MYSTICISM

Bertrand Russell

Bertrand Russell (1872-   ) is one of the most prominent philosophers of the twentieth century, having left his mark on virtually every branch of philosophy.

Ought we to admit that there is available, in support of religion, a source of knowledge which lies outside science and may properly be described as "revelation"? This is a difficult question to argue, because those who believe that truths have been revealed to them profess the same kind of certainty in regard to them that we have in regard to objects of sense. We believe the man who has seen things through the telescope that we have never seen; why, then, they ask, should we not believe them when they report things that are to them equally unquestionable?

It is, perhaps, useless to attempt an argument such as will appeal to the man who has himself enjoyed mystic illumination. But something can be said as to whether we others should accept this testimony. In the first place, it is not subject to the ordinary tests. When a man of science tells us the result of an experiment, he also tells us how the experiment was performed; others can repeat it, and if the result is not confirmed it is not accepted as true; but many men might put themselves into the situation in which the mystic's vision occurred without obtaining the same revelation. To this it may be answered that a man must use the appropriate sense: a telescope is useless to a man who keeps his eyes shut. The argument as to the credibility of the mystic's testimony may be prolonged almost indefinitely. Science should be neutral, since the argument is a scientific one, to be conducted exactly as an argument would be conducted about an uncertain experiment. Science depends upon perception and inference; its credibility is due to the fact that the perceptions are such as any observer can test. The mystic himself may be certain that he *knows,* and has no need of scientific tests; but those who are asked to accept his testimony will subject it to the

From Chapter VII, "Mysticism," of *Religion and Science* (1935). Reprinted by permission of the Oxford University Press.

same kind of scientific tests as those applied to men who say they have been to the North Pole. Science, as such, should have no expectation, positive or negative, as to the result.

The chief argument in favour of the mystics is their agreement with each other. "I know nothing more remarkable," says Dean Inge, "than the unanimity of the mystics, ancient, mediaeval, and modern, Protestant, Catholic, and even Buddhist or Mohammedan, though the Christian mystics are the most trustworthy." I do not wish to underrate the force of this argument, which I acknowledged long ago in a book called *Mysticism and Logic*. The mystics vary greatly in their capacity for giving verbal expression to their experiences, but I think we may take it that those who succeeded best all maintain: (1) that all division and separateness is unreal, and that the universe is a single indivisible unity; (2) that evil is illusory, and that the illusion arises through falsely regarding a part as self-subsistent; (3) that time is unreal, and that reality is eternal, not in the sense of being everlasting, but in the sense of being wholly outside time. I do not pretend that this is a complete account of the matters on which all mystics concur, but the three propositions that I have mentioned may serve as representatives of the whole. Let us now imagine ourselves a jury in a law-court, whose business it is to decide on the credibility of the witnesses who make these three somewhat surprising assertions.

We shall find, in the first place, that, while the witnesses agree up to a point, they disagree totally when that point is passed, although they are just as certain as when they agree. Catholics, but not Protestants, may have visions in which the Virgin appears; Christians and Mohammedans, but not Buddhists, may have great truths revealed to them by the Archangel Gabriel; the Chinese mystics of the Tao tell us, as a direct result of their central doctrine, that all government is bad, whereas most European and Mohammedan mystics, with equal confidence, urge submission to constituted authority. As regards the points where they differ, each group will argue that the other groups are untrustworthy; we might, therefore, if we were content with a mere forensic triumph, point out that most mystics think most other mystics mistaken on most points. They might, however, make this only half a triumph by agreeing on the greater importance of the matters about which they are at one, as compared with those as to which their opinions differ. We will, in any case, assume that they have composed their differences, and concentrated the defence at these three points — namely, the unity of the world, the illusory nature of evil, and the unreality of time. What test can we, as impartial outsiders, apply to their unanimous evidence?

As men of scientific temper, we shall naturally first ask whether there is any way by which we can ourselves obtain the same evidence at first hand. To this we shall receive various answers. We may be told that we are obviously not in a receptive frame of mind, and that we lack the requisite humility; or that fasting and religious meditation are necessary; or (if our witness is Indian or Chinese) that the essential prerequisite is a course of breathing exercises. I think we shall find that the weight of experimental evidence is in favour of this last view, though fasting also has been frequently found effective. As a matter of fact, there is a definite physical discipline, called yoga, which is practised in order to produce the mystic's certainty, and which is recommended with much confidence by those who have tried it.[1] Breathing exercises are its most essential feature, and for our purposes we may ignore the rest.

In order to see how we could test the assertion that yoga gives insight, let us artificially simplify this assertion. Let us suppose that a number of people assure us that if, *for a certain time,* we breathe in a certain way, we shall become convinced that time is unreal. Let us go further, and suppose that, having tried their recipe, we have ourselves experienced a state of mind such as they describe. But now, having returned to our normal mode of respiration, we are not quite sure whether the vision was to be believed. How shall we investigate this question?

First of all, what can be meant by saying that time is unreal? If we really mean what we say, we must mean that such statements as "this is before that" are mere empty noise, like "twas brillig." If we suppose anything less than this — as, for example, that there is a relation between events which puts them in the same order as the relation of earlier and later, but that it is a different relation — we shall not have made any assertion that makes any real change in our outlook. It will be merely like supposing that the Iliad was not written by Homer, but by another man of the same name. We have to suppose that there are no "events" at all; there must be only the one vast whole of the universe, embracing whatever is real in the misleading appearance of a temporal procession. There must be nothing in reality corresponding to the apparent distinction between earlier and later events. To say that we are born, and then grow, and then die, must be just as false as to say that we die, then grow small, and finally are born. The truth of what seems an individual life is merely the illusory isolation of one element in the timeless and indivisible being of the universe. There is no distinction between improvement and deterioration, no difference between sorrows that end in happiness and happiness that ends in sorrow. If you find a corpse with a dagger in it, it makes no difference whether the man died of the wound or the dagger was plunged in after death. Such a view, if true, puts an end, not only to science, but to prudence, hope, and effort; it is incompatible with worldly wisdom, and — what is more important to religion — with morality.

Most mystics, of course, do not accept these conclusions in their entirety, but they urge doctrines from which these conclusions inevitably follow. Thus Dean Inge rejects the kind of religion that appeals to evolution, because it lays too much stress upon a temporal process. "There is no law of progress, and there is no universal progress," he says. And again: "The doctrine of automatic and universal progress, the lay religion of many Vic-

---

[1] As regards yoga in China, see Waley, *The Way and its Power,* pp. 117-18.

torians, labours under the disadvantage of being almost the only philosophical theory which can be definitely disproved." On this matter, which I shall discuss at a later stage, I find myself in agreement with the Dean, for whom, on many grounds, I have a very high respect. But he naturally does not draw from his premises all the inferences which seem to me to be warranted.

It is important not to caricature the doctrine of mysticism, in which there is, I think, a core of wisdom. Let us see how it seeks to avoid the extreme consequences which seem to follow from the denial of time.

The philosophy based upon mysticism has a great tradition, from Parmenides to Hegel. Parmenides says: "What is, is uncreated and indestructible; for it is complete, immovable, and without end. Nor was it ever, nor will it be; for now *it is,* all at once, a continuous one."[2] He introduced into metaphysics the distinction between reality and appearance, or the way of truth and the way of opinion, as he calls them. It is clear that whoever denies the reality of time must introduce some such distinction, since obviously the world *appears* to be in time. It is also clear that, if everyday experience is not to be *wholly* illusory, there must be some relation between appearance and the reality behind it. It is at this point, however, that the greatest difficulties arise: if the relation between appearance and reality is made too intimate, all the unpleasant features of appearance will have their unpleasant counterparts in reality, while if the relation is made too remote, we shall be unable to make inferences from the character of appearance to that of reality, and reality will be left a vague Unknowable, as with Herbert Spencer. For Christians, there is the related difficulty of avoiding pantheism: if the world is *only* apparent, God created nothing, and the reality corresponding to the world is a part of God; but if the world is in any degree real and distinct from God, we abandon the wholeness of everything, which is an essential doctrine of mysticism, and we are compelled to suppose that, in so far as the world is real, the evil which it contains is also real. Such difficulties make thoroughgoing mysticism very difficult for an orthodox Christian. As the Bishop of Birmingham says: "All forms of pantheism . . . as it seems to me, must be rejected because, if man is actually a part of God, the evil in man is also in God."

All this time I have been supposing that we are a jury, listening to the testimony of the mystics, and trying to decide whether to accept or reject it. If, when they deny the reality of the world of sense, we took them to mean "reality" in the ordinary sense of the law-courts, we should have no hesitation in rejecting what they say, since we should find that it runs counter to all other testimony, and even to their own in their mundane moments. We must therefore look for some other sense. I believe that, when the mystics contrast "reality" with "appearance," the word "reality" has not a logical, but an emotional, significance: it means what is, in some sense, important. When it is said that time is "unreal," what should be said is that, in some sense and

_____

[2] Quoted from Burnet's *Early Greek Philosophy,* p. 199.

on some occasions, it is important to conceive the universe as a whole, as the Creator, if He existed, must have conceived it in deciding to create it. When so conceived, all process is within one completed whole; past, present, and future, all exist, in some sense, together, and the present does not have that pre-eminent reality which it has to our usual ways of apprehending the world. If this interpretation is accepted, mysticism expresses an emotion, not a fact; it does not assert anything, and therefore can be neither confirmed nor contradicted by science. The fact that mystics do make assertions is owing to their inability to separate emotional importance from scientific validity. It is, of course, not to be expected that they will accept this view, but it is the only one, so far as I can see, which, while admitting something of their claim, is not repugnant to the scientific intelligence.

The certainty and partial unanimity of mystics is no conclusive reason for accepting their testimony on a matter of fact. The man of science, when he wishes others to see what he has seen, arranges his microscope or telescope; that is to say, he makes changes in the external world, but demands of the observer only normal eyesight. The mystic, on the other hand, demands changes in the observer, by fasting, by breathing exercises, and by a careful abstention from external observation. (Some object to such discipline, and think that the mystic illumination cannot be artificially achieved; from a scientific point of view, this makes their case more difficult to test than that of those who rely on yoga. But nearly all agree that fasting and an ascetic life are helpful.) We all know that opium, hashish, and alcohol produce certain effects on the observer, but as we do not think these effects admirable we take no account of them in our theory of the universe. They may even, sometimes, reveal fragments of truth; but we do not regard them as sources of general wisdom. The drunkard who sees snakes does not imagine, afterwards, that he has had a revelation of a reality hidden from others, though some not wholly dissimilar belief must have given rise to the worship of Bacchus. In our own day, as William James related,[3] there have been people who considered that the intoxication produced by laughing-gas revealed truths which are hidden at normal times. From a scientific point of view, we can make no distinction between the man who eats little and sees heaven and the man who drinks much and sees snakes. Each is in an abnormal physical condition, and therefore has abnormal perceptions. Normal perceptions, since they have to be useful in the struggle for life, must have some correspondence with fact; but in abnormal perceptions there is no reason to expect such correspondence, and their testimony, therefore, cannot outweigh that of normal perception.

The mystic emotion, if it is freed from unwarranted beliefs, and not so overwhelming as to remove a man wholly from the ordinary business of life, may give something of very great value — the same kind of thing, though in a heightened form, that is given by contemplation. Breadth and

[3] See his *Varieties of Religious Experience.* [Above, p. 61.]

calm and profundity may all have their source in this emotion, in which, for the moment, all self-centered desire is dead, and the mind becomes a mirror for the vastness of the universe. Those who have had this experience, and believe it to be bound up unavoidably with assertions about the nature of the universe, naturally cling to these assertions. I believe myself that the assertions are inessential, and that there is no reason to believe them true. I cannot admit any method of arriving at truth except that of science, but in the realm of the emotions I do not deny the value of the experiences which have given rise to religion. Through association with false beliefs, they have led to much evil as well as good; freed from this association, it may be hoped that the good alone will remain.

7

THE CASE
FOR ATHEISM

Ernest Nagel

*Ernest Nagel (1901-   ), a prominent American philosopher of science, is John
Dewey Professor of Philosophy at Columbia University.*

The essays in this book are devoted in the main to the exposition of the
major religious creeds of humanity. It is a natural expectation that this final
paper, even though its theme is so radically different from nearly all of the
others, will show how atheism belongs to the great tradition of religious
thought. Needless to say, this expectation is difficult to satisfy, and did
anyone succeed in doing so he would indeed be performing the neatest con-
juring trick of the week. But the expectation nevertheless does cause me
some embarrassment, which is only slightly relieved by an anecdote Bertrand
Russell reports in his recent book, *Portraits from Memory*. Russell was im-
prisoned during the First World War for pacifistic activities. On entering
the prison he was asked a number of customary questions about himself for
the prison records. One question was about his religion. Russell explained
that he was an agnostic. "Never heard of it," the warden declared. "How
do you spell it?" When Russell told him, the warden observed "Well, there
are many religions, but I suppose they all worship the same God." Russell
adds that this remark kept him cheerful for about a week. Perhaps philosophical atheism also is a religion.

1

I must begin by stating what sense I am attaching to the word "atheism,"
and how I am construing the theme of this paper. I shall understand by
"atheism" a critique and a denial of the major claims of all varieties of
theism. And by theism I shall mean the view which holds, as one writer
has expressed it, "that the heavens and the earth and all that they contain owe

The whole of the essay, "Philosophical Concepts of Atheism," which originally appeared in *Basic Beliefs,* ed. Johnson E. Fairchild, and published by Sheridan House,
Inc. Reprinted by permission of the author and publisher.

their existence and continuance in existence to the wisdom and will of a supreme, self-consistent, omnipotent, omniscient, righteous, and benevolent being, who is distinct from, and independent of, what he has created." Several things immediately follow from these definitions.

In the first place, atheism is not necessarily an irreligious concept, for theism is just one among many views concerning the nature and origin of the world. The denial of theism is logically compatible with a religious outlook upon life, and is in fact characteristic of some of the great historical religions. For as readers of this volume will know, early Buddhism is a religion which does not subscribe to any doctrine about a god; and there are pantheistic religions and philosophies which, because they deny that God is a being separate from and independent of the world, are not theistic in the sense of the word explained above.

The second point to note is that atheism is not to be identified with sheer unbelief, or with disbelief in some particular creed of a religious group. Thus, a child who has received no religious instruction and has never heard about God, is not an atheist — for he is not denying any theistic claims. Similarly in the case of an adult who, if he has withdrawn from the faith of his fathers without reflection or because of frank indifference to any theological issue, is also not an atheist — for such an adult is not challenging theism and is not professing any views on the subject. Moreover, though the term "atheist" has been used historically as an abusive label for those who do not happen to subscribe to some regnant orthodoxy (for example, the ancient Romans called the early Christians atheists, because the latter denied the Roman divinities), or for those who engage in conduct regarded as immoral it is not in this sense that I am discussing atheism.

One final word of preliminary explanation. I propose to examine some *philosophic* concepts of atheism, and I am not interested in the slightest in the many considerations atheists have advanced against the evidences for some particular religious and theological doctrine — for example, against the truth of the Christian story. What I mean by "philosophical" in the present context is that the views I shall consider are directed against any form of theism, and have their origin and basis in a logical analysis of the theistic position, and in a comprehensive account of the world believed to be wholly intelligible without the adoption of a theistic hypothesis.

Theism as I conceive it is a theological proposition, not a statement of a position that belongs primarily to religion. On my view, religion as a historical and social phenomenon is primarily an institutionalized *cultus* or practice, which possesses identifiable social functions and which expresses certain attitudes men take toward their world. Although it is doubtful whether men ever engage in religious practices or assume religious attitudes without some more or less explicit interpretation of their ritual or some rationale for their attitude, it is still the case that it is possible to distinguish religion as a social and personal phenomenon from the theological doctrines which may be developed as justifications for religious practices. Indeed, in some of the great religions of the world the profession of a creed plays a relatively minor role. In short, religion is a form of social communion, a participation in certain kinds of ritual (whether it be a dance, worship, prayer, or the like), and a form of experience (sometimes, though not invariably, directed to a personal confrontation with divine and holy things). Theology is an articulated and, at its best, a rational attempt at understanding these feelings and practices, in the light of their relation to other parts of human experience, and in terms of some hypothesis concerning the nature of things entire.

2

As I see it, atheistic philosophies fall into two major groups: 1) those which hold that the theistic doctrine is meaningful, but reject it either on the ground that, (a) the positive evidence for it is insufficient, or (b) the negative evidence is quite overwhelming; and 2) those who hold that the theistic thesis is not even meaningful, and reject it (a) as just nonsense or (b) as literally meaningless but interpreting it as a symbolic rendering of human ideals, thus reading the theistic thesis in a sense that most believers in theism would disavow. It will not be possible in the limited space at my disposal to discuss the second category of atheistic critiques; and in any event, most of the traditional atheistic critiques of theism belong to the first group.

But before turning to the philosophical examination of the major classical arguments for theism, it is well to note that such philosophical critiques do not quite convey the passion with which atheists have often carried on their analyses of theistic views. For historically, atheism has been, and indeed continues to be, a form of social and political protest, directed as much against institutionalized religion as against theistic doctrine. Atheism has been, in effect, a moral revulsion against the undoubted abuses of the secular power exercised by religious leaders and religious institutions.

Religious authorities have opposed the correction of glaring injustices, and encouraged politically and socially reactionary policies. Religious institutions have been havens of obscurantist thought and centers for the dissemination of intolerance. Religious creeds have been used to set limits to free inquiry, to perpetuate inhumane treatment of the ill and the underprivileged, and to support moral doctrines insensitive to human suffering.

These indictments may not tell the whole story about the historical significance of religion; but they are at least an important part of the story. The refutation of theism has thus seemed to many as an indispensable step not only towards liberating men's minds from superstition, but also towards achieving a more equitable reordering of society. And no account of even the more philosophical aspects of atheistic thought is adequate, which does not give proper recognition to the powerful social motives that actuate many atheistic arguments.

But however this may be, I want now to discuss three classical arguments for the existence of God, arguments which have constituted at least a partial basis for theistic commitments. As long as theism is defended simply as dogma, asserted as a matter of direct revelation or as the deliverance of authority, belief in the dogma is impregnable to rational argument. In fact, however, reasons are frequently advanced in support of the theistic creed, and these reasons have been the subject of acute philosophical critiques.

One of the oldest intellectual defenses of theism is the cosmological argument, also known as the argument from a first cause. Briefly put, the argument runs as follows. Every event must have a cause. Hence an event A must have as cause some event B, which in turn must have a cause C, and so on. But if there is no end to this backward progression of causes, the progression will be infinite; and in the opinion of those who use this argument, an infinite series of actual events is unintelligible and absurd. Hence there must be a first cause, and this first cause is God, the initiator of all change in the universe.

The argument is an ancient one, and is especially effective when stated within the framework of assumptions of Aristotelian physics; and it has impressed many generations of exceptionally keen minds. The argument is nonetheless a weak reed on which to rest the theistic thesis. Let us waive any question concerning the validity of the principle that every event has a cause, for though the question is important its discussion would lead us far afield. However, if the principle is assumed, it is surely incongruous to postulate a first cause as a way of escaping from the coils of an infinite series. For if everything must have a cause, why does not God require one for His own existence? The standard answer is that He does not need any, because He is self-caused. But if God can be self-caused, why cannot the world be self-caused? Why do we require a God transcending the world to bring the world into existence and to initiate changes in it? On the other hand, the supposed inconceivability and absurdity of an infinite series of regressive causes will be admitted by no one who has competent familiarity with the modern mathematical analysis of infinity. The cosmological argument does not stand up under scrutiny.

The second "proof" of God's existence is usually called the ontological argument. It too has a long history going back to early Christian days, though it acquired great prominence only in medieval times. The argument can be stated in several ways, one of which is the following. Since God is conceived to be omnipotent, he is a perfect being. A perfect being is defined as one whose essence or nature lacks no attributes (or properties) whatsoever, one whose nature is complete in every respect. But it is evident that we have an idea of a perfect being, for we have just defined the idea; and since this is so, the argument continues, God who is the perfect being must exist. Why must he? Because his existence follows from his defined nature. For if God lacked the attribute of existence, he would be lacking at least one attribute, and would therefore not be perfect. To sum up, since we have an idea of God as a perfect being, God must exist.

There are several ways of approaching this argument, but I shall consider only one. The argument was exploded by the 18th century philosopher Immanuel Kant. The substance of Kant's criticism is that it is just a confusion to say that existence is an attribute, and that though the *word* "existence" may occur as the grammatical predicate in a sentence no attribute is being predicated of a thing when we say that the thing exists or has existence. Thus, to use Kant's example, when we think of $100 we are thinking of the nature of this sum of money; but the nature of $100 remains the same whether we have $100 in our pockets or not. Accordingly, we are confounding grammar with logic if we suppose that some characteristic is being attributed to the nature of $100 when we say that a hundred dollar bill exists in someone's pocket.

To make the point clearer, consider another example. When we say that a lion has a tawny color, we are predicating a certain attribute of the animal, and similarly when we say that the lion is fierce or is hungry. But when we say the lion exists, all that we are saying is that something is (or has the nature of) a lion; we are not specifying an attribute which belongs to the nature of anything that is a lion. In short, the word "existence" does not signify any attribute, and in consequence no attribute that belongs to the nature of anything. Accordingly, it does not follow from the assumption that we have an idea of a perfect being that such a being exists. For the idea of a perfect being does not involve the attribute of existence as a constituent of that idea, since there is no such attribute. The ontological argument thus has a serious leak, and it can hold no water.

3

The two arguments discussed thus far are purely dialectical, and attempt to establish God's existence without any appeal to empirical data. The next argument, called the argument from design, is different in character, for it is based on what purports to be empirical evidence. I wish to examine two forms of this argument.

One variant of it calls attention to the remarkable way in which different things and processes in the world are integrated with each other, and concludes that this mutual "fitness" of things can be explained only by the assumption of a divine architect who planned the world and everything in it. For example, living organisms can maintain themselves in a variety of environments, and do so in virtue of their delicate mechanisms which adapt the organisms to all sorts of environmental changes. There is thus an intricate pattern of means and ends throughout the animate world. But the existence of this pattern is unintelligible, so the argument runs, except on the hypothesis that the pattern has been deliberately instituted by a Supreme Designer. If we find a watch in some deserted spot, we do not think it came into existence by chance, and we do not hesitate to conclude that an intelligent creature designed and made it. But the world and all its contents exhibit mechanisms and mutual adjustments that are far more complicated and subtle than are those of a watch. Must we not therefore conclude that these things too have a Creator?

The conclusion of this argument is based on an inference from analogy: the watch and the world are alike in possessing a congruence of parts and an adjustment of means to ends; the watch has a watch-maker; hence the world has a world-maker. But is the analogy a good one? Let us once more waive some important issues, in particular the issue whether the universe is the unified system such as the watch admittedly is. And let us concentrate on the question what is the ground for our assurance that watches do not come into existence except through the operations of intelligent manufacturers. The answer is plain. We have never run across a watch which has not been deliberately made by someone. But the situation is nothing like this in the case of the innumerable animate and inanimate systems with which we are familiar. Even in the case of living organisms, though they are generated by their parent organisms, the parents do not "make" their progeny in the same sense in which watchmakers make watches. And once this point is clear, the inference from the existence of living organisms to the existence of a supreme designer no longer appears credible.

Moreover, the argument loses all its force if the facts which the hypothesis of a divine designer is supposed to explain can be understood on the basis of a better supported assumption. And indeed, such an alternative explanation is one of the achievements of Darwinian biology. For Darwin showed that one can account for the variety of biological species, as well as for their adaptations to their environments, without invoking a divine creator and acts of special creation. The Darwinian theory explains the diversity of biological species in terms of chance variations in the structure of organisms, and of a mechanism of selection which retains those variant forms that possess some advantages for survival. The evidence for these assumptions is considerable; and developments subsequent to Darwin have only strengthened the case for a thoroughly naturalistic explanation of the facts of biological adaptation. In any event, this version of the argument from design has nothing to recommend it.

A second form of this argument has been recently revived in the speculations of some modern physicists. No one who is familiar with the facts, can fail to be impressed by the success with which the use of mathematical methods has enabled us to obtain intellectual mastery of many parts of nature. But some thinkers have therefore concluded that since the book of nature is ostensibly written in mathematical language, nature must be the creation of a divine mathematician. However, the argument is most dubious. For it rests, among other things, on the assumption that mathematical tools can be successfully used only if the events of nature exhibit some *special* kind of order, and on the further assumption that if the structure of things were different from what they are mathematical language would be inadequate for describing such structure. But it can be shown that no matter what the world were like — even if it impressed us as being utterly chaotic — it would still possess some order, and would in principle be amenable to a mathematical description. In point of fact, it makes no sense to say that there is absolutely *no* pattern in any conceivable subject matter. To be sure, there are differences in complexities of structure, and if the patterns of events were sufficiently complex we might not be able to unravel them. But however that may be, the success of mathematical physics in giving us some understanding of the world around us does not yield the conclusion that only a mathematician could have devised the patterns of order we have discovered in nature.

4

The inconclusiveness of the three classical arguments for the existence of God was already made evident by Kant, in a manner substantially not different from the above discussion. There are, however, other types of arguments for theism that have been influential in the history of thought, two of which I wish to consider, even if only briefly.

Indeed, though Kant destroyed the classical intellectual foundations for theism, he himself invented a fresh argument for it. Kant's attempted proof is not intended to be a purely theoretical demonstration, and is based on the supposed facts of our moral nature. It has exerted an enormous influence on subsequent theological speculation. In barest outline, the argument is as follows. According to Kant, we are subject not only to physical laws like the rest of nature, but also to moral ones. These moral laws are categorical imperatives, which we must heed not because of their utilitarian consequences, but simply because as autonomous moral agents it is our duty to accept them as binding. However, Kant was keenly aware that though virtue may be its reward, the virtuous man (that is, the man who acts out of a sense of duty and in conformity with the moral law) does not always receive his just desserts in this world; nor did he shut his eyes to the fact that evil men frequently enjoy the best things this world has to offer. In short, virtue does not always reap happiness. Nevertheless, the highest human good is the realization of happiness commensurate with one's virtue; and Kant believed that it is a practical postulate of the moral life to promote this good. But what can guarantee that the highest good is realizable? Such a guarantee can be found only in God, who must therefore exist if the highest good is not to be a fatuous ideal. The existence of an omnipotent, omniscient, and omnibenevolent God is thus postulated as a necessary condition for the possibility of a moral life.

Despite the prestige this argument has acquired, it is difficult to grant it any force. It is easy enough to postulate God's existence. But as Bertrand Russell observed in another connection, postulation has all the advantages of theft over honest toil. No postulation carries with it any assurance that what is postulated is actually the case. And though we may postulate God's existence as a means to guaranteeing the possibility of realizing happiness together with virtue, the postulation establishes neither the actual realizability of this ideal nor the fact of his existence. Moreover, the argument is not made more cogent when we recognize that it is based squarely on the highly dubious conception that considerations of utility and human happiness must not enter into the determination of what is morally obligatory. Having built his moral theory on a radical separation of means from ends, Kant was driven to the desperate postulation of God's existence in order to relate them again. The argument is thus at best a *tour de force,* contrived to remedy a fatal flaw in Kant's initial moral assumptions. It carries no conviction to anyone who does not commit Kant's initial blunder.

One further type of argument, pervasive in much Protestant theological literature, deserves brief mention. Arguments of this type take their point of departure from the psychology of religious and mystical experience. Those who have undergone such experiences, often report that during the experience they feel themselves to be in the presence of the divine and holy, that they lose their sense of self-identity and become merged with some fundamental reality, or that they enjoy a feeling of total dependence upon some ultimate power. The overwhelming sense of transcending one's finitude which characterizes such vivid periods of life, and of coalescing with some ultimate source of all existence, is then taken to be compelling evidence for the existence of a supreme being. In a variant form of this argument, other theologians have identified God as the object which satisfies the commonly experienced need for integrating one's scattered and conflicting impulses into a coherent unity, or as the subject which is of ultimate concern to us. In short, a proof of God's existence is found in the occurrence of certain distinctive experiences.

It would be flying in the face of well-attested facts were one to deny that such experiences frequently occur. But do these facts constitute evidence for the conclusion based on them? Does the fact, for example, that an individual experiences a profound sense of direct contact with an alleged transcendent ground of all reality, constitute competent evidence for the claim that there is such a ground and that it is the immediate cause of the experience? If well-established canons for evaluating evidence are accepted, the answer is surely negative. No one will dispute that many men do have vivid experiences in which such things as ghosts or pink elephants appear before them; but only the hopelessly credulous will without further ado count such experiences as establishing the existence of ghosts and pink elephants. To establish the existence of such things, evidence is required that is obtained under controlled conditions and that can be confirmed by independent inquirers. Again, though a man's report that he is suffering pain may be taken at face value, one cannot take at face value the claim, were he to make it, that it is the food he ate which is the cause (or a contributory cause) of his felt pain — not even if the man were to report a vivid feeling of abdominal disturbance. And similarly, an overwhelming feeling of being in the presence of the Divine is evidence enough for admitting the genuineness of such feeling; it is no evidence for the claim that a supreme being with a substantial existence independent of the experience is the cause of the experience.

5

Thus far the discussion has been concerned with noting inadequacies in various arguments widely used to support theism. However, much atheistic criticism is also directed toward exposing incoherencies in the very thesis of theism. I want therefore to consider this aspect of the atheistic critique, though I will restrict myself to the central difficulty in the theistic position which arises from the simultaneous attribution of omnipotence, omniscience, and omnibenevolence to the Deity. The difficulty is that of reconciling these attributes with the occurrence of evil in the world. Accordingly, the question to which I now turn is whether, despite the existence of evil, it is possible to construct a theodicy which will justify the ways of an infinitely powerful and just God to man.

Two main types of solutions have been proposed for this problem. One way that is frequently used is to maintain that what is commonly called evil is only an illusion, or at worst only the "privation" or absence of good. Accordingly, evil is not "really real," it is only the "negative" side of God's beneficence, it is only the product of our limited intelligence which fails to plumb the true character of God's creative bounty. A sufficient comment on this proposed solution is that facts are not altered or abolished by rebaptizing them. Evil may indeed be only an appearance and not genuine. But this does not eliminate from the realm of appearance the tragedies, the sufferings, and the iniquities which men so frequently endure. And it raises once more, though on another level, the problem of reconciling the fact that there is evil in the realm of appearance with God's alleged omnibenevolence. In any event, it is small comfort to anyone suffering a cruel misfortune for which he is in no way responsible, to be told that what he is undergoing is only the absence of good. It is a gratuitous insult to mankind, a symptom of insensitivity and indifference to human suffering, to be assured that all the miseries and agonies men experience are only illusory.

Another gambit often played in attempting to justify the ways of God to man is to argue that the things called evil are evil only because they are viewed in isolation; they are not evil when viewed in proper perspective and in relation to the rest of creation. Thus, if one attends to but a single instrument in an orchestra, the sounds issuing from it may indeed be harsh and discordant. But if one is placed at a proper distance from the whole orchestra, the sounds of that single instrument will mingle with the sounds issuing from the other players to produce a marvellous bit of symphonic music. Analogously, experiences we call painful undoubtedly occur and are real enough. But the pain is judged to be an evil only because it is experienced in a limited perspective — the pain is there for the sake of a more inclusive good, whose reality eludes us because our intelligences are too weak to apprehend things in their entirety.

It is an appropriate retort to this argument that of course we judge things to be evil in a human perspective, but that since we are not God this is the only proper perspective in which to judge them. It may indeed be the case that what is evil for us is not evil for some other part of creation. However, we are not this other part of creation, and it is irrelevant to argue that were we something other than what we are, our evaluations of what is good and bad would be different. Moreover, the worthlessness of the argument becomes even more evident if we remind ourselves that it is unsupported speculation to suppose that whatever is evil in a finite perspective is good from the purported perspective of the totality of things. For the argument can be turned around: what we judge to be a good is a good only because it is viewed in isolation; when it is viewed in proper perspective, and in relation to the entire scheme of things, it is an evil. This is in fact a standard form of the argument for a universal pessimism. Is it any worse than the similar argument for a universal optimism? The very raising of this question is a *reductio ad absurdum* of the proposed solution to the ancient problem of evil.

I do not believe it is possible to reconcile the alleged omnipotence and omnibenevolence of God with the unvarnished facts of human existence. In point of fact, many theologians have concurred in this conclusion; for in order to escape from the difficulty which the traditional attributes of God present, they have assumed that God is not all powerful, and that there are limits as to what He can do in his efforts to establish a righteous order in the universe. But whether such a modified theology is better off, is doubtful; and in any event, the question still remains whether the facts of human life support the claim that an omnibenevolent Deity, though limited in power, is revealed in the ordering of human history. It is pertinent to note in this connection that though there have been many historians who have made the effort, no historian has yet succeeded in showing to the satisfaction of his professional colleagues that the hypothesis of a Divine Providence is capable of explaining anything which cannot be explained just as well without this hypothesis.

6

This last remark naturally leads to the question whether, apart from their polemics against theism, philosophical atheists have not shared a common set of positive views, a common set of philosophical convictions which set them off from other groups of thinkers. In one very clear sense of this query the answer is indubitably negative. For there never has been what one might call a "school of atheism," in the way in which there has been a Platonic school or even a Kantian school. In point of fact, atheistic critics of theism can be found among many of the conventional groupings of philosophical thinkers — even, I venture to add, among professional theologians in recent years who in effect preach atheism in the guise of language taken bodily from the Christian tradition.

Nevertheless, despite the variety of philosophic positions to which at one time or another in the history of thought atheists have subscribed, it seems to me that atheism is not simply a negative standpoint. At any rate, there is a certain quality of intellectual temper that has characterized, and continues to characterize, many philosophical atheists. (I am excluding from consideration the so-called "village atheist," whose primary concern is to twit and ridicule those who accept some form of theism, or for that matter those who have any religious convictions.) Moreover, their rejection of theism is based not only on the inadequacies they have found in the arguments for theism, but often also on the positive ground that atheism is a corollary to a better supported general outlook upon the nature of things. I want therefore to conclude this discussion with a brief enumeration of some points of positive doctrine to which by and large philosophical atheists seem to me to subscribe. These points fall into three major groups.

In the first place, philosophical atheists reject the assumption that there are disembodied spirits, or that incorporeal entities of any sort can exercise a causal agency. On the contrary, atheists are generally agreed that if we wish to achieve any understanding of what takes place in the universe, we must look to the operations of organized bodies. Accordingly, the various processes taking place in nature, whether animate or inanimate, are to be explained in terms of the properties and structures of identifiable and spatio-temporally located objects. Moreover, the present variety of systems and activities found in the universe is to be accounted for on the basis of the transformations things undergo when they enter into different relations with one another — transformations which often result in the emergence of novel kinds of objects. On the other hand, though things are in flux and undergo alteration, there is no all-encompassing unitary pattern of change. Nature is ineradicably plural, both in respect to the individuals occurring in it as well as in respect to the processes in which things become involved. Accordingly, the human scene and the human perspective are not illusory; and man and his works are no less and no more "real" than are other parts or phases of the cosmos. At the risk of using a possibly misleading characterization, all of this can be summarized by saying that an atheistic view of things is a form of materialism.

In the second place, atheists generally manifest a marked empirical temper, and often take as their ideal the intellectual methods employed in the contemporaneous empirical sciences. Philosophical atheists differ considerably on important points of detail in their account of how responsible claims to knowledge are to be established. But there is substantial agreement among them that controlled sensory observation is the court of final appeal in issues concerning matters of fact. It is indeed this commitment to the use of an empirical method which is the final basis of the atheistic critique of theism. For at bottom this critique seeks to show that we can understand whatever a theistic assumption is alleged to explain, through the use of the proved methods of the positive sciences and without the introduction of empirically unsupported *ad hoc* hypotheses about a Deity. It is pertinent in this connection to recall a familiar legend about the French mathematical physicist Laplace. According to the story, Laplace made a personal presentation of a copy of his now famous book on celestial mechanics to Napoleon. Napoleon glanced through the volume, and finding no reference to the Deity asked Laplace whether God's existence played any role in the analysis. "Sire, I have no need for that hypothesis," Laplace is reported to have replied. The dismissal of sterile hypotheses characterizes not only the work of Laplace; it is the uniform rule in scientific inquiry. The sterility of the theistic assumption is one of the main burdens of the literature of atheism both ancient and modern.

And finally, atheistic thinkers have generally accepted a utilitarian basis for judging moral issues, and they have exhibited a libertarian attitude toward human needs and impulses. The conceptions of the human good they have advocated are conceptions which are commensurate with the actual capacities of mortal men, so that it is the satisfaction of the complex needs of the human creature which is the final standard for evaluating the validity of a moral ideal or moral prescription.

In consequence, the emphasis of atheistic moral reflection has been this-worldly rather than other-worldly, individualistic rather than authoritarian. The stress upon a good life that must be consummated in this world, has made atheists vigorous opponents of moral codes which seek to repress human impulses in the name of some unrealizable other-worldly ideal. The individualism that is so pronounced a strain in many philosophical atheists has made them tolerant of human limitations and sensitive to the plurality of legitimate moral goals. On the other hand, this individualism has certainly not prevented many of them from recognizing the crucial role which institutional arrangements can play in achieving desirable patterns of human living. In consequence, atheists have made important contributions to the development of a climate of opinion favorable to pursuing the values of a liberal civilization and they have played effective roles in attempts to rectify social injustices.

Atheists cannot build their moral outlook on foundations upon which so many men conduct their lives. In particular, atheism cannot offer the incentives to conduct and the consolations for misfortune which theistic religions supply to their adherents. It can offer no hope of personal immortality, no threats of Divine chastisement, no promise of eventual recompense for injustices suffered, no blueprints to sure salvation. For on its view of the place of man in nature, human excellence and human dignity must be achieved within a finite life-span, or not at all, so that the rewards of moral endeavor must come from the quality of civilized living, and not from some source of disbursement that dwells outside of time. Accordingly, atheistic moral reflection at its best does not culminate in a quiescent ideal of human perfection, but is a vigorous call to intelligent activity — activity for the sake of realizing human potentialities and for eliminating whatever stands in the way of such realization. Nevertheless, though slavish resignation to remediable ills is not characteristic of atheistic thought, responsible atheists have never pretended that human effort can invariably achieve the heart's every legitimate desire. A tragic view of life is thus an uneliminable ingredient in atheistic thought. This ingredient does not invite or generally produce lugubrious lamentation. But it does touch the atheist's view of man and his place in nature with an emotion that makes the philosophical atheist a kindred spirit to those who, within the framework of various religious traditions, have developed a serenely resigned attitude toward the inevitable tragedies of the human estate.

8

A CHRISTIAN VIEW
OF THE PROBLEM
OF EVIL

John Hick

John Hick (1922-   ) is Lecturer in Divinity, Cambridge University.

To many, the most powerful positive objection to belief in God is the fact of evil. Probably for most agnostics it is the appalling depth and extent of human suffering, more than anything else, that makes the idea of a loving Creator seem so implausible and disposes them toward one or another of the various naturalistic theories of religion.

As a challenge to theism, the problem of evil has traditionally been posed in the form of a dilemma: if God is perfectly loving, he must wish to abolish evil; and if he is all-powerful, he must be able to abolish evil. But evil exists; therefore God cannot be both omnipotent and perfectly loving.

Certain solutions, which at once suggest themselves, have to be ruled out so far as the Judaic-Christian faith is concerned.

To say, for example (with contemporary Christian Science), that evil is an illusion of the human mind, is impossible within a religion based upon the stark realism of the Bible. Its pages faithfully reflect the characteristic mixture of good and evil in human experience. They record every kind of sorrow and suffering, every mode of man's inhumanity to man and of his painfully insecure existence in the world. There is no attempt to regard evil as anything but dark, menacingly ugly, heart-rending, and crushing. In the Christian scriptures, the climax of this history of evil is the crucifixion of Jesus, which is presented not only as a case of utterly unjust suffering, but as the violent and murderous rejection of God's Messiah. There can be no doubt, then, that for biblical faith, evil is unambiguously evil, and stands in direct opposition to God's will.

Again, to solve the problem of evil by means of the theory (sponsored, for example, by the Boston "Personalist" School)[1] of a finite deity who does the best he can with a material, intractable and co-eternal with himself, is to have abandoned the basic premise of Hebrew-Christian monotheism; for the theory amounts to rejecting belief in the infinity and sovereignty of God.

Indeed, any theory which would avoid the problem of the origin of evil by depicting it as an ultimate constituent of the universe, coordinate with good, has been repudiated in advance by the classic Christian teaching, first developed by Augustine, that evil represents the going wrong of something which in itself is good.[2] Augustine holds firmly to the Hebrew-Christian conviction that the universe is *good* — that is to say, it is the creation of a good God for a good purpose. He completely rejects the ancient prejudice, widespread in his day, that matter is evil. There are, according to Augustine, higher and lower, greater and lesser goods in immense abundance and variety; but everything which has being is good in its own way and degree, except in so far as it may have become spoiled or corrupted. Evil — whether it be an evil will, an instance of pain, or some disorder or decay in nature — has not been set there by God, but represents the distortion of something that is inherently valuable. Whatever exists is, as such, and in its proper place, good; evil is essentially parasitic upon good, being disorder and perversion in a fundamentally good creation. This understanding of evil as something negative means that it is not willed and created by God; but it does not mean (as some have supposed) that evil is unreal and can be disregarded. Clearly, the first effect of this doctrine is to accentuate even more the question of the origin of evil.

Theodicy,[3] as many modern Christian thinkers see it, is a modest enterprise, negative rather than positive in its conclusions. It does not claim to explain, nor to explain away, every instance of evil in human experience, but only to point to certain considerations which prevent the fact of evil (largely incomprehensible though it remains) from constituting a final and insuperable bar to rational belief in God.

In indicating these considerations it will be useful to follow the traditional division of the subject. There is the problem of *moral evil* or wickedness: why does an all-good and all-powerful God permit this? And there is the problem of the *non-moral evil* of suffering or pain, both physical and mental: why has an all-good and all-powerful God created a world in which this occurs?

Christian thought has always considered moral evil in its relation to human freedom and responsibility. To be a person is to be a finite center of freedom, a (relatively) free and self-directing agent responsible for one's own

---

[1] Edgar Brightman's *A Philosophy of Religion* (Englewood Cliffs, N.J.: Prentice-Hall, Inc., 1940), chaps. 8-10, is a classic exposition of one form of this view.

[2] See Augustine's *Confessions,* Book VII, chap. 12; *City of God,* Book XII, chap. 3; *Enchiridion,* chap. 4.

[3] The word "theodicy" from the Greek *theos* (God) and *dike* (righteous), means the justification of God's goodness in face of the fact of evil.

decisions. This involves being free to act wrongly as well as to act rightly. The idea of a person who can be infallibly guaranteed always to act rightly is self-contradictory. There can be no guarantee in advance that a genuinely free moral agent will never choose amiss. Consequently, the possibility of wrongdoing or sin is logically inseparable from the creation of finite persons, and to say that God should not have created beings who might sin amounts to saying that he should not have created people.

.   .   .

An objector might raise the question of whether or not we deny God's omnipotence if we admit that he is unable to create persons who are free from the risks inherent in personal freedom. The answer that has always been given is that to create such beings is logically impossible. It is no limitation upon God's power that he cannot accomplish the logically impossible, since there is nothing here to accomplish, but only a meaningless conjunction of words[4] — in this case "person who is not a person." God is able to create beings of any and every conceivable kind; but creatures who lack moral freedom, however superior they might be to human beings in other respects, would not be what we mean by persons. They would constitute a different form of life which God might have brought into existence instead of persons. When we ask why God did not create such beings in place of persons, the traditional answer is that only persons could, in any meaningful sense, become "children of God," capable of entering into a personal relationship with their Creator by a free and uncompelled response to his love.

.   .   .

The necessary connection between moral freedom and the possibility, now actualized, of sin throws light upon a great deal of the suffering which afflicts mankind. For an enormous amount of human pain arises either from the inhumanity or the culpable incompetence of mankind. This includes such major scourges as poverty, oppression and persecution, war, and all the injustice, indignity, and inequity which occur even in the most advanced societies. These evils are manifestations of human sin. Even disease is fostered to an extent, the limits of which have not yet been determined by psychosomatic medicine, by moral and emotional factors seated both in the individual and in his social environment. To the extent that all of these evils stem from human failures and wrong decisions, their possibility is inherent in the creation of free persons inhabiting a world which presents them with real choices which are followed by real consequences.

We may now turn more directly to the problem of suffering. Even though the major bulk of actual human pain is traceable to man's misused freedom as a sole or part cause, there remain other sources of pain which are entirely independent of the human will, for example, earthquake, hurricane, storm, flood, drought, and blight. In practice, it is often impossible to trace a boundary between the suffering which results from human wickedness and

---

[4] As Aquinas said, ". . . nothing that implies a contradiction falls under the scope of God's omnipotence." *Summa Theologica*, Part I, Question 25, article 4.

folly and that which falls upon mankind from without. Both kinds of suffering are inextricably mingled together in human experience. For our present purpose, however, it is important to note that the latter category does exist and that it seems to be built into the very structure of our world. In response to it, theodicy, if it is wisely conducted, follows a negative path. It is not possible to show positively that each item of human pain serves the divine purpose of good; but, on the other hand, it does seem possible to show that the divine purpose as it is understood in Judaism and Christianity could not be forwarded in a world which was designed as a permanent hedonistic paradise.[5]

An essential premise of this argument concerns the nature of the divine purpose in creating the world. The skeptic's assumption is that man is to be viewed as a completed creation and that God's purpose in making the world was to provide a suitable dwelling-place for this fully-formed creature. Since God is good and loving, the environment which he has created for human life to inhabit is naturally as pleasant and comfortable as possible. The problem is essentially similar to that of a man who builds a cage for some pet animal. Since our world, in fact, contains sources of hardship, inconvenience, and danger of innumerable kinds, the conclusion follows that this world cannot have been created by a perfectly benevolent and all-powerful deity.[6]

Christianity, however, has never supposed that God's purpose in the creation of the world was to construct a paradise whose inhabitants would experience a maximum of pleasure and a minimum of pain. The world is seen, instead, as a place of "soul-making" in which free beings, grappling with the tasks and challenges of their existence in a common environment, may become "children of God" and "heirs of eternal life." A way of thinking theologically of God's continuing creative purpose for man was suggested by some of the early Hellenistic Fathers of the Christian Church, especially Irenaeus. Following hints from St. Paul, Irenaeus taught that man has been made as a person in the image of God but has not yet been brought as a free and responsible agent into the finite likeness of God, which is revealed in Christ.[7] Our world, with all its rough edges, is the sphere in which this second and harder stage of the creative process is taking place.

This conception of the world (whether or not set in Irenaeus' theological framework) can be supported by the method of negative theodicy. Suppose, contrary to fact, that this world were a paradise from which all possibility of pain and suffering were excluded. The consequences would be very far-reaching. For example, no one could ever injure anyone else: the murderer's knife would turn to paper or his bullets to thin air; the bank safe, robbed of a million dollars, would miraculously become filled with another million dollars (without this device, on however large a scale, proving inflationary); fraud, deceit, conspiracy, and treason would somehow always leave

---

[5] From the Greek *hedone*, pleasure.

[6] This is the nature of David Hume's argument in his discussion of the problem of evil in his *Dialogues,* Part XI.

[7] See Irenaeus' *Against Heresies,* Book IV, chaps. 37 and 38.

the fabric of society undamaged. Again, no one would ever be injured by accident: the mountain-climber, steeplejack, or playing child falling from a height would float unharmed tothe ground; the reckless driver would never meet with disaster. There would be no need to work, since no harm could result from avoiding work; there would be no call to be concerned for others in time of need or danger, for in such a world there could be no real needs or dangers.

To make possible this continual series of individual adjustments, nature would have to work by "special providences" instead of running according to general laws which men must learn to respect on penalty of pain or death. The laws of nature would have to be extremely flexible: sometimes gravity would operate, sometimes not; sometimes an object would be hard and solid, sometimes soft. There could be no sciences, for there would be no enduring world structure to investigate. In eliminating the problems and hardships of an objective environment, with its own laws, life would become like a dream in which, delightfully but aimlessly, we would float and drift at ease.[8]

One can at least begin to imagine such a world. It is evident that our present ethical concepts would have no meaning in it. If, for example, the notion of harming someone is an essential element in the concept of a wrong action, in our hedonistic paradise there could be no wrong actions — nor any right actions in distinction from wrong. Courage and fortitude would have no point in an environment in which there is, by definition, no danger or difficulty. Generosity, kindness, the *agape* aspect of love, prudence, unselfishness, and all other ethical notions which presuppose life in a stable environment, could not even be formed. Consequently, such a world, however well it might promote pleasure, would be very ill adapted for the development of the moral qualities of human personality. In relation to this purpose it would be the worst of all possible worlds.

It would seem, then, that an environment intended to make possible the growth in free beings of the finest characteristics of personal life, must have a good deal in common with our present world. It must operate according to general and dependable laws; and it must involve real dangers, difficulties, problems, obstacles, and possibilities of pain, failure, sorrow, frustration, and defeat. If it did not contain the particular trials and perils which — subtracting man's own very considerable contribution — our world contains, it would have to contain others instead.

To realize this is not, by any means, to be in possession of a detailed theodicy. It is to understand that this world, with all its "heartaches and the thousand natural shocks that flesh is heir to," an environment so manifestly not designed for the maximization of human pleasure and the minimization of human pain, may be rather well adapted to the quite different purpose of "soul-making."

---

8 Tennyson's poem, *The Lotus-Eaters,* well expresses the desire (analyzed by Freud as a wish to return to the peace of the womb) for such "dreamful ease."

9

CAN RELIGIOUS BELIEFS BE TESTED EMPIRICALLY?

Antony Flew

Antony Flew (1923-   ), Professor of Philosophy at the University of Keele, Stafford-shire, is identified with the contemporary Oxford style of analytical philosophy.

A

ANTONY FLEW

Let us begin with a parable. It is a parable developed from a tale told by John Wisdom in his haunting and revelatory article 'Gods'.[1] Once upon a time two explorers came upon a clearing in the jungle. In the clearing were growing many flowers and many weeds. One explorer says, 'Some gardener must tend this plot.' The other disagrees, 'There is no gardener.' So they pitch their tents and set a watch. No gardener is ever seen. 'But perhaps he is an invisible gardener.' So they set up a barbed-wire fence. They electrify it. They patrol with bloodhounds. (For they remember how H. G. Wells's *The Invisible Man* could be both smelt and touched though he could not be seen.) But no shrieks ever suggest that some intruder has received a shock. No movement of the wire ever betrays an invisible climber. The bloodhounds never give cry. Yet still the Believer is not convinced. 'But there is a gardener, invisible, intangible, insensible to electric shocks, a gardener who has no scent and makes no sound, a gardener who comes secretly to look after the garden which he loves.' At last the Sceptic despairs, 'But what remains of your original assertion? Just how does what you call

This selection is the opening statement in a symposium, "Theology and Falsification," from *New Essays in Philosophical Theology* (1955), ed. Antony Flew and Alasdair MacIntyre. Reprinted by permission of the author and the publishers, SCM Press, Ltd., and the Macmillan Company.

[1] Proceedings of the Aristotelian Society, 1944-5, reprinted as Ch. X of *Logic and Language*, Vol. I (Blackwell, 1951), and in his *Philosophy and Psychoanalysis* (Blackwell, 1953).

an invisible, intangible, eternally elusive gardener differ from an imaginary gardener or even from no gardener at all?'

In this parable we can see how what starts as an assertion, that something exists or that there is some analogy between certain complexes of phenomena, may be reduced step by step to an altogether different status, to an expression perhaps of a 'picture preference.' The Sceptic says there is no gardener. The Believer says there is a gardener (but invisible, etc.). One man talks about sexual behaviour. Another man prefers to talk of Aphrodite (but knows that there is not really a superhuman person additional to, and somehow responsible for, all sexual phenomena). The process of qualification may be checked at any point before the original assertion is completely withdrawn and something of that first assertion will remain (Tautology). Mr. Wells's invisible man could not, admittedly, be seen, but in all other respects he was a man like the rest of us. But though the process of qualification may be, and of course usually is, checked in time, it is not always judiciously so halted. Someone may dissipate his assertion completely without noticing that he has done so. A fine brash hypothesis may thus be killed by inches, the death by a thousand qualifications.

And in this, it seems to me, lies the peculiar danger, the endemic evil, of theological utterance. Take such utterances as 'God has a plan,' 'God created the world,' 'God loves us as a father loves his children.' They look at first sight very much like assertions, vast cosmological assertions. Of course, this is no sure sign that they either are, or are intended to be, assertions. But let us confine ourselves to the cases where those who utter such sentences intend them to express assertions. (Merely remarking parenthetically that those who intend or interpret such utterances as crypto-commands, expressions of wishes, disguised ejaculations, concealed ethics, or as anything else but assertions, are unlikely to succeed in making them either properly orthodox or practically effective).

Now to assert that such and such is the case is necessarily equivalent to denying that such and such is not the case. Suppose then that we are in doubt as to what someone who gives vent to an utterance is asserting, or suppose that, more radically, we are sceptical as to whether he is really asserting anything at all, one way of trying to understand (or perhaps it will be to expose) his utterance is to attempt to find what he would regard as counting against, or as being incompatible with, its truth. For if the utterance is indeed an assertion, it will necessarily be equivalent to a denial of the negation of that assertion. And anything which would count against the assertion, or which would induce the speaker to withdraw it and to admit that it had been mistaken, must be part of (or the whole of) the meaning of the negation of that assertion. And to know the meaning of the negation of an assertion, is as near as makes no matter, to know the meaning of that assertion. And if there is nothing which a putative assertion denies then there is nothing which it asserts either: and so it is not really an assertion. When the Sceptic in the parable asked the Believer, 'Just how does what you call an invisible, intangible, eternally elusive gardener differ from an imaginary gardener or even from no gardener at all?' he was suggesting that the Believer's earlier statement had been so eroded by qualification that it was no longer an assertion at all.

Now it often seems to people who are not religious as if there was no conceivable event or series of events the occurrence of which would be admitted by sophisticated religious people to be a sufficient reason for conceding 'There wasn't a God after all' or 'God does not really love us then.' Someone tells us that God loves us as a father loves his children. We are reassured. But then we see a child dying of inoperable cancer of the throat. His earthly father is driven frantic in his efforts to help, but his Heavenly Father reveals no obvious sign of concern. Some qualification is made — God's love is 'not a merely human love' or it is 'an inscrutable love,' perhaps — and we realize that such sufferings are quite compatible with the truth of the assertion that 'God loves us as a father (but, of course, . . .).' We are reassured again. But then perhaps we ask: what is this assurance of God's (appropriately qualified) love worth, what is this apparent guarantee really a guarantee against? Just what would have to happen not merely (morally and wrongly) to tempt but also (logically and rightly) to entitle us to say 'God does not love us' or even 'God does not exist'? I therefore put the simple central question, 'What would have to occur or to have occurred to constitute for you a disproof of the love of, or of the existence of, God?'

10

THE VERIFICATION OF
BELIEF IN GOD

John Hick

To ask "Is the existence of God verifiable?" is to pose a question which is too imprecise to be capable of being answered.[1] There are many different concepts of God, and it may be that statements employing some of them are open to verification or falsification while statements employing others of them are not. Again, the notion of verifying is itself by no means perfectly clear and fixed; and it may be that on some views of the nature of verification the existence of God is verifiable, whereas on other views it is not.

Instead of seeking to compile a list of the various different concepts of God and the various possible senses of "verify," I wish to argue with regard to one particular concept of deity, namely the Christian concept, that divine existence is in principle verifiable; and as the first stage of this argument I must indicate what I mean by "verifiable."

I

The central core of the concept of verification, I suggest, is the removal of ignorance or uncertainty concerning the truth of some proposition. That *p*

From "Theology and Verification," originally published in the journal, *Theology Today*, 1960. Pp. 12-31. Reprinted by permission of the author and editor.

[1] In this paper I assume that an indicative sentence expresses a factual assertion if and only if the state in which the universe would be if the putative assertion could correctly be said to be true differs in some experienceable way from the state in which the universe would be if the putative assertion could correctly be said to be false, all aspects of the universe other than that referred to in the putative assertion being the same in either case. This criterion acknowledges the important core of truth in the logical positivist verification principle. "Experienceable" in the above formulation means, in the case of alleged subjective or private facts (*e.g.*, pains, dreams, after-images, etc.), "experienceable by the subject in question" and, in the case of alleged objective or public facts, "capable in principle of being experienced by anyone." My contention is going to be that "God exists" asserts a matter of objective fact.

is verified (whether *p* embodies a theory, hypothesis, prediction, or straight-forward assertion) means that something happens which makes it clear that *p* is true. A question is settled so that there is no longer room for rational doubt concerning it. The way in which grounds for rational doubt are excluded varies, of course, with the subject matter. But the general feature common to all cases of verification is the ascertaining of truth by the removal of grounds for rational doubt. Where such grounds are removed, we rightly speak of verification having taken place.

To characterize verification in this way is to raise the question whether the notion of verification is purely logical or is both logical and psychological. Is the statement that *p* is verified simply the statement that a certain state of affairs exists (or has existed) or is it the statement also that someone is aware that this state of affairs exists (or has existed) and notes that its existence establishes the truth of *p*? A geologist predicts that the earth's surface will be covered with ice in 15 million years time. Suppose that in 15 million years time the earth's surface *is* covered with ice, but that in the meantime the human race has perished, so that no one is left to observe the event or to draw any conclusion concerning the accuracy of the geologist's prediction. Do we now wish to say that his prediction has been verified, or shall we deny that it has been verified, on the ground that there is no one left to do the verifying?

The range of "verify" and its cognates is sufficiently wide to permit us to speak in either way. But the only sort of verification of theological propositions which is likely to interest us is one in which human beings participate. We may therefore, for our present purpose, treat verification as a logico-psychological rather than as a purely logical concept. I suggest, then, that "verify" be construed as a verb which has its primary uses in the active voice: I verify, you verify, we verify, they verify, or have verified. The impersonal passive, it is verified, now becomes logically secondary. To say that *p* has been verified is to say (at least) someone has verified it, often with the implication that his or their report to this effect is generally accepted. But it is impossible, on this usage, for *p* to have been verified without someone having verified it. "Verification" is thus primarily the name for an event which takes place in human consciousness.[2] It refers to an experience, the experience of ascertaining that a given proposition or set of propositions is true. To this extent verification is a psychological notion. But of course it is also a logical notion. For needless to say, not *any* experience is rightly called an experience of verifying *p*. Both logical and psychological conditions must be fulfilled in order for verification to have taken place. In this respect, "verify" is like "know." Knowing is an experience which someone has or under-

---

[2] This suggestion is closely related to Carnap's insistence that, in contrast to "true," "confirmed" is time-dependent. To say that a statement is confirmed, or verified, is to say that it has been confirmed at a particular time — and, I would add, by a particular person. See Rudolf Carnap, "Truth and Confirmation," Feigl and Sellars, *Readings in Philosophical Analysis,* 1949, pp. 119 f.

goes, or perhaps a dispositional state in which someone is, and it cannot take place without someone having or undergoing it or being in it; but not by any means every experience which people have, or every dispositional state in which they are, is rightly called knowing.

With regard to this logico-psychological concept of verification, such questions as the following arise. When A, but nobody else, has ascertained that p is true, can p be said to have been verified; or is it required that others also have undergone the same ascertainment? How public, in other words, must verification be? Is it necessary that p could in principle be verified by anyone, without restriction, even though perhaps only A has in fact verified it? If so, what is meant here by "in principle"; does it signify, for example, that p must be verifiable by anyone who performs a certain operation; and does it imply that to do this is within everyone's power?

These questions cannot, I believe, be given any general answer applicable to all instances of the exclusion of rational doubt. The answers must be derived in each case from an investigation of the particular subject matter. It will be the object of subsequent sections of this article to undertake such an investigation concerning the Christian concept of God.

Verification is often construed as the verification of a prediction. However, verification, as the exclusion of grounds for rational doubt, does not necessarily consist in the proving correct of a prediction; a verifying experience does not always need to have been predicted in order to have the effect of excluding rational doubt. But when we are interested in the verifiability of propositions as the criterion for their having factual meaning, the notion of prediction becomes central. If a proposition contains or entails predictions which can be verified or falsified, its character as an assertion (though not of course its character as a true assertion) is thereby guaranteed.

Such predictions may be and often are conditional. For example, statements about the features of the dark side of the moon are rendered meaningful by the conditional predictions which they entail to the effect that if an observer comes to be in such a position in space, he will make such-and-such observations. It would in fact be more accurate to say that the prediction is always conditional, but that sometimes the conditions are so obvious and so likely to be fulfilled in any case that they require no special mention, while sometimes they require for their fulfillment some unusual expedition or operation. A prediction, for example, that the sun will rise within twenty-four hours is intended unconditionally, at least as concerns conditions to be fulfilled by the observer; he is not required by the terms of the prediction to perform any special operation. Even in this case, however, there is an implied negative condition that he shall not put himself in a situation (such as immuring himself in the depths of a coal mine) from which a sunrise would not be perceptible. Other predictions, however, are explicitly conditional. In these cases it is true for any particular individual that in order to verify the statement in question he must go through some specified course of action. The prediction is to the effect that if you conduct such an experiment you will obtain such a result; for example, if you go into the next room you will have such-and-such visual experiences, and if you then touch the table which you see you will have such-and-such tactual experiences, and so on. The content of the "if" clause is of course always determined by the particular subject matter. The logic of "table" determines what you must do to verify statements about tables; the logic of "molecule" determines what you must do to verify statements about molecules; and the logic of "God" determines what you must do to verify statements about God.

In those cases in which the individual who is to verify a proposition must himself first perform some operation, it clearly cannot follow from the circumstances that the proposition is true that everybody has in fact verified it, or that everybody will at some future time verify it. For whether or not any particular person performs the requisite operation is a contingent matter.

II

What is the relation between verification and falsification? We are all familiar today with the phrase, "theology and falsification." A. G. N. Flew and others,[3] taking their cue from John Wisdom,[4] have raised instead of the question, "What possible experiences would verify 'God exists'?" the matching question, "What possible experiences would falsify 'God exists'? What conceivable state of affairs would be incompatible with the existence of God?" In posing the question in this way it was apparently assumed that verification and falsification are symmetrically related, and that the latter is apt to be the more accessible of the two.

In the most common cases, certainly, verification and falsification are symmetrically related. The logically simplest case of verification is provided by the crucial instance. Here it is integral to a given hypothesis that if, in specified circumstances, *A* occurs, the hypothesis is thereby shown to be true, whereas if *B* occurs the hypothesis is thereby shown to be false. Verification and falsification are also symmetrically related in the testing of such a proposition as "There is a table in the next room." The verifying experiences in this case are experiences of seeing and touching, predictions of which are entailed by the proposition in question, under the proviso that one goes into the next room; and the absence of such experiences in those circumstances serves to falsify the proposition.

But it would be rash to assume, on this basis, that verification and falsification must always be related in this symmetrical fashion. They do not necessarily stand to one another as do the two sides of a coin, so that once the coin is spun it must fall on one side or the other. There are cases in

---

[3] A. G. N. Flew, editor, *New Essays in Philosophical Theology,* 1955, Chapter VI. (See above, p. 97.)

[4] "Gods," *Proceedings of the Aristotelian Society,* 1944-45. Reprinted in A. G. N. Flew, editor, *Logic and Language,* First Series, 1951, and in John Wisdom, *Philosophy and Psycho-Analysis,* 1953.

which verification and falsification each correspond to a side on a different coin, so that one can fail to verify without this failure constituting falsification.

Consider, for example, the proposition that "there are three successive sevens in the decimal determination of π." So far as the value of π has been worked out, it does not contain a series of three sevens, but it will always be true that such a series may occur at a point not yet reached in anyone's calculations. Accordingly, the proposition may one day be verified, if it is true, but can never be falsified, if it is false.

The hypothesis of continued conscious existence after bodily death provides an instance of a different kind of such asymmetry, and one which has a direct bearing upon the theistic problem. This hypothesis has built into it a prediction that one will after the date of one's bodily death have conscious experiences, including the experience of remembering that death. This is a prediction which will be verified in one's own experience if it is true, but which cannot be falsified if it is false. That is to say, it can be false, but *that* it is false can never be a fact which anyone has experientially verified. But this circumstance does not determine the meaningfulness of the hypothesis, since it is also such that if it be true, it will be known to be true.

It is important to remember that we do not speak of verifying logically necessary truths, but only propositions concerning matters of fact. Accordingly verification is not to be identified with the concept of logical certification or proof. The exclusion of rational doubt concerning some matter of fact is not equivalent to the exclusion of the logical possibility of error or illusion. For truths concerning fact are not logically necessary. Their contrary is never self-contradictory. But at the same time the bare logical possibility of error does not constitute ground for rational doubt as to the veracity of our experience. If it did, no empirical proposition could ever be verified, and indeed the notion of empirical verification would be without use and therefore without sense. What we rightly seek, when we desire the verification of a factual proposition, is not a demonstration of the logical impossibility of the proposition being false (for this would be a self-contradictory demand), but such weight of evidence as suffices, in the type of case in question, to exclude rational doubt.

III

These features of the concept of verification — that verification consists in the exclusion of grounds for rational doubt concerning the truth of some proposition; that this means its exclusion from particular minds; that the nature of the experience which serves to exclude grounds for rational doubt depends upon the particular subject matter; that verification is often related to predictions and that such predictions are often conditional; that verification and falsification may be asymmetrically related; and finally, that the verification of a factual proposition is not equivalent to logical certification — are all relevant to the verification of the central religious claim, "God exists."

I wish now to apply these discriminations to the notion of eschatological verification, which has been briefly employed by Ian Crombie in his contribution to *New Essays in Philosophical Theology*,[5] and by myself in *Faith and
Knowledge*.[6] This suggestion has on each occasion been greeted with disapproval by both philosophers and theologians. I am, however, still of the
opinion that the notion of eschatological verification is sound; and further,
that no viable alternative to it has been offered to establish the factual character of theism.

The strength of the notion of eschatological verification is that it is not
an *ad hoc* invention but is based upon an actually operative religious concept of God. In the language of Christian faith, the word "God" stands as
the center of a system of terms, such as Spirit, grace, Logos, incarnation, Kingdom of God, and many more; and the distinctly Christian conception of God
can only be fully grasped in its connection with these related terms.[7] It
belongs to a complex of notions which together constitute a picture of the
universe in which we live, of man's place therein, of a comprehensive divine
purpose interacting with human purposes, and of the general nature of the
eventual fulfillment of that divine purpose. This Christian picture of the universe, entailing as it does certain distinctive expectations concerning the
future, is a very different picture from any that can be accepted by one who
does not believe that the God of the New Testament exists. Further, these
differences are such as to show themselves in human experience. The possibility of experimental confirmation is thus built into the Christian concept
of God; and the notion of eschatological verification seeks to relate this fact
to the logical problem of meaning.

Let me first give a general indication of this suggestion, by repeating a
parable which I have related elsewhere,[8] and then try to make it more precise
and eligible for discussion. Here, first, is the parable.

Two men are travelling together along a road. One of them believes
that it leads to a Celestial City, the other that it leads nowhere; but since
this is the only road there is, both must travel it. Neither has been this way
before, and therefore neither is able to say what they will find around each
next corner. During their journey they meet both with moments of refresh-
ment and delight, and with moments of hardship and danger. All the time
one of them thinks of his journey as a pilgrimage to the Celestial City and
interprets the pleasant parts as encouragements and the obstacles as trials of
his purpose and lessons in endurance, prepared by the king of that city and

[5] *Op. cit.*, p.. 126.

[6] Cornell University Press, 1957, pp. 150-62.

[7] Its clear recognition of this fact, with regard not only to Christianity but to any
religion, is one of the valuable features of Ninian Smart's *Reasons and Faiths* (1958).
He remarks, for example, that "the claim that God exists can only be understood by
reference to many, if not all, other propositions in the doctrinal scheme from which it
is extrapolated" (p. 12).

[8] *Faith and Knowledge*, pp. 150 f.

designed to make of him a worthy citizen of the place when at last he arrives there. The other, however, believes none of this and sees their journey as an unavoidable and aimless ramble. Since he has no choice in the matter, he enjoys the good and endures the bad. But for him there is no Celestial City to be reached, no all-encompassing purpose ordaining their journey; only the road itself and the luck of the road in good weather and in bad.

During the course of the journey the issue between them is not an experimental one. They do not entertain different expectations about the coming details of the road, but only about its ultimate destination. And yet when they do turn the last corner it will be apparent that one of them has been right all the time and the other wrong. Thus although the issue between them has not been experimental, it has nevertheless from the start been a real issue. They have not merely felt differently about the road; for one was feeling appropriately and the other inappropriately in relation to the actual state of affairs. Their opposed interpretations of the road constituted genuinely rival assertions, though assertions whose assertion-status has the peculiar characteristic of being guaranteed retrospectively by a future crux.

This parable has of course (like all parables) strict limitations. It is designed to make only one point: that Christian doctrine postulates an ultimate unambiguous state of existence *in patria* as well as our present ambiguous existence *in via*. There is a state of having arrived as well as a state of journeying, an eternal heavenly life as well as an earthly pilgrimage. The alleged future experience of this state cannot, of course, be appealed to as evidence for theism as a present interpretation of our experience; but it does suffice to render the choice between theism and atheism a real and not a merely empty or verbal choice. And although this does not affect the logic of the situation, it should be added that the alternative interpretations are, more than theoretical, for they render different practical plans and policies appropriate now.

The universe as envisaged by the theist, then, differs as a totality from the universe as envisaged by the atheist. This difference does not, however, from our present standpoint within the universe, involve a difference in the objective content of each or even any of its passing moments. The theist and the atheist do not (or need not) expect different events to occur in the successive details of the temporal process. They do not (or need not) entertain divergent expectations of the course of history viewed from within. But the theist does and the atheist does not expect that when history is completed it will be seen to have led to a particular end-state and to have fulfilled a specific purpose, namely that of creating "children of God."

The idea of an eschatological verification of theism can make sense, however, only if the logically prior idea of continued personal existence after death is intelligible. A desultory debate on this topic has been going on for several years in some of the philosophical periodicals. C. I. Lewis has contended that the hypothesis of immortality "is an hypothesis about our own future experience. And our understanding of what would verify it has no lack of clarity."[9] And Morris Schlick agreed, adding, "We must conclude that immortality, in the sense defined [i.e. 'survival after death,' rather than 'never-ending life'], should not be regarded as a 'metaphysical problem,' but is an empirical hypothesis, because it possesses logical verifiability. It could be verified by following the prescription: 'Wait until you die!' "[10] However, others have challenged this conclusion, either on the ground that the phrase "surviving death" is self-contradictory in ordinary language or, more substantially, on the ground that the traditional distinction between soul and body cannot be sustained.[11] I should like to address myself to this latter view. The only self of which we know, it is said, is the empirical self, the walking, talking, acting, sleeping individual who lives, it may be, for some sixty to eighty years and then dies. Mental events and mental characteristics are analyzed into the modes of behavior and behavioral dispositions of this empirical self. The human being is described as an organism capable of acting in the "high-level" ways which we characterize as intelligent, thoughtful, humorous, calculating, and the like. The concept of mind or soul is thus not the concept of a "ghost in the machine" (to use Gilbert Ryle's loaded phrase[12]), but of the more flexible and sophisticated ways in which human beings behave and have it in them to behave. On this view there is no room for the notion of soul in distinction from body; and if there is no soul in distinction from body, there can be no question of the soul surviving the death of the body. Against this philosophical background the specifically Christian (and also Jewish) belief in the resurrection of the flesh, or body, in contrast to the Hellenic notion of the survival of a disembodied soul, might be expected to have attracted more attention than it has. For it is consonant with the conception of man as an indissoluble psycho-physical unity, and yet it also offers the possibility of an empirical meaning for the idea of "life after death."

Paul is the chief Biblical expositor of the idea of the resurrection of the body.[13] His view, as I understand it, is this. When someone has died he is, apart from any special divine action, extinct. A human being is by nature mortal and subject to annihilation by death. But in fact God, by an act of sovereign power, either sometimes or always resurrects or (better) reconstitutes or recreates him — not, however, as the identical physical organism that he was before death, but as a *soma pneumatikon* ("spiritual body") embodying the dispositional characteristics and memory traces of the deceased physical organism, and inhabiting an environment with which the *soma*

---

[9] "Experience and Meaning," *Philosophical Review,* 1934, reprinted in Feigl and Sellars, *Readings in Philosophical Analysis,* 1949, p. 142.

[10] "Meaning and Verification," *Philosophical Review,* 1936, reprinted in Feigl and Sellars, *op. cit.,* p. 160.

[11] E.g. A. G. N. Flew, "Death," *New Essays in Philosophical Theology;* "Can a man Witness his own Funeral?" *Hibbert Journal,* 1956.

[12] *The Concept of Mind,* 1949, which contains an important exposition of the interpretation of "mental" qualities as characteristics of behavior.

[13] I Cor. 15.

pneumatikon is continuous as the *ante-mortem* body was continuous with our present world. In discussing this notion we may well abandon the word "spiritual," as lacking today any precise established usage, and speak of "resurrection bodies" and of "the resurrection world." The principal questions to be asked concern the relation between the physical world and the resurrection world, and the criteria of personal identity which are operating when it is alleged that a certain inhabitant of the resurrection world is the same person as an individual who once inhabited this world. The first of these questions turns out on investigation to be the more difficult of the two, and I shall take the easier one first.

Let me sketch a very odd possibility (concerning which, however, I wish to emphasize not so much its oddness as its possibility!), and then see how far it can be stretched in the direction of the notion of the resurrection body. In the process of stretching it will become even more odd than it was before; but my aim will be to show that, however odd, it remains within the bounds of the logically possible. This progression will be presented in three pictures, arranged in a self-explanatory order.

First picture: Suppose that at some learned gathering in this country one of the company were suddenly and inexplicably to disappear, and that at the same moment an exact replica of him were suddenly and inexplicably to appear at some comparable meeting in Australia. The person who appears in Australia is exactly similar, as to both bodily and mental characteristics, with the person who disappears in America. There is continuity of memory, complete similarity of bodily features, including even fingerprints, hair and eye coloration and stomach contents, and also of beliefs, habits, and mental propensities. In fact there is everything that would lead us to identify the one who appeared with the one who disappeared, except continuity of occupancy of space. We may suppose, for example, that a deputation of the colleagues of the man who disappeared fly to Australia to interview the replica of him which is reported there, and find that he is in all respects but one exactly as though he had travelled from say, Princeton to Melbourne, by conventional means. The only difference is that he describes how, as he was sitting listening to Dr. Z reading a paper, on blinking his eyes he suddenly found himself sitting in a different room listening to a different paper by an Australian scholar. He asks his colleagues how the meeting had gone after he ceased to be there, and what they had made of his disappearance, and so on. He clearly thinks of himself as the one who was present with them at their meeting in the United States. I suggest that faced with all these circumstances his colleagues would soon, if not immediately, find themselves thinking of him and treating him as the individual who had so inexplicably disappeared from their midst. We should be extending our normal use of "same person" in a way which the postulated facts would both demand and justify if we said that the one who appears in Australia is the same person as the one who disappears in America. The factors inclining us to identify them would far outweigh the factors disinclining us to do this. We should have no reasonable alternative but to extend our usage of "the same person" to cover the strange new case.

Second picture: Now let us suppose that the event in America is not a sudden and inexplicable disappearance, and indeed not a disappearance at all, but a sudden death. Only, at the moment when the individual dies, a replica of him as he was at the moment before his death, complete with memory up to that instant, appears in Australia. Even with the corpse on our hands, it would still, I suggest, be an extension of "same person" required and warranted by the postulated facts, to say that the same person who died has been miraculously recreated in Australia. The case would be considerably odder than in the previous picture, because of the existence of the corpse in America contemporaneously with the existence of the living person in Australia. But I submit that, although the oddness of this circumstance may be stated as strongly as you please, and can indeed hardly be overstated, yet it does not exceed the bounds of the logically possible. Once again we must imagine some of the deceased's colleagues going to Australia to interview the person who has suddenly appeared there. He would perfectly remember them and their meeting, be interested in what had happened, and be as amazed and dumbfounded about it as anyone else; and he would perhaps be worried about the possible legal complications if he should return to America to claim his property; and so on. Once again, I believe, they would soon find themselves thinking of him and treating him as the same person as the dead Princetonian. Once again the factors inclining us to say that the one who died and the one who appeared are the same person would outweigh the factors inclining us to say that they are different people. Once again we should have to extend our usage of "the same person" to cover this new case.

Third picture: My third supposal is that the replica, complete with memory, etc. appears, not in Australia, but as a resurrection replica in a different world altogether, a resurrection world inhabited by resurrected persons. This world occupies its own space, distinct from the space with which we are now familiar. That is to say, an object in the resurrection world is not situated at any distance or in any direction from an object in our present world, although each object in either world is spatially related to each other object in the same world.

Mr. X, then, dies. A Mr. X replica, complete with the set of memory traces which Mr. X had at the last moment before his death, comes into existence. It is composed of other material than physical matter, and is located in a resurrection world which does not stand in any spatial relationship with the physical world. Let us leave out of consideration St. Paul's hint that the resurrection body may be as unlike the physical body as is a full grain of wheat from the wheat seed, and consider the simpler picture in which the resurrection body has the same shape as the physical body.[14]

---

[14] As would seem to be assumed, for example, by Irenaeus (*Adversus Haereses,* Bk. II, Ch. 34, Sec. 1).

In these circumstances, how does Mr. X know that he has been resurrected or recreated? He remembers dying; or rather he remembers being on what he took to be his death-bed, and becoming progressively weaker until, presumably, he lost consciousness. But how does he know that (to put it Irishly) his "dying" proved fatal; and that he did not, after losing consciousness, begin to recover strength, and has now simply waked up?

The picture is readily enough elaborated to answer this question. Mr. X meets and recognizes a number of relatives and friends and historical personages whom he knows to have died; and from the fact of their presence, and also from their testimony that he has only just now appeared in their world, he is convinced that he has died. Evidences of this kind could mount up to the point at which they are quite as strong as the evidence which, in pictures one and two, convince the individual in question that he has been miraculously translated to Australia. Resurrected persons would be individually no more in doubt about their own identity than we are now, and would be able to identify one another in the same kinds of ways, and with a like degree of assurance, as we do now.

If it be granted that resurrected persons might be able to arrive at a rationally founded conviction that their existence is *post-mortem,* how could they know that the world in which they find themselves is in a different space from that in which their physical bodies were? How could such a one know that he is not in a like situation with the person in picture number two, who dies in America and appears as a full-blooded replica in Australia, leaving his corpse in the U.S.A. — except that now the replica is situated, not in Australia, but on a planet of some other star?

It is of course conceivable that the space of the resurrection world should have properties which are manifestly incompatible with its being a region of physical space. But on the other hand, it is not of the essence of the notion of a resurrection world that its space should have properties different from those of physical space. And supposing it not to have different properties, it is not evident that a resurrected individual could learn from any direct observations that he was not on a planet of some sun which is at so great a distance from our own sun that the stellar scenery visible from it is quite unlike that which we can now see. The grounds that a resurrected person would have for believing that he is in a different space from physical space (supposing there to be no discernible difference in spatial properties) would be the same as the grounds that any of us may have now for believing this concerning resurrected individuals. These grounds are indirect and consist in all those considerations (*e.g.,* Luke 16: 26) which lead most of those who consider the question to reject as absurd the possibility of, for example, radio communication or rocket travel between earth and heaven.

V

In the present context my only concern is to claim that this doctrine of the divine creation of bodies, composed of a material other than that of physical matter, which bodies are endowed with sufficient correspondence of characteristics with our present bodies, and sufficient continuity of memory with our present consciousness, for us to speak of the same person being raised up again to life in a new environment, is not self-contradictory. If, then, it cannot be ruled out *ab initio* as meaningless, we may go on to consider whether and how it is related to the possible verification of Christian theism.

So far I have argued that a survival prediction such as is contained in the *corpus* of Christian belief is in principal subject to future verification. But this does not take the argument by any means as far as it must go to succeed. For survival, simply as such, would not serve to verify theism. It would not necessarily be a state of affairs which is manifestly incompatible with the non-existence of God. It might be taken just as a surprising natural fact. The atheist, in his resurrection body, and able to remember his life on earth, might say that the universe has turned out to be more complex, and perhaps more to be approved of, than he had realized. But the mere fact of survival, with a new body in a new environment, would not demonstrate to him that there is a God. It is fully compatible with the notion of survival that the life to come be, so far as the theistic problem is concerned, essentially a continuation of the present life, and religiously no less ambiguous. And in this event, survival after bodily death would not in the least constitute a final verification of theistic faith.

I shall not spend time in trying to draw a picture of resurrection existence which would merely prolong the religious ambiguity of our present life. The important question, for our purpose, is not whether one can conceive of after-life experiences which would *not* verify theism (and in point of fact one can fairly easily conceive them), but whether one can conceive of after-life experiences which *would* serve to verify theism.

I think that we can. In trying to do so I shall not appeal to the traditional doctrine, which figures especially in Catholic and mystical theology, of the Beatific Vision of God. The difficulty presented by this doctrine is not so much that of deciding whether there are grounds for believing it, as of deciding what it means. I shall not, however, elaborate this difficulty, but pass directly to the investigation of a different and, as it seems to me, more intelligible possibility. This is the possibility not of a direct vision of God, whatever that might mean, but of a *situation* which point unambiguously to the existence of a loving God. This would be a situation which, so far as its religious significance is concerned, contrasts in a certain important respect with our present situation. Our present situation is one which in some ways seems to confirm and in other ways to contradict the truth of theism. Some events around us suggest the presence of an unseen benevolent intelligence and others suggest that no such intelligence is at work. Our situation is religiously ambiguous. But in order for us to be aware of this fact we must already have some idea, however vague, of what it would be for our situation to be not ambiguous, but on the contrary wholly evidential of God. I therefore want to try to make clearer this presupposed concept of a religiously unambiguous situation.

There are, I suggest, two possible developments of our experience such that, if they occurred in conjunction with one another (whether in this life or in another life to come), they would assure us beyond rational doubt of the reality of God, as conceived in the Christian faith. These are, *first,* an experience of the fulfillment of God's purpose for ourselves, as this has been disclosed in the Christian revelation; in conjunction, *second,* with an experience of communion with God as he has revealed himself in the person of Christ.

The divine purpose for human life, as this is depicted in the New Testament documents, is the bringing of the human person, in society with his fellows, to enjoy a certain valuable quality of personal life, the content of which is given in the character of Christ — which quality of life (i.e., life in relationship with God, described in the Fourth Gospel as eternal life) is said to be the proper destiny of human nature and the source of man's final self-fulfillment and happiness. The verification situation with regard to such a fulfillment is asymmetrical. On the one hand, so long as the divine purpose remains unfulfilled, we cannot know that it never will be fulfilled in the future, hence no final falsification is possible of the claim that this fulfillment will occur — unless, of course, the prediction contains a specific time clause which, in Christian teaching, it does not. But on the other hand, if and when the divine purpose *is* fulfilled in our own experience, we must be able to recognize and rejoice in that fulfillment. For the fulfillment would not be for us the promised fulfillment without our own conscious participation in it.

It is important to note that one can say this much without being cognizant in advance of the concrete form which such fulfillment will take. The before-and-after situation is analogous to that of a small child looking forward to adult life and then, having grown to adulthood, looking back upon childhood. The child possesses and can use correctly in various contexts the concept of "being grown-up," although he does not know, concretely, what it is like to be grown-up. But when he reaches adulthood he is nevertheless able to know that he has reached it; he is able to recognize the experience of living a grown-up life even though he did not know in advance just what to expect. For his understanding of adult maturity grows as he himself matures. Something similar may be supposed to happen in the case of the fulfillment of the divine purpose for human life. That fulfillment may be as far removed from our present condition as is mature adulthood from the mind of a little child; nevertheless, we possess already a comparatively vague notion of this final fulfillment, and as we move towards it our concept will itself become more adequate; and if and when we finally reach that fulfillment, the problem of recognizing it will have disappeared in the process.

The other feature that must, I suggest, be present in a state of affairs that would verify theism, is that the fulfillment of God's purpose be apprehended *as* the fulfillment of God's purpose and not simply as a natural state of affairs. To this end it must be accompanied by an experience of communion with God as he has made himself known to men in Christ.

The specifically Christian clause, "as he has made himself known to men in Christ," is essential, for it provides a solution to the problem of recognition in the awareness of God. Several writers have pointed out the logical difficulty involved in any claim to have encountered God.[15] How could one know that it was *God* whom one had encountered? God is described in Christian theology in terms of various absolute qualities, such as omnipotence, omnipresence, perfect goodness, infinite love, etc., which cannot as such be observed by us, as can their finite analogues, limited power, local presence, finite goodness, and human love. One can recognize that a being whom one "encounters" has a given finite degree of power, but how does one recognize that he has *un*limited power? How does one observe that an encountered being is *omni*present? How does one perceive that his goodness and love, which one can perhaps see to exceed any human goodness and love, are actually infinite? Such qualities cannot be given in human experience. One might claim, then, to have encountered a Being whom one presumes, or trusts, or hopes to be God; but one cannot claim to have encountered a Being whom one recognized to be the infinite almighty, eternal Creator.

This difficulty is met in Christianity by the doctrine of the Incarnation — although this was not among the considerations which led to the formulation of that doctrine. The idea of incarnation provides answers to the two related questions: "How do we know that God has certain absolute qualities which, by their very nature, transcend human experience?" and "How can there be an eschatological verification of theism which is based upon a recognition of the presence of God in his Kingdom?

In Christianity God is known as "the God and Father of our Lord Jesus Christ."[16] God is the Being about whom Jesus taught; the Being in relation to whom Jesus lived, and into a relationship with whom he brought his disciples; the Being whose *agape* toward men was seen on earth in the life of Jesus. In short, God is the transcendent Creator who has revealed himself in Christ. Now Jesus' teaching about the Father is a part of that self-disclosure, and it is from this teaching (together with that of the prophets who preceded him) that the Christian knowledge of God's transcendent being is derived. Only God himself knows his own infinite nature; and our human belief about that nature is based upon his self-revelation to men in Christ. As Karl Barth expresses it, "Jesus Christ is the knowability of God."[17] Our beliefs about God's infinite being are not capable of observational verification,

---

[15] For example, R. W. Hepburn, *Christianity and Paradox*, 1958, pp. 56 f.
[16] II Cor. 11:31.
[17] *Church Dogmatics*, Vol. II, Pt. I, p. 150.

being beyond the scope of human experience, but they are susceptible of indirect verification by the removal of rational doubt concerning the authority of Christ. An experience of the reign of the Son in the Kingdom of the Father would confirm that authority, and therewith, indirectly, the validity of Jesus' teaching concerning the character of God in his infinite transcendent nature.

The further question as to how an eschatological experience of the Kingdom of God could be known to be such has already been answered by implication. It is God's union with man in Christ that makes possible man's recognition of the fulfillment of God's purpose for man as being indeed the fulfillment of *God's* purpose for him. The presence of Christ in his Kingdom marks this as being beyond doubt the Kingdom of the God and Father of the Lord Jesus Christ.

It is true that even the experience of the realization of the promised Kingdom of God, with Christ reigning as Lord of the New Aeon, would not constitute a logical certification of his claim nor, accordingly, of the reality of God. But this will not seem remarkable to any philosopher in the empiricist tradition, who knows that it is only a confusion to demand that a factual proposition be an analytic truth. A set of expectations based upon faith in the historic Jesus as the incarnation of God, and in his teaching as being divinely authoritative, could be so fully confirmed in *post-mortem* experience as to leave no ground for rational doubt as to the validity of that faith.

SUGGESTED READINGS

1. The Ontological Argument

DESCARTES, RENE. *Meditations,* Part V [in Edwards-Pap, Smart].

HARTSHORNE, CHARLES. *The Logic of Perfection.* La Salle, Ill.: Open Court, 1963.

PLANTINGA, ALVIN (ed.). *The Ontological Argument.* Garden City, N. Y.: Doubleday & Company, Inc., 1965. [A comprehensive collection of writings on the argument, pro and con.]

2. The Cosmological Argument

COPLESTONE, F. C. *Aquinas.* Harmondsworth, England: Penguin Books, 1955. Ch. 3 [in Alston, Edwards-Pap].

GILSON, ETIENNE. *The Philosophy of St. Thomas Aquinas,* trans. EDWARD BULLOUGH. Cambridge, England: W. Heffer, 1925. Chs. 7, 9 [partly in Mandelbaum-Gramlich-Anderson].

HAWKINS, D. J. B. *The Essentials of Theism.* New York: Sheed & Ward, 1949, Ch. 4.

JOYCE, G. H. *The Principles of Natural Theology.* New York: Longmans, Green, 1951, Ch. 3.

TAYLOR, A. E. "The Vindication of Religion," in *Essays Catholic and Critical.* Saffron Walden, England: Society for Promoting Christian Knowledge, 1926. Sec. 1 [in Alston].

3. The Argument from Design

DU NOÜY, LECOMTE. *Human Destiny.* New York: New American Library (Signet Books), 1949.

PALEY, WILLIAM. *Evidences of the Existence and Attributes of the Deity,* 1802 [partly in Edwards Pap].

RUSSELL, BERTRAND. *Religion and Science.* London: Oxford Univ. Press, 1935, Ch. 8.

TENNANT, F. R. *Philosophical Theology.* London: Cambridge Univ. Press, 1928-30. Vol. II, Ch. 4 [in Alston, Hick].

4. Religious Experience

BAILLIE, JOHN. *Our Knowledge of God.* New York: Scribner's, 1939.

BROAD, C. D. *Religion, Philosophy, and Psychical Research.* New York: Harcourt, 1953. Pp. 190-201 [in Alston].

LEUBA, J. H. *The Psychology of Religious Mysticism.* New York: Harcourt, 1925.

MARTIN, C. B. *Religious Belief.* Ithaca, N. Y.: Cornell Univ. Press, 1959. Ch. 5 [in Alston].

OTTO RUDOLF. *The Idea of the Holy,* trans. J. W. HARVEY. London: Oxford Univ. Press, 1923 [partly in Alston].

PRATT, JAMES B. *The Religious Consciousness.* New York: Macmillan, 1920.

STACE, W. T. *Mysticism and Philosophy.* Philadelphia: Lippincott, 1960.

——————. (ed.). *The Teachings of the Mystics.* New York: New American Library (Mentor Books), 1960.

——————. *Time and Eternity.* Princeton, N. J.: Princeton Univ. Press, 1952.

UNDERHILL, EVELYN. *Mysticism.* New York: Dutton, 1930.

5. Criticisms of Arguments for the Existence of God

BROAD, C. D. "Arguments for the Existence of God," in *Religion, Philosophy, and Psychical Research.* New York: Harcourt, 1953.

KANT, IMMANUEL. *Critique of Pure Reason.* Book II, Ch. 3 [partly in Alston].
LAIRD, JOHN. *Theism and Cosmology.* London: Allen & Unwin, 1940.
McTAGGART, J. M. E. *Some Dogmas of Religion.* London: Arnold, 1906.
RUSSELL, BERTRAND. *Why I Am Not a Christian and Other Essays.* New York: Simon & Schuster, 1957. Chs. 1, 13.

6. *Anti-Supernaturalistic Interpretations of Religion*
COMTE, AUGUSTE. *A General View of Positivism,* trans. J. H. BRIDGES. London: Routledge & Kegan Paul, 1880. Ch. 6 [partly in Alston].
DEWEY, JOHN. *A Common Faith.* New Haven, Conn.: Yale Univ. Press, 1934 [partly in Bronstein-Krikorian-Wiener, 3rd ed., Mandelbaum-Gramlich-Anderson].
FEUERBACH, LUDWIG. *The Essence of Christianity,* trans. GEORGE ELIOT. New York: Harper & Row, 1957.
FROMM, ERICH. *Psychoanalysis and Religion.* London: Victor Gollancz, 1951 [partly in Abernethy-Langford, Bronstein-Schulweis].
HUXLEY, JULIAN. *Religion Without Revelation.* New York: New American Library, 1958 [partly in Alston].
SANTAYANA, GEORGE. *Reason in Religion.* New York: Scribner's, 1905. [Partly in Alston, Mandelbaum-Gramlich-Anderson.]
WIEMAN, H. N. *The Source of Human Good.* Chicago: Univ. of Chicago Press, 1946 [partly in Alston].

7. *The Problem of Evil*
HUME, DAVID. *Dialogues Concerning Natural Religion,* Parts 10 and 11 [partly in Alston, Edwards-Pap, Hick, Singer-Ammerman, Sprague-Taylor].
LEIBNIZ, G. W. *On the Ultimate Origination of Things* [partly in Sprague-Taylor].
LEWIS, C. S. *The Problem of Pain.* New York: Macmillan, 1950.
MILL, J. S. "Nature," in *Three Essays on Religion* [partly in Bronstein-Schulweis, Levi, and Randall-Buchler-Shirk].
PIKE, NELSON (ed.). *God and Evil.* Englewood Cliffs, N. J.: Prentice-Hall, 1964. [A collection of writings on the subject.]
ROYCE, JOSIAH. *The Religious Aspect of Philosophy.* New York: Harper & Row, 1958. Ch. 12.
ST. AUGUSTINE. *Confessions,* Bk. VIII [partly in Bronstein-Schulweis].
——————. "On Free Will" [partly in Sprague-Taylor].
——————. *The Enchiridion,* Chs. 10-16 [partly in Hick].
TENNANT, F. R. *Philosophical Theology.* London: Cambridge Univ. Press, 1930. Vol. II, Ch. 7 [partly in Abernethy-Langford, Alston, Bronstein-Schulweis, Hick].

8. *Religious Language*
AYER, A. J. *Language, Truth, and Logic,* 2nd ed. London: Victor Gollancz, 1946. Ch. 6.
DEMOS, RAPHAEL and DUCASSE, C. J. "Are Religious Dogmas Cognitive and Meaningful?" in MORTON WHITE (ed.), *Academic Freedom, Logic, and Religion.* Philadelphia: Univ. of Pennsylvania Press, 1953.
FLEW, ANTONY and MACINTYRE, ALASDAIR (eds.). *New Essays in Philosophical Theology.* London: Student Christian Movement, 1955.
HOOK, SIDNEY (ed.). *Religious Experience and Truth.* New York: New York Univ. Press, 1961. Pts. I, III.
MACINTYRE, ALASDAIR. "The Logical Status of Religious Belief," in *Metaphysical Beliefs.* London: Student Christian Movement, 1957.
MASCALL, E. L. *Existence and Analogy.* London: Longmans, Green, 1949.

MITCHELL, BASIL (ed.). *Faith and Logic.* London: Allen & Unwin, 1957.
ST. THOMAS AQUINAS. *Summa Contra Gentiles,* Bk. I, Chs. 28-34 [in Hick].
—————. *Summa Theologica,* Pt. I, Q. 1 [in Smart], Q. 12.
TILLICH, PAUL. "Religious Symbols and Our Knowledge of God," *Christian Scholar,* Vol. 38 (1955).
WISDOM, JOHN. "Gods," in Antony Flew (ed.), *Essays in Logic and Language,* First Series. Oxford: Basil Blackwell, 1951 [in Abernethy-Langford, Hick, Jarrett-McMurrin].

Part II

VALUE
AND
OBLIGATION

INTRODUCTION

One set of beliefs, the rational appraisal of which is of very great interest, is ethical beliefs. Among "ethical" beliefs philosophers mean to include not only beliefs about what is morally right or wrong, morally obligatory, and what is one's moral duty, but also beliefs about what is a good or desirable or worthwhile thing, or the best, most desirable thing. Examples of statements expressing ethical beliefs in this sense are: "The only thing in life that is really worthwhile for itself is pleasure." "Knowledge and character are desirable not simply as means to happiness, but for themselves." "People should have taken a firmer stand against Hitler (or Senator McCarthy) than they did." "People are morally bound to stick by their promises, no matter what." "A person's moral obligation is always to do whatever will make for the greatest happiness of those his action will affect." "A person has a perfect right to promote his own happiness and interest, irrespective of the effects of his behavior on anyone else."

Can we show, by appeal to observation or truths of reason, that some such beliefs are correct or incorrect? Or can we at least show that every such belief is rationally justified, or rationally unjustified, in some important sense?

A good many people, especially among social scientists, think that the answer to these questions is in the negative. It is convenient to call such persons "sceptics about ethics," if we are careful not to rule out by this terminology the possibility that such persons have strong ethical commitments.

Some persons who are not sceptics in this sense take a view that has much in common with scepticism: they think that some ethical beliefs are correct or rationally justified for some individual or group of individuals, although some conflicting ethical belief is correct or rationally justified for some other individual or group of individuals. For instance, they might think it correct or justified for twentieth-century Englishmen to think it was wrong for Brutus to have stabbed Caesar, whereas it was also correct or justified for contemporary Romans to think it was right for Brutus to stab Caesar. This view may seem queer, but it is widely enough held to deserve a name. We may call it "ethical relativism."

Relativists in this sense differ among themselves on important points. For instance, some relativists think that an *individual person's* values or ethical convictions can be shown to be correct or incorrect; they are correct if and only if they conform with the standards of his social group. (Sometimes this view is defended by arguing that "it is right" just *means* "it is the custom in my social group.") A person's values are thus subject to correction in the way his grammar is. There is nothing inherently wrong about the use of "you is," but if educated people generally say "you are," an individual is mistaken if he says "you is." The same with ethical values. Such relativists do not think there is any comparable way of criticizing the standards of the group. Other relativists, who would reject this view, think that ethical judgments can be validly criticized in a rather different way. They say that an ethical judgment is mistaken if it is not impartial. (This view may be defended by claiming that what "X is wrong" means is "I disapprove of X and my disapproval is impartial.") Thus if I say, for instance, that your son was wrong in striking my son, the statement is incorrect if it expresses an attitude that would have been different had my son done the striking. But, these relativists say, while such criticism can show some ethical judgments to be mistaken (even judgments shared by a whole community or society), it may not succeed, and in fact will not succeed, in showing that one and the same value or moral conviction is correct for everybody, in every case.

Our first reading below is by a social scientist who describes herself as a relativist and has been recognized as one of relativism's leading exponents among social scientists. The second reading is a summary and criticism of both scepticism and relativism (the two views are not distinguished in the article) by a philosopher who is rather sympathetic toward the view. A representative of the sceptical view (Ayer) appears later in our readings; part of Stace's summary is descriptive of views essentially like his.

The popularity of both scepticism and relativism among social scientists and the educated public in recent years is probably a result of emphasis on findings of anthropology and psychology: the finding of anthropology that the values or moral convictions of people differ from one social group to another; and the finding of psychology that values and moral convictions are learned relatively early in life, often simply from the statements of parents or other authoritative persons, and that they are resistant to change. It is not so generally recognized that these findings do not establish either scepticism or relativism. That they do not is clear from a parallel case: people differ greatly in their estimates of extrasensory perception (e.g., water divining), and their beliefs seem to derive largely from the statements of authoritative persons, and to be highly resistant to change. The same, perhaps, with religious beliefs. But we do not infer scepticism or relativism in these cases. Why not? Because the claim that people have the capacity to make certain predictions accurately without the ordinary means of observation is a claim that is clearly true or false, and to which observation and scientific method are relevant, however much confusion there is about the matter.

What is really crucial for the truth of either ethical scepticism or relativism is rather what ethical statements mean (or would be used to mean by people who thought clearly), or how they function, and whether any reasonable support for them is possible, in view of what they mean. We have already noticed that some relativists properly support their views by claims about the meaning of ethical statements. A sceptic who would give his views a sound foundation must do the same. This central question has occupied the center of the stage in moral philosophy for the last three decades. Discussion of it is known as discussion of "meta-ethics" or "critical ethics."

Three main complexes of views have developed about this question, and it has come to be believed that these — with, of course, some variations — are the only possible views. The first is usually called "naturalism." According to it, when we examine what people mean when they make ethical statements, or what they would mean by them if they thought clearly, we find that the meaning of the statements is such that they are obviously true or false, and such that observation and deductive and inductive logic are relevant to finding whether they are true or false. This thesis is defended by both Sharp and James in the readings below; they take somewhat different views, however, about what in particular we should say ethical statements do mean. Naturalists generally have differed among themselves, to a considerable extent, about what ethical statements mean. One example of a naturalist analysis of the meaning of "good" is the view that "is a *good* thing in itself" just means "is a pleasant experience." An example of a naturalist analysis of "right" is the thesis that "is the *right* thing to do" just means "is the thing which, in the circumstances, will produce at least as much net happiness as any other course of action open to the agent." It is quite clear that, if such are the meanings to be assigned to ethical words, ethical statements are true or false, and, in principle, we can determine by observation and the methods of science when things are good or right.

We should notice, however, a rather subtle difference between naturalists. Some, like Sharp, think that what ordinary people *in fact do mean* by ethical terms is the kind of thing the naturalist says is the meaning of these terms. It would be agreed that the man on the street might not think of such a definition of his terms if asked, but it is thought that a reasonable interpretation of what he means, in view of how he actually uses ethical terms and when he retracts ethical statements made, is what the naturalist suggests. Other naturalists, and James among them, are not so optimistic about the meanings of ordinary persons. They rather think that, on reflection, a certain meaning has to be assigned to these terms, if the terms are to have a sensible use — if they are to be used to say something that an intelligent person would want to say. Such forms of naturalism are *proposals* about how ethical terms might well be used. The views are not very different, however, and it is not misleading to classify them all by the one term "naturalism."

It is convenient, although it seems paradoxical, to classify *supernaturalist* views of ethical statements as forms of naturalism in this sense. Let us define a supernaturalist as one who holds that ethical statements assert some fact about a divine being (or beings), which *someone* (perhaps that being itself) could know by observation or the methods of science. Thus, the supernaturalist may say that "is a good thing" means "is something God wants or approves of"; or he may say that "is wrong" means "is an action which God condemns or plans to punish or prohibits or deplores." If he is right, then, again, it is obvious that ethical statements are true or false, for it obviously just is or is not true that there is a divine being who has some such attitude or plan, etc. And *someone* is in a position to determine the truth of any ethical statement by observation and the methods of science — perhaps not we, for according to some views we can know about such matters only by revelation. Some writers, however, think that even we can know something about the intentions of the deity by observation and the methods of science, perhaps by examining the course of history, or at least by inspection of the totality of our knowledge about the universe. In any case, it is helpful to classify this view as a form of naturalism. This theory about ethical statements is criticized by Ewing, below.

The second main view about the nature of ethical statements is usually called "nonnaturalism," and it is represented by Reid's discussion. Nonnaturalists agree with the naturalists on one point: the meaning of ethical statements is such that these statements are clearly either true or false. But they disagree with the naturalist's view about how to decide which they are; they hold that the methods of science are not competent to decide any such thing. They say that if you want to know whether knowledge is worthwhile in itself, or whether the fact that a certain action would be a breach of promise has a tendency to make the action wrong, observation is absolutely useless in trying to find out what you want to know. Why do they say this? It is essential to the naturalist position that ethical statements mean the same as some statement that clearly can be confirmed by the methods of science — say, "Telling a lie in these circumstances is right" being the same as "Telling a lie in these circumstances is the way to maximize the happiness of all concerned." It is because the naturalist affirms this identity of meaning that he says that ethical statements can be confirmed by observation and inductive or deductive logic.

Now, the objection of the nonnaturalist (and, incidentally, of defenders of the noncognitivist view described below) is that this contention is just mistaken. "Is right" and "will maximize the happiness of everyone concerned" are just expressions with *different* meanings, and while *possibly* it is always right to do what will maximize the happiness of everyone involved, it is debatable whether it is, and at any rate it clearly is not self-contradictory to deny it. (It is sometimes suggested that writers are naturalists only because they fallaciously infer, from the fact that, as they think, some general ethical statement is true, it must be self-contradictory to deny it and it is true by definition, given the meaning of ethical words. This alleged fallacy of inference has been called "the naturalistic fallacy" by G. E. Moore, the leading nonnaturalistic critic of naturalism in the present century.) No ethical word (like "good" or "right") means the same as *any* word or phrase designating any property which we can determine to belong to something by observation and the methods of science. It has sometimes been claimed that it is easy to show this by what is called the "open question" argument, which runs as follows: Let *E* stand for any ethical predicate; and let *P* stand for any word or phrase of the kind a naturalist would say gives the meaning of *E*. Now ask yourself: "Is everything that is *E* also *P*? And is everything that is *P* also *E*?" Now, it is said, no matter what word or phrase the naturalist may put for *P*, it will be obvious that it is not self-contradictory to answer these questions in the negative; furthermore, the questions will be intelligible ones requiring ethical reflection for an answer. But, it is argued, if *E* just *meant* the same as *P*, it would obviously be self-contradictory to answer in the negative, and the questions would not be intelligible ones requiring ethical reflection for an answer. Obviously, in the case of "bachelor" and "unmarried male," which do mean roughly the same thing, it clearly *is* self-contradictory to say, "Not everything that is a bachelor is an unmarried male," and it would not be an intelligible question requiring reflection for an answer to ask, "Is every bachelor an unmarried male?" So the nonnaturalist argument runs. Naturalists think it confused and open to objections.

Nonnaturalists, we have said, are like naturalists in thinking that ethical statements are true or false; they also think we can sometimes *know* which they are, although not by observation and the methods of science. We may rightly ask them, then, *how* do we know such things? Usually, their answer is that some general ethical propositions are *truths of reason,* although not analytic ones or truths of logic. They are cases of *a priori synthetic knowledge.* (For an explanation of these terms, see the Introduction to Part V.) Sometimes, however, a different view seems to be held. Sometimes nonnaturalists appear to think that a person can be aware of something's being good, or an action's being right or wrong, not by reason, but by a quasi-observation or "moral sense" — by a kind of direct awareness which is not seeing with the eyes, touch, or knowing by any of the five senses. Reid discusses all these points.

The third main view about the nature of ethical statements we shall call "noncognitivism," and a form of this view is represented by the passage from A. J. Ayer. The noncognitivist agrees with the nonnaturalist that ethical statements are not the sort of statement the truth of which can be assessed by appeal to observation and deductive or inductive logic — in short, by the methods of the scientist. But the reason for this is that he disagrees with both the preceding theories in a very fundamental way: he thinks ethical statements, when we get clear about what they mean or do, are obviously not the kind of thing that is true or false at all; they do not assert any kind of fact about the world. In this respect, ethical statements are rather like "Come to the party!" or "I promise to meet you at eight o'clock" or "I bet you a dollar," all of which are important items in our speech repertory, but none of which *asserts a fact*. On the contrary, the first of these utterances issues an invitation; the second makes a promise; and the third offers (or seals) a bet. But it would be senseless to say of any such remark, "That's true!" The noncognitivist holds that ethical statements are like these utterances in not asserting facts. Only, because of their grammatical form, it is easily supposed that they state facts. (Other statements are like them in this respect: "The faculty will wear academic dress" looks like a fact-stating remark but may be used, not to make a prediction, but to issue an order or request to the faculty.)

Since ethical statements do not assert facts and are neither true nor false, obviously the question of how to determine whether they are true (how we know them) does not arise. What, then, according to writers of this persuasion, is it that ethical statements do? Here there is a good deal of disagreement. It has been said that to make an ethical statement is to issue a disguised *command*. This view is hardly defended today, but a somewhat similar view proposes that to make an ethical statement is to issue a *prescription* for choice or action, with the implication that one would issue the same prescription for all similar cases. According to another view, ethical convictions are essentially attitudes of favoring and disfavoring, and ethical statements are instruments for expressing one's own attitudes and for encouraging the same ones in others. Or it is held that an ethical statement may be an instrument of advice-giving in one context, of exhortation in another, of praise in a third, of condemnation in a fourth, of commendation in a fifth, and so on. In the reading below, Ayer defends the view that the function of ethical statements is to evince feelings of approval or disapproval and to arouse feeling or stimulate action much as commands do. Professor Ayer at present takes a view somewhat more complex than that espoused in the passage reprinted here. Obviously a view like Ayer's leads to scepticism in the sense explained above.

There was a time, a few years ago, when some philosophers thought that discussion of traditional ethical questions — about what is good or right — should be abandoned until the problems about how to confirm ethical statements were definitely solved. Indeed, some philosophers thought that the business of moral philosophy is solely to discuss the meaning and verification of ethical statements — that philosophers should not discuss questions of what *is* good or right at all. However, at the present time many philosophers, if not almost all, have returned to a discussion of the traditional questions, which had been debated for centuries before anyone had raised clearly the questions about meaning and verification.

Let us look at some of the positions held. A discussion of these questions is sometimes called "normative ethics" as contrasted with "meta-ethics." Of course, in these introductory remarks we must discuss the problems of normative ethics without assuming that the problems of meta-ethics have been decided in any particular way.

The problem of the good or the desirable is usually contrasted with the problem of the right or the morally obligatory, and we begin with it. Philosophers have generally thought that the main issue to be decided is what things are worthwhile or good *in themselves* ("intrinsically good," in one terminology), that is, roughly, good or desirable in abstraction from consequences. Undoubtedly, this is the main problem, for if we know what is a good thing in itself, apart from consequences, we can find out which things are good in view of their consequences by learning what their consequences are likely to be (and this we can obviously determine by the methods of science).

It is worth noticing that decisions we must make much more often require us to have made up our minds about what we think worthwhile or good than to have made up our minds about what is wrong or morally obligatory. For the most part, when deliberation about action occurs, it is deliberation to decide what is the best thing to do (either for one's self or one's family, etc.). The most important decisions one makes, about whether or where to continue one's education, or which occupation to take up, or whether and whom to marry, usually raise only questions of what is good or best or most desirable. Of course, decisions that raise moral questions do arise often enough, and these questions always lurk in the background. Doubtless there is always something wrong one might do; and moral issues in the narrow sense can be involved in a decision where to go for one's education (ought one to insist on going to a college one's family cannot afford?) or on a choice of profession (ought one to become a bookie or a narcotics peddler?). But the main issue with most decisions is simply what is the best thing to do from the point of view of one's own welfare or the welfare of one's own family, etc.; or the only issue is what kind of life is a good life, or the best life.

The debates among philosophers about the nature of "the good" have been debates about these questions. So they have attempted to assess, for the status of being worthwhile or desirable in itself, such things as enjoyment, fame, prestige, wealth, knowledge, character, love, friendship, just being alive or conscious, and other things that human beings sometimes find themselves wanting and whose worthwhileness they may question. As representatives of two widely supported traditions on these issues, readings from Aristotle and Smart appear below. They agree on one point — that the good or best life is in some sense a "happy" life; but they differ as to what kind of life is a "happy" one. Smart is in the ancient tradition which holds that only enjoyment of some sort is worthwhile; with qualifications, he identifies a life of enjoyment with the good or best life. Aristotle does not deny enjoyment a place in the good life; indeed, he thinks a good life will be enjoyable to a good man. But he takes a dim view of a life of sensual enjoyments; he thinks the key to understanding what kind of life is good or happy is recognizing that human beings are rational minds, and he infers from this that the kind of life which is most satisfying to a human being is one of reflection on truth, of order and moderation in desire and emotion. The tradition represented by Smart is usually called "hedonism" from the Greek word for "pleasure"; the tradition represented by Aristotle is sometimes called "pluralism," in recognition of the fact that he thinks that different kinds of things (contemplation, moderation in action, and features of character which are "means" between possible extremes) are worthwhile in themselves.

The implications of these different theories for decisions or choices differ less than one might at first suppose, primarily because of the conditions necessary for obtaining enjoyments and the consequences of enjoyments for the possibility of more enjoyments. Hedonists generally think that one maximizes one's enjoyments in the long run by acquiring knowledge, by moderation in indulgence of the appetites, and even by suppression of some appetites. The hedonist Epicurus regarded a diet of bread, milk, and cheese as being as lavish as a rational man would want, and he thought that fame and power, however enjoyable, are apt to produce more frustration and sadness than they ever bring joy.

A larger number of theories must be distinguished when we turn to the question of which actions are right, obligatory, or wrong. The broadest division between theories is between those which hold that rightness (etc.) is fixed by the consequences of an action (or a relevant class of actions) and those which deny that consequences are the only things relevant — a view sometimes called "formalism." The former type of theory we may call "teleologism," from the Greek for "end" or "result." It is not profitable to classify formalist theories into types, but teleological theories are distinguished into egoist theories (which hold that the rightness of an act is fixed by consequences for the agent) and universalist or utilitarian theories (which hold that rightness is fixed by consequences for people generally). If a man is considering whether to seek a divorce, an egoist would say that so doing is right or even obligatory if a divorce will, or probably will, maximize the man's own welfare; whereas the utilitarian will say that it is right to do so only when the welfare of wife, children, and anyone else affected is taken into account, and the total maximized by the course of action in question. Some utilitarians think that matters are rather more complex than this. In order to do justice to the views of these philosophers, we must recognize two types of utilitarians: the act-utilitarian and the rule-utilitarian. The act-utilitarian says that an act is right if and only if *it* will (or probably will) maximize the welfare of everyone concerned or affected, as compared with other acts the agent might perform instead. The rule-utilitarian, in contrast, says that an act is right if and only if it is the one, among those the agent could perform, which it would be best to have *generally,* or *always,* performed in circumstances like the one in question. Or, perhaps better put, the rule-utilitarian thinks an act is right if and only if it would not be forbidden, for circumstances like those in the case at issue, by a moral code the currency of which would have the best consequences for the society of the agent.

In order to see the differences between the theories, consider whether a physician should lie to his patient about the nature of his illness. The egoist will have the easiest time deciding what to do; he need only consider which course of action will benefit the physician most in the long run. The act-utilitarian will say the physician should lie if his doing so will maximize the welfare of everyone concerned (relieve the patient, make life easier in the patient's home, etc.). The rule-utilitarian will say that he should do so only if most good would be done if physicians generally lied to their patients in such circumstances, or (according to the second formulation) if it would do most good for there to be a recognized moral code that permits physicians to lie to their patients in such circumstances. It might well be that a particular lie to a patient would maximize the welfare of all concerned, whereas it would be a bad thing — because the relation of confidence between physician and patient would be destroyed — for physicians generally to lie to their patients in such circumstances, or for it to be recognized as morally unobjectionable for a physician to lie to his patient.

These theories about which acts are right are not committed, as stated, to any particular view about what is intrinsically good, either to hedonism or some type of pluralism. Thus a person who is convinced by one of them will still have to make up his mind about this latter question in order to decide in a concrete case what it is right to do. Thus an egoist might be a hedonist, but he could also be a kind of pluralist.

Among the readings below, a form of egoism is defended by Williams and is criticized by Medlin. A form of act-utilitarianism is espoused by Smart.

Formalism is represented in the readings by Ross and Kant. Ross centers his critical fire on utilitarianism combined with a pluralistic theory of the intrinsic good, since he regards it as the most plausible of the other theories. It should be noted, however, that the various forms of utilitarianism had not been sharply distinguished when he wrote four decades ago, and consequently he discusses only act-utilitarianism. Ross agrees with utilitarianism that the consequences of an action for good or ill are relevant to its rightness, but he thinks that other features of an act besides consequences are also relevant: whether the action would be a breach of faith, an expression of ingratitude, or incompatible with justice. All these features of an act tend to make it wrong (or right), and whether an act in given circumstances is right or wrong is a matter of how weighty these various features are in the particular cases — rather as the resultant force on a body is the sum of the vectors of the forces operating on it.

Kant's theory is further removed from any kind of teleologism, at least as far as express professions go. Kant says that good or ill consequences are totally irrelevant to whether something is right or wrong. His view about when an action is right is rather similar to the Golden Rule: he says roughly that an act is right if and only if its agent is prepared to have that kind of action made universal practice or a "law of nature." (Kant offers two other different formulations of his thesis, which he asserts come to the same thing — although it is highly doubtful that they do.) Thus, for instance, Kant says it is right for a person to lie if and only if he is prepared to have everyone lie in similar circumstances, including those in which *he* is deceived by the lie. Kant thinks that no one is prepared, at least consistently, to espouse a universal practice of suicide, breach of promise, refusal to develop one's own talents, or ignoring others in need, and therefore he concludes that such actions are wrong. Such a theory is certainly not act-utilitarianism, but it is not so different from rule-utilitarianism (which has been much influenced by Kant), since willingness to have some kind of act made a universal practice is at least not far from thinking it will have good consequences for a certain mode of conduct to be generally practised. But Kant's view is certainly not identical with any form of utilitarianism.

All these writers on normative ethics have some view or other on the problems of meta-ethics; the reader may find it interesting to identify these views.

Many people think that, after we have made up our minds about whether a given line of action is morally right or obligatory, there is a further problem outstanding. This is the question of whether it is reasonable for the agent to perform a morally obligatory action if so doing conflicts with his own interests, and if so, why. Obviously this problem hardly arises for the act-egoist, but it can arise for the other types of theory. It has been held by intelligent writers, for instance Plato, that a person can never hurt himself by doing what is right or morally obligatory, but this view seems absurd on the face of it. The last two of our readings, by Baier and Frankena, are attempts to deal with this problem. Obviously a great deal turns on what is meant by acting "reasonably." If to act "reasonably" means to act in a manner calculated to maximize one's own welfare, then it is self-contradictory to say it can be reasonable for a man to do what is morally obligatory when this conflicts with his personal interests. On the other hand, if to act "reasonably" means to act in such a manner as to fulfill one's moral obligations, then it is self-contradictory to say that it could be *un*reasonable for a man to do what is morally obligatory even when this conflicts with his personal welfare. It is, then, crucial to decide what it is to act reasonably.

11 🦎

AN ANTHROPOLOGIST'S
VIEW OF VALUES
AND MORALITY

Ruth Fulton Benedict

Ruth F. Benedict (1887-1948) was Professor of Anthropology at Columbia University.

Modern social anthropology has become more and more a study of the varieties and common elements of cultural environment and the consequences of these in human behavior. For such a study of diverse social orders primitive peoples fortunately provide a laboratory not yet entirely vitiated by the spread of a standardized worldwide civilization. Dyaks and Hopis, Fijians and Yakuts are significant for psychological and sociological study because only among these simpler peoples has there been sufficient isolation to give opportunity for the development of localized social forms. In the higher cultures the standardization of custom and belief over a couple of continents has given a false sense of the inevitability of the particular forms that have gained currency, and we need to turn to a wider survey in order to check the conclusions we hastily base upon this near-universality of familiar customs. Most of the simpler cultures did not gain the wide currency of the one which, out of our experience, we identify with human nature, but this was for various historical reasons, and certainly not for any that gives us as its carriers a monopoly of social good or of social sanity. Modern civilization, from this point of view, becomes not a necessary pinnacle of human achievement but one entry in a long series of possible adjustments.

These adjustments, whether they are in mannerisms like the ways of showing anger, or joy, or grief in any society, or in major human drives like those of sex, prove to be far more variable than experience in any one culture would suggest. In certain fields, such as that of religion or of formal marriage arrangements, these wide limits of variability are well known and can be fairly described. In others it is not yet possible to give a generalized

From Ruth Fulton Benedict, "Anthropology and the Abnormal," *Journal of General Psychology*, X (1934), pp. 59-80. Reprinted by permission of the Journal Press, Provincetown, Mass.

account, but that does not absolve us of the task of indicating the significance of the work that has been done and of the problems that have arisen.

One of these problems relates to the customary modern normal-abnormal categories and our conclusions regarding them. In how far are such categories culturally determined, or in how far can we with assurance regard them as absolute? In how far can we regard inability to function socially as diagnostic of abnormality, or in how far is it necessary to regard this as a function of the culture? . . .

The most spectacular illustrations of the extent to which normality may be culturally defined are those cultures where an abnormality of our culture is the cornerstone of their social structure. It is not possible to do justice to these possibilities in a short discussion. A recent study of an island of northwest Melanesia by Fortune describes a society built upon traits which we regard as beyond the border of paranoia. In this tribe the exogamic groups look upon each other as prime manipulators of black magic, so that one marries always into an enemy group which remains for life one's deadly and unappeasable foes. They look upon a good garden crop as a confession of theft, for everyone is engaged in making magic to induce into his garden the productiveness of his neighbor's; therefore no secrecy in the island is so rigidly insisted upon as the secrecy of a man's harvesting of his yams. Their polite phrase at the acceptance of a gift is, "And if you now poison me, how shall I repay you this present?" Their preoccupation with poisoning is constant; no woman ever leaves her cooking pot for a moment unattended. Even the great affinal economic exchanges that are characteristic of this Melanesian culture area are quite altered in Dobu since they are incompatible with this fear and distrust that pervades the culture. . . . They go farther and people the whole world outside their own quarters with such malignant spirits that all-night feasts and ceremonials simply do not occur here. They have even religiously enforced customs that forbid the sharing of seed even in one family group. Anyone else's food is deadly poison to you, so that communality of stores is out of the question. For some months before harvest the whole society is on the verge of starvation, but if one falls to the temptation and eats up one's seed yams, one is an outcast and a beachcomber for life. There is no coming back. It involves, as a matter of course, divorce and the breaking of all social ties.

Now in this society where no one may work with another and no one may share with another, Fortune describes the individual who was regarded by all his fellows as crazy. He was not one of those who periodically ran amok and, beside himself and frothing at the mouth, fell with a knife upon anyone he could reach. Such behavior they did not regard as putting anyone outside the pale. They did not even put the individuals who were known to be liable to these attacks under any kind of control. They merely fled when they saw the attack coming on and kept out of the way. "He would be all right tomorrow." But there was one man of sunny, kindly disposition who liked work and liked to be helpful. The compulsion was too strong for him to repress it in favor of the opposite tendencies of his culture. Men and women never spoke of him without laughing; he was silly and simple and definitely crazy. Nevertheless, to the ethnologist used to a culture that has, in Christianity, made his type the model of all virtue, he seemed a pleasant fellow.

An even more extreme example, because it is of a culture that has built itself upon a more complex abnormality, is that of the North Pacific Coast of North America. The civilization of the Kwakiutl, at the time when it was first recorded in the last decades of the nineteenth century, was one of the most vigorous in North America. It was built up on an ample economic supply of goods, the fish which furnished their food staple being practically inexhaustible and obtainable with comparatively small labor, and the wood which furnished the material for their houses, their furnishings, and their arts being, with however much labor, always procurable. They lived in coastal villages that compared favorably in size with those of any other American Indians and they kept up constant communication by means of sea-going dug-out canoes.

It was one of the most vigorous and zestful of the aboriginal cultures of North America, with complex crafts and ceremonials, and elaborate and striking arts. It certainly had none of the earmarks of a sick civilization. The tribes of the Northwest Coast had wealth, and exactly in our terms. That is, they had not only a surplus of economic goods, but they made a game of the manipulation of wealth. It was by no means a mere direct transcription of economic needs and the filling of those needs. It involved the idea of capital, of interest, and of conspicuous waste. It was a game with all the binding rules of a game, and a person entered it as a child. His father distributed wealth for him, according to his ability, at a small feast or potlatch, and each gift the receiver was obliged to accept and to return after a short interval with interest that ran to about 100 per cent a year. By the time the child was grown, therefore, he was well launched, a larger potlatch had been given for him on various occasions of exploit or initiation, and he had wealth either out at usury or in his own possession. Nothing in the civilization could be enjoyed without validating it by the distribution of this wealth. Everything that was valued, names and songs as well as material objects were passed down in family lines, but they were always publicly assumed with accompanying sufficient distributions of property. It was the game of validating and exercising all the privileges one could accumulate from one's various forebears, or by gift, or by marriage, that made the chief interest of the culture. Everyone in his degree took part in it, but many, of course, mainly as spectators. In its highest form it was played out between rival chiefs representing not only themselves and their family lines but their communities, and the object of the contest was to glorify oneself and to humiliate one's opponent. On this level of greatness the property involved was no longer represented by blankets, so many thousand of them to a potlatch, but by higher units of value. These higher units were like our bank notes. They were incised copper tablets, each of them named, and having a value that depended upon their illustrious history. This was as high as ten thousand blankets, and to possess one of them, still more to enhance its value at a great potlatch, was one of the greatest glories within the compass of the chiefs of the Northwest Coast. . . .

Every contingency of life was dealt with in . . . two traditional ways. To them the two were equivalent. Whether one fought with weapons or "fought with property," as they say, the same idea was at the bottom of both. In the olden times, they say, they fought with spears, but now they fight with property. One overcomes one's opponents in equivalent fashion in both, matching forces and seeing that one comes out ahead, and one can thumb one's nose at the vanquished rather more satisfactorily at a potlatch than on a battlefield. Every occasion in life was noticed, not in its own terms, as a stage in the sex life of the individual or as a climax of joy or of grief, but as furthering this drama of consolidating one's own prestige and bringing shame to one's guests. Whether it was the occasion of the birth of a child, or a daughter's adolescence, or of the marriage of one's son, they were all equivalent raw material for the culture to use for this one traditionally selected end. They were all to raise one's own personal status and to entrench oneself by the humiliation of one's fellows. A girl's adolescence among the Nootka was an event for which her father gathered property from the time she was first able to run about. When she was adolescent he would demonstrate his greatness by an unheard of distribution of these goods, and put down all his rivals. It was not as a fact of the girl's sex life that it figured in their culture, but as the occasion for a major move in the great game of vindicating one's own greatness and humiliating one's associates.

In their behavior at great bereavements this set of the culture comes out most strongly. Among the Kwakiutl it did not matter whether a relative had died in bed of disease, or by the hand of an enemy; in either case death was an affront to be wiped out by the death of another person. The fact that one had been caused to mourn was proof that one had been put upon. A chief's sister and her daughter had gone up to Victoria, and either because they drank bad whiskey or because their boat capsized they never came back. The chief called together his warriors. "Now, I ask you, tribes, who shall wail? Shall I do it or shall another?" The spokesman answered, of course, "Not you, Chief. Let some other of the tribes." Immediately they set up the war pole to announce their intention of wiping out the injury, and gathered a war party. They set out, and found seven men and two children asleep and killed them. "Then they felt good when they arrived at Sebaa in the evening."

The point which is of interest to us is that in our society those who on that occasion would feel good when they arrived at Sebaa that evening would be the definitely abnormal. There would be some, even in our society, but it is not a recognized and approved mood under the circumstances. On the Northwest Coast those are favored and fortunate to whom that mood under those circumstances is congenial, and those to whom it is repugnant are un-lucky. This latter minority can register in their own culture only by doing violence to their congenial responses and acquiring others that are difficult for them. The person, for instance, who, like a Plains Indian whose wife has been taken from him, is too proud to fight, can deal with the Northwest Coast civilization only by ignoring its strongest bents. If he cannot achieve it, he is the deviant in that culture, their instance of abnormality.

This head-hunting that takes place on the Northwest Coast after a death is no matter of blood revenge or of organized vengeance. There is no effort to tie up the subsequent killing with any responsibility on the part of the victim for the death of the person who is being mourned. A chief whose son has died goes visiting wherever his fancy dictates, and he says to his host, "My prince has died today, and you go with him." Then he kills him. In this, according to their interpretation, he acts nobly because he has not been downed. He has thrust back in return. The whole procedure is meaningless without the fundamental paranoid reading of bereavement. Death, like all the other untoward accidents of existence, confounds man's pride and can only be handled in the category of insults. . . .

These illustrations, which it has been possible to indicate only in the briefest manner, force upon us the fact that normality is culturally defined. An adult shaped to the drives and standards of either of these cultures, if he were transported into our civilization, would fall into our categories of abnormality. He would be faced with the psychic dilemmas of the socially unavailable. In his own culture, however, he is the pillar of society, the end result of socially inculcated mores, and the problem of personal instability in his case simply does not arise.

No one civilization can possibly utilize in its mores the whole potential range of human behavior. Just as there are great numbers of possible pho-netic articulations, and the possibility of language depends on a selection and standardization of a few of these in order that speech communication may be possible at all, so the possibility of organized behavior of every sort, from the fashions of local dress and houses to the dicta of a people's ethics and religion, depends upon a similar selection among the possible behavior traits. In the field of recognized economic obligations or sex tabus this selection is as non-rational and subconscious a process as it is in the field of phonetics. It is a process which goes on in the group for long periods of time and is historically conditioned by innumerable accidents of isolation or of contact of peoples. In any comprehensive study of psychology, the selection that different cul-tures have made in the course of history within the great circumference of potential behavior is of great significance.

Every society, beginning with some slight inclination in one direction or another, carries its preference farther and farther, integrating itself more and more completely upon its chosen basis, and discarding those types of behavior that are uncongenial. Most of those organizations of personality that seem to us most incontrovertibly abnormal have been used by different civilizations in the very foundations of their institutional life. Conversely the most valued traits of our normal individuals have been looked on in differently organized cultures as aberrant. Normality, in short, within a very wide range, is culturally defined. It is primarily a term for the socially elaborated segment of human behavior in any culture; and abnormality, a term for the segment that that particular civilization does not use. The very eyes with which we see the problem are conditioned by the long traditional habits of our own society.

It is a point that has been made more often in relation to ethics than in relation to psychiatry. We do not any longer make the mistake of deriving the morality of our own locality and decade directly from the inevitable constitution of human nature. We do not elevate it to the dignity of a first principle. We recognize that morality differs in every society, and is a convenient term for socially approved habits. Mankind has always preferred to say, "It is morally good," rather than "It is habitual," and the fact of this preference is matter enough for a critical science of ethics. But historically the two phrases are synonymous.

The concept of the normal is properly a variant of the concept of the good. It is that which society has approved. A normal action is one which falls well within the limits of expected behavior for a particular society. Its variability among different peoples is essentially a function of the variability of the behavior patterns that different societies have created for themselves, and can never be wholly divorced from a consideration of culturally institutionalized types of behavior.

Each culture is a more or less elaborate working-out of the potentialities of the segment it has chosen. In so far as a civilization is well integrated and consistent within itself, it will tend to carry farther and farther, according to its nature, its initial impulse toward a particular type of action, and from the point of view of any other culture those elaborations will include more and more extreme and aberrant traits.

Each of these traits, in proportion as it reinforces the chosen behavior patterns of that culture, is for that culture normal. Those individuals to whom it is congenial either congenitally, or as the result of childhood sets, are accorded prestige in that culture, and are not visited with the social contempt or disapproval which their traits would call down upon them in a society that was differently organized. On the other hand, those individuals whose characteristics are not congenial to the selected type of human behavior in that community are the deviants, no matter how valued their personality traits may be in a contrasted civilization. . . .

The problem of understanding abnormal human behavior in any absolute sense independent of cultural factors is still far in the future. The categories of borderline behavior which we derive from the study of the neuroses and psychoses of our civilization are categories of prevailing local types of instability. They give much information about the stresses and strains of Western civilization, but no final picture of inevitable human behavior. Any conclusions about such behavior must await the collection by trained observers of psychiatric data from other cultures. Since no adequate work of the kind has been done at the present time, it is impossible to say what core of definition of abnormality may be found valid from the comparative material. It is as it is in ethics; all our local conventions of moral behavior and of immoral are without absolute validity, and yet it is quite possible that a modicum of what is considered right and what wrong could be disentangled that is shared by the whole human race. When data are available in psychiatry, this minimum definition of abnormal human tendencies will be probably quite unlike our culturally conditioned, highly elaborated psychoses such as those that are described, for instance, under the terms of schizophrenia and manic-depressive.

12

ETHICAL
RELATIVISM:
PROS AND CONS

Walter Terence Stace

W. T. Stace (1886-   ) was a British civil servant in Ceylon (at one time Mayor of Colombo) before joining the Philosophy Department of Princeton University in 1932. He has been president of the American Philosophical Association.

There is an opinion widely current nowadays in philosophical circles which passes under the name of "ethical relativity." Exactly what this phrase means or implies is certainly far from clear. But unquestionably it stands as a label for the opinions of a group of ethical philosophers whose position is roughly on the extreme left wing among the moral theorizers of the day. And perhaps one may best understand it by placing it in contrast with the opposite kind of extreme view against which, undoubtedly, it has arisen as a protest. For among moral philosophers one may clearly distinguish a left and a right wing. Those of the left wing are the ethical relativists. They are the revolutionaries, the clever young men, the up to date. Those of the right wing we may call the ethical absolutists. They are the conservatives and the old-fashioned.

According to the absolutists there is but one eternally true and valid moral code. This moral code applies with rigid impartiality to all men. What is a duty for me must likewise be a duty for you. And this will be true whether you are an Englishman, a Chinaman, or a Hottentot. If cannibalism is an abomination in England or America, it is an abomination in central Africa, notwithstanding that the African may think otherwise. The fact that he sees nothing wrong in his cannibal practices does not make them for him morally right. They are as much contrary to morality for him as they are for us. The only difference is that he is an ignorant savage who does not know this.

The ethical absolutist recognizes as a fact that moral customs and moral ideas differ from country to country and from age to age. This indeed seems manifest and not to be disputed. We think slavery morally wrong, the Greeks thought it morally unobjectionable. The inhabitants of New Guinea

From W. T. Stace, *The Concept of Morals,* The Macmillan Company, New York, 1937. From Chapters 1 and 2. Reprinted by permission of the publisher.

138

certainly have very different moral ideas from ours. But the fact that the Greeks or the inhabitants of New Guinea think something right does not make it right, even for them. Nor does the fact that we think the same things wrong make them wrong. They are *in themselves* either right or wrong. What we have to do is to discover which they are. What anyone thinks makes no difference. It is here just as it is in matters of physical science. We believe the earth to be a globe. Our ancestors may have thought it flat. This does not show that it *was* flat, and is *now* a globe. What it shows is that men having in other ages been ignorant about the shape of the earth have now learned the truth. So if the Greeks thought slavery morally legitimate, this does not indicate that it was for them and in that age morally legitimate, but rather that they were ignorant of the truth of the matter.

The ethical absolutist is not indeed committed to the opinion that his own, or our own, moral code is the true one. Theoretically at least he might hold that slavery is ethically justifiable, that the Greeks knew better than we do about this, that ignorance of the true morality lies with us and not with them. All that he is actually committed to is the opinion that, whatever the true moral code may be, it is always the same for all men in all ages. His view is not at all inconsistent with the belief that humanity has still much to learn in moral matters. If anyone were to assert that in five hundred years the moral conceptions of the present day will appear as barbarous to the people of that age as the moral conceptions of the middle ages appear to us now, he need not deny it. If anyone were to assert that the ethics of Christianity are by no means final, and will be superseded in future ages by vastly nobler moral ideals, he need not deny this either. For it is of the essence of his creed to believe that morality is in some sense objective, not man-made, not produced by human opinion; that its principles are real truths about which men have to learn — just as they have to learn about the shape of the world — about which they may have been ignorant in the past, and about which therefore they may well be ignorant now.

Thus although absolutism is conservative in the sense that it is regarded by the more daring spirits as an out of date opinion, it is not necessarily conservative in the sense of being committed to the blind support of existing moral ideas and institutions. If ethical absolutists are sometimes conservative in this sense too, that is their personal affair. Such conservatism is accidental, not essential to the absolutist's creed. . . .

Any ethical position which denies that there is a single moral standard which is equally applicable to all men at all times may fairly be called a species of ethical relativity. There is not, the relativist asserts, merely one moral law, one code, one standard. There are many moral laws, codes, standards. What morality ordains in one place or age may be quite different from what morality ordains in another place or age. The moral code of Chinamen is quite different from that of Europeans, that of African savages quite different from both. Any morality, therefore, is relative to the age, the place, and the circumstances in which it is found. It is in no sense absolute.

This does not mean merely — as one might at first sight be inclined to suppose — that the very same kind of action which is *thought* right in one country and period may be *thought* wrong in another. This would be a mere platitude, the truth of which everyone would have to admit. Even the absolutist would admit this — would even wish to emphasize it — since he is well aware that different peoples have different sets of moral ideas, and his whole point is that some of these sets of ideas are false. What the relativist means to assert is, not this platitude, but that the very same kind of action which *is* right in one country and period may *be* wrong in another. And this, far from being a platitude, is a very startling assertion.

It is very important to grasp thoroughly the difference between the two ideas. For there is reason to think that many minds tend to find ethical relativity attractive because they fail to keep them clearly apart. It is so very obvious that moral ideas differ from country to country and from age to age. And it is so very easy, if you are mentally lazy, to suppose that to say this means the same as to say that no universal moral standard exists, — or in other words that it implies ethical relativity. We fail to see that the word "standard" is used in two different senses. It is perfectly true that, in one sense, there are many variable moral standards. We speak of judging a man by the standard of his time. And this implies that different times have different standards. And this, of course, is quite true. But when the word "standard" is used in this sense it means simply the set of moral ideas current during the period in question. It means what people *think* right, whether as a matter of fact it *is* right or not. On the other hand when the absolutist asserts that there exists a single universal moral "standard," he is not using the word in this sense at all. He means by "standard" what *is* right as distinct from what people merely think right. His point is that although what people think right varies in different countries and periods, yet what actually is right is everywhere and always the same. And it follows that when the ethical relativist disputes the position of the absolutist and denies that any universal moral standard exists he too means by "standard" what actually is right. . . .

The genuine relativist, then, does not merely mean that Chinamen may think right what French think wrong. He means that what *is* wrong for the Frenchman may *be* right for the Chinaman. And if one enquires how, in those circumstances, one is to know what actually is right in China or in France, the answer comes quite glibly. What is right in China is the same as what people think right in China; and what is right in France is the same as what people think right in France. So that, if you want to know what is moral in any particular country or age all you have to do is to ascertain what are the moral ideas current in that age or country. Those ideas are, *for that age or country,* right. . . .

There are, I think, four main arguments in favour of ethical relativity. The first is that which relies upon the actual varieties of moral "standards" found in the world. It was easy enough to believe in a single absolute morality in older times when there was no anthropology, when all humanity was divided clearly into two groups, Christian peoples and the "heathen." Christian peoples knew and possessed the one true morality. The rest were savages whose moral ideas could be ignored. But all this is changed. Greater knowledge has brought greater tolerance. We can no longer exalt our own morality as alone true, while dismissing all other moralities as false or inferior. The investigations of anthropologists have shown that there exist side by side in the world a bewildering variety of moral codes. On this topic endless volumes have been written, masses of evidence piled up. Anthropologists have ransacked the Melanesian Islands, the jungles of New Guinea, the steppes of Siberia, the deserts of Australia, the forests of central Africa, and have brought back with them countless examples of weird, extravagant, and fantastic "moral" customs with which to confound us. We learn that all kinds of horrible practices are, in this, that, or the other place, regarded as essential to virtue. We find that there is nothing, or next to nothing, which has always and everywhere been regarded as morally good by all men. Where then is our universal morality? Can we, in face of all this evidence, deny that it is nothing but an empty dream?

This argument, taken by itself, is a very weak one. It relies upon a single set of facts — the variable moral customs of the world. But this variability of moral ideas is admitted by both parties to the dispute, and is, capable of ready explanation upon the hypothesis of either party. The relativist says that the facts are to be explained by the non-existence of any absolute moral standard. The absolutist says that they are to be explained by human ignorance of what the absolute moral standard is. And he can truly point out that men have differed widely in their opinions about all manner of topics including the subject-matters of the physical sciences — just as much as they differ about morals. And if the various different opinions which men have held about the shape of the earth do not prove that it has no one real shape, neither do the various opinions which they have held about morality prove that there is no one true morality.

Thus the facts can be explained equally plausibly on either hypothesis. There is nothing in the facts themselves which compels us to prefer the relativistic hypothesis to that of the absolutist. And therefore the argument fails to prove the relativist conclusion. If that conclusion is to be established it must be by means of other considerations.

This is the essential point. But I will add some supplementary remarks. The work of the anthropologists, upon which ethical relativists seem to rely so heavily, has as a matter of fact added absolutely nothing *in principle* to what has always been known about the variability of moral ideas. Educated people have known all along that the Greeks tolerated sodomy, which in modern times has been regarded in some countries as an abominable crime; that the Hindus thought it a sacred duty to burn their widows; that trickery, now thought despicable, was once believed to be a virtue; that terrible torture was thought by our own ancestors only a few centuries ago to be a justifiable weapon of justice; that it was only yesterday that western peoples came to believe that slavery is immoral. Even the ancients knew very well that moral customs and ideas vary — witness the writings of Herodotus. Thus the principle of the variability of moral ideas was well understood long before modern anthropology was ever heard of. Anthropology has added nothing to the knowledge of this principle except a mass of new and extreme examples of it drawn from very remote sources. But to multiply examples of a principle already well known and universally admitted adds nothing to the argument which is built upon that principle. The discoveries of the anthropologists have no doubt been of the highest importance in their own sphere. But in my considered opinion they have thrown no new light upon the special problems of the moral philosopher. . . .

A second argument for relativism is that which asserts that all moral ideas are based upon "emotions." That which men regard with such emotions as resentment and disgust they disapprove and call immoral. That which they view with admiration they approve and call good. But emotions are notoriously variable. What disgusts some people pleases others. What angers one person does not anger another. Hence moral standards will vary with the emotions upon which they are based.

This argument is not approved by all relativists. By Westermarck it is made the mainstay of his position.[1] By Dewey, on the other hand it is belittled as being based upon an out of date dualistic psychology.[2] I do not propose to comment upon it in this chapter.

The third argument in favour of ethical relativity is, I think, an exceedingly powerful and important one. But it depends wholly upon the acceptance of the general philosophical attitude known as "radical empiricism." . . .

Radical empiricists hold that no word has cognitive meaning unless what it refers to, or purports to refer to, is something of a kind whose elements are at least theoretically capable of being directly experienced. Concepts are derived from experience, and therefore must at least refer to the experience from which they have been derived. Or even if we believe, as Kant did, that some concepts are *a priori* and not derived from experience, yet even these concepts apply to experience (or in other words refer to it), and could have no meaning unless we could find in experience something to which they apply. This was implicitly recognized by Kant himself when he wrote the words "concepts without percepts are empty."

The concept "red" has meaning because it refers to the red things which we find in experience. The concept "centaur" has meaning because, although we do not experience centaurs, we do experience men and horses, and the concept "centaur" has no content which is not referable to one or other of these things. But a concept which purported to stand for something the elements of which never have been, and in principle never could be, experi-

[1] Edward Westermarck, *Ethical Relativity.*
[2] John Dewey, *Human Nature and Conduct,* Chap. V.

enced, would be meaningless. It would not really *be* a concept at all. It would be a mere word. Thus though the word "potentiality" may, if properly used, have good meaning, it is sometimes used in a way which has none. Suppose I say "Oaks are potentially present in acorns." If all I intend to assert is that, given certain conditions, oaks grow out of acorns, my statement is meaningful, since the growth of acorns into oaks is an experienceable fact. If what I intend is that a sufficiently powerful microscope would detect a minute oak wrapped up inside the acorn, this is also meaningful (though probably false). For the tiny oak asserted to exist would be *visible,* at least theoretically, and therefore experienceable. But if what is intended is that there is now present in the acorn, not an actually existing oak tree however small, but a "potentially existing" one, then this is meaningless. For what does not actually exist could not conceivably be experienced. The essence of the theory of meaning which radical empiricists hold is that any word which purports to stand for an entity which could not possibly be experienced by any conceivable mind in any conceivable circumstances is entirely meaningless; and that any sentence which affirms the reality or existence of any such entity is also entirely meaningless. Now an entity whose being is not actual but potential could not possibly be experienced by any mind — even by the mind of God. For if it were experienced that very fact would show it to be an *actual* existence. Hence "potential existence" is a very good example of a phrase which, on radical empiricist principles, is quite meaningless.

We have now to apply this theory of meaning to the ethical problem before us. When we do so we find that absolutism involves the use of conceptions which have no meaning, while, on the other hand, the relativist account of morals is wholly meaningful.

The key word of morals is the word "ought." Morality means simply that which men ought to do. But in the light of the empirical criterion of meaning just explained has the word "ought" any meaning? This question presents a real difficulty. For it is obvious that only what *is* is capable of being experienced, and that no being could ever conceivably experience what only ought to be but is not. The difficulty is really identical with that which Hume discovered in the notion of natural, as distinguished from logical, necessity. It is possible to experience something which actually is the case — for example, the fact that the sun rises. But how can one ever experience the fact that anything must *necessarily* be the case — for example that the sun *must* rise? In the same way, no being can ever experience the fact that something *ought* to be the case. But if this is true, it would seem that the word "ought," since its objective referent is not to be found in experience, is meaningless. And in that case morality collapses.

Fortunately there is more to be said. I am going to call all sentences which state that something ought (or ought not) to be the case, or that something ought (or ought not) to be done, by the name "ought sentences." And I am going to call all sentences which merely state that something is (or is not) the case by the name "is sentences." According to what has been said it will then be clear that all "ought" sentences are meaningless, but that "is" sentences are meaningful. If then an "ought" sentence can be wholly translated, without loss of intended content, into an "is" sentence — if the word "ought" can be got rid of from it — it may in that way be shown to have meaning. It may be the case that what is *verbally* an "ought" sentence is in reality, according to its true meaning, an "is" sentence. We may have said that something ought to be the case when what we really mean is only that something is the case. And in that case our sentence will have meaning even though by mistake, or for some convenience of speech, we have used the meaningless word "ought" in it.

This is often the real state of affairs. I say, for example, "You ought not to over-eat." It seems quite clear here that I have left part of my meaning to be understood. What I really mean is "You ought not to over-eat, *if* you wish to retain your health." And this can be translated into "Abstention from over-eating *is* one of the means to health." This is an "is" sentence, and the "ought" sentence "You ought not to over-eat" has been translated into it, thus showing that it possesses meaning. What has really been stated as to the way to retain one's health is a matter of *fact* which is *empirically verifiable*, namely, the fact that over-eating leads to ill-health.

Further examination will show that *hypothetical* "ought" sentences — sentences of the form "*if* you want so and so, then you ought to do so and so" — are all thus translatable into "is" sentences, since they all merely state that the best way of attaining some desired end *is* to adopt such and such means. All such sentences are therefore meaningful. But *categorical* "ought" sentences — which have the form "You absolutely ought to do so and so without any conditions whatsoever" — are not so translatable. There is no way, in them, of getting rid of the word "ought" and replacing it by the word "is." They do not state that something is the case, for example that the best means to some end is to adopt certain measures. They purport to state unconditionally that something absolutely ought to be the case, and the "ought" in them is therefore totally intractable.

Now absolutism implies that moral judgments are categorical. It therefore involves the use of a meaningless conception, that of the absolute and unconditional "ought," and it thereby stands condemned. . . .

When it is said that the word "ought," taken absolutely, is meaningless, it is not of course meant that it conveys no idea whatever to the mind. This would certainly be nonsense, since it would then be impossible to explain how human beings ever came to suppose that it had a meaning. And obviously when a despot issues an absolute command to a subject, the latter does receive some mental impression, usually a very strong one. What is intended by saying that it is meaningless is that it has no *cognitive* meaning, that is, it does not convey any information about the world, it does not make any statement of alleged fact which could be either true or false. In order for a sentence to be either true or false it must at least purport to convey some information. There are many perfectly good sentences in language which do not do this. For example, if I say "May the sun shine on my wedding to-morrow," I am not even pretending to state any kind of fact about the actual state of the weather or about anything else in the world. I am giving expression to a feeling or a hope. And if I say "Go and get my umbrella," here too I am not giving any information about anything, but I am issuing a command. The purpose of such sentences is not to give information but to express emotions or to influence people's actions. Such sentences cannot be said to be strictly true or false, for they do not assert anything to be, or not to be, a fact. Of course it is no doubt a fact that I have the emotion or that I issue the command, but this is not what these sentences specifically say. And these sentences are, therefore, "meaningless" in the technical sense of that term which is employed in the argument which we are discussing. But of course they are not meaningless in the ordinary sense of conveying nothing at all to the minds of their hearers. . . .

The fourth argument in favor of ethical relativity is also a very strong one. And it does not suffer from the disadvantage that it is dependent upon the acceptance of any particular philosophy such as radical empiricism. It makes its appeal to considerations of a quite general character. It consists in alleging that no one has ever been able to discover upon what foundation an absolute morality could rest, or from what source a universally binding moral code could derive its authority.

If, for example, it is an absolute and unalterable moral rule that all men ought to be unselfish, from whence does this *command* issue? For a command it certainly is, phrase it how you please. There is no difference in meaning between the sentence "You ought to be unselfish" and the sentence "Be unselfish." Now a command implies a commander. An obligation implies some authority which obliges. Who is this commander, what this authority? Thus the vastly difficult question is raised of *the basis of moral obligation*. Now the argument of the relativist would be that it is impossible to find any basis for a universally binding moral law; but that it is quite easy to discover a basis for morality if moral codes are admitted to be variable, ephemeral, and relative to time, place, and circumstance.

In this book I am assuming that it is no longer possible to solve this difficulty by saying naïvely that the universal moral law is based upon the uniform commands of God to all men. There will be many, no doubt, who will dispute this. But I am not writing for them. I am writing for those who feel the necessity of finding for morality a basis independent of particular religious dogmas. And I shall therefore make no attempt to argue the matter.

The problem which the absolutist has to face, then, is this. The religious basis of the one absolute morality having disappeared, can there be found for it any other, any secular, basis? If not, then it would seem that we cannot any longer believe in absolutism. We shall have to fall back upon belief in a variety of perhaps mutually inconsistent moral codes operating over restricted areas and limited periods. No one of these will be better, or more true, than any other. Each will be good and true for those living in those areas and periods. We shall have to fall back, in a word, on ethical relativity.

For there is no great difficulty in discovering the foundations of morality, or rather of moralities, if we adopt the relativistic hypothesis. Even if we cannot be quite certain *precisely* what these foundations are — and relativists themselves are not entirely agreed about them — we can at least see in a general way the *sort* of foundations they must have. We can see that the question on this basis is not in principle impossible to answer — although the details may be obscure; while, if we adopt the absolutist hypothesis — so the argument runs — no kind of answer is conceivable at all.

Relativists, speaking generally, offer two different solutions of the problem, either of which, or perhaps some compromise between the two, might be correct. According to some the basis of morality is in "emotion." According to others it is in "customs." I do not intend to examine these rival suggestions in detail. An understanding of the general principles involved in them will be quite sufficient for our purpose.

According to the first view emotions such as that of resentment give rise to the idea that the things or actions resented are immoral and bad. Westermarck, who is the chief exponent of this type of opinion, makes further distinctions. Not any resentment, but only impartial or "disinterested" resentment, is the source of moral disapproval. But with these refinements we need not concern ourselves. We can see, easily enough, that if in one community a particular type of act, say sodomy, comes for any reason — biological, historical, or merely accidental — to be resented by the majority of the members of the group, it will come to be regarded as "wrong" by that group. If in another community no such feeling of resentment or dislike arises, it will be thought to be morally unobjectionable. The sense of moral obligation and the commands of morality, then, have their source in *feelings*. And since the feelings of men, and of different groups of men, are variable, the moral codes which are based upon them will be variable too.

Moreover an emotion is not — at any rate according to the psychology implied by Westermarck's conceptions — anything rational. An emotion, as such, cannot be true or false, right or wrong. It simply *is*. If therefore one group of people feels resentment at murder, while another does not, it cannot be said that the moral ideas of the former are any better or more true or more right than those of the latter. They are simply different. What is right *means* simply what arouses certain kinds of feelings, say those of approval. What is wrong *means* simply what arouses resentment or disapproval. There is consequently no sense in asking whether a race of men is right in approving this or that kind of action. Their approving it is what makes it right. For them, therefore, it *is* right. And if another race disapproves it, then, for that race, it *is* wrong.

According to the other view it is custom which is the source of moral standards and ideas. That is "wrong" in any community which is contrary to the customs of that community. That is "right" which is in accordance with them. A moral standard, in fact, is simply identifiable with the set of customs which are in force in any particular region at any particular time. And as customs are variable, so are moral standards. Here too there can be no question of declaring that one set of customs is morally better than another. For the fact that something is the custom is what makes it morally good. And according to this view the sense of moral obligation is simply the force of social custom making itself felt in the individual consciousness.

These two views are not really incompatible. For customs surely have their roots in men's feelings. And to say that morality is based on customs is in the end the same as to say that it is based on feelings. One view emphasizes the outward behaviour which exhibits itself in customs; the other view emphasizes the inward feelings which give rise to this behaviour. The dispute is a professional one between rival schools of psychology. It does not affect the larger issues with which we are concerned.

No such easy solution of the problem of the basis of moral obligation is open to the absolutist. He believes in moral commands obedience to which is obligatory on all men, whether they know it or not, whatever they feel, and whatever their customs may be. Such uniform obligation cannot be founded upon feelings, because feelings are — or are said to be — variable. And there is no set of customs which is more than local in its operation. The will of God as the source of a universal law is no longer a feasible suggestion. And there is obviously no mundane authority, king, or Pope, or superstate, to which all men admit allegiance, and which could have the recognized right to issue universally binding decrees. Where then is the absolutist to turn for an answer to the question? And if he cannot find out, he will have to admit the claims of the ethical relativist; or at least he will have to give up his own claims.

.   .   .

It is time that we turned our attention from the case in favour of ethical relativity to the case against it. Now the case against it consists, to a very large extent, in urging that, if taken seriously and pressed to its logical conclusion, ethical relativity can only end in destroying the conception of morality altogether, in undermining its practical efficacy, in rendering meaningless many almost universally accepted truths about human affairs, in robbing human beings of any incentive to strive for a better world, in taking the life-blood out of every ideal and every aspiration which has ever ennobled the life of man. In short, the charge against it is that it revolts and outrages man's moral *feelings*.

.   .   .

First of all, then, ethical relativity, in asserting that the moral standards of particular social groups are the only standards which exist, renders meaningless all positions which attempt to compare these standards with one another in respect of their moral worth. And this is a very serious matter indeed. We are accustomed to think that the moral ideas of one nation or social group may be "higher" or "lower" than those of another. We believe, for example, that Christian ethical ideals are nobler than those of the savage races of central Africa. Probably most of us would think that the Chinese moral standards are higher than those of the inhabitants of New Guinea. In short we habitually compare one civilization with another and judge the sets of ethical ideas to be found in them to be some better, some worse. The fact that such judgments are very difficult to make with any justice, and that they are frequently made on very superficial and prejudiced grounds, has no bearing on the question now at issue. The question is whether such judgments have any *meaning*. We habitually assume that they have.

But on the basis of ethical relativity they can have none whatever. For the relativist must hold that there is no *common* standard which can be applied to the various civilizations judged. Any such comparison of moral standards implies the existence of some superior standard which is applicable to both. And the existence of any such standard is precisely what the relativist denies. According to him the Christian standard is applicable only to Christians, the Chinese standard only to Chinese, the New Guinea standard only to the inhabitants of New Guinea. . . .

This in its turn implies that the whole notion of moral *progress* is a sheer delusion. Progress means an advance from lower to higher, from worse to better. But on the basis of ethical relativity it has no meaning to say that the standards of this age are better (or worse) than those of a previous age. For there is no common standard by which both can be measured. Thus it is nonsense to say that the morality of the New Testament is higher than that of the Old. And Jesus Christ, if he imagined that he was introducing into the world a higher ethical standard than existed before his time, was merely deluded. . . .

I come now to a second point. Up to the present I have allowed it to be taken tacitly for granted that, though judgments comparing different races and ages in respect of the worth of their moral codes are impossible for the ethical relativist, yet judgments of comparison between individuals living within the same social group would be quite possible. For individuals living within the same social group would presumably be subject to the same moral code, that of their group, and this would therefore constitute, as between these individuals, a common standard by which they could both be measured. We have not here, as we had in the other case, the difficulty of the absence of any common standard of comparison. It should therefore be possible for the ethical relativist to say quite meaningfully that President Lincoln was a better man than some criminal or moral imbecile of his own time and country, or that Jesus was a better man than Judas Iscariot.

But is even this minimum of moral judgment really possible on relativist grounds? It seems to me that it is not. For when once the whole of humanity is abandoned as the area covered by a single moral standard, what smaller areas are to be adopted as the *loci* of different standards? Where are we to draw the lines of demarcation? We can split up humanity, perhaps, — though the procedure will be very arbitrary — into races, races into nations,

nations into tribes, tribes into families, families into individuals. Where are we going to draw the *moral* boundaries? Does the *locus* of a particular moral standard reside in a race, a nation, a tribe, a family, or an individual? Perhaps the blessed phrase "social group" will be dragged in to save the situation. Each such group, we shall be told, has its own moral code which is, for it, right. But what *is* a "group"? Can anyone define it or give its boundaries? This is the seat of that ambiguity in the theory of ethical relativity to which reference was made on an earlier page.

The difficulty is not, as might be thought, merely an academic difficulty of logical definition. If that were all, I should not press the point. But the ambiguity has practical consequences which are disastrous for morality. No one is likely to say that moral codes are confined within the arbitrary limits of the geographical divisions of countries. Nor are the notions of race, nation, or political state likely to help us. To bring out the essentially practical character of the difficulty let us put it in the form of concrete questions. Does the American nation constitute a "group" having a single moral standard? Or does the standard of what I ought to do change continuously as I cross the continent in a railway train? Do different States of the Union have different moral codes? Perhaps every town and village has its own peculiar standard. This may at first seem reasonable enough. "In Rome do as Rome does" may seem as good a rule in morals at it is in etiquette. But can we stop there? Within the village are numerous cliques each having its own set of ideas. Why should not each of these claim to be bound only by its own special and peculiar moral standards? And if it comes to that, why should not the gangsters of Chicago claim to constitute a group having its own morality, so that its murders and debaucheries mus be viewed as "right" by the only standard which can legitimately be applied to it? And if it be answered that the nation will not tolerate this, that may be so. But this is to put the foundation of right simply in the superior force of the majority. In that case whoever is stronger will be right, however monstrous his ideas and actions. And if we cannot deny to any set of people the right to have its own morality, is it not clear that, in the end, we cannot even deny this right to the individual? Every individual man and woman can put up, on this view, an irrefutable claim to be judged by no standard except his or her own.

If these arguments are valid, the ethical relativist cannot really maintain that there is anywhere to be found a moral standard binding upon anybody against his will. And he cannot maintain that, even within the social group, there is a common standard as between individuals. And if that is so, then even judgments to the effect that one man is morally better than another becomes meaningless. All moral valuation thus vanishes. There is nothing to prevent each man from being a rule unto himself. The result will be moral chaos and the collapse of all effective standards.

13

THE IDEAL
OBSERVER THEORY

Frank Chapman Sharp

F. C. Sharp (1866-1943) was Professor of Philosophy at the University of Wisconsin.

The moral judgment takes the form: Action S is right — or wrong. It thus consists in the application of the predicate "right" to conduct. We have now to inquire into the meaning of this predicate.

The subject matter of our studies is still the man on the street. It is what *he* means by "right" that interests us. And the difficulty we face is that he cannot tell us. Ask him to define the term, and he will not even understand what you are driving at. This difficulty, however, is not one peculiar to the vocabulary of ethics. John Smith cannot tell you what he means by "cause," "probable," or "now"; he cannot give a really satisfactory answer to so apparently simple a question as "What is 'money'?"

This difficulty we can meet today as we met it again and again when we were three years old. We heard the people about us using such terms as "very" or "if"; and we wanted to know what they meant. Undoubtedly we were very far from persistent or systematic in our search for enlightenment; indeed, perhaps we did not *search* at all. But, at any rate, when we had been told that this milk was very hot, this stool very heavy, this glass very easily broken, and that we had been very naughty, the meaning of "very" dawned upon our minds, not in the sense that we could define it but that we could use it intelligently. It is in precisely this same way that we can discover what the layman means by the fundamental terms in the moral vocabulary. We watch his use of them. Thereupon, proceeding one step farther than the child, we generalize our observations and in doing so form a definition.

It is indeed a curious fact that men can go through life using words with a fair degree of definiteness and consistency with no formulated definition before the mind. But it is fact, nonetheless. "I cannot define poetry," says A. E. Housman in effect, "but I know it when I see it. In the same way a terrier cannot define rat, but he knows one when he sees it."

If the analysis of this chapter is correct, "right" must be definable in terms of desire, or approbation, that is to say, in terms of "feeling." When John Smith calls an action "right" or "wrong," however, he means something other than that he happens to feel about it in a certain way at that particular moment. This was clearly pointed out by Hume two hundred years ago and should have become commonplace among moralists by this time. A successful swindle may arouse feelings of very different intensity according to who happens to be the victim — myself, my son, my intimate friend, an acquaintance, a stranger, a foreigner, a man who died a hundred years ago. Indeed, in some of the latter cases the feeling component may drop out entirely. Again, an incident I myself have witnessed, such as an act of malicious cruelty or the bullying of the weak by the strong, makes me feel very different from that about which I have only read or heard. And my feelings in the latter case are likely to depend on the vividness and completeness with which the narrator brings the situation home to my imagination. An incident which I can realize because I have been through just such an experience myself appeals to me far otherwise than one which I know only through having viewed it from the outside. The robbery or oppression of those whom I see from day to day or am personally acquainted with arouses in me far more indignation than if they are merely unknown people living for all practical purposes in a world other than my own. With all these variations in my feelings, I recognize upon reflection that what is really right or wrong in the premises remains unchanged. Wrong does not become innocent or right merely because the act took place a hundred years ago instead of this morning, because I did not happen to see it myself, because I myself have never happened to be in that position, or because one of the persons involved happens to be an acquaintance, a member of my family, or myself.

In view of these facts, we must define "right," if we are to use the term in the sense in which the ordinary man uses it, as *that which arouses approbation under certain conditions.* Accordingly the question arises: What are these conditions?

We shall not expect to discover them by asking John Smith to enumerate and describe them. The man in the street does not carry about with him in his mental kit a set of formulas covering these conditions, any more than when he cuts a corner he says to himself, "A straight line is the shortest distance between two points." That the conditions in question represent real forces may be shown empirically by what John Smith does when in doubt or when he changes his mind or when the correctness of his predication is challenged by others.

In the first place, then, John Smith does not apply the predicates right and wrong to conduct unless he supposes himself to be viewing it from an impersonal standpoint. This means that he supposes, negatively, that his atti-

tude is not determined by his egoistic interests or by any purely personal relations to the parties concerned; positively, that the act is one that he would
approve of anyone's performing under the same conditions. This attitude is
expressed in the familiar maxim: What is right for one is right for everyone
else under the same conditions. This maxim is an analytic, not a synthetic,
proposition. It is no discovery of moralists, least of all of Kant, to whom it is
often attributed, for its governing role in the moral world was noted in effect
by Cumberland and quite explicitly by Clarke before Kant was born. As a
matter of fact, the "discovery" has been made countless millions of times, for
it is a dull-witted seven-year-old who does not remind his parents on occasions
that what they require him to do they are bound to do themselves.

Here, again, enters the all-important distinction between correct and
incorrect moral judgments, or, as I should prefer to say, between valid and
invalid; for, as we have seen in this chapter, John Smith frequently regards
an action as innocent or even obligatory when he profits by it and wrong
when he happens to be the sufferer. In calling it "wrong" instead of "harmful," he implies that it is an act which, performed under the conditions, he
would condemn in anyone, including himself. His supposition being false,
his judgment expresses an opinion which can only be called "incorrect."

As soon as John Smith realizes this lack of impersonality, he recognizes
at once the incorrectness of the judgment and therewith the necessity of
modifying or abandoning it. In a certain city, the university YMCA, having
included a barber shop among the attractions of its new building, engaged
as its manager the popular head-barber of the city's leading "tonsorial parlor";
whereupon the proprietor complained loudly of the action of the association
in attracting his most valuable employee away from him as being "unfair."
When he was reminded that he himself had obtained this same employee
in precisely the same way, by attracting him from another shop by a better
financial offer, nothing more was heard from him on this subject.

Common sense thus recognizes the existence of such a thing as a mistaken moral judgment. Those moralists who ignore this fact thereby show
that their picture of the workings of the moral consciousness is an arbitrary
construction, out of touch with the realities of life.

Impersonality, however, is not the only condition which John Smith
recognizes the moral judgment must meet if it is to conform to the implications involved in this conception of right. The second condition is a consequence of the essential character of the evaluating judgment as such. When
we pass judgment upon anything whatever, whether it be a candidate for
public office or Titian's "Assumption of the Virgin," we suppose that we
know what it is. Really to know what anything is, is to have an apprehension
of its nature, which is at once accurate and complete. In practice, of course,
this ideal is ordinarily incapable of attainment. But, in proportion as we
approach certainty of conviction, our confidence increases that our view possesses an amount of accuracy and completeness such that any correction of or
addition to the data in our possession would make no difference in the con-

clusion reached. And our task is lightened by growing insight into what kinds of data are relevant and what are not. A datum is relevant when its introduction would tend to make any difference in the resulting judgment.

The application of these observations to the moral judgment is obvious. The subject of the moral judgment is voluntary action. A voluntary act is an attempt to produce certain effects. The moral judgment, accordingly, is supposed, with varying degrees of confidence, by the judger to be based upon an accurate and complete knowledge of these effects or upon as much knowledge as would involve no change of opinion if the rest of the effects were displayed accurately and in order before the mind's eye. If this supposition is true, the judgment is in so far forth correct or valid. On the other hand, if the judgment turns on an incomplete or otherwise inaccurate view of these effects, including, of course, a view of the situation in which they operate, it may properly be termed incorrect or invalid, because it is not what the judger supposes it to be.

Observation verifies this analysis. Our study of the causes that lead to the diversities in moral judgments has shown that a leading cause is difference of opinion as to what the consequences of the act will be. And in the majority of instances when John Smith begins to doubt the correctness of one of his past judgments, it is upon the consequences believed to be involved that his decision turns. Under such and such circumstances is a man justified in lying? in breaking a promise or a contract? in helping himself to someone else's property? in giving a dose of poison to a hopeless invalid? in making a true statement injurious to the reputation of a neighbor? in giving money to a street beggar? Whatever decision is reached turns fundamentally upon what are believed to be the good or evil consequences involved.

If, then, we are to conform to the implications of everyday usage in applying the predicates right and wrong to the effects of volitions, we must know what these effects are. Now, knowledge is of two kinds; or, if you prefer, it has two levels. Using Professor James's terminology, one is acquaintance with; the other, knowledge about. The former is given in immediate experience, whether in the world of sense or in the inner world of pleasure, pain, emotion, or desire. It may be re-created, when past, in those persons who are fortunate enough to possess the capacity for full and vivid imagery. We may call this "realization." The second kind, or level, reveals reality through the instrumentality of concepts. Now, the concept is an abstract idea, such as "length" or "walking" or "very." It represents one or a group of aspects torn from the concrete objects that make up the real world and held before the mind in more or less complete isolation from such objects.

The ability to form and use concepts is the most powerful instrument in the possession of the human mind. Among other things, as a constituent of desire it determines the direction of every voluntary action we perform. But, like everything else in the world, the concept has its limitations. In its very nature as an abstraction, it reveals only a part, usually only a very small part, of the object at which it points. It may report truth but never the whole truth. In this respect it is like a map. Show a map of Switzerland to a person who has never been away from a North Dakota prairie or even seen a picture of a mountain. Compare the knowledge thus gained with that of a Swiss who has spent his vacations for many years exploring his native country. Or, again, let some one who has never come in contact with death and has never had to carry crushing financial burdens read in the newspaper that some stranger, formerly a clerk in a certain grocery store, died yesterday after a painful and lingering illness; he was thirty-five years old; a widow and three children survive him. How small a fraction of the grim realities at which these words hint would enter our consciousness!

Quite apart from poverty of detail, conceptual thought, again like a map, has another limitation. It reveals relations but can never reveal the things related. In other words, thought at its best, conceptual thought, merely performs the functions of a mathematical formula. It is a commonplace that a person born blind may know all the laws of light and yet have no acquaintance with color.

Thus, notwithstanding its marvelous range, conceptual thought is a very inadequate substitute for "acquaintance with" as a revelation of reality. There is only one road to genuine acquaintance with the world outside the consciousness of the moment, and it is through imagery, the power to realize. If, then, a moral judgment is to be valid, it must be either a judgment based upon a complete acquaintance with the whole situation in all its relevant details or, since this is rarely or perhaps never attainable, such a judgment as would result from an acquaintance with the whole situation.

The influence of realization upon the processes of moral judgment exhibits itself frequently in those pseudo-moral judgments in which the predicates right and wrong follow the judger's personal interests, and a vivid sense of his own gain or loss eclipses the vague concept of the loss or gain of the other part. Let the other side of the case come home to him and the victim's plight be fully realized, he "changes his mind," thereby bringing his judgment into conformity with his new insight. This phenomenon has been abundantly illustrated in this chapter.

The definition emerging from the preceding analysis is the following: When John Smith calls an action "right," he means that complete acquaintance with its results would evoke impersonal approval. Exchanging the negative term "impersonal" for a positive one, "right" characterizes the kind of action he would want all human beings to perform under the given conditions if he had a complete acquaintance with all the revelant consequences. The evidence for the correctness of this analysis is that when John Smith discovers that he has failed to meet some one of these conditions, he recognizes that his judgment calls for reconsideration.

14

THE GOOD,
OBLIGATION,
AND DESIRE:
A NATURALISTIC VIEW

William James

William James (1842-1910) taught psychology and physiology at Harvard before becoming Professor of Philosophy there in 1880.

. . . There are three questions in ethics which must be kept apart. Let them be called respectively the *psychological* question, the *metaphysical* question, and the *casuistic* question. The psychological question asks after the historical *origin* of our moral ideas and judgments; the metaphysical question asks what the very *meaning* of the words 'good,' 'ill,' and 'obligation' are; the casuistic question asks what is the *measure* of the various goods and ills which men recognize, so that the philosopher may settle the true order of human obligations.

. . .

The next [question] in order is the metaphysical question, of what we mean by the words 'obligation,' 'good,' and 'ill.'

II.

First of all, it appears that such words can have no application or relevancy in a world in which no sentient life exists. Imagine an absolutely material world, containing only physical and chemical facts, and existing from eternity without a God, without even an interested spectator: would there be any sense in saying of that world that one of its states is better than another? Or if there were two such worlds possible, would there be any rhyme or reason in calling one good and the other bad, — good or bad positively, I mean, and apart from the fact that one might relate itself better than the other to the philosopher's private interests? But we must leave these private interests out of the account, for the philosopher is a mental fact, and we are asking whether goods and evils and obligations exist in physical facts *per se*.

From William James, "The Moral Philosopher and the Moral Life," published in the *International Journal of Ethics*, 1891, reprinted in *The Will to Believe* (New York: Longmans, Green, and Co., 1919).

Surely there is no *status* for good and evil to exist in, in a purely insentient world. How can one physical fact, considered simply as a physical fact, be 'better' than another? Betterness is not a physical relation. In its mere material capacity, a thing can no more be good or bad than it can be pleasant or painful. Good for what? Good for the production of another physical fact, do you say? But what in a purely physical universe demands the production of that other fact? Physical facts simply *are* or are *not;* and neither when present or absent, can they be supposed to make demands. If they do, they can only do so by having desires; and then they have ceased to be purely physical facts, and have become facts of conscious sensibility. Goodness, badness, and obligation must be *realized* somewhere in order really to exist; and the first step in ethical philosophy is to see that no merely inorganic 'nature of things' can realize them. Neither moral relations nor the moral law can swing *in vacuo.* Their only habitat can be a mind which feels them; and no world composed of merely physical facts can possibly be a world to which ethical propositions apply.

The moment one sentient being, however, is made a part of the universe, there is a chance for goods and evils really to exist. Moral relations now have their *status,* in that being's consciousness. So far as he feels anything to be good, he *makes* it good. It *is* good, for him; and being good for him, is absolutely good, for he is the sole creator of values in that universe, and outside of his opinion things have no moral character at all.

In such a universe as that it would of course be absurd to raise the question of whether the solitary thinker's judgments of good and ill are true or not. Truth supposes a standard outside of the thinker to which he must conform; but here the thinker is a sort of divinity, subject to no higher judge. Let us call the supposed universe which he inhabits a *moral solitude.* In such a moral solitude it is clear that there can be no outward obligation, and that the only trouble the god-like thinker is liable to have will be over the consistency of his own several ideals with one another. Some of these will no doubt be more pungent and appealing than the rest, their goodness will have a profounder, more penetrating taste; they will return to haunt him with more obstinate regrets if violated. So the thinker will have to order his life with them as its chief determinants, or else remain inwardly discordant and unhappy. Into whatever equilibrium he may settle, though, and however he may straighten out his system, it will be a right system; for beyond the facts of his own subjectivity there is nothing moral in the world.

If now we introduce a second thinker with his likes and dislikes into the universe, the ethical situation becomes much more complex, and several possibilities are immediately seen to obtain.

One of these is that the thinkers may ignore each other's attitude about good and evil altogether, and each continue to indulge his own preferences, indifferent to what the other may feel or do. In such a case we have a world with twice as much of the ethical quality in it as our moral solitude, only it is without ethical unity. The same object is good or bad there, according as you measure it by the view which this one or that one of the thinkers takes. Nor can you find any possible ground in such a world for saying that one thinker's opinion is more correct than the other's, or that either has the truer moral sense. Such a world, in short, is not a moral universe but a moral dualism. Not only is there no single point of view within it from which the values of things can be unequivocally judged, but there is not even a demand for such a point of view, since the two thinkers are supposed to be indifferent to each other's thoughts and acts. Multiply the thinkers into a pluralism, and we find realized for us in the ethical sphere something like that world which the antique sceptics conceived of, — in which individual minds are the measures of all things, and in which no one 'objective' truth, but only a multitude of 'subjective' opinions, can be found.

But this is the kind of world with which the philosopher, so long as he holds to the hope of a philosophy, will not put up. Among the various ideals represented, there must be, he thinks, some which have the more truth or authority; and to these the others *ought* to yield, so that system and subordination may reign. Here in the word 'ought' the notion of *obligation* comes emphatically into view, and the next thing in order must be to make its meaning clear.

Since the outcome of the discussion so far has been to show us that nothing can be good or right except so far as some consciousness feels it to be good or thinks it to be right, we perceive on the very threshold that the real superiority and authority which are postulated by the philosopher to reside in some of the opinions, and the really inferior character which he supposes must belong to others, cannot be explained by any abstract moral 'nature of things' existing antecedently to the concrete thinkers themselves with their ideals. Like the positive attributes good and bad, the comparative ones better and worse must be *realized* in order to be real. If one ideal judgment be objectively better than another, that betterness must be made flesh by being lodged concretely in some one's actual perception. It cannot float in the atmosphere, for it is not a sort of meteorological phenomenon, like the aurora borealis or the zodiacal light. Its *esse* is *percipi*, like the *esse* of the ideals themselves between which it obtains. The philosopher, therefore, who seeks to know which ideal ought to have supreme weight and which one ought to be subordinated, must trace the *ought* itself to the *de facto* constitution of some existing consciousness, behind which, as one of the data of the universe, he as a purely ethical philosopher is unable to go. This consciousness must make the one ideal right by feeling it to be right, the other wrong by feeling it to be wrong. But now what particular consciousness in the universe *can* enjoy this prerogative of obliging others to conform to a rule which it lays down?

If one of the thinkers were obviously divine, while all the rest were human, there would probably be no practical dispute about the matter. The divine thought would be the model, to which the others should conform. But still the theoretic question would remain, What is the ground of the obligation, even here?

In our first essays at answering this question, there is an inevitable tendency to slip into an assumption which ordinary men follow when they are disputing with one another about questions of good and bad. They imagine an abstract moral order in which the objective truth resides; and each tries to prove that this pre-existing order is more accurately reflected in his own ideas than in those of his adversary. It is because one disputant is backed by this overarching abstract order that we think the other should submit. Even so, when it is a question no longer of two finite thinkers, but of God and ourselves, — we follow our usual habit, and imagine a sort of *de jure* relation, which antedates and overarches the mere facts, and would make it right that we should conform our thoughts to God's thoughts, even though he made no claim to that effect, and though we preferred *de facto* to go on thinking for ourselves.

But the moment we take a steady look at the question, *we see not only that without a claim actually made by some concrete person there can be no obligation, but that there is some obligation wherever there is a claim.* Claim and obligation are, in fact, coextensive terms; they cover each other exactly. Our ordinary attitude of regarding ourselves as subject to an overarching system of moral relations, true 'in themselves,' is therefore either an out-and-out superstition, or else it must be treated as a merely provisional abstraction from that real Thinker in whose actual demand upon us to think as he does our obligation must be ultimately based. In a theistic-ethical philosophy that thinker in question is, of course, the Deity to whom the existence of the universe is due.

I know well how hard it is for those who are accustomed to what I have called the superstitious view, to realize that every *de facto* claim creates in so far forth an obligation. We inveterately think that something which we call the 'validity' of the claim is what gives to it its obligatory character, and that this validity is something outside of the claim's mere existence as a matter of fact. It rains down upon the claim, we think, from some sublime dimension of being, which the moral law inhabits, much as upon the steel of the compass-needle the influence of the Pole rains down from out of the starry heavens. But again, how can such an inorganic abstract character of imperativeness, additional to the imperativeness which is in the concrete claim itself, *exist?* Take any demand, however slight, which any creature, however weak, may make. Ought it not, for its own sole sake, to be satisfied? If not, prove why not. The only possible kind of proof you could adduce would be the exhibition of another creature who should make a demand that ran the other way. The only possible reason there can be why any phenomenon ought to exist is that such a phenomenon actually is desired. Any desire is imperative to the extent of its amount; it *makes* itself valid by the fact that it exists at all. Some desires, truly enough, are small desires;

they are put forward by insignificant persons, and we customarily make light of the obligations which they bring. But the fact that such personal demands as these impose small obligations does not keep the largest-obligations from being personal demands.

If we must talk impersonally, to be sure we can say that 'the universe' requires, exacts, or makes obligatory such or such an action, whenever it expresses itself through the desires of such or such a creature. But it is better not to talk about the universe in this personified way, unless we believe in a universal or divine consciousness which actually exists. If there be such a consciousness, then its demands carry the most of obligation simply because they are the greatest in amount. But it is even then not *abstractly* right that we should respect them. It is only *concretely* right, — or right after the fact, and by virtue of the fact, that they are actually made. Suppose we do not respect them, as seems largely to be the case in this queer world. That ought not to be, we say; that is wrong. But in what way is this fact of wrongness made more acceptable or intelligible when we imagine it to consist rather in the laceration of an *à priori* ideal order than in the disappointment of a living personal God? Do we, perhaps, think that we cover God and protect him and make his impotence over us less ultimate, when we back him up with this *à priori* blanket from which he may draw some warmth of further appeal? But the only force of appeal to *us*, which either a living God or an abstract ideal order can wield, is found in the 'everlasting ruby vaults' of our own human hearts, as they happen to beat responsive and not irresponsive to the claim. So far as they do feel it when made by a living consciousness, it is life answering to life. A claim thus livingly acknowledged is acknowledged with a solidity and fullness which no thought of an 'ideal' backing can render more complete; while if, on the other hand, the heart's response is withheld, the stubborn phenomenon is there of an impotence in the claims which the universe embodies, which no talk about an eternal nature of things can glaze over or dispel. An ineffective *à priori* order is as impotent a thing as an ineffective God; and in the eye of philosophy, it is as hard a thing to explain.

We may now consider that what we distinguished as the metaphysical question in ethical philosophy is sufficiently answered, and that we have learned what the words 'good,' 'bad,' and 'obligation' severally mean. They mean no absolute natures, independent of personal support. They are objects of feeling and desire, which have no foothold or anchorage in Being, apart from the existence of actually living minds.

Wherever such minds exist, with judgments of good and ill, and demands upon one another, there is an ethical world in its essential features. Were all other things, gods and men and starry heavens, blotted out from this universe, and were there left but one rock with two loving souls upon it, that rock would have as thoroughly moral a constitution as any possible world which the eternities and immensities could harbor. It would be a tragic constitution, because the rock's inhabitants would die. But while they lived, there would be real good things and real bad things in the universe; there would be obligations, claims, and expectations; obediences, refusals, and disappointments; compunctions and longings for harmony to come again, and inward peace of conscience when it was restored; there would, in short, be a moral life, whose active energy would have no limit but the intensity of interest in each other with which the hero and heroine might be endowed.

We, on this terrestrial globe, so far as the visible facts go, are just like the inhabitants of such a rock. Whether a God exist, or whether no God exist, in yon blue heaven above us bent, we form at any rate an ethical republic here below. And the first reflection which this leads to is that ethics have as genuine and real a foothold in a universe where the highest consciousness is human, as in a universe where there is a God as well. 'The religion of humanity' affords a basis for ethics as well as theism does. Whether the purely human system can gratify the philosopher's demand as well as the other is a different question, which we ourselves must answer ere we close.

III.

The last fundamental question in Ethics was, it will be remembered, the *casuistic* question. Here we are, in a world where the existence of a divine thinker has been and perhaps always will be doubted by some of the lookers-on, and where, in spite of the presence of a large number of ideals in which human beings agree, there are a mass of others about which no general consensus obtains. It is hardly necessary to present a literary picture of this, for the facts are too well known. The wars of the flesh and the spirit in each man, the concupiscences of different individuals pursuing the same unsharable material or social prizes, the ideals which contrast so according to races, circumstances, temperaments, philosophical beliefs, etc., — all form a maze of apparently inextricable confusion with no obvious Ariadne's thread to lead one out. Yet the philosopher, just because he is a philosopher, adds his own peculiar ideal to the confusion (with which if he were willing to be a sceptic he would be passably content), and insists that over all these individual opinions there is a *system of truth* which he can discover if he only takes sufficient pains.

We stand ourselves at present in the place of that philosopher, and must not fail to realize all the features that the situation comports. In the first place we will not be sceptics; we hold to it that there is a truth to be ascertained. But in the second place we have just gained the insight that that truth cannot be a self-proclaiming set of laws, or an abstract 'moral reason,' but can only exist in act, or in the shape of an opinion held by some thinker really to be found. There is, however, no visible thinker invested with authority. Shall we then simply proclaim our own ideals as the lawgiving ones? No; for if we are true philosophers we must throw our own spontaneous ideals, even the dearest, impartially in with that total mass of ideals which are fairly to be judged. But how then can we as philosophers ever find a test; how avoid complete moral scepticism on the one hand, and on the other escape bringing a wayward personal standard of our own along with us, on which we simply pin our faith?

The dilemma is a hard one, nor does it grow a bit more easy as we revolve it in our minds. The entire undertaking of the philosopher obliges him to seek an impartial test. That test, however, must be incarnated in the demand of some actually existent person; and how can he pick out the person save by an act in which his own sympathies and prepossessions are implied?

One method indeed presents itself, and has as a matter of history been taken by the more serious ethical schools. If the heap of things demanded proved on inspection less chaotic than at first they seemed, if they furnished their own relative test and measure, then the casuistic problem would be solved. If it were found that all goods *quâ* goods contained a common essence, then the amount of this essence involved in any one good would show its rank in the scale of goodness, and order could be quickly made; for this essence would be *the* good upon which all thinkers were agreed, the relatively objective and universal good that the philosopher seeks. Even his own private ideals would be measured by their share of it, and find their rightful place among the rest.

Various essences of good have thus been found and proposed as bases of the ethical system. Thus, to be a mean between two extremes; to be recognized by a special intuitive faculty; to make the agent happy for the moment; to make others as well as him happy in the long run; to add to his perfection or dignity; to harm no one; to follow from reason or flow from universal law; to be in accordance with the will of God; to promote the survival of the human species on this planet, — are so many tests, each of which has been maintained by somebody to constitute the essence of all good things or actions so far as they are good.

No one of the measures that have been actually proposed has, however, given general satisfaction. Some are obviously not universally present in all cases, — *e.g.*, the character of harming no one, or that of following a universal law; for the best course is often cruel; and many acts are reckoned good on the sole condition that they be exceptions, and serve not as examples of a universal law. Other characters, such as following the will of God, are unascertainable and vague. Others again, like survival, are quite indeterminate in their consequences, and leave us in the lurch where we most need their help: a philosopher of the Sioux Nation, for example, will be certain to use the survival-criterion in a very different way from ourselves. The best, on the whole, of these marks and measures of goodness seems to be the capacity to bring happiness. But in order not to break down fatally, this test must be taken to cover innumerable acts and impulses that never *aim* at happiness; so that, after all, in seeking for a universal principle we inevitably are carried onward to the *most* universal principle, — that *the essence of good is simply to satisfy demand.* The demand may be for anything under the sun. There is really no more ground for supposing that all our demands can be accounted for by one universal underlying kind of motive than there is ground for supposing that all physical phenomena are cases of a single law. The elementary forces in ethics are probably as plural as those of physics are. The various ideals have no common character apart from the fact that they are ideals. No single abstract principle can be so used as to yield to the philosopher anything like a scientifically accurate and genuinely useful casuistic scale.

A look at another peculiarity of the ethical universe, as we find it, will still further show us the philosopher's perplexities. As a purely theoretical problem, namely, the casuistic question would hardly ever come up at all. If the ethical philosopher were only asking after the best *imaginable* system of goods he would indeed have an easy task; for all demands as such are *primâ facie* respectable, and the best simply imaginary world would be one in which *every* demand was gratified as soon as made. Such a world would, however, have to have a physical constitution entirely different from that of the one which we inhabit. It would need not only a space, but a time, 'of *n*-dimensions,' to include all the acts and experiences incompatible with one another here below, which would then go on in conjunction, — such as spending our money, yet growing rich; taking our holiday, yet getting ahead with our work; shooting and fishing, yet doing no hurt to the beasts; gaining no end of experience, yet keeping our youthful freshness of heart; and the like. There can be no question that such a system of things, however brought about, would be the absolutely ideal system; and that if a philosopher could create universes *à priori,* and provide all the mechanical conditions, that is the sort of universe which he should unhesitatingly create.

But this world of ours is made on an entirely different pattern, and the casuistic question here is most tragically practical. The actually possible in this world is vastly narrower than all that is demanded; and there is always a *pinch* between the ideal and the actual which can only be got through by leaving part of the ideal behind. There is hardly a good which we can imagine except as competing for the possession of the same bit of space and time with some other imagined good. Every end of desire that presents itself appears exclusive of some other end of desire. Shall a man drink and smoke, *or* keep his nerves in condition? — he cannot do both. Shall he follow his fancy for Amelia, *or* for Henrietta? — both cannot be the choice of his heart. Shall he have the dear old Republican party, *or* a spirit of unsophistication in public affairs? — he cannot have both, etc. So that the ethical philosopher's demand for the right scale of subordination in ideals is the fruit of an altogether practical need. Some part of the ideal must be butchered, and he needs to know which part. It is a tragic situation, and no mere speculative conundrum, with which he has to deal. . . .

What can he do, then, it will now be asked, except to fall back on scepticism and give up the notion of being a philosopher at all?

But do we not already see a perfectly definite path of escape which is open to him just because he is a philosopher, and not the champion of one particular ideal? Since everything which is demanded is by that fact a good, must not the guiding principle for ethical philosophy (since all demands conjointly cannot be satisfied in this poor world) be simply to satisfy at all times *as many demands as we can?* That act must be the best act, accordingly, which makes for the *best whole,* in the sense of awakening the least sum of dissatisfactions. In the casuistic scale, therefore, those ideals must be written highest which *prevail at the least cost,* or by whose realization the least possible number of other ideals are destroyed. Since victory and defeat there must be, the victory to be philosophically prayed for is that of the more inclusive side, — of the side which even in the hour of triumph will to some degree do justice to the ideals in which the vanquished party's interests lay. The course of history is nothing but the story of men's struggles from generation to generation to find the more and more inclusive order. *Invent some manner* of realizing your own ideals which will also satisfy the alien demands, — that and that only is the path of peace! Following this path, society has shaken itself into one sort of relative equilibrium after another by a series of social discoveries quite analogous to those of science. Polyandry and polygamy and slavery, private warfare and liberty to kill, judicial torture and arbitrary royal power have slowly succumbed to actually aroused complaints; and though some one's ideals are unquestionably the worse off for each improvement, yet a vastly greater total number of them find shelter in our civilized society than in the old savage ways. So far then, and up to date, the casuistic scale is made for the philosopher already far better than he can ever make it for himself. An experiment of the most searching kind has proved that the laws and usages of the land are what yield the maximum of satisfaction to the thinkers taken all together. The presumption in cases of conflict must always be in favor of the conventionally recognized good. The philosopher must be a conservative, and in the construction of his casuistic scale must put the things most in accordance with the customs of the community on top.

And yet if he be a true philosopher he must see that there is nothing final in any actually given equilibrium of human ideals, but that, as our present laws and customs have fought and conquered other past ones, so they will in their turn be overthrown by any newly discovered order which will hush up the complaints that they still give rise to, without producing others louder still. "Rules are made for man, not man for rules," — that one sentence is enough to immortalize Green's *Prolegomena to Ethics.* And although a man always risks much when he breaks away from established rules and strives to realize a larger ideal whole than they permit, yet the philosopher must allow that it is at all times open to any one to make the experiment, provided he fear not to stake his life and character upon the throw. The pinch is always here. Pent in under every system of moral rules are innumerable persons whom it weighs upon, and goods which it represses; and these are always rumbling and grumbling in the background, and ready for any issue by which they may get free. See the abuses which the institution of private property covers, so that even to-day it is shamelessly asserted among us that one of the prime functions of the national government is to help the adroiter citizens to grow rich. See the unnamed and unnamable sorrows which the tyranny, on the whole so beneficent, of the marriage-institution brings to so many, both of the married and the unwed. See the wholesale loss of opportunity under our *régime* of so-called equality and industrialism, with the drummer and the counter-jumper in the saddle, for so many faculties and graces which could flourish in the feudal world. See our kindliness for the humble and the outcast, how it wars with that stern weeding-out which until now has been the condition of every perfection in the breed. See everywhere the struggle and the squeeze; and everlastingly the problem how to make them less. The anarchists, nihilists, and free-lovers; the free-silverites, socialists, and single-tax men; the free-traders and civil-service reformers; the prohibitionists and anti-vivisectionists; the radical darwinians with their idea of the suppression of the weak, — these and all the conservative sentiments of society arrayed against them, are simply deciding through actual experiment by what sort of conduct the maximum amount of good can be gained and kept in this world. These experiments are to be judged, not *à priori,* but by actually finding, after the fact of their making, how much more outcry or how much appeasement comes about. What closet-solutions can possibly anticipate the result of trials made on such a scale? Or what can any superficial theorist's judgment be worth, in a world where every one of hundreds of ideals has its special champion already provided in the shape of some genius expressly born to feel it, and to fight to death in its behalf? The pure philosopher can only follow the windings of the spectacle, confident that the line of least resistance will always be towards the richer and the more inclusive arrangement, and that by one tack after another some approach to the kingdom of heaven is incessantly made.

IV.

All this amounts to saying that, so far as the casuistic question goes, ethical science is just like physical science, and instead of being deducible all at once from abstract principles, must simply bide its time, and be ready to revise its conclusions from day to day. The presumption of course, in both sciences, always is that the vulgarly accepted opinions are true, and the right casuistic order that which public opinion believes in; and surely it would be folly quite as great, in most of us, to strike out independently and to aim at originality in ethics as in physics. Every now and then, however, some one is born with the right to be original, and his revolutionary thought or action may bear prosperous fruit. He may replace old 'laws of nature' by better ones; he may, by breaking old moral rules in a certain place, bring in a total condition of things more ideal than would have followed had the rules been kept. . . .

15

SUPERNATURALISM
IN ETHICS:
A CRITICISM

Alfred Cyril Ewing

A. C. Ewing (1899-　　) is Reader in Philosophy at Cambridge University.

A metaphysical definition is a definition by reference to the ultimate nature of the real as distinguished from the less ultimate aspect in which reality is conceived as appearing for natural science. Of metaphysical definitions we need only trouble about one here, which is by far the clearest and the best known. I refer to the attempt to define ethical concepts in terms of religion by maintaining that to say something is good or right is to say that it is commanded by God. At first sight it may well seem that such a theory is refuted at once by the mere fact that agnostics and atheists can make rational judgements in ethics, but it will be replied that what even the atheist really has in mind when he thinks of obligation is some confused idea of a command, and that a command implies a commander and a perfect moral law a perfectly good commander on whose mind the whole moral law depends, so that the atheist is inconsistent in affirming the validity of the moral law and yet denying the existence of God. It may be doubted whether this argument, if valid, would make the theological statement an analysis of what the man meant and not rather of the logical consequences of what he meant, but there are other objections to such a definition.

(*a*) If "right" and "good" are themselves defined in terms of the commands of God, God cannot command anything because it is right or good, since this would only mean that He commanded it because He commanded it, and therefore there is no reason whatever for His commands, which become purely arbitrary. It would follow that God might just as rationally will that our whole duty should consist in cheating, torturing and killing

From Alfred Cyril Ewing, *Ethics*, Chapter 6. Copyright 1953 by The Macmillan Company, and used with their permission. Also published by The English Universities Press, Ltd., London, and reprinted with their permission.

people to the best of our ability, and that in that case it would be our duty
to act in his fashion.

(b) And why are we to obey God's commands? Because we ought to
do so? Since "we ought to do A" is held to mean "God commands us to do
A", this can only mean that we are commanded by God to obey God's commands, which supplies no further reason. Because we love God? But this involves the assumptions that we ought to obey God if we love Him, and that
we ought to love Him. So it again presupposes ethical propositions which
cannot without a vicious circle be validated by once more referring to God's
commands. Because God is good? This could only mean that God carries
out His own commands. Because God will punish us if we do not obey Him?
This might be a very good reason from the point of view of self-interest, but
self-interest cannot, as we have seen, be an adequate basis for ethics. Without a prior conception of God being good or His commands being right God
would have no more claim on our obedience than Hitler except that He
would have more power to make things uncomfortable for us if we disobeyed
Him than Hitler ever had, and that is not an ethical reason. A moral obligation cannot be created by mere power and threat of punishment. No doubt
if we first grant the fundamental concepts of ethics, the existence of God may
put us under certain obligations which we otherwise would not have had,
e.g. that of thinking of God, as the existence of a man's parents puts him
under certain obligations under which he would not stand if they were
dead, but we cannot possibly derive all obligations in this fashion from the
concept of God. No doubt, if God is perfectly good, we ought to obey His
will, but how can we know what His will for us is in a particular case without first knowing what we ought to do?

What I have said of course constitutes no objection to the belief in God
or even to the view that we can have a valid argument from ethics to the
existence of God, but these views can be held without holding that our ethical terms have to be defined in terms of God. It has been held that the existence of anything implies the existence of God, but it would not therefore be
concluded that the meaning of all our words includes a reference to God.
Nor is what I have said meant to imply that religion can have no important
bearing on ethics, but I think its influence should lie more in helping people
to bring themselves to do what would be their duty in any case and in influencing the general spirit in which it is done than in prescribing what our duty
is. While it is quite contrary to fact to suggest that an agnostic or atheist
cannot be a good man, the influence in the former respects of religious belief,
whether true or false, cannot be denied to have been exceedingly strong.

Metaphysical definitions, like naturalistic, err in trying to reduce the
"ought" to the "is". Like them they would destroy what Kant calls the
autonomy of ethics by refusing to recognize the uniqueness of its fundamental concepts and trying to reduce it to a mere branch of another study,
in this case not a natural science but metaphysics or theology. The theological definition is more ethical than naturalism only in so far as it covertly rein-

troduces the notion of obligation or goodness thus involving a vicious circle. Indeed it is only plausible because God is already conceived as good. Apart from this it would make duty consist just in obeying the stronger, for if you once exclude the specifically ethical element from the conception of the Deity, God has no claim on us except that of mere power. But it cannot be *morally* obligatory to obey some being just because he is powerful. . . .

16 🦎

NONNATURALISM:
INTUITIVE KNOWLEDGE
OF ETHICAL FACTS

Thomas Reid

*Thomas Reid (1710-1796) was first a minister, then taught philosophy at King's Col-
lege, Aberdeen, and at the University of Glasgow.*

OF THE NOTION OF DUTY, RECTITUDE, MORAL OBLIGATION

A Being endowed with the animal principles of action only, may be capable
of being trained to certain purposes by discipline, as we see many brute-
animals are, but would be altogether incapable of being governed by law.

The subject of law must have the conception of a general rule of conduct, which, without some degree of reason, he cannot have. He must likewise have a sufficient inducement to obey the law, even when his strongest
animal desires draw him the contrary way.

This inducement may be a sense of interest, or a sense of duty, or both
concurring.

These are the only principles I am able to conceive which can reasonably
induce a man to regulate all his actions according to a certain general rule,
or law. They may therefore be justly called the *rational* principles of action,
since they can have no place but in a being endowed with reason, and since
it is by them only, that man is capable either of political or of moral government.

Without them, human life would be like a ship at sea without hands,
left to be carried by winds and tides as they happen. It belongs to the rational
part of our nature to intend a certain port, as the end of the voyage of life;
to take the advantage of winds and tides when they are favourable, and to
bear up against them when they are unfavourable.

A sense of interest may induce us to do this, when a suitable reward
is set before us. But there is a nobler principle in the constitution of man,
which, in many cases, gives a clearer and more certain rule of conduct, than

From Thomas Reid, *Essays on the Active Powers of Man*, first published 1788. Essay
III, Chapters 5 to 7.

a regard merely to interest would give, and a principle, without which man would not be a moral agent.

A man is prudent when he consults his real interest, but he cannot be virtuous, if he has no regard to duty.

I proceed now to consider this regard to duty as a rational principle of action in man, and as that principle alone by which he is capable either of virtue or vice.

I shall first offer some observations with regard to the general notion of duty, and its contrary, or of right and wrong in human conduct; and then consider how we come to judge and determine certain things in human conduct to be right, and others to be wrong.

With regard to the notion or conception of duty, I take it to be too simple to admit of a logical definition.

We can define it only by synonymous words or phrases, or by its properties and necessary concomitants; as when we say that it is what we ought to do, what is fair and honest, what is approvable, what every man professes to be the rule of his conduct, what all men praise, and what is in itself laudable, though no man should praise it.

I observe, in the *next* place, That the notion of duty cannot be resolved into that of interest, or what is most for our happiness.

Every man may be satisfied of this who attends to his own conceptions, and the language of all mankind shews it. When I say this is my interest, I mean one thing; when I say it is my duty, I mean another thing. And though the same course of action, when rightly understood, may be both my duty and my interest, the conceptions are very different. Both are reasonable motives to action, but quite distinct in their nature.

I presume it will be granted, that in every man of real worth, there is a principle of honour, a regard to what is honourable or dishonourable, very distinct from a regard to his interest. It is folly in a man to disregard his interest, but to do what is dishonourable is baseness. The first may move our pity, or, in some cases, our contempt, but the last provokes our indignation.

As these two principles are different in their nature, and not resolvable into one, so the principle of honour is evidently superior in dignity to that of interest.

No man would allow him to be a man of honour, who should plead his interest to justify what he acknowledged to be dishonourable; but to sacrifice interest to honour never costs a blush.

It likewise will be allowed by every man of honour, that this principle is not to be resolved into a regard to our reputation among men, otherwise the man of honour would not deserve to be trusted in the dark. He would have no aversion to lie, or cheat, or play the coward, when he had no dread of being discovered.

I take it for granted, therefore, that every man of real honour feels an abhorrence of certain actions, because they are in themselves base, and feels an obligation to certain other actions, because they are in themselves what honour requires, and this, independently of any consideration of interest or reputation.

This is an immediate moral obligation. This principle of honour, which is acknowledged by all men who pretend to character, is only another name for what we call a regard to duty, to rectitude, to propriety of conduct. It is a moral obligation which obliges a man to do certain things because they are right, and not to do other things because they are wrong.

Ask the man of honour, why he thinks himself obliged to pay a debt of honour? The very question shocks him. To suppose that he needs any other inducement to do it but the principle of honour, is to suppose that he has no honour, no worth, and deserves no esteem.

There is therefore a principle in man, which, when he acts according to it, gives him a consciousness of worth, and when he acts contrary to it, a sense of demerit.

From the varieties of education, of fashion, of prejudices, and of habits, men may differ much in opinion with regard to the extent of this principle, and of what it commands and forbids; but the notion of it, as far as it is carried, is the same in all. It is that which gives a man real worth, and is the object of moral approbation.

Men of rank call it *honour,* and too often confine it to certain virtues that are thought most essential to their rank. The vulgar call it *honesty, probity, virtue, conscience.* Philosophers have given it the names of *the moral sense, the moral faculty, rectitude.*

The universality of this principle in men that are grown up to years of understanding and reflection, is evident. The words that express it, the names of the virtues which it commands, and of the vices which it forbids, the *ought* and *ought not* which express its dictates, make an essential part of every language. The natural affections of respect to worthy characters, of resentment of injuries, of gratitude for favours, of indignation against the worthless, are parts of the human constitution which suppose a right and a wrong in conduct. Many transactions that are found necessary in the rudest societies go upon the same supposition. In all testimony, in all promises, and in all contracts, there is necessarily implied a moral obligation on one party, and a trust in the other, grounded upon this obligation.

The variety of opinions among men in points of morality, is not greater, but, as I apprehend, much less than in speculative points; and this variety is as easily accounted for from the common causes of error, in the one case as in the other; so that it is not more evident, that there is a real distinction between true and false, in matters of speculation, than that there is a real distinction between right and wrong in human conduct. . . .

If we examine the abstract notion of duty, or moral obligation, it appears to be neither any real quality of the action considered by itself, nor of the agent considered without respect to the action, but a certain relation between the one and the other.

When we say a man ought to do such things, the *ought,* which expresses the moral obligation, has a respect, on the one hand, to the person who ought, and, on the other, to the action which he ought to do. Those two correlates are essential to every moral obligation; take away either, and it has no existence. So that, if we seek the place of moral obligation among the categories, it belongs to the category of *relation*.

There are many relations of things, of which we have the most distinct conception, without being able to define them logically. Equality and proportion are relations between quantities, which every man understands, but no man can define.

Moral obligation is a relation of its own kind, which every man understands, but is perhaps too simple to admit of logical definition. Like all other relations, it may be changed or annihilated by a change in any of the two related things, I mean the agent or the action.

Perhaps it may not be improper to point out briefly the circumstances, both in the action and in the agent, which are necessary to constitute moral obligation. The universal agreement of men in these, shews that they have one and the same notion of it.

With regard to the action, it must be a voluntary action . . . of the person obliged, and not of another. There can be no moral obligation upon a man to be six feet high. Nor can I be under a moral obligation that another person should do such a thing. His actions must be imputed to himself, and mine only to me, either for praise or blame.

I need hardly mention, that a person can be under a moral obligation, only to things within the sphere of his natural power.

As to the party obliged, it is evident, there can be no moral obligation upon an inanimate thing. To speak of moral obligation upon a stone or a tree is ridiculous, because it contradicts every man's notion of moral obligation.

The person obliged must have understanding and will, and some degree of active power. He must not only have the natural faculty of understanding, but the means of knowing his obligation. An invincible ignorance of this destroys all moral obligation. . . .

Of the Sense of Duty

We are next to consider, how we learn to judge and determine, that this is right, and that is wrong.

The abstract notion of moral good and ill would be of no use to direct our life, if we had not the power of applying it to particular actions, and determining what is morally good, and what is morally ill.

Some philosophers, with whom I agree, ascribe this to an original power or faculty in man, which they call the *moral sense*, the *moral faculty*, *conscience*. Others think, that our moral sentiments may be accounted for without supposing any original sense or faculty appropriated to that purpose, and go into very different systems to account for them.

I am not, at present, to take any notice of those systems, because the opinion first mentioned seems to me to be the truth, to wit, That, by an original power of the mind, when we come to years of understanding and reflection, we not only have the notions of right and wrong in conduct, but perceive certain things to be right, and others to be wrong.

The name of the *moral sense,* though more frequently given to conscience since Lord SHAFTSBURY and Dr. HUTCHESON wrote, is not new. The *sensus recti et honesti* is a phrase not unfrequent among the ancients, neither is the *sense of duty* among us.

It has got this name of *sense,* no doubt, from some analogy which it is conceived to bear to the external senses. And if we have just notions of the office of the external senses, the analogy is very evident, and I see no reason to take offence, as some have done, at the name of the *moral sense.* . . .

A man who has totally lost the sense of seeing, may retain very distinct notions of the various colours; but he cannot judge of colours, because he has lost the sense by which alone he could judge. By my eyes I not only have the ideas of a square and a circle, But I perceive this surface to be a square, that to be a circle.

By my ear, I not only have the idea of sounds, loud and soft, acute and grave, but I immediately perceive and judge this sound to be loud, that to be soft, this to be acute, that to be grave. Two or more synchronous sounds I perceive to be concordant, others to be discordant.

These are judgments of the senses. They have always been called and accounted such, by those whose minds are not tinctured by philosophical theories. They are the immediate testimony of nature by our senses; and we are so constituted by nature, that we must receive their testimony, for no other reason but because it is given by our senses.

In vain do Sceptics endeavour to overturn this evidence by metaphysical reasoning. Though we should not be able to answer their arguments, we believe our senses still, and rest our most important concerns upon their testimony.

If this be a just notion of our external senses, as I conceive it is, our moral faculty may, I think, without impropriety, be called the *moral sense.*

In its dignity it is, without doubt, far superior to every other power of the mind; but there is this analogy between it and the external senses, That, as by them we have not only the original conceptions of the various qualities of bodies, but the original judgments that this body has such a quality, that such another; so by our moral faculty, we have both the original conceptions of right and wrong in conduct, of merit and demerit, and the original judgments that this conduct is right, that is wrong; that this character has worth, that, demerit.

The testimony of our moral faculty, like that of the external senses, is the testimony of nature, and we have the same reason to rely upon it.

The truths immediately testified by the external senses are the first principles from which we reason, with regard to the material world, and from which all our knowledge of it is deduced.

The truths immediately testified by our moral faculty, are the first principles of all moral reasoning, from which all our knowledge of our duty must be deduced. . . .

All reasoning must be grounded on first principles. This holds in moral reasoning, as in all other kinds. There must therefore be in morals, as in all other sciences, first or self-evident principles, on which all moral reasoning is grounded, and on which it ultimately rests. From such self-evident principles, conclusions may be drawn synthetically with regard to the moral conduct of life; and particular duties or virtues may be traced back to such principles analytically. But, without such principles, we can no more establish any conclusion in morals, than we can build a castle in the air, without any foundation.

An example or two will serve to illustrate this.

It is a first principle in morals. That we ought not to do to another, what we should think wrong to be done to us in like circumstances. If a man is not capable of perceiving this in his cool moments, when he reflects seriously, he is not a moral agent, nor is he capable of being convinced of it by reasoning.

From what topic can you reason with such a man? You may possibly convince him by reasoning, that it is his interest to observe this rule; but this is not to convince him that it is his duty. To reason about justice with a man who sees nothing to be just or unjust; or about benevolence with a man who sees nothing in benevolence preferable to malice, is like reasoning with a blind man about colour, or with a deaf man about sound.

It is a question in morals that admits of reasoning, Whether, by the law of nature, a man ought to have only one wife?

We reason upon this question, by balancing the advantages and disadvantages to the family, and to society in general, that are naturally consequent both upon monogamy and polygamy. And if it can be shewn that the advantages are greatly upon the side of monogamy, we think the point is determined.

But, if a man does not perceive that he ought to regard the good of society, and the good of his wife and children, the reasoning can have no effect upon him, because he denies the first principles upon which it is grounded.

Suppose again, that we reason for monogamy from the intention of nature, discovered by the proportion of males and of females that are born; a proportion which corresponds perfectly with monogamy but by no means with polygamy. This argument can have no weight with a man who does not perceive that he ought to have a regard to the intention of nature.

Thus we shall find that all moral reasonings rest upon one or more first principles of morals, whose truth is immediately perceived without reasoning, by all men come to years of understanding.

And this indeed is common to every branch of human knowledge that deserves the name of science. There must be first principles proper to that science, by which the whole superstructure is supported.

The first principles of all the sciences, must be the immediate dictates of our natural faculties; nor is it possible that we should have any other evidence of their truth. And in different sciences the faculties which dictate their first principles are very different.

The first principles of morals are the immediate dictates of the moral faculty. They shew us, not what man is, but what he ought to be. Whatever is immediately perceived to be just, honest, and honourable, in human conduct, carries moral obligation along with it, and the contrary carries demerit and blame; and, from those moral obligations that are immediately perceived, all other moral obligations must be deduced by reasoning.

He that will judge of the colour of an object, must consult his eyes, in a good light, when there is no medium or contiguous objects that may give it a false tinge. But in vain will he consult every other faculty in this matter.

In like manner, he that will judge of the first principles of morals, must consult his conscience, or moral faculty, when he is calm and dispassionate, unbiassed by interest, affection, or fashion.

As we rely upon the clear and distinct testimony of our eyes, concerning the colours and figures of the bodies about us, we have the same reason to rely with security upon the clear and unbiassed testimony of our conscience, with regard to what we ought, and ought not to do. In many cases, moral worth and demerit are discerned no less clearly by the last of those natural faculties, than figure and colour by the first.

The faculties which nature hath given us, are the only engines we can use to find out the truth. We cannot indeed prove that those faculties are not fallacious, unless GOD should give us new faculties to sit in judgment upon the old. But we are born under a necessity of trusting them.

Every man in his senses believes his eyes, his ears, and his other senses. He believes his consciousness, with respect to his own thoughts and purposes, his memory, with regard to what is past, his understanding, with regard to abstract relations of things, and his taste, with regard to what is elegant and beautiful. And he has the same reason, and, indeed, is under the same necessity of believing the clear and unbiassed dictates of his conscience, with regard to what is honourable and what is base.

OBSERVATIONS CONCERNING CONSCIENCE

I shall now conclude this Essay with some observations concerning this power of the mind which we call *conscience,* by which its nature may be better understood.

The *first* is, That like all our other powers, it comes to maturity by insensible degrees, and may be much aided in its strength and vigour by proper culture. . . .

The seeds, as it were, of moral discernment are planted in the mind by him that made us. They grow up in their proper season, and are at first tender and delicate, and easily warped. Their progress depends very much upon their being duly cultivated and properly exercised.

It is so with the power of reasoning, which all acknowledge to be one of the most eminent natural faculties of man. It appears not in infancy. It springs up, by insensible degrees, as we grow to maturity. But its strength and vigour depend so much upon its being duly cultivated and exercised, that we see many individuals, nay, many nations, in which it is hardly to be perceived.

Our intellectual discernment is not so strong and vigorous by nature, as to secure us from errors in speculation. On the contrary, we see a great part of mankind, in every age, sunk in gross ignorance of things that are obvious to the more enlightened, and fettered by errors and false notions, which the human understanding, duly improved, easily throws off.

It would be extremely absurd, from the errors and ignorance of mankind, to conclude that there is no such thing as truth; or that man has not a natural faculty of discerning it, and distinguishing it from error.

In like manner, our moral discernment of what we ought, and what we ought not to do, is not so strong and vigorous by nature, as to secure us from very gross mistakes with regard to our duty.

In matters of conduct, as well as in matters of speculation, we are liable to be misled by prejudices of education, or by wrong instruction. But, in matters of conduct, we are also very liable to have our judgment warped by our appetites and passions, by fashion, and by the contagion of evil example.

We must not therefore think, because man has the natural power of discerning what is right, and what is wrong, that he has no need of instruction; that this power has no need of cultivation and improvement; that he may safely rely upon the suggestions of his mind, or upon opinions he has got, he knows not how.

What should we think of a man who because he has by nature the power of moving all his limbs, should therefore conclude that he needs not be taught to dance, or to fence, to ride, or to swim? All these exercises are performed by that power of moving our limbs, which we have by nature; but they will be performed very awkwardly and imperfectly by those who have not been trained to them, and practised in them.

It may be observed, That there are truths, both speculative and moral, which a man left to himself would never discover; yet, when they are fairly laid before him, he owns and adopts them, not barely upon the authority of his teacher, but upon their own intrinsic evidence, and perhaps wonders that he could be so blind as not to see them before.

Like a man whose son has been long abroad, and supposed dead. After many years the son returns, and is not known by his father. He would never find that this is his son. But, when he discovers himself, the father soon finds, by many circumstances, that this is his son who was lost, and can be no other person.

Truth has an affinity with the human understanding, which error hath not. And right principles of conduct have an affinity with a candid mind, which wrong principles have not. When they are set before it in a just light, a well disposed mind recognises this affinity, feels their authority, and perceives them to be genuine. It was this, I apprehend, that led PLATO to conceive that the knowledge we acquire in the present state, is only reminiscence of what, in a former state, we were acquainted with.

A man born and brought up in a savage nation, may be taught to pursue injury with unrelenting malice, to the destruction of his enemy. Perhaps when he does so, his heart does not condemn him.

Yet, if he be fair and candid, and, when the tumult of passion is over, have the virtues of clemency, generosity, and forgiveness, laid before him, as they were taught and exemplified by the divine Author of our religion, he will see, that it is more noble to overcome himself, and subdue a savage passion, than to destroy his enemy. He will see, that to make a friend of an enemy, and to overcome evil with good, is the greatest of all victories, and gives a manly and a rational delight, with which the brutish passion of revenge deserves not to be compared. He will see that hitherto he acted like a man to his friends, but like a brute to his enemies; now he knows how to make his whole character consistent, and one part of it to harmonize with another.

He must indeed be a great stranger to his own heart, and to the state of human nature, who does not see that he has need of all the aid which his situation affords him, in order to know how he ought to act in many cases that occur.

17

A NONCOGNITIVE
THEORY

Alfred Jules Ayer

A. J. Ayer (1910-   ) was Professor of Philosophy at the University of London, and since 1946 has been Professor of Philosophy at Oxford University.

There is still one objection to be met before we can claim to have justified our view that all synthetic propositions are empirical hypotheses. This objection is based on the common supposition that our speculative knowledge is of two distinct kinds — that which relates to questions of empirical fact, and that which relates to questions of value. It will be said that "statements of value" are genuine synthetic propositions, but that they cannot with any show of justice be represented as hypotheses, which are used to predict the course of our sensations; and, accordingly, that the existence of ethics and æsthetics as branches of speculative knowledge presents an insuperable objection to our radical empiricist thesis.

In face of this objection, it is our business to give an account of "judgements of value" which is both satisfactory in itself and consistent with our general empiricist principles. We shall set ourselves to show that in so far as statements of value are significant, they are ordinary "scientific" statements; and that in so far as they are not scientific, they are not in the literal sense significant, but are simply expressions of emotion which can be neither true nor false. In maintaining this view, we may confine ourselves for the present to the case of ethical statements. What is said about them will be found to apply, *mutatis mutandis*, to the case of æsthetic statements also.

The ordinary system of ethics, as elaborated in the works of ethical philosophers, is very far from being a homogeneous whole. Not only is it apt to contain pieces of metaphysics, and analyses of non-ethical concepts: its actual ethical contents are themselves of very different kinds. We may divide them, indeed, into four main classes. There are, first of all, propositions

From A. J. Ayer, *Language, Truth and Logic*, Chapter 6. Published by Victor Gollancz, Ltd., London, 1936; and by Dover Publications, Inc., New York, 1936. Reprinted by permission of the publishers.

177

which express definitions of ethical terms, or judgements about the legitimacy or possibility of certain definitions. Secondly, there are propositions describing the phenomena of moral experience, and their causes. Thirdly, there are exhortations to moral virtue. And, lastly, there are actual ethical judgements. It is unfortunately the case that the distinction between these four classes, plain as it is, is commonly ignored by ethical philosophers; with the result that it is often very difficult to tell from their works what it is that they are seeking to discover or prove.

In fact, it is easy to see that only the first of our four classes, namely that which comprises the propositions relating to the definitions of ethical terms, can be said to constitute ethical philosophy. The propositions which describe the phenomena of moral experience, and their causes, must be assigned to the science of psychology, or sociology. The exhortations to moral virtue are not propositions at all, but ejaculations or commands which are designed to provoke the reader to action of a certain sort. Accordingly, they do not belong to any branch of philosophy or science. As for the expressions of ethical judgements, we have not yet determined how they should be classified. But inasmuch as they are certainly neither definitions nor comments upon definitions, nor quotations, we may say decisively that they do not belong to ethical philosophy. A strictly philosophical treatise on ethics should therefore make no ethical pronouncements. But it should, by giving an analysis of ethical terms, show what is the category to which all such pronouncements belong. And this is what we are now about to do.

A question which is often discussed by ethical philosophers is whether it is possible to find definitions which would reduce all ethical terms to one or two fundamental terms. But this question, though it undeniably belongs to ethical philosophy, is not relevant to our present enquiry. We are not now concerned to discover which term, within the sphere of ethical terms, is to be taken as fundamental; whether, for example, "good" can be defined in terms of "right" or "right" in terms of "good," or both in terms of "value." What we are interested in is the possibility of reducing the whole sphere of ethical terms to non-ethical terms. We are enquiring whether statements of ethical value can be translated into statements of empirical fact.

That they can be so translated is the contention of those ethical philosophers who are commonly called subjectivists, and of those who are known as utilitarians. For the utilitarian defines the rightness of actions, and the goodness of ends, in terms of the pleasure, or happiness, or satisfaction, to which they give rise; the subjectivist, in terms of the feelings of approval which a certain person, or group of people, has towards them. Each of these types of definition makes moral judgements into a sub-class of psychological or sociological judgements; and for this reason they are very attractive to us. For, if either was correct, it would follow that ethical assertions were not generically different from the factual assertions which are ordinarily contrasted with them; and the account which we have already given of empirical hypotheses would apply to them also.

Nevertheless we shall not adopt either a subjectivist or a utilitarian analysis of ethical terms. We reject the subjectivist view that to call an action right, or a thing good, is to say that it is generally approved of, because it is not self-contradictory to assert that some actions which are generally approved of are not right, or that some things which are generally approved of are not good. And we reject the alternative subjectivist view that a man who asserts that a certain action is right, or that a certain thing is good, is saying that he himself approves of it, on the ground that a man who confessed that he sometimes approved of what was bad or wrong would not be contradicting himself. And a similar argument is fatal to utilitarianism. We cannot agree that to call an action right is to say that of all the actions possible in the circumstances it would cause, or be likely to cause, the greatest happiness, or the greatest balance of pleasure over pain, or the greatest balance of satisfied over unsatisfied desire, because we find that it is not self-contradictory to say that it is sometimes wrong to perform the action which would actually or probably cause the greatest happiness, or the greatest balance of pleasure over pain, or of satisfied over unsatisfied desire. And since it is not self-contradictory to say that some pleasant things are not good, or that some bad things are desired, it cannot be the case that the sentence "x is good" is equivalent to "x is pleasant," or "x is desired." And to every other variant of utilitarianism with which I am acquainted the same objection can be made. And therefore we should, I think, conclude that the validity of ethical judgements is not determined by the felicific tendencies of actions, any more than by the nature of people's feelings; but that it must be regarded as "absolute" or "intrinsic," and not empirically calculable.

If we say this, we are not, of course, denying that it is possible to invent a language in which all ethical symbols are definable in non-ethical terms, or even that it is desirable to invent such a language and adopt it in place of our own; what we are denying is that the suggested reduction of ethical to non-ethical statements is consistent with the conventions of our actual language. That is, we reject utilitarianism and subjectivism, not as proposals to replace our existing ethical notions by new ones, but as analyses of our existing ethical notions. Our contention is simply that, in our language, sentences which contain normative ethical symbols are not equivalent to sentences which express psychological propositions, or indeed empirical propositions of any kind.

It is advisable here to make it plain that it is only normative ethical symbols, and not descriptive ethical symbols, that are held by us to be indefinable in factual terms. There is a danger of confusing these two types of symbols, because they are commonly constituted by signs of the same sensible form. Thus a complex sign of the form "x is wrong" may constitute a sentence which expresses a moral judgement concerning a certain type of conduct, or it may constitute a sentence which states that a certain type of conduct is repugnant to the moral sense of a particular society. In the latter case, the symbol "wrong" is a descriptive ethical symbol, and the sentence in which it occurs expresses an ordinary sociological proposition; in the former case, the symbol "wrong" is a normative ethical symbol, and the sentence in which it occurs does not, we maintain, express an empirical proposition at all. It is only with normative ethics that we are at present concerned; so that whenever ethical symbols are used in the course of this argument without qualification, they are always to be interpreted as symbols of the normative type.

In admitting that normative ethical concepts are irreducible to empirical concepts, we seem to be leaving the way clear for the "absolutist" view of ethics — that is, the view that statements of value are not controlled by observation, as ordinary empirical propositions are, but only by a mysterious "intellectual intuition." A feature of this theory, which is seldom recognized by its advocates, is that it makes statements of value unverifiable. For it is notorious that what seems intuitively certain to one person may seem doubtful, or even false, to another. So that unless it is possible to provide some criterion by which one may decide between conflicting intuitions, a mere appeal to intuition is worthless as a test of a proposition's validity. But in the case of moral judgements, no such criterion can be given. Some moralists claim to settle the matter by saying that they "know" that their own moral judgements are correct. But such an assertion is of purely psychological interest, and has not the slightest tendency to prove the validity of any moral judgement. For dissentient moralists may equally well "know" that their ethical views are correct. And, as far as subjective certainty goes, there will be nothing to choose between them. When such differences of opinion arise in connection with an ordinary empirical proposition, one may attempt to resolve them by referring to, or actually carrying out, some relevant empirical test. But with regard to ethical statements, there is, on the "absolutist" or "intuitionist" theory, no relevant empirical test. We are therefore justified in saying that on this theory ethical statements are held to be unverifiable. They are, of course, also held to be genuine synthetic propositions.

Considering the use which we have made of the principle that a synthetic proposition is significant only if it is empirically verifiable, it is clear that the acceptance of an "absolutist" theory of ethics would undermine the whole of our main argument. And as we have already rejected the "naturalistic" theories which are commonly supposed to provide the only alternative to "absolutism" in ethics, we seem to have reached a difficult position. We shall meet the difficulty by showing that the correct treatment of ethical statements is afforded by a third theory, which is wholly compatible with our radical empiricism.

We begin by admitting that the fundamental ethical concepts are unanalysable, inasmuch as there is no criterion by which one can test the validity of the judgements in which they occur. So far we are in agreement with the absolutists. But, unlike the absolutists, we are able to give an explanation of this fact about ethical concepts. We say that the reason why they are unanalysable is that they are mere pseudo-concepts. The presence of an ethical symbol in a proposition adds nothing to its factual content. Thus if I say to someone, "You acted wrongly in stealing that money," I am not stating anything more than if I had simply said, "You stole that money." In adding that this action is wrong I am not making any further statement about it. I am simply evincing my moral disapproval of it. It is as if I had said, "You stole that money," in a peculiar tone of horror, or written it with the addition of some special exclamation marks. The tone, or the exclamation marks, adds nothing to the literal meaning of the sentence. It merely serves to show that the expression of it is attended by certain feelings in the speaker.

If now I generalise my previous statement and say, "Stealing money is wrong," I produce a sentence which has no factual meaning — that is, expresses no proposition which can be either true or false. It is as if I had written "Stealing money!!" — where the shape and thickness of the exclamation marks show, by a suitable convention, that a special sort of moral disapproval is the feeling which is being expressed. It is clear that there is nothing said here which can be true or false. Another man may disagree with me about the wrongness of stealing, in the sense that he may not have the same feelings about stealing as I have, and he may quarrel with me on account of my moral sentiments. But he cannot, strictly speaking, contradict me. For in saying that a certain type of action is right or wrong, I am not making any factual statement, not even a statement about my own state of mind. I am merely expressing certain moral sentiments. And the man who is ostensibly contradicting me is merely expressing his moral sentiments. So that there is plainly no sense in asking which of us is in the right. For neither of us is asserting a genuine proposition.

What we have just been saying about the symbol "wrong" applies to all normative ethical symbols. Sometimes they occur in sentences which record ordinary empirical facts besides expressing ethical feeling about those facts: sometimes they occur in sentences which simply express ethical feeling about a certain type of action, or situation, without making any statement of fact. But in every case in which one would commonly be said to be making an ethical judgement, the function of the relevant ethical word is purely "emotive." It is used to express feeling about certain objects, but not to make any assertion about them.

It is worth mentioning that ethical terms do not serve only to express feeling. They are calculated also to arouse feeling, and so to stimulate action. Indeed some of them are used in such a way as to give the sentences in which they occur the effect of commands. Thus the sentence "It is your duty to tell the truth" may be regarded both as the expression of a certain sort of ethical feeling about truthfulness and as the expression of the command "Tell the truth." The sentence "You ought to tell the truth" also involves the command "Tell the truth," but here the tone of the command is less emphatic. In the sentence "It is good to tell the truth" the command has become little more than a suggestion. And thus the "meaning" of the word "good," in its ethical usage, is differentiated from that of the word "duty" or the word "ought." In fact we may define the meaning of the various ethical words in terms both of the different feelings they are ordinarily taken to express, and also the different responses which they are calculated to provoke.

We can now see why it is impossible to find a criterion for determining the validity of ethical judgements. It is not because they have an "absolute" validity which is mysteriously independent of ordinary sense-experience, but because they have no objective validity whatsoever. If a sentence makes no statement at all, there is obviously no sense in asking whether what it says is true or false. And we have seen that sentences which simply express moral judgements do not say anything. They are pure expressions of feelings and as such do not come under the category of truth and falsehood. They are unverifiable for the same reason as a cry of pain or a word of command is unverifiable — because they do not express genuine propositions.

Thus, although our theory of ethics might fairly be said to be radically subjectivist, it differs in a very important respect from the orthodox subjectivist theory. For the orthodox subjectivist does not deny, as we do, that the sentences of a moralizer express genuine propositions. All he denies is that they express propositions of a unique non-empirical character. His own view is that they express propositions about the speaker's feelings. If this were so, ethical judgements clearly would be capable of being true or false. They would be true if the speaker had the relevant feelings and false if he had not. And this is a matter which is, in principle, empirically verifiable. Furthermore they could be significantly contradicted. For if I say, "Tolerance is a virtue," and someone answers, "You don't approve of it," he would, on the ordinary subjectivist theory, be contradicting me. On our theory, he would not be contradicting me, because, in saying that tolerance was a virtue, I should not be making any statement about my own feelings or about anything else. I should simply be evincing my feelings, which is not at all the same thing as saying that I have them.

The distinction between the expression of feeling and the assertion of feeling is complicated by the fact that the assertion that one has a certain feeling often accompanies the expression of that feeling, and is then, indeed, a factor in the expression of that feeling. Thus I may simultaneously express boredom and say that I am bored, and in that case my utterance of the words, "I am bored," is one of the circumstances which make it true to say that I am expressing or evincing boredom. But I can express boredom without actually saying that I am bored. I can express it by my tone and gestures, while making a statement about something wholly unconnected with it, or by an ejaculation, or without uttering any words at all. So that even if the assertion that one has a certain feeling always involves the expression of that feeling, the expression of a feeling assuredly does not always involve the assertion that one has it. And this is the important point to grasp in considering the distinction between our theory and the ordinary subjectivist theory. For whereas the subjectivist holds that ethical statements actually assert the existence of certain feelings, we hold that ethical statements are expressions and excitants of feeling which do not necessarily involve assertions.

We have already remarked that the main objection to the ordinary subjectivist theory is that the validity of ethical judgements is not determined by the nature of their author's feelings. And this is an objection which our theory escapes. For it does not imply that the existence of any feelings is a necessary and sufficient condition of the validity of an ethical judgement. It implies, on the contrary, that ethical judgements have no validity.

There is, however, a celebrated argument against subjectivist theories which our theory does not escape. It has been pointed out by Moore that if ethical statements were simply statements about the speaker's feelings, it would be impossible to argue about questions of value.[1] To take a typical example: if a man said that thrift was a virtue, and another replied that it was a vice, they would not, on this theory, be disputing with one another. One would be saying that he approved of thrift, and the other that *he* didn't; and there is no reason why both these statements should not be true. Now Moore held it to be obvious that we do dispute about questions of value, and accordingly concluded that the particular form of subjectivism which he was discussing was false.

It is plain that the conclusion that it is impossible to dispute about questions of value follows from our theory also. For as we hold that such sentences as "Thrift is a virtue" and "Thrift is a vice" do not express propositions at all, we clearly cannot hold that they express incompatible propositions. We must therefore admit that if Moore's argument really refutes the ordinary subjectivist theory, it also refutes ours. But, in fact, we deny that it does refute even the ordinary subjectivist theory. For we hold that one really never does dispute about questions of value.

This may seem, at first sight, to be a very paradoxical assertion. For we certainly do engage in disputes which are ordinarily regarded as disputes about questions of value. But, in all such cases, we find if we consider the matter closely, that the dispute is not really about a question of value, but about a question of fact. When someone disagrees with us about the moral value of a certain action or type of action, we do admittedly resort to argument in order to win him over to our way of thinking. But we do not attempt to show by our arguments that he has the "wrong" ethical feeling towards a situation whose nature he has correctly apprehended. What we attempt to show is that he is mistaken about the facts of the case. We argue that he has misconceived the agent's motive: or that he has misjudged the effects of the action, or its probable effects in view of the agent's knowledge; or that he has failed to take into account the special circumstances in which the agent was placed. Or else we employ more general arguments about the effects which actions of a certain type tend to produce, or the qualities which are usually manifested in their performance. We do this in the hope that we have only to get our opponent to agree with us about the nature of the

---

[1] Cf. *Philosophical Studies*, "The Nature of Moral Philosophy."

empirical facts for him to adopt the same moral attitude towards them as we do. And as the people with whom we argue have generally received the same moral education as ourselves, and live in the same social order, our expectation is usually justified. But if our opponent happens to have undergone a different process of moral "conditioning" from ourselves, so that, even when he acknowledges all the facts, he still disagrees with us about the moral value of the actions under discussion, then we abandon the attempt to convince him by argument. We say that it is impossible to argue with him because he has a distorted or undeveloped moral sense; which signifies merely that he employs a different set of values from our own. We feel that our own system of values is superior, and therefore speak in such derogatory terms of his. But we cannot bring forward any arguments to show that our system is superior. For our judgement that it is so is itself a judgement of value, and accordingly outside the scope of argument. It is because argument fails us when we come to deal with pure questions of value, as distinct from questions of fact, that we finally resort to mere abuse.

In short, we find that argument is possible on moral questions only if some system of values is presupposed. If our opponent concurs with us in expressing moral disapproval of all actions of a given type *t*, then we may get him to condemn a particular action A, by bringing forward argument to show that A is of type *t*. For the question whether A does or does not belong to that type is a plain question of fact. Given that a man has certain moral principles, we argue that he must, in order to be consistent, react morally to certain things in a certain way. What we do not and cannot argue about is the validity of these moral principles. We merely praise or condemn them in the light of our own feelings.

If anyone doubts the accuracy of this account of moral disputes, let him try to construct even an imaginary argument on a question of value which does not reduce itself to an argument about a question of logic or about an empirical matter of fact. I am confident that he will not succeed in producing a single example. And if that is the case, he must allow that its involving the impossibility of purely ethical arguments is not, as Moore thought, a ground of objection to our theory, but rather a point in favour of it.

Having upheld our theory against the only criticism which appeared to threaten it, we may now use it to define the nature of all ethical enquiries. We find that ethical philosophy consists simply in saying that ethical concepts are pseudo-concepts and therefore unanalysable. The further task of describing the different feelings that the different ethical terms are used to express, and the different reactions that they customarily provoke, is a task for the psychologist. There cannot be such a thing as ethical science, if by ethical science one means the elaboration of a "true" system of morals. For we have seen that, as ethical judgements are mere expressions of feeling, there can be no way of determining the validity of any ethical system, and, indeed, no sense in asking whether any such system is true. All that one may legitimately enquire in this connection is, What are the moral habits of a given person or group of people, and what causes them to have precisely those habits and feelings? And this enquiry falls wholly within the scope of the existing social sciences.

It appears, then, that ethics, as a branch of knowledge, is nothing more than a department of psychology and sociology. And in case anyone thinks that we are overlooking the existence of casuistry, we may remark that casuistry is not a science, but is a purely analytical investigation of the structure of a given moral system. In other words, it is an exercise in formal logic.

When one comes to pursue the psychological enquiries which constitute ethical science, one is immediately enabled to account for the Kantian and hedonistic theories of morals. For one finds that one of the chief causes of moral behavior is fear, both conscious and unconscious, of a god's displeasure, and fear of the enmity of society. And this, indeed, is the reason why moral precepts present themselves to some people as "categorical" commands. And one finds, also, that the moral code of a society is partly determined by the beliefs of that society concerning the conditions of its own happiness — or, in other words, that a society tends to encourage or discourage a given type of conduct by the use of moral sanctions according as it appears to promote or detract from the contentment of the society as a whole. And this is the reason why altruism is recommended in most moral codes and egotism condemned. It is from the observation of this connection between morality and happiness that hedonistic or eudæmonistic theories of morals ultimately spring, just as the moral theory of Kant is based on the fact, previously explained, that moral precepts have for some people the force of inexorable commands. As each of these theories ignores the fact which lies at the root of the other, both may be criticized as being onesided; but this is not the main objection to either of them. Their essential defect is that they treat propositions which refer to the causes and attributes of our ethical feelings as if they were definitions of ethical concepts. And thus they fail to recognize that ethical concepts are pseudo-concepts and consequently indefinable.

As we have already said, our conclusions about the nature of ethics apply to æsthetics also. Aesthetic terms are used in exactly the same way as ethical terms. Such æsthetic words as "beautiful" and "hideous" are employed, as ethical words are employed, not to make statements of fact, but simply to express certain feelings and evoke a certain response. It follows, as in ethics, that there is no sense in attributing objective validity to æsthetic judgements, and no possibility of arguing about questions of value in æsthetics, but only about questions of fact. A scientific treatment of æsthetics would show us what in general were the causes of æsthetic feeling, why various societies produced and admired the works of art they did, why taste varies as it does within a given society, and so forth. And these are ordinary psychological or sociological questions. They have, of course, little or nothing to do with æsthetic criticism as we understand it. But that is because the purpose of æsthetic criticism is not so much to give knowledge as to communicate emotion. The critic, by calling attention to certain features of the work under review, and expressing his own feelings about them, endeavours to make us share his attitude towards the work as a whole. The only relevant propositions that he formulates are propositions describing the nature of the work. And these are plain records of fact. We conclude, therefore, that there is nothing in æsthetics, any more than there is in ethics, to justify the view that it embodies a unique type of knowledge.

18

THE GOOD LIFE
IS RATIONAL ACTIVITY

Aristotle

Aristotle (384-322 B.C.) was a student of Plato, tutor of Alexander of Macedon, founder of a school in Athens known as the Lyceum.

1. The good is what people desire for itself.

If, therefore, among the ends at which our conduct aims there is one which we will for its own sake, whereas we will the other ends only for the sake of this one, and if we do not choose everything for the sake of some other thing — that would clearly be an endless process, making all desire futile and idle —, it is clear that this one ultimate end will be the good, and the greatest good. Then will not a knowledge of this ultimate end be of more than theoretic interest? Will it not also have great practical importance for the conduct of life? Shall we not be more likely to attain our needs if like archers we have a target before us to aim at? If this be so, an attempt must be made to ascertain at all events in outline what precisely this supreme good is, and under which of the theoretical or practical sciences it falls.

2. It is generally thought that the good is happiness, and we need not deny this; but if we accept it, it is a mistake to identify happiness with pleasure, honor, wealth, or having a fine character.

To resume: inasmuch as all study and all deliberate action is aimed at some good object, let us state what is the good which is in our view the aim of political science, and what is the highest of the goods obtainable by action.

Now as far as the name goes there is virtual agreement about this among

From Aristotle, *Ethics for English Readers*, Books I, II, and X, translated by H. Rackham, published by Basil Blackwell, Publisher, Oxford, 1952. Reprinted with the permission of the publisher. These paragraphs have been rearranged in order to present a consecutive discussion. The italicized headings are by the present editors.

the vast majority of mankind. Both ordinary people and persons of trained mind define the good as happiness. But as to what constitutes happiness opinions differ; the answer given by ordinary people is not the same as the verdict of the philosopher. Ordinary men identify happiness with something obvious and visible, such as pleasure or wealth or honour — everybody gives a different definition, and sometimes the same person's own definition alters: when a man has fallen ill he thinks that happiness is health, if he is poor he thinks it is wealth. And when people realise their own ignorance they regard with admiration those who propound some grand theory that is above their heads. The view has been held by some thinkers that besides the many good things alluded to above there also exists something that is good in itself, which is the fundamental cause of the goodness of all the others.

Now to review the whole of these opinions would perhaps be a rather thankless task. It may be enough to examine those that are most widely held, or that appear to have some considerable argument in their favour.

To judge by men's mode of living, the mass of mankind think that good and happiness consist in pleasure, and consequently are content with a life of mere enjoyment. There are in fact three principal modes of life — the one just mentioned, the life of active citizenship and the life of contemplation. The masses, being utterly servile, obviously prefer the life of mere cattle; and indeed they have some reason for this, inasmuch as many men of high station share the tastes of Sardanapalus. The better people, on the other hand, and men of action, give the highest value to honour, since honour may be said to be the object aimed at in a public career. Nevertheless, it would seem that honour is a more superficial thing than the good which we are in search of, because honour seems to depend more on the people who render it than on the person who receives it, whereas we dimly feel that good must be something inherent in oneself and inalienable. Moreover men's object in pursuing honour appears to be to convince themselves of their own worth; at all events they seek to be honoured by persons of insight and by people who are well acquainted with them, and to be honoured for their merit. It therefore seems that at all events in the opinions of these men goodness is more valuable than honour, and probably one may suppose that it has a better claim than honour to be deemed the end at which the life of politics aims. But even virtue appears to lack completeness as an end, inasmuch as it seems to be possible to possess it while one is asleep or living a life of perpetual inactivity, and moreover one can be virtuous and yet suffer extreme sorrow and misfortune; but nobody except for the sake of maintaining a paradox would call a man happy in those circumstances.

The life of money-making is a cramped way of living, and clearly wealth is not the good we are in search of, as it is only valuable as a means to something else. Consequently a stronger case might be made for the objects previously specified, because they are valued for their own sake; but even they appear to be inadequate, although a great deal of discussion has been devoted to them.

3. *Happiness is desired for itself, and never for the sake of anything else; it is sufficient in itself to make life desirable.*

Now the objects at which our actions aim are manifestly several, and some of these objects, for instance money, and instruments in general, we adopt as means to the attainment of something else. This shows that not all the objects we pursue are final ends. But the greatest good manifestly is a final end. Consequently if there is only one thing which is final, that will be the object for which we are now seeking, or if there are several, it will be that one among them which possesses the most complete finality.

Now a thing that is pursued for its own sake we pronounce to be more final than one pursued as a means to some other thing, and a thing that is never desired for the sake of something else we call more final than those which are desired for the sake of something else as well as for their own sake. In fact the absolutely final is something that is always desired on its own account and never as a means for obtaining something else. Now this description appears to apply in the highest degree to happiness, since we always desire happiness for its own sake and never on account of something else; whereas honour and pleasure and intelligence and each of the virtues, though we do indeed desire them on their own account as well, for we should desire each of them even if it produced no external result, we also desire for the sake of happiness, because we believe that they will bring it to us, whereas nobody desires happiness for the sake of those things, nor for anything else but itself.

The same result seems to follow from a consideration of the subject of self-sufficiency, which is felt to be a necessary attribute of the final good. The term self-sufficient denotes not merely being sufficient for oneself alone, as if one lived the life of a hermit, but also being sufficient for the needs of one's parents and children and wife, and one's friends and fellow-countrymen in general, inasmuch as man is by nature a social being.

Yet we are bound to assume some limit in these relationships, since if one extends the connexion to include one's children's children and friends' friends, it will go on *ad infinitum*. But that is a matter which must be deferred for later consideration. Let us define self-sufficiency as the quality which makes life to be desirable and lacking in nothing even when considered by itself; and this quality we assume to belong to happiness. Moreover when we pronounce happiness to be the most desirable of all things, we do not mean that it stands as one in a list of good things — were it so it would obviously be more desirable in combination with even the smallest of the other goods, inasmuch as that addition would increase the total of good, and of two good things the larger must always be the more desirable.

Thus it appears that happiness is something final and complete in itself, as being the aim and end of all practical activities whatever.

4. *In order to acquire a clearer concept of human happiness, we do well to ask whether human beings have a function, as the eye, or a carpenter, has one. What is distinctive in man is reason, so his happiness must be the exercise of reason in living.*

Possibly, however, the student may feel that the statement that happiness is the greatest good is a mere truism, and he may want a clearer explanation of what the precise nature of happiness is. This may perhaps be achieved by ascertaining what is the proper function of man. In the case of flute-players or sculptors or other artists, and generally of all persons who have a particular work to perform, it is felt that their good and their well-being are found in that work. It may be supposed that this similarly holds good in the case of a human being, if we may assume that there is some work which constitutes the proper function of a human being as such. Can it then be the case that whereas a carpenter and a shoemaker have definite functions or businesses to perform, a man as such has none, and is not designed by nature to perform any function? Should we not rather assume that, just as the eye and hand and foot and every part of the body manifestly have functions assigned to them, so also there is a function that belongs to a man, over and above all the special functions that belong to his members? If so, what precisely will that function be? It is clear that the mere activity of living is shared by man even with the vegetable kingdom, whereas we are looking for some function that belongs specially to man. We must therefore set aside the vital activity of nutrition and growth. Next perhaps comes the life of the senses; but this also is manifestly shared by the horse and the ox and all the animals. There remains therefore what may be designated the practical life of the rational faculty.

But the term 'rational' life has two meanings: it denotes both the mere possession of reason, and its active exercise. Let us take it that we here mean the latter, as that appears to be the more proper signification of the term. Granted then that the special function of man is the active exercise of the mind's faculties in accordance with rational principle, or at all events not in detachment from rational principle, and that the function of anything, for example, a harper, is generally the same as the function of a good specimen of that thing, for example a good harper (the specification of the function merely being augmented in the latter case with the statement of excellence — a harper is a man who plays the harp, a good harper one who plays the harp well) — granted, I say, the truth of these assumptions, it follows that the good of man consists in the active exercise of the faculties in conformity with excellence or virtue, or if there are several virtues in conformity with the best and most perfect among them.

Moreover, happiness requires an entire life-time. One swallow does not make a summer, nor does a single fine day; and similarly one day or a brief period of prosperity does not make a man supremely fortunate and happy.

Happiness then we define as the active exercise of the mind in conformity with perfect goodness or virtue.

5. *The rationally ordered life will necessarily be pleasant, but it must be admitted that happiness does also require some external goods.*

In consequence of this their life has no need of pleasure as an external appendage; it contains pleasures within itself. For in addition to what has been said, if a man does not enjoy performing noble actions he is not a good man at all. Nobody would call a man just who did not enjoy acting justly, nor liberal if he did not enjoy acting liberally, and similarly with the other virtues. But if this is so, actions in conformity with virtue will be intrinsically pleasant. Moreover, they are also good and noble; and good and noble in the highest degree, inasmuch as the virtuous man must be a good judge of these matters, and his judgement is as we have said.

Consequently happiness is at once the best and the noblest and the pleasantest thing there is, and these qualities do not exist in separate compartments, as is implied by the inscription at Delos:

> The noblest thing is justice, health the best,
> But getting your desire the pleasantest.

For all these qualities are combined in the highest activities, and it is these activities or the best one among them which according to our definition constitutes happiness. All the same it is manifest that happiness requires external goods in addition, since it is impossible, or at all events difficult, to perform noble actions without resources. Many of them require the aid of friends and of wealth and power in the state. Also a lack of such advantages as good birth or a fine family of children or good looks is a blot on a man's supreme felicity. A very ugly man or one of low birth or without children cannot be classed as completely happy; and still less perhaps can a man whose children or friends are utterly base, or though worthy have died.

6. *Some have thought that sheer pleasure, just as such, is the ultimate good; but this is a mistake.*

It was the opinion of Eudoxus, that pleasure is the good. His reason was as follows. Observation showed him that all creatures, rational and irrational alike, desire to obtain pleasure, and he held the view that in every department of life what is desired is good, and what is most desired is the greatest good. Consequently, he argued, the fact that all things 'gravitate in the direction of' the same object proves that object to be the greatest good for all, inasmuch as everything finds out its own particular good, just as every creature discovers what food is nourishing for it; but that which is good for all things and which all things try to obtain must be *the* good. This argument won acceptance more because of its author's excellence of character than from its own merits.

Eudoxus had the reputation of being an exceptionally temperate man, and so his theory was not supposed to be suggested by love of pleasure but to be a correct statement of the facts.

Eudoxus also held that the truth of this estimate of pleasure is equally attested by considering its opposite. Pain, he argued, was an object of intrinsic aversion to all living things, so that the opposite of pain must be intrinsically desirable. Moreover those things are most desirable which we choose for their own sake and not for the sake of something else, and to this class, he said, pleasure admittedly belongs, because we never ask anybody *why* he wants pleasure: we assume that pleasure is desirable in itself. He also argued that the value of just or temperate conduct is enhanced if we enjoy acting justly or temperately; but a good thing can only be augmented by something else that is good.

But this argument at all events only seems to show that pleasure is *a* good, not that it is a greater good than any other; for every good thing is better and more desirable if some other good thing is added to it than it is by itself. This argument resembles the one used by Plato to prove that the good is not pleasure, since the pleasant life is more desirable if combined with wisdom than it is without it, but if pleasure is improved by combination with something else, pleasure is not the good.

In reply to those who bring forward the degrading pleasures one might say that these are not really pleasant; if they are pleasant to ill-conditioned persons, it must not be thought that they are really pleasant, except to those persons, any more than the things that are wholesome for invalids or that taste sweet or bitter to them, or that look white to people suffering from disease of the eye, are really so. Or one might express the point by saying that, though pleasures are desirable, yet they are not desirable when derived from those sources, just as wealth is desirable, but not if won by treachery, and health, but not at the cost of eating any diet the doctor may prescribe. Or one might say that pleasures differ in kind, those derived from honourable sources not being the same as those from base sources; and that one cannot experience the pleasure of justice without being a just man, nor enjoy music without being a musician, and similarly with the other pleasures.

Moreover the difference that exists between a friend and a flatterer seems to show clearly that pleasure is not a good, or else that there are different kinds of pleasure. A friend is thought to aim at doing good to his associates, but a flatterer at giving them pleasure; to be a flatterer is a reproach, but a friend is praised, because his motives for seeking society are different. Also nobody would like to pass the whole of his life with the intellect of a child, however much pleasure he might get from things that please children, nor to enjoy doing something very disgraceful even though it brought no painful consequences. And there are many things that we should be eager to possess even if they brought us no pleasure, for instance, sight, memory, knowledge, virtue. If these things do as a matter of fact necessarily bring pleasure, that makes no difference; we should prefer to possess them even if we got no pleasure from them.

It seems therefore that pleasure is not the good, and also that not all pleasure is desirable, but that some pleasures of various kinds and derived from various sources are desirable in themselves.

7. *The place of pleasure in the good life is indicated by the fact that pleasure occurs when some sense or faculty is functioning well; pleasure completes this activity. Consequently there are different kinds of pleasure.*

Each of the senses acts in relation to its object, and acts perfectly when in good condition and when directed to the finest of the objects that come under it — this seems to be the best description of a perfect activity, it being assumed that it makes no difference whether we speak of the sense itself acting or the organ which contains it. Consequently each of the senses acts best when its sense-organ is in its best condition and is directed to the best of its objects. And this activity will be the most complete and the most pleasant. For every sensation is accompanied by pleasure, as also are thought and contemplation, and the pleasantest sensation is the most complete. The most complete sensation is that of the sense-organ when in good condition and directed to its worthiest object; and the activity of sensation is completed by the pleasure, though not in the same way as it is completed by the combination of object and sense, both being in good condition, any more than health is the cause of a man's being healthy in the same sense as the doctor is the cause of it.

(It is clear that each of the senses has a particular pleasure corresponding to it; we speak of pleasant sights and sounds as well as of sweet tastes and scents. And it is also clear that the pleasure is greatest when the sense faculty is in the best condition and is directed to the best object; there will always be pleasure when there is an object to cause it and a subject to feel it, if both the object perceived and the percipient organ are good.)

But the pleasure completes the activity not in the way in which it is completed by a fixed disposition of character already present in the agent, but as a supervening consummation, in the same way as a good complexion gives a finishing touch to the young and healthy. Consequently the activity will be attended by pleasure as long as both the object thought of or perceived and the subject discerning or judging are in a proper condition, inasmuch as in any relationship as long as both the passive and the active parties remain the same and stand in the same position as regards each other, the same result is naturally produced.

How is it then that nobody can go on feeling a pleasure continuously? Is it that we grow tired? No human activity can continue working without a break, and consequently pleasure also is not continuous, as it accompanies the exercise of a faculty. Also some things give pleasure when they are new but do not give similar pleasure later, for the same reason; at the outset the mind is stimulated and acts vigorously in regard to the object, just as in the case of sight when people fix their gaze on something very intently. Subsequently however the activity is not so vigorous, but relaxes; and this damps down the pleasure which the activity gives.

This moreover is ground for believing that pleasures vary in specific quality. We feel that different kinds of things must have a different sort of perfection; we see this both with natural objects like animals and trees and with the products of art such as a picture or a statue or a building or an implement. Similarly we feel that the thing which perfects one kind of activity must itself be of a different sort from that which perfects another kind. But the activities of the intellect are different in kind from those of the senses, and also differ among themselves. So also therefore do the pleasures that complete them. . . .

8. *The rationally ordered activity which constitutes happiness is of two kinds: the practical and the purely intellectual or scientific. Rational practical activity consists in the choice of the mean, as determined by a man with practical wisdom.*

In the case of every whole that is divisible into parts, it is possible to take a larger or a smaller share of it, or an equal share; and those amounts may be measured either in relation to the thing itself or in relation to us. I mean that whereas the middle of an object is the point equally distant from each of its extremes, which is one and the same for everybody, the medium quantity in its relation to us is the amount that is not excessive and not deficient, and this is not the same for everybody. For instance, if ten is many and two is few, to take the actual middle amount between them gives six (because 6 is the arithmetic mean between 2 and 10: $6 - 2 = 10 - 6$); but a medium quantity relative to us cannot be arrived at in this same way. For instance, supposing that for an athlete in training ten pounds of food is too large a ration and two pounds too small, the trainer will not necessarily advise six pounds, as possibly that will be too large or too small an allowance for the particular person — a small ration for a Milo but a large one for a novice in athletics; and the same applies to the amount of running or wrestling prescribed in training. This is how every expert avoids excess and deficiency and adopts the middle amount — not the exact half of the object he is dealing with, but a medium quantity in relation to the person concerned.

Such then is the manner in which every kind of skill operates successfully, by looking to the middle point and making its products conform with it. This accounts for the remark commonly made about successful productions, that you cannot take anything away from them or add anything to them. The implication is that excess and deficiency impair excellence, and a middle quantity secures it. If then we are right in saying that good craftsmen when at work keep their eyes fixed on a middle point, and if virtue, no less than nature herself, surpasses all the arts and crafts in accuracy and excellence, it follows that excellence will be the faculty of hitting a middle point. I refer to moral excellence or virtue; and this is concerned with emotions and actions, in which it is possible to have excess, or deficiency, or a medium amount. For instance you can feel either more or less than a moderate amount of fear and boldness, and of desire and anger and pity, and of pleasant or painful emotions generally; and in both cases the feelings will be wrong. But to feel these emotions at the right time and on the right occasion and towards the right people and for the right motives and in the right manner is a middle course, and the best course; and this is the mark of goodness. And similarly there is excess and deficiency or a middle amount in the case of actions. Now it is with emotions and actions that virtue is concerned; excess and deficiency in them are wrong, and a middle amount receives praise and achieves success, both of which are marks of virtue. It follows that virtue is a sort of middle state, in the sense that it aims at the middle.

Moreover, though it is possible to go wrong in many ways (according to the conjecture of the Pythagorean school evil is a property of the infinite and good of the finite), it is only possible to go right in one way:

> Goodness is one, but badness manifold.

This is why to go wrong is easy but to go right difficult; it is easy to miss the target but difficult to hit it. Here then is another reason why vice is a matter of excess and deficiency and virtue a middle state.

It follows that virtue is a fixed quality of the will, consisting essentially in a middle state — middle in relation to ourselves, and as determined by principle, by the standard that a man of practical wisdom would apply. And it is a middle state between two vices, one of excess and one of deficiency: and this in view of the fact that vices either exceed or fall short of the right amount in emotions or actions, whereas virtue ascertains the mean and chooses that. Consequently while in its essence and by the principle defining its fundamental nature virtue is a middle state, in point of excellence and rightness it is an extreme.

But not every action or every emotion admits of a middle state: the very names of some of them suggest wickedness — for instance spite, shamelessness, envy, and among actions, adultery, theft, murder; all of these and similar emotions and actions are blamed as being wicked intrinsically and not merely when practised to excess or insufficiently. Consequently it is not possible ever to feel or commit them rightly: they are always wrong, nor are the qualifications 'well' or 'ill' applicable to them — for instance, you cannot commit adultery with the right woman and at the right time and in the right place: the mere commission of adultery with any woman anywhere at any time is an offence. Similarly, it is equally erroneous to think that there can be a middle amount and an excess and a deficiency of injustice or cowardice or self-indulgence, as that would mean that you can have a medium quantity of excess and deficiency or too much excess or too little deficiency. So just as there is no such thing as an excess or a deficiency of self-control and courage, because in these the middle is in a sense the top point, so there can be no middle amount or excess or deficiency of self-indulgence or cowardice, but actions of that sort however committed are an offence. There is no such thing as a medium amount of excess or deficiency, nor an excessive or insufficient amount of observance of a mean.

It is not enough, however, merely to give a general definition of moral goodness; it is necessary to show how our definition applies to particular virtues. In theories of conduct although general principles have a wider application, particular rules are more accurate, inasmuch as actual conduct deals with particular cases, and theory must be in agreement with these. Let us then take the particular virtues and vices from the diagram.

The middle state as regards fear and boldness is courage. Excessive fearlessness has no name (as is the case with many types of character); excessive boldness is called rashness, and excessive fear and insufficient boldness cowardice.

In regard to pleasure, and in a less degree to pain, the middle state is self-control, and the excess self-indulgence. Persons deficient in sensibility to pleasure are scarcely to be found, so that this class has no recognized name; they may however be called insensitive.

The middle disposition in respect of giving and getting money is liberality; the excess and the deficiency are extravagance and meanness, both of these vices in opposite ways displaying both excess and deficiency — the extravagant man exceeds in spending money and is deficient in acquiring it, and the mean man exceeds in acquiring money but is deficient in spending it.

There are also other dispositions in regard to money — the middle state called munificence (which is not the same as liberality, as munificence is concerned with large sums of money whereas liberality is displayed in dealing with minor amounts), the excess which is tasteless vulgarity and the deficiency shabbiness in the use of money. . . .

9. *The pleasure of virtuous activity is better, indeed in a sense more real, than the pleasure of bad activity.*

Activities differ in moral value. Some are to be adopted, others to be avoided, and others are neutral. And the same is the case with the sort of pleasure they afford, as every activity has a special kind of pleasure connected with it. The pleasure of doing a worthy action is morally good and that of doing a base action is morally evil: in fact even to desire what is honourable is praiseworthy and to desire what is disgraceful is reprehensible; but the pleasures contained in our activities are more intimately connected with them than are the desires which prompt them: these are both separate in time and distinct in nature from the activities themselves, whereas the pleasures are closely united wtih them, and indeed they are so closely linked together as to make it difficult to distinguish the pleasure of doing a thing from the action itself. Nevertheless we must not regard pleasure as actually identical with the sensation or the thought which it accompanies — that would be absurd; although as they occur simultaneously, some people suppose that they are the same thing.

But we hold that in all such matters the thing really is what it appears to be to the good man. And if this rule is sound, as it is generally taken to be, and if the standard of everything is goodness or the good man as such, then the things that appear to him to be pleasures will be real pleasures and the things that he enjoys will be really pleasant. Nor need it surprise us if things which the good man dislikes seem pleasant to some people. Human nature is liable to many corruptions and perversions, and the things referred to are not really pleasant but only pleasant to people who are in a condition to fancy them to be pleasant. It is clear therefore that pleasures which are admittedly disgraceful cannot properly be called pleasant at all, but only pleasant to a corrupt taste.

10. Since the intellect is the highest part of human nature, contemplation must be the most perfect form of happiness.

But if happiness is activity in conformity with virtue, it is reasonable to suppose that it is in conformity with the highest virtue, which must be the virtue belonging to the highest part of our nature. This is our intellect, or whatever part of us is held to be our natural ruler and guide, and to apprehend things noble and divine, as being itself divine, or nearest to the divine of all the parts of our nature. It will consequently be the activity of this part, in conformity with the virtue that belongs to it, which will constitute perfect happiness; and it has already been stated that this activity is the activity of contemplation.

This view may be accepted as in agreement both with the conclusions reached before and with the truth. Contemplation is the highest form of activity, because the intellect is the highest part of our nature, and the things apprehended by it are the highest objects of knowledge. Also it is the most continuous form of activity; we can go on reflecting more continuously than we can pursue any form of practical activity. Moreover we feel that happiness is bound to contain an element of pleasure; but the activity of philosophic contemplation is admittedly the most pleasurable of all the activities in conformity with virtue. Philosophy is thought to comprise pleasures of marvellous purity and permanence; and it is reasonable to hold that the enjoy-

ment of knowledge already acquired is a more pleasant occupation than research directed to the acquirement of new knowledge. Also the activity of
contemplation will be found to possess in the highest degree the quality designated self-sufficiency. It is of course true that the wise man as well as the
just man and those possessing all the other virtues requires the necessities of
life; but given a sufficient supply of these, whereas the just man needs people
towards whom and in partnership with whom he may act justly, and similarly
the self-controlled man and the brave man and the others, the wise man can
practise contemplation by himself, and the wiser he is the better he can do
this. No doubt he can do this better if he has fellow-workers, but nevertheless
he is the most self-sufficient of all men.

It would appear that philosophic speculation is the only occupation that
is pursued for its own sake. It produces no result beyond the act of contemplation itself, whereas from our practical pursuits we look to gain more or less
advantage apart from the activities themselves.

Also happiness is thought to involve leisure. We practice business in
order to gain leisure, and we go to war in order to secure peace. Thus the
practical virtues are exhibited in the activities of politics or of warfare, and the
actions connected with these seem to be essentially unleisurely. Military
activities are entirely a business matter: nobody goes to war for choice, just
in order to have a war, or takes deliberate steps to cause one. A man would
be thought to be an absolutely bloodthirsty person if he made war on a
friendly state in order to bring about battles and bloodshed. The life of active
citizenship also is devoid of leisure; besides the actual business of politics it
aims at winning posts of authority and honour, or at all events at securing
happiness for oneself and one's friends — objects which are clearly not the
same thing as mere political activity in itself. We see therefore that the occu-
pations connected with politics and with war, although standing highest in
nobility and importance among activities in conformity with the virtues, are
devoid of leisure, and are not adopted for their own sakes but as means to
attaining some object outside themselves. But the exercise of the intellect in
contemplation seems to be pre-eminent in point of leisure and to aim at no
result external to itself; the pleasure it contains is inherent, and augments its
activity. Consequently self-sufficiency and leisure, as well as such freedom
from fatigue as lies within the capacity of human nature, and all the other
advantages that we think of as belonging to complete bliss, appear to be contained in this activity. Therefore the activity of contemplation will be the
perfect happiness of man, — provided that it continues throughout a complete
lifetime, since in happiness there must be nothing incomplete.

The following consideration will also show that perfect happiness is
found in contemplation. The gods as we conceive them are supremely blessed
and happy. But what kind of actions must we attribute to them? Just actions?
or would it not be absurd to imagine them as making contracts and repaying
deposits and so on? Then shall we say brave actions — enduring alarms and
facing dangers in a noble cause? Or liberal actions? but who will receive

their gifts? Moreover it is curious to think of the gods as having money or tokens of value. And what would be the meaning in their case of conduct exhibiting self-control? would it not be a poor compliment to the gods to say that they have no base appetites? If we went through the whole list, all the various forms of virtuous conduct would appear to be too trivial to be worthy of divine beings. Nevertheless everybody conceives of the gods as at all events alive, and therefore active, — they are certainly not imagined as always asleep, like Endymion. But take away action, and particularly productive action, and what remains for a living being except contemplation? It follows that the divine activity, since it is supremely blissful, will be the activity of contemplation. Therefore among human activities the one most nearly akin to divine contemplation is the activity that contains the largest amount of happiness.

And it appears that one who lives the life of the mind, and cultivates his intellect and keeps that in its best condition, is the man whom the gods love best. It is the common belief that the gods pay heed to the affairs of men. If this is true, it is reasonable to assume that the gods take pleasure in what is best and most akin to themselves, namely man's intellect, and that they requite with benefits those who pay the highest respect to the life of the mind, because these men care for the things that are dear to themselves and these men act rightly and nobly. But manifestly all these attributes belong in the highest degree to the wise man. He therefore is the man dearest to the gods, and consequently it is he who will presumably be supremely happy. This is another indication that the philosopher is the happiest of mankind.

19

A FORM OF HEDONISM
AND UTILITARIANISM

J. J. C. Smart

J. J. C. Smart (1920-   ) is Professor of Philosophy at the University of Adelaide.

ACT UTILITARIANISM AND RULE UTILITARIANISM

The system of normative ethics which I shall be concerned to defend is, as I have said earlier, *act* utilitarianism, not rule utilitarianism. Act utilitarianism states that the rightness or wrongness of an action is to be judged by the consequences, good and bad, of the action itself. Rule utilitarianism holds that the rightness or wrongness of an action is to be judged by the goodness and badness of the consequences of a rule that everyone should perform the action in like circumstances. There are two sub-varieties of rule utilitarianism according to whether one construes 'rule' here as 'actual rule' or 'possible rule'. With the former, one gets a view like that of S. E. Toulmin,[1] and with the latter, one like Kant's.[2] That is, if it is permissible to interpret Kant's principle 'Act only on that maxim through which you can at the same time will that it should become a universal law' as 'Act only on that maxim which you as a humane and benevolent person would like to see established as a universal law.' Of course Kant would resist this appeal to human feeling, but it seems necessary in order to interpret his doctrine in a plausible way. A subtle version of the Kantian type of rule utilitarianism is given by R. F. Harrod in his 'Utilitarianism Revised.'[3]

From J. J. C. Smart, *An Outline of a System of Utilitarian Ethics,* 1961. Published by the Melbourne University Press, Melbourne, and the Cambridge University Press, Cambridge. Reprinted by permission of the author and publishers.

[1] *The Place of Reason in Ethics* (Cambridge University Press, London, 1960).

[2] Immanuel Kant, *Groundwork of the metaphysic of morals.* Translated from the German in *The Moral Law,* by H. J. Paton (Hutchinson, London, 1948).

[3] *Mind,* vol. 45, 1936, pp. 137-56.

I have argued elsewhere[4] the objections to rule utilitarianism as compared with act utilitarianism.[5] Briefly they boil down to the accusation of rule worship: the rule utilitarian presumably advocates his principle because he is ultimately concerned with human happiness: why then should he advocate abiding by a rule when he knows that it will not in the present case be most beneficial to abide by it? The reply that in most cases it is most beneficial to abide by the rule seems irrelevant. And so is the reply that it would be better that everybody should abide by the rule than that nobody should. This is to suppose that the only alternative to 'everyone does *A*' is 'no-one does *A*'. But clearly we have the possibility 'some people do *A* and some don't'. Hence to refuse to break a generally beneficial rule in those cases in which it is not most beneficial to obey it seems irrational and to be a case of rule worship.

　　The type of utilitarianism which I shall advocate will, then, be act utilitarianism, not rule utilitarianism.

HEDONISTIC AND NON-HEDONISTIC UTILITARIANISM

An act utilitarian judges the rightness or wrongness of actions by the goodness and badness of their consequences. But is he to judge the goodness and badness of the consequences of an action solely by their pleasantness and unpleasantness? Bentham,[6] who thought that quantity of pleasure being equal, the experience of playing pushpin was as good as that of reading poetry, could be classified as a hedonistic act utilitarian. Moore,[7] who believed that some states of mind, such as those of acquiring knowledge, had intrinsic value quite independent of their pleasantness, can be called an ideal utilitarian. Mill seemed to occupy an intermediate position.[8] He held that there are higher and lower pleasures. This seems to imply that pleasure is a necessary condition for goodness but that goodness depends on other qualities of experience than pleasantness and unpleasantness. I propose to call Mill a quasi-ideal utilitarian. For Mill, pleasantness functions like x in the algebraic product $x \times y \times z$. If $x = o$ the product is zero. For Moore pleasantness functions more like x in $(x + 1) \times y \times z$. If $x = o$ the product need not be zero. Of course this is only a very rough analogy.

　　[4] "Extreme and Restricted Utilitarianism," *Philosophical Quarterly*, vol. 6, 1956, pp. 344-54. In this article I used the terms "extreme" and "restricted" instead of "act" and "rule" utilitarianism. I now prefer Brandt's terminology ("act" and "rule").
　　[5] For another discussion of what in effect is the same problem see A. K. Stout's excellent paper 'But suppose everyone did the same', *Australasian Journal of Philosophy*, vol. 32, 1954, pp. 1-29.
　　[6] Jeremy Bentham's most important ethical work is 'An Introduction to the Principles of Morals and Legislation', in *A Fragment on Government and an Introduction to the Principles of Morals and Legislation,* ed. Wilfred Harrison (Blackwell, Oxford, 1948). For the remark on poetry and pushpin see Bentham's *Works* (Tait, Edinburgh, 1843), vol. 2, pp. 253-4.
　　[7] G. E. Moore, *Principia Ethica* (Cambridge University Press, London, 1903).
　　[8] J. S. Mill, *Utilitarianism*, Everyman ed.

What Bentham, Mill and Moore are all agreed on is that the rightness of an action is to be judged solely by consequences, states of affairs brought about by the action. Of course we shall have to be careful here not to construe 'state of affairs' so widely that any ethical doctrine becomes utilitarian. For if we did so we would not be saying anything at all in advocating utilitarianism. If, for example, we allowed 'the state of having just kept a promise' to be a state of affairs brought about by keeping a promise, then a deontologist who said we should keep promises simply because they are promises would be a utilitarian. And we do not wish to allow this.

According to the type of non-cognitivist ethics that I am assuming, the function of the words 'ought' and 'good' is primarily to commend. With 'ought' we commend actions. With 'good' we may commend all sorts of things, but here I am concerned with 'good' as used to commend states of affairs or consequences of actions. Suppose we could know with certainty the total consequences of two alternative actions A and B, and suppose that A and B are the only possible actions open to us. Then in deciding whether we ought to do A or B, the act utilitarian would ask whether the total consequences of A are better than those of B, or vice versa, or whether the total consequences are equal. That is, he commends A rather than B if he thinks that the total consequences of A are better than those of B. But to say 'better' is itself to commend. So the act utilitarian has to do a double evaluation or piece of commending. First of all he has to evaluate consequences. Then on the basis of his evaluation of consequences he has to evaluate the actions A and B which would lead to these two sets of consequences. It is easy to fail to notice that this second evaluation is needed, but we can see that it is necessary if we remind ourselves of the following fact. This is that a non-utilitarian, say a philosopher of the type of Sir David Ross, might agree with us in our evaluation of the relative merits of the total sets of consequences of the actions A and B and yet disagree with us about whether we ought to do A or B. He might agree with us in the evaluation of total consequences but disagree with us in the evaluation of possible actions. He might say: 'The total consequences of A are better than the total consequences of B, but it would be *unjust* to do A, for you *promised* to do B'.

My chief concern in this study is with the *second* type of evaluation: the evaluation of actions. The people I am trying to convert will mostly agree with me about what consequences are good, but will disagree with me about whether we ought always to do that which will produce the best consequences. For a reason, which will appear presently, the differences between ideal and hedonistic utilitarianism in most cases will not lead to a serious disagreement about what ought to be done in practice. In this section, however, I wish to clear the ground by saying something about the *first* type of evaluation, the evaluation of consequences. It is with respect to this evaluation that Bentham, Mill and Moore differ from one another. Let us consider Mill's contention that it is 'better to be Socrates dissatisfied than a fool satisfied.[9] Mill holds that pleasure is not to be our sole criterion for evaluating consequences: the state of mind of Socrates might be less pleasurable than that of the fool, but, according to Mill, Socrates would be happier than the fool.

It is necessary to observe, first of all, that a purely hedonistic utilitarian, like Bentham, might agree with Mill in preferring the experiences of discontented philosophers to those of contented fools. His preference for the philosopher's state of mind however, would not be an *intrinsic* one. He would say that the discontented philosopher is a useful catalyst in society and that the existence of Socrates is responsible for an improvement in the lot of humanity generally. Consider two brothers. One may be of a docile and easy temperament: he may lead a supremely contented and unambitious life, enjoying himself hugely. The other brother may be ambitious, may stretch his talents to the full, may strive for scientific success and academic honours, and may invent something or discover some remedy for disease or improvement in agriculture which will enable innumerable men of easy temperament to lead a contented life, whereas otherwise they would have been thwarted by poverty, disease or hunger. Or he may make some advance in pure science which will later have beneficial practical applications. Or, again, he may write poetry which will solace the leisure hours and stimulate the brains of practical men or scientists, thus indirectly leading to an improvement in society. That is, the pleasures of poetry or mathematics may be *extrinsically* valuable in a way in which those of pushpin or sunbathing may not be. Though the poet or mathematician may be discontented, society as a whole may be the more contented for his presence.

Again, a man who enjoys pushpin is likely eventually to become bored with it, whereas the man who enjoys poetry is likely to retain this interest throughout his life. Moreover the reading of poetry may develop imagination and sensitivity, and so as a result of his interest in poetry a man may be able to do more for the happiness of others than if he had played pushpin and let his brain deteriorate. In short, both for the man immediately concerned and for others, the pleasures of poetry are, to use Bentham's words, more *fecund* than those of pushpin.

Perhaps, then, our preference for poetry over pushpin is not one of intrinsic value, but is merely one of extrinsic value. Perhaps strictly in itself and at a particular moment, a contented sheep is as good as a contented philosopher. However it is hard to agree to this. If we did we should have to agree that the human population ought ideally to be reduced by contraceptive methods and the sheep population more than correspondingly increased. Perhaps just so many humans should be left as could keep innumerable millions

---

[9] Op. cit., p. 9. The problem of the unhappy sage and the happy fool is cleverly stated in Voltaire's 'Histoire d'un bon Bramin', *Choix de Contes*, edited with an introduction and notes by F. C. Green (Cambridge University Press, London, 1951), pp. 245-7.

of placid sheep in contented idleness and immunity from depredations by ferocious animals. Indeed if a contented idiot is as good as a contented philosopher, and if a contented sheep is as good as a contented idiot, a contented fish is as good as a contented sheep, and a contented beetle is as good as a contented fish. Where shall we stop?

Maybe we have gone wrong in talking of pleasure as though it were no more than contentment. Contentment consists roughly in relative absence of unsatisfied desires; pleasure is perhaps something more positive and consists in a balance between absence of unsatisfied desires and presence of satisfied desires. We might put the difference in this way: pure unconsciousness would be a limiting case of contentment, but not of pleasure. A stone has no unsatisfied desires, but then it just has no desires. Nevertheless this consideration will not resolve the disagreement between Bentham and Mill. No doubt a dog has as intense a desire to discover rats as the philosopher has to discover the mysteries of the universe. Mill would wish to say that the pleasures of the philosopher were more valuable intrinsically than those of the dog, however intense these might be.

It appears, then, that many of us may well have a preference not only for enjoyment as such but for certain sorts of enjoyment. And this goes for many of the humane and beneficent readers whom I am addressing. I suspect that they too have an intrinsic preference for the more complex and intellectual pleasures. This is not surprising. We must not underrate the mere brute strength of a hard and fit human being: by any standards man is a large and strong animal. Nevertheless above all else man owes his survival to his superior intelligence. If man were not a species which was inclined above all else to think and strive, we should not be where we are now. And with the increase of modern science we need ever increasing thought and labour to survive. To take only one example, as cures are found for diseases more unfit people survive, more people of poor heredity are propagated, more medical science is required, and so on. We need all the intelligence we can muster to keep one jump ahead of the consequences of our own intelligence. No wonder that many of those who survive have a liking for intelligence and complexity, and this may become increasingly so in future. Perhaps some people may feel that my remarks here are somewhat too complacent, in view of the liking of so many people for low-grade entertainments, such as the allegedly moronic fodder of commercial television. But even the most avid television addict probably enjoys solving practical problems connected with his car, his furniture, or his garden. However unintellectual he might be, he would certainly resent the suggestion that he should, if it were possible, change places with a contented sheep, or even a lively and happy dog. Nevertheless, when all is said and done, we must not disguise the fact that disagreements in ultimate attitude are possible between those who like Mill have, and those who like Bentham have not, an intrinsic preference for the 'higher' pleasures. It is possible for two people to disagree about ultimate ends and yet agree in practice about what ought to be done. It is worth while enquiring how much practical ethics is likely to be affected by the possibility of disagreement over the question of Socrates dissatisfied versus the fool satisfied.

'Not very much', one feels like saying at first. We noted that the most complex and intellectual pleasures are also the most fecund. Poetry elevates the mind, makes one more sensitive, and so harmonizes with various intellectual pursuits, some of which are of practical value. Delight in mathematics is even more obviously, on Benthamite views, a pleasure worth encouraging, for on the progress of mathematics depends the progress of science, practical arts, and the physical and mental well-being of mankind. Even the most hedonistic schoolmaster would prefer to see his boys enjoying poetry and mathematics rather than neglecting these arts for the pleasures of marbles or the tuckshop. Indeed many of the brutish pleasures not only lack fecundity but are actually the reverse of fecund. To enjoy food too much is to end up fat, unhealthy and without zest or vigour. To enjoy drink too much is even worse. In most circumstances of ordinary life the pure hedonist will agree in his practical recommendations with the quasi-ideal utilitarian.

This need not always be so. Recently two psychologists, Olds and Milner, carried out some experiments with rats.[10] Through the skull of each rat they inserted an electrode. These electrodes penetrated to various regions of the brain. In the case of some of these regions the rat showed behavior characteristic of pleasure when a current was passed from the electrode, in others they seemed to show pain, and in others the stimulus seemed neutral. That a stimulus was pleasure-giving was shown by the fact that the rat would learn to pass the current himself by pressing a lever. He would neglect food and make straight for this lever and start stimulating himself. In some cases he would sit there pressing the lever every few seconds for hours on end. This calls up a pleasant picture of the voluptuary of the future, a bald-headed man with a number of electrodes protruding from his skull, one to give the physical pleasure of sex, one for that of eating, one for that of drinking, and so on. Now is this the sort of life that all our ethical planning should culminate in? A few hours' work a week, automatic factories, comfort and security from disease, and hours spent at a switch, continually electrifying various regions of one's brain? Surely not. Men were made for higher things, one can't help wanting to say, even though one knows that men weren't made for anything, but are the products of evolution by natural selection.

It might be said that the objection to continual sensual stimulation of the above sort is that though it would be pleasant in itself it would be infecund of future pleasures. This is certainly so with the ordinary sensual pleasures. Excessive indulgence in the physical pleasures of sex does have a debilitating effect and does interfere with the deeper feelings of romantic

---

10 James Olds and Peter Milner, 'Positive reinforcement produced by electrical stimulation of the septal area and other regions of the rat brain', *J. comp. physiol. Psychol.*, vol. 49, 1954, pp. 419-27; James Olds, 'A preliminary mapping of electrical reinforcing effect in the rat brain', *J. comp. physiol. Psychol.*, vol. 49, 1956, pp. 281-5.

love. But whether stimulation by the electrode method would have this weakening effect and whether it would impair the possibility of future pleasures of the same sort is another matter. For example, there would be no excessive secretion of hormones. The whole biochemical mechanism would, literally, be short-circuited. Maybe, however, a person who stimulated himself by the electrode method would find it so enjoyable that he would neglect all other pursuits. Maybe if everyone became an electrode operator people would lose interest in everything else and the human race would die out.

Suppose, however, that the facts turned out otherwise: that a man could (and would) do his full share of work in the office or the factory and come back in the evening to a few hours contented electrode work, without bad after-effects. This would be his greatest pleasure, and the pleasure would be so great intrinsically and so easily repeatable that its lack of fecundity would not matter. Indeed perhaps by this time human arts, such as medicine, engineering, agriculture and architecture will have been brought to a pitch of perfection sufficient to enable most of the human race to spend most of its time electrode operating, without compensating pains of starvation, disease and squalor. Would this be a satisfactory state of society? Would this be the millennium towards which we have been striving? Surely the pure hedonist would have to say that it was.

It is time, therefore, that we had another look at the concept of happiness. Should we say that the electrode operator was really happy? This is a difficult question to be clear about, for the concept of happiness is a tricky one. But whether we should call the electrode operator 'happy' or not, there is no doubt (a) that he would be *contented* and (b) that he would be *enjoying himself*.

Perhaps a possible reluctance to call the electrode operator 'happy' might come from the following circumstance. The electrode operator might be perfectly contented, might perfectly enjoy his electrode operating, and might not be willing to exchange his lot for any other. And we ourselves, perhaps, once we became electrode operators too, could become perfectly contented and satisfied. But nevertheless, as we are now, we just do not want to become electrode operators. We want other things, perhaps to write a book or get into a cricket team. If someone said 'from tomorrow onwards you are going to be forced to be an electrode operator' we should not be pleased. Maybe from tomorrow onwards, once the electrode work has started, we should be perfectly contented, but we are not contented now at the prospect. We are not satisfied at being told that we would be in a certain state from tomorrow onwards, even though we may know that from tomorrow onwards we shall be perfectly satisfied. All this is psychologically possible. It is just the obverse of a situation that we often find. Thus yesterday, as I first wrote this, I was suspended by cable car half-way up a precipitous mountain. While I was in the cable car and as I looked at the yawning chasm below I fervently wished that I had never come. When I bought the ticket for the cable car I knew that I should shortly be wishing that I had never bought it. And yet

I should have been annoyed if I had been refused it. Again, a man may be very anxious to catch a bus, so as to be in time for a dental appointment, and yet a few minutes later, while the drill is boring into his tooth, wish that he had missed that bus. It is, contrariwise, perfectly possible that I should be annoyed today if told that from tomorrow onwards I should be an electrode addict, even though I knew that from tomorrow onwards I should be perfectly contented.

This, I think, explains part of our hesitancy about whether to call the electrode operator 'happy'. The notion of happiness ties up with that of contentment: to be fairly happy at least involves being fairly contented, though it involves something more as well. Though we should be contented when we became electrode operators, we are not contented now with the prospect that we shall become electrode operators. Similarly if Socrates had become a fool he might thereafter have been perfectly contented. Nevertheless if beforehand he had been told that he would in the future become a fool he would have been even more dissatisfied than in fact he was. This is part of the trouble about the dispute between Bentham and Mill. The case involves the possibility of (a) our being contented if we are in a certain state, and (b) our being contented at the prospect of being so contented. Normally situations in which we should be contented go along with our being contented at the prospect of our getting into such a situation. In the case of the electrode operator and in that of Socrates and the fool we are pulled two ways at once.

Now to call a person 'happy' is to say more than that he is contented for most of the time, or even that he frequently enjoys himself and is rarely discontented or in pain. It is, I think, in part to express a favourable attitude to the idea of such a form of contentment and enjoyment. That is, for A to call B 'happy', A must be contented at the prospect of B being in his present state of mind and at the prospect of A himself, should the opportunity arise, enjoying that sort of state of mind. That is, 'happy' is a word which is mainly descriptive (tied to the concepts of contentment and enjoyment) but is partly evaluative. It is because Mill approves of the 'higher' pleasures, e.g. intellectual pleasures, so much more than he approves of the more simple and brutish pleasures, that, quite apart from consequences and side effects, he can pronounce the man who enjoys the pleasures of philosophic discourse as 'more happy' than the man who gets enjoyment from pushpin or beer drinking. ·

The word 'happy' is not wholly evaluative, for there would be something absurd, as opposed to merely unusual, in calling a man who was in pain, or who was not enjoying himself, or who hardly ever enjoyed himself, or who was in a more or less permanent state of intense dissatisfaction, a 'happy' man. For man to be happy he must, as a minimal condition, be fairly contented and moderately enjoying himself for much of the time. Once this minimal condition is satisfied we can go on to evaluate various type of contentment and enjoyment and to grade them in terms of happiness. Happiness is, of course, a long-term concept in a way that enjoyment is not. We can talk of a man enjoying himself at a quarter past two precisely, but hardly of a man being happy at a quarter past two precisely. Similarly we can talk of it raining at a quarter past two precisely, but hardly about it being a wet climate at a quarter past two precisely. But happiness involves enjoyment at various times, just as a wet climate involves rain at various times.

To be enjoying oneself, Ryle once suggested, is to be doing what you want to be doing and not to be wanting to do anything else,[11] or, more accurately, we might say that one enjoys oneself the more one wants to be doing what one is in fact doing and the less one wants to be doing anything else. A man will not enjoy a round of golf if (a) he does not particularly want to play golf, or (b) though he wants to play golf there is something else he wishes he were doing at the same time, such as buying the vegetables for his wife, filling in his income tax forms, or listening to a lecture on philosophy. Even sensual pleasures come under the same description. For example the pleasure of eating an ice-cream essentially involves having a certain physical sensation, in a way in which the pleasures of golf or symbolic logic do not, but the man who is enjoying an ice-cream can still be said to be doing what he wants to do (have a certain physical sensation) and not to be wanting to do anything else. If his mind is preoccupied with work or if he is conscious of a pressing engagement somewhere else, he will not enjoy the physical sensation, however intense it be, or will not enjoy it very much.

The hedonistic ideal would then appear to reduce to a state of affairs in which each person is enjoying himself. Since, as we noted, a dog may, as far as we can tell, enjoy chasing a ball as much as a mathematician may enjoy solving a problem, we must, if we adopt the purely hedonistic position, defend the higher pleasures on account of their fecundity. And that might not turn out to be a workable defence in a world made safe for electrode operators.

To sum up so far, happiness is partly an evaluative concept, and so the utilitarian maxim 'You ought to maximize happiness' is doubtly evaluative. There is the possibility of an ultimate disagreement between two utilitarians who differ over the question of pushpin versus poetry, or Socrates dissatisfied versus the fool satisfied. The case of the electrode operators shows that two utilitarians might come to advocate very different courses of actions if they differed about what constituted happiness, and this difference between them would be simply an ultimate difference in attitude. (Some other possibilities of the 'science fiction' type will be mentioned briefly in the final section of this study.) So I do not wish to say that the difference in ultimate valuation between a hedonistic and a non-hedonistic utilitarian will *never* lead to differences in practice.

Leaving these more remote possibilities out of account, however, and considering the decisions we have to make at present, the question of whether

---

[11] *The Concept of Mind* (Hutchinson, London, 1949), p. 108.

the 'higher' pleasures should be preferred to the 'lower' ones does seem to be of slight practical importance. There are already perfectly good hedonistic arguments for poetry as against pushpin. As has been pointed out, the more complex pleasures arc incomparably more fecund than the less complex ones: they are not only enjoyable in themselves but are a means to further enjoyment. Still less, on the whole, do they lead to disillusionment, physical deterioration or social disharmony. The connoisseur of poetry may enjoy himself no more than the connoisseur of whisky, but he runs no danger of a headache on the following morning. Moreover the question of whether the general happiness would be increased by replacing most of the human population by a bigger population of contented sheep and pigs is not one which by any stretch of the imagination could become a live issue. Even if we thought, on abstract grounds, that such a replacement would be desirable, we should not have the slightest chance of having our ideas generally adopted.

So much for the issue between Bentham and Mill. What about that between Mill and Moore? Could a pleasurable state of mind have no intrinsic value at all, or perhaps even a *negative* intrinsic value?[12] Are there pleasurable states of mind towards which we have an unfavourable attitude, even though we disregard their consequences? In order to decide this question let us imagine a universe consisting of one sentient being only, who falsely believes that there are other sentient beings and that they are undergoing exquisite torment. So far from being distressed by the thought, he takes a great delight in these imagined sufferings. Is this better or worse than a universe containing no sentient being at all? Is it worse, again, than a universe containing only one sentient being with the same beliefs as before but who sorrows at the imagined tortures of his fellow creatures? I suggest, as against Moore, that the universe containing the deluded sadist is the preferable one. After all he is happy, and since there is no other sentient being, what harm can he do? Moore would nevertheless agree that the sadist was happy, and this shows how happiness, though partly an evaluative concept, is also partly not an evaluative concept.

It is difficult, I admit, not to feel an immediate repugnance at the thought of the deluded sadist. If throughout our childhood we had been given an electric shock whenever we had tasted cheese, then cheese would have been immediately distasteful to us. Our repugnance to the sadist arises, naturally enough, because in our universe sadists invariably do harm. If we lived in a universe in which by some extraordinary laws of psychology a sadist was always confounded by his own knavish tricks and invariably did a great deal of good, then we should feel better disposed towards the sadistic mentality. Even if we could de-condition ourselves from feeling an immediate repugnance to a sadist (as we could de-condition ourselves from a repugnance to cheese by going through a course in which the taste of cheese was invariably associated with a pleasurable stimulus) language might make it

---

12 Cf. G. E. Moore, op. cit., pp. 209-10.

difficult for us to distinguish an extrinsic distaste for sadism, founded on our distaste for the consequences of sadism, from an immediate distaste for sadism as such. Normally when we call a thing 'bad' we mean indifferently to express a dislike for it in itself or to express a dislike for what it leads to. When a state of mind is sometimes extrinsically good and sometimes extrinsically bad, we find it easy to distinguish between our intrinsic and extrinsic preferences for instances of it, but when a state of mind is always, or most always, extrinsically bad, it is easy for us to confuse an extrinsic distaste for it with an intrinsic one. If we allow for this, it does not seem so absurd to hold that there are no pleasures which are intrinsically bad. Pleasures are bad only because they cause harm to the person who has them or to other people. But if anyone likes to disagree with me about this I do not feel very moved to argue the point. Such a disagreement about ultimate ends is not likely to lead to any disagreement in practice. For in all actual cases there are sufficient extrinsic reasons for abhorring sadism and similar states of mind. *Approximate* agreement about ultimate ends is often quite enough for rational and co-operative moral discourse. In practical cases the possibility of factual disagreement about what causes produce what effects is likely to be overwhelmingly more important than disagreement in ultimate ends between hedonistic and ideal utilitarians.

There are of course many valuations other than that of the intrinsic goodness of sadistic pleasures which divide the ideal from the hedonistic utilitarian. For example the ideal utilitarian would hold that an intellectual experience, even though not pleasurable, would be intrinsically good. Once more, however, I think we can convince ourselves that in most cases this disagreement about ends will not lead to disagreement about means. Intellectual experiences are in the hedonistic view extrinsically good. Of course there may be wider issues dividing the hedonistic from the ideal utilitarian, if Moore is the ideal utilitarian. I would argue that Moore's principle of organic unities destroys the essential utilitarianism of his doctrine. He need never disagree in practice, as a utilitarian ought to, with Sir David Ross. Every trick Ross can play with his prima facie duties, Moore can play, in a different way, with his organic unities.

AVERAGE HAPPINESS VERSUS TOTAL HAPPINESS

Another type of ultimate disagreement between utilitarians, whether hedonistic or ideal, arises over whether we should try to maximize the *average* happiness of human beings (or the average goodness of their states of mind) or whether we should try to maximize the *total* happiness or goodness. (I owe this point to Professor A. G. N. Flew.) I have not yet elucidated the concept of total happiness, and you may regard it as a suspect notion. But for present purposes I shall put it in this way: would you be quite indifferent between

(a) a universe containing only one million happy sentient beings, all equally happy, and (b) a universe containing two million happy beings, each neither more nor less happy than any in the first universe? Or would you, as a humane and sympathetic person, give a preference to the second universe? I myself cannot help feeling a preference for the second universe. But if someone feels the other way I do not know how to argue with him. It looks as though we have yet another possibility of disagreement within a general utilitarian framework.

This type of disagreement might have practical relevance. It might be important in discussions of the ethics of birth control. This is not to say that the utilitarian who values total, rather than average, happiness may not have potent arguments in favour of birth control. But he will need more arguments to convince himself than will the other type of utilitarian.

In most cases the difference between the two types of utilitarianism will not lead to disagreement in practice. For in most cases the most effective way to increase the total happiness is to increase the average happiness, and vice versa.

Negative Utilitarianism

K. R. Popper has suggested[13] that we should concern ourselves not so much with the maximization of happiness as with the minimization of suffering. By 'suffering' we must understand misery involving actual pain, not just unhappiness. For otherwise the doctrine becomes unclear. Suppose we found a new university. We may hope that indirectly research will help to minimize pains, but that is not the only reason why we found universities. We do so partly because we want the happiness of understanding the world. But producing the happiness of understanding could equally well be thought of as removing the unhappiness of ignorance.

Let us see what sort of utilitarian position we should develop if we made the minimization of misery our sole ultimate ethical principle. The doctrine of negative utilitarianism, that we should concern ourselves with the minimization of suffering rather than with the maximization of happiness, does seem to be a theoretically possible one. It does, however, have some very curious consequences, which have been pointed out by my brother, R. N. Smart.[14] In virtue of these very curious consequences I doubt whether negative utilitarianism will commend itself to many people, though it is always possible that someone might feel so attracted by the principle that he would accept it in spite of its consequences. For example it is easy to show that a negative utilitarian would have to be in favour of exterminating the human

[13] *The Open Society and its Enemies*, 1st, 2nd and 3rd edition (Routledge and Kegan Paul, London, 1945, 1952, 1957), vol. 1, ch. 5, note 6.
[14] *Mind*, vol. 67, 1958, pp. 542-4.

race. It seems likely that Popper is himself not a utilitarian, and so *a fortiori* not a negative utilitarian. For alongside the negative utilitarian principle he sets two principles, that we should tolerate the tolerant, and that we should resist tyranny.[15] It is hard to see how these principles could be deduced from the negative utilitarian principle, for surely, as my brother has pointed out, on this principle we should approve of a tyrannical but benevolent world exploder. Such a tyrant would prevent infinite future misery.

Though I am not attracted to negative utilitarianism as an ultimate principle, I do concede that the injunction 'worry about removing misery rather than about promoting happiness' has a good deal to recommend it as a subordinate rule of thumb. For in most cases we can do most for our fellow men by trying to remove their miseries. Moreover people will be less ready to agree on what goods they would like to see promoted than they will be to agree on what miseries should be avoided. Mill and Bentham might disagree on whether poetry should be preferred to pushpin, but they would agree that an occasional visit to the dentist is preferable to chronic toothache. While there are so many positive evils in the world there is plenty of scope for co-operative effort among men who may nevertheless disagree to some extent as to what constitute positive goods.

RIGHTNESS AND WRONGNESS OF ACTIONS

I shall now state the act utilitarian doctrine. I shall put it forward in a broadly hedonistic form. If anyone values states of mind such as knowledge independently of their pleasureableness he can make appropriate verbal alterations to convert it from hedonistic to ideal utilitarianism. And I shall not here take sides on the issue between hedonistic and quasi-ideal utilitarianism. I shall concern myself with the evaluation signified by 'ought' in 'one ought to do that which will produce the best consequences', and leave to one side the evaluation signified by the word 'best'.

Let us say, then, that the only reason for performing an action *A* rather than an alternative action *B* is that doing *A* will make mankind (or, perhaps, all sentient beings) happier than will doing *B*. This is so simple and natural a doctrine that we can surely expect that my readers, or at any rate those readers with whom I am interested in talking ethics, will have at least some propensity to agree. For I am talking, as I said earlier, to sympathetic and benevolent men, that is, to men who desire the happiness of mankind. Since they have a favourable attitude to the general happiness, surely they will have a tendency to submit to an ultimate moral principle which does no more than express this attitude. It is true that these men, being human, will also have purely selfish attitudes. Either these attitudes will be in harmony with the

---

[15] Popper, op. cit.

general happiness (in cases where everyone's looking after his own interests promotes the maximum general happiness) or they will not be in harmony with the general happiness, in which case they will largely cancel one another out, and so could not be made the basis of an interpersonal discussion any-way. It is my hypothesis, then, that sympathetic and benevolent people depart from or fail to attain a utilitarian ethical principle only under the stress of tradition, of superstition, or of unsound philosophical reasoning. If this hypothesis should turn out to be correct, then there will be little need to defend the utilitarian position directly, save by stating it in a consistent manner, and by showing that common objections to it are unsound. After all, it expresses an ultimate attitude, not a liking for something merely as a means to something else. Save for attempting to remove confusions and discredit superstitions which may get in the way of clear moral thinking, I cannot appeal to argument and must rest my hopes on the good feeling of my readers. If any reader is not a sympathetic and benevolent man, then of course I can-not expect him to have an ultimate pro-attitude to human happiness in gen-eral.

My ultimate moral principle, let it be remembered, expresses the senti-ment not of altruism but of benevolence, the agent counting himself neither more nor less than any other person. Pure altruism cannot be made the basis of a universal moral discussion in that it would lead different people to dif-ferent and perhaps incompatible courses of action, even though the circum-stances were identical. When two men each try to let the other through a door first a deadlock results. Altruism could hardly commend itself to those of a scientific, and hence universalistic, frame of mind. If you count in my calculations why should I not count in your calculations? And why should I pay more attention to my calculations than to yours? Of course we often tend to praise and honour altruism even more than generalized benevolence. This is because people too often err on the side of selfishness, and so altruism is a fault on the right side. If we can make a man try to be an altruist he may succeed as far as acquiring a generalized benevolence.

Suppose we could predict the future consequences of our actions with certainty. Then it would be possible to say that the total future consequences of action *A* are such-and-such and that the total future consequences of action *B* are so-and-so. In order to help him decide whether to do *A* or *B* we could say to a man: 'Envisage the total consequences of *A,* and think them over carefully and imaginatively. Now envisage the total consequences of *B,* and think them over carefully. As a benevolent and humane man, and thinking of yourself just as one man among others, would you prefer the consequences of *A* or those of *B*?' That is, we are asking for a comparison of one (present and future) *total* situation with another (present and future) *total* situa-tion. So far we are not asking for a *summation* or *calculation* of pleasures or happiness. We are asking only for a comparison of total situations. And it would be absurd to deny that we can frequently make such a com-parison and say that one total situation is better than another. For exam-

ple few people would not prefer a total situation in which a million people are well-fed, well-clothed, free of pain, doing interesting and enjoyable
work, and enjoying the pleasures of conversation, study, business, art, humour,
and so on, to a total situation where there are ten thousand such people only,
or perhaps 999,999 such people plus one man with toothache, or neurotic, or
shivering with cold. In general, we can sum things up by saying that if we
are humane, kindly, benevolent people, we want as many people as possible
now and in the future to be as happy as possible. Someone might object
that we cannot envisage the total future situation, because this stretches into
infinity. In reply to this we may say that it does not stretch into infinity,
as all sentient life on earth will ultimately be extinguished, and furthermore
we do not normally in practice need to consider very remote consequences, as
these in the end approximate rapidly to zero like the furthermost ripples on a
pond after a stone has been dropped into it.

But do the remote consequences of an action diminish to zero? Suppose
two people decide whether to have a child or remain childless. Let us suppose
that they decide to have the child, and that they have a limitless succession
of happy descendants. The remote consequences do not seem to get less.
Not at any rate if these people are Adam and Eve. The difference would be
between the end of the human race and a limitless accretion of human happiness, generation by generation. The Adam and Eve example shows that
the 'ripples on the pond' postulate is not needed in every case for a rational
utilitarian decision. If you had some reason for knowing that every generation would be more happy than not you would not need to be worried that
the remote consequences of your actions would be in detail unknown. The
necessity for the 'ripples in the pond' postulate comes from the fact that we
do not know whether remote consequences will be good or bad. Therefore
we cannot know what to do unless we can assume that remote consequences
can be left out of account. This can often be done. Thus if we consider
two actual parents, instead of Adam and Eve, then they need not worry
about thousands of years hence. Not, at least, if we assume that there will be
ecological forces determining the future population of the world. If these
parents do not have remote descendants, then other people will presumably
have more than they would otherwise. And there is no reason to suppose that
my descendants would be more or less happy than yours. We must note, then,
that unless we are dealing with 'all or nothing' situations (such as the Adam
and Eve one, or that of someone in a position to end human life altogether)
we need some sort of 'ripples in the pond' postulate to make utilitarianism
workable in practice. I do not know how to prove such a postulate, though it
seems plausible enough. If it is not accepted, not only utilitarianism, but also
deontological systems like that of Sir David Ross, who at least admits beneficence as one prima facie duty among the others, will be fatally affected.

Sometimes, of course, more needs to be said. For example one course
of action may make some people very happy and leave the rest as they are or
perhaps slightly less happy. Another course of action may make all men

rather more happy than before but no one very happy. Which course of action makes mankind happier on the whole? Again, one course of action may make it highly probable that everyone will be made a little happier whereas another course of action may give us a much smaller probability that everyone will be made very much happier. In the third place, one course of action may make everyone happy in a pig-like way, whereas another course of action may make a few people happy in a highly complex and intellectual way.

It seems therefore that we have to weigh the maximizing of happiness against equitable distribution, to weigh probabilities with happiness, and to weigh the intellectual and other qualities of states of mind with their pleasurableness. Are we not therefore driven back to the necessity of some calculus of happiness? Can we just say: 'envisage two total situations and tell me which you prefer'? If this were possible, of course there would be no need to talk of summing happiness or of a calculus. All we should have to do would be to put total situations in an order of preference. Since this is not always possible there is a difficulty, to which I shall return shortly.

We have already considered the question of intellectual versus non-intellectual pleasures and activities. This is irrelevant to the present issue because there seems no reason why the ideal or quasi-ideal utilitarian cannot use the method of envisaging total situations just as much as the hedonistic utilitarian. It is just a matter of envisaging various alternative total situations, stretching out into the future, and saying which situation one prefers. The non-hedonistic utilitarian may evaluate the total situations differently from the hedonistic utilitarian, in which case there will be an ultimate ethical disagreement. This possibility of ultimate disagreement is always there, though we have given reasons for suspecting that it will not frequently lead to important disagreement in practice.

Let us now consider the question of equity. Suppose that we have the choice of sending four equally worthy and intelligent boys to a medium-grade public school or of leaving three in an adequate but uninspiring high school and sending one to Eton. (For sake of the example I am making the almost certainly incorrect assumption that Etonians are happier than other public-school boys and that these other public-school boys are happier than high-school boys.) Which course of action makes the most for the happiness of the four boys? Let us suppose that we can neglect complicating factors, such as that the superior Etonian education might lead one boy to develop his talents so much that he will have an extraordinary influence on the well-being of mankind, or that the unequal treatment of the boys might cause jealousy and rift in the family. Let us suppose that the Etonian will be as happy as (we may hope) Etonians usually are, and similarly for the other boys, and let us suppose that remote effects can be neglected. Should we prefer the greater happiness of one boy to the moderate happiness of all four? Clearly one parent may prefer one total situation (one boy at Eton and three at the grammar school) while another may prefer the other total situation (all four at the medium-grade public school). Surely both parents have an equal claim to being sympathetic and benevolent, and yet their difference of opinion here is not founded on an empirical disagreement about facts. I suggest, however, that there are not in fact many cases in which such a disagreement could arise. Probably the parent who wished to send one son to Eton would draw the line at sending one son to Eton plus giving him expensive private tuition during the holidays plus giving his other sons no secondary education at all. It is only within rather small limits that this sort of disagreement about equity can arise. Furthermore the cases in which we can make one person *very* much happier without increasing *general* happiness are rare ones. The law of diminishing returns comes in here. So, in most practical cases, a disagreement about what should be done will be an empirical disagreement of opinion about what total situation is likely to be brought about by an action, and will not be a disagreement about which total situation is preferable. For example the inequalitarian parent would get the other to agree with him if he could convince him that there was a much higher probability of Etonians benefiting the human race, such as by inventing a valuable drug or opening up the mineral riches of Antarctica, than there is of a non-Etonian doing so. (Once more I should like to say that I do not myself take such a possibility very seriously!) I must again stress that since disagreement about what causes produce what effects is in practice so much the more important sort of disagreement, to have intelligent moral discussion with a person we do not in fact need complete agreement with him about ultimate ends: an approximate agreement is sufficient.

Rawls[16] has suggested that we must maximize the general happiness only if we do so in a *fair* way. An *unfair* way of maximizing the general happiness would be to do so by a method which involved making some people less happy than they might be otherwise.[17] As against this suggestion I would make the following rhetorical objection: if it is rational for me to choose the pain of a visit to the dentist in order to prevent the pain of toothache, why is it not rational of me to choose a pain for Jones, similar to that of my visit to the dentist, if that is the only way in which I can prevent a pain, equal to that of my toothache, for Robinson? Such situations continually occur in war, in mining, and in the fight against disease, when we may often find ourselves in the position of having in the general interest to inflict suffering on good and happy men. However I concede that my objections against fairness as an *ultimate* principle must be rhetorical only, and that Rawls's principle could perhaps be incorporated in a restrained system of deontological ethics, which would avoid the artificiality of the usual forms of deontology. There are in any case plenty of good utilitarian reasons for adopting the principle of fairness as an important, but not inviolable, rule of thumb.

16 'Justice as Fairness', *Philosophical Review*, vol. 67, 1958, pp. 164-94.
17 See especially p. 168 of Rawls's article.

We must now deal with the difficulty about probability. We have so far avoided the common objection to utilitarianism that it involves the allegedly absurd notion of a summation or calculus of happiness or goodness. We have done this by using the method of comparing total situations. All we have to do is to envisage two or more total situations and say which we prefer. A purely ordinal, not a quantitative, judgment is all we require. However in taking this position we have oversimplified the matter. Unfortunately we cannot say with certainty what would be the various total situations which could result from our actions. Worse still, we cannot even assign rough probabilities to the total situations as a whole. All we can do is to assign various probabilities to the various possible effects of an action. For example, one course of action may almost certainly lead to a fairly good result next year together with a high probability of a slightly good result the year after, while another action may give a very small probability of a superlatively good result next year with a quite small probability of a moderately good result the year after and a very small but not negligible probability of a rather bad result the year after that. (I am assuming that in both cases the still more remote results become negligible or such as to cancel one another out.) If we had to weight total situations with probabilities, this would give us enough conceptual difficulty, but it now appears that we have to go within total situations and weight different elements within them according to different probabilities. We seem to be driven back towards a calculus.

If it were possible to assign numerical probabilities to the various effects of our actions we could devise a way of applying the total situation method. Suppose that we could say that an action X would either give Smith the pleasure of eating ice-cream with probability 4/5 or the pain of toothache with probability 1/5 and that it would give Jones the pleasure of sympathy with probability 3/5 or the displeasure of envy with probability 2/5 and that no other important results (direct or indirect) would accrue. Suppose that the only alternative action to X is Y and that this has no effect on Smith but causes Jones to go to sleep with probability 3/5 or to go for a walk with probability 2/5 and that no other important results (direct or indirect) would accrue. Then we could say that the total situations we have to imagine and to compare are (a) (for X):four people (just like Smith) eating ice-cream plus one (just like Smith) with toothache plus three sympathetic people (just like Jones) plus two envious people (just like Jones), and (b) (for Y): three people (just like Jones) who are asleep plus two (just like Jones) going for a walk. In the example I have, for convenience, taken all probabilities to be multiples of 1/5. If they did not have common denominators we should have to make them such, by expressing them as multiples of a denominator which is the lowest common multiple of the original denominators.

However it is not usually possible to assign a numerical probability to a particular event. No doubt we could use actuarial tables to ascertain the probability that a friend of ours, who is of a certain age, a certain carefully specified medical history, and a certain occupation, will die within the next year. But can we give a numerical value to the probability that a new war will break out, that a proof of Fermat's theorem will be found, or that our knowledge of genetical linkage in human chromosomes will be much improved in the next five years? Surely it is meaningless to talk of a numerical value for these probabilities, and it is probabilities of this sort with which we have to deal in our moral life.

When, however, we look at the way in which in fact we take some of our ordinary practical decisions we see that there is a sense in which most people think that we can weigh up probabilities and advantages. A man deciding whether to migrate to a tropical country may well say to himself, for example, that he can expect a pleasanter life for himself and his family in that country, unless there is a change in the system of government there, which is not very likely, or unless one of his children catches an epidemic disease, which is perhaps rather more likely, and so on, and thinking over all these advantages and disadvantages and probabilities and improbabilities he may come out with the statement that on the whole it seems preferable for him to go there or with the statement that on the whole it seems preferable for him to stay at home.

If we are able to take account of probabilities in our ordinary prudential decisions it seems idle to say that in the field of ethics, the field of our universal and humane attitudes, we cannot do the same thing, but must rely on some dogmatic morality, in short on some set of rules or rigid criteria. Maybe sometimes we just will be unable to say whether we prefer for humanity an improbable great advantage or a probable small advantage, and in these cases perhaps we shall have to toss a penny in deciding what to do. Maybe we have not any precise methods for deciding what to do, but then our imprecise methods must just serve their turn. We need not on that account be driven into authoritarianism, dogmatism or romanticism.

So, at any rate, it appears at first sight. But if I cannot say any more my position has a serious weakness. My method of developing normative ethics is to appeal to feelings, namely of benevolence, and to reason, in the sense of conceptual clarification and also of empirical enquiry, but not, as so many moralists do, to what the ordinary man says or thinks. The ordinary man is frequently irrational in his moral thinking. And if he can be irrational about morals why cannot he be irrational about probabilities? The fact that the ordinary man thinks that he can weigh up probabilities in making prudential decisions does not mean that there is really any sense in what he is doing. What utilitarianism badly needs, in order to make its theoretical foundations secure, is some method according to which numerical probabilities, even approximate ones, could in theory, though not necessarily always in practice, be assigned to any imagined future event.

D. Davidson and P. Suppes[18] have proposed a method whereby, at any rate in simplified situations, *subjective* probabilities can be given a numerical

---

[18] *Decision Making* (Stanford University Press, Stanford, California, 1957).

value. Their theory was to some extent anticipated in an essay by F. P. Ramsey, in which he tries to show how numbers can be assigned to probabilities in the sense of degrees of belief.[19] This allows us to give a theory of rational, in the sense of *self-consistent,* utilitarian choice, but to make utilitarianism thoroughly satisfactory we need something more. We need a method of assigning numbers to *objective,* not subjective probabilities. Perhaps one method might be to accept the Davidson-Suppes method of assigning subjective probabilities, and define objective probabilities as the subjective probabilities of an unbiassed and far-sighted man. This, however, would require independent criteria for lack of bias and for far-sightedness. I do not know how to do this, but I suspect, from the work that is at present being done on decision-making, that the situation may not be hopeless. But until we have an adequate theory of *objective* probability utilitarianism is not on a secure theoretical basis. Nor, for that matter, is ordinary prudence; nor are deontological systems of ethics, like that of Sir David Ross, which assign some weight to beneficence. And any system of deontological ethics implies some method of weighing up the claims of conflicting prima facie duties, for it is impossible that deontological rules of conduct should *never* conflict, and the rationale of this is even more insecure than is the theory of objective probability.

[19] F. P. Ramsey, *The Foundations of Mathematics* (Routledge and Kegan Paul, London, 1931), Chapter 7.

20

THE RIGHT ACT
IS TO PROMOTE
ONE'S OWN WELFARE:
EGOISM

Gardner Williams

Gardner Williams (1895-   ) is Professor Emeritus of Philosophy at Toledo University.

. . . The good is the satisfactory. The satisfactory is anything which causes a feeling of satisfaction, or any experience which contains this feeling. The good also is equivalently defined as anything which is *needed.* Everyone needs what is satisfactory simply because it is satisfactory. The good is the same as the valuable. It is anything that has value. There are two kinds of good, intrinsic and extrinsic, and two corresponding kinds of value. Intrinsic good has intrinsic or primary value, and extrinsic good has extrinsic or secondary value.

Primary value is the feeling of satisfaction. It is the felt intrinsic satisfactoriness which any experience may have or contain. It, and its opposite, dissatisfaction or intrinsic disvalue, are probably produced by neural processes in the central nervous system. These feelings are not sensations or desires or ideas. They are called, respectively, positive and negative feeling-tone, or positive and negative affects, or pleasure-pain. I do not think that they can be analyzed into simpler experiential elements. Like any ultimate qualities of experience they can be referred to or pointed at. They can not be described. No one could understand what was meant by the words "satisfaction" and "dissatisfaction" if he had never experienced the kinds of consciousness to which these words refer. But everybody has experienced such consciousness. All experience is immediately felt as being either satisfactory or unsatisfactory, and probably almost all is simultaneously felt as being both, in varying proportions. Possibly some experience is absolutely pure joy, and possibly some is pure anguish, but probably very little is pure in either of these senses.

From Gardner Williams, "Individual, Social, and Universal Ethics," *The Journal of Philosophy*, XLV (1948), pp. 645-55. Reprinted by kind permission of the author and of the editors of the *Journal of Philosophy*.

From this meaning of primary value it will follow that our theory may properly be called an *affective axiology*. Feeling-tone or affect is the *axiological absolute*. This feeling is basic in determining all good and evil, though of course it depends for its existence upon the life processes of a biological organism. It is axiologically primary and ultimate, but it is ontologically and metaphysically secondary, dependent, peripheral, and ephemeral.

An *intrinsic good,* we have indicated, is an experience that has primary value. It is any total happy experience as of any given moment. It will be a complex *gestalt* including, in many cases, sensation, imagination, desire, perhaps a rational concept, retrospection, anticipation, and feeling-tone. The *primary value* or feeling-tone is, like each of the other elements, a quality or abstract aspect of the complex total.

An *extrinsic good* is an instrumental good. It has secondary value. It is a cause of intrinsic good. The *secondary value* which it has, and which makes it instrumentally good, is its causal relation to intrinsic good.

This terminology, combined with some sound psychological principles, commits us to a radical individualism. Our theory may properly be called an *affective axiological individualism.* For all intrinsic goods are individual, since they are total complexes of consciousness or experience, which is always individual. The individuality of all experience may be disputed, and it can not be proved beyond peradventure, but it is indicated by the truth that only a biological organism can be conscious. This too may be disputed. Disembodied spirits, or portions of spirits, might exist. But scientific psychology indicates pretty clearly that all consciousness depends for its existence upon the neurones of a biological organism. Then since such organisms are individual, that is, since they are spatially distinct from each other, so are people's consciousnesses, perhaps with the exception of any Siamese twins who might have parts of their central nervous systems in common. Barring such abnormalities, consciousness is in every case tied down to the neurones of an individual, separate, and distinct biological organism. Minds never merge or overlap if persons are not Siamese twins, and they seldom or never do even in these linked organisms. Ideas never fly through the air from one mind to another. The group mind is a fiction, unless it is just the interactions or inter-communication of a number of individual minds. Communication occurs, but it is never a direct contact of mind with mind. It is never intuitive. It is always effected through some physical medium. We must reject the theory of mental telepathy, which is that one mind can apprehend directly the thoughts in other minds. Supposed telepathy is either an unintentional error, or a fraud, or else it is signalling from a distance, through physical media which are not now understood, and which stimulate sense organs which have not yet been located. We must also reject the theory of Platonic universals, the view that one identical universal concept can exist simultaneously or successively in several minds which are located in distinct bodies spatially separated from each other.

If, then, all experience is absolutely individual in its existence, all intrinsic good must be individual, for intrinsic good is experience. Moreover, every primary value must be individual, for it will in every case belong to an individual intrinsic good. Also all instrumental goods are purely individual in the sense that they are good only because of their causal relations to individual intrinsic goods. And secondary values are individual in the sense that they are always causal relations between some instrumental good and an individual intrinsic good.

This value theory is also in some sense relativistic. Its full name is *affective axiological individualistic relativism*. Instrumental goods are relative by definition. They are things causally *related* to some intrinsic goods and values. Secondary value is relative in the sense that it *is* this causal relation. Even intrinsic good is in a sense relative. This may seem like a contradiction in terms, but at least we must recognize that the terminology of relativism applies properly to it, for an intrinsic good is intrinsically good only in and to itself. It has its primary value inside itself. This value may be known and appreciated by others, but the only value that an intrinsic good can actually have to others is an instrumental value. Anything that can be a cause can have instrumental value. An intrinsic good which causes another intrinsic good to exist will have both its own primary value within itself and a secondary value, which is its causal relation to the other intrinsic good. It will be simultaneously both an intrinsic good in itself, and an instrumental good to all individuals in whom it causes satisfaction. It will cause this in the souls of all who sympathize with and love the person that contains it, and in all who are made happy by the knowledge that this person has intrinsic value and is happy. Its ultimate justification or value, from their points of view, depends upon the satisfaction which they feel as a result of it.

All good, then, is relative. Nothing can be good at all unless it is good for at least some one individual. The good, for him, is always what he needs and what satisfies him. This is always determined by his actual individual character or nature. What is good for a canary bird is determined by the nature of the canary bird, and what is good for a man is determined by the nature of the man. Moreover, when something is in fact good for him, there is no logical necessity that it should be good for anybody else. Others may not need it. It may not satisfy them. Their natures may be different from his, by biological inheritance or by training. His good often *is* good for others, but that is because their natures are similar to his, or because they love him, or because his well-being enables him to help them.

This relativistic theory does not mean that there is nothing either good or bad but *thinking* makes it so. Rather the principle is that there is nothing either good or bad but *feeling* makes it so. Feeling, the axiological absolute, however, is not the goal of all desire. Nor ought it to be. The egoistic hedonists were wrong in thinking that it should be. But they were right in thinking that it is the ultimate value and justification of whatever is morally justified and worthy. This affective axiology reiterates what is true in their ancient, oft libelled, and seldom understood doctrine.

This axiological theory is also in the tradition of the interest theory of value, the essential truth of which is that the intrinsic good of any individual is the satisfactions involved in, and resulting from, the fulfillment of his major interests or desires such as love, ambition, and the desires for truth, for beauty, and for sensuous enjoyment.

We now come to the definitions of right and duty. These are equivalent terms. One always has a duty to do what is right, and it is always right for one to do his duty. The meaning of these terms is to be derived from the meanings which we have already found for good and value. An individual always has a duty, from his own point of view, to attain as nearly as possible his highest good. His highest good is that which is most deeply satisfactory to him in the long run. An equivalent statement of this principle of obligation is that he always ought to do what he needs the most. His duty to attain this objective as nearly as possible is a *categorical imperative*. It is unconditionally binding upon him, from his own point of view. Such an imperative is binding, without exception, upon every individual that is capable of experiencing satisfaction or dissatisfaction. This principle of duty is universal and absolute. It is a definition. I think that we ought to adopt this definition because it is the one which will help us the most in understanding man's moral experience.

This theory indicates that there is a plurality of ultimate moral standards, one for each conscious organism, each standard being determined by the individual nature of its organism. What is a duty for one, from his point of view, may be contrary to the duty of another, from the other's point of view; and there is no standard by which either of these duties may be validly proclaimed absolutely right apart from all points of view, or right from every point of view, or right from one absolute point of view. How, then, shall we discover, and how shall we validate, social obligations? I shall maintain that social ethics exists, that it is valid, and that its validity is derived from individual moral imperatives which are ultimate.

An individual has a duty to help others if, when, and because he needs to help them. Helping them is an individual moral imperative of his whenever it will satisfy him most deeply in the long run. In his helpfulness he will be, in part, selfish in the ordinary sense. He will help others as a means to getting help from them in return. This is ethical. No moral taint attaches when he pays his debts and respects his neighbors' rights in order to secure services and consideration for himself. Should he omit to give what society demands of him he will be made to suffer. Society can inflict terrible punishments upon almost anybody. Also it can bestow valuable rewards upon those who coöperate. It is constantly rewarding those who have not broken the law, by letting them circulate about freely and say pretty much what they think. It gives thrilling honors and distinctions to those who are thought to have made outstanding contributions. Each individual ought to try to coöperate and to make a creative contribution partly because he needs to avoid social penalties and to enjoy great social distinction. He needs these rewards because he will be dissatisfied if he does not get them, and because he will be deeply satisfied if he does get them.

Man's duty to help others is, then, based partly on ordinary selfishness. It is also based partly on ordinary unselfishness, benevolence, or love. Love aims ultimately at the welfare of others. When love is combined with the sensuous desires of sex it is called romantic love. But it may exist independently of sex, as in mother-love or in the brotherly love which has always been the leading principle of Christian ethical teaching. *A*'s love for *B* is a desire, located in *A*'s soul, whose objective is *B*'s welfare, considered not as a means to any further end, but as a final goal. *A*'s desire, so to speak, terminates upon its object *B*. *A*'s love is satisfied when *A* can help *B* to be happy and when *A* knows that *B* is happy. Successful love always satisfies the lover. A mother enjoys caring for her children and knowing that they are well-off. She does not aim at this enjoyment. She aims at the children's enjoyment. But the joy or satisfaction which she feels is the intrinsic value of her love to her. From her point of view she ought to lavish her loving care upon her children because *she* enjoys having them happy. The "cause" involved in this "because" is not Aristotle's final cause; it is his formal cause. Her own joy is not her goal. But by definition it characterizes what she ought to do.

The primary value or satisfaction which she experiences is purely selfish in the sense that it is part of herself. Her love too is purely selfish in the sense that it is part of herself, and that its expression is her self-expression. But this is not the ordinary meaning of selfishness. This is a Pickwickian selfishness which consists in being and in expressing one's own individual self. Ordinary selfishness, on the other hand, consists in pursuing one's own future welfare and self-expression as a final objective. This Pickwickian individualistic selfishness is absolutely inescapable as long as one lives. No man can desire or enjoy anything unless it is his individual self that desires and enjoys it. And clearly no moral taint is necessarily involved in this.

In caring for others by reason of selfish prudence one is selfish both in the ordinary and in the Pickwickian senses. In caring for others by reason of one's love, one is selfish only in the Pickwickian sense.

Let us reformulate the ultimate principle of duty so as to include the compelling social obligations which are binding upon each person because of the needs of his own nature. Every individual has a duty, from his own point of view, to attain as nearly as possible (1) his own maximum satisfaction in the long run, (2) that of those whom he loves, to the extent that he loves them, (3) that of those who will help him, to the extent that they will help, and (4) that of those who will coöperate with his institutions, so far as they will coöperate. But clearly his duties, from his own point of view, to attain the second, third, and fourth items, are all due to the fact that these things will be satisfactory to him. They are all obligatory, from his point of view, because of the first item. All duty to others is ultimately analyzable into an individual duty to maximize individual satisfaction.

We must in no way belittle the importance of society in this individualistic theory. When an individual confronts society he should realize that all of the people who make it up generate just as completely autonomous authorities as he does, and he ought to know that the social value of his behavior depends upon their intrinsic satisfactions. Social value, however, *is* always secondary value. The social value of his love for his children is its causal relations to all of the satisfactions which it produces, directly or indirectly, in other people. If his loving care helps to make his children happy, it has a certain social value to them. If it helps to make them useful citizens, it has added social values to many other people who are helped by his children, and whose happiness thus results, indirectly, from his love for his children.

Society is also very important because of the imperious demands which it makes upon every individual member, and because of the tremendous power which it exercises over individual satisfactions, to back up these demands. Society requires that each individual make certain contributions, and that he conform to laws, mores, and folkways. We have already referred to the fact that it often makes individuals happy who contribute and conform, and it often makes individuals miserable who do not. But axiological individualism is not impugned by these facts. Society's demands are only the demands of individuals seeking what will satisfy them. A social demand is, more accurately, just a lot of individual demands. Each of the citizens requires that an individual contribute and conform, largely so that each of the citizens' lives may be safe, prosperous, and happy. And an individual ought in most cases to contribute and conform largely because that will tend to make his own life safe, prosperous, and happy.

Although society is very powerful, still its might does not essentially or necessarily make right. Society's power to punish an individual and to make him miserable does not necessarily make his misery good for him. A man's misery is good for him only if it causes him to be more deeply satisfied later on. Sometimes it does this. It may strengthen his character and discipline his spirit and thus help him eventually to triumph over the obstacles which once blocked his path. This is the redemptive power of suffering. But the fact that the force of society imposes the suffering does not guarantee this blessed eventuality. Force may, of course, make the right exist or cause it to prevail. A social order, which is right for those who benefit from it, is caused to exist by force. It would be destroyed by its enemies if force were not used for its protection. But force will sometimes make the wrong prevail. Not force, but long-range individual satisfaction is the only essential characteristic which necessarily and universally makes a thing right.

The tremendous power which society wields is exerted in the endeavor to bring each individual's right into conformity with society's demands. When it rewards a man for doing what it approves, it makes his doing this very satisfactory to him, and thus in most cases it tends to harmonize his highest good with the highest goods of its other members. When it punishes him for doing what is a wrong to it, it makes this wrong also wrong to him, for his act thus brings suffering to himself. But there are exceptions to this. Sometimes it fails to reward its friends and to punish its enemies. And even when it succeeds, by rewards and punishments, in making social coöperation right for any individual, still this is only Aristotle's efficient making or causing, not his formal or essential making or causing.

Moreover, when society thus succeeds, its success is directly attributable to the natures of the individuals involved. Society can not reward an individual unless he needs what it can give. It could not reward a man who found no joy in honor or status or wealth or security or love. It could not punish an individual who was indifferent to any attempted punishment it might seek to inflict. It could not torture him unless he was an organism capable of experiencing either mental anguish or sensory pain. It can execute him, but if that is just what he desires most, his death will, from his point of view, be a reward and not a punishment.

The worst of all social conflicts, war, can be properly evaluated only from individual points of view. A successful war might be a benefit to most of the people of a nation. It would be, so far as it saved them from slavery or gave them prosperity and freedom. For them it would be good. The same war would be evil to its victims, and possibly to nearly everyone in the defeated country, if, as sometimes happens, most of these folks were enslaved, impoverished, or killed. Then the freedom and prosperity which the victorious power achieved might help to launch it on a career of aggression which might end in disaster for itself three generations hence. Then its original victory will have been good for most of its citizens who were there at the time, but bad for most of their descendants in the third generation. What is good for the individuals of one generation may be bad for those of a later one in the same country, or anywhere else. However, so far as people are not satisfied with a system which protects them but threatens disaster to their descendants, that system is bad for them.

It should be clear that a federal world government ought to be set up. Probably most people now and in the future would live more satisfactory lives if this were done, with representative democracy and with safeguards to individual freedom. Then from these people's points of view, such a state ought to be created. This state would work hardships on some who have vested interests in nationalistic separatism and aggression. For them, the added satisfactions, if any, from world peace would not compensate for the frustrations. From their points of view a world state would be evil. Then it is our duty, from our points of view, to inflict this evil upon them, and to crush their opposition, by force, if we must, and if we can, because to do so would be more deeply satisfactory to us in the long run.

The clash of autonomous individual axiological standards comes out very clearly in crime. Consider a dangerous felon who has been properly sentenced to life imprisonment for murder. Here the highest good of most of the law-abiding citizens demands his incarceration. He must not be allowed to get away with murder. His punishment is required in order to help protect their lives and property. But it might be better for him, from his point of view, to escape. He might be better satisfied. On the other hand, in some cases he would not be better satisfied. Worry and a bad conscience might make such an individual more dissatisfied than if he had stayed in jail. But I think that there are cases where escape would be more satisfactory in the long run for such a felon. A life lived in the open might be happier. If so, to escape would be his duty, — from his own point of view. If maximum individual long-range satisfaction makes duty for decent people it does so for rascals also. It does so for all conscious organisms. The principle is universal.

There are three senses in which genuine universality appears in ethical theory.

First off, as we have already seen, the ultimate principle of individualistic relativism is itself universal by definition.

In a second form, universality is present in ethics, in that, from the point of view of any conscious individual, all things in the universe without exception ought to help him because he needs their help. All of his needs for satisfactory living ought, from his point of view, to be met. From a citizen's point of view a felon ought not to escape, and everything in the universe ought to conspire to prevent him from escaping. But from the culprit's point of view everything and everybody ought to help him escape, if that would be more deeply satisfactory to him in the long run.

Of course a normal citizen will repudiate this latter obligation because it is not imposed upon him by his own point of view. He knows that, as St. Thomas said, he must be true to his *own* highest good, which is God. Also the criminal will repudiate the duty created by the citizen's need. In this ultimate conflict of categorical individual duties, involving, obviously, war in heaven, force determines what is done on earth. The power of organized society will have to be exerted in order to inflict the legal penalty upon the culprit. Force, we have seen, does not determine essentially what ought to be done. The battles of the gods, that is, the final conflicts of human ideals, are not settled by force. They are not settled. The ultimate brittle good of one individual contestant may be in grim, tight-lipped, and unyielding conflict with the ultimate brittle good of another individual contestant.

Men often grasp vaguely the truth that from their own points of view the whole universe ought to help them and ought to further what they are interested in; and then they unwarrantably infer that *apart from any point of view*, that is, objectively, it ought to do so. They have not yet fully grasped that the highest good of one individual may be contrary to the highest good of another. Their thinking is still on the level of the sort of objective ethics which denies axiological individualism. To free oneself from the belief in this kind of objectivity is an indispensable step in ethical enlightenment.

Universality is present in ethics in a third form, in that the truth about every particular good and value is, like all truth, absolutely universal. This will be seen if we compare two propositions:

(1) Criminal A says truly, "It is false that (X) this punishment of A is good for me."
(2) Citizen B says truly, "It is true that (Y) this punishment of A is good for me."

It may seem as if sentences X and Y were one proposition and that this proposition is true for citizen B and false for criminal A. But nothing that is true for one can be false for another, or *vice versa*. Sentences X and Y express different propositions because "me" has a different meaning in each. It means criminal A in X and citizen B in Y. Assuming that criminal A would be better satisfied if he escaped, proposition X is universally false in the sense that whenever anyone asserts exactly that subjective meaning or proposition, namely, that "the punishment of criminal A is good for A," it is false no matter who says it, and no matter what words are used. And proposition Y is universally true in the sense that whenever anyone asserts exactly that meaning, that "the punishment of criminal A is good for citizen B," it is true no matter who says it, and no matter what words are used.

Thus in three senses value, good, and duty are universal; and at the same time, in another sense, without contradiction, they are all purely individual, relative, and thus obviously subjective.

However they are also genuinely objective in another sense, namely, that they are real independently of anyone's cognitive ideas about them. What actually satisfies individual need is good no matter whether anybody knows that it does so or not. The good is the satisfactory and some things really are satisfactory. This doctrine is not nihilism. It shows the invalidity, not of morals, but of prevalent alternative theories about morals. It does this because it reveals the actual ground and nature of all genuine moral obligation.

21

EGOISM CLAIMED
INCONSISTENT

Brian Medlin

Brian Medlin (1927-   ) is a Fellow in New College, Oxford.

I believe that it is now pretty generally accepted by professional philosophers that ultimate ethical principles must be arbitrary. One cannot derive conclusions about what should be merely from accounts of what is the case; one cannot decide how people ought to behave merely from one's knowledge of how they do behave. To arrive at a conclusion in ethics one must have at least one ethical premiss. This premiss, if it be in turn a conclusion, must be the conclusion of an argument containing at least one ethical premiss. And so we can go back, indefinitely but not for ever. Sooner or later, we must come to at least one ethical premiss which is not deduced but baldly asserted. Here we must be a-rational; neither rational nor irrational, for here there is no room for reason even to go wrong.

But the triumph of Hume in ethics has been a limited one. What appears quite natural to a handful of specialists appears quite monstrous to the majority of decent intelligent men. At any rate, it has been my experience that people who are normally rational resist the above account of the logic of moral language, not by argument — for that can't be done — but by tooth and nail. And they resist from the best motives. They see the philosopher wantonly unravelling the whole fabric of morality. If our ultimate principles are arbitrary, they say, if those principles came out of thin air, then anyone can hold any principle he pleases. Unless moral assertions are statements of fact about the world and either true or false, we can't claim that any man is wrong, whatever his principles may be, whatever his behaviour. We have to surrender the luxury of calling one another scoundrels. That this anxiety flourishes because its roots are in confusion is evident when

From Brian Medlin, "Ultimate Principles and Ethical Egoism," *Australasian Journal of Philosophy*, Vol. 35 (1957), pp. 111-18. Reprinted by kind permission of the author and of the editor of the *Australasian Journal of Philosophy*.

we consider that we don't call people scoundrels, anyhow, for being mistaken about their facts. Fools, perhaps, but that's another matter. Nevertheless, it doesn't become us to be high-up. The layman's uneasiness, however irrational it may be, is very natural and he must be reassured.

People cling to objectivist theories of morality from moral motives. It's a very queer thing that by doing so they often thwart their own purposes. There are evil opinions abroad, as anyone who walks abroad knows. The one we meet with most often, whether in pub or parlour, is the doctrine that everyone should look after himself. However refreshing he may find it after the high-minded pomposities of this morning's editorial, the good fellow knows this doctrine is wrong and he wants to knock it down. But while he believes that moral language is used to make statements either true or false, the best he can do is to claim that what the egoist says is false. Unfortunately, the egoist can claim that it's true. And since the supposed fact in question between them is not a publicly ascertainable one, their disagreement can never be resolved. And it is here that even good fellows waver, when they find they have no refutation available. The egoist's word seems as reliable as their own. Some begin half to believe that perhaps it is possible to supply an egoistic basis for conventional morality, some that it may be impossible to supply any other basis. I'm not going to try to prop up our conventional morality, which I fear to be a task beyond my strength, but in what follows I do want to refute the doctrine of ethical egoism. I want to resolve this disagreement by showing that what the egoist says is inconsistent. It is true that there are moral disagreements which can never be resolved, but this isn't one of them. The proper objection to the man who says 'Everyone should look after his own interests regardless of the interest of others' is not that he isn't speaking the truth, but simply that he isn't speaking.

We should first make two distinctions. This done, ethical egoism will lose much of its plausibility.

1. Universal and Individual Egoism

Universal egoism maintains that everyone (including the speaker) ought to look after his own interests and to disregard those of other people except in so far as their interests contribute towards his own.

Individual egoism is the attitude that the egoist is going to look after himself and no one else. The egoist cannot promulgate that he is going to look after himself. He can't even preach that he *should* look after himself and preach this alone. When he tries to convince me that he should look after himself, he is attempting so to dispose me that I shall approve when he drinks my beer and steals Tom's wife. I cannot approve of his looking after himself and himself alone without so far approving of his achieving his happiness, regardless of the happiness of myself and others. So that when he sets out to persuade me that he should look after himself regardless of others, he must also set out to persuade me that I should look after him regardless of myself and others. Very small chance he has! And if the individual egoist cannot promulgate his doctrine without enlarging it, what he has is no doctrine at all.

A person enjoying such an attitude may believe that other people are fools not to look after themselves. Yet he himself would be a fool to tell them so. If he did tell them, though, he wouldn't consider that he was giving them *moral* advice. Persuasion to the effect that one should ignore the claims of morality because morality doesn't pay, to the effect that one has insufficient selfish motive and, therefore, insufficient motive for moral behaviour is not moral persuasion. For this reason I doubt that we should call the individual egoist's attitude an ethical one. And I don't doubt this in the way someone may doubt whether to call the ethical standards of Satan "ethical" standards. A malign morality is none the less a morality for being malign. But the attitude we're considering is one of mere contempt for all moral considerations whatsoever. An indifference to morals may be wicked, but it is not a perverse morality. So far as I am aware, most egoists imagine that they are putting forward a doctrine in ethics, though there may be a few who are prepared to proclaim themselves individual egoists. If the good fellow wants to know how he should justify conventional morality to an individual egoist, the answer is that he shouldn't and can't. Buy your car elsewhere, blackguard him whenever you meet, and let it go at that.

2. Categorical and Hypothetical Egoism

Categorical egoism is the doctrine that we all ought to observe our own interests, *because that is what we ought to do*. For the categorical egoist the egoistic dogma is the ultimate principle in ethics.

The hypothetical egoist, on the other hand, maintains that we all ought to observe our own interest, because. . . . If we want such and such an end, we must do so and so (look after ourselves). The hypothetical egoist is not a real egoist at all. He is very likely an unwitting utilitarian who believes mistakenly that the general happiness will be increased if each man looks wisely to his own. Of course, a man may believe that egoism is enjoined on us by God and he may therefore promulgate the doctrine and observe it in his conduct, not in the hope of achieving thereby a remote end, but simply in order to obey God. But neither is *he* a real egoist. He believes, ultimately, that we should obey God, even should God command us to altruism.

An ethical egoist will have to maintain the doctrine in both its universal and categorical form. Should he retreat to hypothetical egoism he is no longer an egoist. Should he retreat to individual egoism his doctrine, while logically impregnable, is no longer ethical, no longer even a doctrine. He may wish to quarrel with this and if so, I submit peacefully. Let him call himself what he will, it makes no difference. I'm a philosopher, not a rat-catcher, and I don't see it as my job to dig vermin out of such burrows as individual egoism.

Obviously something strange goes on as soon as the ethical egoist tries to promulgate his doctrine. What is he doing when he urges upon his audience that they should each observe his own interests and those interests alone? Is he not acting contrary to the egoistic principle? It cannot be to his advantage to convince them, for seizing always their own advantage they will impair his. Surely if he does believe what he says, he should try to persuade them otherwise. Not perhaps that they should devote themselves to his interests, for they'd hardly swallow that; but that everyone should devote himself to the service of others. But is not to believe that someone should act in a certain way to try to persuade him to do so? Of course, we don't always try to persuade people to act as we think they should act. We may be lazy, for instance. But in so far as we believe that Tom should do so and so, we have a tendency to induce him to do so and so. Does it make sense to say: "Of course you should do this, but for goodness' sake don't?" Only where we mean: "You should do this for certain reasons, but here are even more persuasive reasons for not doing it." If the egoist believes ultimately that others should mind themselves alone, then, he must persuade them accordingly. If he doesn't persuade them, he is no universal egoist. It certainly makes sense to say: "I know very well that Tom should act in such and such a way. But I know also that it's not to my advantage that he should so act. So I'd better dissuade him from it." And this is just what the egoist must say, if he is to consider his own advantage and disregard everyone else's. That is, he must behave as an individual egoist, if he is to be an egoist at all.

He may want to make two kinds of objection here:

1.   That it will not be to his disadvantage to promulgate the doctrine, provided that his audience fully understand what is to their ultimate advantage. This objection can be developed in a number of ways, but I think that it will always be possible to push the egoist into either individual or hypothetical egoism.

2.   That it is to the egoist's advantage to preach the doctrine if the pleasure he gets out of doing this more than pays for the injuries he must endure at the hands of his converts. It is hard to believe that many people would be satisfied with a doctrine which they could only consistently promulgate in very special circumstances. Besides, this looks suspiciously like individual egoism in disguise.

I shall say no more on these two points because I want to advance a further criticism which seems to me at once fatal and irrefutable.

Now it is time to show the anxious layman that we have means of dealing with ethical egoism which are denied him; and denied him by just that objectivism which he thinks essential to morality. For the very fact that our ultimate principles must be arbitrary means they can't be anything we please. Just because they come out of thin air they can't come out of hot air. Because these principles are not propositions about matters of fact and cannot be deduced from propositions about matters of fact, they must be the fruit of our own attitudes. We assert them largely to modify the attitudes of our fellows but by asserting them we express our own desires and purposes. This means that we cannot use moral language cavalierly. Evidently, we cannot say something like 'All human desires and purposes are bad.' This would be to express our own desires and purposes, thereby committing a kind of absurdity. Nor, I shall argue, can we say 'Everyone should observe his own interests regardless of the interests of others.'

Remembering that the principle is meant to be both universal and categorical, let us ask what kind of attitude the egoist is expressing. Wouldn't that attitude be equally well expressed by the conjunction of an infinite number of avowals thus? —

I want myself to come out on top	and	I don't care about Tom, Dick, Harry . . .
and		and
I want Tom to come out on top	and	I don't care about myself, Dick, Harry . . .
and		and
I want Dick to come out on top	and	I don't care about myself, Tom, Harry . . .
and		and
I want Harry to come out on top	and	I don't care about myself, Dick, Tom . . .
etc.		etc.

From this analysis it is obvious that the principle expressing such an attitude must be inconsistent.

But now the egoist may claim that he hasn't been properly understood. When he says 'Everyone should look after himself and himself alone,' he means 'Let each man do what he wants regardless of what anyone else wants.' The egoist may claim that what he values is merely that he and Tom and Dick and Harry should each do what he wants and not care about what anyone else may want and that this doesn't involve his principle in any inconsistency. Nor need it. But even if it doesn't, he's no better off. Just what does he value? Is it the well-being of himself, Tom, Dick and Harry or merely their going on in a certain way regardless of whether or not this is going to promote their well-being? When he urges Tom, say, to do what he wants, is he appealing to Tom's self-interest? If so, his attitude can be expressed thus:

I want myself to be happy		I want myself not to care
and	and	about Tom, Dick,
I want Tom to be happy		Harry . . .

We need go no further to see that the principle expressing such an attitude
must be inconsistent. I have made this kind of move already. What concerns
me now is the alternative position the egoist must take up to be safe from
it. If the egoist values merely that people should go on in a certain way,
regardless of whether or not this is going to promote their well-being, then he
is not appealing to the self-interest of his audience when he urges them to
regard their own interests. If Tom has any regard for himself at all, the
egoist's blandishments will leave him cold. Further, the egoist doesn't even
have his own interest in mind when he says that, like everyone else, he
should look after himself. A funny kind of egoism this turns out to be.

Perhaps now, claiming that he is indeed appealing to the self-interest
of his audience, the egoist may attempt to counter the objection of the previous paragraph. He may move into 'Let each man do what he wants and let
each man disregard what others want when their desires clash with his own.'
Now his attitude may be expressed thus:

I want everyone to be happy		I want everyone to dis-
	and	regard the happiness
		of others when their
		happiness clashes
		with his own.

The egoist may claim justly that a man can have such an attitude and also
that in a certain kind of world such a man could get what he wanted. Our
objection to the egoist has been that his desires are incompatible. And this
is still so. If he and Tom and Dick and Harry did go on as he recommends
by saying 'Let each man disregard the happiness of others, when their happiness conflicts with his own,' then assuredly they'd all be completely miserable.
Yet he wants them to be happy. He is attempting to counter this by saying
that it is merely a fact about the world that they'd make one another miserable
by going on as he recommends. The world could conceivably have been different. For this reason, he says, this principle is not inconsistent. This argument may not seem very compelling, but I advance it on the egoist's behalf
because I'm interested in the reply to it. For now we don't even need to
tell him that the world isn't in fact like that. (What it's like makes no difference.) Now we can point out to him that he is arguing not as an egoist
but as a utilitarian. He has slipped into hypothetical egoism to save his principle from inconsistency. If the world were such that we always made ourselves and others happy by doing one another down, then we could find good
utilitarian reasons for urging that we should do one another down.

If, then, he is to save his principle, the egoist must do one of two things.

He must give up the claim that he is appealing to the self-interest of his audience, that he has even his own interest in mind. Or he must admit that, in the conjunction on page 234, although 'I want everyone to be happy' refers to ends, nevertheless 'I want everyone to disregard the happiness of others when their happiness conflicts with his own' can refer only to means. That is, his so-called ultimate principle is really compounded of a principle and a moral rule subordinate to that principle. That is, he is really a utilitarian who is urging everyone to go on in a certain way so that everyone may be happy. A utilitarian, what's more, who is ludicrously mistaken about the nature of the world. Things being as they are, his moral rule is a very bad one. Things being as they are, it can only be deduced from his principle by means of an empirical premiss which is manifestly false. Good fellows don't need to fear him. They may rest easy that the world is and must be on their side and the best thing they can do is be good.

It may be worth pointing out that objections similar to those I have brought against the egoist can be made to the altruist. The man who holds that the principle 'Let everyone observe the interests of others' is both universal and categorical can be compelled to choose between two alternatives, equally repugnant. He must give up the claim that he is concerned for the well-being of himself and others. Or he must admit that, though 'I want everyone to be happy' refers to ends, nevertheless 'I want everyone to disregard his own happiness when it conflicts with the happiness of others' can refer only to means.

I have said from time to time that the egoistic principle is inconsistent. I have not said it is contradictory. This for the reason that we can, without contradiction, express inconsistent desires and purposes. To do so is not to say anything like 'Goliath was ten feet tall and not ten feet tall.' Don't we all want to eat our cake and have it too? And when we say we do we aren't asserting a contradiction. We are not asserting a contradiction whether we be making an avowal of our attitudes or stating a fact about them. We all have conflicting motives. As a utilitarian exuding benevolence I want the man who mows my landlord's grass to be happy, but as a slug-a-bed I should like to see him scourged. None of this, however, can do the egoist any good. For we assert our ultimate principles not only to express our own attitudes but also to induce similar attitudes in others, to dispose them to conduct themselves as we wish. In so far as their desires conflict, people don't know what to do. And, therefore, no expression of incompatible desires can ever serve for an ultimate principle of human conduct.

22

MANY SELF-EVIDENT OBLIGATIONS

William David Ross

Sir William David Ross (1877-   ) was, until his retirement, Provost of Oriel College, Oxford.

The real point at issue between hedonism and utilitarianism on the one hand and their opponents on the other is not whether 'right' means 'productive of so and so'; for it cannot with any plausibility be maintained that it does. The point at issue is that to which we now pass, viz. whether there is any general character which makes right acts right, and if so, what it is. Among the main historical attempts to state a single characteristic of all right actions which is the foundation of their rightness are those made by egoism and utilitarianism. But I do not propose to discuss these, not because the subject is unimportant, but because it has been dealt with so often and so well already, and because there has come to be so much agreement among moral philosophers that neither of these theories is satisfactory. A much more attractive theory has been put forward by Professor Moore: that what makes actions right is that they are productive of more *good* than could have been produced by any other action open to the agent.

This theory is in fact the culmination of all the attempts to base rightness on productivity of some sort of result. The first form this attempt takes is the attempt to base rightness on conduciveness to the advantage or pleasure of the agent. This theory comes to grief over the fact, which stares us in the face, that a great part of duty consists in an observance of the rights and a furtherance of the interests of others, whatever the cost to ourselves may be. Plato and others may be right in holding that a regard for the rights of others never in the long run involves a loss of happiness for the agent, that "the just life profits a man.' But this, even if true, is irrelevant to the rightness of the act. As soon as a man does an action *because* he thinks he will promote

From W. D. Ross, *The Right and the Good*, published by The Clarendon Press, Oxford, 1930. From Chapter 2. Reprinted by permission of the publisher.

his own interests thereby, he is acting not from a sense of its rightness but from self-interest.

To the egoistic theory hedonistic utilitarianism supplies a much-needed amendment. It points out correctly that the fact that a certain pleasure will be enjoyed by the agent is no reason why he *ought* to bring it into being rather than an equal or greater pleasure to be enjoyed by another, though, human nature being what it is, it makes it not unlikely that he *will* try to bring it into being. But hedonistic utilitarianism in its turn needs a correction. On reflection it seems clear that pleasure is not the only thing in life that we think good in itself, that for instance we think the possession of a good character, or an intelligent understanding of the world, as good or better. A great advance is made by the substitution of 'productive of the greatest good' for 'productive of the greatest pleasure.'

Not only is this theory more attractive than hedonistic utilitarianism, but its logical relation to that theory is such that the latter could not be true unless *it* were true, while it might be true though hedonistic utilitarianism were not. It is in fact one of the logical bases of hedonistic utilitiarianism. For the view that what produces the maximum pleasure is right has for its bases the views (1) that what produces the maximum good is right, and (2) that pleasure is the only thing good in itself. . . . If, therefore, it can be shown that productivity of the maximum good is not what makes all right actions right, we shall *a fortiori* have refuted hedonistic utilitarianism.

When a plain man fulfils a promise because he thinks he ought to do so, it seems clear that he does so with no thought of its total consequences, still less with any opinion that these are likely to be the best possible. He thinks in fact much more of the past than of the future. What makes him think it right to act in a certain way is the fact that he has promised to do so — that and, usually, nothing more. That his act will produce the best possible consequences is not his reason for calling it right. What lends colour to the theory we are examining, then, is not the actions (which form probably a great majority of our actions) in which some such reflection as 'I have promised' is the only reason we give ourselves for thinking a certain action right, but the exceptional cases in which the consequences of fulfilling a promise (for instance) would be so disastrous to others that we judge it right not to do so. It must of course be admitted that such cases exist. If I have promised to meet a friend at a particular time for some trivial purpose, I should certainly think myself justified in breaking my engagement if by doing so I could prevent a serious accident or bring relief to the victims of one. And the supporters of the view we are examining hold that my thinking so is due to my thinking that I shall bring more good into existence by the one action than by the other. A different account may, however, be given of the matter, an account which will, I believe, show itself to be the true one. It may be said that besides the duty of fulfilling promises I have and recognize a duty of relieving distress, and that when I think it right to do the latter at the cost of not doing the former, it is not not because I think I shall produce more good

thereby but because I think it the duty which is in the circumstances more
of a duty. This account surely corresponds much more closely with what we
really think in such a situation. If, so far as I can see, I could bring equal
amounts of good into being by fulfilling my promise and by helping some one
to whom I had made no promise, I should not hesitate to regard the former
as my duty. Yet on the view that what is right is right because it is productive of the most good I should not so regard it.

There are two theories, each in its way simple, that offer a solution of
such cases of conscience. One is the view of Kant, that there are certain
duties of perfect obligation, such as those of fulfilling promises, of paying
debts, of telling the truth, which admit of no exception whatever in favour
of duties of imperfect obligation, such as that of relieving distress. The other
is the view of, for instance, Professor Moore and Dr. Rashdall, that there is
only the duty of producing good, and that all 'conflicts of duties' should be
resolved by asking 'by which action will most good be produced?' But it is
more important that our theory fit the facts than that it be simple, and the
account we have given above corresponds (it seems to me) better than either
of the simpler theories with what we really think, viz. that normally promise-
keeping, for example, should come before benevolence, but that when and
only when the good to be produced by the benevolent act is very great and
the promise comparatively trivial, the act of benevolence becomes our duty.

In fact the theory of 'ideal utilitarianism,' if I may for brevity refer so to
the theory of Professor Moore, seems to simplify unduly our relations to our
fellows. It says, in effect, that the only morally significant relation in which
my neighbours stand to me is that of being possible beneficiaries by my
action.[1] They do stand in this relation to me, and this relation is morally significant. But they may also stand to me in the relation of promisee to prom-
iser, of creditor to debtor, of wife to husband, of child to parent, of friend to
friend, of fellow countryman to fellow countryman, and the like; and each
of these relations is the foundation of a *prima facie* duty, which is more or
less incumbent on me according to the circumstances of the case. When I am
in a situation, as perhaps I always am, in which more than one of these *prima
facie* duties is incumbent on me, what I have to do is to study the situation as
fully as I can until I form the considered opinion (it is never more) that in
the circumstances one of them is more incumbent than any other; then I am
bound to think that to do this *prima facie* duty is my duty *sans phrase* in the
situation.

I suggest '*prima facie* duty' or 'conditional duty' as a brief way of referring to the characteristic (quite distinct from that of being a duty proper)
which an act has, in virtue of being of a certain kind (e.g. the keeping of
a promise), of being an act which would be a duty proper if it were not at
the same time of another kind which is morally significant. Whether an act

---

[1] Some will think it, apart from other considerations, a sufficient refutation of this
view to point out that I also stand in that relation to myself, so that for this view the
distinction of oneself from others is morally insignificant.

is a duty proper or actual duty depends on *all* the morally significant kinds it is an instance of. . . .

There is nothing arbitrary about these *prima facie* duties. Each rests on a definite circumstance which cannot seriously be held to be without moral significance. Of *prima facie* duties I suggest, without claiming completeness or finality for it, the following division.[2]

(1) Some duties rest on previous acts of my own. These duties seem to include two kinds, (*a*) those resting on a promise or what may fairly be called an implicit promise, such as the implicit undertaking not to tell lies which seems to be implied in the act of entering into conversation (at any rate by civilized men), or of writing books that purport to be history and not fiction. These may be called the duties of fidelity. (*b*) Those resting on a previous wrongful act. These may be called the duties of reparation. (2) Some rest on previous acts of other men, i.e. services done by them to me. These may be loosely described as the duties of gratitude. (3) Some rest on the fact or possibility of a distribution of pleasure or happiness (or of the means thereto) which is not in accordance with the merit of the persons concerned; in such cases there arises a duty to upset or prevent such a distribution. These are the duties of justice. (4) Some rest on the mere fact that there are other beings in the world whose condition we can make better in respect of virtue, or of intelligence, or of pleasure. These are the duties of beneficence. (5) Some rest on the fact that we can improve our own condition in respect of virtue or of intelligence. These are the duties of self-improvement. (6) I think that we should distinguish from (4) the duties that may be summed up under the title of 'not injuring others.' No doubt to injure others is incidentally to fail to do them good; but it seems to me clear that non-maleficence is apprehended as a duty distinct from that of beneficence, and as a duty of a more stringent character. It will be noticed that this alone among the types of duty has been stated in a negative way. An attempt might no doubt be made to state this duty, like the others, in a positive way. It might be said that it is really the duty to prevent ourselves from acting either from an inclination to harm others or from an inclination to seek our own pleasure, in doing which we should incidentally harm them. But on reflection it seems clear that the primary duty here is the duty not to harm others, this being a duty whether or not we have an inclination that if followed would lead to

[2] I should make it plain at this stage that I am *assuming* the correctness of some of our main convictions as to *prima facie* duties, or, more strictly, am claiming that we *know* them to be true. To me it seems as self-evident as anything could be, that to make a promise, for instance, is to create a moral claim on us in someone else. Many readers will perhaps say that they do *not* know this to be true. If so, I certainly cannot prove it to them; I can only ask them to reflect again, in the hope that they will ultimately agree that they also know it to be true. The main moral convictions of the plain man seem to me to be, not opinions which it is for philosophy to prove or disprove, but knowledge from the start; and in my own case I seem to find little difficulty in distinguishing these essential convictions from other moral convictions which I also have, which are merely fallible opinions based on an imperfect study of the working for good or evil of certain institutions or types of action.

our harming them; and that when we have such an inclination the primary duty not to harm others gives rise to a consequential duty to resist the inclination. The recognition of this duty of nonmaleficence is the first step on the way to the recognition of the duty of beneficence; and that accounts for the prominence of the commands 'thou shalt not kill,' 'thou shalt not commit adultery,' 'thou shalt not steal,' 'thou shalt not bear false witness,' in so early a code as the Decalogue. But even when we have come to recognize the duty of beneficence, it appears to me that the duty of non-maleficence is recognized as a distinct one, and as *prima facie* more binding. We should not in general consider it justifiable to kill one person in order to keep another alive, or to steal from one in order to give alms to another.

The essential defect of the 'ideal utilitarian' theory is that it ignores, or at least does not do full justice to, the highly personal character of duty. If the only duty is to produce the maximum of good, the question who is to have the good — whether it is myself, or my benefactor, or a person to whom I have made a promise to confer that good on him, or a mere fellow man to whom I stand in no such special relation — should make no difference to my having a duty to produce that good. But we are all in fact sure that it makes a vast difference. . . .

If the objection be made, that this catalogue of the main types of duty is an unsystematic one resting on no logical principle, it may be replied, first, that it makes no claim to being ultimate. It is a *prima facie* classification of the duties which reflection on our moral convictions seems actually to reveal. And if these convictions are, as I would claim that they are, of the nature of knowledge, and if I have not misstated them, the list will be a list of authentic conditional duties, correct as far as it goes though not necessarily complete. The list of *goods* put forward by the rival theory is reached by exactly the same method — the only sound one in the circumstances — viz. that of direct reflection on what we really think. Loyalty to the facts is worth more than a symmetrical architectonic or a hastily reached simplicity. If further reflection discovers a perfect logical basis for this or for a better classification, so much the better.

It may, again, be objected that our theory that there are these various and often conflicting types of *prima facie* duty leaves us with no principle upon which to discern what is our actual duty in particular circumstances. But this objection is not one which the rival theory is in a position to bring forward. For when we have to choose between the production of two heterogeneous goods, say knowledge and pleasure, the 'ideal utilitarian' theory can only fall back on an opinion, for which no logical basis can be offered, that one of the goods is the greater; and this is no better than a similar opinion that one of two duties is the more urgent. And again, when we consider the infinite variety of the effects of our actions in the way of pleasure, it must surely be admitted that the claim which *hedonism* sometimes makes, that it offers a readily applicable criterion of right conduct, is quite illusory.

I am unwilling, however, to content myself with an *argumentum ad*

hominem, and I would contend that in principle there is no reason to anticipate that every act that is our duty is so for one and the same reason. Why
should two sets of circumstances, or one set of circumstances, *not* possess different characteristics, any one of which makes a certain act our *prima facie*
duty? When I ask what it is that makes me in certain cases sure that I have
a *prima facie* duty to do so and so, I find that it lies in the fact that I have
made a promise; when I ask the same question in another case, I find the
answer lies in the fact that I have done a wrong. And if on reflection I find
(as I think I do) that neither of these reasons is reducible to the other, I must
not on any *a priori* ground assume that such a reduction is possible. . . .

It is necessary to say something by way of clearing up the relation between *prima facie* duties and the actual or absolute duty to do one particular
act in particular circumstances. If, as almost all moralists except Kant are
agreed, and as most plain men think, it is sometimes right to tell a lie or to
break a promise, it must be maintained that there is a difference between
prima facie duty and actual or absolute duty. When we think ourselves justified in breaking, and indeed morally obliged to break, a promise in order to
relieve some one's distress, we do not for a moment cease to recognize a *prima
facie* duty to keep our promise, and this leads us to feel, not indeed shame or
repentance, but certainly compunction, for behaving as we do; we recognize,
further, that it is our duty to make up somehow to the promisee for the breaking of the promise. We have to distinguish from the characteristic of being
our duty that of tending to be our duty. Any act that we do contains various
elements in virtue of which it falls under various categories. In virtue of
being the breaking of a promise, for instance, it tends to be wrong; in virtue
of being an instance of relieving distress it tends to be right. Tendency to be
one's duty may be called a parti-resultant attribute, i.e. one which belongs to
an act in virtue of some one component in its nature. *Being* one's duty is a
toti-resultant attribute, one which belongs to an act in virtue of its whole
nature and of nothing less than this. . . .

Another instance of the same distinction may be found in the operation
of natural laws. *Qua* subject to the force of gravitation towards some other
body, each body tends to move in a particular direction with a particular
velocity; but its actual movement depends on *all* the forces to which it is
subject. It is only by recognizing this distinction that we can preserve the
absoluteness of laws of nature, and only by recognizing a corresponding distinction that we can preserve the absoluteness of the general principles of
morality. But an important difference between the two cases must be pointed
out. When we say that in virtue of gravitation a body tends to move in a
certain way, we are referring to a causal influence actually exercised on it
by another body or other bodies. When we say that in virtue of being deliberately untrue a certain remark tends to be wrong, we are referring to no
causal relation, to no relation that involves succession in time, but to such a
relation as connects the various attributes of a mathematical figure. And if
the word 'tendency' is thought to suggest too much a causal relation, it is

better to talk of certain types of act as being *prima facie* right or wrong (or of different persons as having different and possibly conflicting claims upon us), than of their tending to be right or wrong.

Something should be said of the relation between our apprehension of the *prima facie* rightness of certain types of act and our mental attitude towards particular acts. It is proper to use the word 'apprehension' in the former case and not in the latter. That an act, *qua* fulfilling a promise, or *qua* effecting a just distribution of good, or *qua* returning services rendered, or *qua* promoting the good of others, or *qua* promoting the virtue or insight of the agent, is *prima facie* right, is self-evident; not in the sense that it is evident from the beginning of our lives, or as soon as we attend to the proposition for the first time, but in the sense that when we have reached sufficient mental maturity and have given sufficient attention to the proposition it is evident without any need of proof, or of evidence beyond itself. It is self-evident just as a mathematical axiom, or the validity of a form of inference, is evident. The moral order expressed in these propositions is just as much part of the fundamental nature of the universe (and, we may add, of any possible universe in which there were moral agents at all) as is the spatial or numerical structure expressed in the axioms of geometry or arithmetic. In our confidence that these propositions are true there is involved the same trust in our reason that is involved in our confidence in mathematics; and we should have no justification for trusting it in the latter sphere and distrusting it in the former. In both cases we are dealing with propositions that cannot be proved, but that just as certainly need no proof. . . .

Our judgements about our actual duty in concrete situations have none of the certainty that attaches to our recognition of the general principles of duty. A statement is certain, i.e. is an expression of knowledge, only in one or other of two cases: when it is either self-evident, or a valid conclusion from self-evident premisses. And our judgements about our particular duties have neither of these characters. (1) They are not self-evident. Where a possible act is seen to have two characteristics, in virtue of one of which it is *prima facie* right, and in virtue of the other *prima facie* wrong, we are (I think) well aware that we are not certain whether we ought or ought not to do it; that whether we do it or not, we are taking a moral risk. We come in the long run, after consideration, to think one duty more pressing than the other, but we do not feel certain that it is so. And though we do not always recognize that a possible act has two such characteristics, and though there *may* be cases in which it has not, we are never certain that any particular possible act has not, and therefore never certain that it is right, nor certain that it is wrong. For, to go no further in the analysis, it is enough to point out that any particular act will in all probability in the course of time contribute to the bringing about of good or of evil for many human beings and thus have a *prima facie* rightness or wrongness of which we know nothing. (2) Again, our judgements about our particular duties are not logical conclusions from self-evident premisses. The only possible premisses would be the general principles stating their *prima facie* rightness or wrongness *qua* having the different characteristics they do have; and even if we could (as we cannot) apprehend the extent to which an act will tend on the one hand, for example, to bring about advantages for our benefactors, and on the other hand to bring about disadvantages for fellow men who are not our benefactors, there is no principle by which we can draw the conclusion that it is on the whole right or on the whole wrong. In this respect the judgement as to the rightness of a particular act is just like the judgement as to the beauty of a particular natural object or work of art. A poem is, for instance, in respect of certain qualities beautiful and in respect of certain others not beautiful; and our judgement as to the degree of beauty it possesses on the whole is never reached by logical reasoning from the apprehension of its particular beauties or particular defects. Both in this and in the moral case we have more or less probable opinions which are not logically justified conclusions from the general principles that are recognized as self-evident.

There is therefore much truth in the description of the right act as a fortunate act. If we cannot be certain that it is right, it is our good fortune if the act we do is the right act. This consideration does not, however, make the doing of our duty a mere matter of chance. There is a parallel here between the doing of duty and the doing of what will be to our personal advantage. We never *know* what act will in the long run be to our advantage. Yet it is certain that we are more likely in general to secure our advantage if we estimate to the best of our ability the probable tendencies of our actions in this respect, than if we act on caprice. And similarly we are more likely to do our duty if we reflect to the best of our ability on the *prima facie* rightness or wrongness of various possible acts in virtue of the characteristics we perceive them to have, than if we act without reflection. With this greater likelihood we must be content.

Many people would be inclined to say that the right act for me is not that whose general nature I have been describing, viz. that which if I were omniscient I should see to be my duty, but that which on all the evidence available to me I should think to be my duty. But suppose that from the state of partial knowledge in which I think act A to be my duty, I could pass to a state of perfect knowledge in which I saw act B to be my duty, should I not say 'act B was the right act for me to do'? I should no doubt add 'though I am not to be blamed for doing act A.' But in adding this, am I not passing from the question 'what is right' to the question 'what is morally good'? At the same time I am not making the *full* passage from the one notion to the other; for in order that the act should be morally good, or an act I am not to be blamed for doing, it must not merely be the act which it is reasonable for me to think my duty; it must also be done for that reason, or from some other morally good motive. Thus the conception of the right act as the act which it is reasonable for me to think my duty is an unsatisfactory compromise between the true notion of the right act and the notion of the morally good action.

The general principles of duty are obviously not self-evident from the beginning of our lives. How do they come to be so? The answer is, that they come to be self-evident to us just as mathematical axioms do. We find by experience that this couple of matches and that couple make four matches, that this couple of balls on a wire and that couple make four balls; and by reflection on these and similar discoveries we come to see that it is of the nature of two and two to make four. In a precisely similar way, we see the *prima facie* rightness of an act which would be the fulfilment of a particular promise, and of another which would be the fulfilment of another promise, and when we have reached sufficient maturity to think in general terms, we apprehend *prima facie* rightness to belong to the nature of any fulfilment of promise. What comes first in time is the apprehension of the self-evident *prima facie* rightness of an individual act of a particular type. From this we come by reflection to apprehend the self-evident general principle of *prima facie* duty. From this, too, perhaps along with the apprehension of the self-evident *prima facie* rightness of the same act in virtue of its having another characteristic as well, and perhaps in spite of the apprehension of its *prima facie* wrongness in virtue of its having some third characteristic, we come to believe something not self-evident at all, but an object of probable opinion, viz. that this particular act is (not *prima facie* but) actually right. . . .

Supposing it to be agreed, as I think on reflection it must, that no one *means* by 'right' just 'productive of the best possible consequences,' or 'optimific,' the attributes 'right' and 'optimific' might stand in either of two kinds of relation to each other. (1) They might be so related that we could apprehend *a priori*, either immediately or deductively, that any act that is optimific is right and any act that is right is optimific, as we can apprehend that any triangle that is equilateral is equiangular and *vice versa*. Professor Moore's view is, I think, that the coextensiveness of 'right' and 'optimific' is apprehended immediately. He rejects the possibility of any proof of it. Or (2) the two attributes might be such that the question whether they are invariably connected had to be answered by means of an inductive inquiry. Now at first sight it might seem as if the constant connexion of the two attributes could be immediately apprehended. It might seem absurd to suggest that it could be right for any one to do an act which would produce consequences less good than those which would be produced by some other act in his power. Yet a little thought will convince us that this is not absurd. The type of case in which it is easiest to see that this is so is, perhaps, that in which one has made a promise. In such a case we all think that *prima facie* it is our duty to fulfill the promise irrespective of the precise goodness of the total consequences. And though we do not think it is necessarily our actual or absolute duty to do so, we are far from thinking that any, even the slightest, gain in the value of the total consequences will necessarily justify us in doing something else instead. Suppose, to simplify the case by abstraction, that the fulfilment of a promise to A would produce 1,000 units of good[3] for him, but that by doing some other act I could produce 1,001 units of good for B, to whom I have made no promise, the other consequences of the two acts being of equal value; should we really think it self-evident that it was our duty to do the second act and not the first? I think not. We should, I fancy, hold that only a much greater disparity of value between the total consequences would justify us in failing to discharge our *prima facie* duty to A. After all, a promise is a promise, and is not to be treated so lightly as the theory we are examining would imply. What, exactly, a promise is, is not so easy to determine, but we are surely agreed that it constitutes a serious moral limitation to our freedom of action. To produce the 1,001 units of good for B rather than fulfil our promise to A would be to take, not perhaps our duty as philanthropists too seriously, but certainly our duty as makers of promises too lightly. . . .

Such instances — and they might easily be added to — make it clear that there is no self-evident connexion between the attributes 'right' and 'optimific.' The theory we are examining has a certain attractiveness when applied to our decision that a particular act is our duty (though I have tried to show that it does not agree with our actual moral judgements even here). But it is not even plausible when applied to our recognition of *prima facie* duty. For if it were self-evident that the right coincides with the optimific, it should be self-evident that what is *prima facie* right is *prima facie* optimific. But whereas we are certain that keeping a promise is *prima facie* right, we are not certain that it is *prima facie* optimific (though we are perhaps certain that it is *prima facie* bonific). Our certainty that it is *prima facie* right depends not on its consequences but on its being the fulfilment of a promise. The theory we are examining involves too much difference between the evident ground of our conviction about *prima facie* duty and the alleged ground of our conviction about actual duty.

I conclude that the attributes 'right' and 'optimific' are not identical, and that we do not know either by intuition, by deduction, or by induction that they coincide in their application, still less that the latter is the foundation of the former. It must be added, however, that if we are ever under no special obligation such as that of fidelity to a promisee or of gratitude to a benefactor, we ought to do what will produce most good; and that even when we are under a special obligation the tendency of acts to promote general good is one of the main factors in determining whether they are right.

In what has preceded, a good deal of use has been made of 'what we really think' about moral questions; a certain theory has been rejected because

---

[3] I am assuming that good is objectively quantitative, but not that we can accurately assign an exact quantitative measure to it. Since it is of a definite amount, we can make the *supposition* that its amount is so-and-so, though we cannot with any confidence *assert* that it is.

it does not agree with what we really think. It might be said that this is in principle wrong; that we should not be content to expound what our present moral consciousness tells us but should aim at a criticism of our existing moral consciousness in the light of theory. Now I do not doubt that the moral consciousness of men has in detail undergone a good deal of modification as regards the things we think right, at the hands of moral theory. But if we are told, for instance, that we should give up our view that there is a special obligatoriness attaching to the keeping of promises because it is self-evident that the only duty is to produce as much good as possible, we have to ask ourselves whether we really, when we reflect, *are* convinced that this is self-evident, and whether we really *can* get rid of our view that promise-keeping has a bindingness independent of productiveness of maximum good. In my own experience I find that I cannot, in spite of a very genuine attempt to do so; and I venture to think that most people will find the same, and that just because they cannot lose the sense of special obligation, they cannot accept as self-evident, or even as true, the theory which would require them to do so. In fact it seems, on reflection, self-evident that a promise, simply as such, is something that *prima facie* ought to be kept, and it does *not*, on reflection, seem self-evident that production of maximum good is the only thing that makes an act obligatory. And to ask us to give up at the bidding of a theory our actual apprehension of what is right and what is wrong seems like asking people to repudiate their actual experience of beauty, at the bidding of a theory which says 'only that which satisfies such and such conditions can be beautiful.' If what I have called our actual apprehension is (as I would maintain that it is) truly an apprehension, i.e. an instance of knowledge, the request is nothing less than absurd.

I would maintain, in fact, that what we are apt to describe as 'what we think' about moral questions contains a considerable amount that we do not think but know, and that this forms the standard by reference to which the truth of any moral theory has to be tested, instead of having itself to be tested by reference to any theory. I hope that I have in what precedes indicated what in my view these elements of knowledge are that are involved in our ordinary moral consciousness.

It would be a mistake to found a natural science on 'what we really think,' i.e. on what reasonably thoughtful and well-educated people think about the subjects of the science before they have studied them scientifically. For such opinions are interpretations, and often misinterpretations, of sense-experience; and the man of science must appeal from these to sense-experience itself, which furnishes his real data. In ethics no such appeal is possible. We have no more direct way of access to the facts about rightness and goodness and about what things are right or good, than by thinking about them; the moral convictions of thoughtful and well-educated people are the data of ethics just as sense-perceptions are the data of a natural science. Just as some of the latter have to be rejected as illusory, so have some of the former; but as the latter are rejected only when they are in conflict with other more accurate sense-perceptions, the former are rejected only when they are in conflict with other convictions which stand better the test of reflection. The existing body of moral convictions of the best people is the cumulative product of the moral reflection of many generations, which has developed an extremely delicate power of appreciation of moral distinctions; and this the theorist cannot afford to treat with anything other than the greatest respect. The verdicts of the moral consciousness of the best people are the foundation on which he must build; though he must first compare them with one another and eliminate any contradictions they may contain.

23

RIGHT ACTS MUST
BE UNIVERSALIZABLE

Immanuel Kant

Immanuel Kant (1724-1804), the most influential philosopher of the modern period, was professor at the University of Königsberg.

. . . Unless we wish to deny to the concept of morality all truth and all relation to a possible object, we cannot dispute that its law is of such widespread significance as to hold, not merely for men, but for all *rational beings as such* — not merely subject to contingent conditions and exceptions, but *with absolute necessity*. It is therefore clear that no experience can give us occasion to infer even the possibility of such apodeictic laws. For by what right can we make what is perhaps valid only under the contingent conditions of humanity into an object of unlimited reverence as a universal precept for every rational nature? And how could laws for determining *our* will be taken as laws for determining the will of a rational being as such — and only because of this for determining ours — if these laws were merely empirical and did not have their source completely *a priori* in pure, but practical, reason?

What is more, we cannot do morality a worse service than by seeking to derive it from examples. Every example of it presented to me must first itself be judged by moral principles in order to decide if it is fit to serve as an original example — that is, as a model: it can in no way supply the prime source for the concept of morality. Even the Holy One of the gospel must first be compared with our ideal of moral perfection before we can recognize him to be such. He also says of himself: 'Why callest thou me (whom thou seest) good? There is none good (the archetype of the good) but one, that is, God (whom thou seest not).' But where do we get the concept of God as the highest good? Solely from the *Idea* of moral perfection, which reason traces *a priori* and conjoins inseparably with the concept of a free will. Imita-

From Immanual Kant, *The Fundamental Principles of the Metaphysic of Morals*, translated by H. J. Paton, 1948. Published by the Hutchinson Publishing Group Ltd., London, and by Harper Torchbooks, New York. Reprinted by permission of the Hutchinson Publishing Group, Ltd. The foregoing volume is a translation of Immanuel Kant, *Grundlegung zur Metaphsik der Sitten*, first published in 1785.

tion has no place in morality, and examples serve us only for encouragement. . . .

From these considerations the following conclusions emerge. All moral concepts have their seat and origin in reason completely *a priori,* and indeed in the most ordinary human reason just as much as in the most highly speculative: they cannot be abstracted from any empirical, and therefore merely contingent, knowledge. In this purity of their origin is to be found their very worthiness to serve as supreme practical principles, and everything empirical added to them is just so much taken away from their genuine influence and from the absolute value of the corresponding actions. It is not only a requirement of the utmost necessity in respect of theory, where our concern is solely with speculation, but is also of the utmost practical importance, to draw these concepts and laws from pure reason, to set them forth pure and unmixed, and indeed to determine the extent of this whole practical, but pure, rational knowledge — that is, to determine the whole power of pure practical reason. We ought never — as speculative philosophy does allow and even at times finds necessary — to make principles depend on the special nature of human reason. Since moral laws have to hold for every rational being as such, we ought rather to derive our principles from the general concept of a rational being as such, and on this basis to expound the whole of ethics — which requires anthropology for its *application* to man — at first independently as pure philosophy, that is, entirely as metaphysics (which we can very well do in this wholly abstract kind of knowledge). We know well that without possessing such a metaphysics it is a futile endeavour, I will not say to determine accurately for speculative judgement the moral element of duty in all that accords with duty — but that it is impossible, even in ordinary and practical usage, particularly in that of moral instruction, to base morals on their genuine principles and so to bring about pure moral dispositions and engraft them on men's minds for the highest good of the world.

In this task of ours we have to progress by natural stages, not merely from ordinary moral judgement (which is here worthy of great respect) to philosophical judgement, . . . but from popular philosophy, which goes no further than it can get by fumbling about with the aid of examples, to metaphysics. (This no longer lets itself be held back by anything empirical, and indeed — since it must survey the complete totality of this kind of knowledge — goes right to Ideas, where examples themselves fail.) For this purpose we must follow — and must portray in detail — the power of practical reason from the general rules determining it right up to the point where there springs from it the concept of duty.

[*Imperatives in general*]

Everything in nature works in accordance with laws. Only a rational being has the power to act *in accordance with his idea* of laws — that is, in accordance with principles — and only so has he a *will.* Since *reason* is required in order to derive actions from laws, the will is nothing but practical reason. If reason infallibly determines the will, then in a being of this kind the actions which are recognized to be objectively necessary are also subjectively necessary — that is to say, the will is then a power to choose *only that* which reason independently of inclination recognizes to be practically necessary, that is, to be good. But if reason solely by itself is not sufficient to determine the will; if the will is exposed also to subjective conditions (certain impulsions) which do not always harmonize with the objective ones; if, in a word, the will is not *in itself* completely in accord with reason (as actually happens in the case of men); then actions which are recognized to be objectively necessary are subjectively contingent, and the determining of such a will in accordance with objective laws is *necessitation*. That is to say, the relation of objective laws to a will not good through and through is conceived as one in which the will of a rational being, although it is determined by principles of reason, does not necessarily follow these principles in virtue of its own nature.

The conception of an objective principle so far as this principle is necessitating for a will is called a command (of reason), and the formula of this command is called an *Imperative*.

All imperatives are expressed by an '*ought*' (*Sollen*). By this they mark the relation of an objective law of reason to a will which is not necessarily determined by this law in virtue of its subjective constitution (the relation of necessitation). They say that something would be good to do or to leave undone; only they say it to a will which does not always do a thing because it has been informed that this is a good thing to do. . . .

A perfectly good will would thus stand quite as much under objective laws (laws of the good), but it could not on this account be conceived as *necessitated* to act in conformity with law, since of itself, in accordance with its subjective constitution, it can be determined only by the concept of the good. Hence for the *divine* will, and in general for a *holy* will, there are no imperatives: '*I ought*' is here out of place, because '*I will*' is already of itself necessarily in harmony with the law. Imperatives are in consequence only formulae for expressing the relation of objective laws of willing to the subjective imperfection of the will of this or that rational being — for example, of the human will.

[Classification of imperatives]

All *imperatives* command either *hypothetically* or *categorically*. Hypothetical imperatives declare a possible action to be practically necessary as a means to the attainment of something else that one wills (or that one may will). A categorical imperative would be one which represented an action as objectively necessary in itself apart from its relation to a further end. . . . [Hence] if the action would be good solely as a means to *something else*, the imperative is *hypothetical*; if the action is represented as good *in itself* and therefore as necessary, in virtue of its principle, for a will which of itself accords with reason, then the imperative is *categorical*.

An imperative therefore tells me which of my possible actions would be good; and it formulates a practical rule for a will that does not perform an action straight away because the action is good — whether because the subject does not always know that it is good or because, even if he did know this, he might still act on maxims contrary to the objective principles of practical reason.

A hypothetical imperative thus says only that an action is good for some purpose or other, either *possible* or *actual*. In the first case it is a *problematic* practical principle; in the second case an *assertoric* practical principle. A categorical imperative, which declares an action to be objectively necessary in itself without reference to some purpose — that is, even without any further end — ranks as an *apodeictic* practical principle. . . .

All sciences have a practical part consisting of problems which suppose that some end is possible for us and of imperatives which tell us how it is to be attained. Hence the latter can in general be called imperatives of *skill*. Here there is absolutely no question about the rationality or goodness of the end, but only about what must be done to attain it. A prescription required by a doctor in order to cure his man completely and one required by a poisoner in order to make sure of killing him are of equal value so far as each serves to effect its purpose perfectly. Since in early youth we do not know what ends may present themselves to us in the course of life, parents seek above all to make their children learn things *of many kinds;* they provide carefully for *skill* in the use of means to all sorts of *arbitrary* ends, of none of which can they be certain that it could not in the future become an actual purpose of their ward, while it is always *possible* that he might adopt it. Their care in this matter is so great that they commonly neglect on this account to form and correct the judgement of their children about the worth of the things which they might possibly adopt as ends.

There is, however, one end that can be presupposed as actual in all rational beings (so far as they are dependent beings to whom imperatives apply); and thus there is one purpose which they not only *can* have, but which we can assume with certainty that they all *do* have by a natural necessity — the purpose, namely, of *happiness*. A hypothetical imperative which affirms the practical necessity of an action as a means to the furtherance of happiness is *assertoric*. We may represent it, not simply as necessary to an uncertain, merely possible purpose, but as necessary to a purpose which we can presuppose *a priori* and with certainty to be present in every man because it belongs to his very being. Now skill in the choice of means to one's own greatest well-being can be called *prudence* in the narrowest sense. Thus an imperative concerned with the choice of means to one's own happiness — that is, a precept of prudence — still remains *hypothetical*: an action is commanded, not absolutely, but only as a means to a further purpose.

Finally, there is an imperative which, without being based on, and conditioned by, any further purpose to be attained by a certain line of conduct, enjoins this conduct immediately. This imperative is *categorical*. It is concerned, not with the matter of the action and its presumed results, but with its form and with the principle from which it follows; and what is essentially good in the action consists in the mental disposition, let the consequences be what they may. This imperative may be called the imperative of *morality.* . . .

[*How are imperatives possible?*]

The question now arises 'How are all these imperatives possible?' This question does not ask how we can conceive the execution of an action commanded by the imperative, but merely how we can conceive the necessitation of the will expressed by the imperative in setting us a task. How an imperative of skill is possible requires no special discussion. Who wills the end, wills (so far as reason has decisive influence on his actions) also the means which are indispensably necessary and in his power. So far as willing is concerned, this proposition is analytic: for in my willing of an object as an effect there is already conceived the causality of myself as an acting cause — that is, the use of means; and from the concept of willing an end the imperative merely extracts the concept of actions necessary to this end. (Synthetic propositions are required in order to determine the means to a proposed end, but these are concerned, not with the reason for performing the act of will, but with the cause which produces the object.) That in order to divide a line into two equal parts on a sure principle I must from its ends describe two intersecting arcs — this is admittedly taught by mathematics only in synthetic propositions; but when I know that the aforesaid effect can be produced only by such an action, the proposition 'If I fully will the effect, I also will the action required for it' is analytic; for it is one and the same thing to conceive something as an effect possible in a certain way through me and to conceive myself as acting in the same way with respect to it. . . .

[With the] categorical imperative or law of morality the reason for our difficulty (in comprehending its possibility) is a very serious one. We have here a synthetic *a priori* practical proposition,[2] and since in theoretical knowledge there is so much difficulty in comprehending the possibility of propositions of this kind, it may readily be gathered that in practical knowledge the difficulty will be no less.

[*The Formula of Universal Law*]

In this task we wish first to enquire whether perhaps the mere concept of a categorical imperative may not also provide us with the formula containing the only proposition that can be a categorical imperative; for even when

---

[2] Without presupposing a condition taken from some inclination I connect an action with the will *a priori* and therefore necessarily (although only objectively so — that is, only subject to the Idea of a reason having full power over all subjective impulses to action). Here we have a practical proposition in which the willing of an action is not derived analytically from some other willing already presupposed (for we do not possess any such perfect will), but is on the contrary connected immediately with the concept of the will of a rational being as something which is not contained in this concept.

we know the purport of such an absolute command, the question of its possibility will still require a special and troublesome effort, which we postpone to the final chapter.

When I conceive a *hypothetical* imperative in general, I do not know beforehand what it will contain — until its condition is given. But if I conceive a *categorical* imperative, I know at once what it contains. For since besides the law this imperative contains only the necessity that our maxim[3] should conform to this law, while the law, as we have seen, contains no condition to limit it, there remains nothing over to which the maxim has to conform except the universality of a law as such; and it is this conformity alone that the imperative properly asserts to be necessary.

There is therefore only a single categorical imperative and it is this: '*Act only on that maxim through which you can at the same time will that it should become a universal law.*'

Now if all imperatives of duty can be derived from this one imperative as their principle, then even although we leave it unsettled whether what we call duty may not be an empty concept, we shall still be able to show at least what we understand by it and what the concept means.

[*The Formula of the Law of Nature*]

Since the universality of the law governing the production of effects constitutes what is properly called *nature* in its most general sense (nature as regards its form) — that is, the existence of things so far as determined by universal laws — the universal imperative of duty may also run as follows: '*Act as if the maxim of your action were to become through your will a universal law of nature.*'

[*Illustrations*]

We will now enumerate a few duties, following their customary division into duties towards self and duties towards others and into perfect and imperfect duties.

1. A man feels sick of life as the result of a series of misfortunes that has mounted to the point of despair, but he is still so far in possession of his reason as to ask himself whether taking his own life may not be contrary to his duty to himself. He now applies the test 'Can the maxim of my action really become a universal law of nature?' His maxim is 'From self-love I make it my principle to shorten my life if its continuance threatens more evil than it promises pleasure.' The only further question to ask is whether this principle of self-love can become a universal law of nature. It is then seen at

---

[3] A *maxim* is a subjective principle of action and must be distinguished from an *objective principle* — namely, a practical law. The former contains a practical rule determined by reason in accordance with the conditions of the subject (often his ignorance or again his inclinations): it is thus a principle on which the subject *acts*. A law, on the other hand, is an objective principle valid for every rational being; and it is a principle on which he *ought to act* — that is, an imperative.

once that a system of nature by whose law the very same feeling whose function (*Bestimmung*) is to stimulate the furtherance of life should actually destroy life would contradict itself and consequently could not subsist as a system of nature. Hence this maxim cannot possibly hold as a universal law of nature and is therefore entirely opposed to the supreme principle of all duty.

2. Another finds himself driven to borrowing money because of need. He well knows that he will not be able to pay it back; but he sees too that he will get no loans unless he gives a firm promise to pay it back within a fixed time. He is inclined to make such a promise; but he has still enough conscience to ask 'Is it now unlawful and contrary to duty to get out of difficulties in this way?' Supposing, however, he did resolve to do so, the maxim of his action would run thus: 'Whenever I believe myself short of money, I will borrow money and promise to pay it back, though I know that this will never be done.' Now this principle of self-love or personal advantage is perhaps quite compatible with my own entire future welfare; only there remains the question 'Is it right?' I therefore transform the demand of self-love into a universal law and frame my question thus: 'How would things stand if my maxim became a universal law?' I then see straight away that this maxim can never rank as a universal law of nature and be self-consistent, but must necessarily contradict itself. For the universality of a law that every one believing himself to be in need can make any promise he pleases with the intention not to keep it would make promising, and the very purpose of promising, itself impossible, since no one would believe he was being promised anything, but would laugh at utterances of this kind as empty shams.

3. A third finds in himself a talent whose cultivation would make him a useful man for all sorts of purposes. But he sees himself in comfortable circumstances, and he prefers to give himself up to pleasure rather than to bother about increasing and improving his fortunate natural aptitudes. Yet he asks himself further 'Does my maxim of neglecting my natural gifts, besides agreeing in itself with my tendency to indulgence, agree also with what is called duty?' He then sees that a system of nature could indeed always subsist under such a universal law, although (like the South Sea Islanders) every man should let his talents rust and should be bent on devoting his life solely to idleness, indulgence, procreation, and, in a word, to enjoyment. Only he cannot possibly *will* that this should become a universal law of nature or should be implanted in us as such a law by a natural instinct. For as a rational being he necessarily wills that all his powers should be developed, since they serve him, and are given him, for all sorts of possible ends.

4. Yet a *fourth* is himself flourishing, but he sees others who have to struggle with great hardships (and whom he could easily help); and he thinks 'What does it matter to me? Let every one be as happy as Heaven wills or as he can make himself; I won't deprive him of anything; I won't even envy him; only I have no wish to contribute anything to his well-being or to his support in distress!' Now admittedly ·if such an attitude were

a universal law of nature, mankind could get on perfectly well — better no doubt than if everybody prates about sympathy and goodwill, and even takes pains, on occasion, to practise them, but on the other hand cheats where he can, traffics in human rights, or violates them in other ways. But although it is possible that a universal law of nature could subsist in harmony with this maxim, yet it is impossible to *will* that such a principle should hold everywhere as a law of nature. For a will which decides in this way would be in conflict with itself, since many a situation might arise in which the man needed love and sympathy from others, and in which, by such a law of nature sprung from his own will, he would rob himself of all hope of the help he wants for himself.

[*The canon of moral judgement*]

These are some of the many actual duties — or at least of what we take to be such — whose derivation from the single principle cited above leaps to the eye. We must *be able to will* that a maxim of our action should become a universal law — this is the general canon for all moral judgement of action. Some actions are so constituted that their maxim cannot even be *conceived* as a universal law of nature without contradiction, let alone be *willed* as what *ought* to become one. In the case of others we do not find this inner impossibility, but it is still impossible to *will* that their maxim should be raised to the universality of a law of nature, because such a will would contradict itself. It is easily seen that the first kind of action is opposed to strict or narrow (rigorous) duty, the second only to wider (meritorious) duty; and thus that by these examples all duties — so far as the type of obligation is concerned (not the object of dutiful action) — are fully set out in their dependence on our single principle.

If we now attend to ourselves whenever we transgress a duty, we find that we in fact do not will that our maxim should become a universal law — since this is impossible for us — but rather that its opposite should remain a law universally: we only take the liberty of making an *exception* to it for ourselves (or even just for this once) to the advantage of our inclination. . . .

We have thus at least shown this much — that if duty is a concept which is to have meaning and real legislative authority for our actions, this can be expressed only in categorical imperatives and by no means in hypothetical ones. At the same time — and this is already a great deal — we have set forth distinctly, and determinately for every type of application, the content of the categorical imperative, which must contain the principle of all duty (if there is to be such a thing at all). But we are still not so far advanced as to prove *a priori* that there actually is an imperative of this kind — that there is a practical law which by itself commands absolutely and without any further motives, and that the following of this law is duty. . . .

Our question therefore is this: 'Is it a necessary law *for all rational beings* always to judge their actions by reference to those maxims of which they can themselves will that they should serve as universal laws?' If there is such a law, it must already be connected (entirely *a priori*) with the concept of the will of a rational being as such. But in order to discover this connexion we must, however much we may bristle, take a step beyond it — that is, into metaphysics, although into a region of it different from that of speculative philosophy, namely, the metaphysic of morals. . . . Here . . . we are discussing objective practical laws, and consequently the relation of a will to itself as determined solely by reason. Everything related to the empirical then falls away of itself; for if *reason entirely by itself* determines conduct (and it is the possibility of this which we now wish to investigate), it must necessarily do so *a priori*.

[*The Formula of the End in Itself*]

The will is conceived as a power of determining oneself to action in *accordance with the idea of certain laws*. And such a power can be found only in rational beings. Now what serves the will as a subjective ground of its self-determination is an *end;* and this, if it is given by reason alone, must be equally valid for all rational beings. What, on the other hand, contains merely the ground of the possibility of an action whose effect is an end is called a *means*. The subjective ground of a desire is an *impulsion (Triebfeder);* the objective ground of a volition is a *motive (Bewegungsgrund)*. Hence the difference between subjective ends, which are based on impulsions, and objective ends, which depend on motives valid for every rational being. Practical principles are *formal* if they abstract from all subjective ends; they are *material,* on the other hand, if they are based on such ends and consequently on certain impulsions. Ends that a rational being adopts arbitrarily as *effects* of his action (material ends) are in every case only relative; for it is solely their relation to special characteristics in the subject's power of appetition which gives them their value. Hence this value can provide no universal principles, no principles valid and necessary for all rational beings and also for every volition — that is, no practical laws. Consequently all these relative ends can be the ground only of hypothetical imperatives.

Suppose, however, there were something *whose existence* has *in itself* an absolute value, something which as *an end in itself* could be a ground of determinate laws; then in it, and in it alone, would there be the ground of a possible categorical imperative — that is, of a practical law.

Now I say that man, and in general every rational being, *exists* as an end in himself, *not merely as a means* for arbitrary use by this or that will: he must in all his actions, whether they are directed to himself or to other rational beings, always be viewed *at the same time as an end*. All the objects of inclination have only a conditioned value; for if there were not these inclinations and the needs grounded on them, their object would be valueless. Inclinations themselves, as sources of needs, are so far from having an absolute value to make them desirable for their own sake that it must rather be the universal wish of every rational being to be wholly free from them. Thus the value of all objects that can *be produced* by our action is always conditioned. Beings whose existence depends, not on our will, but on nature, have none the less, if they are non-rational beings, only a relative value as means and are consequently called *things*. Rational beings, on the other hand, are called *persons* because their nature already marks them out as ends in themselves — that is, as something which ought not to be used merely as a means — and consequently imposes to that extent a limit on all arbitrary treatment of them (and is an object of reverence). Persons therefore, are not merely subjective ends whose existence as an object of our actions has a value *for us*: they are *objective ends* — that is, things whose existence is in itself an end, and indeed an end such that in its place we can put no other end to which they should serve *simply* as means; for unless this is so, nothing at all of *absolute* value would be found anywhere. But if all value were conditioned — that is, contingent — then no supreme principle could be found for reason at all.

If then there is to be a supreme practical principle and — so far as the human will is concerned — a categorical imperative, it must be such that from the idea of something which is necessarily an end for every one because it is an *end in itself* it forms an *objective* principle of the will and consequently can serve as a practical law. The ground of this principle is: *Rational nature exists as an end in itself*. This is the way in which a man necessarily conceives his own existence: it is therefore so far a *subjective* principle of human actions. But it is also the way in which every other rational being conceives his existence on the same rational ground which is valid also for me; hence it is at the same time an *objective* principle, from which, as a supreme practical ground, it must be possible to derive all laws for the will. The practical imperative will therefore be as follows: *Act in such a way that you always treat humanity, whether in your own person or in the person of any other, never simply as a means, but always at the same time as an end.* We will now consider whether this can be carried out in practice.

[*Illustrations*]

Let us keep to our previous examples.

First, as regards the concept of necessary duty to oneself, the man who contemplates suicide will ask 'Can my action be compatible with the Idea of humanity *as an end in itself?*' If he does away with himself in order to escape from a painful situation, he is making use of a person merely as *a means* to maintain a tolerable state of affairs till the end of his life. But man is not a thing — not something to be used *merely* as a means: he must always in all his actions be regarded as an end in himself. Hence I cannot dispose of man in my person by maiming, spoiling, or killing. (A more precise determination of this principle in order to avoid all misunderstanding — for example, about having limbs amputated to save myself or about exposing my life to danger in order to preserve it, and so on — I must here forego: this question belongs to morals proper.)

Secondly, so far as necessary or strict duty to others is concerned, the man who has a mind to make a false promise to others will see at once that he is intending to make use of another man *merely as a means* to an end he does not share. For the man whom I seek to use for my own purposes by such a promise cannot possibly agree with my way of behaving to him, and so cannot himself share the end of the action. This incompatibility with the principle of duty to others leaps to the eye more obviously when we bring in examples of attempts on the freedom and property of others. For then it is manifest that a violator of the rights of man intends to use the person of others merely as a means without taking into consideration that, as rational beings, they ought always at the same time to be rated as ends — that is, only as beings who must themselves be able to share in the end of the very same action.

Thirdly, in regard to contingent (meritorious) duty to oneself, it is not enough that an action should refrain from conflicting with humanity in our own person as an end in itself: it must also *harmonize with this end*. Now there are in humanity capacities for greater perfection which form part of nature's purpose for humanity in our person. To neglect these can admittedly be compatible with the *maintenance* of humanity as an end in itself, but not with the *promotion* of this end.

Fourthly, as regards meritorious duties to others, the natural end which all men seek is their own happiness. Now humanity could no doubt subsist if everybody contributed nothing to the happiness of others but at the same time refrained from deliberately impairing their happiness. This is, however, merely to agree negatively and not positively with *humanity as an end in itself* unless every one endeavours also, so far as in him lies, to further the ends of others. For the ends of a subject who is an end in himself must, if this conception is to have its *full* effect in me, be also, as far as possible, *my* ends.

24

IT IS RATIONAL
TO ACT MORALLY

Kurt Baier

Kurt Baier (1917-   ) is Professor of Philosophy at the University of Pittsburgh.

THE SUPREMACY OF MORAL REASONS

Are moral reasons really superior to reasons of self-interest as we all believe? Do we really have reason on our side when we follow moral reasons against self-interest? What reasons could there be for being moral? Can we really give an answer to "Why should we be moral?" It is obvious that all these questions come to the same thing. When we ask, "Should we be moral?" or "Why should we be moral?" or "Are moral reasons superior to all others?" we ask to be shown the reason for being moral. What is this reason?

Let us begin with a state of affairs in which reasons of self-interest are supreme. In such a state everyone keeps his impulses and inclinations in check when and only when they would lead him into behavior detrimental to his own interest. Everyone who follows reason will discipline himself to rise early, to do his exercises, to refrain from excessive drinking and smoking, to keep good company, to marry the right sort of girl, to work and study hard in order to get on, and so on. However, it will often happen that people's interests conflict. In such a case, they will have to resort to ruses or force to get their own way. As this becomes known, men will become suspicious, for they will regard one another as scheming competitors for the good things in life. The universal supremacy of the rules of self-interest must lead to what Hobbes called the state of nature. At the same time, it will be clear to everyone that universal obedience to certain rules overriding self-interest would produce a state of affairs which serves everyone's interest much better than his unaided pursuit of it in a state where everyone does the same. Moral rules are universal rules designed to override those of self-interest when following the latter is harmful to others. "Thou shalt not kill," "Thou shalt not lie," "Thou shalt not steal" are rules which forbid the inflicting of harm on someone else even when this might be in one's interest.

The very *raison d'être* of a morality is to yield reasons which overrule the reasons of self-interest in those cases when everyone's following self-interest would be harmful to everyone. Hence moral reasons are superior to all others.

"But what does this mean?" it might be objected. "If it merely means that we do so regard them, then you are of course right, but your contention is useless, a mere point of usage. And how could it mean any more? If it means that we not only do so regard them, but *ought* so to regard them, then there must be *reasons* for saying this. But there could not be any reasons for it. If you offer reasons of self-interest, you are arguing in a circle. Moreover, it cannot be true that it is always in my interest to treat moral reasons as superior to reasons of self-interest. If it were, self-interest and morality could never conflict, but they notoriously do. It is equally circular to argue that there are moral reasons for saying that one ought to treat moral reasons as superior to reasons of self-interest. And what other reasons are there?"

The answer is that we are now looking at the world from the point of view of *anyone*. We are not examining particular alternative courses of action before this or that person; we are examining two alternative worlds, one in which moral reasons are always treated by everyone as superior to reasons of self-interest and one in which the reverse is the practice. And we can see that the first world is the better world, because we can see that the second world would be the sort which Hobbes describes as the state of nature.

This shows that I ought to be moral, for when I ask the question "What ought I to do?" I am asking, "Which is the course of action supported by the best reasons?" But since it has just been shown that moral reasons are superior to reasons of self-interest, I have been given a reason for being moral, for following moral reasons rather than any other, namely, they are better reasons than any other.

But is this always ·so? Do we have a reason for being moral whatever the conditions we find ourselves in? Could there not be situations in which it is not true that we have reasons for being moral, that, on the contrary, we have reasons for ignoring the demands of morality? Is not Hobbes right in saying that in a state of nature the laws of nature, that is, the rules of morality, bind only *in foro interno*?

Hobbes argues as follows.

(i) To live in a state of nature is to live outside society. It is to live in conditions in which there are no common ways of life and, therefore, no reliable expectations about other people's behavior other than that they will follow their inclination or their interest.

(ii) In such a state reason will be the enemy of co-operation and mutual trust. For it is too risky to hope that other people will refrain from protecting their own interests by the preventive elimination of probable or even possible dangers to them. Hence reason will counsel everyone to avoid these risks by preventive action. But this leads to war.

(iii) It is obvious that everyone's following self-interest leads to a state of affairs which is desirable from no one's point of view. It is, on the contrary, desirable that everybody should follow rules overriding self-interest whenever that is to the detriment of others. In other words, it is desirable to bring about a state of affairs in which all obey the rules of morality.

(iv) However, Hobbes claims that in the state of nature it helps nobody if a single person or a small group of persons begins to follow the rules of morality, for this could only lead to the extinction of such individuals or groups. In such a state, it is therefore contrary to reason to be moral.

(v) The situation can change, reason can support morality, only when the presumption about other people's behavior is reversed. Hobbes thought that this could be achieved only by the creation of an absolute ruler with absolute power to enforce his laws. We have already seen that this is not true and that it is quite different if people live in a society, that is, if they have common ways of life, which are taught to all members and somehow enforced by the group. Its members have reason to expect their fellows generally to obey its rules, that is, its religion, morality, customs, and law, even when doing so is not, on certain occasions, in their interest. Hence they too have reason to follow these rules.

Is this argument sound? One might, of course, object to step (i) on the grounds that this is an empirical proposition for which there is little or no evidence. For how can we know whether it is true that people in a state of nature would follow only their inclinations or, at best, reasons of self-interest, when nobody now lives in that state or has ever lived in it?

However, there is some empirical evidence to support this claim. For in the family of nations, individual states are placed very much like individual persons in a state of nature. The doctrine of the sovereignty of nations and the absence of an effective international law and police force are a guarantee that nations live in a state of nature, without commonly accepted rules that are somehow enforced. Hence it must be granted that living in a state of nature leads to living in a state in which individuals act either on impulse or as they think their interest dictates. For states pay only lip service to morality. They attack their hated neighbors when the opportunity arises. They start preventive wars in order to destroy the enemy before he can deliver his knockout blow. Where interests conflict, the stronger party usually has his way, whether his claims are justified or not. And where the relative strength of the parties is not obvious, they usually resort to arms in order to determine "whose side God is on." Treaties are frequently concluded but, morally speaking, they are not worth the paper they are written on. Nor do the partners regard them as contracts binding in the ordinary way, but rather as public expressions of the belief of the governments concerned that for the time being their alliance is in the interest of the allies. It is well understood that such treaties may be canceled before they reach their predetermined end or simply broken when it suits one partner. In international affairs, there are very few examples of *Nibelungentreue,* although statesmen whose countries have profited from keeping their treaties usually make such high moral claims.

It is, moreover, difficult to justify morality in international affairs. For suppose a highly moral statesman were to demand that his country adhere to a treaty obligation even though this meant its ruin or possibly its extinction. Suppose he were to say that treaty obligations are sacred and must be kept whatever the consequences. How could he defend such a policy? Perhaps one might argue that someone has to make a start in order to create mutual confidence in international affairs. Or one might say that setting a good example is the best way of inducing others to follow suit. But such a defense would hardly be sound. The less skeptical one is about the genuineness of the cases in which nations have adhered to their treaties from a sense of moral obligation, the more skeptical one must be about the effectiveness of such examples of virtue in effecting a change of international practice. Power politics still govern in international affairs.

We must, therefore, grant Hobbes the first step in his argument and admit that in a state of nature people, as a matter of psychological fact, would not follow the dictates of morality. But we might object to the next step that knowing this psychological fact about other people's behavior constitutes a reason for behaving in the same way. Would it not still be immoral for anyone to ignore the demands of morality even though he knows that others are likely or certain to do so, too? Can we offer as a justification for morality the fact that no one is entitled to do wrong just because someone else is doing wrong? This argument begs the question whether it *is* wrong for anyone in this state to disregard the demands of morality. It cannot be wrong to break a treaty or make preventive war if we have no reason to obey the moral rules. For to say that it is wrong to do so is to say that we ought not to do so. But if we have no reason for obeying the moral rule, then we have no reason overruling self-interest, hence no reason for keeping the treaty when keeping it is not in our interest, hence it is not true that we have a reason for keeping it, hence not true that we ought to keep it, hence not true that it is wrong not to keep it.

I conclude that Hobbes's argument is sound. Moralities are systems of principles whose acceptance by everyone as overruling the dictates of self-interest is in the interest of everyone alike, though following the rules of a morality is not of course identical with following self-interest. If it were, there could be no conflict between a morality and self-interest and no point in having moral rules overriding self-interest. Hobbes is also right in saying that the application of this system of rules is in accordance with reason only in social conditions, that is, when there are well-established ways of behavior.

The answer to our question "Why should we be moral?" is therefore as follows. We should be moral because being moral is following rules designed to overrule self-interest whenever it is in the interest of everyone alike that everyone should set aside his interest. It is not self-contradictory to say this, because it may be in one's interest *not* to follow one's interest at times. We have already seen that enlightened self-interest acknowledges this point. But while enlightened self-interest does not require any genuine sacrifice from anyone, morality does. In the interest of the possibility of the good life for everyone, voluntary sacrifices are sometimes required from everybody. Thus, a person might do better for himself by following enlightened self-interest rather than morality. It is not possible, however, that *everyone* should do better for himself by following enlightened self-interest rather than morality. The best possible life *for everyone* is possible only by everyone's following the rules of morality, that is, rules which quite frequently may require individuals to make genuine sacrifices.

It must be added to this, however, that such a system of rules has the support of reason only where people live in societies, that is, in conditions in which there are established common ways of behavior. Outside society, people have no reason for following such rules, that is, for being moral. In other words, outside society, the very distinction between right and wrong vanishes.

25

REASONS FOR
ACTING MORALLY

William K. Frankena

W. K. Frankena (1907-   ) is Professor of Philosophy at the University of Michigan.

Another problem that remains has been mentioned before. Why should we be moral? Why should we take part in the moral institution of life? Why should we adopt the moral point of view? We have already seen that the question, "Why should . . .?" is ambiguous, and may be a request either for motivation or for justification. Here, then, one may be asking for (1) the motives for doing what is morally right, (2) a justification for doing what is morally right, (3) motivation for adopting the moral point of view and otherwise subscribing to the moral institution of life, or (4) a justification of morality and the moral point of view. It is easy to see the form which an answer to a request for (1) and (3) must take; it will consist in pointing out the various prudential and non-prudential motives for doing what is right or for enrolling in the moral institution of life. Most of these are familiar or readily thought of and need not be detailed here. A request for (2) might be taken as a request for a moral justification for doing what is right. Then, the answer is that doing what is morally right does not need a justification, since the justification has already been given in showing that it is right. Under these circumstances, a request for (2) is like asking, "Why morally ought I to do what is morally right?" A request for (2) may also, however, be meant as a demand for a nonmoral justification of doing what is morally right; then, the answer to it will be like the answer to a request for (4). For a request for (4), being a request for reasons for subscribing to the moral way of thinking, judging, and living, must be a request for a nonmoral justification of morality. What will this be like?

There seem to be two questions here. First, why should *society* adopt such an institution as morality? Why should it foster such a system for the

From William K. Frankena, *Ethics.* © 1963. From Chapter 6. Reprinted by permission of Prentice-Hall, Inc.

guidance of conduct in addition to convention, law, and prudence? To this the answer is clear. The conditions of a satisfactory human life for people living in groups could hardly obtain otherwise. The alternatives would seem to be either a state of nature in which all or most of us would be worse off than we are, even *if* Hobbes is wrong in thinking that life in such a state would be "solitary, poor, nasty, brutish, and short," or a leviathan civil state more totalitarian than any yet dreamed of, one in which the laws would cover all aspects of life and every possible deviation by the individual would be closed off by an effective threat of force.

The other question concerns what nonmoral reasons (not just motives) there are for an *individual's* adopting the moral way of thinking and living. To some extent, the answer has just been given, but only to some extent. For on reading the last paragraph an individual might say, "Yes. This shows that society requires morality and even that it is to my advantage to have others adopt the moral way of life. But it does not show that I should adopt it. And it is no use arguing on moral grounds that I should. I want a nonmoral justification for thinking I should." Now, if this means that he wants to be shown that it is always to his advantage — that is, that his life will invariably be better or, at least, not worse in the nonmoral sense of better — if he thoroughly adopts the moral way of life, then I doubt that his demand can always be met. Through the use of various familiar arguments, one can show that the moral way of life is pretty likely to be to his advantage, but one must admit in all honesty that one who takes the moral road may be called upon to make a sacrifice and, hence, may not have as good a life in the nonmoral sense as he would otherwise have had.

It does not follow that one cannot justify the ways of morality to an individual, although it may follow that one cannot justify morality to some individuals. For nonmoral justification is not necessarily egoistic or prudential. If A asks B why he, A, should be moral, B may reply by asking A to try to decide in a rational way what kind of a life he wishes to live or what kind of a person he wishes to be. That is, he may ask A what way of life he would choose if he were to choose rationally, or in other words, freely, impartially, and in full knowledge of what it is like to live the various alternative ways of life, including the moral one. B may then be able to convince A, when he is calm and cool in this way, that the way of life he prefers, all things considered, includes the moral way of life. If so, then he has justified the moral way of life to A.

Of course, A may refuse to be rational, calm, and cool. He may retort, "But why should I be rational?" If this was his posture in originally asking for justification, he had no business asking for it. For one can only ask for justification if one is willing to be rational. One cannot consistently ask for reasons unless one is ready to accept reasons of some sort. Even in asking, "Why should I be rational?" one is implicitly committing oneself to rationality; for such a commitment is, at least, part of the connotation of the word "should."

Perhaps A has yet one more question: "What justification has society in demanding that I adopt the moral way of life, and in punishing me if I do not?" But this is a moral question; and A can hardly expect it to be allowed that society is justified in doing this to A only if it can show that doing so is to A's advantage. However, if A is asking whether society is morally justified in requiring of him at least a certain minimal subscription to the moral institution of life, then the answer surely is that society sometimes is justified in this, as we saw before. But, as we also saw, society must be careful here. For it is itself morally required to respect the individual's autonomy and liberty, and in general to treat him justly; and it must remember that morality is made to minister to the good lives of individuals and not to interfere with them any more than is necessary. Morality is made for man, not man for morality.

SUGGESTED READINGS

General Books on Ethics

BRANDT, R. B. *Ethical Theory*. Englewood Cliffs, N.J.: Prentice-Hall, Inc., 1959.
DEWEY, JOHN. *Theory of the Moral Life*. New York: Holt, Rinehart and Winston, Inc., 1960.
EWING, A. C. *Ethics*. New York: The Macmillan Company, 1953.
FRANKENA, W. K. *Ethics*. Englewood Cliffs, N.J.: Prentice-Hall, Inc., 1963.
GARNETT, A. C. *The Moral Nature of Man*. New York: Ronald Press Co., 1952.
HOSPERS, JOHN. *Human Conduct*. New York: Harcourt, Brace & World, Inc., 1961.
NOWELL-SMITH, P. H. *Ethics*. Baltimore: Penguin Books, 1954.
SIDGWICK, HENRY. *The Methods of Ethics*. London: Macmillan and Co., Ltd., 1922.
STACE, W. T. *The Concept of Morals*. New York: The Macmillan Company, 1937.
ZINK, S. The Concepts of Ethics. New York: St. Martin's Press, 1962.

Ethical Relativism

ASCH, S. E. *Social Psychology*. Englewood Cliffs, N.J.: Prentice-Hall, Inc., 1952. Chap. 13. [Reprinted in Brandt.]
BRANDT, R. B. *Ethical Theory*. Englewood Cliffs, N.J.: Prentice-Hall, Inc., 1959. Chaps. 5, 6, 11.
———. *Hopi Ethics: A Theoretical Analysis*. Chicago: The University of Chicago Press, 1954. Chap. 16, 87-90.
FIRTH, R. *Elements of Social Organization*. London: Watts & Co., 1951. Chap. 6.
GINSBERG, M. *Essays in Sociology and Social Philosophy*, vol. I. London: William Heinemann, Ltd., 1956. Chaps. 7 and 8.
HERSKOVITS, M. *Man and His Works*. New York: Alfred A. Knopf, Inc., 1948. Chap. 5.
LINTON, RALPH. "The Problem of Universal Values," in R. F. SPENCER, ed., *Method and Perspective in Anthropology*. Minneapolis: University of Minnesota Press, 1954. [Reprinted in Brandt, *Value and Obligation*.]
MACBEATH, A. *Experiments in Living*. London: Macmillan & Co., Ltd., 1952.
SUMNER, W. G. *Folkways*. Boston: Ginn & Co., 1934. [Excerpted in Brandt and Johnson.]
TAYLOR, P. "Four Types of Ethical Relativism," *Philosophical Review* 63 (1954), 500-16.
———. "Social Science and Ethical Relativism," *Journal of Philosophy* 55 (1958), 32-43.
WESTERMARCK, E. *The Origins and Development of the Moral Ideas*. Vol. I. New York: The Macmillan Company, 1906. Chaps. 1 to 5.

Theology and Ethics

AUGUSTINE, ST. "The Morals of the Catholic Church." In *Basic Writings of Saint Augustine,* ed., WHITNEY J. OATES. New York: Random House, 1948. [Excerpted in Brandt, and Johnson, *Ethics*.]
BRANDT, R. B. *Ethical Theory*. Englewood Cliffs, N.J.: Prentice-Hall, Inc., 1959. Chap. 4.
BRUNNER, EMIL. *The Divine Imperative*. Philadelphia: Westminster Press, 1947. [Excerpted in Johnson, *Ethics,* and Dewey-Gramlich-Loftsgordon.]
HOSPERS, JOHN. *Human Conduct*. New York: Harcourt, Brace & World, Inc., 1961, 246-56.
MORTIMER, R. C. *Christian Ethics*. London: Hutchinson's University Library, 1950.

PLATO. *Euthyphro,* in *Plato on the Trial and Death of Socrates,* trans. by LANE
    COOPER. Ithaca, N.Y.: Cornell University Press, 1941. [Reprinted in Brandt.]
RASHDALL, H. *Conscience and Christ.* London: Gerald Duckworth & Co., Ltd., 1933.
THOMAS, GEORGE W. *Christian Ethics and Moral Philosophy.* New York: Charles
    Scribner's Sons, 1955. [Excerpt in Brandt.]

Intuitionist or Rationalist Views

BROAD, C. D. *Five Types of Ethical Theory.* New York: Humanities Press, Inc., 1956,
    266-73.
EWING, A. C. *Ethics.* New York: The Macmillan Company, 1947. Chaps. 6 and 7.
    [Excerpt in Ekman.]
MOORE, G. E. *Principia Ethica.* Cambridge: Cambridge University Press, 1929. [Ex-
    cerpts in Dewey-Gramlich-Loftsgordon; Melden; Pap and Edwards.]
PRICE, RICHARD. *A Review of the Principle Questions in Morals.* Oxford: The Claren-
    don Press, 1948. [Excerpted in Brandt.]
PRICHARD, H. A. "Does Moral Philosophy Rest on a Mistake?" *Mind,* 21 (1912).
    [Reprinted in Sellars and Hospers; Dewey-Gramlich-Loftsgordon.]
Critics:
BRANDT, R. B. *Ethical Theory.* Englewood Cliffs, N. J.: Prentice-Hall, Inc., 1959.
    Chap. 8.
FRANKENA, W. K. *Ethics.* Englewood Cliffs, N. J.: Prentice-Hall, Inc., 1963, 85-88.
NOWELL-SMITH, P. H. *Ethics.* Baltimore: Penguin Books, 1954. Chaps. 2-4.
STRAWSON, P. F. "Ethical Intuitionism," *Philosophy,* 24 (1949), 23-33. [Excerpted
    in Brandt; Hospers and Sellars.]

Naturalism

FIRTH, R. "Ethical Absolutism and the Ideal Observer," *Philosophy and Phenomeno-
    logical Research* 12 (1952), 317-45.
HUME, DAVID. *Enquiry Concerning the Principles of Morals.* Many editions. [Ex-
    cerpted in Melden; Brandt; Johnson; Ekman; Dewey-Gramlich-Anderson.]
    (May be classified as a noncognitive theory.)
LEWIS, C. I. *Analysis of Knowledge and Valuation.* La Salle, Ill.: Open Court Publish-
    ing Company, 1946. Chaps. 12, 13, 16, 17.
PERRY, R. B. *Realms of Value: A Critique of Human Civilization.* Cambridge, Mass.:
    Harvard University Press, 1954. [Excerpts in Brandt; Johnson; Dewey-
    Gramlich-Loftsgordon.]
SPARSHOTT, F. E. *An Inquiry Into Goodness.* Chicago: University of Chicago Press,
    1958.
Critics:
BRANDT, R. B. *Ethical Theory.* Englewood Cliffs, N. J.: Prentice-Hall, Inc., 1959.
    Chap. 7.
EDWARDS, PAUL. *The Logic of Moral Discourse.* Glencoe, Ill.: The Free Press, 1955.
    Chap. 2.
EWING, A. C. *Ethics.* New York: The Macmillan Company, 1953. Chap. 6.
———. *The Definition of Good.* New York: The Macmillan Company, 1947. Chaps.
    1 and 2.
HARE, R. M. *The Language of Morals.* Oxford: The Clarendon Press, 1952. Chap. 5.
RUSSELL, BERTRAND. "The Elements of Ethics," originally in *Philosophical Essays.*
    London, George Allen & Unwin, Ltd., 1910. [Reprinted in Sellars and
    Hospers.]

Noncognitive Theories

HARE, R. M. *Freedom and Reason.* Oxford: The Clarendon Press, 1963. Chap. 6.
NOWELL-SMITH, P. H. *Ethics.* Baltimore: Penguin Books, 1954. [Excerpts in Brandt;
    Johnson *Selections.*]

RUSSELL, B. *Religion and Science.* New York: Henry Holt & Company, Inc., 1935. Chap. 9. [Reprinted in Brandt; Edwards and Pap.]

STEVENSON, C. L. "The Emotive Meaning of Ethical Terms," *Mind* 46 (1937), 14-31. [Reprinted in Ekman; Johnson *Selections;* Dewey-Gramlich-Loftsgordon.]

———. "The Nature of Ethical Disagreement," *Sigma,* vols. 1-2n, Nos. 8-9, 1947-48. [Reprinted in Sellars-Hospers; Brandt.]

———. "The Emotive Conception of Ethics and its Cognitive Implications," Philosophical Review 59 (1950), 291-304.

———. *Ethics and Language.* New Haven: Yale University Press, 1944. Chaps. 1, 2, 4-7, 9. [Excerpt in Ekman.]

Critics:

AIKEN, HENRY. "Emotive 'Meanings' and Ethical Terms," *Journal of Philosophy* 41 (1944), 456-70.

BRANDT, R. B. "The Emotive Theory of Ethics," *Philosophical Review,* LIX (1950), 305-18.

———. *Ethical Theory.* Englewood Cliffs, N.J.: Prentice-Hall, Inc., 1959. Chap. 9.

FALK, W. D. "Goading and Guiding," *Mind* 62 (1953), 145-69. [Reprinted in Ekman.]

LADD, JOHN. "Value Judgments, Emotive Meaning and Attitudes," *Journal of Philosophy,* XLVI (1949), 119-29.

KERNER, GEORGE. *The Revolution in Ethical Theory.* New York: Oxford University Press, 1966.

Hedonism and Pluralism

Hedonists:

BENTHAM, JEREMY. *Principles of Morals and Legislation.* Many editions. [Excerpts in Melden; Brandt; Dewey-Gramlich-Loftsgordon.]

BLAKE, R. "Why Not Hedonism?" *Ethics* 37 (1926), 1-18.

EPICURUS. From DIOGENES LAERTIUS, *Lives of Eminent Philosophers,* trans. by R. D. Hicks, Cambridge, Mass.: Harvard University Press, 1925. [Excerpts in Brandt; Johnson; Melden.]

MILL, J. S. *Utilitarianism.* Many editions. [Excerpts in Brandt; Melden; Johnson.]

SHARP, F. C. *Ethics.* New York: Appleton-Century Company, 1928. Chap. 19.

SIDGWICK, HENRY. *Methods of Ethics.* London: Macmillan & Co., Ltd., 1922. Bk. III, Chap. 14. [Excerpt in Melden.]

Critics and Pluralists:

BRANDT, R. B. *Ethical Theory.* Englewood Cliffs, N.J.: Prentice-Hall, Inc., 1959. Chaps. 12 and 13.

BROAD, C. D. *Five Types of Ethical Theory.* New York: Harcourt, Brace & World, Inc., 1934, 180-91. [Reprinted in Brandt.]

CARRITT, E. F. *Ethical and Political Thinking.* Oxford: Clarendon Press, 1947. Chap. 8.

EWING, A. C. *Ethics.* New York: The Macmillan Company, 1953. Chap. 3.

HOSPERS, JOHN. *Human Conduct.* New York: Harcourt, Brace & World, Inc., 1961. Chap. 3.

MOORE, G. E. *Principia Ethica.* Cambridge: Cambridge University Press, 1929. Sections 36-57. [Excerpts in Johnson, *Ethics.*]

———. *Ethics.* Oxford: Oxford University Press, 1949. Chaps. 1 and 2.

NIETZSCHE, F. *Beyond Good and Evil,* trans. HELEN ZIMMERN. London: George Allen & Unwin, Ltd., 1924. [Excerpts in Brandt; Dewey-Gramlich-Loftsgordon; Johnson.]

RICE, P. *On the Knowledge of Good and Evil.* New York: Random House, 1955. Chap. 11 and 266-78.

Ross, W. D. *The Right and the Good.* Oxford: The Clarendon Press, 1930. Chap. 5. [Reprinted in Brandt.]

Egoism

Hobbes, Thomas. *Leviathan.* First published 1651; many editions. [Excerpts in Johnson *Selections.*]
————. *Philosophical Rudiments Concerning Government and Society.* Reprinted in Sir William Molesworth, ed., *The English Works of Thomas Hobbes.* London: Bohn, 1841. [Excerpt in Brandt.]
Hospers, J. "Baier and Medlin on Ethical Egoism," *Philosophical Studies* 12: 10-16.
Critics:
Brandt, R. B. *Ethical Theory.* Englewood Cliffs, N.J.: Prentice-Hall, Inc., 1959. Chap. 14.
Broad, C. D. *Five Types of Ethical Theory.* New York: Humanities Press, Inc., 1956, 161-77.
Butler, Joseph. *Fifteen Sermons upon Human Nature.* First published 1726. Many editions. [Excerpts in Brandt; Johnson; Melden.]
Ewing, A. C. *Ethics.* New York: The Macmillan Company, 1953. Chap. 2.
Frankena, W. K. *Ethics.* Englewood Cliffs, N.J.: Prentice-Hall, Inc., 1963. Chap. 2.
Hospers, John. *Human Conduct.* New York: Harcourt, Brace & World, Inc., 1961. Chap. 4.
Kading, D. and Kramer, M. "Mr. Hospers' Defense of Impersonal Egoism," *Philosophical Studies* 15 (1964), 44-46.
Sharp, F. C. *Ethics.* New York: D. Appleton-Century Company, 1928. Chaps. 22 and 23.

Utilitarianism

Classical Utilitarianism:
Bentham, Jeremy. *Principles of Morals and Legislation.* Many editions. [Excerpts in Melden; Brandt; Dewey-Gramlich-Loftsgordon.]
Mill, J. S. *Utilitarianism.* Many editions. [Excerpts in Brandt; Melden; Johnson.]
Sidgwick, Henry. *Methods of Ethics.* London: Macmillan & Co., Ltd., 1922. Bk. I, Chap. 9; Bk. II, Chap. 1; Bk. III, Chaps. 11, 13; Bk. IV, Chaps. 2-5. Analyzed in C. D. Broad, *Five Types of Ethical Theory,* New York: Harcourt, Brace & World, Inc., 1934. Chap. 6.

Rule-Utilitarianism:
Baier, Kurt. *The Moral Point of View.* Ithaca: Cornell University Press, 1958. Chap. 8.
Brandt, R. B. "Toward a Credible Form of Utilitarianism," in H. Castaneda and G. Nakhnikian, eds., *Morality and the Language of Conduct,* Detroit: Wayne State University Press, 1963.
Harrison, J. "Utilitarianism, Universalization, and Our Duty To Be Just," *Proceedings,* The Aristotelian Society, 1952-53.
Mabbott, J. D. "Moral Rules," *Proceedings of the British Academy,* 39 (1953), 97-117.
Nowell-Smith, P. H. *Ethics.* Baltimore: Penguin Books, 1954. Chaps. 15 and 16.
Rawls, John. "Two Concepts of Rules," *Philosophical Review* 64 (1955), 3-32. [Excerpts in Brandt.]
Urmson, J. O. "The Interpretation of the Philosophy of J. S. Mill," *Philosophical Quarterly* 3 (1953), 33-40.

Discussions and Critics:
Brandt, R. B. *Ethical Theory.* Englewood Cliffs, N.J.: Prentice-Hall, Inc., 1959. Chap. 15.
Ewing, A. C. *Ethics.* New York: The Macmillan Company, 1947. Chap. 5.

FRANKENA, W. K. *Ethics*. Englewood Cliffs, N.J.: Prentice-Hall, Inc., 1963. Chap. 3.

HOSPERS, JOHN. *Human Conduct*. New York: Harcourt, Brace & World, Inc., 1961. Chaps. 12-17.

SINGER, M. G. *Generalization in Ethics*. New York: Alfred A. Knopf, 1961.

Why Be Moral?

BRANDT, R. B. *Ethical Theory*. Englewood Cliffs, N.J.: Prentice-Hall, Inc., 1959, 375-78.

HOSPERS, JOHN. *Human Conduct*. New York: Harcourt, Brace & World, Inc., 1961, 174-98.

MELDEN, A. I. "Why Be Moral?" *Journal of Philosophy* 45 (1948), 449-56.

NIELSEN, KAIS. "Is 'Why Should I Be Moral?' an Absurdity?" *Australasian Journal of Philosophy* 36 (1958), 25-31. [Reprinted in Ekman.]

SCRIVEN, MICHAEL. *Primary Philosophy*. New York: McGraw-Hill Book Company, 1966, 238-59.

SINGER, M. G. *Generalization in Ethics*. New York: Alfred A. Knopf, 1961, 319-27.

STACE, W. T. *The Concept of Morals*. New York: The Macmillan Company, 1937. Chaps. 11 and 12.

TAYLOR, PAUL. *Normative Discourse*. Englewood Cliffs, N.J.: Prentice-Hall, Inc., 1961, 164-88.

Part III

FREE WILL
AND
DETERMINISM

INTRODUCTION

There are many situations in which it seems obvious that a man has a free choice between two or more alternatives, where it is *possible* to him to choose either. In normal circumstances, if I am offered a job I am free to either take it or not take it; neither possibility is closed off to me in advance. And yet this apparently obvious fact seems to be contradicted by an almost equally deep-rooted conviction that everything that happens, including human choices, is causally determined to happen just as it does happen. If I hold a ball aloft in still air and then release it, it *must* drop. Only one direction is possible for it. The gravitational forces acting on it uniquely determine a downward motion. According to the widely accepted thesis of determinism, exactly the same thing is true of human choices and actions, although the causal determinants here are much more complex and not so open to our inspection. In the case of the job offer, if one had an adequate knowledge of my desires, scruples, principles, predilections, sentiments, etc., knew all the pressures operating on me, and also knew the general laws in accordance with which choices are determined by combinations of such factors, he would see that the decision I made was just as rigidly determined by its causes as was the falling of the ball. But if this is so, then my supposition that I had a choice in the matter would seem to be illusory. Only one of the alternatives was a real possibility, even though I did not know in advance which that was.

The free will problem is the problem of what to do about the apparent conflict between these fundamental convictions. In surveying the problem our first task is to get clearer about the content of each of these convictions and the reasons for holding it.

As an initial formulation of the belief in free will, we may offer the following:

There are situations in which *there is more than one action that a person can*

275

perform. Hence when he performs one of these actions, he can be said to have acted freely, and it remains true that he could have done otherwise.

There are many alternate ways of expressing the underlined phrase. For example:

> *More than one action is a real possibility for the person.*
> *More than one action is within the person's power.*
> *The person has a real choice between alternatives.*

As we shall see, one of the chief points at issue concerns the precise interpretation of the key phrases in this formulation, "can perform," "real possibility," and "could have done otherwise." But anyone who believes in free will, will subscribe to the above formulation in some sense.

The reasons usually offered in support of the free will thesis fall under two main headings. First there is the well-nigh irresistible conviction one has in situations of choice that more than one alternative is open to one. If I am trying to decide whether to accept a certain job offer, I am unable to take seriously the idea that only one alternative is open; indeed the very possibility of deliberation depends on my supposing that there is more than one action I *can* choose to perform. Deliberation is trying to decide which action to perform. If I supposed that only one alternative was a real possibility, I would not consider myself faced with a plurality from which a choice is necessary. This almost universal and well-nigh irresistible sense of freedom is particularly stressed by Campbell (Reading 28), but it is also recognized by Hobart (Reading 29).

Free will is also defended as a necessary presupposition of moral responsibility. When I hold a person morally responsible for something, when I praise or blame someone for what he did (praise A for having visited B in the hospital or blame him for having lied to me), I presuppose that it was *in his power* to do something other than what he did. If I supposed that no other outcome was possible in each case, then I would no more feel justified in praising or blaming him than I would feel justified in praising him for being light-skinned or blaming him for knocking me over because the crowd irresistibly shoved him against me. In these latter cases the characteristic or occurrence cannot be put down to his merit or demerit, and this is just because there were no alternatives within the power of the agent.

As an initial formulation of determinism we may offer the following:

> Every event is uniquely determined to happen just as it does happen by the causes operating on it.

Now unlike the case of the free will thesis, the precise interpretation of determinism, though a very complex matter and one on which there are differences of opinion, is not a major bone of contention within the free will problem. Hence we can proceed without more ado to deeper questions as to the import of the deterministic thesis.

The formulation given above, which is a natural one, suggests the notion of an event being *forced* or *compelled* to happen just as it does. The terminology seems congenial so long as we stick to the model of one physical object producing effects by striking another physical object, as when a window is broken by a rock striking it. However, most contemporary philosophers do not find this account illuminating even for these cases, largely because it throws no light on how we tell what causes what. Why suppose that the window was caused to break by the rock hitting it, rather than by, for example, the breeze blowing against it? It is not that we see the rock *compelling* or *necessitating* the window to break. Our real basis for picking out the rock as the cause is our knowledge of what *generally* happens in *like* circumstances. It is generally true that when a hard object like this rock, which is traveling as fast as this one was traveling, hits a window like this one, the window breaks. But it is not generally true that when a breeze like this one blows against a window like this, the window breaks. We assign causes in particular cases by reference to the general regularities we know to hold. Most contemporary philosophers follow Hume (see Reading 48) in basing their analysis of the concept of causal determination on these considerations. To say that one event, *A* (the window breaking), was causally determined by another event, *B* (the impact of the rock on the window), is to say that invariably events like *B* will be followed by events like *A*, and hence that one who has discovered this general regularity would be able infallibly to predict *A* from *B*. In Hume's words: ". . . we know nothing farther of causation of any kind, than merely the constant conjunction of objects and the consequent inference of the mind from one to another . . ." In line with this approach we may reformulate determinism in a more illuminating manner as follows:

> Every event is of some kind, *A*, such that there is a universally true generalization (law of nature) according to which events of another kind, *B*, are invariably followed by *A*'s. (This makes it possible in principle to predict an *A* if we know that a *B* has occurred.)

What reasons are there to accept determinism, as so understood? Holbach (Reading 27) talks as if the position is self-evident, but it seems that once we clear our minds of preconceptions, indeterminism is as clearly conceivable as determinism. Hume (Reading 26), on the other hand, with a modesty befitting a more empirical philosopher, argues that *in fact* there is as much uniformity in the ways in which men's actions flow from their dispositions, motives, etc., as there is in the way motions are determined by physical forces. This seems to be more to the point. The real strength of the deterministic position lies in the fact that a number of fairly dependable uniformities have actually been discovered, and that more and more are being discovered as science progresses. The extent of this achievement should not be overstated. In many areas, most notably in the field of human behavior, we are very far from being able to give precise statements of invariable regularities. (A person who wants very much [how much?] to go to Europe will accept the offer of a free trip, unless he has an obligation to do something else at the same time and has a strong sense of duty [how strong?] or unless there is something incompatible that he wants to do more, or unless he has a strong fear of the consequences of going, or unless . . .) Nevertheless, the achievements we do have to our credit give us some ground for supposing that where we cannot formulate invariable regularities the fault lies in us rather than in our subject matter.

The difficulties of assessing empirical evidence for such a sweeping hypothesis as determinism are so great that many determinists prefer to construe the thesis as an *assumption,* which is justified by the fact that it is a necessary presupposition of the scientific enterprise. If we did not suppose that events are causally determined, we would not persevere in the task of discovering the causal determinants of events of various sorts. There is no doubt that the assumption of determinism has in fact often been in the background of scientific inquiry. But there are two difficulties with this. First, as Eddington brings out in Reading 30, it is quite possible to do scientific research on the assumption that probability laws (according to which a given set of conditions simply give different probabilities to different outcomes, rather than uniquely determining any one) are the most that can be found. Second, and most crucial philosophically, even if determinism were a necessary presupposition of scientific research, that would not in itself be a sufficient reason for accepting determinism. The thesis that some people are possessed by the devil is a necessary presupposition of witch hunts (in the literal sense of the term), but it is no more respectable for that. If determinism is in a different position, it is because the actual results of scientific research have given us some reason to suppose that causal determinants are always there to be found.

We can now proceed to consider the main positions on the free will problem. If one accepts the prima facie incompatibility between free will and determinism, then he will (1) either reject free will in order to retain determinism (*Necessitarianism*) or (2) reject determinism in order to retain free will (*Libertarianism*). A given philosopher's choice will depend on which thesis he takes to be most strongly supported. Finally (3) there is the position that, contrary to first appearances, free will and determinism are not inconsistent and hence no choice between them is necessary (*Reconcilism*). We shall now consider these positions in turn.

Since we have already set out the grounds of free will and of determinism, the main points to bring out concerning (1) and (2) are the ways in which each of them tries to counter the arguments that support what is being rejected. (There is also the question of their common assumption, that free will and determinism are inconsistent; we shall discuss that in connection with the reconcilist position.) Necessitarianism is represented by Holbach (Reading 27). (Hospers, Reading 32, comes close, but, as we shall see, his position is not unambiguously so classifiable.) In rejecting free will the Necessitarian dismisses the subjective sense of freedom of choice as an illusion generated by our ignorance of the complex network of causal factors. I think that a number of different items on the menu are all real possibilities for me at this moment, only because, given the limited powers of the human mind and the imperfect state of psychology, I am unable to trace the operations of the desires, aversions, and beliefs that determine my choice. To the second main support for free will (that it is presupposed by moral responsibility) there are two possible reactions. On the one hand, the Necessitarian may simply draw the inference that the whole practice of holding men responsible is one that should be abandoned since it rests on the mistaken assumption of free will. (Hospers approximates this position, with qualifications to be noted below.) On the other hand, he may try to reinterpret such activities as holding persons responsible, and praising and blaming them, as justified solely in terms of their consequences, in which case they would no longer rest on a free will assumption. In that case his position on this point should merge into that of the reconcilist, who claims that these activities presuppose free will in his sense (in which it is compatible with determinism). The deterministic interpretation of responsibility will be set out below in discussing the reconcilist position.

Moving to position (2), there are two quite different ways in which Libertarians react to the arguments for determinism. The more common position is that represented by Campbell. He does not question the strength of the general case for determinism; rather he limits himself to arguing that the reasons for free will are so strong as to require us to make an exception for human choice. Indeed Campbell himself is willing to abandon even most voluntary actions to causal determination, insisting on an exceptional status only for those special cases in which a person feels a conflict between an obligation and what he would otherwise be most inclined to do. We are thus left with a picture of a world governed by inexorable causes, except for those very special occasions on which a man is struggling with moral temptation.

Benn and Peters (Reading 31), although not taking a Libertarian position themselves, give aid and comfort to the position by arguing for a more sweeping exemption of human action from causal determination. They point out features of human action which, so they claim, prevent any causal explanation from being a complete explanation of any action. This position is presently the center of lively controversy in philosophy. (For further references, see the bibliography.)

The other libertarian reaction is exemplified by Eddington. He attacks determinism on its home ground — the physical sciences. He calls attention to recent developments in the physics of subatomic phenomena which suggest that the ultimate laws governing physical occurrences are of a probability or statistical form, rather than an absolute form. That is, given circumstances C_1, C_2, . . . the laws tell us not unqualifiedly what will happen, but rather what is most likely to happen, or more precisely, that a given event, E_1, has a probability of, say, .999. According to this view, it is not just that this is the best approximation we have been able to make so far to the way things really are; it is rather that this is all there is to be discovered. The nature of things leaves it (at least a little) open in each case exactly what is going to happen. The causal factors in operation make one outcome most likely, perhaps enormously most likely, but they do not rule out the possibility of other outcomes. This view holds out an attractive prospect of accommodating a belief in a plurality of open possibilities at the moment of choice, without requiring us to suppose that psychological laws are of a radically different kind from those operative elsewhere in nature. It should be noted that this interpretation of contemporary quantum physics, and the applicability of these considerations to the phenomena of choice, are highly controversial matters. (See suggested readings at the end of this chapter.)

The Reconcilist position (3) has been taken by a number of eminent philosophers, including Hobbes, Locke, and Mill. In our selections it is briefly stated by Hume and set out in detail by Hobart.

It may seem incredible to the reader that anyone should suppose free will and determinism to be compatible. Free will involves the existence of plurality of alternatives, any one of which was a real possibility at the time of choice, while according to determinism only the one that was chosen was a real possibility. It seems obvious that the positions are mutually inconsistent. To see how anyone could suppose them to be consistent, we shall have to go back to our formulation of the free will thesis. We shall see that the crucial terms in that formulation conceal an ambiguity, and that whether free will and determinism are incompatible depends on how that ambiguity is resolved.

According to the free will thesis, as formulated above, there are situations in which there is more than one action that a person *can* perform, so that after he performs one of them it remains true that he *could* have done something else instead. Now the Necessitarian and the Libertarian, who share the assumption that free will and determinism are inconsistent, understand "can" and "could" in this context to imply *causal possibility*. That is, on their understanding, to say that I can either accept or reject the job offer is to imply that the either action is left open by whatever causes are operative in the situation (desires, fears, social pressures, etc.); both actions are causally possible. Similarly, to say, after the fact, that I *could* have done something other than I did is to imply that the relevant factors did not causally rule out some other action. We may term this understanding of "can" and "could" the "categorical" interpretation, following Campbell's terminology ("causal interpretation" would be a happier terminological choice); and the kind of freedom that consists in the fact that more than one action is causally possible in a given situation, *A,* we may term "contra-causal freedom" or "freedom from determinism." (Analogous interpretations can be given for the other crucial terms: "real possibility," "real choice," and "within the person's power," but for simplicity of exposition we shall confine our attention to "can" and "could.") If we adopt this very natural way of understanding these terms, then free will and determinism are in flat contradiction, for the former asserts and the latter denies the existence of a plurality of causal possibilities of action in certain situations.

However, this is not the only sense that can reasonably be attached to "can" and "could" in such contexts. To see another possibility, let us contrast X missing class because he went to a cinema instead, with Y missing class because he was held prisoner elsewhere under lock and key. Here it seems obviously correct to contrast these cases by saying that X could have done otherwise, but that Y could not; X missed class freely, he had a choice; Y had no choice, he couldn't help himself. Now in what sense are the crucial terms like "could" being used in this contrast? Are we using them in the categorical sense? Are we saying that Y's, but not X's, skipping class was uniquely determined by causes? Not at all, says the Reconcilist. We do not have to settle the question of what is or is not causally determined in order to make this contrast. All that we have to know is that X was able to carry out a decision to come to class if such a decision was made, whereas Y was not able to carry out any such decision. Thus the essential difference between the two cases is the extent to which they allow for alternative decisions to be implemented, if they were made. This makes it appear that "could have done otherwise" is being used in this context to mean "had the power to do otherwise if one decided (chose) to," or more simply "would have done otherwise if one had decided (chosen) to do otherwise." We may term this sense of "could" ("can") the "hypothetical" sense, and the corresponding type of freedom "freedom from constraint." (Again we can give corresponding interpretations for other terms involved, like "had a choice" and "real possibility," but again we will stick to "can" and "could" in order to simplify the exposition.) To be free in this sense is to be in a position to implement whatever decisions one makes (or at least to be in a position to implement more than one such decision). It carries no implication at all as to what is or is not causally determined. The class skipping of X could be as rigidly determined as you like by his desires, fears, etc., and it could still be true that he cuts class of his own free will, in the (hypothetical) sense that he could have attended class instead had he chosen to do so. The distinction between free and unfree, on this interpretation, is not a distinction between caused and uncaused, but between the operation of different classes of causes. A free act is one in which choice is efficacious. Thus if we give the hypothetical interpretation to the crucial terms in the free will thesis it is clearly not inconsistent with determinism.

It is not enough for the reconcilist to point out that one can interpret "can" in the hypothetical sense, or even to show that it is sometimes so used. To make out his case he must show that "can," and the other terms, should be interpreted this way in the free will thesis. And to do that he must show that whatever solid reasons there are for accepting the free will thesis support the thesis interpreted in this way. Discussion on this point is heavily concentrated on the second main reason, that free will is a presupposition of persons' responsibility for their actions. The first main reason, our immediate conviction of being able to choose more than one alternative, is too inarticulate to afford much scope for argumentation. Campbell claims that in situations of moral temptation, what we are convinced of is that we have the capacity to go counter to the strongest causal influences, while Hobart maintains that this sense of alternative possibilities is simply the sense that "I can do whatever I decide to do." These opposing claims having been made, one is hard put to find any basis for adjudicating the dispute. The experience in question is too immediate to display any features supporting the one interpretation or the other. On the question of responsibility, however, there is more to be said.

Campbell and Hobart agree that one can justifiably hold a person responsible for what he did only if he acted freely (could have done otherwise, etc.). Furthermore, they agree that persons often act freely in the hypothetical sense. (Campbell, of course, asserts, while Hobart denies or doubts, that persons sometimes act freely in the categorical sense.) But they disagree on whether freedom in the hypothetical sense is sufficient as a basis for responsibility, Hobart answering this in the affirmative, Campbell in the negative.

The Reconcilist argues first that the basis we actually use for deciding whether to hold people responsible is the presence or absence of freedom in this sense. In the cases cited earlier, I would hold X responsible for missing class, but not Y. Again, if a burglar breaks into your house, he will be held responsible for having violated your rights, whereas if someone is picked up by a tornado and deposited in your back yard, he will not. Our basis for making these discriminations, says the Reconcilist, is simply that in the first case, but not the second, the person could have done otherwise, in the hypothetical sense of "could." That is all we need to assure ourselves of to determine whether to impute responsibility. The burglar could have done otherwise, in the sense that if he had decided not to break into your house he would not have done so; whereas this is not true of the tornado victim. He could decide as often as he pleased, while sailing through the air, not to enter your back yard, but the outcome would not be affected in the slightest. This is all we need to know. In particular, we do not also need to go into the question of whether the burglar's action was causally determined by certain psychological factors; that inquiry would have no relevance here.

To this argument the Libertarian replies that although we do not normally look into the question of causal determination before assigning responsibility, that is because we work with an unquestioned assumption that, except in unusual circumstances, human actions are not causally determined, and that if we come to doubt this assumption, we would begin to have doubts about any ascriptions of responsibility. It would seem that doubt about contracausal freedom has this effect in some cases (e.g., Hospers), but not in others (e.g., Hobart). So it is difficult to assess this reply by the Libertarian.

The Reconcilist does not confine himself to pointing out how we in fact proceed in assigning responsibility. He also has an analysis of the concept of responsibility in terms of which he can argue that freedom from constraint is a sufficient basis. What holding a person responsible for an action amounts to, says the Reconcilist, is taking it to be appropriate to praise or blame (reward or punish) him for his action. Hence the question as to when a man is responsible is just the question as to when he is appropriately praised or blamed. But this is to be settled in terms of the intended effect of praise or blame, which is to influence the man's future action, to make it more, or less, likely that he will act in a like manner in the future. Now if X's trip to the cinema, instead of to class, was causally determined, that will do nothing to prevent my blaming him from having its intended effect of making it less likely that he will cut class in the future. It is a fact about human nature that praise and blame, in favorable circumstances, tend to affect the likelihood of future actions; this fact is in no way dependent on the action for which one is blamed being causally indetermined. On the other hand, praise and blame have no function where the action was not free from constraint. Blaming the tornado victim could not possibly make it less likely that he would intrude on a neighbor the next time he was picked up by a tornado. Thus a consideration of the nature of responsibility gives us grounds for holding that hypothetical, but not categorical, freedom is a necessary condition of responsibility.

The Libertarian rejoinder consists of two points. First he denies that responsibility can be equated with the probable *effectiveness* of praise and blame (or reward and punishment) on future behavior. One may attempt to mold the future actions of a dog by rewards and punishments, but one does not hold a dog (morally) responsible for what he does in the way one holds a man responsible. What is distinctive of moral responsibility, claims the Libertarian, is that the presupposition of contra-causal freedom is built into it.

His second argument is, perhaps, a more fundamental one. Even if X was free in cutting class in the sense that *if* he had chosen to come to class nothing would have prevented him from doing so, that does not show that he can be held responsible for cutting class, unless he could have chosen to come to class. More generally, the fact that one could have done otherwise *if* he had chosen to do otherwise, does not show that his action was free in any way that makes him responsible for what he did, unless it is also the case that he could have *chosen* otherwise.

There are stronger and weaker forms of Reconcilism. Hobart's version is one that, while including the position we have been presenting, goes beyond it in claiming that determinism is a necessary condition for free will. This is less widely accepted than the mere compatibility thesis. The usual reason offered in its support is that given by Hobart, viz., that an action which is not causally determined by the character of the agent (together with the situation in which he is acting) cannot be said to have stemmed from *him,* from the particular person that he is, and hence is not anything for which *he* can be held responsible. If it is causally determined by something independent of his character it is certainly not his act, while if it is not causally determined at all, it is a chance happening and again something for which he cannot be held responsible. However, the last step in this argument depends on regarding chance as the only alternative to causal determination. This ignores the possibility, brought out by Eddington, that human choice may be governed by probability laws that make the action influenced but not necessitated by the agent's character.

Hospers, in Reading 32, while not denying that the senses of "free" and "can" brought out by Hobart are important ones, suggests some serious qualifications in the Reconcilist position. First he argues that psychoanalytic insights into neurotic behavior show that being able to do otherwise, in the hypothetical sense, is not sufficient for responsibility, even if we have a Utilitarian criterion for responsibility (a man is responsible if and only if praise or blame is likely to be effective). Considering a neurotic woman who is driven by unconscious guilt to subject herself to a succession of sadistic men, it may be true that she could avoid getting involved with a given man *if she chose to do so* (and so is free in the hypothetical sense); but blame is still doomed to ineffectiveness because it will not touch the unconscious motives that are responsible for her behavior. In an illuminating discussion of responsibility Hospers suggests that we add, as another necessary condition for responsibility, the possibility of rational control of one's actions. Second, he argues that there is a deeper sense in which determinism would imply that even those who satisfy these stronger conditions are not responsible for their actions. For whether their actions stem from rational deliberation, impulse, unconscious desires, or whatever, the factors that determine the actions were in turn determined by something previous, and those in turn . . . It is clear that in tracing back this chain we will eventually arrive at a time prior to the birth of the person in question. Thus determinism implies that given certain conditions that obtained prior to my birth, it is causally impossible that I should be doing anything other than what I am doing now. But obviously I couldn't have done anything about those conditions, even in the Reconcilist's sense of "could," since I was not around to do anything about them. But it seems unwarranted to hold anyone responsible for anything that follows necessarily from conditions that he was unable to do anything about.

Thus, according to Hospers, if determinism is true, we are often practically justified in holding people responsible, though not as often as we suppose, and not as often as Hobart's criterion would imply. However, there is a deeper sense of "responsible" in which the Libertarian is justified in holding that if determinism is true no one is responsible for any of his actions.

26

THE CASE FOR
DETERMINISM

David Hume

It might reasonably be expected, in questions which have been canvassed and disputed with great eagerness, since the first origin of science and philosophy, that the meaning of all the terms, at least, should have been agreed upon among the disputants, and our inquiries, in the course of two thousand years, been able to pass from words to the true and real subject of the controversy. For how easy may it seem to give exact definitions of the terms employed in reasoning, and make these definitions, not the mere sound of words, the object of future scrutiny and examination? But if we consider the matter more narrowly, we shall be apt to draw a quite opposite conclusion. From this circumstance alone, that a controversy has been long kept on foot, and remains still undecided, we may presume that there is some ambiguity in the expression, and that the disputants affix different ideas to the terms employed in the controversy. For as the faculties of the mind are supposed to be naturally alike in every individual — otherwise nothing could be more fruitless than to reason or dispute together — it were impossible, if men affix the same ideas to their terms, that they could so long form different opinions of the same subject, especially when they communicate their views, and each party turn themselves on all sides, in search of arguments which may give them the victory over their antagonists. It is true, if men attempt the discussion of questions which lie entirely beyond the reach of human capacity, such as those concerning the origin of worlds, or the economy of the intellectual system or region of spirits, they may long beat the air in their fruitless contests, and never arrive at any determinate conclusion. But if the question regard any subject of common life and experience, nothing, one would think, could preserve the dispute so long undecided, but some ambiguous expres-

This selection is Part I of Section VIII, "Of Liberty and Necessity," of *An Inquiry Concerning Human Understanding,* a work first published in 1748.

sions, which keep the antagonists still at a distance, and hinder them from grappling with each other.

This has been the case in the long disputed question concerning liberty and necessity; and to so remarkable a degree, that, if I be not much mistaken, we shall find that all mankind, both learned and ignorant, have always been of the same opinion with regard to this subject, and that a few intelligible definitions would immediately have put an end to the whole controversy. I own, that this dispute has been so much canvassed on all hands, and has led philosophers into such a labyrinth of obscure sophistry, that it is no wonder if a sensible reader indulge his ease so far as to turn a deaf ear to the proposal of such a question, from which he can expect neither instruction nor entertainment. But the state of the argument here proposed may, perhaps, serve to renew his attention, as it has more novelty, promises at least some decision of the controversy, and will not much disturb his ease by any intricate or obscure reasoning.

I hope, therefore, to make it appear, that all men have ever agreed in the doctrine both of necessity and of liberty, according to any reasonable sense which can be put on these terms, and that the whole controversy has hitherto turned merely upon words. We shall begin with examining the doctrine of necessity.

It is universally allowed, that matter, in all its operations, is actuated by a necessary force, and that every natural effect is so precisely determined by the energy of its cause, that no other effect, in such particular circumstances, could possibly have resulted from it. The degree and direction of every motion is, by the laws of nature, prescribed with such exactness, that a living creature may as soon arise from the shock of two bodies, as motion, in any other degree or direction, than what is actually produced by it. Would we, therefore, form a just and precise idea of *necessity,* we must consider whence that idea arises, when we apply it to the operation of bodies.

It seems evident, that if all the scenes of nature were continually shifted in such a manner, that no two events bore any resemblance to each other, but every object was entirely new, without any similitude to whatever had been seen before, we should never, in that case, have attained the least idea of necessity, or of a connexion among these objects. We might say, upon such a supposition, that one object or event has followed another, not that one was produced by the other. The relation of cause and effect must be utterly unknown to mankind. Inference and reasoning concerning the operations of nature would, from that moment, be at an end; and the memory and senses remain the only canals by which the knowledge of any real existence could possibly have access to the mind. Our idea, therefore, of necessity and causation, arises entirely from the uniformity observable in the operations of nature, where similar objects are constantly conjoined together, and the mind is determined by custom to infer the one from the appearance of the other. These two circumstances form the whole of that necessity which we ascribe to matter. Beyond the constant *conjunction* of similar objects, and the consequent *inference* from one to the other, we have no notion of any necessity of connexion.

If it appear, therefore, that all mankind have ever allowed, without any doubt or hesitation, that these two circumstances take place in the voluntary actions of men, and in the operations of mind, it must follow, that all mankind have ever agreed in the doctrine of necessity, and that they have hitherto disputed, merely for not understanding each other.

As to the first circumstances, the constant and regular conjunction of similar events, we may possibly satisfy ourselves by the following considerations. It is universally acknowledged, that there is a great uniformity among the actions of men, in all nations and ages, and that human nature remains still the same in its principles and operations. The same motives always produce the same actions; the same events follow from the same causes. Ambition, avarice, self-love, vanity, friendship, generosity, public spirit; these passions, mixed in various degrees, and distributed through society, have been, from the beginning of the world, and still are, the source of all the actions and enterprises which have ever been observed among mankind. Would you know the sentiments, inclinations, and course of life of the Greeks and Romans? Study well the temper and actions of the French and English: You cannot be much mistaken in transferring to the former *most* of the observations which you have made with regard to the latter. Mankind are so much the same, in all times and places, that history informs us of nothing new or strange in this particular. Its chief use is only to discover the constant and universal principles of human nature, by showing men in all varieties of circumstances and situations, and furnishing us with materials from which we may form our observations, and become acquainted with the regular springs of human action and behaviour. These records of wars, intrigues, factions, and revolutions, are so many collections of experiments, by which the politician or moral philosopher fixes the principles of his science, in the same manner as the physician or natural philosopher becomes acquainted with the nature of plants, minerals, and other external objects, by the experiments which he forms concerning them. Nor are the earth, water, and other elements, examined by Aristotle and Hippocrates, more like to those which at present lie under our observation, than the men described by Polybius and Tacitus are to those who now govern the world.

Should a traveller, returning from a far country, bring us an account of men wholly different from any with whom we were ever acquainted, men who were entirely divested of avarice, ambition, or revenge, who knew no pleasure but friendship, generosity, and public spirit, we should immediately, from these circumstances, detect the falsehood, and prove him a liar, with the same certainty as if he had stuffed his narration with stories of centaurs and dragons, miracles and prodigies. And if we would explode any forgery in history, we cannot make use of a more convincing argument than to prove, that the actions ascribed to any person are directly contrary to the course of nature, and that no human motives, in such circumstances, could ever induce

him to such a conduct. The veracity of Quintus Curtius is as much to be suspected, when he describes the supernatural courage of Alexander, by which
he was hurried on singly to attack multitudes, as when he describes his
supernatural force and activity, by which he was able to resist them. So readily and universally do we acknowledge a uniformity in human motives and
actions, as well as in the operations of body.

Hence, likewise, the benefit of that experience, acquired by long life and
a variety of business and company, in order to instruct us in the principles of
human nature, and regulate our future conduct, as well as speculation. By
means of this guide we mount up to the knowledge of men's inclinations and
motives, from their actions, expressions, and even gestures; and again descend
to the interpretation of their actions, from our knowledge of their motives and
inclinations. The general observations, treasured up by a course of experience, give us the clue of human nature, and teach us to unravel all its intrica-
cies. Pretexts and appearances no longer deceive us. Public declarations
pass for the specious colouring of a cause. And though virtue and honour
be allowed their proper weight and authority, that perfect disinterestedness,
so often pretended to, is never expected in multitudes and parties, seldom in
their leaders; and scarcely even in individuals of any rank or station. But
were there no uniformity in human actions, and were every experiment,
which we could form of this kind, irregular and anomalous, it were impossible
to collect any general observations concerning mankind; and no experience,
however accurately digested by reflection, would ever serve to any purpose.
Why is the aged husbandman more skilful in his calling than the young
beginner, but because there is a certain uniformity in the operation of the
sun, rain, and earth, towards the production of vegetables; and experience
teaches the old practitioner the rules by which this operation is governed and
directed?

We must not, however, expect that this uniformity of human actions
should be carried to such a length, as that all men, in the same circumstances,
will always act precisely in the same manner, without making any allowance
for the diversity of characters, prejudices, and opinions. Such a uniformity,
in every particular, is found in no part of nature. On the contrary, from
observing the variety of conduct in different men, we are enabled to form a
greater variety of maxims, which still suppose a degree of uniformity and
regularity.

Are the manners of men different in different ages and countries? We
learn thence the great force of custom and education, which mould the human
mind from its infancy, and form it into a fixed and established character. Is
the behaviour and conduct of the one sex very unlike that of the other? It
is thence we become acquainted with the different characters which Nature
has impressed upon the sexes, and which she preserves with constancy and
regularity. Are the actions of the same person much diversified in the different
periods of his life, from infancy to old age? This affords room for many

general observations concerning the gradual change of our sentiments and inclinations, and the different maxims which prevail in the different ages of human creatures. Even the characters which are peculiar to each individual have a uniformity in their influence; otherwise our acquaintance with the persons, and our observations of their conduct, could never teach us their dispositions, or serve to direct our behaviour with regard to them.

I grant it possible to find some actions, which seem to have no regular connexion with any known motives, and are exceptions to all the measures of conduct which have ever been established for the government of men. But if we could willingly know what judgment should be formed of such irregular and extraordinary actions, we may consider the sentiments, commonly entertained with regard to those irregular events which appear in the course of nature, and the operations of external objects. All causes are not conjoined to their usual effects with like uniformity. An artificer, who handles only dead matter, may be disappointed of his aim, as well as the politician, who directs the conduct of sensible and intelligent agents.

The vulgar, who take things according to their first appearance, attribute the uncertainty of events to such an uncertainty in the causes, as makes the latter often fail of their usual influence; though they meet with no impediment in their operation. But philosophers, observing that, almost in every part of nature, there is contained a vast variety of springs and principles, which are hid, by reason of their minuteness or remoteness, find, that it is at least possible the contrariety of events may not proceed from any contingency in the cause, but from the secret operation of contrary causes. This possibility is converted into certainty by further observation, when they remark that, upon an exact scrutiny, a contrariety of effects always betrays a contrariety of causes, and proceeds from their mutual opposition. A peasant can give no better reason for the stopping of any clock or watch, than to say that it does not commonly go right: But an artist easily perceives, that the same force in the spring or pendulum has always the same influence on the wheels; but fails of its usual effect, perhaps by reason of a grain of dust, which puts a stop to the whole movement. From the observation of several parallel instances, philosophers form a maxim, that the connexion between all causes and effects is equally necessary, and that its seeming uncertainty in some instances proceeds from the secret opposition of contrary causes.

Thus, for instance, in the human body, when the usual symptoms of health or sickness disappoint our expectation; when medicines operate not with their wonted powers; when irregular events follow from any particular cause: the philosopher and physician are not surprised at the matter, nor are ever tempted to deny, in general, the necessity and uniformity of those principles, by which the animal economy is conducted. They know that a human body is a mighty complicated machine: That many secret powers lurk in it, which are altogether beyond our comprehension: That to us it must often appear very uncertain in its operations: And that therefore the irregular events, which outwardly discover themselves, can be no proof that the laws of Nature are not observed with the greatest regularity in its internal operations and government.

The philosopher, if he be consistent, must apply the same reasonings to the actions and volitions of intelligent agents. The most irregular and unexpected resolutions of men may frequently be accounted for by those who know every particular circumstance of their character and situation. A person of an obliging disposition gives a peevish answer: But he has the toothache, or has not dined. A stupid fellow discovers an uncommon alacrity in his carriage: But he has met with a sudden piece of good fortune. Or even when an action, as sometimes happens, cannot be particularly accounted for, either by the person himself or by others; we know, in general, that the characters of men are, to a certain degree, inconstant and irregular. There is, in a manner, the constant character of human nature; though it be applicable, in a more particular manner, to some persons who have no fixed rule for their conduct, but proceed in a continued course of caprice and inconstancy. The internal principles and motives may operate in a uniform manner, notwithstanding these seeming irregularities; in the same manner as the winds, rains, clouds, and other variations of the weather are supposed to be governed by steady principles; though not easily discoverable by human sagacity and inquiry.

Thus it appears, not only that the conjunction between motives and voluntary actions is as regular and uniform as that between the cause and effect in any part of nature; but also that this regular conjunction has been universally acknowledged among mankind, and has never been the subject of dispute, either in philosophy or common life. Now, as it is from past experience that we draw all inferences concerning the future, and as we conclude that objects will always be conjoined together, which we find to have always been conjoined; it may seem superfluous to prove, that this experienced uniformity in human actions is a source whence we draw *inferences* concerning them. But in order to throw the argument into a greater variety of lights, we shall also insist, though briefly, on this latter topic.

The mutual dependence of men is so great in all societies, that scarce any human action is entirely complete in itself, or is performed without some reference to the actions of others, which are requisite to make it answer fully the intention of the agent. The poorest artificer, who labours alone, expects at least the protection of the magistrate, to insure him the enjoyment of the fruits of his labour. He also expects, that when he carries his goods to market, and offers them at a reasonable price, he shall find purchasers; and shall be able, by the money he acquires, to engage others to supply him with those commodities which are requisite for his subsistence. In proportion as men extend their dealings, and render their intercourse with others more complicated, they always comprehend in their schemes of life a greater variety of voluntary actions, which they expect, from the proper motives, to cooperate with their own. In all these conclusions, they take their measures from past experience, in the same manner as in their reasonings concerning external objects; and firmly believe that men, as well as all the elements, are to continue in their operations the same that they have ever found them. A manufacturer reckons upon the labour of his servants for the execution of any work, as much as upon the tools which he employs, and would be equally surprised were his expectations disappointed. In short, this experimental inference and reasoning concerning the actions of others, enters so much into human life, that no man, while awake, is ever a moment without employing it. Have we not reason, therefore, to affirm, that all mankind have always agreed in the doctrine of necessity, according to the foregoing definition and explication of it?

Nor have philosophers ever entertained a different opinion from the people in this particular. For, not to mention, that almost every action of their life supposes that opinion, there are even few of the speculative parts of learning to which it is not essential. What would become of *history*, had we not a dependence on the veracity of the historian, according to the experience which we have had of mankind? How could *politics* be a science, if laws and forms of government had not a uniform influence upon society? Where would be the foundation of *morals*, if particular characters had no certain or determinate power to produce particular sentiments, and if these sentiments had no constant operation on actions? And with what pretence could we employ our *criticism* upon any poet or polite author, if we could not pronounce the conduct and sentiments of his actors, either natural or unnatural, to such characters, and in such circumstances? It seems almost impossible, therefore, to engage either in science or action of any kind, without acknowledging the doctrine of necessity, and this *inference*, from motives to voluntary actions; from characters to conduct.

And, indeed, when we consider how aptly *natural* and *moral* evidence link together, and form only one chain of argument, we shall make no scruple to allow that they are of the same nature, and derived from the same principles. A prisoner who has neither money nor interest, discovers the impossibility of his escape, as well when he considers the obstinacy of the gaoler, as the walls and bars with which he is surrounded; and, in all attempts for his freedom, chooses rather to work upon the stone and iron of the one, than upon the inflexible nature of the other. The same prisoner, when conducted to the scaffold, foresees his death as certainly from the constancy and fidelity of his guards, as from the operation of the axe or wheel. His mind runs along a certain train of ideas: The refusal of the soldiers to consent to his escape; the action of the executioner; the separation of the head and body; bleeding, convulsive motions, and death. Here is a connected chain of natural causes and voluntary actions; but the mind feels no difference between them, in passing from one link to another, nor is less certain of the future event, than if it were connected with the objects present to the memory or senses, by a train of causes cemented together by what we are pleased to call a *physical* necessity. The same experienced union has the same effect on the mind, whether the united objects be motives, volition, and actions; or figure and motion. We may change the names of things, but their nature and their operation on the understanding never change.

[Were a man, whom I know to be honest and opulent, and with whom I lived in intimate friendship, to come into my house, where I am surrounded with my servants, I rest assured, that he is not to stab me before he leaves it, in order to rob me of my silver standish; and I no more suspect this event than the falling of the house itself, which is new, and solidly built and founded. — *But he may have been seized with a sudden and unknown frenzy.* — So may a sudden earthquake arise, and shake and tumble my house about my ears. I shall therefore change the suppositions. I shall say, that I know with certainty, that he is not to put his hand into the fire, and hold it there till it be consumed: And this event I think I can foretell with the same assurance, as that, if he throw himself out of the window, and meet with no obstruction, he will not remain a moment suspended in the air. No suspicion of an unknown frenzy can give the least possibility to the former event, which is so contrary to all the known principles of human nature. A man who at noon leaves his purse full of gold on the pavement at Charing-Cross, may as well expect that it will fly away like a feather, as that he will find it untouched an hour after. Above one half of human reasonings contain inferences of a similar nature, attended with more or less degrees of certainty, proportioned to our experience of the usual conduct of mankind in such particular situations.] [1]

I have frequently considered, what could possibly be the reason why all mankind, though they have ever, without hesitation, acknowledged the doctrine of necessity in their whole practice and reasoning, have yet discovered such a reluctance to acknowledge it in words, and have rather shown a propensity, in all ages, to profess the contrary opinion. The matter, I think, may be accounted for after the following manner. If we examine the operations of body, and the production of effects from their causes, we shall find, that all our faculties can never carry us farther in our knowledge of this relation, than barely to observe, that particular objects are *constantly conjoined* together, and that the mind is carried, by a *customary transition,* from the appearance of the one to the belief of the other. But though this conclusion concerning human ignorance be the result of the strictest scrutiny of this subject, men still entertain a strong propensity to believe, that they penetrate farther into the powers of nature, and perceive something like a necessary connexion between the cause and the effect. When, again, they turn their reflections towards the operations of their own minds, and *feel* no such connexion of the motive and the action; they are thence apt to suppose, that there is a difference betwen the effects, which result from material force, and those which arise from thought and intelligence. But, being once convinced, that we know nothing farther of causation of any kind, than merely the *constant*

---

[1] This paragraph occurs only in the last corrected Edition of 1777.—O.

conjunction of objects, and the consequent *inference* of the mind from one to another, and finding that these two circumstances are universally allowed to have place in voluntary actions; we may be more easily led to own the same necessity common to all causes. And though this reasoning may contradict the systems of many philosophers, in ascribing necessity to the determinations of the will, we shall find, upon reflection, that they dissent from it in words only, not in their real sentiments Necessity, according to the sense in which it is here taken, has never yet been rejected, nor can ever, I think, be rejected by any philosopher. It may only, perhaps, be pretended, that the mind can perceive, in the operations of matter, some farther connexion between the cause and effect, and a connexion that has not place in the voluntary actions of intelligent beings. Now, whether it be so or not, can only appear upon examination; and it is incumbent on these philosophers to make good their assertion, by defining or describing that necessity, and pointing it out to us in the operations of material causes.

It would seem, indeed, that men begin at the wrong end of this question concerning liberty and necessity, when they enter upon it by examining the faculties of the soul, the influence of the understanding, and the operations of the will. Let them first discuss a more simple question, namely, the operations of body and brute unintelligent matter; and try whether they can there form any idea of causation and necessity, except that of a constant conjunction of objects, and subsequent inference of the mind from one to another. If these circumstances form, in reality, the whole of that necessity which we conceive in matter, and if these circumstances be also universally acknowledged to take place in the operations of the mind, the dispute is at an end; at least, must be owned to be thenceforth merely verbal. But as long as we will rashly suppose, that we have some farther idea of necessity and causation in the operations of external objects; at the same time that we can find nothing farther in the voluntary actions of the mind; there is no possibility of bringing the question to any determinate issue, while we proceed upon so erroneous a supposition. The only method of undeceiving us is to mount up higher; to examine the narrow extent of science when applied to material causes; and to convince ourselves, that all we know of them is the constant conjunction and inference above mentioned. We may, perhaps, find that it is with difficulty we are induced to fix such narrow limits to human understanding: But we can afterwards find no difficulty when we come to apply this doctrine to the actions of the will. For as it is evident that these have a regular conjunction with motives and circumstances and character, and as we always draw inferences from one to the other, we must be obliged to acknowledge in words, that necessity which we have already avowed in every deliberation of our lives, and in every step of our conduct and behaviour.[2]

---

[2] The prevalence of the doctrine of liberty may be accounted for from another cause, viz. a false sensation, or seeming experience, which we have, or may have, of liberty or indifference in many of our actions. The necessity of any action, whether of matter or of mind, is not, properly speaking, a quality in the agent, but in any

But to proceed in this reconciling project with regard to the question of liberty and necessity; the most contentious question of metaphysics, the most contentious science: it will not require many words to prove, that all mankind have ever agreed in the doctrine of liberty, as well as in that of necessity, and that the whole dispute, in this respect also, has been hitherto merely verbal. For what is meant by liberty, when applied to voluntary actions? We cannot surely mean, that actions have so little connexion with motives, inclinations, and circumstances, that one does not follow with a certain degree of uniformity from the other, and that one affords no inference by which we can conclude the existence of the other. For these are plain and acknowledged matters of fact. By liberty, then, we can only mean *a power of acting or not acting according to the determinations of the will;* that is, if we choose to remain at rest, we may; if we choose to move, we also may. Now this hypothetical liberty is universally allowed to belong to every one who is not a prisoner and in chains. Here then is no subject of dispute.

Whatever definition we may give of liberty, we should be careful to observe two requisite circumstances; *first,* that it be consistent with plain matter of fact; *secondly,* that it be consistent with itself. If we observe these circumstances, and render our definition intelligible, I am persuaded that all mankind will be found of one opinion with regard to it.

It is universally allowed, that nothing exists without a cause of its existence; and that chance, when strictly examined, is a mere negative word, and means not any real power which has any where a being in nature. But it is pretended that some causes are necessary, some not necessary. Here then is the advantage of definitions. Let any one *define* a cause, without compre-

---

thinking or intelligent being, who may consider the action; and it consists chiefly in the determination of his thoughts to infer the existence of that action from some preceding objects; as liberty, when opposed to necessity, is nothing but the want of that determination, and a certain looseness or indifference, which we feel in passing, or not passing, from the idea of one object to that of any succeeding one. Now we may observe, that though, in *reflecting* on human actions, we seldom feel such a looseness or indifference, but are commonly able to infer them with considerable certainty from their motives, and from the dispositions of the agent; yet it frequently happens, that in *performing* the actions themselves, we are sensible of something like it: And as all resembling objects are readily taken for each other, this has been employed as a demonstrative and even intuitive proof of human liberty. We feel that our actions are subject to our will on most occasions; and imagine we feel, that the will itself is subject to nothing, because, when by a denial of it we are provoked to try, we feel that it moves easily every way, and produces an image of itself (or a *Velleity,* as it is called in the schools), even on that side on which it did not settle. This image, or faint motion, we persuade ourselves, could at that time have been completed into the thing itself; because, should that be denied, we find, upon a second trial, that at present it can. We consider not, that the fantastical desire of shewing liberty is here the motive of our actions. And it seems certain, that however we may imagine we feel a liberty within ourselves, a spectator can commonly infer our actions from our motives and character; and even where he cannot, he concludes in general that he might, were he perfectly acquainted with every circumstance of our situation and temper, and the most secret springs of our complexion and disposition. Now this is the very essence of necessity, according to the foregoing doctrine.

hending, as a part of the definition, a *necessary connexion* with its effect; and let him show distinctly the origin of the idea expressed by the definition, and I shall readily give up the whole controversy. But if the foregoing explication of the matter be received, this must be absolutely impracticable. Had not objects a regular conjunction with each other, we should never have entertained any notion of cause and effect; and this regular conjunction produces that inference of the understanding, which is the only connexion that we can have any comprehension of. Whoever attempts a definition of cause, exclusive of these circumstances, will be obliged either to employ unintelligible terms, or such as are synonymous to the term which he endeavours to define. And if the definition above mentioned be admitted, liberty, when opposed to necessity, not to constraint, is the same thing with chance, which is universally allowed to have no existence.

27

DETERMINISM
RULES OUT
FREE WILL

Baron D'Holbach

Baron P. H. D. d'Holbach (1725-1789) was a leading figure in the French enlightenment.

Those who have pretended that the *soul* is distinguished from the body, is immaterial, draws its ideas from its own peculiar source, acts by its own energies, without the aid of any exterior object, have, by a consequence of their own system, enfranchised it from those physical laws according to which all beings of which we have a knowledge are obliged to act. They have believed that the soul is mistress of its own conduct, is able to regulate its own peculiar operations, has the faculty to determine its will by its own natural energy; in a word, they have pretended that man is a *free agent*.

It has been already sufficiently proved that the soul is nothing more than the body considered relatively to some of its functions more concealed than others: it has been shown that this soul, even when it shall be supposed immaterial, is continually modified conjointly with the body, is submitted to all its motion, and that without this it would remain inert and dead: that, consequently, it is subjected to the influence of those material and physical causes which give impulse to the body; of which the mode of existence, whether habitual or transitory, depends upon the material elements by which it is surrounded, that form its texture, constitute its temperament, enter into it by means of the aliments, and penetrate it by their subtility. The faculties which are called *intellectual,* and those qualities which are styled *moral,* have been explained in a manner purely physical and natural. In the last place it has been demonstrated that all the ideas, all the systems, all the affections, all the opinions, whether true or false, which man forms to himself, are to be attributed to his physical and material senses. Thus man is a being purely physical; in whatever manner he is considered, he is connected to universal nature, and submitted to the necessary and immutable laws that she imposes

From Chapter XI, "Of the System of Man's Free Agency," of *The System of Nature* (1770). The translation is by H. D. Robinson.

on all the beings she contains, according to their peculiar essences or to the respective properties with which, without consulting them, she endows each particular species. Man's life is a line that nature commands him to describe upon the surface of the earth, without his ever being able to swerve from it, even for an instant. He is born without his own consent; his organization does in nowise depend upon himself; his ideas come to him involuntarily; his habits are in the power of those who cause him to contract them; he is unceasingly modified by causes, whether visible or concealed, over which he has no control, which necessarily regulate his mode of existence, give the hue to his way of thinking, and determine his manner of acting. He is good or bad, happy or miserable, wise or foolish, reasonable or irrational, without his will being for any thing in these various states. Nevertheless, in despite of the shackles by which he is bound, it is pretended he is a free agent, or that independent of the causes by which he is moved, he determines his own will, and regulates his own condition.

However slender the foundation of this opinion, of which every thing ought to point out to him the errour, it is current at this day and passes for an incontestable truth with a great number of people, otherwise extremely enlightened; it is the basis of religion, which, supposing relations between man and the unknown being she has placed above nature, has been incapable of imagining how man could either merit reward or deserve punishment from this being, if he was not a free agent. Society has been believed interested in this system; because an idea has gone abroad, that if all the actions of man were to be contemplated as necessary, the right of punishing those who injure their associates would no longer exist. At length human vanity accommodated itself to a hypothesis which, unquestionably, appears to distinguish man from all other physical beings, by assigning to him the special privilege of a total independence of all other causes, but of which a very little reflection would have shown him the impossibility.

. . .

The will, as we have elsewhere said, is a modification of the brain, by which it is disposed to action, or prepared to give play to the organs. This will is necessarily determined by the qualities, good or bad, agreeable or painful, of the object or the motive that acts upon his senses, or of which the idea remains with him, and is resuscitated by his memory. In consequence, he acts necessarily, his action is the result of the impulse he receives either from the motive, from the object, or from the idea which has modified his brain, or disposed his will. When he does not act according to this impulse, it is because there comes some new cause, some new motive, some new idea, which modifies his brain in a different manner, gives him a new impulse, determines his will in another way, by which the action of the former impulse is suspended: thus, the sight of an agreeable object, or its idea, determines his will to set him in action to procure it; but if a new object or a new idea more powerfully attracts him, it gives a new direction to his will, annihilates the effect of the former, and prevents the action by which it was to be procured. This is the mode in which reflection, experience, reason, necessarily arrests or suspends the action of man's will: without this he would of necessity have followed the anterior impulse which carried him towards a then desirable object. In all this he always acts according to necessary laws, from which he has no means of emancipating himself.

If when tormented with violent thirst, he figures to himself in idea, or really perceives a fountain, whose limpid streams might cool his feverish want, is he sufficient master of himself to desire or not to desire the object competent to satisfy so lively a want? It will no doubt be conceded, that it is impossible he should not be desirous to satisfy it; but it will be said — if at this moment it is announced to him that the water he so ardently desires is poisoned, he will, notwithstanding his vehement thirst, abstain from drinking it: and it has, therefore, been falsely concluded that he is a free agent. The fact, however, is, that the motive in either case is exactly the same: his own conservation. The same necessity that determined him to drink before he knew the water was deleterious, upon this new discovery equally determines him not to drink; the desire of conserving himself either annihilates or suspends the former impulse; the second motive becomes stronger than the preceding, that is, the fear of death, or the desire of preserving himself, necessarily prevails over the painful sensation caused by his eagerness to drink: but, it will be said, if the thirst is very parching, an inconsiderate man without regarding the danger will risk swallowing the water. Nothing is gained by this remark: in this case the anterior impulse only regains the ascendency; he is persuaded that life may possibly be longer preserved, or that he shall derive a greater good by drinking the poisoned water than by enduring the torment, which, to his mind, threatens instant dissolution: thus the first becomes the strongest and necessarily urges him on to action. Nevertheless, in either case, whether he partakes of the water, or whether he does not, the two actions will be equally necessary; they will be the effect of that motive which finds itself most puissant; which consequently acts in the most coercive manner upon his will.

This example will serve to explain the whole phenomena of the human will. This will, or rather the brain, finds itself in the same situation as a bowl, which, although it has received an impulse that drives it forward in a straight line, is deranged in its course whenever a force superior to the first obliges it to change its direction. The man who drinks the poisoned water appears a madman; but the actions of fools are as necessary as those of the most prudent individuals. The motives that determine the voluptuary and the debauchee to risk their health, are as powerful, and their actions are as necessary, as those which decide the wise man to manage his. But, it will be insisted, the debauchee may be prevailed on to change his conduct: this does not imply that he is a free agent; but that motives may be found sufficiently powerful to annihilate the effect of those that previously acted upon him; then these new motives determine his will to the new mode of conduct he may adopt as necessarily as the former did to the old mode.

Man is said to *deliberate*, when the action of the will is suspended; this

happens when two opposite motives act alternately upon him. *To deliberate,*
is to hate and to love in succession; it is to be alternately attracted and repelled;
it is to be moved, sometimes by one motive, sometimes by another. Man only
deliberates when he does not distinctly understand the quality of the objects
from which he receives impulse, or when experience has not sufficiently apprised him of the effects, more or less remote, which his actions will produce.
He would take the air, but the weather is uncertain; he deliberates in consequence; he weighs the various motives that urge his will to go out or to stay
at home; he is at length determined by that motive which is most probable;
this removes his indecision, which necessarily settles his will, either to remain
within or to go abroad: his motive is always either the immediate or ultimate
advantage he finds, or thinks he finds, in the action to which he is persuaded.

Man's will frequently fluctuates between two objects, of which either
the presence or the ideas move him alternately: he waits until he has contemplated the objects, or the ideas they have left in his brain which solicit him to
different actions; he then compares these objects or ideas; but even in the
time of deliberation, during the comparison, pending these alternatives of love
and hatred which succeed each other, sometimes with the utmost rapidity, he
is not a free agent for a single instant; the good or the evil which he believes
he finds successively in the objects, are the necessary motives of these momentary wills; of the rapid motion of desire or fear, that he experiences as
long as his uncertainty continues. From this it will be obvious that deliberation is necessary; that uncertainty is necessary; that whatever part he takes, in
consequence of this deliberation, it will always necessarily be that which he
has judged, whether well or ill, is most probable to turn to his advantage.

When the soul is assailed by two motives that act alternately upon it,
or modify it successively, it deliberates; the brain is in a sort of equilibrium,
accompanied with perpetual oscillations, sometimes towards one object, sometimes towards the other, until the most forcible carries the point, and thereby
extricates it from this state of suspense, in which consists the indecision of his
will. But when the brain is simultaneously assailed by causes equally strong
that move it in opposite directions, agreeable to the general law of all bodies
when they are struck equally by contrary powers, it stops, it is in *nisu;* it is
neither capable to will nor to act; it waits until one of the two causes has obtained sufficient force to overpower the other; to determine its will; to attract
it in such a manner that it may prevail over the efforts of the other cause.

This mechanism, so simple, so natural, suffices to demonstrate why uncertainty is painful, and why suspense is always a violent state for man. The
brain, an organ so delicate and so mobile, experiences such rapid modifications
that it is fatigued; or when it is urged in contrary directions, by causes equally
powerful, it suffers a kind of compression, that prevents the activity which is
suitable to the preservation of the whole, and which is necessary to procure
what is advantageous to its existence. This mechanism will also explain the
irregularity, the indecision, the inconstancy of man, and account for that conduct which frequently appears an inexplicable mystery, and which is, indeed,

the effect of the received systems. In consulting experience, it will be found that the soul is submitted to precisely the same physical laws as the material body. If the will of each individual, during a given time, was only moved by a single cause or passion, nothing would be more easy than to foresee his actions; but his heart is frequently assailed by contrary powers, by adverse motives, which either act on him simultaneously or in succession; then his brain, attracted in opposite directions, is either fatigued, or else tormented by a state of compression, which deprives it of activity. Sometimes it is in a state of incommodious inaction; sometimes it is the sport of the alternate shocks it undergoes. Such, no doubt, is the state in which man finds himself when a lively passion solicits him to the commission of crime, whilst fear points out to him the danger by which it is attended: such, also, is the condition of him whom remorse, by the continued labour of his distracted soul, prevents from enjoying the objects he has criminally obtained.

.   .   .

Choice by no means proves the free agency of man: he only deliberates when he does not yet know which to choose of the many objects that move him, he is then in an embarrassment, which does not terminate until his will is decided by the greater advantage he believes he shall find in the object he chooses, or the action he undertakes. From whence it may be seen, that choice is necessary, because he would not determine for an object, or for an action, if he did not believe that he should find in it some direct advantage. That man should have free agency it were needful that he should be able to will or choose without motive, or that he could prevent motives coercing his will. Action always being the effect of his will once determined, and as his will cannot be determined but by a motive which is not in his own power, it follows that he is never the master of the determination of his own peculiar will; that consequently he never acts as a free agent. It has been believed that man was a free agent because he had a will with the power of choosing; but attention has not been paid to the fact that even his will is moved by causes independent of himself; is owing to that which is inherent in his own organization, or which belongs to the nature of the beings acting on him.†
Is he the master of willing not to withdraw his hand from the fire when he fears it will be burnt? Or has he the power to take away from fire the property which makes him fear it? Is he the master of not choosing a dish of meat, which he knows to be agreeable or analogous to his palate; of not preferring it to that which he knows to be disagreeable or dangerous? It is always accord-

---

† Man passes a great portion of his life without even willing. His will depends on the motive by which he is determined. If he were to render an exact account of every thing he does in the course of each day — from rising in the morning to lying down at night — he would find that not one of his actions have been in the least voluntary; that they have been mechanical, habitual, determined by causes he was not able to foresee; to which he was either obliged to yield, or with which he was allured to acquiesce: he would discover, that all the motives of his labours, of his amusements, of his discourses, of his thoughts, have been necessary; that they have evidently either seduced him or drawn him along.

ing to his sensations, to his own peculiar experience, or to his suppositions, that he judges of things, either well or ill; but whatever may be his judgment, it depends necessarily on his mode of feeling, whether habitual or accidental, and the qualities he finds in the causes that move him, which exist in despite of himself.

.   .   .

It has been believed that man was a free agent, because it has been imagined that his soul could at will recall ideas which sometimes suffice to check his most unruly desires. Thus, the idea of a remote evil, frequently prevents him from enjoying a present and actual good: thus remembrance, which is an almost insensible or slight modification of his brain, annihilates, at each instant, the real objects that act upon his will. But he is not master of recalling to himself his ideas at pleasure; their association is independent of him; they are arranged in his brain in despite of him and without his own knowledge, where they have made an impression more or less profound; his memory itself depends upon his organization; its fidelity depends upon the habitual or momentary state in which he finds himself; when his will is vigorously determined to some object or idea that excites a very lively passion in him, those objects or ideas that would be able to arrest his action, no longer present themselves to his mind; in those moments his eyes are shut to the dangers that menace him; of which the idea ought to make him forbear; he marches forwards headlong towards the object by whose image he is hurried on; reflection cannot operate upon him in any way; he sees nothing but the object of his desires; the salutary ideas which might be able to arrest his progress disappear, or else display themselves either too faintly or too late to prevent his acting. Such is the case with all those who, blinded by some strong passion, are not in a condition to recall to themselves those motives, of which the idea alone, in cooler moments, would be sufficient to deter them from proceeding; the disorder in which they are, prevents their judging soundly; renders them incapable of foreseeing the consequences of their actions; precludes them from applying to their experience; from making use of their reason; natural operations which suppose a justness in the manner of associating their ideas, but to which their brain is then not more competent, in consequence of the momentary delirium it suffers, than their hand is to write whilst they are taking violent exercise.

Man's mode of thinking is necessarily determined by his manner of being; it must therefore depend on his natural organization, and the modification his system receives independently of his will. From this, we are obliged to conclude, that his thoughts, his reflections, his manner of viewing things, of feeling, of judging, of combining ideas, is neither voluntary nor free. In a word, that his soul is neither mistress of the motion excited in it, nor of representing to itself, when wanted, those images or ideas that are capable of counterbalancing the impulse it receives. This is the reason, why man, when in a passion, ceases to reason; at that moment reason is as impossible to be heard, as it is during an ecstacy, or in a fit of drunkenness. The wicked are never more than men who are either drunk or mad; if they reason, it is not until tranquillity is re-established in their machine; then, and not till then, the tardy ideas that present themselves to their mind enable them to see the consequence of their actions, and give birth to ideas that bring on them that trouble, which is designated *shame, regret, remorse.*

The errours of philosophers on the free agency of man, have arisen from their regarding his will as the *primum mobile,* the original motive of his actions; for want of recurring back, they have not perceived the multiplied, the complicated causes which, independently of him, give motion to the will itself; or which dispose and modify his brain, whilst he himself is purely passive in the motion he receives. Is he the master of desiring or not desiring an object that appears desirable to him? Without doubt it will be answered, no: but he is the master of resisting his desire, if he reflects on the consequences. But, I ask, is he capable of reflecting on these consequences, when his soul is hurried along by a very lively passion, which entirely depends upon his natural organization, and the causes by which he is modified? Is it in his power to add to these consequences all the weight necessary to counterbalance his desire? Is he the master of preventing the qualities which render an object desirable from residing in it? I shall be told: he ought to have learned to resist his passions; to contract a habit of putting a curb on his desires. I agree to it without any difficulty. But in reply, I again ask, is his nature susceptible of this modification? Does his boiling blood, his unruly imagination, the igneous fluid that circulates in his veins, permit him to make, enable him to apply true experience in the moment when it is wanted? And even when his temperament has capacitated him, has his education, the examples set before him, the ideas with which he has been inspired in early life, been suitable to make him contract this habit of repressing his desires? Have not all these things rather contributed to induce him to seek with avidity, to make him actually desire those objects which you say he ought to resist.

In despite of these proofs of the want of free agency in man, so clear to unprejudiced minds, it will, perhaps, be insisted upon with no small feeling of triumph, that if it be proposed to any one, to move or not to move his hand, an action in the number of those called *indifferent,* he evidently appears to be the master of choosing; from which it is concluded that evidence has been offered of his free agency. The reply is, this example is perfectly simple; man in performing some action which he is resolved on doing, does not by any means prove his free agency: the very desire of displaying this quality, excited by the dispute, becomes a necessary motive, which decides his will either for the one or the other of these actions: what deludes him in this instance, or that which persuades him he is a free agent at this moment, is, that he does not discern the true motive which sets him in action, namely, the desire of convincing his opponent: if in the heat of the dispute he insists and asks, "Am I not the master of throwing myself out of the window?" I shall answer him, no; that whilst he preserves his reason there is no probability that the desire of proving his free agency, will become a motive sufficiently power-ful to make him sacrifice his life to the attempt: if, notwithstanding this, to prove he is a free agent, he should actually precipitate himself from the win-dow, it would not be a sufficient warranty to conclude he acted freely, but rather that it was the violence of his temperament which spurred him on to this folly. Madness is a state, that depends upon the heat of the blood, not upon the will. A fanatic or a hero, braves death as necessarily as a more phlegmatic man or a coward flies from it.*

It is said that free agency is the absence of those obstacles competent to oppose themselves to the actions of man, or to the exercise of his faculties: it is pretended that he is a free agent whenever, making use of these faculties, he produces the effect he has proposed to himself. In reply to this reasoning, it is sufficient to consider that it in nowise depends upon himself to place or remove the obstacles that either determine or resist him; the motive that causes his action is no more in his own power than the obstacle that impedes him, whether this obstacle or motive be within his own machine or exterior of his person: he is not master of the thought presented to his mind, which determines his will; this thought is excited by some cause independent of himself.

To be undeceived on the system of his free agency, man has simply to re-cur to the motive by which his will is determined; he will always find this motive is out of his own control. It is said: that in consequence of an idea to which the mind gives birth, man acts freely if he encounters no obstacle. But the question is, what gives birth to this idea in his brain? was he the master either to prevent it from presenting itself, or from renewing itself in his brain? Does not this idea depend either upon objects that strike him exteriorly and in despite of himself, or upon causes, that without his knowl-edge, act within himself and modify his brain? Can he prevent his eyes, cast without design upon any object whatever, from giving him an idea of this object, and from moving his brain? He is not more master of the obstacles; they are the necessary effects of either interior or exterior causes, which always act according to their given properties. A man insults a coward, this neces-sarily irritates him against his insulter, but his will cannot vanquish the ob-stacle that cowardice places to the object of his desire, because his natural con-

---

* There is, in point of fact, no difference between the man that is cast out of the window by another, and the man who throws himself out of it, except that the impulse in the first instance comes immediately from without, whilst that which determines the fall in the second case, springs from within his own peculiar machine, having its more remote cause also exterior. When Mutius Scaevola held his hand in the fire, he was as much acting under the influence of necessity (caused by interior motives) that urged him to this strange action, as if his arm had been held by strong men: pride, despair, the desire of braving his enemy, a wish to astonish him, an anxiety to intimidate him, &c., were the invisible chains that held his hand bound to the fire. The love of glory, enthusiasm for their country, in like manner caused Codrus and Decius to devote themselves for their fellow-citizens. The Indian Colanus and the philosopher Peregrinus were equally obliged to burn themselves, by desire of exciting the astonishment of the Grecian assembly.

formation, which does not depend upon himself, prevents his having courage. In this case, the coward is insulted in despite of himself; and against his will is obliged patiently to brook the insult he has received.

The partisans of the system of free agency appear ever to have confounded constraint with necessity. Man believes he acts as a free agent, every time he does not see any thing that places obstacles to his actions; he does not perceive that the motive which causes him to will, is always necessary and independent of himself. A prisoner loaded with chains is compelled to remain in prison; but he is not a free agent in the desire to emancipate himself; his chains prevent him from acting, but they do not prevent him from willing; he would save himself if they would loose his fetters; but he would not save himself as a free agent; fear or the idea of punishment would be sufficient motives for his action.

Man may, therefore, cease to be restrained, without, for that reason, becoming a free agent: in whatever manner he acts, he will act necessarily, according to motives by which he shall be determined. He may be compared to a heavy body that finds itself arrested in its descent by any obstacle whatever: take away this obstacle, it will gravitate or continue to fall; but who shall say this dense body is free to fall or not? Is not its descent the necessary effect of its own specific gravity? The virtuous Socrates submitted to the laws of his country, although they were unjust; and though the doors of his jail were left open to him, he would not save himself; but in this he did not act as a free agent: the invisible chains of opinion, the secret love of decorum, the inward respect for the laws, even when they are iniquitous, the fear of tarnishing his glory, kept him in his prison; they were motives sufficiently powerful with this enthusiast for virtue, to induce him to wait death with tranquillity; it was not in his power to save himself, because he could find no potential motive to bring him to depart, even for an instant, from those principles to which his mind was accustomed.

Man, it is said, frequently acts against his inclination, from whence it is falsely concluded he is a free agent; but when he appears to act contrary to his inclination, he is always determined to it by some motive sufficiently efficacious to vanquish this inclination. A sick man, with a view to his cure, arrives at conquering his repugnance to the most disgusting remedies: the fear of pain, or the dread of death, then become necessary motives; consequently this sick man cannot be said to act freely.

When it is said, that man is not a free agent, it is not pretended to compare him to a body moved by a simple impulsive cause: he contains within himself causes inherent to his existence; he is moved by an interior organ, which has its own peculiar laws, and is itself necessarily determined in consequence of ideas formed from perceptions resulting from sensations which it receives from exterior objects. As the mechanism of these sensations, of these perceptions, and the manner they engrave ideas on the brain of man, are not known to him; because he is unable to unravel all these motions; because he cannot perceive the chain of operations in his soul, or the motive principle that acts within him, he supposes himself a free agent; which, literally translated, signifies, that he moves himself by himself; that he determines himself without cause: when he rather ought to say, that he is ignorant how or for why he acts in the manner he does. It is true the soul enjoys an activity peculiar to itself; but it is equally certain that this activity would never be displayed, if some motive or some cause did not put it in a condition to exercise itself: at least it will not be pretended that the soul is able either to love or to hate without being moved, without knowing the objects, wihout having some idea of their qualities. Gunpowder has unquestionably a particular activity, but this activity will never display itself, unless fire be applied to it; this, however, immediately sets it in motion.

It is the great complication of motion in man, it is the variety of his action, it is the multiplicity of causes that move him, whether simultaneously or in continual succession, that persuades him he is a free agent: if all his motions were simple, if the causes that move him did not confound themselves with each other, if they were distinct, if his machine were less complicated, he would perceive that all his actions were necessary, because he would be enabled to recur instantly to the cause that made him act. A man who should be always obliged to go towards the west, would always go on that side; but he would feel that, in so going, he was not a free agent: if he had another sense, as his actions or his motion, augmented by a sixth, would be still more varied and much more complicated, he would believe himself still more a free agent than he does with his five senses.

It is, then, for want of recurring to the causes that move him; for want of being able to analyze, from not being competent to decompose the complicated motion of his machine, that man believes himself a free agent; it is only upon his own ignorance that he founds the profound yet deceitful notion he has of his free agency; that he builds those opinions which he brings forward as a striking proof of his pretended freedom of action. If, for a short time, each man was willing to examine his own peculiar actions, search out their true motives to discover their concatenation, he would remain convinced that the sentiment he has of his natural free agency, is a chimera that must speedily be destroyed by experience.

Nevertheless it must be acknowledged that the multiplicity and diversity of the causes which continually act upon man, frequently without even his knowledge, render it impossible, or at least extremely difficult for him to recur to the true principles of his own peculiar actions, much less the actions of others: they frequently depend upon causes so fugitive, so remote from their effects, and which, superficially examined, appear to have so little analogy, so slender a relation with them, that it requires singular sagacity to bring them into light. This is what renders the study of the moral man a task of such difficulty; this is the reason why his heart is an abyss, of which it is frequently impossible for him to fathom the depth. He is then obliged to content himself with a knowledge of the general and necessary laws by which the human heart is regulated: for the individuals of his own species these laws are pretty nearly the same; they vary only in consequence of the organization that is peculiar to each, and of the modification it undergoes: this, however, cannot be rigorously the same in any two. It suffices to know, that by his essence, man tends to conserve himself, and to render his existence happy: this granted, whatever may be his actions, if he recur back to this first principle, to this general, this necessary tendency of his will, he never can be deceived with regard to his motives.

28

FREE WILL
RULES OUT
DETERMINISM

C. A. Campbell

C. A. Campbell (1897-   ) is Professor Emeritus at the University of Glasgow.

1. During the greater part of the last lecture, which was concerned with the defence of the notion of self-activity and with the classification of its main species, we were operating on the very threshold of the problem of Free Will; and in its later stages, particularly in connection with the analysis of moral-decision activity, we may perhaps be judged to have passed beyond the threshold. The present lecture, in which we address ourselves formally to the Free Will problem, is in fact so closely continuous with its predecessor that I should wish the two lectures to be regarded as constituting, in a real sense, a single unit.

In the later, more constructive part of my programme today this intimate dependence upon what has gone before will become very apparent. My initial task, however, must be one of elucidation and definition. The general question I have to try to answer, a question which is very far indeed from admitting of a ready answer, is, What precisely *is* the Free Will problem?

It is something of a truism that in philosophic enquiry the exact formulation of a problem often takes one a long way on the road to its solution. In the case of the Free Will problem I think there is a rather special need of careful formulation. For there are many sorts of human freedom; and it can easily happen that one wastes a great deal of labour in proving or disproving a freedom which has almost nothing to do with the freedom which is at issue in the traditional problem of Free Will. The abortiveness of so much of the argument for and against Free Will in contemporary philosophical literature seems to me due in the main to insufficient pains being taken over the preliminary definition of the problem. There is, indeed, one outstanding ex-

From Lecture IX, "Has the Self 'Free Will'?" of *On Selfhood and Godhood* (1957). Reprinted by permission of the publisher, George Allen & Unwin, Ltd.)

ception, Professor Broad's brilliant inaugural lecture entitled, 'Determinism, Indeterminism, and Libertarianism',[1] in which forty-three pages are devoted to setting out the problem, as against seven of its solution! I confess that the solution does not seem to myself to follow upon the formulation quite as easily as all that:[2] but Professor Broad's eminent example fortifies me in my decision to give here what may seem at first sight a disproportionate amount of time to the business of determining the essential characteristics of the kind of freedom with which the traditional problem is concerned.

Fortunately we can at least make a beginning with a certain amount of confidence. It is not seriously disputable that the kind of freedom in question is the freedom which is commonly recognised to be in some sense a precondition of moral responsibility. Clearly, it is on account of this integral connection with moral responsibility that such exceptional importance has always been felt to attach to the Free Will problem. But in what precise sense is free will a precondition of moral responsibility, and thus a postulate of the moral life in general? This is an exceedingly troublesome question; but until we have satisfied ourselves about the answer to it, we are not in a position to state, let alone decide, the question whether 'Free Will' in its traditional, ethical, significance is a reality.

Our first business, then, is to ask, exactly what kind of freedom is it which is required for moral responsibility? And as to method of procedure in this inquiry, there seems to me to be no real choice. I know of only one method that carries with it any hope of success; viz. the critical comparison of those acts for which, on due reflection, we deem it proper to attribute moral praise or blame to the agents, with those acts for which, on due reflection, we deem such judgments to be improper. The ultimate touchstone, as I see it, can only be our moral consciousness as it manifests itself in our more critical and considered moral judgments. The 'linguistic' approach by way of the analysis of moral *sentences* seems to me, despite its present popularity, to be an almost infallible method for reaching wrong results in the moral field; but I must reserve what I have to say about this for the next lecture.

2. The first point to note is that the freedom at issue (as indeed the very name 'Free *Will* Problem' indicates) pertains primarily not to overt acts but to inner acts. The nature of things has decreed that, save in the case of one's self, it is only overt acts which one can directly observe. But a very little reflection serves to show that in our moral judgments upon others their overt acts are regarded as significant only in so far as they are the expression of inner acts. We do not consider the acts of a robot to be morally responsible acts; nor do we consider the acts of a man to be so save in so far as they are distinguishable from those of a robot by reflecting an inner life of choice. Similarly, from the other side, if we are satisfied (as we may on occasion be, at least in the case of ourselves) that a person has definitely elected to follow

---

[1] Reprinted in *Ethics and the History of Philosophy, Selected Essays.*
[2] I have explained the grounds for my dissent from Broad's final conclusions on pp. 27 ff. of *In Defence of Free Will* (Jackson Son & Co., 1938).

a course which he believes to be wrong, but has been prevented by external circumstances from translating his inner choice into an overt act, we still regard him as morally blameworthy. Moral freedom, then, pertains to *inner* acts.

The next point seems at first sight equally obvious and uncontroversial; but, as we shall see, it has awkward implications if we are in real earnest with it (as almost nobody is). It is the simple point that the act must be one of which the person judged can be regarded as the *sole* author. It seems plain enough that if there are any *other* determinants of the act, external to the self, to that extent the act is not an act which the *self* determines, and to that extent not an act for which the self can be held morally responsible. The self is only part-author of the act, and his moral responsibility can logically extend only to those elements within the act (assuming for the moment that these can be isolated) of which he is the *sole* author.

The awkward implications of this apparent truism will be readily appreciated. For, if we are mindful of the influences exerted by heredity and environment, we may well feel some doubt whether there is any act of will at all of which one can truly say that the self is sole author, sole determinant. No man has a voice in determining the raw material of impulses and capacities that constitute his hereditary endowment, and no man has more than a very partial control of the material and social environment in which he is destined to live his life. Yet it would be manifestly absurd to deny that these two factors do constantly and profoundly affect the nature of a man's choices. That this is so we all of us recognise in our moral judgments when we 'make allowances', as we say, for a bad heredity or a vicious environment, and acknowledge in the victim of them a diminished moral responsibility for evil courses. Evidently we do *try*, in our moral judgments, however crudely, to praise or blame a man only in respect of that of which we can regard him as *wholly* the author. And evidently we do recognise that, for a man to be the author of an act in the full sense required for moral responsibility, it is not enough merely that he 'wills' or 'chooses' the act: since even the most unfortunate victim of heredity or environment does, as a rule, 'will' what he does. It is significant, however, that the ordinary man, though well enough aware of the influence upon choices of heredity and environment, does not feel obliged thereby to give up his assumption that moral predicates *are* somehow applicable. Plainly he still believes that there is *something* for which a man is morally responsible, something of which we can fairly say that he is the sole author. *What is this something?* To that question common-sense is not ready with an explicit answer — though an answer is, I think, implicit in the line which its moral judgments take. I shall do what I can to give an explicit answer later in this lecture. Meantime it must suffice to observe that, if we are to be true to the deliverances of our moral consciousness, it is very difficult to deny that *sole* authorship is a necessary condition of the morally responsible act.

Thirdly we come to a point over which much recent controversy has raged. We may approach it by raising the following question. Granted an act of which the agent is sole author, does this 'sole authorship' suffice to make the act a morally free act? We may be inclined to think that it does, until we contemplate the possibility that an act of which the agent is sole author might conceivably occur as a necessary expression of the agent's nature; the way in which, e.g. some philosophers have supposed the Divine act of creation to occur. This consideration excites a legitimate doubt; for it is far from easy to see how a person can be regarded as a proper subject for moral praise or blame in respect of an act which he *cannot help* performing — even if it be his own 'nature' which necessitates it. Must we not recognise it as a condition of the morally free act that the agent 'could have acted otherwise' than he in fact did? It is true, indeed, that we sometimes praise or blame a man for an act about which we are prepared to say, in the light of our knowledge of his established character, that he 'could no other'. But I think that a little reflection shows that in such cases we are not praising or blaming the man strictly for what he does *now* (or at any rate we ought not to be), but rather for those past acts of his which have generated the firm habit of mind from which his *present* act follows 'necessarily'. In other words, our praise and blame, so far as justified, are really retrospective, being directed not to the agent *qua* performing *this* act, but to the agent *qua* performing those past acts which have built up his present character, and in respect to which we presume that he *could* have acted otherwise, that there really *were* open possibilities before him. These cases, therefore, seem to me to constitute no valid exception to what I must take to be the rule, viz. that a man can be morally praised or blamed for an act only if he could have acted otherwise.

Now philosophers today are fairly well agreed that it is a postulate of the morally responsible act that the agent 'could have acted otherwise' in *some* sense of that phrase. But sharp differences of opinion have arisen over the way in which the phrase ought to be interpreted. There is a strong disposition to water down its apparent meaning by insisting that it is not (as a postulate of moral responsibility) to be understood as a straightforward categorical proposition, but rather as a disguised hypothetical proposition. All that we really require to be assured of, in order to justify our holding X morally responsible for an act, is, we are told, that X could have acted otherwise *if* he had *chosen* otherwise (Moore, Stevenson); or perhaps that X could have acted otherwise *if* he had had a different character, or *if* he had been placed in different circumstances.

I think it is easy to understand, and even, in a measure, to sympathise with, the motives which induce philosophers to offer these counter-interpretations. It is not just the fact that 'X could have acted otherwise', as a bald categorical statement, is incompatible with the universal sway of causal law — though this is, to some philosophers, a serious stone of stumbling. The more widespread objection is that it at least looks as though it were incompatible with that causal continuity of an agent's character with his conduct which is implied when we believe (surely with justice) that we can often tell the sort of thing a man will do from our knowledge of the sort of man he is.

We shall have to make our accounts with that particular difficulty later. At this stage I wish merely to show that neither of the hypothetical propositions suggested — and I think the same could be shown for *any* hypothetical alternative — is an acceptable substitute for the categorical proposition 'X could have acted otherwise' as the presupposition of moral responsibility.

Let us look first at the earlier suggestion — 'X could have acted otherwise *if* he had chosen otherwise'. Now clearly there are a great many acts with regard to which we are entirely satisfied that the agent is thus situated. We are often perfectly sure that — for this is all it amounts to — if X had chosen otherwise, the circumstances presented no external obstacle to the translation of that choice into action. For example, we often have no doubt at all that X, who in point of fact told a lie, could have told the truth *if* he had so chosen. But does our confidence on this score allay all legitimate doubts about whether X is really blameworthy? Does it entail that X is free in the sense required for moral responsibility? Surely not. The obvious question immediately arises: 'But *could* X have *chosen* otherwise than he did?' It is doubt about the true answer to *that* question which leads most people to doubt the reality of moral responsibility. Yet on this crucial question the hypothetical proposition which is offered as a sufficient statement of the condition justifying the ascription of moral responsibility gives us no information whatsoever.

Indeed this hypothetical substitute for the categorical 'X could have acted otherwise' seems to me to lack all plausibility unless one contrives to forget why it is, after all, that we ever come to feel fundamental doubts about man's moral responsibility. Such doubts are born, surely, when one becomes aware of certain reputable world-views in religion or philosophy, or of certain reputable scientific beliefs, which in their several ways imply that man's actions are necessitated, and thus could not be otherwise than they in fact are. But clearly a doubt so based is not even touched by the recognition that a man could very often act otherwise *if* he so chose. That proposition is entirely compatible with the necessitarian theories which generate our doubt: indeed it is this very compatibility that has recommended it to some philosophers, who are reluctant to give up either moral responsibility or Determinism. The proposition which we *must* be able to affirm if moral praise or blame of X is to be justified is the categorical proposition that X could have acted otherwise because — not if — he could have chosen otherwise; or, since it is essentially the inner side of the act that matters, the proposition simply that X could have chosen otherwise.

For the second of the alternative formulae suggested we cannot spare more than a few moments. But its inability to meet the demands it is required to meet is almost transparent. 'X could have acted otherwise', as a statement of a precondition of X's moral responsibility, really means (we are told) 'X could have acted otherwise *if* he were differently constituted, or *if* he had been placed in different circumstances'. It seems a sufficient reply to this to point out that the person whose moral responsibility is at issue is X; a specific individual, in a specific set of circumstances. It is totally irrelevant to X's moral responsibility that we should be able to say that some person differently constituted from X, or X in a different set of circumstances, could have done something different from what X did.

3. Let me, then, briefly sum up the answer at which we have arrived to our question about the kind of freedom required to justify moral responsibility. It is that a man can be said to exercise free will in a morally significant sense only in so far as his chosen act is one of which he is the sole cause or author, and only if — in the straightforward, categorical sense of the phrase — he 'could have chosen otherwise'.

I confess that this answer is in some ways a disconcerting one, disconcerting, because most of us, however objective we are in the actual conduct of our thinking, would *like* to be able to believe that moral responsibility is real: whereas the freedom required for moral responsibility, on the analysis we have given, is certainly far more difficult to establish than the freedom required on the analyses we found ourselves obliged to reject. If, e.g. moral freedom entails only that I could have acted otherwise *if* I had chosen otherwise, there is no real 'problem' about it at all. I am 'free' in the normal case where there is no external obstacle to prevent my translating the alternative choice into action, and not free in other cases. Still less is there a problem if all that moral freedom entails is that I could have acted otherwise *if* I had been a differently constituted person, or been in different circumstances. Clearly I am *always* free in *this* sense of freedom. But, as I have argued, these so-called 'freedoms' fail to give us the pre-conditions of moral responsibility, and hence leave the freedom of the traditional free-will problem, the freedom that people are really concerned about, precisely where it was.

5. That brings me to the second, and more constructive, part of this lecture. From now on I shall be considering whether it is reasonable to believe that man does in fact possess a free will of the kind specified in the first part of the lecture. If so, just how and where within the complex fabric of the volitional life are we to locate it? — for although free will must presumably belong (if anywhere) to the volitional side of human experience, it is pretty clear from the way in which we have been forced to define it that it does not pertain simply to volition as such; not even to all volitions that are commonly dignified with the name of 'choices'. It has been, I think, one of the more serious impediments to profitable discussion of the Free Will problem that Libertarians and Determinists alike have so often failed to appreciate the comparatively narrow area within which the free will that is necessary to 'save' morality is required to operate. It goes without saying that this failure has been gravely prejudicial to the case for Libertarianism. I attach a good deal of importance, therefore, to the problem of locating free will correctly

within the volitional orbit. Its solution forestalls and annuls, I believe, some of the more tiresome clichés of Determinist criticism.

We saw earlier that Common Sense's practice of 'making allowances' in its moral judgments for the influence of heredity and environment indicates Common Sense's conviction, both that a just moral judgment must discount determinants of choice over which the agent has no control, and also (since it still accepts moral judgments as legitimate) that *something* of moral relevance survives which can be regarded as genuinely self-originated. We are now to try to discover what this 'something' is. And I think we may still usefully take Common Sense as our guide. Suppose one asks the ordinary intelligent citizen *why* he deems it proper to make allowances for X, whose heredity and/or environment are unfortunate. He will tend to reply, I think, in some such terms as these: that X has more and stronger temptations to deviate from what is right than Y or Z, who are normally circumstanced, so that he must put forth *a stronger moral effort* if he is to achieve the same level of external conduct. The intended implication seems to be that X is just as morally praiseworthy as Y or Z *if* he exerts an equivalent moral effort, even though he may not thereby achieve an equal success in conforming his will to the 'concrete' demands of duty. And this implies, again, Common Sense's belief that *in moral effort* we have something for which a man is responsible *without qualification*, something that is *not* affected by heredity and environment but depends *solely* upon the self itself.

Now in my opinion Common Sense has here, in principle, hit upon the one and only defensible answer. Here, and here alone, so far as I can see, in the act of deciding whether to put forth or withhold the moral effort required to resist temptation and rise to duty, is to be found an act which is free in the sense required for moral responsibility; an act of which the self is sole author, and of which it is true to say that 'it could be' (or, after the event, 'could have been') 'otherwise'. Such is the thesis which we shall now try to establish.

6. The species of argument appropriate to the establishment of a thesis of this sort should fall, I think, into two phases. First, there should be a consideration of the evidence of the moral agent's own inner experience. What *is* the act of moral decision, and what does it imply, from the standpoint of the actual participant? Since there is no way of knowing the act of moral decision — or for that matter any other form of activity — except by actual participation in it, the evidence of the subject, or agent, is on an issue of this kind of palmary importance. It can hardly, however, be taken as in itself conclusive. For even if that evidence should be overwhelmingly to the effect that moral decision does have the characteristics required by moral freedom, the question is bound to be raised — and in view of considerations from other quarters pointing in a contrary direction is *rightly* raised — Can we *trust* the evidence of inner experience? That brings us to what will be the second phase of the argument. We shall have to go on to show, if we are to make good our case,

that the extraneous considerations so often supposed to be fatal to the belief in moral freedom are in fact innocuous to it.

In the light of what was said in the last lecture about the self's experience of moral decision as a *creative* activity, we may perhaps be absolved from developing the first phase of the argument at any great length. The appeal is throughout to one's own experience in the actual taking of the moral decision in the situation of moral temptation. 'Is it possible', we must ask, 'for anyone so circumstanced to *dis*believe that we could be deciding otherwise?' The answer is surely not in doubt. When we decide to exert moral effort to resist a temptation, we feel quite certain that we *could* withhold the effort; just as, if we decide to withhold the effort and yield to our desires, we feel quite certain that we *could* exert it — otherwise we should not blame ourselves afterwards for having succumbed. It may be, indeed, that this conviction is mere self-delusion. But that is not at the moment our concern. It is enough at present to establish that the act of deciding to exert or to withhold moral effort, as we know it from the inside in actual moral living, belongs to the category of acts which 'could have been otherwise'.

Mutatis mutandis, the same reply is forthcoming if we ask, 'Is it possible for the moral agent in the taking of his decision to *dis*believe that he is the *sole* author of that decision?' Clearly he cannot disbelieve that it is *he* who takes the decision. That, however, is not in itself sufficient to enable him, on reflection, to regard himself as *solely* responsible for the act. For his 'character' as so far formed might conceivably be a factor in determining it, and no one can suppose that the constitution of his 'character' is uninfluenced by circumstances of heredity and environment with which *he* has nothing to do. But as we pointed out in the last lecture, the very essence of the moral decision as it is experienced is that it is a decision whether or not to *combat* our strongest desire, and our strongest desire *is* the expression in the situation of our character as so far formed. Now clearly our character cannot be a factor in determining the decision whether or not to *oppose* our character. I think we are entitled to say, therefore, that the act of moral decision is one in which the self is for itself not merely 'author' but 'sole author'.

7. We may pass on, then, to the second phase of our constructive argument; and this will demand more elaborate treatment. Even if a moral agent *qua* making a moral decision in the situation of 'temptation' cannot help believing that he has free will in the sense at issue — a moral freedom between real alternatives, between genuinely open possibilities — are there, nevertheless, objections to a freedom of this kind so cogent that we are bound to distrust the evidence of 'inner experience'?

I begin by drawing attention to a simple point whose significance tends, I think, to be under-estimated. If the phenomenological analysis we have offered is substantially correct, no one while functioning as a moral agent can help believing that he enjoys free will. Theoretically he may be completely convinced by Determinist arguments, but when actually confronted with a personal situation of conflict between duty and desire he is quite certain that it lies with him here and now whether or not he will rise to duty. It follows that if Determinists could produce convincing theoretical arguments against a free will of this kind, the awkward predicament would ensue that man has to deny as a theoretical being what he has to assert as a practical being. Now I think the Determinist ought to be a good deal more worried about this than he usually is. He seems to imagine that a strong case on general theoretical grounds is enough to prove that the 'practical' belief in free will, even if inescapable for us as practical beings, is mere illusion. But in fact it proves nothing of the sort. There is no reason whatever why a belief that we find ourselves obliged to hold *qua* practical beings should be required to give way before a belief which we find ourselves obliged to hold *qua* theoretical beings; or, for that matter, *vice versa*. All that the theoretical arguments of Determinism can prove, unless they are reinforced by a refutation of the phenomenological analysis that supports Libertarianism, is that there is a radical conflict between the theoretical and the practical sides of man's nature, an antimony at the very heart of the self. And this is a state of affairs with which no one can easily rest satisfied. I think therefore that the Determinist ought to concern himself a great deal more than he does with phenomenological analysis, in order to show, if he can, that the assurance of free will is not really an inexpugnable element in man's practical consciousness. There is just as much obligation upon him, convinced though he may be of the soundness of his theoretical arguments, to expose the errors of the Libertarian's phenomenological analysis, as there is upon us, convinced though we may be of the soundness of the Libertarian's phenomenological analysis, to expose the errors of the Determinist's theoretical arguments.

8. However, we must at once begin the discharge of our own obligation. The rest of this lecture will be devoted to trying to show that the arguments which seem to carry most weight with Determinists are, to say the least of it, very far from compulsive.

Fortunately a good many of the arguments which at an earlier time in the history of philosophy would have been strongly urged against us make almost no appeal to the bulk of philosophers today, and we may here pass them by. That applies to any criticism of 'open possibilities' based on a metaphysical theory about the nature of the universe as a whole. Nobody today *has* a metaphysical theory about the nature of the universe as a whole! It applies also, with almost equal force, to criticisms based upon the universality of causal law as a supposed postulate of science. There have always been, in my opinion, sound philosophic reasons for doubting the validity, as distinct from the convenience, of the causal postulate in its universal form, but at the present time, when scientists themselves are deeply divided about the need for postulating causality even within their own special field, we shall do better to concentrate our attention upon criticisms which are more confidently advanced. I propose to ignore also, on different grounds, the type of criticism of free will that is sometimes advanced from the side of religion, based upon religious postulates of Divine Omnipotence and Omniscience. So far as I can see, a postulate of human freedom is every bit as necessary to meet certain religious demands (e.g. to make sense of the 'conviction of sin'), as postulates of Divine Omniscience and Omnipotence are to meet certain other religious demands. If so, then it can hardly be argued that religious experience as such tells more strongly against than for the position we are defending; and we may be satisfied, in the present context, to leave the matter there. It will be more profitable to discuss certain arguments which contemporary philosophers do think important, and which recur with a somewhat monotonous regularity in the literature of anti-Libertarianism.

These arguments can, I think, be reduced in principle to no more than two: first, the argument from 'predictability'; second, the argument from the alleged meaninglessness of an act supposed to be the self's act and yet not an expression of the self's character. Contemporary criticism of free will seems to me to consist almost exclusively of variations of these two themes. I shall deal with each in turn.

9. On the first we touched in passing at an earlier stage. Surely it is beyond question (the critical urges) that when we know a person intimately we can foretell with a high degree of accuracy how he will respond to at least a large number of practical situations. One feels safe in predicting that one's dog-loving friend will not use his boot to repel the little mongrel that comes yapping at his heels; or again that one's wife will not pass with incurious eyes (or indeed pass at all) the new hat-shop in the city. So to behave would not be (as we say) 'in character'. But, so the criticism runs, you with your doctrine of 'genuinely open possibilities', of a free will by which the self can diverge from its own character, remove all rational basis from such prediction. You require us to make the absurd supposition that the success of countless predictions of the sort in the past has been mere matter of chance. If you *really* believed in your theory, you would not be surprised if tomorrow your friend with the notorious horror of strong drink should suddenly exhibit a passion for whisky and soda, or if your friend whose taste for reading has hitherto been satisfied with the sporting columns of the newspapers should be discovered on a fine Saturday afternoon poring over the works of Hegel. But of course you *would* be surprised. Social life would be sheer chaos if there were not well-grounded social expectations; and social life is not sheer chaos. Your theory is hopelessly wrecked upon obvious facts.

Now whether or not this criticism holds good against some versions of Libertarian theory I need not here discuss. It is sufficient if I can make it clear that against the version advanced in this lecture, according to which free will is localised in a relatively narrow field of operation, the criticism has no relevance whatsoever.

Let us remind ourselves briefly of the setting within which, on our view, free will functions. There is X, the course which we believe we ought to follow, and Y, the course towards which we feel our desire is strongest. The freedom which we ascribe to the agent is the freedom to put forth or refrain from putting forth the moral effort required to resist the pressure of desire and do what he thinks he ought to do.

But then there is surely an immense range of practical situations — covering by far the greater part of life — in which there is no question of a conflict within the self between what he most desires to do and what he thinks he ought to do? Indeed such conflict is a comparatively rare phenomenon for the majority of men. Yet over that whole vast range there is nothing whatever in our version of Libertarianism to prevent our agreeing that character determines conduct. In the absence, real or supposed, of any 'moral' issue, what a man chooses will be simply that course which, after such reflection as seems called for, he deems most likely to bring him what he most strongly desires; and that is the same as to say the course to which his present character inclines him.

Over by far the greater area of human choices, then, our theory offers no more barrier to successful prediction on the basis of character than any other theory. For where there is no clash of strongest desire with duty, the free will we are defending has no business. There is just nothing for it to do.

But what about the situations — rare enough though they may be — in which there *is* this clash and in which free will does therefore operate? Does our theory entail that there at any rate, as the critic seems to suppose, 'anything may happen'?

Not by any manner of means. In the first place, and by the very nature of the case, the range of the agent's possible choices is bounded by what he thinks he ought to do on the one hand, and what he most strongly desires on the other. The freedom claimed for him is a freedom of decision to make or withhold the effort required to do what he thinks he ought to do. There is no question of a freedom to act in some 'wild' fashion, out of all relation to his characteristic beliefs and desires. This so-called 'freedom of caprice', so often charged against the Libertarian, is, to put it bluntly, a sheer figment of the critic's imagination, with no *habitat* in serious Libertarian theory. Even in situations where free will does come into play it is perfectly possible, on a view like ours, given the appropriate knowledge of a man's character, to predict within certain limits how he will respond.

But 'probable' prediction in such situations can, I think, go further than this. It is obvious that where desire and duty are at odds, the felt 'gap' (as it were) between the two may vary enormously in breadth in different cases. The moderate drinker and the chronic tippler may each want another glass, and each deem it his duty to abstain, but the felt gap between desire and duty in the case of the former is trivial beside the great gulf which is felt to separate them in the case of the latter. Hence it will take a far harder moral effort for the tippler than for the moderate drinker to achieve the same external result of abstention. So much is matter of common agreement. And we are entitled, I think, to take it into account in prediction, on the simple principle that the harder the moral effort required to resist desire the less likely it is to occur. Thus in the example taken, most people would predict that the tippler will very probably succumb to his desires, whereas there is a reasonable likelihood that the moderate drinker will make the comparatively slight effort needed to resist them. So long as the prediction does not pretend to more than a measure of probability, there is nothing in our theory which would disallow it.

I claim, therefore, that the view of free will I have been putting forward is consistent with predictability of conduct on the basis of character over a very wide field indeed. And I make the further claim that that field will cover all the situations in life concerning which there is any empirical evidence that successful prediction is possible.

10. Let us pass on to consider the second main line of criticism. This is, I think, much the more illuminating of the two, if only because it compels the Libertarian to make explicit certain concepts which are indispensable to him, but which, being desperately hard to state clearly, are apt not to be stated at all. The critic's fundamental point might be stated somewhat as follows:

'Free will as you describe it is completely unintelligible. On your own showing no *reason* can be given, because there just *is* no reason, why a man decides to exert rather than to withhold moral effort, or *vice versa*. But such an act — or more properly, such an "occurrence" — it is nonsense to speak of as an act of a *self*. If there is nothing in the self's character to which it is, even in principle, in any way traceable, the self has nothing to do with it. Your so-called "freedom", therefore, so far from supporting the self's moral responsibility, destroys it as surely as the crudest Determinism could do.'

If we are to discuss this criticism usefully, it is important, I think, to begin by getting clear about two different senses of the word 'intelligible'.

If, in the first place, we mean by an 'intelligible' act one whose occurrence is in principle capable of being inferred, since it follows necessarily from something (though we may not know in fact from what), then it is certainly true that the Libertarian's free will is unintelligible. But that is only saying, is it not, that the Libertarian's 'free' act is not an act which follows necessarily from something! This can hardly rank as a *criticism* of Libertarianism. It is just a description of it. That there can be nothing unintelligible in *this* sense is precisely what the Determinist has got to *prove*.

Yet it is surprising how often the critic of Libertarianism involves himself in this circular mode of argument. Repeatedly it is urged against the Libertarian, with a great air of triumph, that on his view he can't say *why* I now decide to rise to duty, or now decide to follow my strongest desire in defiance of duty. Of course he can't. If he could he wouldn't *be* a Libertarian. To 'account for' a 'free' act is a contradiction in terms. A free will is *ex hypothesi* the sort of thing of which the request for an *explanation* is absurd. The assumption that an explanation must be in principle possible for the act of moral decision deserves to rank as a classic example of the ancient fallacy of 'begging the question'.

But the critic usually has in mind another sense of the word 'unintelligible'. He is apt to take it for granted that an act which is unintelligible in the *above* sense (as the morally free act of the Libertarian undoubtedly is) is unintelligible in the *further* sense that we can attach no meaning to it. And this is an altogether more serious matter. If it could really be shown that the Libertarian's 'free will' were unintelligible in this sense of being meaningless, that, for myself at any rate, would be the end of the affair. Libertarianism would have been conclusively refuted.

But it seems to me manifest that this can *not* be shown. The critic has allowed himself, I submit, to become the victim of a widely accepted but fundamentally vicious assumption. He has assumed that whatever is meaningful must exhibit its meaningfulness to those who view it from the standpoint of external observation. Now if one chooses thus to limit one's self to the rôle of external observer, it is, I think, perfectly true that one can attach no meaning to an act which is the act of something we call a 'self' and yet follows from nothing in that self's character. But then *why should we* so limit ourselves, when what is under consideration is a subjective activity? For the apprehension of subjective acts there is *another* standpoint available, that of *inner experience,* of the practical consciousness in its actual functioning. If our free will should turn out to be something to which we can attach a meaning from *this* standpoint, no more is required. And no more ought to be expected. For I must repeat that only from the inner standpoint of living experience *could* anything of the nature of 'activity' be directly grasped. Observation from without is in the nature of the case impotent to apprehend the active *qua* active. We can from without observe sequences of states. If into these we read activity (as we sometimes do), this can only be on the basis of what we discern in ourselves from the inner standpoint. It follows that if anyone insists upon taking his criterion of the meaningful simply from the standpoint of external observation, he is really deciding in advance of the evidence that the notion of activity, and *a fortiori* the notion of a free will, is 'meaningless'. He looks for the free act through a medium which is in the nature of the case incapable of revealing it, and then, because inevitably he doesn't find it, he declares that it doesn't exist!

But if, as we surely ought in this context, we adopt the inner standpoint, then (I am suggesting) things appear in a totally different light. From the inner standpoint, it seems to me plain, there is no difficulty whatever in attaching meaning to an act which is the self's act and which nevertheless does not follow from the self's character. So much I claim has been established by the phenomenological analysis, in this and the previous lecture, of the act of moral decision in face of moral temptation. It is thrown into particularly clear relief where the moral decision is to make the moral effort required to rise to duty. For the very function of moral effort, as it appears to the agent engaged in the act, is to enable the self to act against the line of least resistance, against the line to which his character as so far formed most strongly inclines him. But if the self is thus conscious here of *combating* his formed character, he surely cannot possibly suppose that the act, although his own act, *issues from* his formed character? I submit, therefore, that the self knows very well indeed — from the inner standpoint — what is meant by an act which is the *self's* act and which nevertheless does not follow from the self's *character*.

What this implies — and it seems to me to be an implication of cardinal importance for any theory of the self that aims at being more than superficial — is that the nature of the self is for itself something more than just its character as so far formed. The 'nature' of the self and what we commonly call the 'character' of the self are by no means the same thing, and it is utterly vital that they should not be confused. The 'nature' of the self comprehends, but is not without remainder reducible to, its 'character'; it must, if we are to be true to the testimony of our experience of it, be taken as including *also* the authentic creative power of fashioning and re-fashioning 'character'.

The misguided, and as a rule quite uncritical, belittlement, of the evidence offered by inner experience has, I am convinced, been responsible for more bad argument by the opponents of Free Will than has any other single factor. How often, for example, do we find the Determinist critic saying, in effect, '*Either* the act follows necessarily upon precedent states, *or* it is a mere matter of chance and accordingly of no moral significance'. The disjunction is invalid, for it does not exhaust the possible alternatives. It seems to the critic to do so only because he *will* limit himself to the standpoint which is proper, and indeed alone possible, in dealing with the physical world, the standpoint of the external observer. If only he would allow himself to assume the standpoint which is not merely proper for, but necessary to, the apprehension of subjective activity, the inner standpoint of the practical consciousness in its actual functioning, he would find himself obliged to recognise the falsity of his disjunction. Reflection upon the act of moral decision as apprehended from the inner standpoint would force him to recognise a *third* possibility, as remote from chance as from necessity, that, namely, of *creative activity,* in which (as I have ventured to express it) nothing determines the act save the agent's doing of it.

11. There we must leave the matter. But as this lecture has been, I know, somewhat densely packed, it may be helpful if I conclude by reminding you, in bald summary, of the main things I have been trying to say. Let me set them out in so many successive theses.

1. The freedom which is at issue in the traditional Free Will problem is the freedom which is presupposed in moral responsibility.

2. Critical reflection upon carefully considered attributions of moral responsibility reveals that the only freedom that will do is a freedom which

pertains to inner acts of choice, and that these acts must be acts (*a*) of which the self is *sole* author, and (*b*) which the self could have performed otherwise.

3. From phenomenological analysis of the situation of moral temptation we find that the self as engaged in this situation is inescapably convinced that it possesses a freedom of precisely the specified kind, located in the decision to exert or withhold the moral effort needed to rise to duty where the pressure of its desiring nature is felt to urge it in a contrary direction.

Passing to the question of the *reality* of this moral freedom which the moral agent believes himself to possess, we argued:

4. Of the two types of Determinist criticism which seem to have most influence today, that based on the predictability of much human behaviour fails to touch a Libertarianism which confines the area of free will as above indicated. Libertarianism so understood is compatible with all the predictability that the empirical facts warrant. And:

5. The second main type of criticism, which alleges the 'meaninglessness' of an act which is the self's act and which is yet not determined by the self's character, is based on a failure to appreciate that the standpoint of inner experience is not only legitimate but indispensable where what is at issue is the reality and nature of a subjective activity. The creative act of moral decision is inevitably meaningless to the mere external observer; but from the inner standpoint it is as real, and as significant, as anything in human experience.

29

THE HARMONY
OF FREE WILL
AND DETERMINISM

R. E. Hobart

The thesis of this article is that there has never been any ground for the controversy between the doctrine of free will and determinism, that it is based upon a misapprehension, that the two assertions are entirely consistent, that one of them strictly implies the other, that they have been opposed only because of our natural want of the analytical imagination. In so saying I do not tamper with the meaning of either phrase. That would be unpardonable. I mean free will in the natural and usual sense, in the fullest, the most absolute sense in which for the purposes of the personal and moral life the term is ever employed. I mean it as implying responsibility, merit and demerit, guilt and desert. I mean it as implying, after an act has been performed, that one "could have done otherwise" than one did. I mean it as conveying these things also, not in any subtly modified sense but in exactly the sense in which we conceive them in life and in law and in ethics. These two doctrines have been opposed because we have not realised that free will can be analysed without being destroyed, and that determinism is merely a feature of the analysis of it. And if we are tempted to take refuge in the thought of an "ultimate", an "innermost" liberty that eludes the analysis, then we have implied a deterministic basis and constitution for this liberty as well. For such a basis and constitution lie in the idea of liberty.

. . . .

I am not maintaining that determinism is true; only that it is true in so far as we have free will. That we are free in willing is, broadly speaking, a fact of experience. That broad fact is more assured than any philosophical analysis. It is therefore surer than the deterministic analysis of it, entirely

From "Free Will as Involving Determination and Inconceivable Without It," first published in *Mind*, Vol. XLIII, No. 169, January, 1934. Pp. 1-27, *passim*. Reprinted by permission of the editor of *Mind*.

adequate as that in the end appears to be. But it is not here affirmed that there are no small exceptions, no slight undetermined swervings, no ingredient of absolute chance. All that is here said is that such absence of determination, if and so far as it exists, is no gain to freedom, but sheer loss of it; no advantage to the moral life, but blank subtraction from it. — When I speak below of "the indeterminist" I mean the libertarian indeterminist, that is, him who believes in free will and holds that it involves indetermination.

By the analytical imagination is meant, of course, the power we have, not by nature but by training, of realising that the component parts of a thing or process, taken together, each in its place, with their relations, are identical with the thing or process itself. If it is "more than its parts", then this "more" will appear in the analysis. It is not true, of course, that all facts are susceptible of analysis, but so far as they are, there is occasion for the analytical imagination. We have been accustomed to think of a thing or a person as a whole, not as a combination of parts. We have been accustomed to think of its activities as the way in which, as a whole, it naturally and obviously behaves. It is a new, an unfamiliar and an awkward act on the mind's part to consider it, not as one thing acting in its natural manner, but as a system of parts that work together in a complicated process. Analysis often seems at first to have taken away the individuality of the thing, its unity, the impression of the familiar identity. For a simple mind this is strikingly true of the analysis of a complicated machine. The reader may recall Paulsen's ever significant story about the introduction of the railway into Germany. When it reached the village of a certain enlightened pastor, he took his people to where a locomotive engine was standing, and in the clearest words explained of what parts it consisted and how it worked. He was much pleased by their eager nods of intelligence as he proceeded. But on his finishing they said: "Yes, yes, Herr Pastor, but there's a horse inside, isn't there?" They could not *realise* the analysis. They were wanting in the analytical imagination. Why not? They had never been trained to it. It is in the first instance a great effort to think of all the parts working together to produce the simple result that the engine glides down the track. It is easy to think of a horse inside doing all the work. A horse is a familiar totality that does familiar things. They could no better have grasped the physiological analysis of a horse's movements had it been set forth to them.

．　　．　　．

Now the position of the indeterminist is that a free act of will is the act of the self. The self becomes through it the author of the physical act that ensues. This volition of the self causes the physical act but it is not in its turn caused, it is "spontaneous". To regard it as caused would be determinism. The causing self to which the indeterminist here refers is to be conceived as distinct from character; distinct from temperament, wishes, habits, impulses. He emphasises two things equally: the physical act springs from the self through its volition, and it does not spring merely from character, it is not simply the result of character and circumstances. If we ask, "Was there anything that induced the self thus to act?" we are answered in effect, "Not definitively. The self feels motives but its act is not determined by them. It can choose between them."

The next thing to notice is that this position of the indeterminist is taken in defence of moral conceptions. There would be no fitness, he says, in our reproaching ourselves, in our feeling remorse, in our holding ourselves or anyone guilty, if the act in question were not the act of the self instead of a product of the machinery of motives.

We have here one of the most remarkable and instructive examples of something in which the history of philosophy abounds — of a persistent, an age-long deadlock due solely to the indisposition of the human mind to look closely into the meaning of its terms.

How do we reproach ourselves? We say to ourselves, "How negligent of me!" "How thoughtless!" "How selfish!" "How hasty and unrestrained!" "That I should have been capable even for a moment of taking such a petty, irritated view!" etc. In other words, we are attributing to ourselves at the time of the act, in some respect and measure, a bad character, and regretting it. And that is the entire point of our self-reproach. We are turning upon ourselves with disapproval and it may be with disgust; we wish we could undo what we did in the past, and, helpless to do that, feel a peculiar thwarted poignant anger and shame at ourselves that we *had it in us* to perpetrate the thing we now condemn. It is self we are reproaching, *i.e.,* self that we are viewing as bad in that it produced bad actions. Except in so far as what-it-is produced these bad actions, there is no ground for reproaching it (calling it bad) and no meaning in doing so. All self-reproach is self-judging, and all judging is imputing a character. We are blaming ourselves. If spoken, what we are thinking would be dispraise. And what are praise and dispraise? Always, everywhere, they are *descriptions* of a person (more or less explicit) with favourable or unfavourable feeling of what is described, — descriptions in terms of value comporting fact, or of fact comporting value, or of both fact and value. In moral instances they are descriptions of his character. We are morally characterising him in our minds (as above) with appropriate feelings. We are attributing to him the character that we approve and like and wish to see more of, or the contrary. All the most intimate terms of the moral life imply that the act has proceeded from *me,* the distinctive me, from the manner of man I am or was. And this is the very thing on which the libertarian lays stress. What the indeterminist prizes with all his heart, what he stoutly affirms and insists upon, is precisely what he denies, namely, that I, the concrete and specific moral being, am the author, the source of my acts. For, of course, that is determinism. To say that they come from the self is to say that they are determined by the self — the moral self, the self with a moral quality. He gives our preferrings the bad name of the machinery of motives, but they are just what we feel in ourselves when we decide. When he maintains that the self at the moment of decision may act to some extent independently of motives, *and is good or bad according as it acts in this direction or that,* he is simply setting up one character within another, he is separating the self from what he understands by the person's character as at first mentioned, only thereupon to attribute to it a character of its own, *in that he judges it good or bad.*

The whole controversy is maintained by the indeterminist in order to defend the validity of the terms in which we morally judge, — for example, ourselves. But the very essence of all judgment, just so far as it extends, asserts determination.

If in conceiving the self you detach it from all motives or tendencies, what you have is not a morally admirable or condemnable, not a morally characterisable self at all. Hence it is not subject to reproach. You cannot call a self good because of its courageous free action, and then deny that its action was determined by its character. In calling it good because of that action you have implied that the action came from its goodness (which means its good character) and was a sign thereof. By their fruits ye shall know them. The indeterminist appears to imagine that he can distinguish the moral "I" from all its propensities, regard its act as arising in the moment undetermined by them, and yet can then (for the first time, in his opinion, with propriety!) ascribe to this "I" an admirable quality. At the very root of his doctrine he contradicts himself. How odd that he never catches sight of that contradiction! He fights for his doctrine in order that he may call a man morally good, on account of his acts, with some real meaning; and his doctrine is that a man's acts (precisely so far as "free" or undetermined) do not come from his goodness. So they do not entitle us to call him good. He has taken his position in defence of moral conceptions, and it is fatal to all moral conceptions.

We are told, however, that it is under determinism that we should have no right any more to praise or to blame. At least we could not do so in the old sense of the terms. We might throw words of praise to a man, or throw words of blame at him, because we know from observation that they will affect his action; but the old light of meaning in the terms has gone out. Well, all we have to do is to keep asking what this old meaning was. We praise a man by saying that he is a good friend, or a hard worker, or a competent man of business, or a trusty assistant, or a judicious minister, or a gifted poet, or one of the noblest of men — one of the noblest of characters! In other words, he is a being with such and such qualities. If it is moral praise, he is a being with such and such tendencies to bring forth good acts. If we describe a single act, saying, for instance: "Well done!" we mean to praise the person for the act as being the author of it. It is he who has done well and proved himself capable of doing so. If the happy act is accidental we say that no praise is deserved for it. If a person is gratified by praise it is because of the estimate of him, in some respect or in general, that is conveyed. Praise (once again) means description, with expressed or implied admiration. If any instance of it can be found which does not consist in these elements our analysis fails. "Praise the Lord, O my soul, *and forget not all His benefits"*, —

and the Psalm goes on to tell His loving and guarding acts toward human-
kind. To praise the Lord is to tell His perfections, especially the perfections of
His character. This is the old light that has always been in words of praise
and there appears no reason for its going out.

Indeterminism maintains that we need not be impelled to action by our
wishes, that our active will need not be determined by them. Motives "incline without necessitating." We choose amongst the ideas of action before
us, but need not choose solely according to the attraction of desire, in however
wide a sense that word is used. Our inmost self may rise up in its autonomy
and moral dignity, independently of motives, and register its sovereign decree.

Now, *in so far* as this "interposition of the self" is undetermined, the act
is not *its* act, it does not issue from any concrete continuing self; it is born at
the moment, of nothing, hence it expresses no quality; it bursts into being from
no source. The self does not register *its* decree, for the decree is not the product of just that *"it."* The self does not rise up in *its* moral dignity, for dignity
is the quality of an enduring being, influencing its actions, and therefore expressed by them, and that would be determination. *In proportion* as an act of
volition starts of itself without cause it is exactly, so far as the freedom of the
individual is concerned, as if it had been thrown into his mind from without
— "suggested" to him — by a freakish demon. It is exactly like it in this respect, that in neither case does the volition arise from what the man is, cares
for or feels allegiance to; it does not come out of him. *In proportion* as it is undetermined, it is just as if his legs should suddenly spring up and carry him off
where he did not prefer to go. Far from constituting freedom, that would mean,
in the exact measure in which it took place, the loss of freedom. It would be
an interference, and an utterly uncontrollable interference, with his power
of acting as he prefers. In fine, then, *just so far* as the volition is undetermined, the self can neither be praised nor blamed for it, since it is not the
act of the self.

The principle of free will says: "*I* produce my volitions". Determinism
says: "My volitions are produced by *me*." Determinism is free will expressed
in the passive voice.

After all, it is plain what the indeterminists have done. It has not
occurred to them that our free will may be resolved into its component elements. (Thus far a portion only of this resolution has been considered.)
When it is thus resolved they do not recognize it. The analytical imagination
is considerably taxed to perceive the identity of the free power that we feel
with the component parts that analysis shows us. We are gratified by their
nods of intelligence and their bright, eager faces as the analysis proceeds, but
at the close are a little disheartened to find them falling back on the innocent
supposition of a horse inside that does all the essential work. They forget
that they may be called upon to analyse the horse. They solve the problem by
forgetting analysis. The solution they offer is merely: "There is a self inside
which does the deciding." Or, let us say, it is as if the *Pfarrer* were explaining the physiology of a horse's motion. They take the whole thing to be

analysed, imagine a duplicate of it reduced in size, so to speak, and place this duplicate-self inside as an explanation — making it the elusive source of the "free decisions." They do not see that they are merely pushing the question a little further back, since the process of deciding, with its constituent factors, must have taken place within that inner self. Either it decided in a particular way because, on the whole, it preferred to decide in that way, or the decision was an underived event, a rootless and sourceless event. It is the same story over again. In neither case is there any gain in imagining a second self inside, however wonderful and elusive. Of course, it is the first alternative that the indeterminist is really imagining. If you tacitly and obscurely conceive the self as deciding *its own way*, i.e., according to its preference, but never admit or recognise this, then you can happily remain a libertarian indeterminist; but upon no other terms. In your theory there is a heart of darkness.

Freedom. — In accordance with the genius of language, free will means freedom of persons in willing, just as "free trade" means freedom of persons (in a certain respect) in trading. The freedom of anyone surely always implies his possession of a power, and means the absence of any interference (whether taking the form of restraint or constraint) with his exercise of that power. Let us consider this in relation to freedom in willing.

"Can". — We say, "I can will this or I can will that, whichever I choose." Two courses of action present themselves to my mind. I think of their consequences, I look on this picture and on that, one of them commends itself more than the other, and I will an act that brings it about. I knew that I could choose either. That means that I had the power to choose either.

What is the meaning of "power?" A person has a power if it is a fact that when he sets himself in the appropriate manner to produce a certain event that event will actually follow. I have the power to lift the lamp; that is, if I grasp it and exert an upward pressure with my arm, *it will rise.* I have the power to will so and so; that is, if I want, that act of will will take place. That and none other is the meaning of power, is it not? A man's being in the proper active posture of body or of mind is the cause, and the sequel in question will be the effect. (Of course, it may be held that the sequel not only does but must follow, in a sense opposed to Hume's doctrine of cause. Very well; the question does not here concern us.)

Thus power depends upon, or rather consists in, a law. The law in question takes the familiar form that if something happens a certain something else will ensue. If A happens then B will happen. The law in this case is that if the man definitively so desires then volition will come to pass. There is a series, wish — will — act. The act follows according to the will (that is a law, — I do not mean an underived law) and the will follows according to the wish (that is another law). A man has the power (sometimes) to act as he wishes. He has the power (whenever he is not physically bound or held) to act as he wills. He has the power always (except in certain morbid states) to will as he wishes. All this depends upon the laws of his being.

Wherever there is a power there is a law. In it the power wholly consists. A man's power to will as he wishes is simply the law that his will follows his wish.

What, again, does freedom mean? It means the absence of any interference with all this. Nothing steps in to prevent my exercising my power.[1]

All turns on the meaning of "can." "I can will either this or that" means, I am so constituted that if I definitively incline to this, the appropriate act of will will take place, and if I definitively incline to that, the appropriate act of will will take place. The law connecting preference and will exists, and there is nothing to interfere with it. My free power, then, is not an exemption from law but in its inmost essence an embodiment of law.

Thus it is true, after the act of will, that I could have willed otherwise. It is most natural to add, "if I had wanted to"; but the addition is not required. The point is the meaning of "could." I could have willed whichever way I pleased. I had the power to will otherwise, there was nothing to prevent my doing so, and I should have done so if I had wanted. If someone says that the wish I actually had prevented my willing otherwise, so that I could not have done it, he is merely making a slip in the use of the word "could." He means, that wish could not have produced anything but this volition. But "could" is asserted not of the wish (a transient fact to which power in this sense is not and should not be ascribed) but of the person. And the person *could* have produced something else than that volition. He could have produced any volition he wanted; he had the power to do so.

But the objector will say, "The person as he was at the moment — the person as animated by that wish — could not have produced any other volition." Oh, yes, he could. "Could" has meaning not as applied to a momentary actual phase of a person's life, but to the person himself of whose life that is but a phase; and it means that (even at that moment) he had the power to will just as he preferred. *The idea of power, because it is the idea of a law, is hypothetical, carries in itself hypothesis as part of its very intent and meaning — "if he should prefer this, if he should prefer that", — and therefore can be truly applied to a person irrespective of what at the moment he does prefer. It remains hypothetical even when applied.*[2] This very peculiarity of its meaning is the whole point of the idea of power. It is just

---

[1] A word as to the relation of power and freedom. Strictly power cannot exist without freedom, since the result does not follow without it. Freedom on the other hand is a negative term, meaning the absence of something, and implies a power only because that whose absence it signifies is interference, which implies something to be interfered with. Apart from this peculiarity of the term itself, there might be freedom without any power. Absence of interference (of what would be interference if there were a power) might exist in the absence of a power; a man might be free to do something because there was nothing to interfere with his doing it, but might have no power to do it. Similarly and conveniently we may speak of a power as existing though interfered with; that is, the law may exist that would constitute a power if the interference were away.

[2] I am encouraged by finding in effect the same remark in Prof. G. E. Moore's *Ethics*, ch. vi., at least as regards what he terms one sense of the word "could." I should hazard saying, the only sense in this context.

because determinism is true, because a law obtains, that one "could have done otherwise."

Sidgwick set over against "the formidable array of cumulative evidence" offered for determinism the "affirmation of consciousness" "that I can now choose to do" what is right and reasonable, "however strong may be my inclination to act unreasonably."[3] But it is not against determinism. It is a true affirmation (surely not of immediate consciousness but of experience), the affirmation of my power to will what I deem right, however intense and insistent my desire for the wrong. I can will anything, and can will effectively anything that my body will enact. I can will it despite an inclination to the contrary of any strength you please — strength as felt by me before decision. We all know cases where we have resisted impulses of great strength in this sense and we can imagine them still stronger. I have the power to do it, and shall do it, shall exercise that power, if I prefer. Obviously in that case (be it psychologically remarked) my solicitude to do what is right will have proved itself even stronger (as measured by ultimate tendency to prevail, though not of necessity by sensible vividness or intensity) than the inclination to the contrary, for that is what is meant by my preferring to do it. I am conscious that the field for willing is open; I can will anything that I elect to will. Sidgwick did not analyse the meaning of "can," that is all. He did not precisely catch the outlook of consciousness when it says, "I can." He did not distinguish the function of the word, which is to express the availability of the alternatives I see when, before I have willed, and perhaps before my preference is decided, I look out on the field of conceivable volition. He did not recognize that I must have a word to express my power to will as I please, quite irrespective of what I shall please, and that "can" is that word. It is no proof that I cannot do something to point out that I shall not do it if I do not prefer. A man, let us say, can turn on the electric light; but he will not turn it on if he walks away from it; though it is still true that he can turn it on. When we attribute power to a man we do not mean that something will accomplish itself without his wanting it to. That would never suggest the idea of power. We mean that if he makes the requisite move the thing will be accomplished. It is part of the idea that the initiative shall rest with him. The initiative for an act of will is a precedent phase of consciousness that we call the definitive inclination, or, in case of conflict, the definitive preference for it. If someone in the throes of struggle with temptation says to himself, "I can put this behind me," he is saying truth and precisely the pertinent truth. He is bringing before his mind the act of will, unprevented, quite open to him, that would deliver him from what he deems noxious. It may still happen that the noxiousness of the temptation does not affect him so powerfully as its allurement, and that he succumbs. It is no whit less true, according to determinism, that he could have willed otherwise. To analyse the fact expressed by "could" is not to destroy it.

But it may be asked, "Can I will in opposition to my strongest desire

---

[3] *Methods of Ethics*, 7th ed., 65.

at the moment when it is strongest?" If the words "at the moment when it is strongest" qualify "can," the answer has already been given. If they qualify "will," the suggestion is a contradiction in terms. Can I turn-on-the-electric-light-at-a-moment-when-I-am-not-trying-to-do-so? This means, if I try to turn on the light at a moment when I am not trying to, will it be turned on? A possible willing as I do not prefer to will is not a power on my part, hence not to be expressed by "I can."

Everybody knows that we often will what we do not want to will, what we do not prefer. But when we say this we are using words in another sense than that in which I have just used them. In *one* sense of the words, whenever we act we are doing what we prefer, on the whole, in view of all the circumstances. We are acting for the greatest good or the least evil or a mixture of these. In the *other* and more usual sense of the words, we are very often doing what we do not wish to do, *i.e.*, doing some particular thing we do not wish because we are afraid of the consequences or disapprove of the moral complexion of the particular thing we do wish. We do the thing that we do not like because the other thing has aspects that we dislike yet more. We are still doing what we like best on the whole. It is again a question of the meaning of words.

.   .   .

Compulsion. — The indeterminist conceives that according to determinism the self is carried along by wishes to acts which it is thus necessitated to perform. This mode of speaking distinguishes the self from the wishes and represents it as under their dominion. This is the initial error. This is what leads the indeterminist wrong on all the topics of his problem. And the error persists in the most recent writings. In fact, the moral self is the wishing self. The wishes are its own. It cannot be described as under their dominion, for it has no separate predilections to be overborne by them; they themselves are its predilections. To fancy that because the person acts according to them he is compelled, a slave, the victim of a power from whose clutches he cannot extricate himself, is a confusion of ideas, a mere slip of the mind. The answer that has ordinarily been given is surely correct; all compulsion is causation, but not all causation is compulsion. Seize a man and violently force him to do something, and he is compelled — also caused — to do it. But induce him to do it by giving him reasons and his doing it is caused but not compelled.

Passivity. — We have to be on our guard even against conceiving the inducement as a cause acting like the impact of a billiard ball, by which the self is precipitated into action like a second billiard ball, as an effect. The case is not so simple. Your reasons have shown him that his own preferences require the action. He does it of his own choice; he acts from his own motives in the light of your reasons. The sequence of cause and effect goes on within the self, with contributory information from without.

It is not clarifying to ask, "Is a volition free or determined?" It is the person who is free, and his particular volition that is determined. Freedom is something that we can attribute only to a continuing being, and he can have it only so far as the particular transient volitions within him are determined. (According to the strict proprieties of language, it is surely events that are caused, not things or persons; a person or thing can be caused or determined only in the sense that its beginning to be, or changes in it, are caused or determined.)

It is fancied that, owing to the "necessity" with which an effect follows upon its cause, if my acts of will are caused I am not free in thus acting. Consider an analogous matter. When I move I use ligaments. "Ligament" means that which binds, and a ligament does bind bones together. But *I* am not bound. *I* (so far as my organism is concerned) am rendered possible by the fact that my bones are bound one to another; that is part of the secret of my being able to act, to move about and work my will. If my bones ceased to be bound one to another I should be undone indeed. The human organism is detached, but it is distinctly important that its component parts shall not be detached. Just so my free power of willing is built up of tight cause-and-effect connections. The point is that when I employ the power thus constituted nothing determines the particular employment of it but *me*. Each particular act of mine is determined from outside itself, *i.e.*, by a cause, a prior event. But not from outside me. I, the possessor of the power, am not in my acts passively played upon by causes outside me, but am enacting my own wishes in virtue of a chain of causation within me. What is needed is to distinguish broadly between a particular effect, on the one hand, and, on the other, the detached, continuous life of a mental individual and his organism; a life reactive, but reacting according to its own nature.

What makes the other party uncontrollably reject all this — let us never forget — is the words. They smell of sordid detail, of unwinsome psychological machinery. They are not bathed in moral value, not elevated and glowing. In this the the opponents' instinct is wholly right; only when they look for the value they fail to focus their eyes aright. It is in the whole act and the whole trait and the whole being that excellence and preciousness inhere; analysis must needs show us elements which, taken severally, are without moral expressiveness; as would be even the celestial anatomy of an angel appearing on earth. The analytic imagination, however, enables us to see the identity of the living fact in its composition with the living fact in its unity and integrity. Hence we can resume the thought of it as a unit and the appropriate feelings without fancying that analysis threatens them or is at enmity with them.

. . .

Prediction. — If we knew a man's character thoroughly and the circumstances that he would encounter, determinism (which we are not here completely asserting) says that we could foretell his conduct. This is a thought that repels many libertarians. Yet to predict a person's conduct need not be repellent. If you are to be alone in a room with £1000 belonging to another on the table and can pocket it without anyone knowing the fact, and if I predict that you will surely *not* pocket it, that is not an insult. I say, I know you, I know your character; you will not do it. But if I say that you are "a free being" and that I really do not know whether you will pocket it or not, that is rather an insult. On the other hand, there are cases where prediction is really disparaging. If I say when you make a remark, "I knew you were going to say that," the impression is not agreeable. My exclamation seems to say that your mind is so small and simple that one can predict its ideas. That is the real reason why people resent in such cases our predicting their conduct; that if present human knowledge, which is known to be so limited, can foresee their conduct, it must be more naive and stereotyped than they like to think it. It is no reflection upon the human mind or its freedom to say that one who knew it through and through (a human impossibility) could foreknow its preferences and its spontaneous choice. It is of the very best of men that even we human beings say, "I am sure of him." It has perhaps in this controversy hardly been observed how much at this point is involved, how far the question of prediction reaches. The word "reliable" or "trustworthy" is a prediction of behaviour. Indeed, all judgment of persons whatever, in the measure of its definitude, is such a prediction.

Material Fate. — The philosopher in the old story, gazing at the stars, falls into a pit. We have to notice the pitfall in our subject to which, similarly occupied, Prof. Eddington has succumbed.

"What significance is there in my mental struggle to-night whether I shall or shall not give up smoking, if the laws which govern the matter of the physical universe already pre-ordain for the morrow a configuration of matter consisting of pipe, tobacco, and smoke connected with my lips?"[4]

No laws, according to determinism, pre-ordain such a configuration, unless I give up the struggle. Let us put matter aside for the moment, to return to it. Fatalism says that my morrow is determined no matter how I struggle. This is of course a superstition. Determinism says that my morrow is determined through my struggle. There is this significance in my mental effort, that it is deciding the event. The stream of causation runs through my deliberations and decision, and, if it did not run as it does run, the event would be different. The past cannot determine the event except through the present. And no past moment determined it any more truly than does the present moment. In other words, each of the links in the causal chain must be in its place. Determinism (which, the reader will remember, we have not here taken for necessarily true in all detail) says that the coming result is "pre-ordained" (literally, caused) at each stage, and therefore the whole following series for to-morrow may be described as already determined; so that did we know all about the struggler, how strong of purpose he was and how he was influenced (which is humanly impossible) we could tell what he would do. But for the struggler this fact (supposing it to be such) is not pertinent. If, believing it, he ceases to struggle, he is merely revealing

---

[4] *Philosophy,* Jan., 1933, p. 41.

that the forces within him have brought about that cessation. If on the other hand he struggles manfully he will reveal the fact that they have brought about his success. Since the causation of the outcome works through his struggle in either case equally, it cannot become for him a moving consideration in the struggle. In it the question is, "Shall I do this or that?" It must be answered in the light of what there is to recommend to me this or that. To this question the scientific truth (according to determinism) that the deliberation itself is a play of causation is completely irrelevant; it merely draws the mind delusively away from the only considerations that concern it.

. . .

Self as Product and Producer. — We can at this stage clearly see the position when a certain very familiar objection is raised. "How can any one be praised or blamed if he was framed by nature as he is, if heredity and circumstance have given him his qualities? A man can surely be blamed only for what he does himself, and he did not make his original character; he simply found it on his hands." A man is to be blamed only for what he does himself, for that alone tells what he is. He did not make his character; no, but he made his acts. Nobody blames him for making such a character, but only for making such acts. And to blame him for that is simply to say that he is a bad act-maker. If he thinks the blame misapplied he has to prove that he is not that sort of an act-maker. Are we to be told that we may not recognise what he is, with appropriate feelings of its quality, because he did not create himself — a mere contortion and intussusception of ideas? The moral self cannot be *causa sui*. To cause his original self a man must have existed before his original self. Is there something humiliating to him in the fact that he is not a contradiction in terms? If there were a being who made his "original character," and made a fine one, and we proceeded to praise him for it, our language would turn out to be a warm ascription to him of a still earlier character, so that the other would not have been original at all. To be praised or blamed you have to be; and be a particular person; and the praise or blame is telling what kind of a person you are. There is no other meaning to be extracted from it. Of course, a man does exist before his later self, and in that other sense he can be a moral *causa sui*. If by unflagging moral effort he achieves for himself better subsequent qualities, what can merit praise but the ingredient in him of aspiration and resolution that was behind the effort? If he should even remake almost his whole character, still there would be a valiant remnant that had done it. These are commonplaces, precisely of the moral outlook upon life. When we come to the moral fountainhead we come to what the man is, at a particular time, as measured by what he does or is disposed to do with his power of volition.

. . .

The indeterminist, we noticed, requires a man to be "an absolute moral source" if we are to commend him. Well, if he were so, what could we say about him but what kind of a source he was? And he is so in fact. Suppose now that this source has in turn a source — or that it has not! Does that (either way) change what it is?

"But moral severity! How can we justly be severe toward a mere fact in nature — in human nature?" Because it is evil; because it must be checked. If somebody takes pleasure in torturing an innocent person, we spring to stop the act; to hold back the perpetrator, if need be with violence; to deter him from doing it again, if need be with violence; to warn any other possible perpetrators: "This shall not be done; we are the enemies of this conduct; this is evil conduct." At what could we be indignant but at a fact in somebody's human nature? Our severity and enmity are an active enmity to the evil; they are all part of that first spring to stop the act. "Society is opposed in every possible manner to such cruelty. You shall be made to feel that society is so, supposing that you cannot be made to feel yourself the vileness of the act." It does not remove our sense of its vileness to reflect that he was acting according to his nature. That is very precisely why we are indignant at him. We intend to make him feel that his nature is in that respect evil and its expression insufferable. We intend to interfere with the expression of his nature. That what he did proceeded from it is not a disturbing and pause-giving consideration in the midst of our conduct, but the entire basis of it. The very epithet "vile" assumes that his behaviour arose from an intention and a moral quality in the man. How can we justly be severe? Because he *ought* to be checked and deterred, made to feel the moral estimate of what he has been doing. This we consider more fully under the topic of Desert.

Compare a case where the wrongdoing, whatever it be, is one's own. Catch a man in a moment of fierce self-reproach, and bring the objection above before him. Would it relieve him of his feeling? It would be an irrelevant frivolity to him. He is shocked at a wrong that was done and at himself for doing it; he repents of the acts of will that brought it about; he would gladly so change himself as never to do the like again; he is ready to "beat himself with rods." With all that the metaphysical entanglement has simply nothing to do.

.   .   .

"Still, does not determinism force us to face a fact in some sort new to us, that the offending person came to act so from natural causes; and does not that of necessity alter somewhat our attitude or state of mind about moral judgment?" Why, the fact is not new at all. In daily life we are all determinists, just as we are all libertarians. We are constantly attributing behaviour to the character, the temperament, the peculiarities of the person and expecting him to behave in certain fashions. The very words of our daily converse, as we have so amply observed, are full of determinism. And we see nothing inconsistent in being aware at the same time that he is free in choosing his course, as we know ourselves to be. We merely form expectations as to what he *will* freely choose. Nor do we see anything inconsistent in blaming him. At the very moment when we do so we often shake our heads over the environment or mode of life or ill-omened pursuits that have brought him to such ways and to being a blameworthy person.

.   .   .

To be sure, determinism as a philosophic doctrine, determinism so named, may come as a new and repellent idea to us. We have been thinking in the right terms of thought all the while, but we did not identify them with terms of causation; when the philosophical names are put upon them we recoil, not because we have a false conception of the facts, but a false conception of the import of the philosophical terms. When we feel that somebody could have done otherwise but chose to do a wrong act knowingly, then we one and all feel that he is culpable and a proper object of disapproval, as we ought to feel. We merely have not been schooled enough in the application of general terms to call the course of mental events within him causation. So again, goodness consists in qualities, but the qualities express themselves in choosing, which is unfettered and so often trembles in the balance; when we are suddenly confronted with the abstract question, "Can we be blamed for a quality we did not choose?" the colours run and the outlines swim a little; some disentanglement of abstract propositions is required, though we think aright in practice on the concrete cases. So all that philosophic determinism "forces us to face" is the meaning of our terms.

No, it is the opposite doctrine that must revolutionise our attitude toward moral judgments. If it is true, we must come to see that no moral severity towards the helpless subject of an act of will that he suddenly finds discharging itself within him, though not emanating from what he is or prefers, can be deserved or relevant. To comprehend all is to pardon all — so far as it is undetermined. Or, rather, not to pardon but to acquit of all.

However, in face of the actual facts, there is something that does bring us to a larger than the usual frame of mind about indignation and punishment and the mood of severity. And that is thought, sympathetic thought, any thought that enters with humane interest into the inner lives of others and pursues in imagination the course of them. In an outbreak of moral indignation we are prone to take little cognizance of that inner life. We are simply outraged by a noxious act and a noxious trait (conceived rather objectively and as it concerns the persons affected) and feel that such act should not be and that such a trait should be put down. The supervening of a sympathetic mental insight upon moral indignation is not a displacement, but the turning of attention upon facts that call out other feelings too. To comprehend all is neither to pardon all nor to acquit of all; overlooking the disvalue of acts and intentions would not be comprehension; but it is to appreciate the human plight; the capacity for suffering, the poor contracted outlook, the plausibilities that entice the will. This elicits a sympathy or concern co-existing with disapproval. That which is moral in moral indignation and behind it, if we faithfully turn to it and listen, will not let us entirely wash our hands even of the torturer, his feelings and his fate; certainly will not permit us to take satisfaction in seeing him in turn tortured, merely for the torture's sake. His act was execrable because of its effect on sentient beings, but he also is a sentient being. The humanity that made us reprobate his crime has not ceased to have jurisdiction. The morality that hates the sin has in that very fact the secret of its undiscourageable interest in the sinner. We come, not to discredit indignation and penalty, nor to tamper with their meaning, but to see their office and place in life and the implications wrapped up in their very fitness. Of this more presently.

Responsibility. — Again, it is said that determinism takes from man all responsibility. As regards the origin of the term, a man is responsible when he is the person to respond to the question why the act was performed, how it is to be explained or justified. That is what he must answer; he is answerable for the act. It is the subject of which he must give an account; he is accountable for the act. The act proceeded from him. He is to say whether it proceeded consciously. He is to give evidence that he did or did not know the moral nature of the act and that he did or did not intend the result. He is to say how he justifies it or if he can justify it. If the act proceeded from him by pure accident, if he can show that he did the damage (if damage it was) by brushing against something by inadvertence, for example, then he has not to respond to the question what he did it for — he is not consciously responsible — nor how it is justified — he is not morally responsible, though of course he may have been responsible in these respects for a habit of carelessness.

But why does the peculiar moral stain of guilt or ennoblement of merit belong to responsibility? If an act proceeds from a man and not merely from his accidental motion but from his mind and moral nature, we judge at once that like acts may be expected from him in the future. The colour of the act for good or bad is reflected on the man. We see him now as a living source of possible acts of the same kind. If we must be on our guard against such acts we must be on our guard against such men. If we must take steps to defend ourselves against such acts we must take steps to defend ourselves against such men. If we detest such acts, we must detest that tendency in such men which produced them. He is guilty in that he knowingly did evil, in that the intentional authorship of evil is in him. Because the act proceeded in every sense from him, for that reason he is (so far) to be accounted bad or good according as the act is bad or good, and he is the one to be punished if punishment is required. And that is moral responsibility.

But how, it is asked, can I be responsible for what I will if a long train of past causes has made me will it — the old query asked anew in relation to another category, responsibility, which must be considered separately. Is it not these causes that are "responsible" for my act — to use the word in the only sense, says the objector, that seems to remain for it?

The parent past produced the man, none the less the man is responsible for his acts. We can truly say that the earth bears apples, but quite as truly that trees bear apples. The earth bears the apples by bearing trees. It does not resent the claim of the trees to bear the apples, or try to take the business out of the trees' hands. Nor need the trees feel their claim nullified by the earth's part in the matter. There is no rivalry between them. A man is a being with free will and responsibility; where this being came from, I repeat, is another story. The past finished its functions in the business when it generated him as he is. So far from interfering with him and coercing him the past does not even exist. If we could imagine it as lingering on into the present, standing over against him and stretching out a ghostly hand to stay his arm, then indeed the past would be interfering with his liberty and responsibility. But so long as it and he are never on the scene together they cannot wrestle; the past cannot overpower him. The whole alarm is an evil dream, a nightmare due to the indigestion of words. The past has created, and left extant, a free-willed being.

Desert. — But we have not come to any final clearness until we see how a man can be said to *deserve* anything when his acts flow from his wishes, and his wishes flow from other facts further up the stream of his life. There is a peculiar element in the idea of deserving. This is the element of "ought." A man deserves punishment or reward if society ought to give it to him; he deserves the punishment or reward that he ought to receive. We cannot say universally that he deserves what he ought to receive, but only when it is a question of reward or punishment.

What treatment a man should receive from society as a result of wrong-doing is a question of ethics. It is widely held that an evildoer deserves punishment, not only for the defence of society but because there is an ultimate fitness in inflicting natural evil for moral evil. This, as we know, has been maintained by determinists. Since the idea of desert collapses altogether on the indeterminist's conception of conduct, this theory of the ground of desert cannot be said to be logically bound up with indeterminism. For my own part, however, owing to reasons for which I have no space here, I cannot hold the theory. I believe that the ideal ends of the administration of justice are (1) to see that all possible restitution is made, (2) to see as far as possible that the malefactor does not repeat the act, and (3) so far as possible to render the act less likely on the part of others. And these ends should be sought by means that will accomplish them. Morality is humane. It is animated by good will toward humanity. Our instinctive impulse to retaliation must be interpreted with a view to its function in society, and so employed and regulated to the best purpose. Being a part of the defensive and fighting instinct, its functional aim is evidently to destroy or check the threatening source of evil — to destroy the culprit or change his temper. Our common and natural notion of desert is in harmony with either of these views; only on the second it receives a supplement, a purposive interpretation.

We discover punishment not only in combat but in nature at large. If a child puts its hand into flames it is burnt. After that it puts its hand into flames no more. Nature teaches us to respect her by punishments that deter. Society, to preserve itself, must find deterrents to administer to men. It must say, "I'll teach you not to do that." Already nature has taught it such deterrents. Society must shape men's actions or at least rough-hew them, to the extent of striking off certain jagged and dangerous edges, and the most obvious way to do so is by penalties. A secondary way is by rewards, and these nature has taught also.

When a man needlessly injures others, society by punishment injures him. It administers to him a specimen of what he has given to others. "This," it says, "is the nature of your act; to give men suffering like this. They rebel at it as you rebel at this. You have to be made more acutely conscious of the other side; the side of the feelings and the forces that you have outraged. You have to be made to feel them recoil upon you, that you may know that they are there. You have to be made to respect them in advance. And others like-minded to respect them in some degree better by seeing how they recoil upon you."

But this is only a method of working upon him and them; it is justified by effectiveness alone. It supposes two things; that society has been just in the first instance to these men themselves, that is, that they were not drawn by unjust conditions of life into the acts for which they are made to suffer; and that the suffering will in fact improve their conduct or that of others. The truth is that society often punishes when it is itself the greater male-factor, and that the penalty, instead of reforming, often confirms the crim-inality. It is due to nothing but the crude state of civilisation that we have added so little of a more sagacious and effectual mode of influencing criminals and preventing crime than the original and natural method of hitting back.

Out of this situation arises a subsidiary sense of deserving. A man may be said to deserve a punishment in the sense that, in view of the offence, it is not too severe to give him if it would work as above conceived; though if we believe it will not so work it ought not to be given him.

.   .   .

If the general view here taken, which seems forced upon us in the prosaic process of examining words, is correct, then as we look back over the long course of this controversy and the false antithesis that has kept it alive, how can we help exclaiming, "What waste!" Waste is surely the tragic fact above all in life; we contrast it with the narrow areas where reason and its economy of means to ends in some measure reign. But here is huge waste in the region of reasoning itself, the enemy in the citadel. What ingenuity, what resource in fresh shifts of defence, what unshaken loyalty to inward repugnances, what devotion to ideal values, have here been expended in blind opposition instead of analysis. The cause of determinism, seeming to deny freedom, has appeared as the cause of reason, of intelligence itself, and the cause of free will, seeming to exclude determination, has appeared that of morals. The worst waste is the clash of best things. In our subject it is time this waste should end. Just as we find that morality requires intelligence to give effect and remains rudimentary and largely abortive till it places the conscience of the mind in the foreground, so we find that determinism and the faith in freedom meet and are united in the facts, and that the long enmity has been a bad dream.

30

THE NEW INDETERMINISM IN PHYSICS

Arthur Eddington

Arthur Eddington (1882-1944) was an eminent British astronomer and physicist who was quite concerned with the application of scientific developments to philosophical problems.

Ten years ago practically every physicist of repute was, or believed himself to be, a determinist, at any rate so far as inorganic phenomena are concerned. He believed he had come across a scheme of strict causality regulating the sequence of phenomena. It was considered to be the primary aim of science to fit as much of the universe as possible into such a scheme; so that, as a working belief if not as a philosophical conviction, the causal scheme was always held to be applicable in default of overwhelming evidence to the contrary. In fact, the methods, definitions and conceptions of physical science were so much bound up with the hypothesis of strict causality that the limits (if any) of the scheme of causal law were looked upon as the ultimate limits of physical science. No serious doubt was entertained that this determinism covered all inorganic phenomena. How far it applied to living or conscious matter or to consciousness itself was a matter of individual opinion; but there was naturally a reluctance to accept any restriction of an outlook which had proved so successful over a wide domain.

Then rather suddenly determinism faded out of theoretical physics. Its exit has been received in various ways. Some writers are incredulous and cannot be persuaded that determinism has really been eliminated from the present foundations of physical theory. Some think that it is no more than a domestic change in physics, having no reactions on general philosophic thought. Some decide cynically to wait and see if determinism fades in again.

The rejection of determinism is in no sense an abdication of scientific method. It is rather the fruition of a scientific method which had grown up under the shelter of the old causal method and has now been found to have a wider range. It has greatly increased the power and precision of the

From Chapter IV, "The Decline of Determinism," of *New Pathways in Science.* Reprinted by permission of the publisher, Cambridge University Press.

mathematical theory of observed phenomena. On the other hand I cannot agree with those who belittle the philosophical significance of the change. The withdrawal of physical science from an attitude it had adopted consistently for more than 200 years is not to be treated lightly; and it provokes a reconsideration of our views as to one of the most perplexing problems of our existence.

In a subject which arouses so much controversy it seems well to make clear at the outset certain facts regarding the extent of the change as to which there has frequently been a misunderstanding. Firstly, it is not suggested that determinism has been disproved. What we assert is that physical science is no longer based on determinism. Is it difficult to grasp this distinction? If I were asked whether astronomy has disproved the doctrine that "the moon is made of green cheese" I might have some difficulty in finding really conclusive evidence; but I could say unhesitatingly that the doctrine is not the basis of present-day selenography. Secondly, the denial of determinism, or as it is often called "the law of causality," does not mean that it is denied that effects may proceed from causes. The common regular association of cause and effect is a matter of experience; the law of causality is an extreme generalisation suggested by this experience. Such generalisations are always risky. To suppose that in doubting the generalisation we are denying the experience is like supposing that a person who doubts Newton's (or Einstein's) law of gravitation denies that apples fall to the ground. The first criterion applied to any theory, deterministic or indeterministic, is that it must account for the regularities in our sensory experience — notably our experience that certain effects regularly follow certain causes. Thirdly, the admission of indeterminism in the physical universe does not immediately clear up all the difficulties — not even all the physical difficulties — connected with Free Will. But it so far modifies the problem that the door is not barred and bolted for a solution less repugnant to our deepest intuitions than that which has hitherto seemed to be forced upon us.

Let us be sure that we agree as to what is meant by determinism. I quote three definitions or descriptions for your consideration. The first is by a mathematician (Laplace):

> We ought then to regard the present state of the universe as the effect of its antecedent state and the cause of the state that is to follow. An intelligence, who for a given instant should be acquainted with all the forces by which Nature is animated and with the several positions of the entities composing it, if further his intellect were vast enough to submit those data to analysis, would include in one and the same formula the movements of the largest bodies in the universe and those of the lightest atom. Nothing would be uncertain for him; the future as well as the past would be present to his eyes. The human mind in the perfection it has been able to give to astronomy affords a feeble outline of such an intelligence. . . . All its efforts in the search for truth tend to approximate without limit to the intelligence we have just imagined.

The second is by a philosopher (C. D. Broad):

"Determinism" is the name given to the following doctrine. Let S be any substance, Ψ any characteristic, and t any moment. Suppose that S is in fact in the state σ with respect to Ψ at t. Then the compound supposition that everything else in the world should have been exactly as it in fact was, and that S should instead have been in one of the other two alternative states with respect to Ψ is an impossible one. [The three alternative states (of which σ is one) are: to have the characteristic Ψ, not to have it, and to be changing.]

The third is by a poet (Omar Khayyam):

> With Earth's first Clay They did the Last Man's knead,
> And then of the Last Harvest sow'd the Seed:
> Yea, the first Morning of Creation wrote
> What the Last Dawn of Reckoning shall read.

I regard the poet's definition as my standard. There is no doubt that his words express what is in our minds when we refer to determinism. In saying that the physical universe as now pictured is not a universe in which "the first morning of creation wrote what the last dawn of reckoning shall read," we make it clear that the abandonment of determinism is no technical quibble but is a fundamental change of outlook. The other two definitions need to be scrutinised suspiciously; we are afraid there may be a catch in them. In fact I think there is a catch in them.*

It is important to notice that all three definitions introduce the time element. Determinism postulates not merely causes but *pre-existing* causes. Determinism means predetermination. Hence in any argument about determinism the dating of the alleged causes is all-important; we must challenge them to produce their birth-certificates.

In the passage quoted from Laplace a definite aim of science is laid down. Its efforts "tend to approximate without limit to the intelligence we have just imagined," i.e. an intelligence who from the present state of the universe could foresee the whole of future progress down to the lightest atom. This aim was accepted without question until recent times. But the practical development of science is not always in a direct line with its ultimate aims; and about the middle of the nineteenth century there arose a branch of physics (thermodynamics) which struck out in a new direction. Whilst striving to perfect a system of law that would predict what *certainly* will happen, physicists also became interested in a system which predicts what *probably* will happen. Alongside the superintelligence imagined by Laplace for whom "nothing would be uncertain" was placed an intelligence for whom nothing would be certain but some things would be exceedingly probable. If we could say of this latter being that for him *all* the events of the future were

---

* The catch that I suspect in Broad's definition is that it seems to convey no meaning without further elucidation of what is meant by the supposition being an *impossible* one. He does not mean impossible because it involves a logical contradiction. The supposition is not rejected as being contrary to logic nor as contrary to fact, but for a third reason undefined.

known with exceedingly high probability, it would be mere pedantry to distinguish him from Laplace's being who is supposed to know them with certainty. Actually, however, the new being is supposed to have glimpses of the future of varying degrees of probability ranging from practical certainty to entire indefiniteness according to his particular field of study. Generally speaking his predictions never approach certainty unless they refer to an average of a very large number of individual entities. Thus the aim of science to approximate to this latter intelligence is by no means equivalent to Laplace's aim. I shall call the aim defined by Laplace the *primary* aim, and the new aim introduced in the science of thermodynamics the *secondary* aim.

We must realise that the two aims are distinct. The prediction of what will probably occur is not a half-way stage in the prediction of what will certainly occur. We often solve a problem approximately, and subsequently proceed to second and third approximations, perhaps finally reaching an exact solution. But here the probable prediction is an end in itself; it is not an approximate attempt at a certain prediction. The methods differ fundamentally, just as the method of diagnosis of a doctor who tells you that you have just three weeks to live differs from that of a Life Insurance Office which tells you that your expectation of life is 18.7 years. We can, of course, occupy ourselves with the secondary aim without giving up the primary aim as an ultimate goal; but a survey of the present state of progress of the two aims produces a startling revelation.

The formulae given in modern textbooks on quantum theory — which are continually being tested by experiment and used to open out new fields of investigation — are exclusively concerned with probabilities and averages. This is quite explicit. The "unknown quantity" which is chased from formula to formula is a probability or averaging factor. The quantum theory therefore contributes to the secondary aim, but adds nothing to the primary Laplacian aim which is concerned with causal certainty. But further it is now recognised that the classical laws of mechanics and electromagnetism (including the modifications introduced by relativity theory) are simply the limiting form assumed by the formulae of quantum theory when the number of individual quanta or particles concerned is very large. This connection is known as Bohr's Correspondence Principle. The classical laws are not a fresh set of laws, but are a particular adaptation of the quantum laws. So they also arise from the secondary scheme. We have already mentioned that it is when a very large number of individuals are concerned that the predictions of the secondary scheme have a high probability approaching certainty. Consequently the domain of the classical laws is just that part of the whole domain of secondary law in which the probability is so high as to be practically equivalent to certainty. That is how they came to be mistaken for causal laws whose operation is definitely certain. Now that their statistical character is recognised they are lost to the primary scheme. When Laplace put forward his ideal of a completely deterministic scheme he thought he already had the nucleus of such a scheme in the laws of mechanics and astronomy. That nucleus has now been transferred to the secondary scheme. Nothing is left of the old scheme of causal law, and we have not yet found the beginnings of a new one.

Measured by advance towards the secondary aim, the progress of science has been amazingly rapid. Measured by advance towards Laplace's aim its progress is just *nil*.

Laplace's aim has lapsed into the position of other former aims of science — the discovery of the elixir of life, the philosopher's stone, the North-West Passage — aims which were a fruitful inspiration in their time. We are like navigators on whom at last it has dawned that there are other enterprises worth pursuing besides finding the North-West Passage. I need hardly say that there are some old mariners who regard these new enterprises as a temporary diversion and predict an early return to the "true aim of geographical exploration."

II

Let us examine how the new aim of physics originated. We observe certain regularities in the course of phenomena and formulate these as laws of Nature. Laws can be stated positively or negatively, "Thou shalt" or "Thou shalt not." For the present purpose we shall formulate them negatively. Here are two regularities in the sensory experience of most of us:

(*a*) We never come across equilateral triangles whose angles are unequal.

(*b*) We never come across thirteen hearts in a hand dealt to us at Bridge.

In our ordinary outlook we explain these regularities in fundamentally different ways. We say that the first holds because a contrary experience is *impossible*; the second because a contrary experience is *too improbable*.

This distinction is theoretical. There is nothing in the observations themselves to suggest to which type a particular observed regularity belongs. We recognise that "impossible" and "too improbable" are both adequate explanations of any observed uniformity of experience; and formerly physics rather haphazardly explained some uniformities one way and others the other way. But now the whole of physical law (so far discovered) is found to be comprised in the secondary scheme which deals only with probabilities; and the only reason assigned for any regularity is that the contrary is too improbable. Our failure to find equilateral triangles with unequal angles is because such triangles are too improbable. Of course, I am not here referring to the theorem of pure geometry; I am speaking of a regularity of sensory experience and refer therefore to whatever measurement is supposed to confirm this property of equilateral triangles as being true of actual experience. Our measurements regularly confirm it to the highest accuracy attainable, and no doubt will always do so; but according to the present physical theory that is because a failure could only occur as the result of an extremely unlikely coincidence in the behaviour of the vast number of particles concerned in the apparatus of measurement.

The older view, as I have said, recognised two types of natural law. The earth keeps revolving round the sun because it is impossible that it should run away. That is the primary or deterministic type. Heat flows from a hot body to a cold body because it is too improbable that it should flow the other way. That is the secondary or statistical type. On the modern theory both regularities belong to the statistical type — it is too improbable that the earth should run away from the sun.*

So long as the aim of physics is to bring to light a deterministic scheme, the pursuit of secondary law is a blind alley since it leads only to probabilities. The determinist is not content with a law which ordains that, given reasonable luck, the fire will warm me; he agrees that that is the probable event, but adds that somewhere at the base of physics there are other laws which ordain just what the fire will do to me, luck or no luck.

To borrow an analogy from genetics, determinism is a *dominant character*. Granting a system of primary law, we can (and indeed must) have secondary indeterministic laws derivable from it stating what will probably happen under that system. So for a long time determinism watched with equanimity the development within itself of a subsidiary indeterministic system of law. What matter? Deterministic law remains dominant. It was not foreseen that the child would grow to supplant its parent. There is a game called "Think of a number." After doubling, adding, and other calculations, there comes the direction "Take away the number you first thought of." Determinism is now in the position of the number we first thought of.

The growth of secondary law whilst still under the dominant deterministic scheme was remarkable, and whole sections of physics were transferred to it. There came a time when in the most progressive branches of physics it was used exclusively. The physicist might continue to profess allegiance to primary law but he ceased to use it. Primary law was the gold stored in the vaults; secondary law was the paper currency actually used. But everyone still adhered to the traditional view that paper currency needs to be backed by gold. As physics progressed the occasions when the gold was actually produced became rarer until they ceased altogether. Then it occurred to some of us to question whether there still was a hoard of gold in the vaults or whether its existence was a mythical tradition. The dramatic ending of the story would be that the vaults were opened and found to be empty. The actual ending is not quite so simple. It turns out that the key has been lost, and no one can say for certain whether there is any gold in the vaults or not. But I think it is clear that, with either termination, present-day physics is *off the gold standard*.

---

* "Impossible" therefore disappears from our vocabulary except in the sense of involving a logical contradiction. But the logical contradiction or impossibility is in the description, not in the phenomenon which it attempts but (on account of the contradiction) fails to describe.

III

The nature of the indeterminism now admitted in the physical world will be considered in more detail in the next chapter. I will here content myself with an example showing its order of magnitude. Laplace's ideal intelligence could foresee the future positions of objects from the heaviest bodies to the lightest atoms. Let us then consider the lightest particle we know, viz. the electron. Suppose that an electron is given a clear course (so that it is not deflected by any unforeseen collisions) and that we know all that can be known about it at the present instant. How closely can we foretell its position one second later? The answer is that (in the most favourable circumstances) we can predict its position to within about 1½ inches — not closer. That is the nearest we can approximate to Laplace's super-intelligence. The error is not large if we recall that during the second covered by our prediction the electron may have travelled 10,000 miles or more.

The uncertainty would, however, be serious if we had to calculate whether the electron would hit or miss a small target such as an atomic nucleus. To quote Prof. Born: "If Gessler had ordered William Tell to shoot a hydrogen atom off his son's head by means of an α particle and had given him the best laboratory instruments in the world instead of a cross-bow, Tell's skill would have availed him nothing. Hit or miss would have been a matter of chance."

For contrast take a mass of .001 milligram — which must be nearly the smallest mass handled macroscopically. The indeterminacy is much smaller because the mass is larger. Under similar conditions we could predict the position of this mass a thousand years hence to within $\frac{1}{5000}$ of a millimetre.

This indicates how the indeterminism which affects the minutest constituents of matter becomes insignificant in ordinary mechanical problems, although there is no change in the basis of the laws. It may not at first be apparent that the indeterminacy of 1½ inches in the position of the electron after the lapse of a second is of any great practical importance either. It would not often be important for an electron pursuing a straight course through empty space; but the same indeterminism occurs whatever the electron is doing. If it is pursuing an orbit in an atom, long before the second has expired the indeterminacy amounts to atomic dimension; that is to say, we have altogether lost track of the electron's position in the atom. Anything which depends on the relative location of electrons in an atom is unpredictable more than a minute fraction of a second ahead.

For this reason the break-down of an atomic nucleus, such as occurs in radio-activity, is not predetermined by anything in the existing scheme of physics. All that the most complete theory can prescribe is how frequently configurations favouring an explosion will occur on the average; the individual occurrences of such a configuration are unpredictable. In the solar system we can predict fairly accurately how many eclipses of the sun (i.e.

how many recurrences of a special configuration of the earth, sun and moon)
will happen in a thousand years; or we can predict fairly accurately the date
and time of each particular eclipse. The theory of the second type of prediction is not an elaboration of the theory of the first; the occurrence of individual eclipses depends on celestial mechanics, whereas the frequency of
eclipses is purely a problem of geometry. In the atom, which we have compared to a miniature solar system, there is nothing corresponding to celestial
mechanics — or rather mechanics is stifled at birth by the magnitude of the
indeterminacy — but the geometrical theory of frequency of configurations
remains analogous.

The future is never entirely determined by the past, nor is it ever entirely detached. We have referred to several phenomena in which the future
is *practically determined;* the break-down of a radium nucleus is an example
of a phenomenon in which the future is *practically detached* from the past.

But, you will say, the fact that physics assigns no characteristic to the
radium nucleus predetermining the date at which it will break up, only
means that that characteristic has not yet been discovered. You readily agree
that we cannot predict the future in all cases; but why blame Nature rather
than our own ignorance? If the radium atom were an exception, it would be
natural to suppose that there is a determining characteristic which, when it is
found, will bring it into line with other phenomena. But the radio-active
atom was not brought forward as an exception; I have mentioned it as an
extreme example of that which applies in greater or lesser degree to all kinds
of phenomena. There is a difference between explaining away an exception
and explaining away a rule.

The persistent critic continues, "You are evading the point. I contend
that there are characteristics unknown to you which completely predetermine
not only the time of break-up of the radio-active atom but all physical phenomena. How do you know that there are not? You are not omniscient." I
can understand the casual reader raising this question; but when a man of
scientific training asks it, he wants shaking up and waking. Let us try the
effect of a story.

About the year 2000, the famous archaeologist Prof. Lambda discovered
an ancient Greek inscription which recorded that a foreign prince, whose
name was given as Κανδείκλης, came with his followers into Greece and
established his tribe there. The Professor anxious to identify the prince, after
exhausting other sources of information, began to look through the letters C
and K in the *Encyclopaedia Athenica*. His attention was attracted by an article on Canticles who it appeared was the son of Solomon. Clearly that was
the required identification; no one could doubt that Κανδείκλης was the Jewish
Prince Canticles. His theory attained great notoriety. At that time the
Great Powers of Greece and Palestine were concluding an Entente and the
Greek Prime Minister in an eloquent peroration made touching reference to
the newly discovered historical ties of kinship between the two nations. Some
time later Prof. Lambda happened to refer to the article again and discovered

that he had made an unfortunate mistake; he had misread "Son of Solomon" for "Song of Solomon". The correction was published widely, and it might have been supposed that the Canticles theory would die a natural death. But no: Greeks and Palestinians continued to believe in their kinship, and the Greek Minister continued to make perorations. Prof. Lambda one day ventured to remonstrate with him. The Minister turned on him severely, "How do you know that Solomon had not a son called Canticles? You are not omniscient". The Professor, having reflected on the rather extensive character of Solomon's matrimonial establishment, found it difficult to reply.

. . .

I have already said that determinism is not disproved by physics. But it is the determinist who puts forward a positive proposal and the onus of proof is on him. He wishes to base on our ordinary experience of the sequence of cause and effect a wide generalisation called the Principle of Causality. Since physics to-day represents this experience as the result of statistical laws without any reference to the principle of causality, it is obvious that the generalisation has nothing to commend it so far as observational evidence is concerned. The indeterminists therefore regard it as they do any other entirely unsupported hypothesis. It is part of the tactics of the advocate of determinism to turn our unbelief in his conjecture into a positive conjecture of our own — a sort of Principle of Uncausality. The indeterminist is sometimes said to postulate "something like free-will" in the individual atoms. *Something like* is conveniently vague; the various mechanisms used in daily life have their obstinate moods and may be said to display something like free-will. But if it is suggested that we postulate psychological characters in the individual atoms of the kind which appear in our minds as human free-will, I deny this altogether. We do not discard one rash generalisation only to fall into another equally rash.

IV

When determinism was believed to prevail in the physical world, the question naturally arose, how far did it govern human activities? The question has often been confused by assuming that human activity belongs to a totally separate sphere — a mental sphere. But man has a body as well as a mind. The movements of his limbs, the sound waves which issue from his lips, the twinkle in his eye, are all phenomena of the physical world, and unless expressly excluded would be predetermined along with other physical phenomena. We can, if we like, distinguish two forms of determinism: (1) The scheme of causal law predetermines all human thought, emotions and volitions; (2) it predetermines human actions but not human motives and volitions. The second seems less drastic and probably commends itself to the liberal-minded, but the concession really amounts to very little. Under it a man can think what he likes, but he can only say that which the laws of physics preordain.

The essential point is that, if determinism is to have any definable meaning, the domain of deterministic law must be a closed system; that is to say, all the data used in predicting must themselves be capable of being predicted. Whatever predetermines the future must itself be predetermined by the past. The movements of human bodies are part of the complete data of prediction of future states of the material universe; and if we include them for this purpose we must include them also as data which (it is asserted) can be predicted.

.   .   .

The revolution of theory which has expelled determinism from present-day physics has therefore the important consequence that it is no longer necessary to suppose that human actions are completely predetermined. Although the door of human freedom is opened, it is not flung wide open; only a chink of daylight appears. But I think this is sufficient to justify a reorientation of our attitude to the problem. If our new-found freedom is like that of the mass of .001 mgm., which is only allowed to stray $\frac{1}{5000}$ mm. in a thousand years, it is not much to boast of. The physical results do not spontaneously suggest any higher degree of freedom than this. But it seems to me that philosophical, psychological, and in fact commonsense arguments for greater freedom are so cogent that we are justified in trying to prise the door further open now that it is not actually barred. How can this be done without violence to physics?

If we could attribute the large-scale movements of our bodies to the "trigger action" of the unpredetermined behaviour of a few key atoms in our brain cells the problem would be simple; for individual atoms have wide indeterminacy of behaviour. It is obvious that there is a great deal of trigger action in our bodily mechanism, as when the pent up energy of a muscle is released by a minute physical change in a nerve; but it would be rash to suppose that the physical controlling cause is contained in the configuration of a few dozen atoms. I should conjecture that the smallest unit of structure in which the physical effects of volition have their origin contains many billions of atoms. If such a unit behaved like an inorganic system of similar mass the indeterminacy would be insufficient to allow appreciable freedom. My own tentative view is that this "conscious unit" does in fact differ from an inorganic system in having a much higher indeterminacy of behaviour — simply because of the unitary nature of that which in reality it represents, namely the Ego.

We have to remember that the physical world of atoms, electrons, quanta, etc., is the abstract symbolic representation of something. Generally we do not know anything of the background of the symbols — we do not know the inner nature of what is being symbolised. But at a point of contact of the physical world with consciousness, we have acquaintance with the conscious unity — the self or mind — whose physical aspect and symbol is the brain cell. Our method of physical analysis leads us to dissect this cell into atoms similar to the atoms in any non-conscious region of the world. But whereas in other regions each atom (so far as its behaviour is indeterminate) is governed independently by chance, in the conscious cell the behaviour symbolises a single volition of the spirit and not a conflict of billions of independent impulses. It seems to me that we must attribute some kind of unitary behaviour to the physical terminal of consciousness, otherwise the physical symbolism is not an appropriate representation of the mental unit which is being symbolised.

We conclude then that the activities of consciousness do not violate the laws of physics, since in the present indeterministic scheme there is freedom to operate within them.

. . .

The two aspects of human freedom on which I would lay most stress are *responsibility* and *self-understanding*. The nature of responsibility brings us to a well-known dilemma which I am no more able to solve than hundreds who have tried before me. How can we be responsible for our own good or evil nature? We feel that we can to some extent change our nature; we can reform or deteriorate. But is not the reforming or deteriorating impulse also in our nature? Or, if it is not in us, how can we be responsible for it? I will not add to the many discussions of this difficulty, for I have no solution to suggest. I will only say that I cannot accept as satisfactory the solution sometimes offered, that responsibility is a self-contradictory illusion. The solution does not seem to me to fit the data. Just as a theory of matter has to correspond to our perceptions of matter so a theory of the human spirit has to correspond to our inner perception of our spiritual nature. And to me it seems that responsibility is one of the fundamental facts of our nature. If I can be deluded over such a matter of immediate knowledge — the very nature of the being that I myself am — it is hard to see where any trustworthy beginning of knowledge is to be found.

. . .

I do not think we can take liberties with that immediate self-knowledge of consciousness by which we are aware of ourselves as responsible, truth-seeking, reasoning, striving. The external world is not what it seems; we can transform our conception of it as we will provided that the system of signals passing from it to the mind is conserved. But as we draw nearer to the source of all knowledge the stream should run clearer. At least that is the hypothesis that the scientist is compelled to make, else where shall he start to look for truth? The Problem of Experience becomes unintelligible unless it is considered as the quest of a responsible, truth-seeking, reasoning spirit. These characteristics of the spirit therefore become the first datum of the problem.

The conceptions of physics are becoming difficult to understand. First relativity theory, then quantum theory and wave mechanics, have transformed the universe, making it seem fantastic to our minds. And perhaps the end is not yet. But there is another side to the transformation. Naïve realism, materialism, and mechanistic conceptions of phenomena were simple to understand; but I think that it was only by closing our eyes to the essential nature of conscious experience that they could be made to seem credible. These revolutions of scientific thought are clearing up the deeper contradictions between life and theoretical knowledge. The latest phase with its release from determinism is one of the greatest steps in the reconciliation. I would even say that in the present indeterministic theory of the physical universe we have reached something which a reasonable man might *almost* believe.

31

DETERMINISM
AND THE CONCEPT
OF ACTION

S. I. Benn and R. S. Peters

S. I. Benn (1920-   ) is Senior Fellow in Philosophy at the Australian National University, Canberra. R. S. Peters (1919-   ) is Professor of the Philosophy of Education at the University of London.

Determinism to a scientist conveys the general proposition that every event has a cause. Whether this general proposition is true is a very difficult question to decide, but it is certainly assumed to be true by most scientists. To say that an event has a cause is to say that there are universal laws together with statements about initial conditions prevailing at particular times, and that from these two together we can predict an event which we call an 'effect'. For example, given that under the conditions x,y,z, iron expands when it is heated, and given that the conditions x,y,z, prevail and that this is a case of iron being heated, we can make the prediction that iron will expand. Here we have a typical causal relation. The so-called 'cause' is then the event referred to in the statement of initial conditions. And these conditions are regarded as being *sufficient* to explain the effect, if it is a full-blooded causal *explanation*.

Have we such relations in human affairs? The initial difficulty about saying that we have is that it is difficult to maintain that there are any psychological or sociological laws which would enable us to make such definite predictions. There are also difficulties connected with our knowledge of particular situations which constitute the initial conditions; for when we are dealing with stones and bodies falling, their past history is scarcely part of the present situation. But when we are dealing with human beings, their past history is very much part of the present situation, and it is very difficult to know whether a given case is really of the type to which the particular law we have in mind applies. Nevertheless, there are some generalizations in psychology and the social sciences which are reasonably well established.

From Chapter IX, "Freedom and Responsibility," of *Social Principles and the Democratic State* (1959). Reprinted by permission of the publisher, George Allen & Unwin, Ltd., London.

351

They do not enable us to make detailed predictions; they merely enable us to state the sort of thing that will *tend* to happen under certain typical conditions. In this respect psychology is in no worse plight than other sciences like meteorology. The difficulties arise from the complexity of the subject-matter, and, it might be argued, can be remedied in time.

If, however, we look more closely at these so-called laws in psychology we find, in the main, that they do not give sufficient explanations of human *actions,* of what human beings do deliberately, knowing what they are doing and for which they can give reasons. Freud's brilliant discoveries, for instance, were not of the causes of *actions* like signing contracts or shooting pheasants; rather they were of things that *happen* to a man like dreams, hysteria, and slips of the tongue. These might be called 'passions' more appropriately than 'actions', and in this respect they are similar to what we call 'fits of passion' or 'gusts of emotion'. Men do not dream or forget a name 'on purpose' any more than they are deliberately subject to impulses or gusts of emotion. One class of laws in psychology, then, gives causal explanations which seem sufficient to account for what *happens* to a man, but not for what he does.

There is another class of laws, however, which concern not what happens to men, but what they do — their actions, performances and achievements. But such laws state necessary rather than sufficient conditions. We have in mind here the contributions made by physiological psychologists and those who have studied cognitive skills like learning, remembering, and perceiving. Part of what we mean by such terms is that human beings attain a norm or standard. Remembering is not just a psychological process; for to remember is to be *correct* about what happened in the past. Knowing is not just a mental state; it is to be sure that we are *correct* and to have *good grounds* for our conviction. To perceive something is to be *right* in our claims about what is before our eyes; to learn something is to *improve* at something or to get something *right*. All such concepts have norms written into them. In a similar way, as we have previously argued, a human action is typically something done in order to bring about a result or in accordance with a standard. Such actions can be said to be done more or less intelligently and more or less correctly only because of the norms defining what are ends and what are efficient and correct means to them. It follows that a psychologist who claims that such performances depend on antecedent physiological conditions or mental processes, can at the most be stating necessary conditions. For processes, of themselves, are not appropriately described as correct or incorrect, intelligent or stupid. They only become so in the context of standards laid down by men. As Protagoras taught, nature knows no norms. It may well be true that a man cannot remember without part of his brain being stimulated, or that learning is a function, in part, of antecedent 'tension'. But the very meaning of 'remembering' and 'learning' precludes a sufficient explanation in these sorts of naturalistic terms.

Furthermore the problem of the freedom of the will arose mainly in connection with a type of action that is palpably different from a mere movement or process — an action that is preceded by deliberation and choice. For, roughly speaking, a 'willed action' was usually taken to mean one in which we think before we act, when we make up our minds in terms of considerations which are relevant to the matter in hand before we act. There are difficulties about developing causal laws for actions of this type which are additional to those already stated about actions in general. Such difficulties are similar to those which the social scientist, as well as the psychologist, has in predicting what human beings will do. This is connected with the fact that into the human being's deliberations about what he is going to do will be introduced considerations about what he is likely to do, which the social scientist may have published. A scientist may discover a causal law connecting the properties of clover with a certain effect upon the digestive organs of sheep. But, when he publishes his findings, the sheep cannot take account of them and modify their behaviour accordingly. But with men it is different. Many causal connections discovered by psychologists may only hold good provided that the people whose actions are predicted in accordance with the law remain ignorant of what it asserts. And it is practically impossible to ensure that this is the case. So, if people know the causes on which a prediction of a certain type of behaviour is based, and if they deliberate before acting they may do something different from what is predicted, just because they recognize these causes. A prediction may thus be valid only on the assumption that the people concerned remain unconscious of the causes on which it is based. Otherwise it may be no more than a warning.

But why cannot causal explanations *also* be given of such informed deliberations which precede actions? We are here confronted with the difficulty of accounting for *logical* thought in causal terms, of giving a causal explanation for rational actions done after deliberation which involves logically relevant considerations. This is an extreme case of the difficulty already cited of giving sufficient explanations in causal terms for actions and performances which involve norms and standards. Yet, as has already been pointed out, such premeditated actions are particularly important in the free-will controversy, as the exercise of 'will' has usually been associated with rational deliberation before acting. When a man is solving a geometrical problem and his thoughts are proceeding in accordance with certain logical canons, it is logically absurd to suggest that any causal explanation in terms of movements in his brain, his temperament, his bodily state, and so on, is sufficient *by itself* to explain the movement of his thought. For logical canons are normative and cannot be sufficiently explained in terms of states and processes which are not. Of course there are any number of necessary conditions which must be taken account of. A man cannot think *without* a brain, for instance. But any *sufficient* explanation would have to take account of the *reasons* for his actions. We would have to know the rules of chess, for instance, which gave some *point* to a chess-player's move. Indeed we would only ask for the cause of a chess-player's behaviour if he did something which could not be explained in terms of the rules of chess and the objective at which he was aiming.

If, for instance, he refrained from taking his opponent's queen, when this was the obvious and the best move, he might ask 'What made him do that?' and we would be asking for a causal explanation, like 'he was tired'. But this would now be an explanation of what *happened* to him, not of what he did deliberately. We would not ask for such an explanation if there was an obvious reason for his move.*

   This example can be generalized and the point made that behaviour is usually explicable not because we know its causes, but because people act in accordance with certain known rules and conventions and adopt appropriate means to objectives which are accepted as legitimate goals. We know why a parson is mounting the pulpit not because we know much about the causes of his behaviour but because we know the conventions governing church services. We would only ask what were the causes of his behaviour if he fainted when he peered out over the congregation or if something similar *happened* to him. Most of our explanations of human behaviour are couched in terms of a purposive, rule-following model, not in causal terms. Moral behaviour, above all other sorts, falls into this purposive, rule-following category. For, as Aristotle put it in his Ethics,† it is not a man's passions which are the object of moral appraisal nor his capacity to be subject to such passions; rather we praise or blame a man for what he does about his passions, for the extent to which he controls or fails to control them in various situations. Deliberation and choice may not precede every action, but habits are set up as a result of such deliberation and choice. It is for the exercise of such habits that men are praised and blamed — for the ends which they seek and for the means which they adopt to bring about their ends. Punishment, too, as we have pointed out, presupposes that men can foresee the consequences of their actions and that they can learn to avoid those to which penalties are attached. Praise and blame, reward and punishment, act as rudders to steer human actions precisely because men deliberate and choose and can be influenced by considerations of consequences. There is a radical difference between actions of this sort and cases where things happen to a man — where he acts 'on impulse', has a dream, a vision, or lapse of memory, or where he is afflicted by a feeling of nausea or hysterical paralysis. Questions of the 'freedom of the will' do not arise where things happen to a man; only where a man acts and can be praised or blamed, punished or rewarded for what he does. Yet it is precisely in these cases of human actions, as distinct from passions, that causal explanations seem inappropriate as sufficient explanations.

---

   * Of course the category of 'action' is much wider than that of premeditated action, though it may be co-extensive with that of 'rationality.' For this covers the sort of things for which a man could have a reason — i.e. which fall under what we call the purposive rule-following model. Premeditated action is a particular case of action where action is *preceded* by rehearsals and deliberation; but often reasons can be given by people for what they do even though they do not deliberate *before* they act.

   † Aristotle, *Nichomachean Ethics*.

Two sorts of objection might be mounted against this attempt to limit the role of causal explanations of human behaviour. In the first place it might be said that by substituting concepts like rule-following and the pursuit of objectives we were in fact introducing other sorts of causes. Now the word 'cause' can be used in this very wide sense. But the terminological question is largely irrelevant; for two sorts of explanations which are logically quite different would then be included under the enlarged concept of 'cause'. To follow rules, to take steps which are seen to be necessary to reach some sort of objective, to see the point of something, these may be 'causes'; but they are causes in quite a different sense of 'cause' from things like stomach contractions, brain lesions, acute pains, and so on. The types of explanation must be distinguished whether we use the term 'cause' to cover both or not. And certainly seeing the point of something is quite different — even if it is called a 'cause' — from the causes prevalent in the physical world. In the early days of the determinist controversy philosophers like Spinoza and Kant used the term 'self-determined' to distinguish rational actions from those which could be explained in terms of mechanical causes like movements of the brain and body. Indeed Kant's suggestion that man lives in two worlds, and is subject to two different sorts of causation, is a metaphysical way of bringing out the logical distinction between these two sorts of explanation.

The second objection is the suggestion that all reasons might be rationalizations — a smoke screen for what we are going to do anyway. We are, as it were, pushed by causes in the mechanical, physical sense, whatever we do; but sometimes we throw up an elaborate smokescreen of excuses which make no difference to what we in fact do. If, however, we say that *all* reasons are rationalizations, we make no difference between the behaviour of an obsessive or a compulsive and that of a rational man. If a compulsive believes that his hands are covered in blood and spends his time continually washing them, no relevant considerations will make any difference to his behaviour. All the known tests fail to show blood; yet he still goes on washing his hands. But a civil servant making a complex decision about policy does not proceed like this. He will change his mind and alter policy in the light of relevant considerations. Indeed it is only because people *sometimes* alter their behaviour because of relevant considerations that it makes any *sense* to talk of rationalizations as well as of reasons. A term like 'rationalization', which casts aspersions on the reasons given for action, is a verbal parasite. It flourishes because there *are* cases of genuine reasons with which rationalizations can be contrasted. Thus even if all behaviour has causes, in the sense of *necessary* conditions, there are objections to saying that all behaviour — especially rational behaviour — can be *sufficiently* explained by causes of the sort suggested by physical scientists, and by mechanistic philosophers like Hobbes.

32

PSYCHOANALYSIS AND
MORAL RESPONSIBILITY

John Hospers

John Hospers (1918-   ) is Professor of Philosophy at Brooklyn College.

. . . As a preparation for developing my own views on the subject, I want to mention a factor that I think is of enormous importance and relevance: namely, unconscious motivation. There are many actions — not those of an insane person (however the term "insane" be defined), nor of a person ignorant of the effects of his action, nor ignorant of some relevant fact about the situation, nor in any obvious way mentally deranged — for which human beings in general and the courts in particular are inclined to hold the doer responsible, and for which, I would say, he should not be held responsible. The deed may be planned, it may be carried out in cold calculation, it may spring from the agent's character and be continuous with the rest of his behavior, and it may be perfectly true that he could have done differently *if* he had wanted to; nonetheless his behavior was brought about by unconscious conflicts developed in infancy, over which he had no control and of which (without training in psychiatry) he does not even have knowledge. He may even *think* he knows why he acted as he did, he may *think* he has conscious control over his actions, he may even *think* he is fully responsible for them; but he is not. Psychiatric casebooks provide hundreds of examples. The law and common sense, though puzzled sometimes by such cases, are gradually becoming aware that they exist; but at this early stage countless tragic blunders still occur because neither the law nor the public in general is aware of the genesis of criminal actions. The mother blames her daughter for choosing the wrong men as candidates for husbands; but though the daughter thinks she is choosing freely and spends a considerable amount of time "deciding" among them, the identification with her sick father, resulting

From "What Means This Freedom?" first published in *Determinism and Freedom in the Age of Modern Science*, ed. Sidney Hook. Reprinted by permission of the author and the publisher, New York University Press.

from Oedipal fantasies in early childhood, prevents her from caring for any but sick men, twenty or thirty years older than herself. Blaming her is beside the point; she cannot help it, and she cannot change it. Countless criminal acts are thought out in great detail; yet the participants are (without their own knowledge) acing out fantasies, fears, and defenses from early childhood, over whose coming and going they have no conscious control.

Now, I am not saying that none of these persons should be in jails or asylums. Often society must be protected against them. Nor am I saying that people should cease the practices of blaming and praising, punishing and rewarding; in general these devices are justified by the results — although very often they have practically no effect; the deeds are done from inner compulsion, which is not lessened when the threat of punishment is great. I am only saying that frequently persons we think responsible are not properly to be called so; we mistakenly think them responsible because we assume they are like those in whom no unconscious drive (toward this type of behavior) is present, and that their behavior can be changed by reasoning, exhorting, or threatening.

I

I have said that these persons are not responsible. But what is the criterion for responsibility? Under precisely what conditions is a person to be held morally responsible for an action? Disregarding here those conditions that have to do with a person's *ignorance* of the situation or the effects of his action, let us concentrate on those having to do with his "inner state." There are several criteria that might be suggested:

1. The first idea that comes to mind is that responsibility is determined by the presence or absence of *premeditation* — the opposite of "premeditated" being, presumably, "unthinking" or "impulsive." But this will not do — both because some acts are not premeditated but responsible, and because some are premeditated and not responsible.

Many acts we call responsible can be as unthinking or impulsive as you please. If you rush across the street to help the victim of an automobile collision, you are (at least so we would ordinarily say) acting responsibly, but you did not do so out of premeditation; you saw the accident, you didn't think, you rushed to the scene without hesitation. It was like a reflex action. But you acted responsibly: unlike the knee jerk, the act was the result of past training and past thought about situations of this kind; that is why you ran to help instead of ignoring the incident or running away. When something done originally from conviction or training becomes habitual, it becomes *like* a reflex action. As Aristotle said, virtue should become second nature through habit: a virtuous act should be performed *as if* by instinct; this, far from detracting from its moral worth, testifies to one's mastery of the desired type of behavior; one does not have to make a moral effort each time it is repeated.

There are also premeditated acts for which, I would say, the person is not responsible. Premeditation, especially when it is so exaggerated as to issue in no action at all, can be the result of neurotic disturbance or what we sometimes call an emotional "block," which the person inherits from long-past situations. In Hamlet's revenge on his uncle (I use this example because it is familiar to all of us), there was no lack, but rather a surfeit, of premeditation; his actions were so exquisitely premeditated as to make Freud and Dr. Ernest Jones look more closely to find out what lay behind them. The very premeditation camouflaged unconscious motives of which Hamlet himself was not aware. I think this is an important point, since it seems that the courts often assume that premeditation is a criterion of responsibility. If failure to kill his uncle had been considered a crime, every court in the land would have convicted Hamlet. Again: a woman's decision to stay with her husband in spite of endless "mental cruelty" is, if she is the victim of an unconscious masochistic "will to punishment," one for which she is not responsible; she is the victim and not the agent, no matter how profound her conviction that she is the agent; she is caught in a masochistic web (of complicated genesis) dating back to babyhood, perhaps a repetition of a comparable situation involving her own parents, a repetition-compulsion that, as Freud said, goes "beyond the pleasure principle." Again: a criminal whose crime was carefully planned step by step is usually considered responsible, but as we shall see in later examples, the overwhelming impulse toward it, stemming from an unusually humiliating ego defeat in early childhood, was as compulsive as any can be.

2. Shall we say, then, that a person is not responsible for his act unless he can *defend it with reasons?* I am afraid that this criterion is no better than the previous one. First, intellectuals are usually better at giving reasons than nonintellectuals, and according to this criterion would be more responsible than persons acting from moral conviction not implemented by reasoning; yet it is very doubtful whether we should want to say that the latter are the more responsible. Second, the giving of reasons itself may be suspect. The reasons may be rationalizations camouflaging unconscious motives of which the agent knows nothing. Hamlet gave many reasons for not doing what he felt it was his duty to do: the time was not right, his uncle's soul might go to heaven, etc. His various "reasons" contradicted one another, and if an overpowering compulsion had not been present, the highly intellectual Hamlet would not have been taken in for a moment by these rationalizations. The real reason, the Oedipal conflict that made his uncle's crime the accomplishment of his own deepest desire, binding their fates into one and paralyzing him into inaction was unconscious and of course unknown to him. One's intelligence and reasoning power do not enable one to escape from unconsciously motivated behavior; it only gives one greater facility in rationalizing that behavior; one's intelligence is simply used in the interests of the neurosis — it is pressed into service to justify with reasons what one does quite independently of the reasons.

If these two criteria are inadequate, let us seek others.

3. Shall we say that a person is responsible for his action unless it is the *result of unconscious forces* of which he knows nothing? Many psychoanalysts would probably accept this criterion. If it is not largely reflected in the language of responsibility as ordinarily used, this may be due to ignorance of fact: most people do not know that there are such things as unconscious motives and unconscious conflicts causing human beings to act. But it may be that if they did, perhaps they would refrain from holding persons responsible for certain actions.

I do not wish here to quarrel with this criterion of responsibility. I only want to point out the fact that if this criterion is employed a far greater number of actions will be excluded from the domain of responsibility than we might at first suppose. Whether we are neat or untidy, whether we are selfish or unselfish, whether we provoke scenes or avoid them, even whether we can exert our powers of will to change our behavior — all these may, and often do, have their source in our unconscious life.

4. Shall we say that a person is responsible for his act unless it is *compelled*? Here we are reminded of Aristotle's assertion (*Nicomachean Ethics,* Book III) that a person is responsible for his act except for reasons of either ignorance or compulsion. Ignorance is not part of our problem here (unless it is unconsciously induced ignorance of facts previously remembered and selectively forgotten — in which case the forgetting is again compulsive), but compulsion is. How will compulsion do as a criterion? The difficulty is to state just what it means. When we say an act is compelled in a psychological sense, our language is metaphorical — which is not to say that there is no point in it or that, properly interpreted, it is not true. Our actions are compelled in a literal sense if someone has us in chains or is controlling our bodily movements. When we say that the storm compelled us to jettison the cargo of the ship (Aristotle's example), we have a less literal sense of compulsion, for at least it is open to us to go down with the ship. When psychoanalysts say that a man was compelled by unconscious conflicts to wash his hands constantly, this is also not a literal use of "compel"; for nobody forces his hands under the tap. Still, it is a typical example of what psychologists call *compulsive* behavior: it has unconscious causes inaccessible to introspection, and moreover nothing can change it — it is as inevitable for him to do it as it would be if someone were forcing his hands under the tap. In this it is exactly like the action of a powerful external force; it is just as little within one's conscious control.

In its area of application this interpretation of responsibility comes to much the same as the previous one. And this area is very great indeed. For if we cannot be held responsible for the infantile situations (in which we were after all passive victims), then neither, it would seem, can we be held responsible for compulsive actions occurring in adulthood that are inevitable consequences of those infantile situations. And, psychiatrists and psychoanalysts tell us, actions fulfilling this description are characteristic of all people some of the time and some people most of the time. Their occurrence, once the infantile events have taken place, is inevitable, just as the explosion is inevitable once the fuse has been lighted; there is simply more "delayed action" in the psychological explosions than there is in the physical ones.

(I have not used the word "inevitable" here to mean "causally determined," for according to such a definition every event would be inevitable if one accepted the causal principle in some form or other; and probably nobody except certain philosophers uses "inevitable" in this sense. Rather, I use "inevitable" in its ordinary sense of "cannot be avoided." To the extent, therefore, that adult neurotic manifestations *can* be avoided, once the infantile patterns have become set, the assertion that they are inevitable is not true.)

5. There is still another criterion, which I prefer to the previous ones, by which a man's responsibility for an act can be measured: the degree to which that act can (or could have been) *changed by the use of reasons.* Suppose that the man who washes his hands constantly does so, he says, for hygienic reasons, believing that if he doesn't do so he will be poisoned by germs. We now convince him, on the best medical authority, that his belief is groundless. Now, the test of his responsibility is whether the changed belief will result in changed behavior. If it does not, as with the compulsive hand washer, he is not acting responsibly, but if it does, he is. It is not the *use* of reasons, but their *efficacy in changing behavior,* that is being made the criterion of responsibility. And clearly in neurotic cases no such change occurs; in fact, this is often made the defining characteristic of neurotic behavior: it is unchangeable by any rational considerations.

II

I have suggested these criteria to distinguish actions for which we can call the agent responsible from those for which we cannot. Even persons with extensive knowledge of psychiatry do not, I think, use any one of these criteria to the exclusion of the others; a conjunction of two or more may be used at once. But however they may be combined or selected in actual application, I believe we can make the distinction along some such lines as we have suggested.

But is there not still another possible meaning of "responsibility" that we have not yet mentioned? Even after we have made all of the above distinctions, there remains a question in our minds whether we are, in the final analysis, *responsible for any of our actions at all.* The issue may be put this way: How can anyone be responsible for his actions, since they grow out of his character, which is shaped and molded and made what it is by influences — some hereditary, but most of them stemming from early parental environment — that were not of his own making or choosing? This question, I believe, still troubles many people who would agree to all the distinctions we have just made but still have the feeling that "this isn't all." They have the uneasy suspicion that there is a more ultimate sense, a "deeper" sense, in which we are *not* responsible for our actions, since we are not responsible for the character out of which those actions spring. This, of course, is the sense Professor Edwards was describing.

Let us take as an example a criminal who, let us say, strangled several persons and is himself now condemned to die in the electric chair. Jury and public alike hold him fully responsible (at least they utter the words "he is responsible"), for the murders were planned down to the minutest detail, and the defendant tells the jury exactly how he planned them. But now we find out how it all came about; we learn of parents who rejected him from babyhood, of the childhood spent in one foster home after another, where it was always plain to him that he was not wanted; of the constantly frustrated early desire for affection, the hard shell of nonchalance and bitterness that he assumed to cover the painful and humiliating fact of being unwanted, and his subsequent attempts to heal these wounds to his shattered ego through defensive aggression.

> The criminal is the most passive person in this world, helpless as a baby in his motorically inexpressible fury. Not only does he try to wreak revenge on the mother of the earliest period of his babyhood; his criminality is based on the inner feeling of being incapable of making the mother even feel that the child seeks revenge on her. The situation is that of a dwarf trying to annoy a giant who superciliously refuses to see these attempts. . . . Because of his inner feeling of being a dwarf, the criminotic uses, so to speak, dynamite. Of that the giant must take cognizance. True, the "revenge" harms the avenger. He may be legally executed. However, the primary inner aim of forcing the giant to acknowledge the dwarf's fury is fulfilled.[1]

The poor victim is not conscious of the inner forces that exact from him this ghastly toll; he battles, he schemes, he revels in pseudo-aggression, he is miserable, but he does not know what works within him to produce these catastrophic acts of crime. His aggressive actions are the wriggling of a worm on a fisherman's hook. And if this is so, it seems difficult to say any longer, "He is responsible." Rather, we shall put him behind bars for the protection of society, but we shall no longer flatter our feeling of moral superiority by calling him personally responsible for what he did.

Let us suppose it were established that a man commits murder only if, sometime during the previous week, he has eaten a certain combination of foods — say, tuna fish salad at a meal also including peas, mushroom soup, and blueberry pie. What if we were to track down the factors common to all murders committed in this country during the last twenty years and found this factor present in all of them, and only in them? The example is of course empirically absurd; but may it not be that there is *some* combination of factors that regularly leads to homicide, factors such as are described in general terms in the above quotation? (Indeed the situation in the quotation is less

---

[1] Edmund Bergler, *The Basic Neurosis* (New York: Grune and Stratton, 1949), p. 305.

fortunate than in our hypothetical example, for it is easy to avoid certain foods once we have been warned about them, but the situation of the infant is thrust on him; something has already happened to him once and for all, before he knows it has happened.) When such specific factors are discovered, won't they make it clear that it is foolish and pointless, as well as immoral, to hold human beings responsible for crimes? Or, if one prefers biological to psychological factors, suppose a neurologist is called in to testify at a murder trial and produces X-ray pictures of the brain of the criminal; anyone can see, he argues, that the *cella turcica* was already calcified at the age of nineteen; it should be a flexible bone, growing, enabling the gland to grow.[2] All the defendant's disorders might have resulted from this early calcification. Now, this particular explanation may be empirically false; but who can say that no such factors, far more complex, to be sure, exist?

When we know such things as these, we no longer feel so much tempted to say that the criminal is responsible for his crime; and we tend also (do we not?) to excuse him — not legally (we still confine him to prison) but morally; we no longer call him a monster or hold him personally responsible for what he did. Moreover, we do this in general, not merely in the case of crime: "You must excuse Grandmother for being irritable; she's really quite ill and is suffering some pain all the time." Or: "The dog always bites children after she's had a litter of pups; you can't blame her for it: she's not feeling well, and besides she naturally wants to defend them." Or: "She's nervous and jumpy, but do excuse her: she has a severe glandular disturbance."

Let us note that the more *thoroughly* and *in detail* we know the causal factors leading a person to behave as he does, the more we tend to exempt him from responsibility. When we know nothing of the man except what we see him do, we say he is an ungrateful cad who expects much of other people and does nothing in return, and we are usually indignant. When we learn that his parents were the same way and, having no guilt feelings about this mode of behavior themselves, brought him up to be greedy and avaricious, we see that we could hardly expect him to have developed moral feelings in this direction. When we learn, in addition, that he is not aware of being ungrateful or selfish, but unconsciously represses the memory of events unfavorable to himself, we feel that the situation is unfortunate but "not really his fault." When we know that this behavior of his, which makes others angry, occurs more constantly when he feels tense or insecure, and that he now feels tense and insecure, and that relief from pressure will diminish it, then we tend to "feel sorry for the poor guy" and say he's more to be pitied than censured. We no longer want to say that he is personally responsible; we might rather blame nature or his parents for having given him an unfortunate constitution or temperament.

> In recent years a new form of punishment has been imposed on middle-aged and elderly parents. Their children, now in their twenties, thirties or even

[2] Meyer Levin, *Compulsion* (New York: Simon and Schuster, 1956), p. 403.

forties, present them with a modern grievance: "My analysis proves that *you* are responsible for my neurosis." Overawed by these authoritative statements, the poor tired parents fall easy victims to the newest variations on the scapegoat theory.

In my opinion, this senseless cruelty — which disinters educational sins which had been burned for decades, and uses them as the basis for accusations which the victims cannot answer — is unjustified. Yes "the truth loves to be centrally located" (Melville), and few parents — since they are human — have been perfect. But granting their mistakes, they acted as *their* neurotic difficulties forced them to act. To turn the tables and declare the children not guilty because of the *impersonal* nature of their own neuroses, while at the same time the parents are *personally* blamed, is worse than illogical; it is profoundly unjust.[3]

And so, it would now appear, neither of the parties is responsible: "they acted as their neurotic difficulties forced them to act." The patients are not responsible for their neurotic manifestations, but then neither are the parents responsible for theirs; and so, of course, for their parents in turn, and theirs before them. It is the twentieth-century version of the family curse, the curse on the House of Atreus.

"But," a critic complains, "it's immoral to exonerate people indiscriminately in this way. I might have thought it fit to excuse somebody because he was born on the other side of the tracks, if I didn't know so many bank presidents who were also born on the other side of the tracks." Now, I submit that the most immoral thing in this situation is the critic's caricature of the conditions of the excuse. Nobody is excused merely because he was born on the other side of the tracks. But if he was born on the other side of the tracks *and* was a highly narcissistic infant to begin with *and* was repudiated or neglected by his parents *and* . . . (here we list a finite number of conditions), and if this complex of factors is *regularly* followed by certain behavior traits in adulthood, and moreover *unavoidably* so — that is, they occur no matter what he or anyone else tries to do — then we excuse him morally and say he is not responsible for his deed. If he is not responsible for *A,* a series of events occurring in his babyhood, then neither is he responsible for *B,* a series of things he does in adulthood, provided that *B* inevitably — that is, unavoidably — follows upon the occurrence of *A.* And according to psychiatrists and psychoanalysts, this often happens.

But one may still object that so far we have talked only about neurotic behavior. Isn't nonneurotic or normal or not unconsciously motivated (or whatever you want to call it) behavior still within the area of responsibility? There are reasons for answering "No" even here, for the normal person no more than the neurotic one has caused his own character, which makes him what he is. Granted that neurotics are not responsible for their behavior (that part of it which we call neurotic) because it stems from undigested infantile conflicts that they had no part in bringing about, and that are external to them just as surely as if their behavior had been forced on them by a malevo-

---

[3] Edmund Bergler, *The Superego* (New York: Grune and Stratton, 1952), p. 320.

lent deity (which is indeed one theory on the subject); but the so-called normal person is equally the product of causes in which his volition took no part. And if, unlike the neurotic's, his behavior is changeable by rational considerations, and if he has the will power to overcome the effects of an unfortunate early environment, this again is no credit to him; he is just lucky. If energy is available to him in a form in which it can be mobilized for constructive purposes, this is no credit to him, for this too is part of his psychic legacy. Those of us who can discipline ourselves and develop habits of concentration of purpose tend to blame those who cannot, and call them lazy and weak-willed; but what we fail to see is that they literally *cannot* do what we expect; if their psyches were structured like ours, they could, but as they are burdened with a tyrannical super-ego (to use psychoanalytic jargon for the moment), and a weak defenseless ego whose energies are constantly consumed in fighting endless charges of the superego, they simply cannot do it, and it is irrational to expect it of them. We cannot with justification blame them for their inability, any more than we can congratulate ourselves for our ability. This lesson is hard to learn, for we constantly and naïvely assume that other people are constructed as we ourselves are.

For example: A child raised under slum conditions, whose parents are socially ambitious and envy families with money, but who nevertheless squander the little they have on drink, may simply be unable in later life to mobilize a drive sufficient to overcome these early conditions. Common sense would expect that he would develop the virtue of thrift; he would make quite sure that he would never again endure the grinding poverty he had experienced as a child. But in fact it is not so: the exact conditions are too complex to be specified in detail here, but when certain conditions are fulfilled (concerning the subject's early life), he will always thereafter be a spendthrift, and no rational considerations will be able to change this. He will listen to the rational considerations and see the force of these, but they will not be able to change him, even if he tries; he cannot change his wasteful habits any more than he can lift the Empire State Building with his bare hands. We moralize and plead with him to be thrifty, but we do not see how strong, how utterly overpowering, and how constantly with him, is the opposite drive, which is so easily manageable with us. But he is possessed by the all-consuming, all-encompassing urge to make the world see that he belongs, that he has arrived, that he is just as well off as anyone else, that the awful humiliations were not real, that they never actually occurred, for isn't he now able to spend and spend? The humiliation must be blotted out; and conspicuous, fleshy, expensive, and wasteful buying will do this; it shows the world what the world must know! True, it is only for the moment; true, it is in the end self-defeating, for wasteful consumption is the best way to bring poverty back again; but the person with an overpowering drive to mend a lesion to his narcissism cannot resist the avalanche of that drive with his puny rational consideration. A man with his back against the wall and a gun at his throat doesn't think of what may happen ten years hence. (Consciously, of course, he knows nothing of this drive; all that appears to consciousness is its shattering effects; he knows only that he must keep on spending — not why — and that he is unable to resist.) He hasn't in him the psychic capacity, the energy to stem the tide of a drive that at that moment is all-powerful. We, seated comfortably away from this flood, sit in judgment on him and blame him and exhort him and criticize him; but he, carried along by the flood, cannot do otherwise than he does. He may fight with all the strength of which he is capable, but it is not enough. And we, who are rational enough at least to exonerate a man in a situation of "overpowering impulse" when we recognize it to be one, do not even recognize this as an example of it; and so, in addition to being swept away in the flood that childhood conditions rendered inevitable, he must also endure our lectures, our criticisms, and our moral excoriation.

But, one will say, he could have overcome his spendthrift tendencies; some people do. Quite true: some people do. They are lucky. They have it in them to overcome early deficiencies by exerting great effort, and they are capable of exerting the effort. Some of us, luckier still, can overcome them with but little effort; and a few, the luckiest, haven't the deficiencies to overcome. It's all a matter of luck. The least lucky are those who can't overcome them, even with great effort, and those who haven't the ability to exert the effort.

But, one persists, it isn't a matter simply of luck; it *is* a matter of effort. Very well then, it's a matter of effort; without exerting the effort you may not overcome the deficiency. But whether or not you are the kind of person who has it in him to exert the effort is a matter of luck.

All this is well known to psychoanalysts. They can predict, from minimal cues that most of us don't notice, whether a person is going to turn out to be lucky or not. "The analyst," they say, "must be able to use the residue of the patient's unconscious guilt so as to remove the symptom or character trait that creates the guilt. The guilt must not only be present, but *available* for use, *mobilizable*. If it is used up (absorbed) in criminal activity, or in an excessive amount of self-damaging tendencies, then it cannot be used for therapeutic purposes, and the prognosis is negative." Not all philosophers will relish the analyst's way of putting the matter, but at least as a physician he can soon detect whether the patient is lucky or unlucky — and he knows that whichever it is, it *isn't the patient's fault.* The patient's conscious volition cannot remedy the deficiency. Even whether he will co-operate with the analyst is really out of the patient's hands: if he continually projects the denying-mother fantasy on the analyst and unconsciously identifies him always with the cruel, harsh forbidder of the nursery, thus frustrating any attempt at impersonal observation, the sessions are useless; yet if it happens that way, he can't help that either. That fatal projection is not under his control; whether it occurs or not depends on how his unconscious identifications have developed since his infancy. He can try, yes — but the ability to try enough for the therapy to have effect is also beyond his control; the capacity to try more than just so much is either there or it isn't — and either way "it's in the lap of the gods."

The position, then, is this: if we *can* overcome the effects of early environment, the ability to do so is itself a product of the early environment. We did not give ourselves this ability; and if we lack it we cannot be blamed for not having it. Sometimes, to be sure, moral exhortation brings out an ability that is there but not being used, and in this lies its *occasional utility*; but very often its use is pointless, because the ability is not there. The only thing that can overcome a desire, as Spinoza said, is a stronger contrary desire; and many times there simply is no wherewithal for producing a stronger contrary desire. Those of us who do have the wherewithal are lucky.

There is one possible practical advantage in remembering this. It may prevent us (unless we are compulsive blamers) from indulging in righteous indignation and committing the sin of spiritual pride, thanking God that we are not as this publican here. And it will protect from our useless moralizings those who are least equipped by nature for enduring them. As with responsibility, so with deserts. Someone commits a crime and is punished by the state; "he deserved it," we say self-righteously — as if we were moral and he immoral, when in fact we are lucky and he is unlucky — forgetting that there, but for the grace of God and a fortunate early environment, go we. Or, as Clarence Darrow said in his speech for the defense in the Loeb-Leopold case:

> I do not believe that people are in jail because they deserve to be. . . . I know what causes the emotional life. . . . I know it is practically left out of some. Without it they cannot act with the rest. They cannot feel the moral shocks which safeguard others. Is [this man] to blame that his machine is imperfect? Who is to blame? I do not know. I have never in my life been interested so much in fixing blame as I have in relieving people from blame. I am not wise enough to fix it.[4]

---

[4] Levin, *op. cit.*, pp. 439-40, 469.

SUGGESTED READINGS

1. General Discussions of the Free Will Problem

BEROFSKY, BERNARD (ed.). *Free Will and Determinism*. New York: Harper & Row, 1966.

BROAD, C. D. *Determinism, Indeterminism, and Libertarianism*. New York: Macmillan, 1934.

HOOK, SIDNEY (ed.). *Determinism and Freedom*. New York: New York Univ. Press, 1961.

LEHRER, KEITH (ed.). *Freedom and Determinism*. New York: Random House, 1966.

MORGENBESSER, SIDNEY, and WALSH, JAMES (eds.). *Free Will*. Englewood Cliffs, N.J.: Prentice-Hall, 1962.

PEARS, DAVID F. (ed.). *Freedom and the Will*. New York: St. Martin's Press, 1963.

2. Libertarianism

CAMPBELL, C. A. *In Defense of Free Will*. Glasgow: Glasgow Univ. Press, 1934 [partly in Brandt, Singer-Ammerman].

———. "Is Free Will a Pseudo-Problem?" *Mind*, Vol. 60 (1951) [partly in Edwards-Pap].

FOOT, PHILIPPA. "Free Will as Involving Determinism," *Philosophical Review*, Vol. 66 (1957).

HARTMANN, NICOLAI. *Ethics*. London: Allen & Unwin, 1932. Vol. III.

JAMES, WILLIAM. "The Dilemma of Determinism," in *The Will to Believe and Other Essays*. London: Longmans, Green, 1931 [partly in Edwards-Pap, Mandelbaum-Gramlich-Anderson].

LEWIS, H. D. *Morals and Revelation*. London: Allen & Unwin, 1951.

3. Reconcilism

BRANDT, R. B. *Ethical Theory*. Englewood Cliffs, N. J.: Prentice-Hall, 1959. Ch. 20.

HOBBES, THOMAS. "Of Liberty and Necessity."

LOCKE, JOHN. *Essay Concerning Human Understanding*, Bk. II, Ch. 21.

MILL, J. S. *A System of Logic*, Bk. VI, Ch. 2 [in Edwards-Pap, Randall-Buchler-Shirk, Singer-Ammerman].

———. *An Examination of Sir William Hamilton's Philosophy*. Ch. 26.

MOORE, G. E. *Ethics*. London: Oxford Univ. Press, 1912. Ch. 6.

NOWELL-SMITH, P. H. *Ethics*. London: Penguin Books, 1954. Chs. 19, 20.

ROSS, W. D. *Foundations of Ethics*. Oxford: Clarendon Press, 1931. Ch. 10.

SCHLICK, MORITZ. *Problems of Ethics*, tr. DAVID RYNIN. Englewood Cliffs, N. J.: Prentice-Hall, 1939. Ch. 7.

STEVENSON, C. L. *Ethics and Language*. New Haven, Conn.: Yale Univ. Press, 1944. Ch. 14.

4. Determinism, Pro and Con

BERGSON, HENRI. *Time and Free Will*. New York: Macmillan, 1921.

NAGEL, ERNEST. *The Structure of Science*. New York: Harcourt, 1961. Ch. 10.

PAP, ARTHUR. *An Introduction to the Philosophy of Science*. New York: Free Press, 1962. Ch. 17.

PEIRCE, C. S. "The Doctrine of Necessity Examined," in M. R. COHEN, ed., *Chance, Love, and Logic*. New York: Harcourt, 1923.

RUSSELL, BERTRAND. "On the Notion of Cause," in *Mysticism and Logic*. London: Longmans, Green, 1918. Ch. 9.

———. *Our Knowledge of the External World*. New York: Norton, 1929. Ch. 8. 1962. Ch. 17.

5. *Indeterminism in Recent Physics*

EDDINGTON, SIR ARTHUR. *The Nature of the Physical World.* New York: Macmillan, 1928. Ch. 14.

PLANCK, MAX. *Where Is Science Going?* tr. JAMES MURPHY. New York: Norton, 1932. Chs. 4, 5 [in Sprague-Taylor].

RUSSELL, BERTRAND. *Religion and Science.* London: Oxford Univ. Press, 1935. Ch. 6.

STEBBING, SUSAN L. *Philosophy and the Physicists.* London: Methuen, 1937. Part III.

6. *Determinism and the Concept of Action*

ALSTON, W. P. "Wants, Actions, and Causal Explanations," in H. N. CASTANEDA, ed., *Intentionality, Minds, and Perception.* Detroit: Wayne State Univ. Press, 1966.

DAVIDSON, DONALD. "Actions, Reasons, and Causes," *Journal of Philosophy,* Vol. 60 (1963).

MACINTYRE, A. C. "Determinism," *Mind,* Vol. 66 (1957).

MELDEN, A. I. *Free Action.* London: Routledge & Kegan Paul, 1961.

7. *Responsibility*

FEINBERG, JOEL. "Problematic Responsibility in Law and Morals," *Philosophical Review,* Vol. 71 (1962).

HART, H. L. A. "The Ascription of Responsibility and Rights," in ANTHONY FLEW, ed., *Essays in Logic and Language,* First Series. Oxford: Basil Blackwell, 1951.

MANDELBAUM, MAURICE. "Determinism and Moral Responsibility," *Ethics.* Vol. 71 (1960).

MORRIS, HERBERT (ed.). *Freedom and Responsibility: Readings in Philosophy and Law.* Stanford, Calif.: Stanford Univ. Press, 1961.

NOWELL-SMITH, P. H. "Free Will and Moral Responsibility," *Mind,* Vol. 57 (1944). [Partly in Brandt, Sprague-Taylor].

Part IV

MIND
AND
BODY

INTRODUCTION

Men have always been fascinated by questions about their own nature, and philosophers have given their attention to a number of questions in this area. These have included (1) the nature of the mind, or consciousness, and its relation to the body; (2) what makes one remain the same person through time (criteria of personal identity); (3) whether a person survives bodily death; (4) how to differentiate a person into parts or aspects, such as thought, feeling, and will, or reason and passion; (5) what the fundamental human motives or needs are; (6) whether man ever has free choice between alternatives. This Part comprises discussions of the first three problems. The fifth is touched on in Part II, while Part III is devoted to the sixth.

First we turn to the mind-body problem. A human being exhibits a kind of complexity that is shared by nothing else in our world. The characteristics he possesses, and the states and processes he undergoes, fall into two fundamentally different classes. On the one hand, there are those which the person in question knows about in a way radically different from that in which anyone else knows about them. This group includes thoughts, feelings, beliefs, and desires. If anyone else is to find out what I am thinking, feeling, or wanting, he has to do so by observing my behavior, including verbal behavior elicited by the question, "What are you thinking about?" Unless his beliefs on this matter are grounded in observation of my behavior, he could not claim to *know* what I was thinking, etc. At most he would be making a lucky guess. But no such restriction is placed on my knowledge of such matters. I don't have to watch what I am doing, or listen to what I am saying, in order to tell what I am thinking or feeling. I don't have to do anything at all; I just know, simply by virtue of the fact that I am thinking or feeling that. Thus my way of knowing such facts is not only different from anyone else's; it is also superior. It is *immediate* knowledge, in the sense of not being based on something else I know.

371

The other class is made up of facts about a person that he knows, if at all, in the same way as anyone else. This would include, e.g., being six feet tall, having well-developed muscles, and secreting gastric juices. I do not have any specially "privileged" access to these facts as I have to facts concerning what I am thinking or feeling. If I am to find out how tall I am, or whether gastric juices are being secreted, I have to resort to the same techniques anyone else would employ to find out. I have to juxtapose my body to some measuring instrument in the first case and employ standard biochemical tests in the second case. We may term states and characteristics of the first sort "mental," those of the second sort "physical."

In distinguishing between mind and body in Reading 33, Descartes does not put the matter in quite this way. Indeed he could not; since he is making the distinction while still holding in doubt the existence of other persons, he could hardly rely on the difference between the way he knows certain facts about himself and the way others do so. He draws the distinction in terms of a difference between the ways in which *he* knows mental and bodily facts about *himself,* the point being that his knowledge of the former is not subject to doubt in the way knowledge of the latter is. Nevertheless, his ground for the distinction can be seen to be closely allied to ours. If my knowledge of my own mental processes is indubitable it is because it is immediate knowledge in the sense brought out above, i.e., because it is not based on other beliefs and hence lacks that source of vulnerability.

But although the mental and the physical aspects of man seem to be radically different in the way specified, they are at the same time intimately interconnected. For one thing they are aspects of one and the same being. At least our whole way of talking and thinking about man is based on the assumption that this is so. It is one and the same person, John Jones, who is both six feet tall and mentally depressed, who is both digesting his food and thinking about the Viet Nam war. Moreover it is not just that these aspects happen to exist side by side in the same substance; they influence each other in a variety of important respects. One's conscious sensations — visual, auditory, etc. — depend on physical processes in the sense organs and the brain. One's emotional feelings and states of mind are affected by glandular secretions. On the other side, anxieties and anger can affect the operations of the circulatory and digestive systems, even to the extent of giving rise to "psychosomatic" disease. And a conscious decision to go to the grocery store gives rise to a complicated series of bodily movements. If one is to develop an adequate conception of human nature, one must find a way of conceiving the mental and physical aspects of man so that their interrelations are made intelligible without denying or ignoring their differences. We shall find that the difficulties of getting these two sides of the matter together have often led theorists to slight or ignore either the differences between mind or body or their intimate interconnection.

Since the seventeenth century philosophical thought has been dominated by a view that places heavy stress on the distinction between the mental and physical, the dualist (two-substance) view of Descartes. Descartes, following the tradition of Plato rather than that of Aristotle, thinks of an embodied human being as a temporary conjunction of two substances: a material substance, the body, which has physical properties, including position and extension in space; and a nonmaterial substance, the mind, which is not located in space at all, and which has consciousness rather than spatial extension as its essential nature. Each of these substances is inherently capable of existing "on its own," although under the conditions of our earthly life they operate in close dependence on each other. Most subsequent thought on the topic has been taken up either with extending and modifying the Cartesian position or with reacting against it in a variety of ways. It is noteworthy that several of our selections make explicit reference to Descartes, particularly Readings 34, 36, and 38.

In Descartes' own time, and in the succeeding two centuries, the main dissatisfaction with the position has been the feeling that it made causal interaction between mind and body unintelligible. It seems inconceivable that a physical body should be set in motion except by impact from another physical body. But then if we construe a conscious decision as a nonphysical activity of a substance that does not have position in space or undergo motion through space, it would be inconceivable that a decision should cause the body to move. And, going in the reverse direction, it has seemed equally inconceivable to many thinkers that physical processes could produce conscious thoughts, feelings, and sensations in an immaterial substance. How could the motions of material bodies affect anything other than the other material bodies they encounter?

The force of these objections has been and still is a matter of controversy. The claim that causal interaction between physical and nonphysical substances is inconceivable rests on the assumption that causal interaction requires an "intelligible bond" between cause and effect, some grasp of *how* the cause brings about the effect. But, according to Hume's widely accepted analysis of causation (see Reading 48), any fundamental mode of causation is equally unintelligible in the last analysis. It is just a brute fact about the world that some kinds of events regularly lead to other kinds of events. To be sure, we can reduce the number of mysteries by showing that the enormous superficial diversity of causal relations can be analyzed in terms of a few basic ones. Thus the rusting of iron in damp air, the moving of leaves in the wind, the explosion of a stick of dynamite, and the growth of a bush look very different. But by getting down to a molecular level of analysis, we can represent all these processes as more or less complicated chains of the alteration of the position and motion of bodies (including very minute bodies) through their impact on each other. But when we then turn our attention to this basic mode of interaction to which the others have been reduced, and ask *how* it is that one body affects the position and velocity of another through impact, we find no more basic mode of causation to which this one can be reduced. We can only say that the world happens to be such that physical impact has this kind of result, and that's that. But then why should we not suppose that mind-body interaction is another such ultimate mode of causality, one which simply has to be accepted as a fact without further explanation? Why suppose that there is only one such mode, and if there could be more than one, why should not mind-body interaction be one of the others?

Whatever the merits of the case, it was often supposed during the seventeenth and eighteenth centuries that causal interaction between a physical and a nonphysical substance is impossible, and in line with this conviction many attempts were made to modify the Cartesian position so that such interaction was not assumed. The smallest deviation from Descartes is to be found in parallelism, which preserves the two-substance view but avoids causal interaction through postulating a "pre-established harmony" which ensures that the mental and bodily states of a person are related as they would be if they influenced each other, even though no actual causal interaction occurs. Each person is "programmed" in advance (and these "programs" are all adjusted to each other and to the "programs" for things in the environment) so that mental and bodily states succeed each other in accordance with discernible regularities. This view has the disadvantage, common to all "as if" positions, of running the risk of being only verbally different from the corresponding "really is" position. If whenever certain bodily processes take place the person has a certain conscious thought, and if whenever he makes a decision to raise his arm (and he is not paralyzed, etc.) his arm rises, then what could be meant by saying that there is not really any causal interaction, although things are proceeding "as if" there were? We could find a difference only if we could specify some feature of a "real" causal interaction over and above the regularity of the succession; if no such additional feature can be specified, parallelism is just interactionism that is unwilling to face the facts.

Another historically important attempt to avoid the difficulties of interactionism was the "double aspect" view, the most famous exponent of which was Benedict Spinoza. Instead of construing man as composed of two substances, a mind and a body, Spinoza thinks of him as a single substance with two "aspects," bodily and mental, each of which is autonomous in that any feature of that aspect can be adequately explained in terms of factors within that aspect. (Spinoza even holds that the entire universe is a single substance, but for our present concerns we may ignore that side of his philosophy.) Thus we can regard bodily states and processes as caused purely "mechanistically" by other bodily states and processes, while mental states are caused purely by other mental states. Nevertheless, there are regularities in the ways in which bodily and mental states of the same person are related to each other because each mental state has a corresponding physical state that is just another "side" or "aspect" of the same state and vice versa. There is no problem of causal interaction because the conscious sensation and the neural excitation in the brain, e.g., are the same thing viewed in different ways. One and the same thing cannot causally interact with itself. The main disadvantage of this view, apart from difficulties in giving a literal rendering of the metaphor of "aspects," is the fact that it implies a thoroughgoing "pan-psychism," that is, a mental aspect for every physical state of affairs. It is clear that some mental states, such as sensations, occur because of physical occurrences outside the body, such as the reflection of light from physical substances. Hence, if we are to maintain that every mental state can be explained purely in terms of other mental states, we must postulate mental "aspects" for all those occurrences that are responsible for a given conscious sensation, and also mental aspects for all those occurrences that are responsible for the afore-mentioned aspects, and so on indefinitely. This implication was recognized by Spinoza, who took the entire universe to be a single substance, which possessed a "complete" set of physical states and, correspondingly, a "complete" set of mental states.

A more radical break with Cartesianism is found in Berkeley's rejection of material substance. If, with Berkeley, we hold that the only substances are mental substances, then construing physical bodies as patterns of sensations in minds, including the divine mind, we obviously have no problem of mind-body interaction. Since this position does not play a large role in contemporary thinking about the mind-body problem, we shall not discuss it further here. Selection #57 may be consulted for an exposition of the reasons that led Berkeley to this view.

Thus far we have been considering reactions to Cartesianism that share with it the view that conscious states are states of an immaterial substance, but during the last century this position has increasingly lost ground in favor of a more materialist view. Materialism, as a general metaphysical position, is the view that nothing exists except physical bodies (i.e., things that have mass, spatial dimensions, and whatever other characteristics are taken as definitive of bodies in the current state of physical science), their properties, states, and activities. As applied to the problem of human nature, it is the view that a man is simply a special kind of physical substance, and that's all. This, like Berkeley's position, is a monism (*one* kind of substance) in contrast to the Cartesian dualism, but it moves away from Descartes in the opposite direction, so to speak. The main considerations supporting this trend have been the following:

(1) With the flowering of physical science the scientific imagination was captured by the vision of an all-embracing scheme of physical law in terms of which everything in the world can be understood. The movements of the planets can be mathematically explained and predicted in terms of a few measurable variables — position, momentum, mass. As the basic concepts and principles of physical science came to be applied to more and more phenomena, including biological processes, it came to seem increasingly plausible that all phenomena can be handled in the same terms, although admittedly we are far from actually being able to do so at the present time. But this is possible only if all phenomena, including conscious thought and feeling, can be described in physical terms. Thus the dream of an all-

embracing unified physical science carries with it a commitment to a material-ist philosophy.

(2) This general materialistic predilection has been reinforced by more specific advances in our understanding of the material basis of consciousness. Descartes himself had made sufficient advances in physiology to become con-vinced that the lower animals could be conceived as purely physical mech-anisms, so that he felt no need to postulate conscious states in order to explain their behavior. With man, on the other hand, he could hardly deny the existence of states of consciousness, and, for reasons presented in Reading 33, he felt constrained to attribute such states to a nonmaterial substance. And indeed until further advances were made in the psychophysiology of the brain and nervous system, the *identification* of thought and feeling with physical processes was at least as speculative as any alternative hypothesis.

We have always had some knowledge of the physiological conditions of perception and bodily sensation, but prior to the nineteenth century one was not contravening any empirical facts if he held that thought, imagination, and feeling were the activity of a nonmaterial substance that, in these func-tions, made use of no material organs at all. Of course there had been materialists, from the fifth-century B.C. Greek philosopher, Democritus, down through eighteenth-century French enlightenment figures, like Cabanis, who held that the brain secretes ideas just as the liver secretes bile; but these thinkers could point to little direct empirical support. In the nine-teenth and twentieth centuries, however, our understanding of the physio-logical basis of the higher mental processes has greatly increased, even though our knowledge of the minute structure of brain processes is still rudi-mentary. Some of these advances are made explicit in Huxley's essay (Read-ing 34), but since his time much more has been accomplished. Through observation of persons who have lost or damaged parts of their brains, and through artificial stimulation of parts of the brain, we have been able to locate the brain regions responsible for such functions as memory, emotion, and abstract thought. More recently, investigators have discovered differ-ences in patterns of brain activity in dreams and in dreamless sleep. At pres-ent it is generally assumed that every distinguishable conscious state has as a necessary condition some specifiable kind of brain process, even though we are a long way from spelling out such conditions in detail. Given this assumption, the only question remaining is as to whether the conscious state is identical with the corresponding brain process.

The conception of mental processes as operations of a physical mech-anism has received additional support from the dramatic postwar develop-ments in computers that carry out, or at least simulate, many distinctively human mental operations. These advances in engineering have provided a fresh perspective on the mind-body problem. If it is possible in principle for a computer to think and feel, doesn't that show that conscious states are purely physical in character? Or does it mean, rather, that when a mech-anism has become sufficiently complicated for such operations to be carried out, a mental substance has been generated? This fascinating area is explored by Türing in Reading 37.

(3) The positive drives toward materialism just presented have been reinforced by difficulties in the conception of mental substance over and above the problems about interaction. One of these has to do with the program of an unrestricted application of scientific method. When one comes to the scientific investigation of thoughts, memories, emotions, and other mental phenomena, there are forces which will push one in the direction of a materialist conception of one's subject matter even if one does not begin with a predilection for the concepts of physical science. It is essential to scientific method, as it has developed in modern times, that empirical data be publicly accessible. This is necessary in order that one investigator's observations be checkable by other investigators; this possibility is one of the distinctive features of the method of science. As we saw above, mental states are distinguished from bodily states precisely by the fact that each of them is directly accessible to one and only one person. Hence if they are thought of as entities that are distinct from the physical states underlying them, they are in principle shut off from public observation, the latter being restricted to their conditions or their manifestations in behavior.

In the nineteenth century a school of psychology grew up which attempted a scientific investigation of conscious states and processes conceived as observable only by the introspection of their possessors, but the project has largely been abandoned by psychologists just because of the impossibility of getting any check on the accuracy of the observers. When the question is, e.g., whether thought can occur without images, and some subjects introspectively report imageless thought whereas others do not, it is impossible to choose between the hypothesis that some people engage in imageless thought and others do not, and the hypothesis that some of the subjects are mistaken in their reports. The latter possibility cannot be checked just because A's thoughts, conceived mentalistically, can be observed only by A. It is clear that a materialistic conception of mental states which would render them, at least in principle, open to public observation, would remove this bar to scientific investigation.

(4) Apart from the quest for scientific knowledge, it has been felt by many philosophers that the Cartesian theory fails to account for the fact that we do have knowledge of one another's mental states. If I can never observe any mental states other than my own, what reason can I have to suppose that there are any others? To be sure, I can observe other bodies behaving in ways similar to the way in which I behave when, e.g., I feel depressed. But if I can never check the assumption that such behavior is correlated with feelings of depression in these other cases, as well as in my own, doesn't this assumption remain forever an unverified speculation? I can ask the other person whether he feels depressed on these occasions, but the interpretation of his responses is going to raise exactly the same problems. Perhaps these puzzles would be lessened by construing mental states so that they are, in

principle, open to public observation. This line of argument is represented
in the selection from Ryle (Reading 36). It should not be supposed, however, that there is any general agreement among philosophers that our knowledge of one another's mental states cannot be explained on a Cartesian theory.
On the contrary, the topic is a matter of intense controversy. For some
recent discussions consult the bibliography to this section.

If a man is simply a special kind of physical body, how are we to make
room for the special features of conscious states which, as we saw above,
seem to sharply distinguish them from obviously bodily states? Here different
forms of materialism give divergent answers.

The least radical deviation from Descartes in a materialist direction is
epiphenomenalism, represented in our readings by Huxley (34). The epiphenomenalist does not deny that conscious states and processes constitute
a distinct, nonphysical type of existence; hence he is not a materialist in the
strict sense. What he does deny is that conscious states are states of any
continuing substance that has any effect on anything. Thoughts and feelings are just momentary occurrences that have no permanent foothold in
reality; they are transient by-products (epiphenomena) that are "given off"
by certain kinds of neural processes in the brain but do not in turn have any
effect on processes in the body or anything else. When we suppose that a
conscious decision led to some bodily movement, it is really the neural processes
in the brain responsible for that spurt of consciousness that really brought
about the bodily movement in question. Consciousness itself is jut a "lyric
cry in the midst of business."

Epiphenomenalism is in many ways an unsatisfactory halfway house. It
avoids any difficulties there may be in the action of mind on body, and
it leaves the way clear for a purely mechanistic account of behavior. But
it is left with a unique and rather mysterious mode of causality — the
generation of the nonphysical by the physical. Moreover it leaves conscious
states themselves as unsusceptible as ever to scientific treatment, though
the epiphenomenalist may argue that since they have no influence on anything else, that does not matter. Moreover Huxley is in no better position
than the Cartesian to explain our knowledge of each other's mental states,
nor is he significantly better off in the matter of ontological economy, unless
one wishes to maintain that an extra category of momentary states is less
wasteful than an extra kind of substance. It would seem that epiphenomenalism would be indicated as an alternative to Cartesianism only if a strict
materialism were untenable.

Interpretations of mental states given by more full-blooded materialist
conceptions of man are themselves of two quite different kinds. Even on a
dualist view of an up-to-date kind, conscious states have bodily causes (viz.,
neural processes in the brain), and bodily consequences (viz., dispositions
to react to situations in one way rather than another). If we are looking
for something physical with which it would be plausible to identify a mental
state, we might well look in either direction. The first tack is taken by

physiological materialism; the second by behaviorism. Consider a belief, e.g., a belief that it is going to rain tomorrow. A physiological materialist would identify this with some state of the brain, while a behaviorist would identify it with the person's disposition or tendency to behave in one way rather than another in certain conditions (for example, his tendency to take an umbrella with him if he is going for a walk tomorrow).

First, let us consider behaviorism. In the sense in which we are using the term, behaviorism is a metaphysical theory as to the nature of mental states, and as such it must be distinguished from other views that go under the same name. In particular it must be distinguished from what may be termed "methodological behaviorism," the view that overt behavior (plus features of the physical environment) provides the only legitimate data for a science of psychology. (The basic reason for this position is the need for publicly accessible data in science, mentioned above.) Thus if, in studying human motivation, we want to compare the strength of our subjects' desire for some goal such as recognition, we will look for indications in patterns of their behavior, e.g., what they say when asked to make up a story around a certain picture, rather than asking them to introspect and tell us how strong their desire is. This view is widely accepted by psychologists, and is reflected in the current conception of psychology as "the science of behavior." A commitment to methodological behaviorism involves only a restriction as to the conduct of certain scientific investigations; it carries no commitment as to the *nature* of mental states. There is, to be sure, a tendency for methodological behaviorists to construe mental states as behavioral dispositions, since this provides the simplest way of connecting mental states with the kind of data to which they are restricted; but this is by no means necessary. Many psychologists who accept the restriction to behavioral data are more inclined to epiphenomenalism or physiological materialism in their interpretation of the nature of conscious states.

In addition to boosts from the behaviorist movement in psychology, metaphysical behaviorism has seemed attractive to some philosophers because it makes short work of the problem of our knowledge of other minds. If mental states *are* behavioral tendencies, then there is no puzzle as to how I get from observations of your behavior to beliefs about your mental states. Moreover, suppose we accept an extreme form of the verifiability principle of meaning (Reading 46), according to which the meaning of a statement simply consists of the empirical evidence that would support it. Then since the only evidence I can have for statements about your mental states consists in pieces of your behavior, it follows that all I can mean when I talk about your mental states is something about your behavior, or tendencies thereto. These latter considerations led Carnap and Hempel to embrace behaviorism in the early days of the logical positivist movement. (See bibliography for references.) Although Gilbert Ryle's book, *The Concept of Mind,* from which Reading 36 is drawn, does not set forth a thoroughgoing behaviorism, it does tend in that direction, and it has exerted a powerful influence by way of showing that our ordinary concepts of mental states are dispositional in character to a much greater extent than has usually been recognized.

Despite its attractions behaviorism is accepted by few philosophers today. This is largely because behaviorists have had little success in specifying what behavioral dispositions particular mental states might be identical with. For some, e.g., mental images, there are no plausible suggestions. What behavioral tendencies would a person have if and only if a picture of a sunny beach came before his mind's eye? And even for the more favorable cases, like beliefs and desires, it seems that in order to make a disposition coextensive with a given mental state we will have to include specifications of other mental states in that disposition. Believing that rain is imminent will not involve a disposition to carry an umbrella unless I *want* to stay dry. For further difficulties in behaviorism, see Ewing's discussion in Reading 38.

This leaves us with physiological materialism, the view set forth by U. T. Place in Reading 35. At this point, it will be in order to mention another distinction within materialism that cuts across those already mentioned. In both physiological materialism and behaviorism, the mind-matter identity may be claimed to hold logically because of the nature of the concepts or the meanings of the words involved, like the identity of my only uncle and my parents' only male sibling. Or it may be claimed to hold only as a matter of fact, like the identity of my only uncle and the man from whom I inherited my fortune. Here, unlike the first case, there is nothing in the meanings of these terms (the concepts) which makes them refer to the same individual, but in fact it happens to be one and the same man who is my only uncle and who left me a fortune. Behaviorism has generally been put forward, at least by philosophers, as a matter of logical identity, while physiological materialism has not; but either position could conceivably be held in either form. Critics of physiological materialism often take that position to be claiming a logical identity; they take pains to point out (what is surely correct) that words like "think" and "feel" are not synonymous with any terms for states of or processes in the brain. However, it would seem that the position has rarely, if ever, been advanced in that form, although prior to the present century the two modes of identity have rarely been explicitly distinguished in discussions of the subject. Be that as it may, Place and other recent philosophical exponents of physiological materialism, under the label "identity theory," have been careful to dissociate themselves from the claim to a logical identity.

If freed from commitment to a logical identity, physiological materialism seems to be in a stronger position than behaviorism. To be sure it still lacks a detailed empirical basis; we are in no position to specify just what kind of neural structure or process a given thought, feeling, or belief *is*. What we actually have in the way of empirical data is a set of relatively crude correlations of the following sorts: if a certain part of the brain is functioning, a certain kind of mental function (e.g., memory) is carried on; if that part of the brain is not functioning, that kind of mental function is not being exercised, at least not to its full extent. This leaves us a long way from being able to, for example, specify in neural terms the difference between thinking about the war in Viet Nam and thinking about the National League pennant race. Nevertheless, the fact that we are continually making progress in the direction of more detailed correlations, plus the fact of our general success in science in explaining things in terms of physical operations, gives us substantial grounds for supposing that there are detailed correlations between variations in neural processes in the brain and variations in the contents of consciousness, and that such correlations will be gradually uncovered in the course of scientific inquiry.

Of course the admission of such correlations does not necessarily carry with it a commitment to materialism. Such correlations could be the result of interaction between a mental substance and a material substance, and epiphenomenalism is another view that can take account of such correlations. Nevertheless, there is no doubt that physiological materialism represents the simplest way of taking account of such correlations; if we have the nervous system on our hands anyway, and if mental states precisely mirror variations in the nervous system, we will obtain the most economical scheme by simply identifying the mental states with the corresponding states of the nervous system rather than postulating a distinct realm of mental states.

On the other hand, economy is not the only relevant consideration. It is reasonable to seek the simplest scheme that will take account of all the facts, but we must take care lest preoccupation with metaphysical economy lead us to ignore some of the relevant facts. Are there any facts that stand in the way of the identification? First, what about the epistemological difference between mind and body with which we introduced the subject, viz., the fact that mental states, unlike bodily states, are known immediately by one and only one person. Does this not show that mental states are distinguishable from any states of the body? Descartes thought so. In Reading 33 he argues that since he was able to doubt that any body exists (including of course his own nervous system) while being unable to doubt that his mind exists, this shows that the mind is distinct from the body. However, in Arnauld's criticism of this argument, also included in Reading 33, he points out that the fact that I can doubt that the triangle before me has the square of its hypotenuse equal to the sum of the square of its legs, while being unable to doubt that it is a right triangle, does not show that these matters are really distinct. Descartes does not have a convincing reply to this criticism. We may generalize Arnauld's point as follows. The fact that I acquire knowledge of a and b in different ways does not suffice to show that a and b are different things. For if I get knowledge of them in different ways, it must be that I come to know a as having one property, P, and b as having another property, Q. But then *if* P and Q are compatible, in the sense that it is in principle possible for them to qualify the same thing (like being tall and being green), a and b still may be identical for anything I have shown.

The question is really one as to the compatibility of the properties I know *a* and *b* as having via these different ways of knowing; the issue is not settled simply by pointing to the difference in the ways of knowing.

Thus the fact that there is unique private access to mental states but not to bodily states establishes a difference between the characteristic of being a mental state and the characteristic of being a bodily state. But it does not show that one and the same entity cannot have both these characteristics. It looks as though most, if not all, of the arguments against materialism exhibit the same defect. Thus Ewing argues in Reading 38 that one can know from experience that a conscious state, like a felt pain, is very different from any physiological state or process. (Ewing does not distinguish between behaviorism and physiological materialism.) What this appeal to experience shows is that the felt quality which marks pain off from other feelings is a different quality from any we attribute to something in thinking of it as a physiological state. This still leaves open the question as to whether it is possible for one and the same thing to have both kinds of qualities. Again it is argued that physiological states and processes have spatial location while conscious states do not; hence they cannot be identical. But to this the materialist can reply that all we are entitled to claim about conscious states on this score is that when we are thinking of a state as a thought or a feeling we do not ascribe a spatial location to it. But this does not rule out the possibility that it may have a spatial location, for all that.

Despite the weakness of these antimaterialist arguments, it still remains possible that there are fundamental characteristics of mental and of bodily states that are mutually incompatible. More exploration of this issue is needed.

The second philosophical problem about human nature represented in this section is the problem of personal identity through time — what makes John Jones today the same person as John Jones yesterday, last week, or ten years ago. In the ordinary conduct of life this does not appear to be a serious difficulty, but there are more or less out-of-the-way problematic situations that reveal the need for, and the difficulty of, specifying just what it takes for a person at one time to be the same as a person at another time. In Reading 10 Hick brings out one such context, the problem of immortality. If I claimed to be a reincarnation of, and hence the same person as, Napoleon, what considerations would be relevant to deciding this question? What would it take to make me the same person as Napoleon? The same problem arises in a more difficult form when we think of the possibility that a disembodied spirit might *be* Napoleon. Cases of "multiple personality" and cases where a person has been altered radically through brain surgery provide other contexts in which the question of the criteria of personal identity takes on urgency.

Of course different positions on the mind-body problem will have different implications for this problem. For a materialist the question of personal identity will be just a special case of the general problem of the sameness of a physical body through time, while a Cartesian dualist will have to address himself to the question of what makes a nonmaterial substance retain its identity through time as the same substance. Nevertheless, to a certain extent the problem can be discussed without reliance on a prior resolution of the mind-body problem, and the selections from Locke and Reid illustrate that possibility. Locke argues, in effect, that even if a man is composed of a mental *and* a bodily substance, it is not the persistence of the same mental substance that makes a man the same person he was previously, but rather continuity of memory. Even if the spiritual substance that is conjoined with my body is the same one (whatever that means) as the one that was conjoined with the body of Napoleon, that does not make me the same person as the victor of Austerlitz, provided I have no consciousness of doing any of the things Napoleon did. This is essentially a "verifiability principle" (see Reading 46) approach to the matter. Locke asks, "What do we take as *showing* that the person in front of me is or is not the same as the person who came to my house yesterday morning?" His answer to this question is that our working criterion is the possibility of memory. If the person in front of me can remember coming to my house yesterday morning, then he is the same person; if not, not. Locke then goes on to argue that since this is all we have to go on, we may as well simply say that this is what personal identity consists in, and drop as so much excess baggage the notion of a continuance of the same immaterial substance. Thus, although Locke himself holds onto Cartesian dualism as an account of the make-up of man, his claim that a consideration of spiritual substance is of no importance for the concept of personal identity has the effect of ejecting that concept from the limelight.

In Reading 40 Reid trenchantly points out some of the weaknesses of Locke's position. It is clear that I (i.e., one and the same person as the person I am now) have done and experienced various things in the past that I cannot now remember doing and experiencing, whereas the Lockean theory, if strictly applied, would imply that nothing I cannot now remember doing was done by me. Indeed Locke's theory would imply that virtually no adult has any early childhood, for virtually no adult can remember anything he did or experienced during his first year of life. Reid's alternative to Locke is a retreat to the notion of continued existence of an immaterial substance, but he does nothing to counter Locke's criticisms of that criterion. He neither shows how we can tell when the immaterial substance is the same one, nor does he answer Locke's doubts as to whether this is what the continued existence of the same person amounts to. It would be desirable to move beyond Locke by supplementing his account of the criteria we actually use to test personal identity. This would presumably involve bringing out the ways in which bodily identity is combined with the possibility of memory, continuity of personality traits, and perhaps other considerations in a complex criterion. The discussion by Hick in Reading 10, although it falls short of carrying out any such program, does represent a contemporary attempt to bring out some of the complexities of the problem.

The third and last philosophical problem about man represented in this section is the question of the ultimate destiny of the individual person, the problem of immortality. Here the dependence on the resolution of the mind-body problem is even closer, although the situation is not so simple as might at first appear. One might think that materialism (and epiphenomenalism) rule out immortality, while dualism allows for the possibility (or even requires it), but the interrelations are more complicated than that. For one thing, a great deal hangs on the kind of immortality that is in question. Under the influence of Platonism and Cartesianism we have become accustomed to thinking of immortality simply as a disembodied existence of an immaterial soul after the dissolution of the body, forgetting that the dominant conception in the Jewish and early Christian tradition is that of the miraculous resurrection of the body at some future date. It is noteworthy that the classic Christian creeds make no mention at all of the "immortality of the soul," though they do affirm belief in the "resurrection of the body." Now although materialism and epiphenomenalism do plainly rule out the possibility of the existence of a conscious person without a body, they plainly do not rule out the possibility that each person might have his body miraculously reconstituted at some time after his death and thereby resume his existence as the same person. The question of what it would take to make a human body existing at some time after my death the same body as the one I possess now is an obscure one, but at least nothing in the general doctrine of materialism rules out the possibility. In the course of the development of Christian theology under the influence of Greek philosophy the two conceptions of immortality were interrelated, so that the orthodox view became that after death the soul enjoyed a disembodied existence until the Day of Judgment, at which time each soul was provided with a reconstituted body; only after this reunion with its body is it able to carry on a fully human existence. Both in this form of orthodoxy, and in more modern forms of Christianity in which the belief in resurrection has been quietly swept under the rug, the belief in the *possibility* of disembodied existence plays a fundamental role, and so it is of religious as well as of philosophical importance to consider what can be said for and against it.

In Reading 42 Russell gives the standard argument against this possibility, from a materialist, or epiphenomenalist, position. (It is not made clear in this selection which position Russell is taking, though judging from his other works, epiphenomenalism seems the more plausible interpretation.) If conscious states are either states of the nervous system or just by-products given off by processes in the nervous system, when the nervous system is no longer functioning the series of conscious states will not continue, and the person will no longer be in existence. In Reading 41 William James argues, on the other hand, that the empirical facts of psycho-physical correlation do not themselves rule out continued disembodied existence. James's own alternative to epiphenomenalism is a rather weird one, involving the notion of an immaterial "reservoir" of consciousness, from which portions seep through into the individual as a result of physical processes in his brain. However, the basic point James is making is independent of this theory; in fact it is essentially the same point as the one we made earlier in this introduction, when we pointed out that the empirical correlations between mental states and neural states are quite compatible with dualism as well as with materialism and epiphenomenalism. James is simply extending this point to its bearing on the problem of immortality. Since the empirical facts in question do not suffice to establish materialism (or epiphenomenalism) they do no suffice to rule out the possibility of immortality.

Our selections on the subject of immortality are confined to a consideration of the bearing of different theories of the mind on the question of the *possibility* of immortality. This is the aspect of the subject which is of most general philosophical interest, but of course even if it is established that immortality is not ruled out by what is known about human nature, the question still remains as to whether it is an actual fact, and one may well seek rational grounds for deciding this question. Philosophers have tried to establish the reality of immortality on the basis of general philosophical considerations. Thus it has been argued, from a dualist standpoint, that since the soul is an immaterial substance, it does not have spatially distinguished parts, and since a thing can be destroyed only by its parts being separated from each other, the soul is, therefore, indestructible. Immanuel Kant criticized this argument by pointing out that one can conceive other modes of destruction which would be possible for a substance not extended in space, e.g., having its intensity of consciousness permanently reduced to zero. Kant himself put forward a moral argument for immortality, which runs roughly as follows. Each person has an absolute obligation to perfect himself morally; this is possible only if one has an indefinitely long time in which to complete the job; therefore . . . The tricky thing about this argument is that one could just as reasonably turn it around and argue that since one does not exist for an indefinitely long time, one cannot have an absolute obligation to perfect oneself, however much it might seem at first that one does. In the light of the history of these and other philosophical arguments, the prospects of establishing immortality on the basis of general philosophical considerations does not seem promising. Assurance of immortality, if available at all, would have to come from more special sources, such as religious revelation, or the experiences of those who claim to have received messages from the surviving spirits of deceased human beings.

33

MAN AS
TWO SUBSTANCES

René Descartes

René Descartes (1596-1650) has, more than any other man, shaped the course of modern philosophy. He made signal contributions to mathematics and physical science as well as to philosophy.

MEDITATION II

Of the nature of the human mind, and that it is more easily known than the body.

The Meditation of yesterday filled my mind with so many doubts that it is no longer in my power to forget them. And yet I do not see in what manner I can resolve them; and, just as if I had all of a sudden fallen into very deep water, I am so disconcerted that I can neither make certain of setting my feet on the bottom, nor can I swim and so support myself on the surface. I shall nevertheless make an effort and follow anew the same path as that on which I yesterday entered, i.e. I shall proceed by setting aside all that in which the least doubt could be supposed to exist, just as if I had discovered that it was absolutely false; and I shall ever follow in this road until I have met with something which is certain, or at least, if I can do nothing else, until I have learned for certain that there is nothing in the world that is certain. Archimedes, in order that he might draw the terrestrial globe out of its place, and transport it elsewhere, demanded only that one point should be fixed and immoveable; in the same way I shall have the right to conceive high hopes if I am happy enough to discover one thing only which is certain and indubitable.

I suppose, then, that all the things that I see are false; I persuade myself that nothing has ever existed of all that my fallacious memory represents to me. I consider that I possess no senses; I imagine that body, figure, extension,

This selection is taken from the second and sixth of the *Meditations,* a work first published in 1641, and from the objections to this work collected from various eminent thinkers of the time and answered by Descartes. The translation is by E. S. Haldane and G. R. T. Ross.

movement and place are but the fiction of my mind. What, then, can be esteemed as true? Perhaps nothing at all, unless that there is nothing in the world that is certain.

But how can I know there is not something different from those things that I have just considered, of which one cannot have the slightest doubt? Is there not some God, or some other being by whatever name we call it, who puts these reflections into my mind? That is not necessary, for is it not possible that I am capable of producing them myself? I myself, am I not at least something? But I have already denied that I had senses and body. Yet I hesitate, for what follows from that? Am I so dependent on body and senses that I cannot exist without these? But I was persuaded that there was nothing in all the world, that there was no heaven, no earth, that there were no minds, nor any bodies: was I not then likewise persuaded that I did not exist? Not at all; of a surety I myself did exist since I persuaded myself of something [or merely because I thought of something]. But there is some deceiver or other, very powerful and very cunning, who ever employs his ingenuity in deceiving me. Then without doubt I exist also if he deceives me, and let him deceive me as much as he will, he can never cause me to be nothing so long as I think that I am something. So that after having reflected well and carefully examined all things, we must come to the definite conclusion that this proposition: I am, I exist, is necessarily true each time that I pronounce it, or that I mentally conceive it.

But I do not yet know clearly enough what I am, I who am certain that I am; and hence I must be careful to see that I do not imprudently take some other object in place of myself, and thus that I do not go astray in respect of this knowledge that I hold to be the most certain and most evident of all that I have formerly learned. That is why I shall now consider anew what I believed myself to be before I embarked upon these last reflections; and of my former opinions I shall withdraw all that might even in a small degree be invalidated by the reasons which I have just brought forward, in order that there may be nothing at all left beyond what is absolutely certain and indubitable.

What then did I formerly believe myself to be? Undoubtedly I believed myself to be a man. But what is a man? Shall I say a reasonable animal? Certainly not; for then I should have to inquire what an animal is, and what is reasonable; and thus from a single question I should insensibly fall into an infinitude of others more difficult; and I should not wish to waste the little time and leisure remaining to me in trying to unravel subtleties like these. But I shall rather stop here to consider the thoughts which of themselves spring up in my mind, and which were not inspired by anything beyond my own nature alone when I applied myself to the consideration of my being. In the first place, then, I considered myself as having a face, hands, arms, and all that system of members composed of bones and flesh as seen in a corpse which I designated by the name of body. In addition to this I considered that I was nourished, that I walked, that I felt, and that I thought, and I referred all these actions to the soul: but I did not stop to consider what the soul was, or if I did stop, I imagined that it was something extremely rare and subtle like a wind, a flame, or an ether, which was spread throughout my grosser parts. As to body I had no manner of doubt about its nature, but thought I had a very clear knowledge of it; and if I had desired to explain it according to the notions that I had then formed of it, I should have described it thus: By the body I understand all that which can be defined by a certain figure: something which can be confined in a certain place, and which can fill a space in such a way that every other body will be excluded from it; which can be perceived either by touch, or by sight, or by hearing, or by taste, or by smell: which can be moved in many ways not, in truth, by itself but by something which is foreign to it, by which it is touched [and from which it receives impressions]: for to have the power of self-movement, as also of feeling or of thinking, I did not consider to appertain to the nature of body: on the contrary, I was rather astonished to find that faculties similar to them existed in some bodies.

But what am I, now that I suppose that there is a certain genius which is extremely powerful, and, if I may say so, malicious, who employs all his powers in deceiving me? Can I affirm that I possess the least of all those things which I have just said pertain to the nature of body? I pause to consider, I revolve all these things in my mind, and I find none of which I can say that it pertains to me. It would be tedious to stop to enumerate them. Let us pass to the attributes of soul and see if there is any one which is in me? What of nutrition or walking [the first mentioned]? But if it is so that I have no body it is also true that I can neither walk nor take nourishment. Another attribute is sensation. But one cannot feel without body, and besides I have thought I perceived many things during sleep that I recognised in my waking moments as not having been experienced at all. What of thinking? I find here that thought is an attribute that belongs to me; it alone cannot be separated from me. I am, I exist, that is certain. But how often? Just when I think; for it might possibly be the case if I ceased entirely to think, that I should likewise cease altogether to exist. I do not now admit anything which is not necessarily true: to speak accurately I am not more than a thing which thinks, that is to say a mind or a soul, or an understanding, or a reason, which are terms whose significance was formerly unknown to me. I am, however, a real thing and really exist; but what thing? I have answered: a thing which thinks.

And what more? I shall exercise my imagination [in order to see if I am not something more]. I am not a collection of members which we call the human body: I am not a subtle air distributed through these members, I am not a wind, a fire, a vapour, a breath, nor anything at all which I can imagine or conceive; because I have assumed that all these were nothing. Without changing that supposition I find that I only leave myself certain of the fact that I am somewhat. But perhaps it is true that these same things which I supposed were non-existent because they are unknown to me, are really not different from the self which I know. I am not sure about this, I shall not dispute about it now; I can only give judgment on things that are known to me. I know that I exist, and I inquire what I am, I whom I know to exist. But it is very certain that the knowledge of my existence taken in its precise significance does not depend on things whose existence is not yet known to me; consequently it does not depend on those which I can feign in imagination. And indeed the very term *feign* in imagination proves to me my error, for I really do this if I image myself a something, since to imagine is nothing else than to contemplate the figure or image of a corporeal thing. But I already know for certain that I am, and that it may be that all these images, and, speaking generally, all things that relate to the nature of body are nothing but dreams [and chimeras]. For this reason I see clearly that I have as little reason to say, 'I shall stimulate my imagination in order to know more distinctly what I am,' than if I were to say, 'I am now awake, and I perceive somewhat that is real and true: but because I do not yet perceive it distinctly enough, I shall go to sleep of express purpose, so that my dreams may represent the perception with greatest truth and evidence.' And, thus, I know for certain that nothing of all that I can understand by means of my imagination belongs to this knowledge which I have of myself, and that it is necessary to recall the mind from this mode of thought with the utmost diligence in order that it may be able to know its own nature with perfect distinctness.

But what then am I? A thing which thinks. What is a thing which thinks? It is a thing which doubts, understands, [conceives], affirms, denies, wills, refuses, which also imagines and feels.

Certainly it is no small matter if all these things pertain to my nature. But why should they not so pertain? Am I not that being who now doubts nearly everything, who nevertheless understands certain things, who affirms that one only is true, who denies all the others, who desires to know more, is averse from being deceived, who imagines many things, sometimes indeed despite his will, and who perceives many likewise, as by the intervention of the bodily organs? Is there nothing in all this which is as true as it is certain that I exist, even though I should always sleep and though he who has given me being employed all his ingenuity in deceiving me? Is there likewise any one of these attributes which can be distinguished from my thought, or which might be said to be separated from myself? For it is so evident of itself that it is I who doubts, who understands, and who desires, that there is no reason here to add anything to explain it. And I have certainly the power of imagining likewise; for although it may happen (as I formerly supposed) that none of the things which I imagine are true, nevertheless this power of imagining does not cease to be really in use, and it forms part of my thought. Finally, I am the same who feels, that is to say, who perceives certain things, as by the organs of sense, since in truth I see light, I hear noise, I feel heat. But it will be said that these phenomena are false and that I am dreaming. Let it be so; still it is at least quite certain that it seems to me that I see light, that

I hear noise and that I feel heat. That cannot be false; properly speaking it is what is in me called feeling; and used in this precise sense that is no other thing than thinking.

·   ·   ·

MEDITATION VI

Of the existence of material things, and of the real distinction between the soul and body of man.

. . . it is right that I should at the same time investigate the nature of sense perception, and that I should see if from the ideas which I apprehend by this mode of thought, which I call feeling, I cannot derive some certain proof of the existence of corporeal objects.

And first of all I shall recall to my memory those matters which I hitherto held to be true, as having perceived them through the senses, and the foundations on which my belief has rested; in the next place I shall examine the reasons which have since obliged me to place them in doubt; in the last place I shall consider which of them I must now believe.

First of all, then, I perceived that I had a head, hands, feet, and all other members of which this body — which I considered as a part, or possibly even as the whole, of myself — is composed. Further I was sensible that this body was placed amidst many others, from which it was capable of being affected in many different ways, beneficial and hurtful, and I remarked that a certain feeling of pleasure accompanied those that were beneficial, and pain those which were harmful. And in addition to this pleasure and pain, I also experienced hunger, thirst, and other similar appetites, as also certain corporeal inclinations towards joy, sadness, anger, and other similar passions. And outside myself, in addition to extension, figure, and motions of bodies, I remarked in them hardness, heat, and all other tactile qualities, and, further, light and colour, and scents and sounds, the variety of which gave me the means of distinguishing the sky, the earth, the sea, and generally all the other bodies, one from the other. And certainly, considering the ideas of all these qualities which presented themselves to my mind, and which alone I perceived properly or immediately, it was not without reason that I believed myself to perceive objects quite different from my thought, to wit, bodies from which those ideas proceeded; for I found by experience that these ideas presented themselves to me without my consent being requisite, so that I could not perceive any object, however desirous I might be, unless it were present to the organs of sense; and it was not in my power not to perceive it, when it was present. And because the ideas which I received through the senses were much more lively, more clear, and even, in their own way, more distinct than any of those which I could of myself frame in meditation, or than those I found impressed on my memory, it appeared as though they could not have proceeded from my mind, so that they must necessarily have been produced in me by some other things. And having no knowledge of those objects excepting the knowledge which the ideas themselves gave me, nothing was more likely to occur to my mind than that the objects were similar to the ideas which were caused. And because I likewise remembered that I had formerly made use of my senses rather than my reason, and recognised that the ideas which I formed of myself were not so distinct as those which I perceived through the senses, and that they were most frequently even composed of portions of these last, I persuaded myself easily that I had no idea in my mind which had not formerly come to me through the senses. Nor was it without some reason that I believed that this body (which by a certain special right I call my own) belonged to me more properly and more strictly than any other; for in fact I could never be separated from it as from other bodies; I experienced in it and on account of it all my appetites and affections, and finally I was touched by the feeling of pain and the titillation of pleasure in its parts, and not in the parts of other bodies which were separated from it. But when I inquired, why, from some, I know not what, painful sensations, there follows sadness of mind, and from the pleasurable sensation there arises joy, or why this mysterious pinching of the stomach which I call hunger causes me to desire to eat, and dryness of throat causes a desire to drink, and so on, I could give no reason excepting that nature taught me so; for there is certainly no affinity (that I at least can understand) between the craving of the stomach and the desire to eat, any more than between the perception of whatever causes pain and the thought of sadness which arises from this perception. And in the same way it appeared to me that I had learned from nature all the other judgments which I formed regarding the objects of my senses, since I remarked that these judgments were formed in me before I had the leisure to weigh and consider any reasons which might oblige me to make them.

But afterwards many experiences little by little destroyed all the faith which I had rested in my senses; for I from time to time observed that those towers which from afar appeared to me to be round, more closely observed seemed square, and that colossal statues raised on the summit of these towers, appeared as quite tiny statues when viewed from the bottom; and so in an infinitude of other cases I found error in judgments founded on the external senses. And not only in those founded on the external senses, but even in those founded on the internal as well; for is there anything more intimate or more internal than pain? And yet I have learned from some persons whose arms or legs have been cut off, that they sometimes seemed to feel pain in the part which had been amputated, which made me think that I could not be quite certain that it was a certain member which pained me, even although I felt pain in it. And to those grounds of doubt I have lately added two others, which are very general; the first is that I never have believed myself to feel anything in waking moments which I cannot also sometimes believe myself to feel when I sleep, and as I do not think that these things which I seem to feel in sleep, proceed from objects outside of me, I do not see any reason why I should have this belief regarding objects which I seem to perceive while awake. The other was that being still ignorant, or rather supposing myself to be ignorant, of the author of my being, I saw nothing to prevent me from having been so constituted by nature that I might be deceived even in matters which seemed to me to be most certain. And as to the grounds on which I was formerly persuaded of the truth of sensible objects, I had not much trouble in replying to them. For since nature seemed to cause me to lean towards many things from which reason repelled me, I did not believe that I should trust much to the teachings of nature. And although the ideas which I receive by the senses do not depend on my will, I did not think that one should for that reason conclude that they proceeded from things different from myself, since possibly some faculty might be discovered in me — though hitherto unknown to me — which produced them.

But now that I begin to know myself better, and to discover more clearly the author of my being, I do not in truth think that I should rashly admit all the matters which the senses seem to teach us, but, on the other hand, I do not think that I should doubt them all universally.

And first of all, because I know that all things which I apprehend clearly and distinctly can be created by God as I apprehend them, it suffices that I am able to apprehend one thing apart from another clearly and distinctly in order to be certain that the one is different from the other, since they may be made to exist in separation at least by the omnipotence of God; and it does not signify by what power this separation is made in order to compel me to judge them to be different: and, therefore, just because I know certainly that I exist, and that meanwhile I do not remark that any other thing necessarily pertains to my nature or essence, excepting that I am a thinking thing, I rightly conclude that my essence consists solely in the fact that I am a thinking thing [or a substance whose whole essence or nature is to think]. And although possibly (or rather certainly, as I shall say in a moment) I possess a body with which I am very intimately conjoined, yet because, on the one side, I have a clear and distinct idea of myself inasmuch as I am only a thinking and unextended thing, and as, on the other, I possess a distinct idea of body, inasmuch as it is only an extended and unthinking thing, it is certain that this I [that is to say, my soul by which I am what I am], is entirely and absolutely distinct from my body, and can exist without it.

I further find in myself faculties employing modes of thinking peculiar to themselves, to wit, the faculties of imagination and feeling, without which I can easily conceive myself clearly and distinctly as a complete being; while, on the other hand, they cannot be so conceived apart from me, that is without an intelligent substance in which they reside, for [in the notion we have of these faculties, or, to use the language of the Schools] in their formal concept, some kind of intellection is comprised, from which I infer that they are distinct from me as its modes are from a thing. I observe also in me some other faculties such as that of change of position, the assumption of different figures and such like, which cannot be conceived, any more than can the preceding, apart from some substance to which they are attached, and consequently cannot exist without it; but it is very clear that these faculties, if it be true that they exist, must be attached to some corporeal or extended substance, and not to an intelligent substance, since in the clear and distinct conception of these there is some sort of extension found to be present, but no intellection at all. There is certainly further in me a certain passive faculty of perception, that is, of receiving and recognising the ideas of sensible things, but this would be useless to me [and I could in no way avail myself of it], if there were not either in me or in some other thing another active faculty capable of forming and producing these ideas. But this active faculty cannot exist in me [inasmuch as I am a thing that thinks] seeing that it does not presuppose thought, and also that those ideas are often produced in me without my contributing in any way to the same, and often even against my will; it is thus necessarily the case that the faculty resides in some substance different from me in which all the reality which is objectively in the ideas that are produced by this faculty is formally or eminently contained, as I remarked before. And this substance is either a body, that is, a corporeal nature in which there is contained formally [and really] all that which is objectively [and by representation] in those ideas, or it is God Himself, or some other creature more noble than body in which that same is contained eminently. But, since God is no deceiver, it is very manifest that He does not communicate to me these ideas immediately and by Himself, nor yet by the intervention of some creature in which their reality is not formally, but only eminently, contained. For since He has given me no faculty to recognise that this is the case, but, on the other hand, a very great inclination to believe [that they are sent to me or] that they are conveyed to me by corporeal objects, I do not see how He could be defended from the accusation of deceit if these ideas were produced by causes other than corporeal objects. Hence we must allow that corporeal things exist. However, they are perhaps not exactly what we perceive by the senses, since this comprehension by the senses is in many instances very obscure and confused, but we must at least admit that all things which I conceive in them clearly and distinctly, that is to say, all things which, speaking generally, are comprehended in the object of pure mathematics, are truly to be recognised as external objects.

As to other things, however, which are either particular only, as, for example, that the sun is of such and such a figure, etc., or which are less clearly and distinctly conceived such as light, sound, pain and the like, it is certain that although they are very dubious and uncertain, yet on the sole ground that God is not a deceiver, and that consequently He has not permitted any falsity to exist in my opinion which He has not likewise given me the faculty of correcting, I may assuredly hope to conclude that I have within me the means of arriving at the truth even here. And first of all there is no doubt that in all things which nature teaches me there is some truth contained; for by nature, considered in general, I now understand no other thing than either God Himself or else the order and disposition which God has established in created things; and by my nature in particular I understand no other thing than the complexus of all the things which God has given me.

But there is nothing which this nature teaches me more expressly [nor more sensibly] than that I have a body which is adversely affected when I feel pain, which has need of food or drink when I experience the feelings of hunger and thirst, and so on; nor can I doubt there being some truth in all this.

Nature also teaches me by these sensations of pain, hunger, thirst, etc., that I am not only lodged in my body as a pilot in a vessel, but that I am very closely united to it, and so to speak so intermingled with it that I seem to compose with it one whole. For if that were not the case, when my body is hurt, I, who am merely a thinking thing, should not feel pain, for I should perceive this wound by the understanding only, just as the sailor perceives by sight when something is damaged in his vessel; and when my body has need of drink or food, I should clearly understand the fact without being warned of it by confused feelings of hunger and thirst. For all these sensations of hunger, thirst, pain, etc. are in truth none other than certain confused modes of thought which are produced by the union and apparent intermingling of mind and body.

.   .   .

. . . in the first place, there is a great difference between mind and body, inasmuch as body is by nature always divisible, and the mind is entirely indivisible. For, as a matter of fact, when I consider the mind, that is to say, myself inasmuch as I am only a thinking thing, I cannot distinguish in myself any parts, but apprehend myself to be clearly one and entire; and although the whole mind seems to be united to the whole body, yet if a foot, or an arm, or some other part, is separated from my body, I am aware that nothing has been taken away from my mind. And the faculties of willing, feeling, conceiving, etc. cannot be properly speaking said to be its parts, for it is one and the same mind which employs itself in willing and in feeling and understanding. But it is quite otherwise with corporeal or extended objects, for there is not one of these imaginable by me which my mind cannot easily divide into parts, and which consequently I do not recognise as being divisible; this would be sufficient to teach me that the mind or soul of man is entirely different from the body, if I had not already learned it from other sources.

I further notice that the mind does not receive the impressions from all parts of the body immediately, but only from the brain, or perhaps even from one of its smallest parts, to wit, from that in which the common sense is said to reside, which, whenever it is disposed in the same particular way, conveys the same thing to the mind, although meanwhile the other portions of the body may be differently disposed, as is testified by innumerable experiments which it is unnecessary here to recount.

I notice, also, that the nature of body is such that none of its parts can be moved by another part a little way off which cannot also be moved in the same way by each one of the parts which are between the two, although this more remote part does not act at all. As, for example, in the cord *ABCD* [which is in tension] if we pull the last part D, the first part A will not be moved in any way differently from what would be the case if one of the intervening parts B or C were pulled, and the last part D were to remain unmoved. And in the same way, when I feel pain in my foot, my knowledge of physics teaches me that this sensation is communicated by means of nerves dispersed through the foot, which, being extended like cords from there to the brain, when they are contracted in the foot, at the same time contract the inmost portions of the brain which is their extremity and place of origin, and then excite a certain movement which nature has established in order to cause the mind to be affected by a sensation of pain represented as existing in the foot. But because these nerves must pass through the tibia, the thigh, the loins, the back and the neck, in order to reach from the leg to the brain, it may happen that although their extremities which are in the foot are not affected, but only certain ones of their intervening parts [which pass by the loins or the neck], this action will excite the same movement in the brain that might have been excited there by a hurt received in the foot, in consequence of which the mind will necessarily feel in the foot the same pain as if it had received a hurt. And the same holds good of all the other perceptions of our senses.

I notice finally that since each of the movements which are in the portion of the brain by which the mind is immediately affected brings about one particular sensation only, we cannot under the circumstances imagine anything more likely than that this movement, amongst all the sensations which it is capable of impressing on it, causes mind to be affected by that one which is best fitted and most generally useful for the conservation of the human body when it is in health. But experience makes us aware that all the feelings with which nature inspires us are such as I have just spoken of; and there is therefore nothing in them which does not give testimony to the power and goodness of the God [who has produced them]. Thus, for example, when the nerves which are in the feet are violently or more than usually moved, their movement, passing through the medulla of the spine to the inmost parts of the brain, gives a sign to the mind which makes it feel somewhat, to wit, pain, as though in the foot, by which the mind is excited to do its utmost to remove the cause of the evil as dangerous and hurtful to the foot. It is true that God could have constituted the nature of man in such a way that this same movement in the brain would have conveyed something quite different to the mind; for example, it might have produced consciousness of itself either in so far as it is in the brain, or as it is in the foot, or as it is in some other place between the foot and the brain, or it might finally have produced consciousness of anything else whatsoever; but none of all this would have contributed so well to the conservation of the body. Similarly, when we desire to drink, a certain dryness of the throat is produced which moves its nerves, and by their means the internal portions of the brain; and this movement causes in the mind the sensation of thirst, because in this case there is nothing more useful to us than to become aware that we have need to drink for the conservation of our health; and the same holds good in other instances.

From this it is quite clear that, notwithstanding the supreme goodness of God, the nature of man, inasmuch as it is composed of mind and body, cannot be otherwise than sometimes a source of deception. For if there is any cause which excites, not in the foot but in some part of the nerves which are extended between the foot and the brain, or even in the brain itself, the same movement which usually is produced when the foot is detrimentally affected, pain will be experienced as though it were in the foot, and the sense will thus naturally be deceived; for since the same movement in the brain is capable of causing but one sensation in the mind, and this sensation is much more frequently excited by a cause which hurts the foot than by another existing in some other quarter, it is reasonable that it should convey to the mind pain in the foot rather than in any other part of the body. And although the parchedness of the throat does not always proceed, as it usually does, from the fact that drinking is necessary for the health of the body, but sometimes comes from quite a different cause, as is the case with dropsical patients, it is yet much better that it should mislead on this occasion than if, on the other hand, it were always to deceive us when the body is in good health; and so on in similar cases.

· · ·

Objection by Thomas Hobbes

I am a thing that thinks; *quite correct. From the fact that I think, or have an image, whether sleeping or waking, it is inferred that I am exercising thought, for* I think and I am exercising thought *mean the same thing. From the fact that I am exercising thought it follows that* I am, *since that which thinks is not nothing. But, where it is added,* this is the mind, the spirit, the understanding, the reason, *a doubt arises. For it does not seem to be good reasoning to say:* I am exercising thought, *hence* I am thought; *or* I am using my intellect, *hence* I am intellect. *For in the same way I might say,* I am walking; *hence* I am the walking. *It is hence an assumption on the part of M. Descartes that that which understands is the same as the exercise of understanding which is an act of that which understands, or, at least, that that which understands is the same as the understanding, which is a power possessed by that which thinks. Yet all Philosophers distinguish a subject from its faculties and activities, i.e. from its properties and essences; for the entity itself is one thing, its essence another. Hence it is possible for a thing that thinks to be the subject of the mind, reason, or understanding, and hence to be something corporeal; and the opposite of this has been assumed, not proved. Yet this inference is the basis of the conclusion that M. Descartes seems to wish to establish.*

· · ·

Reply by Descartes

Where I have said, *this is the mind, the spirit, the intellect, or the reason,* I understood by these names not merely faculties, but rather what is endowed with the faculty of thinking; and this sense the two former terms commonly, the latter frequently bear. But I used them in this sense so expressly and in so many places that I cannot see what occasion there was for any doubt about their meaning.

Further, there is here no parity between walking and thinking; for walking is usually held to refer only to that action itself, while thinking applies now to the action, now to the faculty of thinking, and again to that in which the faculty exists.

A thing that thinks, he says, may be something corporeal; and the opposite of this has been assumed; not proved. But really I did not assume the opposite, neither did I use it as a basis for my argument; I left it wholly undetermined until Meditation VI, in which its proof is given.

. . . it is certain that no thought can exist apart from a thing that thinks; no activity, no accident can be without a susbtance in which to exist. Moreover, since we do not apprehend the substance itself immediately through itself, but by means only of the fact that it is the subject of certain activities, it is highly rational, and a requirement forced on us by custom, to give diverse names to those substances that we recognize to be the subjects of clearly diverse activities or accidents, and afterwards to inquire whether those diverse names refer to one and the same or to diverse things. But there are *certain* activities, which we call *corporeal,* e.g. magnitude, figure, motion, and all those that cannot be thought of apart from extension in space; and the substance in which they exist is called *body.* It cannot be pretended that the substance that is the subject of figure is different from that which is the subject of spatial motion, etc., since all these activities agree in presupposing extension. Further, there are other activities, which we call *thinking* activities, e.g. understanding, willing, imagining, feeling, etc., which agree in falling under the description of thought, perception, or consciousness. The substance in which they reside we call a *thinking thing* or *the mind,* or any other name we care, provided only we do not confound it with corporeal substance, since thinking activities have no affinity with corporeal activities, and thought, which is the common nature in which the former agree, is totally different from extension, the common term for describing the latter.

But after we have formed two distinct concepts of those two substances, it is easy, from what has been said in the sixth Meditation, to determine whether they are one and the same or distinct.

Objection by Antoine Arnauld

. . . let us discover how we can demonstrate the fact that our mind is [distinct and] separate from our body.

I am able to doubt whether I have a body, nay, whether any body exists at all; yet I have no right to doubt whether I am, or exist, so long as I doubt or think.

Hence I, who doubt and think, am not a body; otherwise in entertaining doubt concerning body, I should doubt about myself.

Nay, even though I obstinately maintain that no body at all exists, the position taken up is unshaken: I am something, hence I am not a body.

This is really very acute, but someone could bring up the objection which our author urges against himself; the fact that I doubt about body or deny that body exists, does not bring it about that no body exists. Hence perhaps it happens that these very things which I suppose to be nothing, because they are unknown to me, yet do not in truth differ from that self which I do know. I know nothing about it, *he says,* I do not dispute this matter; [I can judge only about things that are known to me.] I know that I exist; I enquire who I, the known self, am; it is quite certain that the knowledge of this self thus precisely taken, does not depend on those things of the existence of which I am not yet acquainted.

But he admits in consonance with the argument laid down in the Method, that the proof has proceeded only so far as to exclude from the nature of the human mind whatsoever is corporeal, not from the point of view of the ultimate truth, but relatively only to his consciousness (the meaning being that nothing at all was known to him to belong to his essential nature, beyond the fact that he was a thinking being). *Hence it is evident from this reply that the argument is exactly where it was, and that therefore the problem which he promises to solve remains entirely untouched. The problem is:* how it follows, from the fact that one is unaware that anything else [(except the fact of being a thinking thing)] belongs to one's essence, that nothing else really belongs to one's essence. *But, not to conceal my dullness, I have been unable to discover in the whole of Meditation II where he has shown this. Yet so far as I can conjecture, he attempts this proof in Meditation VI, because he believes that it is dependent on the possession of the clear knowledge of God to which in Meditation II he has not yet attained. Here is his proof:*

Because I know that all the things I clearly and distinctly understand can be created by God just as I conceive them to exist, it is sufficient for me to be able to comprehend one thing clearly and distinctly apart from another, in order to be sure that the one is diverse from the other, because at least God can isolate them; and it does not matter by what power that isolation is effected, in order that I may be obliged to think them different from one another. Hence because, on the one hand, I have a clear and distinct idea of myself in so far as I am a thinking being, and not extended, and on the other hand, a distinct idea of body, in so far as it is only an extended thing, not one that thinks, it is certain that I am in reality distinct from my body and can exist apart from it.

Here we must halt awhile; for on these few words the whole of the difficulty seems to hinge.

Firstly, in order to be true, the major premiss of that syllogism must be held to refer to the adequate notion of a thing (i.e., the notion which comprises everything which may be known of the thing), not to any notion, even a clear and distinct one.

.   .   .

But, if anyone casts doubt on the (minor) premiss here assumed, and contends that it is merely that your conception is inadequate when you conceive yourself [(i.e. your mind)] as being a thinking but not an extended thing, and similarly when you conceive yourself [(i.e. your body)] as being an extended and not a thinking thing, we must look for its proof in the previous part of the argument. For I do not reckon a matter like this to be so clear as to warrant us in assuming it as an indemonstrable first principle and in dispensing with proof.

Now as to the first part of the statement, namely, that you completely understand what body is, merely by thinking that it is extended, has figure, can move, etc., and by denying of it everything which belongs to the nature of mind, *this is of little value. For one who contends that the human mind is corporeal does not on that account believe that every body is a mind. Hence body would be so related to mind as genus is to species. But the genus can be conceived without the species, even although one deny of it whatsoever is proper and peculiar to the species; whence comes the common dictum of Logicians, 'the negation of the species does not negate the genus.' Thus, I can conceive figure without conceiving any of the attributes proper to the circle. Therefore, we must prove over and above this that the mind can be completely and adequately conceived apart from the body.*

I can discover no passage in the whole work capable of effecting this proof, save the proposition laid down at the outset: —I can deny that there is any body or that any extended thing exists, but yet it is certain that I exist, so long as I make this denial, or think; hence I am a thing that thinks and not a body, and the body does not pertain to the knowledge of myself.

But the only result that I can see to give, is that a certain knowledge of myself be obtained without a knowledge of the body. But it is not yet quite clear to me that this knowledge is complete and adequate, so as to make me sure that I am not in error in excluding the body from my essence. I shall explain by means of an example: —

Let us assume that a certain man is quite sure that the angle in a semicircle is a right angle and that hence the triangle made by this angle and the diameter is right-angled; but suppose he questions and has not yet firmly apprehended, nay, let us imagine that, misled by some fallacy, he denies that the square on its base is equal to the squares on the sides of the right-angled tri-

angle. Now, according to our author's reasoning, he will see himself confirmed in his false belief. For, *he will argue,* while I clearly and distinctly perceive that this triangle is right-angled, I yet doubt whether the square on its base is equal to the square on its sides. Hence the equality of the square on the base to those on the sides does not belong to its essence.

Further, even though I deny that the square on its base is equal to the squares on its sides, I yet remain certain that it is right-angled, and the knowledge that one of its angles is a right angle remains clear and distinct in my mind; and this remaining so, not God himself could cause it not to be right-angled.

Hence, that of which I doubt, or the removal of which leaves me with the idea still, cannot belong to its essence.

Besides, since I know that all things I clearly and distinctly understand can be created by God just as I conceive them to exist, it is sufficient for me, in order to be sure that one thing is distinct from another, to be able to comprehend the one clearly and distinctly apart from the other, because it can be isolated by God. *But I clearly and distinctly understand that this triangle is right-angled, without comprehending that the square on its base is equal to the squares on its sides. Hence God at least can create a right-angled triangle, the square on the base of which is not equal to the squares on its sides.*

I do not see what reply can here be made, except that the man in question does not perceive clearly that the triangle is right-angled. But whence do I obtain any perception of the nature of my mind clearer than that which he has of the nature of the triangle? He is as sure that the triangle in a semicircle has one right angle (which is the notion of a right-angled triangle) as I am in believing that I exist because I think.

Hence, just as a man errs in not believing that the equality of the square on its base to the square on its sides belong to the nature of that triangle, which he clearly and distinctly knows to be right-angled, so why am I not perhaps in the wrong in thinking that nothing else belongs to my nature, which I clearly and distinctly know to be something that thinks, except the fact that I am this thinking being? Perhaps it also belongs to my essence to be something extended.

·   ·   ·

Reply by Descartes

But it can nowise be maintained that, in the words of M. Arnauld, *body is related to mind as genus is to species;* for, although the genus can be apprehended apart from this or that specific difference, the species can by no means be thought apart from the genus.

For, to illustrate, we easily apprehend figure, without thinking at all of a circle (although that mental act is not distinct unless we refer to some specific figure, and it does not give us a complete thing, unless it embraces the nature of the body); but we are cognisant of no specific difference belonging to the circle, unless at the same time we think of figure.

But mind can be perceived clearly and distinctly, or sufficiently so to let it be considered to be a complete thing without any of those forms or attributes by which we recognize that body is a substance, as I think I have sufficiently shown in the Second Meditation; and body is understood distinctly and as a complete thing apart from the attributes attaching to the mind.

Nevertheless M. Arnauld here urges that *although a certain notion of myself can be obtained without a knowledge of the body, it yet does not thence result that this knowledge is complete and adequate, so as to make me sure that I am not in error in excluding the body from my essence.* He elucidates his meaning by taking as an illustration the triangle inscribed in a semicircle, which we can clearly and distinctly know to be right-angled, though we do not know, or even deny, that the square on its base is equal to the squares on its sides; and nevertheless we cannot thence infer that we can have a [right-angled] triangle, the square on the base of which is not equal to the squares on the sides.

But, as to this illustration, the example differs in many respects from the case in hand.

For firstly, although perhaps a triangle may be taken in the concrete as a substance possessing triangular shape, certainly the property of having the square on the base equal to the squares on the sides is not a substance; so too, neither can either of these two things be understood to be a complete thing in the sense in which *Mind and Body* are; indeed, they cannot be called *things* in the sense in which I used the word when I said *that I might comprehend one thing* (i.e. one complete thing) *apart from the other, etc.* as is evident from the succeeding words — *Besides, I discover in myself faculties, etc.* For I did not assert these faculties to be *things*, but distinguished them accurately from things or substances.

Secondly, although we can clearly and distinctly understand that the triangle in the semicircle is right-angled, without noting that the square on its base equals those on its sides, we yet cannot clearly apprehend a triangle in which the square on the base is equal to those on the sides, without at the same time perceiving that it is right-angled. But we do clearly and distinctly perceive mind without body and body without mind.

Thirdly, although our concept of the triangle inscribed in the semicircle may be such as not to comprise the equality between the square on its base and those on its sides, it cannot be such that no ratio between the square on the base and those on the sides is held to prevail in the triangle in question; and hence, so long as we remain ignorant of what the ratio is, nothing can be denied of the triangle other than what we clearly know not to belong to it: but to know this is the case of the equality of the ratio is entirely impossible. Now, on the other hand, there is nothing included in the concept of body that belongs to the mind; and nothing in that of mind that belongs to the body.

Therefore, though I said that *it was sufficient to be able to apprehend one thing clearly and distinctly apart from another, etc.*, we cannot go on to complete the argument thus: — *but I clearly and distinctly apprehend this triangle, etc.* Firstly, because the ratio between the square on the base and those on the sides is not a complete thing. Secondly, because that ratio is clearly understood only in the case of the right-angled triangle. Thirdly, because the triangle itself cannot be distinctly apprehended if the ratio between the squares on the base and on the sides is denied.

But now I must explain how it is that, *from the mere fact that I apprehend one substance clearly and distinctly apart from another, I am sure that the one excludes the other.*

Really the notion of *substance* is just this — that which can exist by itself, without the aid of any other substance. No one who perceives two substances by means of two diverse concepts ever doubts that they are really distinct.

Consequently, if I had not been in search of a certitude greater than the vulgar, I should have been satisfied with showing in the Second Meditation that *Mind* was apprehended as a thing that subsists, although nothing belonging to the body be ascribed to it, and conversely that *Body* was understood to be something subsistent without anything being attributed to it that pertains to the mind. And I should have added nothing more in order to prove that there was a real distinction between mind and body: because commonly we judge that all things stand to each other in respect to their actual relations in the same way as they are related in our consciousness. But, since one of those hyperbolical doubts adduced in the First Meditation went so far as to prevent me from being sure of this very fact (viz. that things are in their true nature exactly as we perceive them to be), so long as I supposed that I had no knowledge of the author of my being, all that I have said about God and about truth in the Third, Fourth and Fifth Meditations serves to further the conclusion as to the real distinction between *mind* and *body,* which is finally completed in Meditation VI.

My opponent, however, says, *I apprehend the triangle inscribed in the semicircle without knowing that the square on its base is equal to the squares on the sides.* True, that triangle may indeed be apprehended although there is no thought of the ratio prevailing between the squares on the base and sides; but we can never think that this ratio must be denied. It is quite otherwise in the case of the mind where, not only do we understand that it exists apart from the body, but also that all the attributes of body may be denied of it; for reciprocal exclusion of one another belongs to the nature of substances.

34

THE DEPENDENCE
OF CONSCIOUSNESS
ON THE BRAIN

T. H. Huxley

*T. H. Huxley (1825-1895) was an English biologist who is best known to history for
his effective defence of the Darwinian theory of evolution.*

But there remains a doctrine to which Descartes attached great weight, so
that full acceptance of it became a sort of note of a thoroughgoing Cartesian,
but which, nevertheless, is so opposed to ordinary prepossessions that it attained more general notoriety, and gave rise to more discussion, than almost
any other Cartesian hypothesis. It is the doctrine that brute animals are mere
machines or automata, devoid not only of reason, but of any kind of consciousness. . . .

Descartes' line of argument is perfectly clear. He starts from reflex
action in man, from the unquestionable fact that, in ourselves, co-ordinate,
purposive, actions may take place, without the intervention of consciousness
or volition, or even contrary to the latter. As actions of a certain degree of
complexity are brought about by mere mechanism, why may not actions of
still greater complexity be the result of a more refined mechanism? What
proof is there that brutes are other than a superior race of marionettes, which
eat without pleasure, cry without pain, desire nothing, know nothing, and
only simulate intelligence as a bee simulates a mathematician?

The Port Royalists adopted the hypothesis that brutes are machines, and
are said to have carried its practical applications so far as to treat domestic
animals with neglect, if not with actual cruelty. As late as the middle of the
eighteenth century, the problem was discussed very fully and ably by Bouil-
lier, in his "Essai philosophique sur l'Ame des Bêtes," while Condillac deals
with it in his "Traité des Animaux;" but since then it has received little attention. Nevertheless, modern research has brought to light a great multitude

From the essay, "On the Hypothesis That Animals Are Automata and Its History,"
first published in 1874 and reprinted in the collection of Huxley's essays, *Methods
and Results*.

of facts, which not only show that Descartes' view is defensible, but render it far more defensible than it was in his day.

It must be premised, that it is wholly impossible absolutely to prove the presence or absence of consciousness in anything but one's own brain, though, by analogy, we are justified in assuming its existence in other men. Now if, by some accident, a man's spinal cord is divided, his limbs are paralyzed, so far as his volition is concerned, below the point of injury; and he is incapable of experiencing all those states of consciousness which, in his uninjured state, would be excited by irritation of those nerves which come off below the injury. If the spinal cord is divided in the middle of the back, for example, the skin of the feet may be cut, or pinched, or burned, or wetted with vitriol, without any sensation of touch, or of pain, arising in consciousness. So far as the man is concerned, therefore, the part of the central nervous system which lies beyond the injury is cut off from consciousness. It must indeed be admitted, that, if any one think fit to maintain that the spinal cord below the injury is conscious, but that it is cut off from any means of making its consciousness known to the other consciousness in the brain, there is no means of driving him from his position by logic. But assuredly there is no way of proving it, and in the matter of consciousness, if in anything, we may hold by the rule, "De non apparentibus et de non existentibus eadem est ratio." However near the brain the spinal cord is injured, consciousness remains intact, except that the irritation of parts below the injury is no longer represented by sensation. On the other hand, pressure upon the anterior division of the brain, or extensive injuries to it, abolish consciousness. Hence, it is a highly probable conclusion, that consciousness in man depends upon the integrity of the anterior division of the brain, while the middle and hinder divisions of the brain,[1] and the rest of the nervous centres, have nothing to do with it. And it is further highly probable, that what is true for man is true for other vertebrated animals.

We may assume, then, that in a living vertebrated animal, any segment of the cerebro-spinal axis (or spinal cord and brain) separated from that anterior division of the brain which is the organ of consciousness, is as completely incapable of giving rise to consciousness as we know it to be incapable of carrying out volitions. Nevertheless, this separated segment of the spinal cord is not passive and inert. On the contrary, it is the seat of extremely remarkable powers. In our imaginary case of injury, the man would, as we have seen, be devoid of sensation in his legs, and would not have the least power of moving them. But, if the soles of his feet were tickled, the legs would be drawn up just as vigorously as they would have been before the injury. We know exactly what happens when the soles of the feet are tickled; a molecular change takes place in the sensory nerves of the skin, and

---

[1] Not to be confounded with the anterior middle and hinder parts of the hemisphere of the cerebrum.

is propagated along them and through the posterior roots of the spinal nerves, which are constituted by them, to the grey matter of the spinal cord. Through that grey matter the molecular motion is reflected into the anterior roots of the same nerves, constituted by the filaments which supply the muscles of the legs, and, travelling along these motor filaments, reaches the muscles, which at once contract, and cause the limbs to be drawn up.

In order to move the legs in this way, a definite co-ordination of muscular contractions is necessary; the muscles must contract in a certain order and with duly proportioned force; and moreover, as the feet are drawn away from the source of irritation, it may be said that the action has a final cause, or is purposive.

Thus it follows, that the grey matter of the segment of the man's spinal cord, though it is devoid of consciousness, nevertheless responds to a simple stimulus by giving rise to a complex set of muscular contractions, co-ordinated towards a definite end, and serving an obvious purpose.

If the spinal cord of a frog is cut across, so as to provide us with a segment separated from the brain, we shall have a subject parallel to the injured man, on which experiments can be made without remorse; as we have a right to conclude that a frog's spinal cord is not likely to be conscious, when a man's is not.

Now the frog behaves just as the man did. The legs are utterly paralysed, so far as voluntary movement is concerned; but they are vigorously drawn up to the body when any irritant is applied to the foot. But let us study our frog a little farther. Touch the skin of the side of the body with a little acetic acid, which gives rise to all the signs of great pain in an uninjured frog. In this case, there can be no pain, because the application is made to a part of the skin supplied with nerves which come off the cord below the point of section; nevertheless, the frog lifts up the limb of the same side, and applies the foot to rub off the acetic acid, and, what is still more remarkable, if the limb be held so that the frog cannot use it, it will, by and by, move the limb of the other side, turn it across the body, and use it for the same rubbing process. It is impossible that the frog, if it were in its entirety and could reason, should perform actions more purposive than these: and yet we have most complete assurance that, in this case, the frog is not acting from purpose, has no consciousness, and is a mere insensible machine.

But now suppose that, instead of making a section of the cord in the middle of the body, it has been made in such a manner as to separate the hindermost division of the brain from the rest of the organ, and suppose the foremost two-thirds of the brain entirely taken away. The frog is then absolutely devoid of any spontaneity; it sits upright in the attitude which a frog habitually assumes; and it will not stir unless it is touched; but it differs from the frog which I have just described in this, that, if it be thrown into the water, it begins to swim, and swims just as well as the perfect frog does. But swimming requires the combination and successive co-ordination of a great number of muscular actions. And we are forced to conclude, that the impression made upon the sensory nerves of the skin of the frog by the contact with the water into which it is thrown, causes the transmission to the central nervous apparatus of an impulse which sets going a certain machinery by which all the muscles of swimming are brought into play in due co-ordination. If the frog be stimulated by some irritating body, it jumps or walks as well as the complete frog can do. The simple sensory impression, acting through the machinery of the cord, gives rise to these complex combined movements.

It is possible to go a step farther. Suppose that only the anterior division of the brain — so much of it as lies in front of the "optic lobes" — is removed. If that operation is performed quickly and skilfully, the frog may be kept in a state of full bodily vigour for months, or it may be for years; but it will sit unmoved. It sees nothing; it hears nothing. It will starve sooner than feed itself, although food put into its mouth is swallowed. On irritation, it jumps or walks; if thrown into the water it swims. If it be put on the hand, it sits there, crouched, perfectly quiet, and would sit there for ever. If the hand be inclined very gently and slowly, so that the frog would naturally tend to slip off, the creature's fore paws are shifted on to the edge of the hand, until he can just prevent himself from falling. If the turning of the hand be slowly continued, he mounts up with great care and deliberation, putting first one leg forward and then another, until he balances himself with perfect precision upon the edge; and if the turning of the hand is continued, he goes through the needful set of muscular operations, until he comes to be seated in security, upon the back of the hand. The doing of all this requires a delicacy of coordination, and a precision of adjustment of the muscular apparatus of the body, which are only comparable to those of a rope-dancer. To the ordinary influences of light, the frog, deprived of its cerebral hemispheres, appears to be blind. Nevertheless, if the animal be put upon a table, with a book at some little distance between it and the light, and the skin of the hinder parts of its body is then irritated, it will jump forward, avoiding the book by passing to the right or left of it. Therefore, although the frog appears to have no sensation of light, visible objects act through its brain upon the motor mechanism of its body.

It is obvious, that had Descartes been acquainted with these remarkable results of modern research, they would have furnished him with far more powerful arguments than he possessed in favour of his view of the automatism of brutes. The habits of a frog, leading its natural life, involve such simple adaptations to surrounding conditions, that the machinery which is competent to do so much without the intervention of consciousness, might well do all. And this argument is vastly strengthened by what has been learned in recent times of the marvellously complex operations which are performed mechanically, and to all appearance without consciousness, by men, when, in consequence of injury or disease, they are reduced to a condition more or less comparable to that of a frog, in which the anterior part of the brain has been removed. A case has recently been publishd by an eminent French physician, Dr. Mesnet, which illustrates this condition so remarkably, that I make no apology for dwelling upon it at considerable length.[2]

A sergeant of the French army, F——, twenty-seven years of age, was wounded during the battle of Bazeilles, by a ball which fractured his left parietal bone. He ran his bayonet through the Prussian soldier who wounded him, but almost immediately his right arm became paralysed; after walking about two hundred yards, his right leg became similarly affected, and he lost his senses. When he recovered them, three weeks afterwards, in hospital at Mayence, the right half of the body was completely paralysed, and remained in this condition for a year. At present, the only trace of the paralysis which remains is a slight weakness of the right half of the body. Three or four months after the wound was inflicted, periodical disturbances of the functions of the brain made their appearance, and have continued ever since. The disturbances last from fifteen to thirty hours; the intervals at which they occur being from fifteen to thirty days.

For four years, therefore, the life of this man has been divided into alternating phases — short abnormal states intervening between long normal states.

In the periods of normal life, the ex-sergeant's health is perfect; he is intelligent and kindly, and performs, satisfactorily, the duties of a hospital attendant. The commencement of the abnormal state is ushered in by uneasiness and a sense of weight about the forehead, which the patient compares to the constriction of a circle of iron; and, after its termination, he complains, for some hours, of dulness and heaviness of the head. But the transition from the normal to the abnormal state takes place in a few minutes, without convulsions or cries, and without anything to indicate the change to a bystander. His movements remain free and his expression calm, except for a contraction of the brow, an incessant movement of the eyeballs, and a chewing motion of the jaws. The eyes are wide open, and their pupils dilated. If the man happens to be in a place to which he is accustomed, he walks about as usual; but, if he is in a new place, or if obstacles are intentionally placed in his way, he stumbles gently against them, stops, and then, feeling over the objects with his hands, passes on one side of them. He offers no resistance to any change of direction which may be impressed upon him, or to the forcible acceleration or retardation of his movements. He eats, drinks, smokes, walks about, dresses and undresses himself, rises and goes to bed at the accustomed hours. Nevertheless, pins may be run into his body, or strong electric shocks sent through it, without causing the least indication of pain; no odorous substance, pleasant or unpleasant, makes the least impression; he eats and drinks with avidity whatever is offered, and takes asafœtida, or

---

[2] "De l'Automatisme de la Mémoire et du Souvenir, dans le Somnambulisme pathologique." Par le Dr. E. Mesnet, Médecin de l'Hôpital Saint-Antoine. *L'Union Médicale,* Juillet 21 et 23, 1874. My attention was first called to a summary of this remarkable case, which appeared in the *Journal des Débats* for the 7th of August, 1874, by my friend General Strachey, F.R.S.

vinegar, or quinine, as readily as water; no noise affects him; and light in-fluences him only under certain conditions. Dr. Mesnet remarks, that the sense of touch alone seems to persist, and indeed to be more acute and delicate than in the normal state: and it is by means of the nerves of touch, almost exclusively, that his organism is brought into relation with the external world. Here a difficulty arises. It is clear from the facts detailed, that the nervous apparatus by which, in the normal state, sensations of touch are excited, is that by which external influences determine the movements of the body, in the abnormal state. But does the state of consciousness, which we term a tactile sensation, accompany the operation of this nervous apparatus in the abnormal state? or is consciousness utterly absent, the man being reduced to an insensible mechanism?

It is impossible to obtain direct evidence in favour of the one conclusion or the other; all that can be said is, that the case of the frog shows that the man may be devoid of any kind of consciousness.

. . .

The ex-sergeant has a good voice, and had, at one time, been employed as a singer at a café. In one of his abnormal states he was observed to begin humming a tune. He then went to his room, dressed himself carefully, and took up some parts of a periodical novel, which lay on his bed, as if he were trying to find something. Dr. Mesnet, suspecting that he was seeking his music, made up one of these into a roll and put it into his hand. He appeared satisfied, took his cane and went down stairs to the door. He Dr. Mesnet turned him round, and he walked quite contentedly, in the opposite direction, towards the room of the concierge. The light of the sun shining through a window now happened to fall upon him, and seemed to suggest the footlights of the stage on which he was accustomed to make his appearance. He stopped, opened his roll of imaginary music, put himself into the attitude of a singer, and sang, with perfect execution, three songs, one after the other. After which he wiped his face with his handkerchief and drank, without a grimace, a tumbler of strong vinegar and water which was put into his hand.

An experiment which may be performed upon the frog deprived of the fore part of its brain, well known as Göltz's "Quak-versuch," affords a parallel to this performance. If the skin of a certain part of the back of such a frog is gently stroked with the finger, it immediately croaks. It never croaks unless it is so stroked, and the croak always follows the stroke, just as the sound of a repeater follows the touching of the spring. In the frog, this "song" is innate — so to speak *à priori* — and depends upon a mechanism in the brain gov-erning the vocal apparatus, which is set at work by the molecular change set up in the sensory nerves of the skin of the back by the contact of a foreign body.

In man there is also a vocal mechanism, and the cry of an infant is in the same sense innate and *à priori,* inasmuch as it depends on an organic relation between its sensory nerves and the nervous mechanism which governs the vocal apparatus. Learning to speak, and learning to sing, are processes by which the vocal mechanism is set to new tunes. A song which has been learned has its molecular equivalent, which potentially represents it in the brain, just as a musical box, wound up, potentially represents an overture. Touch the stop and the overture begins; send a molecular impulse along the proper afferent nerve and the singer begins his song.

Again, the manner in which the frog, though apparently insensible to light, is yet, under some circumstances, influenced by visual images, finds a singular parallel in the case of the ex-sergeant.

Sitting at a table, in one of his abnormal states, he took up a pen, felt for paper and ink, and began to write a letter to his general, in which he recommended himself for a medal, on account of his good conduct and courage. It occurred to Dr. Mesnet to ascertain experimentally how far vision was concerned in this act of writing. He therefore interposed a screen between the man's eyes and his hands; under these circumstances he went on writing for a short time, but the words became illegible, and he finally stopped, without manifesting any discontent. On the withdrawal of the screen he began to write again where he had left off. The substitution of water for ink in the inkstand had a similar result. He stopped, looked at his pen, wiped it on his coat, dipped it in the water, and began again with the same effect.

On one occasion, he began to write upon the topmost of ten superimposed sheets of paper. After he had written a line or two, this sheet was suddenly drawn away. There was a slight expression of surprise, but he continued his letter on the second sheet exactly as if it had been the first. This operation was repeated five times, so that the fifth sheet contained nothing but the writer's signature at the bottom of the page. Nevertheless, when the signature was finished, his eyes turned to the top of the blank sheet, and he went through the form of reading over what he had written, a movement of the lips accompanying each word; moreover, with his pen, he put in such corrections as were needed, in that part of the blank page which corresponded with the position of the words which required correction, in the sheets which had been taken away. If the five sheets had been transparent, therefore, they would, when superposed, have formed a properly written and corrected letter.

Immediately after he had written his letter, F—— got up, walked down to the garden, made himself a cigarette, lighted and smoked it. He was about to prepare another, but sought in vain for his tobacco-pouch, which had been purposely taken away. The pouch was now thrust before his eyes and put under his nose, but he neither saw nor smelt it; yet, when it was placed in his hand, he at once seized it, made a fresh cigarette, and ignited a match to light the latter. The match was blown out, and another lighted match placed close before his eyes, but he made no attempt to take it; and, if his cigarette was lighted for him, he made no attempt to smoke. All this time the eyes were vacant, and neither winked, nor exhibited any contraction of the pupils. From these and other experiments, Dr. Mesnet draws the conclusion that his patient sees some things and not others; that the sense of sight is accessible to all things which are brought into relation with him by the sense of touch, and, on the contrary, insensible to things which lie outside this relation. He sees the match he holds and does not see any other.

Just so the frog "sees" the book which is in the way of his jump, at the same time that isolated visual impressions take no effect upon him.

As I have pointed out, it is impossible to prove that F—— is absolutely unconscious in his abnormal state, but it is no less impossible to prove the contrary; and the case of the frog goes a long way to justify the assumption that, in the abnormal state, the man is a mere insensible machine.

If such facts as these had come under the knowledge of Descartes, would they not have formed an apt commentary upon that remarkable passage in the "Traité de l'Homme," which I have quoted elsewhere, but which is worth repetition? —

> "All the functions which I have attributed to this machine (the body), as the digestion of food, the pulsation of the heart and of the arteries; the nutrition and the growth of the limbs; respiration, wakefulness, and sleep; the reception of light, sounds, odours, flavours, heat, and such like qualities, in the organs of the external senses; the impression of the ideas of these in the organ of common sensation and in the imagination; the retention of the impression of these ideas on the memory; the internal movements of the appetites and the passions; and lastly the external movements of all the limbs, which follow so aptly, as well the action of the objects which are presented to the senses, as the impressions which meet in the memory, that they imitate as nearly as possible those of a real man; I desire, I say, that you should consider that these functions in the machine naturally proceed from the mere arrangement of its organs, neither more nor less than do the movements of a clock, or other automaton, from that of its weights and its wheels; so that, so far as these are concerned, it is not necessary to conceive any other vegetative or sensitive soul, nor any other principle of motion or of life, than the blood and the spirits agitated by the fire which burns continually in the heart, and which is no wise essentially different from all the fires which exist in inanimate bodies."

And would Descartes not have been justified in asking why we need deny that animals are machines, when men, in a state of unconsciousness, perform, mechanically, actions as complicated and as seemingly rational as those of any animals?

But though I do not think that Descartes' hypothesis can be positively refuted, I am not disposed to accept it. The doctrine of continuity is too well established for it to be permissible to me to suppose that any complex natural phenomenon comes into existence suddenly, and without being preceded by simpler modifications; and very strong arguments would be needed to prove that such complex phenomena as those of consciousness, first make their appearance in man. We know, that, in the individual man, consciousness grows from a dim glimmer to its full light, whether we consider the infant advancing in years, or the adult emerging from slumber and swoon. We know, further, that the lower animals possess, though less developed, that part of the brain which we have every reason to believe to be the organ of consciousness in man; and as, in other cases, function and organ are proportional, so we have a right to conclude it is with the brain; and that the brutes, though they may not possess our intensity of consciousness, and though, from the absence of language, they can have no trains of thoughts, but only trains of feelings, yet have a consciousness which, more or less distinctly, foreshadows our own.

I confess that, in view of the struggle for existence which goes on in the animal world, and of the frightful quantity of pain with which it must be accompanied, I should be glad if the probabilities were in favour of Descartes' hypothesis; but, on the other hand, considering the terrible practical consequences to domestic animals which might ensue from any error on our part, it is as well to err on the right side, if we err at all, and deal with them as weaker brethren, who are bound, like the rest of us, to pay their toll for living, and suffer what is needful for the general good. As Hartley finely says, "We seem to be in the place of God to them;" and we may justly follow the precedents He sets in nature in our dealings with them.

But though we may see reason to disagree with Descartes' hypothesis that brutes are unconscious machines, it does not follow that he was wrong in regarding them as automata. They may be more or less conscious, sensitive, automata; and the view that they are such conscious machines is that which is implicitly, or explicitly, adopted by most persons. When we speak of the actions of the lower animals being guided by instinct and not by reason, what we really mean is that, though they feel as we do, yet their actions are the results of their physical organisation. We believe, in short, that they are machines, one part of which (the nervous system) not only sets the rest in motion, and co-ordinates its movements in relation with changes in surrounding bodies, but is provided with special apparatus, the function of which is the calling into existence of those states of consciousness which are termed sensations, emotions, and ideas. I believe that this generally accepted view is the best expression of the facts at present known.

It is experimentally demonstrable — any one who cares to run a pin into himself may perform a sufficient demonstration of the fact — that a mode of motion of the nervous system is the immediate antecedent of a state of consciousness. All but the adherents of "Occasionalism," or of the doctrine of "Pre-established Harmony" (if any such now exist), must admit that we have as much reason for regarding the mode of motion of the nervous system as the cause of the state of consciousness, as we have for regarding any event as the cause of another. How the one phenomenon causes the other we know, as much or as little, as in any other case of causation; but we have as much right to believe that the sensation is an effect of the molecular change, as we have to believe that motion is an effect of impact; and there is as much propriety in saying that the brain evolves sensation, as there is in saying that an iron rod, when hammered, evolves heat.

As I have endeavoured to show, we are justified in supposing that something analogous to what happens in ourselves takes place in the brutes, and that the affections of their sensory nerves give rise to molecular changes in the brain, which again give rise to, or evolve, the corresponding states of consciousness. Nor can there be any reasonable doubt that the emotion of brutes, and such ideas as they possess, are similarly dependent upon molecular brain changes. Each sensory impression leaves behind a record in the structure of the brain — an "ideagenous" molecule, so to speak, which is competent, under certain conditions, to reproduce, in a fainter condition, the state of consciousness which corresponds with that sensory impression; and it is these "ideagenous molecules" which are the physical basis of memory.

It may be assumed, then, that molecular changes in the brain are the causes of all the states of consciousness of brutes. Is there any evidence that these states of consciousness may, conversely, cause those molecular changes which give rise to muscular motion? I see no such evidence. The frog walks, hops, swims, and goes through his gymnastic performances quite as well without consciousness, and consequently without volition, as with it; and, if a frog, in his natural state, possesses anything corresponding with what we call volition, there is no reason to think that it is anything but a concomitant of the molecular changes in the brain which form part of the series involved in the production of motion.

The consciousness of brutes would appear to be related to the mechanism of their body simply as a collateral product of its working, and to be as completely without any power of modifying that working as the steam-whistle which accompanies the work of a locomotive engine is without influence upon its machinery. Their volition, if they have any, is an emotion indicative of physical changes, not a cause of such changes.

This conception of the relations of states of consciousness with molecular changes in the brain . . . does not prevent us from ascribing free will to brutes. For an agent is free when there is nothing to prevent him from doing that which he desires to do. If a greyhound chases a hare, he is a free agent, because his action is in entire accordance with his strong desire to catch the hare; while so long as he is held back by the leash he is not free, being prevented by external force from following his inclination. And the ascription of freedom to the greyhound under the former circumstances is by no means inconsistent with the other aspect of the facts of the case — that he is a machine impelled to the chase, and caused, at the same time, to have the desire to catch the game by the impression which the rays of light proceeding from the hare make upon his eyes, and through them upon his brain.

Much ingenious argument has at various times been bestowed upon the question: How is it possible to imagine that volition, which is a state of consciousness, and, as such, has not the slightest community of nature with matter in motion, can act upon the moving matter of which the body is composed, as it is assumed to do in voluntary acts? But if, as is here suggested, the voluntary acts of brutes — or, in other words, the acts which they desire to perform — are as purely mechanical as the rest of their actions, and are simply accompanied by the state of consciousness called volition, the inquiry, so far as they are concerned, becomes superfluous. Their volitions do not enter into the chain of causation of their actions at all.

The hypothesis that brutes are conscious automata is perfectly consistent with any view that may be held respecting the often discussed and curious question whether they have souls or not; and, if they have souls, whether those souls are immortal or not. It is obviously harmonious with the most literal adherence to the text of Scripture concerning "the beast that perisheth"; but it is not inconsistent with the amiable conviction ascribed by Pope to his "untutored savage," that when he passes to the happy hunting-grounds in the sky, "his faithful dog shall bear him company." If the brutes have consciousness and no souls, then it is clear that, in them, consciousness is a direct function of material changes; while, if they possess immaterial subjects of consciousness, or souls, then, as consciousness is brought into existence only as the consequence of molecular motion of the brain, it follows that it is an indirect product of material changes. The soul stands related to the body as the bell of a clock to the works, and consciousness answers to the sound which the bell gives out when it is struck.

Thus far I have strictly confined myself to the problem with which I proposed to deal at starting — the automatism of brutes. The question is, I believe, a perfectly open one, and I feel happy in running no risk of either Papal or Presbyterian condemnation for the views which I have ventured to put forward. And there are so very few interesting questions which one is, at present, allowed to think out scientifically — to go as far as reason leads, and stop where evidence comes to an end — without speedily being deafened by the tattoo of "the drum ecclesiastic" — that I have luxuriated in my rare freedom, and would now willingly bring this disquisition to an end if I could hope that other people would go no farther. Unfortunately, past experience debars me from entertaining any such hope, even if

> ". . . . that drum's discordant sound
> Parading round and round and round,"

were not, at present, as audible to me as it was to the mild poet who ventured to express his hatred of drums in general, in that well-known couplet.

It will be said, that I mean that the conclusions deduced from the study of the brutes are applicable to man, and that the logical consequences of such application are fatalism, materialism, and atheism — whereupon the drums will beat the *pas de charge.*

One does not do battle with drummers; but I venture to offer a few remarks for the calm consideration of thoughtful persons, untrammelled by foregone conclusions, unpledged to shore-up tottering dogmas, and anxious only to know the true bearings of the case.

It is quite true that, to the best of my judgment, the argumentation which applies to brutes holds equally good of men; and, therefore, that all states of consciousness in us, as in them, are immediately caused by molecular changes of the brain-substance. It seems to me that in men, as in brutes, there is no proof that any state of consciousness is the cause of change in the motion of the matter of the organism. If these positions are well based, it follows that our mental conditions are simply the symbols in consciousness of the changes which take place automatically in the organism; and that, to take an extreme illustration, the feeling we call volition is not the cause of a voluntary act, but the symbol of that state of the brain which is the immediate cause of that act. We are conscious automata, endowed with free will in the only intelligible sense of that much-abused term — inasmuch as in many respects we are able to do as we like — but none the less parts of the great series of causes and effects which, in unbroken continuity, composes that which is, and has been, and shall be — the sum of existence.

As to the logical consequences of this conviction of mine, I may be permitted to remark that logical consequences are the scarecrows of fools and the beacons of wise men. The only question which any wise man can ask himself, and which any honest man will ask himself, is whether a doctrine is true or false. Consequences will take care of themselves; at most their importance can only justify us in testing with extra care the reasoning process from which they result.

So that if the view I have taken did really and logically lead to fatalism, materialism, and atheism, I should profess myself a fatalist, materialist, and atheist; and I should look upon those who, while they believed in my honesty of purpose and intellectual competency, should raise a hue and cry against me, as people who by their own admission preferred lying to truth, and whose opinions therefore were unworthy of the smallest attention.

But, as I have endeavoured to explain on other occasions, I really have no claim to rank myself among fatalistic, materialistic, or atheistic philosophers. Not among fatalists, for I take the conception of necessity to have a logical, and not a physical foundation; not among materialists, for I am utterly incapable of conceiving the existence of matter if there is no mind in which to picture that existence; not among atheists, for the problem of the ultimate cause of existence is one which seems to me to be hopelessly out of reach of my poor powers. Of all the senseless babble I have ever had occasion to read, the demonstrations of these philosophers who undertake to tell us all about the nature of God would be the worst, if they were not surpassed by the still greater absurdities of the philosophers who try to prove that there is no God.

35

CONSCIOUS STATES
ARE
BRAIN PROCESSES

U. T. Place

The thesis that consciousness is a process in the brain is put forward as a reasonable scientific hypothesis, not to be dismissed on logical grounds alone. The conditions under which two sets of observations are treated as observations of the same process, rather than as observations of two independent correlated processes, are discussed. It is suggested that we can identify consciousness with a given pattern of brain activity, if we can explain the subject's introspective observations by reference to the brain processes with which they are correlated. It is argued that the problem of providing a physiological explanation of introspective observations is made to seem more difficult than it really is by the 'phenomenological fallacy', the mistaken idea that descriptions of the appearances of things are descriptions of the actual state of affairs in a mysterious internal environment.

I. Introduction

The view that there exists a separate class of events, mental events, which cannot be described in terms of the concepts employed by the physical sciences no longer commands the universal and unquestioning acceptance amongst philosophers and psychologists which it once did. Modern physicalism, however, unlike the materialism of the seventeenth and eighteenth centuries, is behaviouristic. Consciousness on this view is either a special type of behaviour, 'sampling' or 'running-back-and-forth' behaviour as Tolman (1932, p. 206) has it, or a disposition to behave in a certain way, an itch for example being a temporary propensity to scratch. In the case of cognitive concepts like 'knowing', 'believing', 'understanding', 'remembering' and volitional con-

The whole of the article, "Is Consciousness a Brain Process?" first published in the *British Journal of Psychology*, February, 1956. Reprinted by permission of the author and editor.

cepts like 'wanting' and 'intending', there can be little doubt, I think, that an analysis in terms of dispositions to behave (Wittgenstein, 1953; Ryle, 1949) is fundamentally sound. On the other hand, there would seem to be an intractable residue of concepts clustering around the notions of consciousness, experience, sensation and mental imagery, where some sort of inner process story is unavoidable (Place, 1954). It is possible, of course, that a satisfactory behaviouristic account of this conceptual residuum will ultimately be found. For our present purposes, however, I shall assume that this cannot be done and that statements about pains and twinges, about how things look, sound and feel, about things dreamed of or pictured in the mind's eye, are statements referring to events and processes which are in some sense private or internal to the individual of whom they are predicated. The question I wish to raise is whether in making this assumption we are inevitably committed to a dualist position in which sensations and mental images form a separate category of processes over and above the physical and physiological processes with which they are known to be correlated. I shall argue that an acceptance of inner processes does not entail dualism and that the thesis that consciousness is a process in the brain cannot be dismissed on logical grounds.

II. THE 'IS' OF DEFINITION AND THE 'IS' OF COMPOSITION

I want to stress from the outset that in defending the thesis that consciousness is a process in the brain, I am not trying to argue that when we describe our dreams, fantasies and sensations we are talking about processes in our brains. That is, I am not claiming that statements about sensations and mental images are reducible to or analysable into statements about brain processes, in the way in which 'cognition statements' are analysable into statements about behaviour. To say that statements about consciousness are statements about brain processes is manifestly false. This is shown (*a*) by the fact that you can describe your sensations and mental imagery without knowing anything about your brain processes or even that such things exist, (*b*) by the fact that statements about one's consciousness and statements about one's brain processes are verified in entirely different ways and (*c*) by the fact that there is nothing self-contradictory about the statement 'X has a pain but there is nothing going on in his brain'. What I do want to assert, however, is that the statement 'consciousness is a process in the brain', although not necessarily true, is not necessarily false. 'Consciousness is a process in the brain', on my view is neither self-contradictory nor self-evident; it is a reasonable scientific hypothesis, in the way that the statement 'lightning is a motion of electric charges' is a reasonable scientific hypothesis.

The all but universally accepted view that an assertion of identity between consciousness and brain processes can be ruled out on logical grounds alone, derives, I suspect, from a failure to distinguish between what we may call the 'is' of definition and the 'is' of composition. The distinction I have in mind here is the difference between the function of the word 'is' in statements like 'a square is an equilateral rectangle', 'red is a colour', 'to understand an instruction is to be able to act appropriately under the appropriate circumstances', and its function in statements like 'his table is an old packing case', 'her hat is a bundle of straw tied together with a string', 'a cloud is a mass of water droplets or other particles in suspension'. These two types of 'is' statement have one thing in common. In both cases it makes sense to add the qualification 'and nothing else'. In this they differ from those statements in which the 'is' is an 'is' of predication; the statements 'Toby is 80 years old and nothing else', 'her hat is red and nothing else' or 'giraffes are tall and nothing else', for example, are nonsense. This logical feature may be described by saying that in both cases both the grammatical subject and the grammatical predicate are expressions which provide an adequate characterization of the state of affairs to which they both refer.

In another respect, however, the two groups of statements are strikingly different. Statements like 'a square is an equilateral rectangle' are necessary statements which are true by definition. Statements like 'his table is an old packing case', on the other hand, are contingent statements which have to be verified by observation. In the case of statements like 'a square is an equilateral rectangle' or 'red is a colour', there is a relationship between the meaning of the expression forming the grammatical predicate and the meaning of the expression forming the grammatical subject, such that whenever the subject expression is applicable the predicate must also be applicable. If you can describe something as red then you must also be able to describe it as coloured. In the case of statements like 'his table is an old packing case', on the other hand, there is no such relationship between the meanings of the expressions 'his table' and 'old packing case'; it merely so happens that in this case both expressions are applicable to and at the same time provide an adequate characterization of the same object. Those who contend that the statement 'consciousness is a brain process' is logically untenable base their claim, I suspect, on the mistaken assumption that if the meanings of two statements or expressions are quite unconnected, they cannot both provide an adequate characterization of the same object or state of affairs: if something is a state of consciousness, it cannot be a brain process, since there is nothing self-contradictory in supposing that someone feels a pain when there is nothing happening inside his skull. By the same token we might be led to conclude that a table cannot be an old packing case, since there is nothing self-contradictory in supposing that someone has a table, but is not in possession of an old packing case.

III. The Logical Independence of Expressions and the Ontological Independence of Entities

There is, of course, an important difference between the table/packing case and the consciousness/brain process in that the statement 'his table is an old packing case' is a particular proposition which refers only to one particular case, whereas the statement 'consciousness is a process in the brain' is a general or universal proposition applying to all states of consciousness whatever. It is fairly clear, I think, that if we lived in a world in which all tables without exception were packing cases, the concepts of 'table' and 'packing case' in our language would not have their present logically independent status. In such a world a table would be a species of packing case in much the same way that red is a species of colour. It seems to be a rule of language that whenever a given variety of object or state of affairs has two characteristics or sets of characteristics, one of which is unique to the variety of object or state of affairs in question, the expression used to refer to the characteristic or set of characteristics which defines the variety of object or state of affairs in question will always entail the expression used to refer to the other characteristic or set of characteristics. If this rule admitted of no exception it would follow that any expression which is logically independent of another expression which uniquely characterizes a given variety of object or state of affairs, must refer to a characteristic or set of characteristics which is not normally or necessarily associated with the object or state of affairs in question. It is because this rule applies almost universally, I suggest, that we are normally justified in arguing from the logical independence of two expressions to the ontological independence of the states of affairs to which they refer. This would explain both the undoubted force of the argument that consciousness and brain processes must be independent entities because the expressions used to refer to them are logically independent and, in general, the curious phenomenon whereby questions about the furniture of the universe are often fought and not infrequently decided merely on a point of logic.

The argument from the logical independence of two expressions to the ontological independence of the entities to which they refer breaks down in the case of brain processes and consciousness, I believe, because this is one of a relatively small number of cases where the rule stated above does not apply. These exceptions are to be found, I suggest, in those cases where the operations which have to be performed in order to verify the presence of the two sets of characteristics inhering in the subject or state of affairs in question can seldom if ever be performed simultaneously. A good example here is the case of the cloud and the mass of droplets or other particles in suspension. A cloud is a large semi-transparent mass with a fleecy texture suspended in the atmosphere whose shape is subject to continual and kaleidoscopic change. When observed at close quarters, however, it is found to consist of a mass of tiny particles, usually water droplets, in continuous motion. On the basis of this second observation we conclude that a cloud is a mass of tiny particles and nothing else. But there is no logical connexion in our language between a cloud and a mass of tiny particles; there is nothing self-contradictory in talking about a cloud which is not composed of tiny particles in suspension. There is no contradiction involved in supposing that clouds consist of a dense mass of fibrous tissue; indeed, such a consistency seems to be implied by many of the functions performed by clouds in fairy stories and mythology. It is clear from this that the terms 'cloud' and 'mass of tiny particles in suspension' mean quite different things. Yet we do not conclude from this that there must be two things, the mass of particles in suspension and the cloud. The reason for this, I suggest, is that although the characteristics of being a cloud and being a mass of tiny particles in suspension are invariably associated, we never make the observations necessary to verify the statement 'that is a cloud' and those necessary to verify the statement 'this is a mass of tiny particles in suspension' at one and the same time. We can observe the micro-structure of a cloud only when we are enveloped by it, a condition which effectively prevents us from observing those characteristics which from a distance lead us to describe it as a cloud. Indeed, so disparate are these two experiences that we use different words to describe them. That which is a cloud when we observe it from a distance becomes a fog or mist when we are enveloped by it.

IV. When Are Two Sets of Observations Observations of the Same Event?

The example of the cloud and the mass of tiny particles in suspension was chosen because it is one of the few cases of a general proposition involving what I have called the 'is' of composition which does not involve us in scientific technicalities. It is useful because it brings out the connexion between the ordinary everyday cases of the 'is' of composition like the table/packing case example and the more technical cases like 'lightning is a motion of electric charges' where the analogy with the consciousness/brain process case is most marked. The limitation of the cloud/tiny particles in suspension case is that it does not bring out sufficiently clearly the crucial problem of how the identity of the states of affairs referred to by the two expressions is established. In the cloud case the fact that something is a cloud and the fact that something is a mass of tiny particles in suspension are both verified by the normal processes of visual observation. It is arguable, moreover, that the identity of the entities referred to by the two expressions is established by the continuity between the two sets of observations as the observer moves towards or away from the cloud. In the case of brain processes and consciousness there is no such continuity between the two sets of observations involved. A closer introspective scrutiny will never reveal the passage of nerve impulses over a thousand synapses in the way that a closer scrutiny of a cloud will reveal a mass of tiny particles in suspension. The operations required to verify statements about consciousness and statements about brain processes are fundamentally different.

To find a parallel for this feature we must examine other cases where an identity is asserted between something whose occurrence is verified by the ordinary processes of observation and something whose occurrence is established by special scientific procedures. For this purpose I have chosen the case where we say that lightning is a motion of electric charges. As in the case of consciousness, however closely we scrutinize the lightning we shall never be able to observe the electric charges, and just as the operations for determining the nature of one's state of consciousness are radically different from those involved in determining the nature of one's brain processes, so the operations for determining the occurrence of lightning are radically different from those involved in determining the occurrence of a motion of electric charges. What is it, therefore, that leads us to say that the two sets of observations are observations of the same event? It cannot be merely the fact that the two sets of observations are systematically correlated such that whenever there is lightning there is always a motion of electric charges. There are innumerable cases of such correlations where we have no temptation to say that the two sets of observations are observations of the same event. There is a systematic correlation, for example, between the movement of the tides and the stages of the moon, but this does not lead us to say that records of tidal levels are records of the moon's stages or vice versa. We speak rather of a causal connexion between two independent events or processes.

The answer here seems to be that we treat the two sets of observations as observations of the same event, in those cases where the technical scientific observations set in the context of the appropriate body of scientific theory provide an immediate explanation of the observations made by the man in the street. Thus we conclude that lightning is nothing more than a motion of electric charges, because we know that a motion of electric charges through the atmosphere, such as occurs when lightning is reported, gives rise to the type of visual stimulation which would lead an observer to report a flash of lightning. In the moon/tide case, on the other hand, there is no such direct causal connexion between the stages of the moon and the observations made by the man who measures the height of the tide. The causal connexion is between the moon and the tides, not between the moon and the measurement of the tides.

V. The Physiological Explanation of Introspection and the Phenomenological Fallacy

If this account is correct, it should follow that in order to establish the identity of consciousness and certain processes in the brain, it would be necessary to show that the introspective observations reported by the subject can be accounted for in terms of processes which are known to have occurred in his brain. In the light of this suggestion it is extremely interesting to find that when a physiologist as distinct from a philosopher finds it difficult to see how consciousness could be a process in the brain, what worries him is not any supposed self-contradiction involved in such an assumption, but the apparent impossibility of accounting for the reports given by the subject of his conscious process in terms of the known properties of the central nervous system.

Sir Charles Sherrington has posed the problem as follows: 'The chain of events stretching from the sun's radiation entering the eye to, on the one hand, the contraction of the pupillary muscles, and on the other, to the electrical disturbances in the brain-cortex are all straightforward steps in a sequence of physical "causation", such as, thanks to science, are intelligible. But in the second serial chain there follows on, or attends, the stage of brain-cortex reaction an event or set of events quite inexplicable to us, which both as to themselves and as to the causal tie between them and what preceded them science does not help us; a set of events seemingly incommensurable with any of the events leading up to it. The self "sees" the sun; it senses a two-dimensional disc of brightness, located in the "sky", this last a field of lesser brightness, and overhead shaped as a rather flattened dome, coping the self and a hundred other visual things as well. Of hint that this is within the head there is none. Vision is saturated with this strange property called "projection", the unargued inference that what it sees is at a "distance" from the seeing "self". Enough has been said to stress that in the sequence of events a step is reached where a physical situation in the brain leads to a psychical, which however contains no hint of the brain or any other bodily part. . . . The supposition has to be, it would seem, two continuous series of events, one physico-chemical, the other psychical, and at times interaction between them' (Sherrington, 1947, pp. xx-xxi).

Just as the physiologist is not likely to be impressed by the philosopher's contention that there is some self-contradiction involved in supposing consciousness to be a brain process, so the philosopher is unlikely to be impressed by the considerations which lead Sherrington to conclude that there are two sets of events, one physico-chemical, the other psychical. Sherrington's argument for all its emotional appeal depends on a fairly simple logical mistake, which is unfortunately all too frequently made by psychologists and physiologists and not infrequently in the past by the philosophers themselves. This logical mistake, which I shall refer to as the 'phenomenological fallacy', is the mistake of supposing that when the subject describes his experience, when he describes how things look, sound, smell, taste or feel to him, he is describing the literal properties of objects and events on a peculiar sort of internal cinema or television screen, usually referred to in the modern psychological literature as the 'phenomenal field'. If we assume, for example, that when a subject reports a green after-image he is assserting the occurrence inside himself of an object which is literally green, it is clear that we have on our hands an entity for which there is no place in the world of physics. In the case of the green after-image there is no green object in the subject's environment corresponding to the description that he gives. Nor is there anything green in his brain; certainly there is nothing which could have emerged when he reported the appearance of the green after-image. Brain processes are not the sort of things to which colour concepts can be properly applied.

The phenomenological fallacy on which this argument is based depends on the mistaken assumption that because our ability to describe things in our environment depends on our consciousness of them, our descriptions of

desc thing
not consciousness

things are primarily descriptions of our conscious experience and only secondarily, indirectly and inferentially descriptions of the objects and events in our environments. It is assumed that because we recognize things in our environment by their look, sound, smell, taste and feel, we begin by describing their phenomenal properties, i.e. the properties of the looks, sounds, smells, tastes and feels which they produce in us, and infer their real properties from their phenomenal properties. In fact, the reverse is the case. We begin by learning to recognize the real properties of things in our environment. We learn to recognize them, of course, by their look, sound, smell, taste and feel; but this does not mean that we have to learn to describe the look, sound, smell, taste and feel of things before we can describe the things themselves. Indeed, it is only after we have learnt to describe the things in our environment that we can learn to describe our consciousness of them. We describe our conscious experience not in terms of the mythological 'phenomenal properties' which are supposed to inhere in the mythological 'objects' in the mythological 'phenomenal field', but by reference to the actual physical properties of the concrete physical objects, events and processes which normally, though not perhaps in the present instance, give rise to the sort of conscious experience which we are trying to describe. In other words when we describe the after-image as green, we are not saying that there is something, the after-image, which is green, we are saying that we are having the sort of experience which we normally have when, and which we have learnt to describe as looking at a green patch of light.

Once we rid ourselves of the phenomenological fallacy we realize that the problem of explaining introspective observations in terms of brain processes is far from insuperable. We realize that there is nothing that the introspecting subject says about his conscious experiences which is inconsistent with anything the physiologist might want to say about the brain processes which cause him to describe the environment and his consciousness of that environment in the way he does. When the subject describes his experience by saying that a light which is in fact stationary, appears to move, all the physiologist or physiological psychologist has to do in order to explain the subject's introspective observations, is to show that the brain process which is causing the subject to describe his experience in this way, is the sort of process which normally occurs when he is observing an actual moving object and which therefore normally causes him to report the movement of an object in his environment. Once the mechanism whereby the individual describes what is going on in his environment has been worked out, all that is required to explain the individual's capacity to make introspective observations is an explanation of his ability to discriminate between those cases where his normal habits of verbal description are appropriate to the stimulus situation and those cases where they are not and an explanation of how and why, in those cases where the appropriateness of his normal descriptive habits is in doubt, he learns to issue his ordinary descriptive protocols preceded by a qualificatory phrase like 'it appears', 'seems', 'looks', 'feels', etc.

36

MIND AS BEHAVIORAL DISPOSITION

Gilbert Ryle

Gilbert Ryle (1900-   ), one of the leaders of the postwar "Oxford School" of analytical philosophy, is Waynflete Professor of Metaphysical Philosophy at the University of Oxford and a long-time editor of Mind.

THE CARTESIAN THEORY

There is a doctrine about the nature and place of minds which is so prevalent among theorists and even among laymen that it deserves to be described as the official theory. Most philosophers, psychologists and religious teachers subscribe, with minor reservations, to its main articles and, although they admit certain theoretical difficulties in it, they tend to assume that these can be overcome without serious modifications being made to the architecture of the theory. It will be argued here that the central principles of the doctrine are unsound and conflict with the whole body of what we know about minds when we are not speculating about them.

The official doctrine, which hails chiefly from Descartes, is something like this. With the doubtful exceptions of idiots and infants in arms every human being has both a body and a mind. Some would prefer to say that every human being is both a body and a mind. His body and his mind are ordinarily harnessed together, but after the death of the body his mind may continue to exist and function.

Human bodies are in space and are subject to the mechanical laws which govern all other bodies in space. Bodily processes and states can be inspected by external observers. So a man's bodily life is as much a public affair as are the lives of animals and reptiles and even as the careers of trees, crystals and planets.

But minds are not in space, nor are their operations subject to mechani-

From Chapters I and II of *The Concept of Mind* (1949). Reprinted by permission of the publishers, the Hutchinson Publishing Group, Ltd., London, and Barnes & Noble, New York. Sub-headings added by the editors.

cal laws. The workings of one mind are not witnessable by other observers; its career is private. Only I can take direct cognisance of the states and processes of my own mind. A person therefore lives through two collateral histories, one consisting of what happens in and to his body, the other consisting of what happens in and to his mind. The first is public, the second private. The events in the first history are events in the physical world, those in the second are events in the mental world.

It has been disputed whether a person does or can directly monitor all or only some of the episodes of his own private history; but, according to the official doctrine, of at least some of these episodes he has direct and unchallengeable cognisance. In consciousness, self-consciousness and introspection he is directly and authentically apprised of the present states and operations of his mind. He may have great or small uncertainties about concurrent and adjacent episodes in the physical world, but he can have none about at least part of what is momentarily occupying his mind.

It is customary to express this bifurcation of his two lives and of his two worlds by saying that the things and events which belong to the physical world, including his own body, are external, while the workings of his own mind are internal. This antithesis of outer and inner is of course meant to be construed as a metaphor, since minds, not being in space, could not be described as being spatially inside anything else, or as having things going on spatially inside themselves. But relapses from this good intention are common and theorists are found speculating how stimuli, the physical sources of which are yards or miles outside a person's skin, can generate mental responses inside his skull, or how decisions framed inside his cranium can set going movements of his extremities.

Even when 'inner' and 'outer' are construed as metaphors, the problem how a person's mind and body influence one another is notoriously charged with theoretical difficulties. What the mind wills, the legs, arms and the tongue execute; what affects the ear and the eye has something to do with what the mind perceives; grimaces and smiles betray the mind's moods and bodily castigations lead, it is hoped, to moral improvement. But the actual transactions between the episodes of the private history and those of the public history remain mysterious, since by definition they can belong to neither series. They could not be reported among the happenings described in a person's autobiography of his inner life, but nor could they be reported among those described in some one else's biography of that person's overt career. They can be inspected neither by introspection nor by laboratory experiment. They are theoretical shuttlecocks which are forever being bandied from the physiologist back to the psychologist and from the psychologist back to the physiologist.

Underlying this partly metaphorical representation of the bifurcation of a person's two lives there is a seemingly more profound and philosophical assumption. It is assumed that there are two different kinds of existence or status. What exists or happens may have the status of physical existence, or it may have the status of mental existence. Somewhat as the faces of coins are either heads or tails, or somewhat as living creatures are either male or female, so, it is supposed, some existing is physical existing, other existing is mental existing. It is a necessary feature of what has physical existence that it is in space and time, it is a necessary feature of what has mental existence that it is in time but not in space. What has physical existence is composed of matter, or else is a function of matter; what has mental existence consists of consciousness, or else is a function of consciousness.

There is thus a polar opposition between mind and matter, an opposition which is often brought out as follows. Material objects are situated in a common field, known as 'space', and what happens to one body in one part of space is mechanically connected with what happens to other bodies in other parts of space. But mental happenings occur in insulated fields, known as 'minds', and there is, apart maybe from telepathy, no direct causal connection between what happens in one mind and what happens in another. Only through the medium of the public physical world can the mind of one person make a difference to the mind of another. The mind is its own place and in his inner life each of us lives the life of a ghostly Robinson Crusoe. People can see, hear and jolt one another's bodies, but they are irremediably blind and deaf to the workings of one another's minds and inoperative upon them.

What sort of knowledge can be secured of the workings of a mind? On the one side, according to the official theory, a person has direct knowledge of the best imaginable kind of the workings of his own mind. Mental states and processes are (or are normally) conscious states and processes, and the consciousness which irradiates them can engender no illusions and leaves the door open for no doubts. A person's present thinkings, feelings and willings, his perceivings, rememberings and imaginings are intrinsically 'phosphorescent'; their existence and their nature are inevitably betrayed to their owner. The inner life is a stream of consciousness of such a sort that it would be absurd to suggest that the mind whose life is that stream might be unaware of what is passing down it.

True, the evidence adduced recently by Freud seems to show that there exist channels tributary to this stream, which run hidden from their owner. People are actuated by impulses the existence of which they vigorously disavow; some of their thoughts differ from the thoughts which they acknowledge; and some of the actions which they think they will to perform they do not really will. They are thoroughly gulled by some of their own hypocrisies and they successfully ignore facts about their mental lives which on the official theory ought to be patent to them. Holders of the official theory tend, however, to maintain that anyhow in normal circumstances a person must be directly and authentically seized of the present state and workings of his own mind.

Besides being currently supplied with these alleged immediate data of consciousness, a person is also generally supposed to be able to exercise from time to time a special kind of perception, namely inner perception, or introspection. He can take a (non-optical) 'look' at what is passing in his mind. Not only can he view and scrutinize a flower through his sense of sight and listen to and discriminate the notes of a bell through his sense of hearing; he can also reflectively or introspectively watch, without any bodily organ of sense, the current episodes of his inner life. This self-observation is also commonly supposed to be immune from illusion, confusion or doubt. A mind's reports of its own affairs have a certainty superior to the best that is possessed by its reports of matters in the physical world. Sense-perceptions can, but consciousness and introspection cannot, be mistaken or confused.

On the other side, one person has no direct access of any sort to the events of the inner life of another. He cannot do better than make problematic inferences from the observed behaviour of the other person's body to the states of mind which, by analogy from his own conduct, he supposes to be signalised by that behaviour. Direct access to the workings of a mind is the privilege of that mind itself; in default of such privileged access, the workings of one mind are inevitably occult to everyone else. For the supposed arguments from bodily movements similar to their own to mental workings similar to their own would lack any possibility of observational corroboration. Not unnaturally, therefore, an adherent of the official theory finds it difficult to resist this consequence of his premises, that he has no good reason to believe that there do exist minds other than his own. Even if he prefers to believe that to other human bodies there are harnessed minds not unlike his own, he cannot claim to be able to discover their individual characteristics, or the particular things that they undergo and do. Absolute solitude is on this showing the ineluctable destiny of the soul. Only our bodies can meet.

As a necessary corollary of this general scheme there is implicitly prescribed a special way of construing our ordinary concepts of mental powers and operations. The verbs, nouns and adjectives, with which in ordinary life we describe the wits, characters and higher-grade performances of the people with whom we have to do, are required to be construed as signifying special episodes in their secret histories, or else as signifying tendencies for such episodes to occur. When someone is described as knowing, believing or guessing something, as hoping, dreading, intending or shirking something, as designing this or being amused at that, these verbs are supposed to denote the occurrence of specific modifications in his (to us) occult stream of consciousness. Only his own privileged access to this stream in direct awareness and introspection could provide authentic testimony that these mental-conduct verbs were correctly or incorrectly applied. The onlooker, be he teacher, critic, biographer or friend, can never assure himself that his comments have any vestige of truth. Yet it was just because we do in fact all know how to make such comments, make them with general correctness and correct them when they turn out to be confused or mistaken, that philosophers found it necessary to construct their theories of the nature and place of minds. Finding mental-conduct concepts being regularly and effectively used, they properly sought to fix their logical geography. But the logical geography officially recommended would entail that there could be no regular or effective use of these mental-conduct concepts in our descriptions of, and prescriptions for, other people's minds.

Such in outline is the official theory. I shall often speak of it, with deliberate abusiveness, as 'the dogma of the Ghost in the Machine'. I hope to prove that it is entirely false, and false not in detail but in principle. It is not merely an assemblage of particular mistakes. It is one big mistake and a mistake of a special kind. It is, namely, a category-mistake. It represents the facts of mental life as if they belonged to one logical type or category (or range of types or categories), when they actually belong to another.

. . .

In this chapter I try to show that when we describe people as exercising qualities of mind, we are not referring to occult episodes of which their overt acts and utterances are effects; we are referring to those overt acts and utterances themselves. There are, of course, differences, crucial for our inquiry, between describing an action as performed absent-mindedly and describing a physiologically similar action as done on purpose, with care or with cunning. But such differences of description do not consist in the absence or presence of an implicit reference to some shadow-action covertly prefacing the overt action. They consist, on the contrary, in the absence or presence of certain sorts of testable explanatory-cum-predictive assertions.

INTELLIGENCE IS AN EXERCISE OF ABILITIES, NOT A SERIES OF INNER ACTS

The mental-conduct concepts that I choose to examine first are those which belong to that family of concepts ordinarily surnamed 'intelligence'. Here are a few of the more determinate adjectives in this family: 'clever', 'sensible', 'careful', 'methodical', 'inventive', 'prudent', 'acute', 'logical', 'witty', 'observant', 'critical', 'experimental', 'quick-witted', 'cunning', 'wise', 'judicious' and 'scrupulous'. When a person is deficient in intelligence he is described as 'stupid' or else by more determinate epithets such as 'dull', 'silly', 'careless', 'unmethodical', 'uninventive', 'rash', 'dense', 'illogical', 'humourless', 'unobservant', 'uncritical', 'unexperimental', 'slow', 'simple', 'unwise' and 'injudicious'.

. . .

When a person is described by one or other of the intelligence-epithets such as 'shrewd' or 'silly', 'prudent' or 'imprudent', the description imputes to him not the knowledge, or ignorance, of this or that truth, but the ability, or inability, to do certain sorts of things. Theorists have been so preoccupied with the task of investigating the nature, the source and the credentials of the theories that we adopt that they have for the most part ignored the question what it is for someone to know how to perform tasks. In ordinary life, on the contrary, as well as in the special business of teaching, we are much more concerned with people's competences than with their cognitive repertoires, with the operations than with the truths that they learn. . . .

What is involved in our descriptions of people as knowing how to make and appreciate jokes, to talk grammatically, to play chess, to fish, or to argue? Part of what is meant is that, when they perform these operations, they tend to perform them well, i.e. correctly or efficiently or successfully. Their performances come up to certain standards, or satisfy certain criteria. But this is not enough. The well-regulated clock keeps good time and the well-drilled circus seal performs its tricks flawlessly, yet we do not call them 'intelligent'. We reserve this title for the persons responsible for their performances. To be intelligent is not merely to satisfy criteria, but to apply them; to regulate one's actions and not merely to be well-regulated. A person's performance is described as careful or skilful, if in his operations he is ready to detect and correct lapses, to repeat and improve upon successes, to profit from the examples of others and so forth. He applies criteria in performing critically, that is, in trying to get things right.

This point is commonly expressed in the vernacular by saying that an action exhibits intelligence, if, and only if, the agent is thinking what he is doing while he is doing it, and thinking what he is doing in such a manner that he would not do the action so well if he were not thinking what he is doing. This popular idiom is sometimes appealed to as evidence in favour of the intellectualist legend. Champions of this legend are apt to try to reassimilate knowing *how* to knowing *that* by arguing that intelligent performance involves the observance of rules, or the application of criteria. It follows that the operation which is characterised as intelligent must be preceded by an intellectual acknowledgment of these rules or criteria; that is, the agent must first go through the internal process of avowing to himself certain propositions about what is to be done ('maxims', 'imperatives' or 'regulative propositions' as they are sometimes called); only then can he execute his performance in accordance with those dictates. He must preach to himself before he can practise. The chef must recite his recipes to himself before he can cook according to them; the hero must lend his inner ear to some appropriate moral imperative before swimming out to save the drowning man; the chess-player must run over in his head all the relevant rules and tactical maxims of the game before he can make correct and skillful moves. To do something thinking what one is doing is, according to this legend, always to do two things; namely, to consider certain appropriate propositions, or prescriptions, and to put into practice what these propositions or prescriptions enjoin. It is to do a bit of theory and then to do a bit of practice.

Certainly we often do not only reflect before we act but reflect in order to act properly. The chess-player may require some time in which to plan his moves before he makes them. Yet the general assertion that all intelligent performance requires to be prefaced by the consideration of appropriate propositions rings unplausibly, even when it is apologetically conceded that the required consideration is often very swift and may go quite unmarked by the agent. I shall argue that the intellectualist legend is false and that when we describe a performance as intelligent, this does not entail the double operation of considering and executing.

．　．　．

ABSURDITY OF THE CARTESIAN (INNER ACT) THEORY OF INTELLIGENCE

The crucial objection to the intellectualist legend is this. The consideration of propositions is itself an operation the execution of which can be more or less intelligent, less or more stupid. But if, for any operation to be intelligently executed, a prior theoretical operation had first to be performed and performed intelligently, it would be a logical impossibility for anyone ever to break into the circle.

Let us consider some salient points at which this regress would arise. According to the legend, whenever an agent does anything intelligently, his act is preceded and steered by another internal act of considering a regulative proposition appropriate to his practical problem. But what makes him consider the one maxim which is appropriate rather than any of the thousands which are not? Why does the hero not find himself calling to mind a cooking-recipe, or a rule of Formal Logic? Perhaps he does, but then his intellectual process is silly and not sensible. Intelligently reflecting how to act is, among other things, considering what is pertinent and disregarding what is inappropriate. Must we then say that for the hero's reflections how to act to be intelligent he must first reflect how best to reflect how to act? The endlessness of this implied regress shows that the application of the criterion of appropriateness does not entail the occurrence of a process of considering this criterion.

．　．　．

To put it quite generally, the absurd assumption made by the intellectualist legend is this, that a performance of any sort inherits all its title to intelligence from some anterior internal operation of planning what to do. Now very often we do go through such a process of planning what to do, and, if we are silly, our planning is silly, if shrewd, our planning is shrewd. It is also notoriously possible for us to plan shrewdly and perform stupidly, i.e. to flout our precepts in our practice. By the original argument, therefore, our intellectual planning process must inherit its title to shrewdness from yet another interior process of planning to plan, and this process could in its turn be silly or shrewd. The regress is infinite, and this reduces to absurdity the theory that for an operation to be intelligent it must be steered by a prior intellectual operation. What distinguishes sensible from silly operations is not their parentage but their procedure, and this holds no less for intellectual than for practical performances. 'Intelligent' cannot be defined in terms of 'intellectual' or 'knowing *how*' in terms of 'knowing *that*'; 'thinking what I am doing' does not connote 'both thinking what to do and doing it'. When I do something intelligently, i.e. thinking what I am doing, <u>I am doing one thing and not two</u>. My performance has a special procedure or manner, not special antecedents.

.   .   .

The cleverness of the clown may be exhibited in his tripping and tumbling. He trips and tumbles just as clumsy people do, except that he trips and tumbles on purpose and after much rehearsal and at the golden moment and where the children can see him and so as not to hurt himself. The spectators applaud his skill at seeming clumsy, but what they applaud is not some extra hidden performance executed 'in his head'. It is his visible performance that they admire, but they admire it not for being an effect of any hidden internal causes but for being an exercise of a skill. Now a skill is not an act. It is therefore neither a witnessable nor an unwitnessable act. To recognise that a performance is an exercise of a skill is indeed to appreciate it in the light of a factor which could not be separately recorded by a camera. But the reason why the skill exercised in a performance cannot be separately recorded by a camera is not that it is an occult or ghostly happening, but that it is not a happening at all. It is a disposition, or complex of dispositions, and a disposition is a factor of the wrong logical type to be seen or unseen, recorded or unrecorded. Just as the habit of talking loudly is not itself loud or quiet, since it is not the sort of term of which 'loud' and 'quiet' can be predicated, or just as a susceptibility to headaches is for the same reason not itself unendurable or endurable, so the skills, tastes and bents which are exercised in overt or internal operations are not themselves overt or internal, witnessable or unwitnessable. The traditional theory of the mind has misconstrued the type-distinction between disposition and exercise into its mythical bifurcation of unwitnessable mental causes and their witnessable physical effects.

INTELLIGENCE AS A COMPLEX KIND OF DISPOSITION

The ability to apply rules is the product of practice. It is therefore tempting to argue that competences and skills are just habits. They are certainly second natures or acquired dispositions, but it does not follow from this that they are mere habits. <u>Habits are one sort</u>, but not the only sort, <u>of second nature</u>, and it will be argued later that the common assumption that <u>all second natures are mere habits obliterate</u>s distinctions which are of cardinal importance for the inquiries in which we are engaged.

The ability to give by rote the correct solutions of multiplication problems differs in certain important respects from the ability to solve them by calculating. When we describe someone as doing something by pure or blind habit, we mean that he does it automatically and without having to mind what he is doing. He does not exercise care, vigilance, or criticism. After the toddling-age we walk on pavements without minding our steps. But a mountaineer walking over ice-covered rocks in a high wind in the dark does not move his limbs by blind habit; he thinks what he is doing, he is ready for emergencies, he economises in effort, he makes tests and experiments; in short he walks with some degree of skill and judgment. If he makes a mistake, he is inclined not to repeat it, and if he finds a new trick effective he is inclined to continue to use it and to improve on it. He is concomitantly walking and teaching himself how to walk in conditions of this sort. It is of the essence of merely habitual practices that one performance is a replica of its predecessors. It is of the essence of intelligent practices that one performance is modified by its predecessors. The agent is still learning.

There is a further important difference between habits and intelligent capacities, to bring out which it is necessary to say a few words about the logic of dispositional concepts in general.

When we describe glass as brittle, or sugar as soluble, we are using dispositional concepts, the logical force of which is this. The brittleness of glass does not consist in the fact that it is at a given moment actually being shivered. It may be brittle without ever being shivered. To say that it is brittle is to say that if it ever is, or ever had been, struck or strained, it would fly, or have flown, into fragments. To say that sugar is soluble is to say that it would dissolve, or would have dissolved, if immersed in water.

A statement ascribing a dispositional property to a thing has much, though not everything, in common with a statement subsuming the thing under a law. To possess a dispositional property is not to be in a particular state, or to undergo a particular change; it is to be bound or liable to be in a particular state, or to undergo a particular change, when a particular condition is realised. The same is true about specifically human dispositions such as qualities of character. My being an habitual smoker does not entail that I am at this or that moment smoking; it is my permanent proneness to smoke when I am not eating, sleeping, lecturing or attending funerals, and have not quite recently been smoking.

In discussing dispositions it is initially helpful to fasten on the simplest models, such as the brittleness of glass or the smoking habit of a man. For in describing these dispositions it is easy to unpack the hypothetical proposition implicitly conveyed in the ascription of the dispositional properties. To be brittle is just to be bound or likely to fly into fragments in such and such conditions; to be a smoker is just to be bound or likely to fill, light and draw on a pipe in such and such conditions. These are simple, single-track dispositions, the actualisations of which are nearly uniform.

But the practice of considering such simple models of dispositions, though initially helpful, leads at a later stage to erroneous assumptions. There are many dispositions the actualisations of which can take a wide and perhaps unlimited variety of shapes; many disposition-concepts are determinable concepts. When an object is described as hard, we do not mean only that it would resist deformation; we mean also that it would, for example, give out a sharp sound if struck, that it would cause us pain if we came into sharp contact with it, that resilient objects would bounce off it, and so on indefinitely. If we wished to unpack all that is conveyed in describing an animal as gregarious, we should similarly have to produce an infinite series of different hypothetical propositions.

Now the higher-grade dispositions of people with which this inquiry is largely concerned are, in general, not single-track dispositions, but dispositions the exercises of which are indefinitely heterogeneous. When Jane Austen wished to show the specific kind of pride which characterised the heroine of 'Pride and Prejudice', she had to represent her actions, words, thoughts and feelings in a thousand different situations. There is no one standard type of action or reaction such that Jane Austen could say 'My heroine's kind of pride was just the tendency to do this, whenever a situation of that sort arose'.

.   .   .   .

In judging that someone's performance is or is not intelligent, we have, as has been said, in a certain manner to look beyond the performance itself. For there is no particular overt or inner performance which could not have been accidentally or 'mechanically' executed by an idiot, a sleepwalker, a man in panic, absence of mind or delirium or even, sometimes, by a parrot. But in looking beyond the performance itself, we are not trying to pry into some hidden counterpart performance enacted on the supposed secret stage of the agent's inner life. We are considering his abilities and propensities of which this performance was an actualisation. Our inquiry is not into causes (and *a fortiori* not into occult causes), but into capacities, skills, habits, liabilities and bents. We observe, for example, a soldier scoring a bull's eye. Was it luck or was it skill? If he has the skill, then he can get on or near the bull's eye again, even if the wind strengthens, the range alters and the target moves. Or if his second shot is an outer, his third, fourth and fifth shots will probably creep nearer and nearer to the bull's eye. He generally checks his breathing before pulling the trigger, as he did on this occasion; he is ready to advise his neighbour what allowances to make for refraction, wind, etc. Marksmanship is a complex of skills, and the question whether he hit the bull's eye by luck or from good marksmanship is the question whether or not he has the skills, and, if he has, whether he used them by making his shot with care, self-control, attention to the conditions and thought of his instructions.

To decide whether his bull's eye was a fluke or a good shot, we need and he himself might need to take into account more than this one success. Namely, we should take into account his subsequent shots, his past record, his explanations or excuses, the advice he gave to his neighbour and a host of other clues of various sorts. There is no one signal of a man's knowing how to shoot, but a modest assemblage of heterogeneous performances generally suffices to establish beyond reasonable doubt whether he knows how to shoot or not. Only then, if at all, can it be decided whether he hit the bull's eye because he was lucky, or whether he hit it because he was marksman enough to succeed when he tried.

A drunkard at the chessboard makes the one move which upsets his opponent's plan of campaign. The spectators are satisfied that this was due not to cleverness but to luck, if they are satisfied that most of his moves made in this state break the rules of chess, or have no tactical connection with the position of the game, that he would not be likely to repeat this move if the tactical situation were to recur, that he would not applaud such a move if made by another player in a similar situation, that he could not explain why he had done it or even describe the threat under which his King had been.

Their problem is not one of the occurrence or non-occurrence of ghostly processes, but one of the truth or falsehood of certain 'could' and 'would' propositions and certain other particular applications of them. For, roughly, the mind is not the topic of sets of untestable categorical propositions, but the topic of sets of testable hypothetical and semi-hypothetical propositions. The difference between a normal person and an idiot is not that the normal person is really two persons while the idiot is only one, but that the normal person can do a lot of things which the idiot cannot do; and 'can' and 'cannot' are not occurrence words but modal words. Of course, in describing the moves actually made by the drunk and the sober players, or the noises actually uttered by the idiotic and the sane men, we have to use not only 'could' and 'would' expressions, but also 'did' and 'did not' expressions. The drunkard's move was made recklessly and the sane man was minding what he was saying. In Chapter V I shall try to show that the crucial differences between such occurrence reports as 'he did it recklessly' and 'he did it on purpose' have to be elucidated not as differences between simple and composite occurrence reports, but in quite another way.

Knowing *how*, then, is a disposition, but not a single-track disposition like a reflex or a habit. Its exercises are observances of rules or canons or the applications of criteria, but they are not tandem operations of theoretically avowing maxims and then putting them into practice. Further, its exercises can be overt or covert, deeds performed or deeds imagined, words spoken aloud or words heard in one's head, pictures painted on canvas or pictures in the mind's eye. Or they can be amalgamations of the two.

.   .   .

Summary

The central point that is being laboured in this chapter is of considerable importance. It is an attack from one flank upon the category-mistake which underlies the dogma of the ghost in the machine. In unconscious reliance upon this dogma theorists and laymen alike constantly construe the adjectives by which we characterise performances as ingenious, wise, methodical, careful, witty, etc. as signalising the occurrence in someone's hidden stream of consciousness of special processes functioning as ghostly harbingers or more specifically as occult causes of the performances so characterised. They postulate an internal shadow-performance to be the real carrier of the intelligence ordinarily ascribed to the overt act, and think that in this way they explain what makes the overt act a manifestation of intelligence. They have described the overt act as an effect of a mental happening, though they stop short, of course, before raising the next question — what makes the postulated mental happenings manifestations of intelligence and not mental deficiency.

In opposition to this entire dogma, I am arguing that in describing the workings of a person's mind we are not describing a second set of shadowy operations. We are describing certain phases of his one career; namely we are describing the ways in which parts of his conduct are managed. The sense in which we 'explain' his actions is not that we infer to occult causes, but that we subsume under hypothetical and semi-hypothetical propositions. The explanation is not of the type 'the glass broke because a stone hit it', but more nearly of the different type 'the glass broke when the stone hit it, because it was brittle'. It makes no difference in theory if the performances we are appraising are operations executed silently in the agent's head, such as what he does, when duly schooled to it, in theorising, composing limericks or solving anagrams. Of course it makes a lot of difference in practice, for the examiner cannot award marks to operations which the candidate successfully keeps to himself.

But when a person talks sense aloud, ties knots, feints or sculpts, the actions which we witness are themselves the things which he is intelligently doing, though the concepts in terms of which the physicist or physiologist would describe his actions do not exhaust those which would be used by his pupils or his teachers in appraising their logic, style or technique. He is bodily active and he is mentally active, but he is not being synchronously active in two different 'places,' or with two different 'engines.' There is the one activity, but it is one susceptible of and requiring more than one kind of explanatory description. Somewhat as there is no aerodynamical or physiological difference between the description of one bird as 'flying south' and of another as 'migrating,' though there is a big biological difference between these descriptions, so there need be no physical or physiological differences between the descriptions of one man as gabbling and another talking sense, though the rhetorical and logical differences are enormous.

The statement 'the mind is its own place,' as theorists might construe it, is not true, for the mind is not even a metaphorical 'place.' On the contrary, the chessboard, the platform, the scholar's desk, the judge's bench, the lorry-driver's seat, the studio and the football field are among its places. These are where people work and play stupidly or intelligently. 'Mind' is not the name of another person, working or frolicking behind an impenetrable screen; it is not the name of another place where work is done or games are played; and it is not the name of another tool with which work is done, or another appliance with which games are played.

37

CAN MACHINES THINK?

A. M. Türing

1. The Imitation Game

I propose to consider the question, 'Can machines think?' This should begin with definitions of the meaning of the terms 'machine' and 'think.' The definitions might be framed so as to reflect so far as possible the normal use of the words, but this attitude is dangerous. If the meaning of the words 'machine' and 'think' are to be found by examining how they are commonly used it is difficult to escape the conclusion that the meaning and the answer to the question, 'Can machines think?' is to be sought in a statistical survey such as a Gallup poll. But this is absurd. Instead of attempting such a definition I shall replace the question by another, which is closely related to it and is expressed in relatively unambiguous words.

The new form of the problem can be described in terms of a game which we call the 'imitation game.' It is played with three people, a man (A), a woman (B), and an interrogator (C) who may be of either sex. The interrogator stays in a room apart from the other two. The object of the game for the interrogator is to determine which of the other two is the man and which is the woman. He knows them by labels X and Y, and at the end of the game he says either 'X is A and Y is B' or 'X is B and Y is A.' The interrogator is allowed to put questions to A and B thus:

C: Will X please tell me the length of his or her hair?

Now suppose X is actually A, then A must answer. It is A's object in the game to try and cause C to make the wrong identification. His answer might therefore be

From "Computing Machinery and Intelligence," first published in *Mind*, Vol. LIX, No. 236, October, 1950. Pp. 433-460, *passim*. Reprinted by permission of the editor of *Mind*.

'My hair is shingled, and the longest strands are about nine inches long.'

In order that tones of voice may not help the interrogator the answers should be written, or better still, typewritten. The ideal arrangement is to have a teleprinter communicating between the two rooms. Alternatively the question and answers can be repeated by an intermediary. The object of the game for the third player (B) is to help the interrogator. The best strategy for her is probably to give truthful answers. She can add such things as 'I am the woman, don't listen to him!' to her answers, but it will avail nothing as the man can make similar remarks.

We now ask the question, 'What will happen when a machine takes the part of A in this game?' Will the interrogator decide wrongly as often when the game is played like this as he does when the game is played between a man and a woman? These questions replace our original, 'Can machines think?'

2. Critique of the New Problem

As well as asking, 'What is the answer to this new form of the question,' one may ask, 'Is this new question a worthy one to investigate?' This latter question we investigate without further ado, thereby cutting short an infinite regress.

The new problem has the advantage of drawing a fairly sharp line between the physical and the intellectual capacities of a man. No engineer or chemist claims to be able to produce a material which is indistinguishable from the human skin. It is possible that at some time this might be done, but even supposing this invention available we should feel there was little point in trying to make a 'thinking machine' more human by dressing it up in such artificial flesh. The form in which we have set the problem reflects this fact in the condition which prevents the interrogator from seeing or touching the other competitors, or hearing their voices. Some other advantages of the proposed criterion may be shown up by specimen questions and answers. Thus:

Q: Please write me a sonnet on the subject of the Forth Bridge.
A: Count me out on this one. I never could write poetry.

Q: Add 34957 to 70764.
A: (Pause about 30 seconds and then give answer as) 105621.

Q: Do you play chess?
A: Yes.

Q: I have K at my K1, and no other pieces. You have only K at K6 and R at R1. It is your move. What do you play?
A: (After a pause of 15 seconds) R-R8 mate.

The question and answer method seems to be suitable for introducing almost any one of the fields of human endeavour that we wish to include. We do not wish to penalise the machine for its inability to shine in beauty competitions, nor to penalise a man for losing in a race against an aeroplane. The conditions of our game make these disabilities irrelevant. The 'witnesses' can brag, if they consider it advisable, as much as they please about their charms, strength or heroism, but the interrogator cannot demand practical demonstrations.

.   .   .

3. The Machines Concerned in the Game

The question which we put in §1 will not be quite definite until we have specified what we mean by the word 'machine.' It is natural that we should wish to permit every kind of engineering technique to be used in our machines. We also wish to allow the possibility than an engineer or team of engineers may construct a machine which works, but whose manner of operation cannot be satisfactorily described by its constructors because they have applied a method which is largely experimental. Finally, we wish to exclude from the machines men born in the usual manner. It is difficult to frame the definitions so as to satisfy those three conditions. One might for instance insist that the team of engineers should be all of one sex, but this would not really be satisfactory, for it is probably possible to rear a complex individual from a single cell of the skin (say) of a man. To do so would be a feat of biological technique deserving of the very highest praise, but we would not be inclined to regard it as a case of 'constructing a thinking machine.' This prompts us to abandon the requirement that every kind of technique should be permitted. We are the more ready to do so in view of the fact that the present interest in 'thinking machines' has been aroused by a particular kind of machine, usually called an 'electronic computer' or 'digital computer'. Following this suggestion we only permit digital computers to take part in our game.

This restriction appears at first sight to be a very drastic one. I shall attempt to show that it is not so in reality. To do this necessitates a short account of the nature and properties of these computers.

It may also be said that this identification of machines with digital computers, like our criterion for 'thinking', will only be unsatisfactory if (contrary to my belief), it turns out that digital computers are unable to give a good showing in the game.

There are already a number of digital computers in working order, and it may be asked, 'Why not try the experiment straight away? It would be easy to satisfy the conditions of the game. A number of interrogators could be used, and statistics compiled to show how often the right identification was given'. The short answer is that we are not asking whether all digital computers would do well in the game nor whether the computers at present available would do well, but whether there are imaginable computers which would do well. But this is only the short answer. We shall see this question in a different light later.

4. Digital Computers

The idea behind digital computers may be explained by saying that these machines are intended to carry out any operations which could be done by a human computer. The human computer is supposed to be following fixed rules; he has no authority to deviate from them in any detail. We may suppose that these rules are supplied in a book, which is altered whenever he is put on to a new job. He has also an unlimited supply of paper on which he does his calculations. He may also do his multiplications and additions on a 'desk machine', but this is not important.

If we use the above explanation as a definition we shall be in danger of circularity of argument. We avoid this by giving an outline of the means by which the desired effect is achieved. A digital computer can usually be regarded as consisting of three parts:

> (i) Store.
> (ii) Executive unit.
> (iii) Control.

The store is a store of information, and corresponds to the human computer's paper, whether this is the paper on which he does his calculations or that on which his book of rules is printed. In so far as the human computer does calculations in his head a part of the store will correspond to his memory.

The executive unit is the part which carries out the various individual operations involved in a calculation. What these individual operations are will vary from machine to machine. Usually fairly lengthy operations can be done such as 'Multiply 3510675445 by 7076345687' but in some machines only very simple ones such as 'Write down 0' are possible.

We have mentioned that the 'book of rules' supplied to the computer is replaced in the machine by a part of the store. It is then called the 'table of instructions'. It is the duty of the control to see that these instructions are obeyed correctly and in the right order. The control is so constructed that this necessarily happens.

The information in the store is usually broken up into packets of moderately small size. In one machine, for instance, a packet might consist of ten decimal digits. Numbers are assigned to the parts of the store in which the various packets of information are stored, in some systematic manner. A typical instruction might say —

'Add the number stored in position 6809 to that in 4302 and put the result back into the latter storage position'.

Needless to say it would not occur in the machine expressed in English. It would more likely be coded in a form such as 6809430217. Here 17 says which of various possible operations is to be performed on the two numbers. In this case the operation is that described above, *viz.* 'Add the number. . . .' It will be noticed that the instruction takes up 10 digits and so forms one packet of information, very conveniently. The control will normally take the instructions to be obeyed in the order of the positions in which they are stored, but occasionally an instruction such as

'Now obey the instruction stored in position 5606, and continue from there'
may be encountered, or again

'If position 4505 contains 0 obey next the instruction stored in 6707, otherwise continue straight on.'

Instructions of these latter types are very important because they make it possible for a sequence of operations to be repeated over and over again until some condition is fulfilled, but in doing so to obey, not fresh instructions on each repetition, but the same ones over and over again. To take a domestic analogy. Suppose Mother wants Tommy to call at the cobbler's every morning on his way to school to see if her shoes are done, she can ask him afresh every morning. Alternatively she can stick up a notice once and for all in the hall which he will see when he leaves for school and which tells him to call for the shoes, and also to destroy the notice when he comes back if he has the shoes with him.

The reader must accept it as a fact that digital computers can be constructed, and indeed have been constructed, according to the principles we have described, and that they can in fact mimic the actions of a human computer very closely.

The book of rules which we have described our human computer as using is of course a convenient fiction. Actual human computers really remember what they have got to do. If one wants to make a machine mimic the behaviour of the human computer in some complex operation one has to ask him how it is done, and then translate the answer into the form of an instruction table. Constructing instruction tables is usually described as 'programming'. To 'programme a machine to carry out the operation A' means to put the appropriate instruction table into the machine so that it will do A.

An interesting variant on the idea of a digital computer is a 'digital computer with a random element'. These have instructions involving the throwing of a die or some equivalent electronic process; one such instruction might for instance be, 'Throw the die and put the resulting number into store 1000'. Sometimes such a machine is described as having free will (though I would not use this phrase myself). It is not normally possible to determine from observing a machine whether it has a random element, for a similar effect can be produced by such devices as making the choices depend on the digits of the decimal for π.

Most actual digital computers have only a finite store. There is no theoretical difficulty in the idea of a computer with an unlimited store. Of course only a finite part can have been used at any one time. Likewise only a finite amount can have been constructed, but we can imagine more and more being added as required. Such computers have special theoretical interest and will be called infinitive capacity computers.

The idea of a digital computer is an old one. Charles Babbage, Lucasian Professor of Mathematics at Cambridge from 1828 to 1839, planned such a machine, called the Analytical Engine, but it was never completed. Although Babbage had all the essential ideas, his machine was not at that time such a very attractive prospect. The speed which would have been available would be definitely faster than a human computer but something like 100 times slower than the Manchester machine, itself one of the slower of the modern machines. The storage was to be purely mechanical, using wheels and cards.

The fact that Babbage's Analytical Engine was to be entirely mechanical will help us to rid ourselves of a superstition. Importance is often attached to the fact that modern digital computers are electrical, and that the nervous system also is electrical. Since Babbage's machine was not electrical, and since all digital computers are in a sense equivalent, we see that this use of electricity cannot be of theoretical importance. Of course electricity usually comes in where fast signalling is concerned, so that it is not surprising that we find it in both these connections. In the nervous system chemical phenomena are at least as important as electrical. In certain computers the storage system is mainly acoustic. The feature of using electricity is thus seen to be only a very superficial similarity. If we wish to find such similarities we should look rather for mathematical analogies of function.

5. Universality of Digital Computers

The digital computers considered in the last section may be classified amongst the 'discrete state machines'. These are the machines which move by sudden jumps or clicks from one quite definite state to another. These states are sufficiently different for the possibility of confusion between them to be ignored. Strictly speaking there are no such machines. Everything really moves continuously. But there are many kinds of machine which can profitably be *thought of* as being discrete state machines. For instance in considering the switches for a lighting system it is a convenient fiction that each switch must be definitely on or definitely off. There must be intermediate positions, but for most purposes we can forget about them. As an example of a discrete state machine we might consider a wheel which clicks round through 120°

once a second, but may be stopped by a lever which can be operated from outside; in addition a lamp is to light in one of the positions of the wheel. This machine could be described abstractly as follows. The internal state of the machine (which is described by the position of the wheel) may be q_1, q_2 or q_3. There is an input signal i_0 or i_1 (position of lever). The internal state at any moment is determined by the last state and input signal according to the table

Last State

		q_1	q_2	q_3
	i_0	q_2	q_3	q_1
Input				
	i_1	q_1	q_2	q_3

The output signals, the only externally visible indication of the internal state (the light) are described by the table

State	q_1	q_2	q_3
Output	o_0	o_0	o_1

This example is typical of discrete state machines. They can be described by such tables provided they have only a finite number of possible states.

It will seem that given the initial state of the machine and the input signals it is always possible to predict all future states. This is reminiscent of Laplace's view that from the complete state of the universe at one moment of time, as described by the positions and velocities of all particles, it should be possible to predict all future states. The prediction which we are considering is, however, rather nearer to practicability than that considered by Laplace. The system of the 'universe as a whole' is such that quite small errors in the initial conditions can have an overwhelming effect at a later time. The displacement of a single electron by a billionth of a centimetre at one moment might make the difference between a man being killed by an avalanche a year later, or escaping. It is an essential property of the mechanical systems which we have called 'discrete state machines' that this phenomenon does not occur. Even when we consider the actual physical machines instead of the idealised machines, reasonably accurate knowledge of the state at one moment yields reasonably accurate knowledge any number of steps later.

As we have mentioned, digital computers fall within the class of discrete state machines. But the number of states of which such a machine is capable is usually enormously large. For instance, the number for the machine now working at Manchester is about $2^{165,000}$, *i.e.* about $10^{50,000}$. Compare this with our example of the clicking wheel described above, which had three states.

It is not difficult to see why the number of states should be so immense. The computer includes a store corresponding to the paper used by a human computer. It must be possible to write into the store any one of the combinations of symbols which might have been written on the paper. For simplicity suppose that only digits from 0 to 9 are used as symbols. Variations in handwriting are ignored. Suppose the computer is allowed 100 sheets of paper each containing 50 lines each with room for 30 digits. Then the number of states is $10^{100 \times 50 \times 30}$, *i.e.* $10^{150,000}$. This is about the number of states of three Manchester machines put together. The logarithm to the base two of the number of states is usually called the 'storage capacity' of the machine. Thus the Manchester machine has a storage capacity of about 165,000 and the wheel machine of our example about 1.6. If two machines are put together their capacities must be added to obtain the capacity of the resultant machine. This leads to the possibility of statements such as 'The Manchester machine contains 64 magnetic tracks each with a capacity of 2560, eight electronic tubes with a capacity of 1280. Miscellaneous storage amounts to about 300 making a total of 174,380.'

Given the table corresponding to a discrete state machine it is possible to predict what it will do. There is no reason why this calculation should not be carried out by means of a digital computer. Provided it could be carried out sufficiently quickly the digital computer could mimic the behavior of any discrete state machine. The imitation game could then be played with the machine in question (as B) and the mimicking digital computer (as A) and the interrogator would be unable to distinguish them. Of course the digital computer must have an adequate storage capacity as well as working sufficiently fast. Moreover, it must be programmed afresh for each new machine which it is desired to mimic.

This special property of digital computers, that they can mimic any discrete state machine, is described by saying that they are *universal* machines. The existence of machines with this property has the important consequence that, considerations of speeds apart, it is unnecessary to design various new machines to do various computing processes. They can all be done with one digital computer, suitably programmed for each case. It will be seen that as a consequence of this all digital computers are in a sense equivalent.

We may now consider again the point raised at the end of §3. It was suggested tentatively that the question, 'Can machines think?' should be replaced by 'Are there imaginable digital computers which would do well in the imitation game?' If we wish we can make this superficially more general and ask 'Are there discrete state machines which would do well?' But in view of the universality property we see that either of these questions is equivalent to this, 'Let us fix our attention on one particular digital computer C. Is it true that by modifying this computer to have an adequate storage, suitably increasing its speed of action, and providing it with an appropriate programme, C can be made to play satisfactorily the part of A in the imitation game, the part of B being taken by a man?'

6. Contrary Views on the Main Question

We may now consider the ground to have been cleared and we are ready to proceed to the debate on our question, 'Can machines think?' and the variant of it quoted at the end of the last section. We cannot altogether abandon the original form of the problem, for opinions will differ as to the appropriateness of the substitution and we must at least listen to what has to be said in this connexion.

It will simplify matters for the reader if I explain first my own beliefs in the matter. Consider first the more accurate form of the question. I believe that in about fifty years' time it will be possible to programme computers, with a store capacity of about 10^9, to make them play the imitation game so well that an average interrogator will not have more than 70 per cent. chance of making the right identification after five minutes of questioning. The original question, 'Can machines think?' I believe to be too meaningless to deserve discussion. Nevertheless I believe that at the end of the century the use of words and general educated opinion will have altered so much that one will be able to speak of machines thinking without expecting to be contradicted. I believe further that no useful purpose is served by concealing these beliefs. The popular view that scientists proceed inexorably from well-established fact to well-established fact, never being influenced by any unproved conjecture, is quite mistaken. Provided it is made clear which are proved facts and which are conjectures, no harm can result. Conjectures are of great importance since they suggest useful lines of research.

I now proceed to consider opinions opposed to my own.

· · ·

(4) *The Argument from Consciousness.* This argument is very well expressed in Professor Jefferson's Lister Oration for 1949, from which I quote. "Not until a machine can write a sonnet or compose a concerto because of thoughts and emotions felt, and not by the chance fall of symbols, could we agree that machine equals brain — that is, not only write it but know that it had written it. No mechanism could feel (and not merely artificially signal, an easy contrivance) pleasure at its successes, grief when its valves fuse, be warmed by flattery, be made miserable by its mistakes, be charmed by sex, be angry or depressed when it cannot get what it wants."

This argument appears to be a denial of the validity of our test. According to the most extreme form of this view the only way by which one could be sure that a machine thinks is to *be* the machine and to feel oneself thinking. One could then describe these feelings to the world, but of course no one would be justified in taking any notice. Likewise according to this view the only way to know that a *man* thinks is to be that particular man. It is in fact the solipsist point of view. It may be the most logical view to hold but it makes communication of ideas difficult. A is liable to believe 'A thinks but B does not' whilst B believes 'B thinks but A does not'. Instead of arguing continually over this point it is usual to have the polite convention that everyone thinks.

I am sure that Professor Jefferson does not wish to adopt the extreme and solipsist point of view. Probably he would be quite willing to accept the imitation game as a test. The game (with the player B omitted) is frequently used in practice under the name of *viva voce* to discover whether some one really understands something or has 'learnt it parrot fashion'. Let us listen in to a part of such a *viva voce*:

Interrogator: In the first line of your sonnet which reads 'Shall I compare thee
    to a summer's day', would not 'a spring day' do as well or better?
Witness: It wouldn't scan.
Interrogator: How about 'a winter's day'. That would scan all right.
Witness: Yes, but nobody wants to be compared to a winter's day.
Interrogator: Would you say Mr. Pickwick reminded you of Christmas?
Witness: In a way.
Interrogator: Yet Christmas is a winter's day, and I do not think Mr. Pickwick would mind the comparison.
Witness: I don't think you're serious. By a winter's day one means a typical winter's day, rather than a special one like Christmas.

And so on. What would Professor Jefferson say if the sonnet-writing machine was able to answer like this in the *vive voce*? I do not know whether he would regard the machine as 'merely artificially signalling' these answers, but if the answers were as satisfactory and sustained as in the above passage I do not think he would describe it as 'an easy contrivance'. This phrase is, I think, intended to cover such devices as the inclusion in the machine of a record of someone reading a sonnet, with appropriate switching to turn it on from time to time.

In short then, I think that most of those who support the argument from consciousness could be persuaded to abandon it rather than be forced into the solipsist position. They will then probably be willing to accept our test.

I do not wish to give the impression that I think there is no mystery about consciousness. There is, for instance, something of a paradox connected with any attempt to localise it. But I do not think these mysteries necessarily need to be solved before we can answer the question with which we are concerned in this paper.

(5) *Arguments from Various Disabilities.* These arguments take the form, "I grant you that you can make machines do all the things you have mentioned but you will never be able to make one to do X". Numerous features X are suggested in this connexion. I offer a selection:

Be kind, resourceful, beautiful, friendly (p. 445), have initiative, have a sense of humour, tell right from wrong, make mistakes (p. 445), fall in love, enjoy strawberries and cream (p. 445), make some one fall in love with it, learn from experience (pp. 460 f.), use words properly, be the subject of its own thought (p. 446), have as much diversity of behaviour as a man, do something really new (p. 447). (Some of these disabilities are given special consideration as indicated by the page numbers.)

No support is usually offered for these statements. I believe they are mostly founded on the principles of scientific induction. A man has seen thousands of machines in his lifetime. From what he sees of them he draws a number of general conclusions. They are ugly, each is designed for a very limited purpose, when required for a minutely different purpose they are useless, the variety of behaviour of any one of them is very small, etc., etc. Naturally he concludes that these are necessary properties of machines in general. Many of these limitations are associated with the very small storage capacity of most machines. (I am assuming that the idea of storage capacity is extended in some way to cover machines other than discrete-state machines. The exact definition does not matter as no mathematical accuracy is claimed in the present discussion.) A few years ago, when very little had been heard of digital computers, it was possible to elicit much incredulity concerning them, if one mentioned their properties without describing their construction. That was presumably due to a similar application of the principle of scientific induction. These applications of the principle are of course largely unconscious. When a burnt child fears the fire and shows that he fears it by avoiding it, I should say that he was applying scientific induction. (I could of course also describe his behaviour in many other ways.) The works and customs of mankind do not seem to be very suitable material to which to apply scientific induction. A very large part of space-time must be investigated, if reliable results are to be obtained. Otherwise we may (as most English children do) decide that everybody speaks English, and that it is silly to learn French.

There are, however, special remarks to be made about many of the disabilities that have been mentioned. The inability to enjoy strawberries and cream may have struck the reader as frivolous. Possibly a machine might be made to enjoy this delicious dish, but any attempt to make one do so would be idiotic. What is important about this disability is that it contributes to some of the other disabilities, *e.g.* to the difficulty of the same kind of friendliness occurring between man and machine as between white man and white man, or between black man and black man.

The claim that "machines cannot make mistakes" seems a curious one. One is tempted to retort, "Are they any the worse for that?" But let us adopt a more sympathetic attitude, and try to see what is really meant. I think this criticism can be explained in terms of the imitation game. It is claimed that the interrogator could distinguish the machine from the man simply by setting them a number of problems in arithmetic. The machine would be unmasked because of its deadly accuracy. The reply to this is simple. The machine (programmed for playing the game) would not attempt to give the *right* answers to the arithmetic problems. It would deliberately introduce mistakes in a manner calculated to confuse the interrogator. A mechanical fault would probably show itself through an unsuitable decision as to what sort of a mistake to make in the arithmetic. Even this interpretation of the criticism is not sufficiently sympathetic. But we cannot afford the space to go into it much further. It seems to me that this criticism depends on a confusion between two kinds of mistake. We may call them 'errors of functioning' and 'errors of conclusion'. Errors of functioning are due to some mechanical or electrical fault which causes the machine to behave otherwise than it was designed to do. In philosophical discussions one likes to ignore the possibility of such errors; one is therefore discussing ' abstract machines'. These abstract machines are mathematical fictions rather than physical objects. By definition they are incapable of errors of functioning. In this sense we can truly say that 'machines can never make mistakes'. Errors of conclusion can only arise when some meaning is attached to the output signals from the machine. The machine might, for instance, type out mathematical equations, or sentences in English. When a false proposition is typed we say that the machine has committed an error of conclusion. There is clearly no reason at all for saying that a machine cannot make this kind of mistake. It might do nothing but type out repeatedly '10 = 1'. To take a less perverse example, it might have some method for drawing conclusions by scientific induction. We must expect such a method to lead occasionally to erroneous results.

The claim that a machine cannot be the subject of its own thought can of course only be answered if it can be shown that the machine has *some* thought with *some* subject matter. Nevertheless, 'the subject matter of a machine's operations' does seem to mean something, at least to the people who deal with it. If, for instance, the machine was trying to find a solution of the equation $x^2 - 40x - 1 = 0$ one would be tempted to describe this equation as part of the machine's subject matter at that moment. In this sort of sense a machine undoubtedly can be its own subject matter. It may be used to help in making up its own programmes, or to predict the effect of alterations in its own structure. By observing the results of its own behaviour it can modify its own programmes so as to achieve some purpose more effectively. These are possibilities of the near future, rather than Utopian dreams.

The criticism that a machine cannot have much diversity of behaviour is just a way of saying that it cannot have much storage capacity. Until fairly recently a storage capacity of even a thousand digits was very rare.

The criticisms that we are considering here are often disguised forms of the argument from consciousness. Usually if one maintains that a machine *can* do one of these things, and describes the kind of method that the machine could use, one will not make much of an impression. It is thought that the method (whatever it may be, for it must be mechanical) is really rather base. Compare the parenthesis in Jefferson's statement quoted on p. 443.

(6) *Lady Lovelace's Objection*. Our most detailed information of Babbage's Analytical Engine comes from a memoir by *Lady Lovelace*. In it she

states, "The Analytical Engine has no pretensions to *originate* anything. It can do *whatever we know how to order it* to perform" (her italics). This statement is quoted by *Hartree* . . . who adds: "This does not imply that it may not be possible to construct electronic equipment which will 'think for itself', or in which, in biological terms, one could set up a conditioned reflex, which would serve as a basis for 'learning'. Whether this is possible in principle or not is a stimulating and exciting question, suggested by some of these recent developments. But it did not seem that the machines constructed or projected at the time had this property".

I am in thorough agreement with Hartree over this. It will be noticed that he does not assert that the machines in question had not got the property, but rather that the evidence available to Lady Lovelace did not encourage her to believe that they had it. It is quite possible that the machines in question had in a sense got this property. For suppose that some discrete-state machine has the property. The Analytical Engine was a universal digital computer, so that, if its storage capacity and speed were adequate, it could by suitable programming be made to mimic the machine in question. Probably this argument did not occur to the Countess or to Babbage. In any case there was no obligation on them to claim all that could be claimed.

This whole question will be considered again under the heading of learning machines.

A variant of Lady Lovelace's objection states that a machine can 'never do anything really new'. This may be parried for a moment with the saw, 'There is nothing new under the sun'. Who can be certain that 'original work' that he has done was not simply the growth of the seed planted in him by teaching, or the effect of following well-known general principles. A better variant of the objection says that a machine can never 'take us by surprise'. This statement is a more direct challenge and can be met directly. Machines take me by surprise with great frequency. This is largely because I do not do sufficient calculation to decide what to expect them to do, or rather because although I do a calculation, I do it in a hurried, slipshod fashion, taking risks. Perhaps I say to myself, 'I suppose the voltage here ought to be the same as there: anyway let's assume it is.' Naturally I am often wrong, and the result is a surprise for me for by the time the experiment is done these assumptions have been forgotten. These admissions lay me open to lectures on the subject of my vicious ways, but do not throw any doubt on my credibility when I testify to the surprises I experience.

I do not expect this reply to silence my critic. He will probably say that such surprises are due to some creative mental act on my part, and reflect no credit on the machine. This leads us back to the argument from consciousness, and far from the idea of surprise. It is a line of argument we must consider closed, but it is perhaps worth remarking that the appreciation of something as surprising requires as much of a 'creative mental act' whether the surprising event originates from a man, a book, a machine or anything else.

The view that machines cannot give rise to surprises is due, I believe, to a fallacy to which philosophers and mathematicians are particularly subject. This is the assumption that as soon as a fact is presented to a mind all consequences of that fact spring into the mind simultaneously with it. It is a very useful assumption under many circumstances, but one too easily forgets that it is false. A natural consequence of doing so is that one then assumes that there is no virtue in the mere working out of consequences from data and general principles.

(7) *Argument from Continuity in the Nervous System.* The nervous system is certainly not a discrete-state machine. A small error in the information about the size of a nervous impulse impinging on a neuron, may make a large difference to the size of the outgoing impulse. It may be argued that, this being so, one cannot expect to be able to mimic the behaviour of the nervous system with a discrete-state system.

It is true that a discrete-state machine must be different from a continuous machine. But if we adhere to the conditions of the imitation game, the interrogator will not be able to take any advantage of this difference. The situation can be made clearer if we consider some other simpler continuous machine. A differential analyser will do very well. (A differential analyser is a certain kind of machine not of the discrete-state type used for some kinds of calculation.) Some of these provide their answers in a typed form, and so are suitable for taking part in the game. It would not be possible for a digital computer to predict exactly what answers the differential analyser would give to a problem, but it would be quite capable of giving the right sort of answer. For instance, if asked to give the value of π (actually about 3·1416) it would be reasonable to choose at random between the values 3·12, 3·13, 3·14, 3·15, 3·16, with the probabilities of 0·05, 0·15, 0·55, 0·19, 0·06 (say). Under these circumstances it would be very difficult for the interrogator to distinguish the differential analyser from the digital computer.

(8) *The Argument from Informality of Behavior.* It is not possible to produce a set of rules purporting to describe what a man should do in every conceivable set of circumstances. One might for instance have a rule that one is to stop when one sees a red traffic light, and to go if one sees a green one, but what if by some fault both appear together? One may perhaps decide that it is safest to stop. But some further difficulty may well arise from this decision later. To attempt to provide rules of conduct to cover every eventuality, even those arising from traffic lights, appears to be impossible. With all this I agree.

From this it is argued that we cannot be machines. I shall try to reproduce the argument, but I fear I shall hardly do it justice. It seems to run something like this. 'If each man had a definite set of rules of conduct by which he regulated his life he would be no better than a machine. But there are no such rules, so men cannot be machines.' The undistributed middle is glaring. I do not think the argument is ever put quite like this, but I believe this is the argument used nevertheless. There may however be a certain confusion between 'rules of conduct' and 'laws of behaviour' to cloud the issue. By 'rules of conduct' I mean precepts such as 'Stop if you see red lights,' on which one can act, and of which one can be conscious. By 'laws of behaviour' I mean laws of nature as applied to a man's body such as 'if you pinch him he will squeak.' If we substitute 'laws of behaviour which regulate his life' for 'laws of conduct by which he regulates his life' in the argument quoted the undistributed middle is no longer insuperable. For we believe that it is not only true that being regulated by laws of behaviour implies being some sort of machine (though not necessarily a discrete-state machine), but that conversely being such a machine implies being regulated by such laws. However, we cannot so easily convince ourselves of the absence of complete laws of behaviour as of complete rules of conduct. The only way we know of for finding such laws is scientific observation, and we certainly know of no circumstances under which we could say. 'We have searched enough. There are no such laws.'

We can demonstrate more forcibly that any such statement would be unjustified. For suppose we could be sure of finding such laws if they existed. Then given a discrete machine it should certainly be possible to discover by observation sufficient about it to predict its future behaviour, and this within a reasonable time, say a thousand years. But this does not seem to be the case. I have set up on the Manchester computer a small programme using only 1000 units of storage, whereby the machine applied with one sixteen figure number replies with another within two seconds. I would defy anyone to learn from these replies sufficient about the programme to be able to predict any replies to untried values.

. . . .

7. Learning Machines

The reader will have anticipated that I have no very convincing arguments of a positive nature to support my views. If I had I should not have taken such pains to point out the fallacies in contrary views. Such evidence as I have I shall now give.

. . .

The only really satisfactory support that can be given for the view expressed at the beginning of §6, will be that provided by waiting for the end of the century and then doing the experiment described. But what can we say in the meantime? What steps should be taken now if the experiment is to be successful?

As I have explained, the problem is mainly one of programming. Advances in engineering will have to be made too, but it seems unlikely that these will not be adequate for the requirements. Estimates of the storage capacity of the brain vary from 10^{10} to 10^{15} binary digits. I incline to the lower values and believe that only a very small fraction is used for the higher types of thinking. Most of it is probably used for the retention of visual impressions. I should be surprised if more than 10^9 was required for satisfactory playing of the imitation game, at any rate against a blind man. (Note — The capacity of the *Encyclopaedia Britannica,* 11th edition, is 2×10^9.) A storage capacity of 10^7 would be a very practicable possibility even by present techniques. It is probably not necessary to increase the speed of operations of the machines at all. Parts of modern machines which can be regarded as analogues of nerve cells work about a thousand times faster than the latter. This should provide a 'margin of safety' which could cover losses of speed arising in many ways. Our problem then is to find out how to programme these machines to play the game. At my present rate of working I produce about a thousand digits of programme a day, so that about sixty workers, working steadily through the fifty years might accomplish the job, if nothing went into the waste-paper basket. Some more expeditious method seems desirable.

In the process of trying to imitate an adult human mind we are bound to think a good deal about the process which has brought it to the state that it is in. We may notice three components,

(*a*) The initial state of the mind, say at birth,

(*b*) The education to which it has been subjected,

(*c*) Other experience, not to be described as education, to which it has been subjected.

Instead of trying to produce a programme to simulate the adult mind, why not rather try to produce one which simulates the child's? If this were then subjected to an appropriate course of education one would obtain the adult brain. Presumably the child-brain is something like a note-book as one buys it from the stationers. Rather little mechanisms, and lots of blank sheets. (Mechanism and writing are from our point of view almost synonymous.) Our hope is that there is so little mechanism in the child-brain that something like it can be easily programmed. The amount of work in the education we can assume, as a first approximation, to be much the same as for the human child.

We have thus divided our problem into two parts. The child-programme and the education process. These two remain very closely connected. We cannot expect to find a good child-machine at the first attempt. One must experiment with teaching one such machine and see how well it learns. One can then try another and see if it is better or worse. There is an obvious connection between this process and evolution, by the identifications

Structure of the child machine	= Hereditary material
Changes ” ”	= Mutations
Natural selection	= Judgment of the experimenter

One may hope, however, that this process will be more expeditious than evolution. The survival of the fittest is a slow method for measuring advantages. The experimenter, by the exercise of intelligence, should be able to speed it up. Equally important is the fact that he is not restricted to random mutations. If he can trace a cause for some weakness he can probably think of the kind of mutation which will improve it.

It will not be possible to apply exactly the same teaching process to the machine as to a normal child. It will not, for instance, be provided with legs, so that it could not be asked to go out and fill the coal scuttle. Possibly it might not have eyes. But however well these deficiencies might be overcome by clever engineering, one could not send the creature to school without the other children making excessive fun of it. It must be given some tuition. We need not be too concerned about the legs, eyes, etc. The example of Miss *Helen Keller* shows that education can take place provided that communication in both directions between teacher and pupil can take place by some means or other.

We normally associate punishments and rewards with the teaching process. Some simple child-machines can be constructed or programmed on this sort of principle. The machine has to be so constructed that events which shortly preceded the occurrence of a punishment-signal are unlikely to be repeated, whereas a reward-signal increased the probability of repetition of the events which led up to it. These definitions do not presuppose any feelings on the part of the machine. I have done some experiments with one such child-machine, and I succeeded in teaching it a few things, but the teaching method was too unorthodox for the experiment to be considered really successful.

The use of punishments and rewards can at best be a part of the teaching process. Roughly speaking, if the teacher has no other means of communicating to the pupil, the amount of information which can reach him does not exceed the total number of rewards and punishments applied. By the time a child has learnt to repeat 'Casabianca' he would probably feel very sore indeed, if the text could only be discovered by a 'Twenty Questions' technique, every 'NO' taking the form of a blow. It is necessary therefore to have some other 'unemotional' channels of communication. If these are available it is possible to teach a machine by punishments and rewards to obey orders given in some language, *e.g.* a symbolic language. These orders are to be transmitted through the 'unemotional' channels. The use of this language will diminish greatly the number of punishments and rewards required.

Opinions may vary as to the complexity which is suitable in the child machine. One might try to make it as simple as possible consistently with the general principles. Alternatively one might have a complete system of logical inference 'built in.'[1] In the latter case the store would be largely occupied with definitions and propositions. The propositions would have various kinds of status, *e.g.* well-established facts, conjectures, mathematically proved theorems, statements given by an authority, expressions having the logical

---

[1] Or rather 'programmed in' for our child-machine will be programmed in a digital computer. But the logical system will not have to be learnt.

form of proposition but not belief-value. Certain propositions may be described as 'imperatives.' The machine should be so constructed that as soon as an imperative is classed as 'well-established' the appropriate action automatically takes place. To illustrate this, suppose the teacher says to the machine, 'Do your homework now.' This may cause "Teacher says 'Do your homework now'" to be included amongst the well-established facts. Another such fact might be, "Everything that teacher says is true." Combining these may eventually lead to the imperative, 'Do your homework now,' being included amongst the well-established facts, and this, by the construction of the machine, will mean that the homework actually gets started, but the effect is very satisfactory. The processes of inference used by the machine need not be such as would satisfy the most exacting logicians. There might for instance be no hierarchy of types. But this need not mean that type fallacies will occur, any more than we are bound to fall over unfenced cliffs. Suitable imperatives (expressed *within* the systems, not forming part of the rules *of* the system) such as 'Do not use a class unless it is a subclass of one which has been mentioned by teacher,' can have a similar effect to 'Do not go too near the edge.'

The imperatives that can be obeyed by a machine that has no limbs are bound to be of a rather intellectual character, as in the example (doing homework) given above. Important amongst such imperatives will be ones which regulate the order in which the rules of the logical system concerned are to be applied. For at each stage when one is using a logical system, there is a very large number of alternatives steps, any of which one is permitted to apply, so far as obedience to the rules of the logical system is concerned. These choices make the difference between a brilliant and a footling reasoner, not the difference between a sound and a fallacious one. Propositions leading to imperatives of this kind might be "When Socrates is mentioned, use the syllogism in Barbara" or "If one method has been proved to be quicker than another, do not use the slower method." Some of these may be 'given by authority,' but others may be produced by the machine itself, *e.g.* by scientific induction.

The idea of a learning machine may appear paradoxical to some readers. How can the rules of operation of the machine change? They should describe completely how the machine will react whatever its history might be, whatever changes it might undergo. The rules are thus quite time-invariant. This is quite true. The explanation of the paradox is that the rules which get changed in the learning process are of a rather less pretentious kind, claiming only an ephemeral validity. The reader may draw a parallel with the Constitution of the United States.

An important feature of a learning machine is that its teacher will often be very largely ignorant of quite what is going on inside, although he may still be able to some extent to predict his pupil's behaviour. This should apply most strongly to the later education of a machine arising from a child-machine of well-tried design (or programme). This is in clear contrast with normal procedure when using a machine to do computations: one's object is then to have a clear mental picture of the state of the machine at each moment in the computation. This object can only be achieved with a struggle. The view that 'the machine can only do what we know how to order it to do,' appears strange in face of this. Most of the programmes which we can put into the machine will result in its doing something that we cannot make sense of at all, or which we regard as completely random behaviour. Intelligent behaviour presumably consists in a departure from the completely disciplined behaviour involved in computation, but a rather slight one, which does not give rise to random behaviour, or to pointless repetitive loops. Another important result of preparing our machine for its part in the imitation game by a process of teaching and learning is that 'human fallibility' is likely to be omitted in a rather natural way, *i.e.* without special 'coaching.' (The reader should reconcile this with the point of view on pp. 445-446.) Processes that are learnt do not produce a hundred per cent. certainty of result; if they did they could not be unlearnt.

It is probably wise to include a random element in a learning machine . . . (see p. 443). A random element is rather useful when we are searching for a solution of some problem. Suppose for instance we wanted to find a number between 50 and 200 which was equal to the square of the sum of its digits, we might start at 51 then try 52 and go on until we got a number that worked. Alternatively we might choose numbers at random until we got a good one. This method has the advantage that it is unnecessary to keep track of the values that have been tried, but the disadvantage that one may try the same one twice, but this is not very important if there are several solutions. The systematic method has the disadvantage that there may be an enormous block without any solutions in the region which has to be investigated first. Now the learning process may be regarded as a search for a form of behaviour which will satisfy the teacher (or some other criterion.) Since there is probably a very large number of satisfactory solutions the random method seems to be better than the systematic. It should be noticed that it is used in the analogous process of evolution. But there the systematic method is not possible. How could one keep track of the different genetical combinations that had been tried, so as to avoid trying them again?

We may hope that machines will eventually compete with men in all purely intellectual fields. But which are the best ones to start with? Even this is a difficult decision. Many people think that a very abstract activity, like the playing of chess, would be best. It can also be maintained that it is best to provide the machine with the best sense organs that money can buy, and then teach it to understand and speak English. This process could follow the normal teaching of a child. Things would be pointed out and named, etc. Again I do not know what the right answer is, but I think both approaches should be tried.

We can only see a short distance ahead, but we can see plenty there that needs to be done.

38

A REAFFIRMATION
OF DUALISM

A. C. Ewing

A. C. Ewing (1899-   ) is Reader in Moral Science in the University of Cambridge.

PRIMARY CERTAINTY OF EXPERIENCE REPLY
TO BEHAVIOURISM

The discussion of physical objects should have been sufficient to counteract the assertion that their existence is the chief and primary certainty. The primary certainty is experience, and this is not a physical object but something mental. When I think I perceive a physical object, it is conceivable that I might be dreaming, but I could not even dream that I existed without existing. And here by 'I' is meant my mind, not my body. It might conceivably be a mere dream or illusion even that I had a body, but it could not be an illusion or dream that I thought, at least in the wide sense of the term in which I am always thinking of something when I am awake at all. And similarly it could not be an illusion that I experienced. For to believe or even doubt that I am thinking or experiencing, I must already think and experience. This is the famous argument used by Descartes: I think, therefore I am (*cogito, ergo sum*). We may grant that the argument as he used it went rather too far. He talked as if it established a permanent self, while all it does establish is the present existence of a thought as experience. But with the appropriate limitations the argument is valuable as showing the primary certainty of experience against those who are disposed to talk as if matter alone were real.

Of course what we cannot practically help holding as certain is not limited to what can be theoretically proved such, but if we are to get back to the ultimate foundations of belief and knowledge we should ask what is

From Chapter V, "Mind," of *The Fundamental Questions of Philosophy* (1951), published by Routledge & Kegan Paul, Ltd., London, and by The Macmillan Company, New York. Reprinted by permission of the publishers.

logically certain. This falls into two classes, (1) Certain *a priori* propositions which could not be denied without logical absurdity, like the law of contradiction or the law of excluded middle. (2) My own present existence as a thinking being. The certainty has, however, a different foundation in the two cases. We can see that the laws of logic could not conceivably be false, but it is quite conceivable that I should not have existed. My father might well have never met my mother. What is inconceivable is that I could deny or doubt my existence without existing, and therefore for me, but only for me, such a denial or doubt would be self-contradictory. But the *logically* certain need not be co-extensive with the certain. Besides what is logically certain there are a number of immediately known propositions which we can regard as absolutely certain although there would be no self-contradiction in our denying them. In this class I put more specific propositions based on introspection. I cannot see any self-contradiction in supposing that I might make mistakes in introspection, and there is therefore no *logical* absurdity in supposing that I might be mistaken now when I judge that I feel warm or that I have a visual presentation of a table. But I still cannot help being absolutely certain of the truth of these propositions and I do not think that I ought to be otherwise. I should not say this of all judgements of introspection, but I should certainly say it of some. Again I cannot help being absolutely certain of the truth of some (though by no means all) of my judgements of memory. As we have seen, it is however hardly possible to claim this absolute certainty for judgements about physical objects, and, as we shall see, there are similar difficulties in claiming it for judgements about minds other than one's own.

Descartes' assertion *Cogito, ergo sum,* is commonly regarded as the beginning of modern philosophy and in particular as initiating the subjective tendency which has been so characteristic of subsequent philosophical developments. Since his time philosophers have tended more than in earlier days before looking outwards first to look inwards in order to form a decision as to the human capacity for knowledge, and this tendency has often been carried much too far. But he was fundamentally right as to the starting-point, though not as to the way in which he used it. It has been objected that the *cogito* implies the existence of something thought as much as of a thinker, but there is nothing in the argument which proves that what is thought need be independent of the thinker. It might be just a mental image dependent on my imagining it for its existence.

Descartes' argument brings out the absurdity of 'behaviourism' as a philosophy. Some psychologists, who call themselves 'behaviourists,' have tried to explain away the concept of mind or even mental events in psychology altogether and substitute for it the concept of behaviour studied as a physical process. Probably most of them merely mean that the observation of outward behaviour and not introspection provides the most useful way of acquiring data in psychology, but some would go further and put forward their behaviourism as a philosophy and not merely a methodology of psychology.

In that case their position can easily be seen to be untenable. Such philosophical behaviourism may mean one of two things. (1) It may mean that there are no mental events at all. But in that case no one can possibly believe behaviourism to be true, for believing itself is a mental event. (2) It may mean that there are mental events but these are simply to be identified with physiological events. The kind of physiological events with which behaviourists identify thinking are usually movements of the vocal organs. People often, when they think, move these as they do when they talk, only less markedly, and behaviourists have advanced the view that this is what always happens when we think, and further that this is just what thinking is. Nineteenth-century materialists were on the other hand inclined to identify thinking, and mental events generally, with processes in the central nervous system or brain. In order to refute such views I shall suggest your trying an experiment. Heat a piece of iron red-hot, then put your hand on it, and note carefully what you feel. You will have no difficulty in observing that it is quite different from anything which a physiologist could observe, whether he considered your outward behaviour or your brain processes. The throb of pain experienced will not be in the least like either the act of withdrawing your hand or the movement of your vocal organs to say whatever you do say, nor would it be like anything described in textbooks of physiology as happening in the nervous system or brain. I do not say that it does not happen in the brain, but it is quite distinct from anything that other people could observe if they looked into your brain. The behaviourists pride themselves on being empiricists, but in maintaining their view they are going clean contrary to experience. We know by experience what feeling pain is like and we know by experience what the physiological reactions to it are, and the two are totally unlike. We know by experience what thinking is, and we know by experience what movements of our vocal organs are, and we see the two to be totally unlike. It is not a question of *a priori* speculative metaphysics whether mental and physiological events are to be distinguished. The difference is as plainly marked and as much an empirical matter as that between a sight and a sound. The physiological and the mental characteristics I have mentioned may conceivably belong to the same substance — I shall discuss that question in the next chapter — but at least they are different in qualities, indeed as different in kind as any two sets of qualities. The element of truth in behaviourism is that I can only acquire knowledge about other minds through their bodily behaviour, including under that what they say about themselves. But it is only because I interpret their behaviour in terms of my own immediate experience of my mental states, not my body, that it can give me information of a psychological kind at all.

We should not regard the conception of the mind as a metaphysical hypothesis concerning what lies behind experience, but rather as the conception of the different experiences of ourselves or some other person as related in a single whole. In this sense its existence cannot be denied. A distinction has been made, chiefly by theologians, between mind, soul and spirit, but this distinction has been avoided by most philosophers and 'mind' used to cover the whole of the man's inner nature and not merely his more intellectual side.

Different Elements in the Mind

Now what do we find in our experience? Into what elements is it analysable? In the first place we discover a number of sensuous elements the qualities of which resemble rather those of physical objects as conceived by common sense, than those attributable to mind as such. I am referring to sensa and images. These may be regarded as mind-dependent, but not as qualities of the mind. When I look at the sky on a clear day my mind is not blue, when I hear the din of a big railway station my mind is not loud. We must remember here the distinction already pointed out between 'sensation' as signifying 'sensing' and 'sensation' as signifying 'what is sensed.' The former but not the latter is an attribute of mind. But certainly, even if they are not attributes of mind, the investigation of the sensa and images we have under certain conditions, is a major part of the work of psychology. Further they, or at least images, are very closely linked with our processes of thought. It may be doubted whether we can think in the least definitely without using some sort of imagery. Words themselves are after all sensuous images of black marks on paper or of sounds.

Turning to the more specifically mental side of ourselves, we find that it has been subjected to a threefold classification, represented by the distinction between affective, cognitive, and conative. By the affective side of our nature is meant the feeling side, by the cognitive side the side concerned with knowing, believing, reasoning, perceiving, by the conative side that concerned with acting, willing, striving, desiring. We must not, however, think of it as if the three sides operated quite separately. On the contrary practically all mental processes involve all three at once. Except perhaps when we are half asleep there are probably no times in our life when we are only feeling beings, and certainly none when we are only cognitive or conative beings, since the feeling element at least must always be present. Thus having an emotion like anger or fear involves at once having more or less strong feelings, striving in a certain direction, e.g. to escape or get the better of our opponent (conative), and recognizing the situation as one of a certain character (cognitive). Cognition is essentially linked up with conation in the form of striving to attain some end by the cognition, if only the end of discovering truth for its own sake, and in the form of voluntarily turning the attention in certain directions. Attention in its turn is bound up with 'interest,' and interest with feeling pleasure or its opposite in a pursuit.

On the other hand, while the three sides of mental activity mostly involve each other, a thinker may emphasize one in preference to the others, and this variation in relative emphasis is one of the chief sources of difference between philosophers. Those who emphasize the cognitive element most are apt to think of reality as primarily something satisfying the intellect, and so as a rational system in which there is a reason for everything or for most things of importance, and the different parts are all logically connected. Others make cognition subject to the conative side and insist that cognitions are always primarily means to a practical end. They exalt the importance of will at the expense of reason both in their estimate of man and in their view of reality in general. The most fundamentally real thing to them is given in the awareness of activity. Thirdly, the philosophers who derive knowledge exclusively or almost exclusively from sense-experience might be described as making the affective element predominant, since sensations are in my opinion best classified as feelings.[1] Hume's psychology would be a good example of one which tends to reduce everything to feelings. Similarly, in the realm of moral philosophy we can distinguish those who make the chief good a cognitive state, whether that of contemplation of the supreme being or simply that of having clear ideas in general; those like Kant who find the chief good in a state of the moral will; and those who find it in the feeling of happiness or pleasure. But it seems more likely that a right view will do justice to all three sides of our nature.

Some philosophers, while accepting images and sensa, have denied the existence of mental acts or processes like knowing, believing, willing, etc., on the ground that these are not accessible to introspection. The trouble is that we cannot introspectively detect such acts by themselves, but that seems to be because they are essentially bound up with some object. We cannot know without knowing something, believe without believing something, will without willing something, etc. If so it is not to be expected that we can introspect these activities by themselves, but we can still have an idea of what they are like because we can see the distinction between willing and not willing something, or that between believing and doubting the same thing. It does not matter if we cannot observe some attribute, A, by itself; we can still know what it is like if we can observe the difference between AB and CB, and this is how we know what it is like, e.g. to believe. That we cannot give an adequate account of the self in terms of images and sensa alone may be shown by, for instance, taking the case of thought. One can go a certain distance in the interpretation of thought by means of images, but in very many cases the only discernible images are words. You may be able to think about physical things by forming images of them, but if you open a book on philoosphy or economics at almost any page, you will not find a sentence the content of which is capable of being imaged. This being so, we are dependent on words for thinking about such topics. It seems to be a psychological necessity to have some sort of sensuous picture in our mind, but we cannot produce pictures that are like the objects about which we think, therefore we employ

---

[1] Many psychologists, however, classify them as cognitions.

verbal images which can be used to represent some fact without needing to be like what they represent. A person who wishes to deny any mental events or processes over and above sensa and images will therefore have to maintain that thinking about philosophy is reducible simply to a combination of verbal images. Now he may be right indeed in maintaining that verbal images are a necessary condition of such thinking, but he cannot be right in maintaining that they are also a sufficient condition. For he will then not be able to make any distinction between a set of words about an abstract topic which we understand and a string of nonsense syllables. If we were dealing with physical objects we could often analyse the meaning in terms of non-verbal images, but this is not always the case even here. The meaning of most scientific theories could not be expressed adequately in terms of images of physical objects and even in cases where propositions about physical objects could be thus expressed we may understand them perfectly well without in fact using the imagery. Some people very rarely use any but verbal images. In any case, as I have said, in e.g. philosophy and economics (or even politics) the meaning of most statements cannot possibly be expressed in terms of sensuous imagery which is like the subject-matter of our thought. Yet we can understand some statements in philosophy and economics. Therefore understanding is something mental which cannot possibly be explained entirely in terms of images. It cannot be explained entirely in terms of verbal imagery, for we must make a distinction between using verbal imagery and understanding it; and, as we have seen, it cannot be explained in terms of non-verbal.

Attempts have also been made to analyse belief in terms of behaviour, thus excluding the need to posit any specific mental act or attitude of belief. On this view to believe that A is B is to act as if A were B. The view is, however, in my opinion, open to several very serious objections. Firstly, what can be meant by 'acting as if A were B?' Surely nothing but acting as if we believed A to be B, in which case belief is being defined in terms of itself. If A were B without our believing it to be so, it would not alter our actions though it might alter their effects. Secondly, I often have beliefs on which I never act. In such cases the theory can only be maintained by referring to hypothetical action. But I can tell whether I believe something without first having to decide how I should act under certain hypothetical circumstances which may never be realized at all. I know immediately in many cases that I believe something on which I am not at present acting, but it cannot be a matter of immediate knowledge how one would act if something were to happen which in fact has not happened. For instance I believe that Chimborazo is the highest mountain of the Andes, and I should therefore refrain from trying to climb it if I were in that neighbourhood because I should think it too formidable a task. But I surely cannot identify the belief with this hypothetical fact. That I should not try to climb Chimborazo is an inference and not anything immediately known at all, further it is an inference from my belief about the height of Chimborazo as premise. It already presupposes the latter belief, which therefore cannot be defined in terms of it. And the same with all propositions about future or possible actions based on a belief. We cannot avoid these criticisms by identifying the action with repeating to oneself or others the words which we say express the belief. For we might do that without having the belief. Thirdly, the theory does not allow for human folly and immorality. We often hold a belief quite genuinely and yet because of some strong desire which carries us against reason do not act as if it were true.

It seems equally impossible to analyse desiring, willing, liking, etc., in terms of imagery. So we have two very different kinds of attributes given in our immediate experience: specifically mental attributes and the attributes of sensa and images. I should say that the latter kind could and the former could not be conceived as existing unexperienced, but the idealist would contradict the first part of this statement. However, no sensible person would deny the second part and say that, e.g. pleasure and pain could exist unexperienced.

When we start talking about the more specifically mental side it is disappointing how little philosophy and psychology can say about it. This is largely because we very soon arrive at characteristics which we can know by experience but cannot define further. Analysis presupposes unanalysable characteristics and we very soon reach these in the process. The unanalysable is of course not the unknowable, it is what we know well enough by experience but cannot explain in terms of anything else so that a person could understand what it was like if he had never had the experience.

DISPOSITIONAL PROPERTIES

The terms applied to the mind both in psychology and in ordinary non-scientific conversation are, however, by no means limited to actual characteristics. They commonly refer to dispositions or capacities. For example, if I talk about somebody's 'beliefs', I am certainly not committing myself to the view that he is at the time I speak actually thinking of what I say he believes. I am sure that I am right in saying that Churchill believes the present government to be bad for Britain, but for anything I know Churchill may be asleep at the moment or thinking about something quite different. Therefore, though I use the present tense, I am not speaking about the actual present state of mind of Churchill. I am speaking about a disposition, by which is meant that I am saying something about not what he necessarily does now think but what he would think if his attention were turned to the subject. Most of the psychological terms we use stand for dispositions and not actual states of mind. When we speak of a person knowing, desiring, fearing, valuing something, we do not ordinarily mean that he is at the moment we speak in a state of actual desire, fear, etc., but that he has a disposition (tendency) to be so in regard to the object in question. (No doubt we must distinguish between long- and short-term dispositions, e.g. he is afraid of dogs and he is afraid that he will not be able to go out to-day.) But dispositional terms have to be defined in terms of actual states. In order to understand what 'believe' in the dispositional sense means we have to know from experience in ourselves what an actual state of coming to believe is like, to understand what 'fear' in the dispositional sense is we must know what it is like to feel an actual emotion of fear, etc. It follows that we cannot explain psychological events by referring to dispositions. To explain a man's bad temper by a disposition to get angry is only to say that he does easily get angry. The only utility in talking like this is that it distinguishes the man's general bent from circumstances for which we can assign more specific causes. For instance, it implies that a particular outburst of bad temper on the part of the man is not to be explained adequately by saying that he was tired out and therefore 'not himself' or that the occasion, though trivial, was for him associated with some more important desire the frustation of which in most normal men would give rise to some symptoms like bad temper. It is important to realize that when we talk about dispositions we are only saying what a man does or would do, thinks or would think, feels or would feel under certain circumstances. For it is all too easy to suppose that when we have referred a psychological event to a disposition we have given an explanation of it as we have when we refer a physical event to some physical machinery. The difference between the two cases is that we can form an idea of what the physical machinery is like even when it is not producing the event in question. Physical machinery can be observed when it is not working, but psychological cannot be. The only way in which we can think of a disposition is as a law determining or inclining us to have certain experiences and perform certain actions. There may be an actually existent basis for the law in the mind, but if so we cannot say what it is like. We can only form an idea of the mind in terms of introspectively observable events, and we cannot introspectively observe our dispositions but only their manifestations in experience. A disposition, as we know it, can only be expressed in terms of a hypothetical proposition, i.e. I shall do and feel so and so if . . . , and is not anything that actually exists in between its manifestations. It is to psychology what a law is to physical science, except that it does not allow of precise mathematical calculation and that a man's dispositions are laws peculiar to him, not common to everybody. Of course the acquiring of even a long-term disposition can sometimes be explained, e.g. by experiences in early childhood, but in order to explain it we have to fall back on more permanent and general dispositions, e.g. the 'instincts.' The ideal of psychology as a science would be to explain all dispositions peculiar to an individual by deduction from dispositions common to all men together with the peculiar environment or physiological heredity of the individual man. Whether we think this ideal could conceivably ever be attained will depend on our views on issues such as determinism and pre-existence, but no doubt a great deal may be done in this way.

39 🙣

MEMORY AS THE
BASIS OF
PERSONAL IDENTITY

John Locke

*John Locke (1632-1706) was one of the major figures in the British empiricist move-
ment. He had a great influence on political thought, as well as on epistemology and
psychology.*

9. *Personal identity* — This being premised, to find wherein personal identity consists, we must consider what "person" stands for; which, I think,
is a thinking intelligent being, that has reason and reflection, and can consider
itself as itself, the same thinking thing, in different times and places; which
it does only by that consciousness which is inseparable from thinking, and it
seems to me essential to it: it being impossible for any one to perceive, without perceiving that he does perceive. When we see, hear, smell, taste, feel,
meditate, or will any thing, we know that we do so. Thus it is always as to
our present sensations and perceptions: and by this every one is to himself that
which he calls "self;" it not being considered, in this case, whether the same
self be continued in the same or diverse substances. For since consciousness
always accompanies thinking, and it is that that makes every one to be what
he calls "self," and thereby distinguishes himself from all other thinking
things; in this alone consists personal identity, *i.e.,* the sameness of a rational
being: and as far as this consciousness can be extended backwards to any
past action or thought, so far reaches the identity of that person; it is the
same self now it was then; and it is by the same self with this present one
that now reflects on it, that that action was done.

10. *Consciousness makes personal identity.* — But it is farther inquired,
whether it be the same identical substance? This, few would think they had
reason to doubt of, if these perceptions, with their consciousness, always
remained present in the mind, whereby the same thinking thing would be
always consciously present, and, as would be thought, evidently the same to
itself. But that which seems to make the difficulty is this, that this consciousness being interrupted always by forgetfulness, there being no moment of our

This selection comprises Sections 9-16, 20, and 22 of Book II, Chapter 27, of the
Essay Concerning Human Understanding, a work first published in 1690.

lives wherein we have the whole train of all our past actions before our eyes in one view; but even the best memories losing the sight of one part whilst they are viewing another; and we sometimes, and that the greatest part of our lives, not reflecting on our past selves, being intent on our present thoughts, and, in sound sleep, having no thoughts at all, or, at least, none with that consciousness which remarks our waking thoughts: I say, in all these cases, our consciousness being interrupted, and we losing the sight of our past selves, doubts are raised whether we are the same thinking thing, *i. e.,* the same substance, or no? which, however reasonable or unreasonable, concerns not personal identity at all: the question being, what makes the same person? and not, whether it be the same identical substance which always thinks in the same person? which in this case matters not at all; different substances, by the same consciousness (where they do partake in it), being united into one person, as well as different bodies by the same life are united into one animal, whose identity is preserved, in that change of substances, by the unity of one continued life. For it being the same consciousness that makes a man be himself to himself, personal identity depends on that only, whether it be annexed only to one individual substance, or can be continued in a succession of several substances. For as far as any intelligent being can repeat the idea of any past action with the same consciousness it had of it at first, and with the same consciousness it has of any present action; so far it is the same personal self. For it is by the consciousness it has of its present thoughts and actions that it is self to itself now, and so will be the same self, as far as the same consciousness can extend to actions past or to come; and would be by distance of time, or change of substance, no more two persons than a man be two men, by wearing other clothes today than he did yesterday, with a long or short sleep between: the same consciousness uniting those distant actions into the same person, whatever substances contributed to their production.

11. *Personal identity in change of substances.* — That this is so, we have some kind of evidence in our very bodies, all whose particles — whilst vitally united to this same thinking conscious self, so that we feel when they are touched, and are affected by and conscious of good or harm that happens to them — are a part of ourselves; *i. e.,* of our thinking conscious self. Thus the limbs of his body is to every one a part of himself: he sympathises and is concerned for them. Cut off an hand and thereby separate it from that consciousness he had of its heat, cold, and other affections, and it is then no longer a part of that which is himself, any more than the remotest part of matter. Thus we see the substance, whereof personal self consisted at one time, may be varied at another, without the change of personal identity; there being no question about the same person, though the limbs, which but now were a part of it, be cut off.

12. *Whether in the change of thinking substances.* — But the question is, Whether, if the same substance which thinks be changed, it can be the same person, or remaining the same, it can be different persons?

And to this I answer, First, This can be no question at all to those who place thought in a purely material, animal constitution, void of an immaterial substance. For, whether their supposition be true or no, it is plain they conceive personal identity preserved in something else than identity of substance; as animal identity is preserved in identity of life, and not of substance. And therefore those who place thinking in an immaterial substance only, before they can come to deal with these men, must show why personal identity cannot be preserved in the change of immaterial substances, or variety of particular immaterial substances, as well as animal identity is preserved in the change of material substances, or variety of particular bodies: unless they will say, it is one immaterial spirit that makes the same life in brutes, as it is one immaterial spirit that makes the same person in men, which the Cartesians at least will not admit, for fear of making brutes thinking things too.

13. But next, as to the first part of the question, Whether, if the same thinking substance (supposing immaterial substances only to think) be changed, it can be the same person? I answer, That cannot be resolved but by those who know what kind of substances they are that do think, and whether the consciousness of past actions can be transferred from one thinking substance to another. I grant, were the same consciousness the same individual action, it could not; but it being but a present representation of a past action, why it may not be possible that *that* may be represented to the mind to have been *which* really never was, will remain to be shown. And therefore how far the consciousness of past actions is annexed to any individual agent, so that another cannot possibly have it, will be hard for us to determine, till we know what kind of action it is that cannot be done without a reflex act of perception accompanying it, and how performed by thinking substances who cannot think without being conscious of it. But that which we call "the same consciousness" not being the same individual act, why one intellectual substance may not have represented to it as done by itself what it never did, and was perhaps done by some other agent; why, I say, such a representation may not possibly be without reality of matter of fact, as well as several representations in dreams are, which yet, whilst dreaming, we take for true, will be difficult to conclude from the nature of things. And that it never is so, will by us (till we have clearer views of the nature of thinking substances) be best resolved into the goodness of God, who, as far as the happiness or misery of any of his sensible creatures is concerned in it, will not by a fatal error of theirs transfer from one to another that consciousness which draws reward or punishment with it. How far this may be an argument against those who would place thinking in a system of fleeting animal spirits, I leave to be considered. But yet, to return to the question before us, it must be allowed, that if the same consciousness (which, as has been shown, is quite a different thing from the same numerical figure or motion in body) can be transferred from one thinking substance to another, it will be possible that two thinking substances may make but one person. For the same conscious-

ness being preserved, whether in the same or different substances, the personal identity is preserved.

14.   As to the second part of the question, Whether, the same immaterial substance remaining, there may be two distinct persons? Which question seems to me to be built on this, Whether the same immaterial being, being conscious of the actions of its past duration, may be wholly stripped of all the consciousness of its past existence, and lose it beyond the power of ever retrieving again; and so, as it were, beginning a new account from a new period, have a consciousness that cannot reach beyond this new state? All those who hold pre-existence are evidently of this mind, since they allow the soul to have no remaining consciousness of what it did in that pre-existent state, either wholly separate from body, or informing any other body; and if they should not, it is plain experience would be against them. So that personal identity reaching no farther than consciousness reaches, a pre-existent spirit not having continued so many ages in a state of silence, must needs make different persons. Suppose a Christian, Platonist, or Pythagorean, should, upon God's having ended all his works of creation the seventh day, think his soul hath existed ever since; and should imagine it has revolved in several human bodies, as I once met with one who was persuaded his had been the soul of Socrates: (how reasonably I will not dispute: this I know, that in the post he filled, which was no inconsiderable one, he passed for a very rational man; and the press has shown that he wanted not parts or learning:) would any one say, that he, being not conscious of any of Socrates's actions or thoughts, could be the same person with Socrates? Let any one reflect upon himself, and conclude, that he has in himself an immaterial spirit, which is that which thinks in him, and in the constant change of his body keeps him the same; and is that which he calls himself; let him also suppose it to be the same soul that was in Nestor or Thersites, at the siege of Troy, (for souls being, as far as we know any thing of them, in their nature indifferent to any parcel of matter, the supposition has no apparent absurdity in it,) which it may have been as well as it is now the soul of any other man: but he now having no consciousness of any of the actions either of Nestor or Thersites, does or can he conceive himself the same person with either of them? Can he be concerned in either of their actions? attribute them to himself, or think them his own, more than the actions of any other man that ever existed? So that this consciousness not reaching to any of the actions of either of those men, he is no more one self with either of them, than if the soul or immaterial spirit that now informs him had been created and began to exist when it began to inform his present body, though it were ever so true that the same spirit that informed Nestor's or Thersites's body were numerically the same that now informs his. For this would no more make him the same person with Nestor, than if some of the particles of matter that were once a part of Nestor were now a part of this man; the same immaterial substance, without the same consciousness, no more making

the same person by being united to any body, than the same particle of matter, without consciousness, united to any body, makes the same person. But let him once find himself conscious of any of the actions of Nestor, he then finds himself the same person with Nestor.

15.   And thus we may be able, without any difficulty, to conceive the same person at the resurrection, though in a body not exactly in make or parts the same which he had here, the same consciousness going along with the soul that inhabits it. But yet the soul alone, in the change of bodies, would scarce to any one, but to him that makes the soul the man, be enough to make the same man. For, should the soul of a prince, carrying with it the consciousness of the prince's past life, enter and inform the body of a cobbler, as soon as deserted by his own soul, every one sees he would be the same person with the prince, accountable only for the prince's actions: but who would say it was the same man? The body too goes to the making of the man, and would, I guess, to every body determine the man in this case, wherein the soul, with all its princely thoughts about it, would not make another man; but he would be the same cobbler to every one besides himself. I know that, in the ordinary way of speaking, the same person and the same man stand for one and the same thing. And, indeed, every one will always have a liberty to speak as he pleases, and to apply what articulate sounds to what ideas he thinks fit, and change them as often as he pleases. But yet, when we will inquire what makes the same spirit, man, or person, we must fix the ideas of spirit, man, or person in our minds; and having resolved with ourselves what we mean by them, it will not be hard to determine in either of them, or the like, when it is the same and when not.

16. *Consciousness makes the same person.* — But though the same immaterial substance or soul does not alone, wherever it be, and in whatsoever state, make the same man; yet it is plain, consciousness, as far as ever it can be extended, should it be to ages past, unites existences and actions, very remote in time, into the same person, as well as it does the existence and actions of the immediately preceding moment: so that whatever has the consciousness of present and past actions is the same person to whom they both belong. Had I the same consciousness that I saw the ark and Noah's flood, as that I saw an overflowing of the Thames last winter, or as that I write now, I could no more doubt that I who write this now, that saw the Thames overflowed last winter, and that viewed the flood at the general deluge, was the same self, place that self in what substance you please, than that I who write this am the same myself now whilst I write (whether I consist of all the same substance, material or immaterial, or no) that I was yesterday. For, as to this point of being the same self, it matters not whether this present self be made up of the same or other substances, I being as much concerned and as justly accountable for any action was done a thousand years since, appropriated to me now by this self-consciousness, as I am for what I did the last moment.

.   .   .

20. But yet possibly it will still be objected, "Suppose I wholly lose the memory of some parts of my life, beyond the possibility of retrieving them, so that perhaps I shall never be conscious of them again; yet am I not the same person that did those actions, had those thoughts, that I was once conscious of, though I have now forgot them?" To which I answer, That we must here take notice what the word "I" is applied to; which in this case, is the man only. And the same man being presumed to be the same person, "I" is easily here supposed to stand also for the same person. But if it be possible for the same man to have distinct incommunicable consciousnesses at different times, it is past doubt the same man would at different times make different persons; which, we see, is the sense of mankind in the solemnest declaration of their opinions, human laws not punishing the mad man for the sober man's actions, nor the sober man for what the mad man did, thereby making them two persons; which is somewhat explained by our way of speaking in English, when we say, "Such an one is not himself, or is beside himself;" in which phrases it is insinuated as if those who now or, at least, first used them, thought that self was changed, the self-same person was no longer in that man.

· · ·

22. "But is not a man drunk and sober the same person? Why else is he punished for the fact he commits when drunk, though he be never afterwards conscious of it?" Just as much the same person as a man that walks and does other things in his sleep is the same person, and is answerable for any mischief he shall do in it. Human laws punish both with a justice suitable to their way of knowledge; because in these cases they cannot distinguish certainly what is real, what counterfeit; and so the ignorance in drunkenness or sleep is not admitted as a plea. For, though punishment be annexed to personality, and personality to consciousness, and the drunkard perhaps be not conscious of what he did; yet human judicatures justly punish him, because the fact is proved against him, but want of consciousness cannot be proved for him. But in the great day, wherein the secrets of all hearts shall be laid open, it may be reasonable to think, no one shall be made to answer for what he knows nothing of; but shall receive his doom, his conscience accusing or excusing.

40

A CRITIQUE
OF LOCKE
ON PERSONAL IDENTITY

Thomas Reid

Thomas Reid (1710-1796) was the founder of the Scottish "common sense" school of philosophy. He was Professor of Moral Philosophy in the University of Glasgow.

1. *Of Identity in General.*] The conviction which every man has of his identity, as far back as his memory reaches, needs no aid of philosophy to strengthen it; and no philosophy can weaken it, without first producing some degree of insanity.

The philosopher, however, may very properly consider this conviction as a phenomenon of human nature worthy of his attention. If he can discover its cause, an addition is made to his stock of knowledge; if not, it must be held as a part of our original constitution, or an effect of that constitution produced in a manner unknown to us.

That we may form as distinct a notion as we are able of this phenomenon of the human mind, it is proper to consider what is meant by identity in general, what by our own personal identity, and how we are led into that invincible belief and conviction which every man has of his own personal identity, as far as his memory reaches.

Identity in general I take to be a relation between a thing which is known to exist at one time, and a thing which is known to have existed at another time. If you ask whether they are one and the same, or two different things, every man of common sense understands the meaning of your question perfectly. Whence we may infer with certainty, that every man of common sense has a clear and distinct notion of identity.

If you ask a definition of identity, I confess I can give none; it is too simple a notion to admit of logical definition: I can say it is a relation, but I cannot find words to express the specific difference between this and other relations, though I am in no danger of confounding it with

This selection is the whole of Chapter III, "Of the Nature and Origin of Our Notion of Personal Identity," of Essay III from *Essays on the Intellectual Powers of Man* (1785).

any other. I can say that diversity is a contrary relation, and that similitude and dissimilitude are another couple of contrary relations, which every man easily distinguishes in his conception from identity and diversity.

I see evidently that identity supposes *an uninterrupted continuance of existence*. That which has ceased to exist cannot be the same with that which afterwards begins to exist; for this would be to suppose a being to exist after it ceased to exist, and to have had existence before it was produced, which are manifest contradictions. Continued uninterrupted existence is therefore necessarily implied in identity. Hence we may infer, that identity cannot, in its proper sense, be applied to our pains, our pleasures, our thoughts, or any operation of our minds. The pain felt this day is not the same individual pain which I felt yesterday, though they may be *similar* in kind and degree, and have the same cause. The same may be said of every feeling, and of every operation of mind. They are all successive in their nature, like time itself, no two moments of which can be the same moment. It is otherwise with the parts of absolute space. They always are, and were, and will be the same. So far, I think, we proceed upon clear ground in fixing the notion of identity in general.

II. *Nature and Origin of our Idea of Personal Identity.*] It is perhaps more difficult to ascertain with precision the meaning of *personality;* but it is not necessary in the present subject: it is sufficient for our purpose to observe, that all mankind place their personality in something that *cannot be divided, or consist of parts.* A part of a person is a manifest absurdity. When a man loses his estate, his health, his strength, he is still the same person, and has lost nothing of his personality. If he has a leg or an arm cut off, he is the same person he was before. The amputated member is no part of his person, otherwise it would have a right to a part of his estate, and be liable for a part of his engagements. It would be entitled to a share of his merit and demerit, which is manifestly absurd. A person is something indivisible, and is what Leibniz calls a *monad*.

My personal identity, therefore, implies the continued existence of that indivisible thing which I call *myself.* Whatever this self may be, it is something which thinks, and deliberates, and resolves, and acts, and suffers. I am not thought, I am not action, I am not feeling; I am something that thinks, and acts, and suffers. My thoughts, and actions, and feelings, change every moment; they have no continued, but a successive, existence; but that *self,* or *I,* to which they belong, is permanent, and has the same relation to all the succeeding thoughts, actions, and feelings which I call mine.

Such are the notions that I have of my personal identity. But perhaps it may be said, this may all be fancy without reality. How do you know, — what evidence have you, — that there is such a permanent self which has a claim to all the thoughts, actions, and feelings which you call yours?

To this I answer, that the proper evidence I have of all this is *remembrance.* I remember that twenty years ago I conversed with such a person; I remember several things that passed in that conversation: my memory testifies, not only that this was done, but that it was done by me who now remember it. If it was done by me, I must have existed at that time, and continued to exist from that time to the present: if the identical person whom I call myself had not a part in that conversation, my memory is fallacious; it gives a distinct and positive testimony of what is not true. Every man in his senses believes what he distinctly remembers, and every thing he remembers convinces him that he existed at the time remembered.

Although memory gives the most irresistible evidence of my being the identical person that did such a thing, at such a time, I may have other good evidence of things which befell me, and which I do not remember: I know who bare me, and suckled me, but I do not remember these events.

It may here be observed, (though the observation would have been unnecessary, if some great philosophers had not contradicted it,) that it is not my remembering any action of mine that *makes* me to be the person who did it. This remembrance makes me to *know* assuredly that I did it; *but I might have done it, though I did not remember it.* That relation to me, which is expressed by saying that *I did it,* would be the same, though I had not the least remembrance of it. To say that my remembering that I did such a thing, or, as some choose to express it, my being conscious that I did it, makes me to have done it, appears to me as great an absurdity as it would be to say, that my belief that the world was created made it to be created.

When we pass judgment on the identity of other persons than ourselves, we proceed upon other grounds, and determine from a variety of circumstances, which sometimes produce the firmest assurance, and sometimes leave room for doubt. The identity of persons has often furnished matter of serious litigation before tribunals of justice. But no man of a sound mind ever doubted of his own identity, as far as he distinctly remembered.

The identity of a person is a perfect identity: wherever it is real, it admits of no degrees; and it is impossible that a person should be in part the same, and in part different; because a person is a *monad,* and is not divisible into parts. The evidence of identity in other persons than ourselves does indeed admit of all degrees, from what we account certainty, to the least degree of probability. But still it is true, that the same person is perfectly the same, and cannot be so in part, or in some degree only.

For this cause, I have first considered personal identity, as that which is perfect in its kind, and the natural measure of that which is imperfect.

We probably at first derive our notion of identity from that natural conviction which every man has from the dawn of reason of *his own* identity and continued existence. The operations of our minds are all successive, and have no continued existence. But the thinking being has a continued existence, and we have an invincible belief, that it remains the same when all its thoughts and operations change.

Our judgments of the identity of objects of sense seem to be formed much upon the same grounds as our judgments of the identity of *other per-*

sons than ourselves. Wherever we observe great *similarity,* we are apt to presume identity, if no reason appears to the contrary. Two objects ever so like, when they are perceived at the same time, cannot be the same; but if they are presented to our senses at different times, we are apt to think them the same, merely from their similarity.

Whether this be a natural prejudice, or from whatever cause it proceeds, it certainly appears in children from infancy; and when we grow up, it is confirmed in most instances by experience: for we rarely find two individuals of the same species that are not distinguishable by obvious differences. A man challenges a thief whom he finds in possession of his horse or his watch, only on similarity. When the watchmaker swears that he sold this watch to such a person, his testimony is grounded on similarity. The testimony of witnesses to the identity of a person is commonly grounded on no other evidence.

Thus it appears, that the evidence we have of our own identity, as far back as we remember, is totally of a different kind from the evidence we have of the identity of other persons, or of objects of sense. The first is grounded on *memory,* and gives undoubted certainty. The last is grounded on *similarity,* and on other circumstances, which in many cases are not so decisive as to leave no room for doubt.

It may likewise be observed, that the identity of *objects of sense* is never perfect. All bodies, as they consist of innumerable parts that may be disjoined from them by a great variety of causes, are subject to continual changes of their substance, increasing, diminishing, changing insensibly. When such alterations are gradual, because language could not afford a different name for every different state of such a changeable being, it retains the same name, and is considered as the same thing. Thus we say of an old regiment, that it did such a thing a century ago, though there now is not a man alive who then belonged to it. We say a tree is the same in the seed-bed and in the forest. A ship of war, which has successively changed her anchors, her tackle, her sails, her masts, her planks, and her timbers, while she keeps the same name, is the same.

The identity, therefore, which we ascribe to bodies, whether natural or artificial, is not perfect identity; it is rather something which, for the conveniency of speech, we call identity. It admits of a great change of the subject, providing the change be *gradual;* sometimes, even of a total change. And the changes which in common language are made consistent with identity differ from those that are thought to destroy it, not in *kind,* but in *number* and *degree.* It has no fixed nature when applied to bodies; and questions about the identity of a body are very often questions about words. But identity, when applied to persons, has no ambiguity, and admits not of degrees, or of more and less. It is the foundation of all rights and obligations, and of all accountableness; and the notion of it is fixed and precise.

III. *Strictures on Locke's Account of Personal Identity.*] In a long chapter, *Of Identity and Diversity*, Mr. Locke has made many ingenious and just observations, and some which I think cannot be defended. I shall only take notice of the account he gives of our own personal identity. His doctrine upon this subject has been censured by Bishop Butler, in a short essay subjoined to his *Analogy*, with whose sentiments I perfectly agree.

Identity, as has been observed, supposes the continued existence of the being of which it is affirmed, and therefore can be applied only to things which have a continued existence. While any being continues to exist, it is the same being; but two beings which have a different beginning or a different ending of their existence cannot possibly be the same. To this, I think, Mr. Locke agrees.

He observes, very justly, that, to know what is meant by the same person, we must consider what the word *person* stands for; and he defines a person to be an intelligent being, endowed with reason and with consciousness, which last he thinks inseparable from thought. From this definition of a person, it must necessarily follow, that, while the intelligent being continues to exist and to be intelligent, it must be the *same* person. To say that the intelligent being is the person, and yet that the person ceases to exist while the intelligent being continues, or that the person continues while the intelligent being ceases to exist, is to my apprehension a manifest contradiction.

One would think that the definition of a person should perfectly ascertain the *nature* of personal identity, or wherein it consists, though it might still be a question how we come *to know and be assured of* our personal identity.

Mr. Locke tells us, however, "that personal identity, that is, the sameness of a rational being, *consists in consciousness alone*, and, as far as this consciousness can be extended backwards to any past action or thought, so far reaches the identity of that person. So that whatever has the consciousness of present and past actions is the same person to whom they belong."

This doctrine has some strange consequences, which the author was aware of. (1.) Such as, that if the same consciousness can be transferred from one intelligent being to another, which he thinks we cannot show to be impossible, *then two or twenty intelligent beings may be the same person.* (2.) And if the intelligent being may lose the consciousness of the actions done by him, which surely is possible, then he is not the person that did those actions; so that *one intelligent being may be two or twenty different persons,* if he shall so often lose the consciousness of his former actions.

(3.) There is another consequence of this doctrine, which follows no less necessarily, though Mr. Locke probably did not see it. It is, *that a man may be, and at the same time not be, the person that did a particular action.* Suppose a brave officer to have been flogged when a boy at school for robbing an orchard, to have taken a standard from the enemy in his first campaign, and to have been made a general in advanced life; suppose, also, which must be admitted to be possible, that, when he took the standard, he was conscious of his having been flogged at school, and that, when made a general, he was conscious of his taking the standard, but had absolutely lost the consciousness of his flogging. These things being supposed, it follows, from Mr. Locke's doctrine, that he who was flogged at school is the same person who took the standard, and that he who took the standard is the same person who was made a general. Whence it follows, if there be any truth in logic, that the general is the same person with him who was flogged at school. But the general's consciousness does not reach so far back as his flogging; therefore, according to Mr. Locke's doctrine, he is not the person who was flogged. Therefore the general is, and at the same time is not, the same person with him who was flogged at school.

Leaving the consequences of this doctrine to those who have leisure to trace them, we may observe, with regard to the doctrine itself, —

First, that Mr. Locke attributes to consciousness the conviction we have of our past actions, as if a man may now be conscious of what he did twenty years ago. It is impossible to understand the meaning of this, unless by *consciousness* he meant *memory,* the only faculty by which we have an immediate knowledge of our past actions.

Sometimes, in popular discourse, a man says he is conscious that he did such a thing, meaning that he distinctly remembers that he did it. It is unnecessary, in common discourse, to fix accurately the limits between consciousness and memory. This was formerly shown to be the case with regard to sense and memory: and therefore distinct remembrance is sometimes called sense, sometimes consciousness, without any inconvenience. But this ought to be avoided in philosophy, otherwise we confound the different powers of the mind, and ascribe to one what really belongs to another. If a man can be conscious of what he did twenty years or twenty minutes ago, there is no use for memory, nor ought we to allow that there is any such faculty. The faculties of consciousness and memory are chiefly distinguished by this, that the first is an immediate knowledge of the present, the second an immediate knowledge of the past.

When, therefore, Mr. Locke's notion of personal-identity is properly expressed, it is, that personal identity *consists in distinct remembrance;* for, even in the popular sense, to say that I am conscious of a past action means nothing else than that I distinctly remember that I did it.

Secondly, it may be observed, that, in this doctrine, not only is consciousness confounded with memory, but, which is still more strange, *personal identity* is confounded with *the evidence which we have of our personal identity.*

It is very true, that my remembrance that I did such a thing is the evidence I have that I am the identical person who did it. And this, I am apt to think, Mr. Locke meant. But to say that my remembrance that I did such a thing, or my consciousness, *makes* me the person who did it, is, in my apprehension, an absurdity too gross to be entertained by any man who attends to the meaning of it; for it is to attribute to memory or consciousness a strange magical power of producing its object, though that object must have existed before the memory or consciousness which produced it. Consciousness is the testimony of one faculty; memory is the testimony of another faculty; and to say that the testimony is the cause of the thing testified, this surely is absurd, if any thing be, and could not have been said by Mr. Locke, if he had not confounded the testimony with the thing testified.

When a horse that was stolen is found and claimed by the owner, the only evidence he can have, or that a judge or witnesses can have, that this is the very identical horse which was his property, is similitude. But would it not be ridiculous from this to infer that the identity of a horse *consists* in similitude only? The only *evidence* I have that I am the identical person who did such actions is, that I remember distinctly I did them; or, as Mr. Locke expresses it, I am conscious I did them. To infer from this, that personal identity consists in consciousnesss, is an argument which, if it had any force, would prove the identity of a stolen horse to consist solely in similitude.

Thirdly, is it not strange that the sameness or identity of a person should consist in a thing *which is continually changing,* and is not any two minutes the same?

Our consciousness, our memory, and every operation of the mind, are still flowing like the water of a river, or like time itself. The consciousness I have this moment can no more be the same consciousness I had last moment, than this moment can be the last moment. Identity can only be affirmed of things which have a continued existence. Consciousness, and every kind of thought, are transient and momentary, and have no continued existence; and, therefore, if personal identity consisted in consciousness, it would certainly follow, that *no man is the same person any two moments of his life;* and as the right and justice of reward and punishment are founded on personal identity, no man could be responsible for his actions.

But though I take this to be the unavoidable consequence of Mr. Locke's doctrine concerning personal identity, and though some persons may have liked the doctrine the better on this account, I am far from imputing any thing of this kind to Mr. Locke. He was too good a man not to have rejected with abhorrence a doctrine which he believed to draw this consequence after it.

Fourthly, there are many expressions used by Mr. Locke, in speaking of personal identity, which to me are altogether unintelligible, unless we suppose that he confounded that sameness or identity which we ascribe to an individual with the identity which, in common discourse, is often ascribed to many individuals of the same species.

When we say that pain and pleasure, consciousness and memory, are the same in all men, this sameness can only mean similarity, or sameness *of kind.* That the pain of one man can be the same individual pain with that of another man is no less impossible, than that one man should be another man: the pain felt by me yesterday can no more be the pain I feel to-day, than yesterday can be this day; and the same thing may be said of every passion and of every operation of the mind. The same kind or species of operation may be in different men, or in the same man at different times; but it is impossible that the same individual operation should be in different men, or in the same man at different times.

When Mr. Locke, therefore, speaks of "the same consciousness being continued through a succession of different substances"; when he speaks of "repeating the idea of a past action, with the same consciousness we had of it at the first," and of "the same consciousness extending to actions past and to come"; these expressions are to me unintelligible, unless he means not the same individual consciousness, but a consciousness that is similar, or of the same kind. If our personal identity consists in consciousness, as this consciousness cannot be the same individually any two moments, but only of the *same kind*, it would follow, that we are not for any two moments the same individual persons, but the same *kind* of persons. As our consciousness sometimes ceases to exist, as in sound sleep, our personal identity must cease with it. Mr. Locke allows, that the same thing cannot have two beginnings of existence, so that our identity would be irrecoverably gone every time we ceased to think, if it was but for a moment.

41

SCIENCE AND IMMORTALITY: A POSITIVE REPORT

William James

(See Reading 5 for biographical note.)

.   .   .

These points are both of them in the nature of replies to objections, to difficulties which our modern culture finds in the old notion of a life hereafter, — difficulties that I am sure rob the notion of much of its old power to draw belief, in the scientifically cultivated circles to which this audience belong.

The first of these difficulties is relative to the absolute dependence of our spiritual life, as we know it here, upon the brain. One hears not only physiologists, but numbers of laymen who read the popular science books and magazines, saying all about us, How can we believe in life hereafter when Science has once for all attained to proving, beyond possibility of escape, that our inner life is a function of that famous material, the so-called 'gray matter' of our cerebral convolutions? How can the function possibly persist after its organ has undergone decay?

Thus physiological psychology is what is supposed to bar the way to the old faith. And it is now as a physiological psychologist that I ask you to look at the question with me a little more closely.

It is indeed true that physiological science has come to the conclusion cited; and we must confess that in so doing she has only carried out a little farther the common belief of mankind. Every one knows that arrests of brain development occasion imbecility, that blows on the head abolish memory or consciousness, and that brain-stimulants and poisons change the quality of our ideas. The anatomists, physiologists, and pathologists have only shown this generally admitted fact of a dependence to be detailed and minute. What the laboratories and hospitals have lately been teaching us is not only that thought in general is one of the brain's functions, but that the various special forms of thinking are functions of special portions of the brain. When we

From a lecture given by James in the series of Ingersoll Lectures on Immortality, entitled *Human Immortality: Two Supposed Objections to the Doctrine* (1899).

are thinking of things seen, it is our occipital convolutions that are active; when of things heard, it is a certain portion of our temporal lobes; when of things to be spoken, it is one of our frontal convolutions. Professor Flechsig of Leipzig (who perhaps more than any one may claim to have made the subject his own) considers that in other special convolutions those processes of association go on, which permit the more abstract processes of thought, to take place. I could easily show you these regions if I had a picture of the brain. Moreover, the diminished or exaggerated associations of what this author calls the *Körperfühlsphäre* with the other regions, accounts, according to him, for the complexion of our emotional life, and eventually decides whether one shall be a callous brute or criminal, an unbalanced sentimentalist, or a character accessible to feeling, and yet well poised. Such special opinions may have to be corrected; yet so firmly established do the main positions worked out by the anatomists, physiologists, and pathologists of the brain appear, that the youth of our medical schools are everywhere taught unhesitatingly to believe them. The assurance that observation will go on to establish them ever more and more minutely is the inspirer of all contemporary research. And almost any of our young psychologists will tell you that only a few belated scholastics, or possibly some crack-brained theosophist or psychical researcher, can be found holding back, and still talking as if mental phenomena might exist as independent variables in the world.

For the purposes of my argument, now, I wish to adopt this general doctrine as if it were established absolutely, with no possibility of restriction. During this hour I wish you also to accept it as a postulate, whether you think it incontrovertibly established or not; so I beg you to agree with me to-day in subscribing to the great psycho-physiological formula: *Thought is a function of the brain.*

The question is, then, Does this doctrine logically compel us to disbelieve in immortality? Ought it to force every truly consistent thinker to sacrifice his hopes of an hereafter to what he takes to be his duty of accepting all the consequences of a scientific truth?

Most persons imbued with what one may call the puritanism of science would feel themselves bound to answer this question with a yes. If any medically or psychologically bred young scientists feel otherwise, it is probably in consequence of that incoherency of mind of which the majority of mankind happily enjoy the privilege. At one hour scientists, at another they are Christians or common men, with the will to live burning hot in their breasts; and, holding thus the two ends of the chain, they are careless of the intermediate connection. But the more radical and uncompromising disciple of science makes the sacrifice, and, sorrowfully or not, according to his temperament, submits to giving up his hopes of heaven.

This, then, is the objection to immortality; and the next thing in order for me is to try to make plain to you why I believe that it has in strict logic no deterrent power. I must show you that the fatal consequence is not coercive, as is commonly imagined; and that, even though our soul's life (as here below it is revealed to us) may be in literal strictness the function of a brain that perishes, yet it is not at all impossible, but on the contrary quite possible, that the life may still continue when the brain itself is dead.

The supposed impossibility of its continuing comes from too superficial a look at the admitted fact of functional dependence. The moment we inquire more closely into the notion of functional dependence, and ask ourselves, for example, how many kinds of functional dependence there may be, we immediately perceive that there is one kind at least that does not exclude a life hereafter at all. The fatal conclusion of the physiologist flows from his assuming off-hand another kind of functional dependence, and treating it as the only imaginable kind.

When the physiologist who thinks that his science cuts off all hope of immortality pronounces the phrase, "Thought is a function of the brain," he thinks of the matter just as he thinks when he says, "Steam is a function of the tea-kettle," "Light is a function of the electric circuit," "Power is a function of the moving waterfall." In these latter cases the several material objects have the function of inwardly creating or engendering their effects, and their function must be called *productive* function. Just so, he thinks, it must be with the brain. Engendering consciousness in its interior, much as it engenders cholesterin and creatin and carbonic acid, its relation to our soul's life must also be called productive function. Of course, if such production be the function, then when the organ perishes, since the production can no longer continue, the soul must surely die. Such a conclusion as this is indeed inevitable from that particular conception of the facts.

But in the world of physical nature productive function of this sort is not the only kind of function with which we are familiar. We have also releasing or permissive function; and we have transmissive function.

The trigger of a crossbow has a releasing function: it removes the obstacle that holds the string, and lets the bow fly back to its natural shape. So when the hammer falls upon a detonating compound. By knocking out the inner molecular obstructions, it lets the constituent gases resume their normal bulk, and so permits the explosion to take place.

In the case of a colored glass, a prism, or a refracting lens, we have transmissive function. The energy of light, no matter how produced, is by the glass sifted and limited in color, and by the lens or prism determined to a certain path and shape. Similarly, the keys of an organ have only a transmisssive function. They open successively the various pipes and let the wind in the air-chest escape in various ways. The voices of the various pipes are constituted by the columns of air trembling as they emerge. But the air is not engendered in the organ. The organ proper, as distinguished from its air-chest, is only an apparatus for letting portions of it loose upon the world in these peculiarly limited shapes.

My thesis now is this: that, when we think of the law that thought is a function of the brain, we are not required to think of productive function only; *we are entitled also to consider permissive or transmissive function.* And this the ordinary psycho-physiologist leaves out of his account.

Suppose, for example, that the whole universe of material things — the furniture of earth and choir of heaven — should turn out to be a mere surface-veil of phenomena, hiding and keeping back the world of genuine realities. Such a supposition is foreign neither to common sense nor to philosophy. Common sense believes in realities behind the veil even too superstitiously; and idealistic philosophy declares the whole world of natural experience, as we get it, to be but a time-mask, shattering or refracting the one infinite Thought which is the sole reality into those millions of finite streams of consciousness known to us as our private selves.

> "Life, like a dome of many-colored glass,
> Stains the white radiance of eternity."

Suppose, now, that this were really so, and suppose, moreover, that the dome, opaque enough at all times to the full super-solar blaze, could at certain times and places grow less so, and let certain beams pierce through into this sublunary world. These beams would be so many finite rays, so to speak, of consciousness, and they would vary in quantity and quality as the opacity varied in degrees. Only at particular times and places would it seem that, as a matter of fact, the veil of nature can grow thin and rupturable enough for such effects to occur. But in those places gleams, however finite and unsatisfying, of the absolute life of the universe, are from time to time vouchsafed. Glows of feeling, glimpses of insight, and streams of knowledge and perception float into our finite world.

Admit now that *our brains* are such thin and half-transparent places in the veil. What will happen? Why, as the white radiance comes through the dome, with all sorts of straining and distortion imprinted on it by the glass, or as the air now comes through my glottis determined and limited in its force and quality of its vibrations by the peculiarities of those vocal chords which form its gate of egress and shape it into my personal voice, even so the genuine matter of reality, the life of souls as it is in its fullness, will break through our several brains into this world in all sorts of restricted forms, and with all the imperfections and queernesses that characterize our finite individualities here below.

According to the state in which the brain finds itself, the barrier of its obstructiveness may also be supposed to rise or fall. It sinks so low, when the brain is in full activity, that a comparative flood of spiritual energy pours over. At other times, only such occasional waves of thought as heavy sleep permits get by. And when finally a brain stops acting altogether, or decays, that special stream of consciousness which it subserved will vanish entirely from this natural world. But the sphere of being that supplied the consciousness would still be intact; and in that more real world with which, even whilst here, it was continuous, the consciousness might, in ways unknown to us, continue still.

You see that, on all these suppositions, our soul's life, as we here know it, would none the less in literal strictness be the function of the brain. The brain would be the independent variable, the mind would vary dependently on it. But such dependence on the brain for this natural life would in no wise make immortal life impossible, — it might be quite compatible with supernatural life behind the veil hereafter.

As I said, then, the fatal consequence is not coercive, the conclusion which materialism draws being due solely to its one-sided way of taking the word 'function.' And whether we care or not for immortality in itself, we ought, as mere critics doing police duty among the vagaries of mankind, to insist on the illogicality of a denial based on the flat ignoring of a palpable alternative. How much more ought we to insist, as lovers of truth, when the denial is that of such a vital hope of mankind!

In strict logic, then, the fangs of cerebralistic materialism are drawn. My words ought consequently already to exert a releasing function on your hopes. You *may* believe henceforward, whether you care to profit by the permission or not. But, as this is a very abstract argument, I think it will help its effect to say a word or two about the more concrete conditions of the case.

All abstract hypotheses sound unreal; and the abstract notion that our brains are colored lenses in the wall of nature, admitting light from the super-solar source, but at the same time tingeing and restricting it, has a thoroughly fantastic sound. What is it, you may ask, but a foolish metaphor? And how can such a function be imagined? Isn't the common materialistic notion vastly simpler? Is not consciousness really more comparable to a sort of steam, or perfume, or electricity, or nerveglow, generated on the spot in its own peculiar vessel? Is it not more rigorously scientific to treat the brain's function as function of production?

The immediate reply is, that, if we are talking of science positively understood, function can mean nothing more than bare concomitant variation. When the brain-activities change in one way, consciousness changes in another; when the currents pour through the occipital lobes, consciousness *sees* things; when through the lower frontal region, consciousness *says* things to itself; when they stop, she goes to sleep, etc. In strict science, we can only write down the bare fact of concomitance; and all talk about either production or transmission, as the mode of taking place, is pure superadded hypothesis, and metaphysical hypothesis at that, for we can frame no more notion of the details on the one alternative than on the other. Ask for any indication of the exact process either of transmission or of production, and Science confesses her imagination to be bankrupt. She has, so far, not the least glimmer of a conjecture or suggestion, — not even a bad verbal metaphor or pun to offer. *Ignoramus, ignorabimus,* is what most physiologists, in the words of one of their number, will say here. The production of such a thing as consciousness in the brain, they will reply with the late Berlin professor of physiology, is the absolute world-enigma, — something so paradoxical and abnormal as to be a stumbling block to Nature, and almost a self-contradiction. Into the mode of production of steam in a tea-kettle we have conjectural insight, for the terms that change are physically homogeneous one with another, and we can easily imagine the case to consist of nothing but alterations of molecular motion. But in the production of consciousness by the brain, the terms are heterogeneous natures altogether; and as far as our understanding goes, it is as great a miracle as if we said, Thought is 'spontaneously generated,' or 'created out of nothing.'

The theory of production is therefore not a jot more simple or credible in itself than any other conceivable theory. It is only a little more popular. All that one need do, therefore, if the ordinary materialist should challenge one to explain how the brain *can* be an organ for limiting and determining to a certain form a consciousness elsewhere produced, is to retort with a *tu quoque*, asking him in turn to explain how it can be an organ for producing consciousness out of whole cloth. For polemic purposes, the two theories are thus exactly on a par.

But if we consider the theory of transmission in a wider way, we see that it has certain positive superiorities, quite apart from its connection with the immortality question.

Just how the process of transmission may be carried on, is indeed unimaginable; but the outer relations, so to speak, of the process, encourage our belief. Consciousness in this process does not have to be generated *de novo* in a vast number of places. It exists already, behind the scenes, coeval with the world. The transmission-theory not only avoids in this way multiplying miracles, but it put itself in touch with general idealistic philosophy better than the production-theory does. It should always be reckoned a good thing when science and philosophy thus meet.

It puts itself also in touch with the conception of a 'threshold,' — a word with which, since Fechner wrote his book called 'Psychophysik,' the so-called 'new Psychology' has rung. Fechner imagines as the condition of consciousness a certain kind of psycho-physical movement, as he terms it. Before consciousness can come, a certain degree of activity in the movement must be reached. This requisite degree is called the 'threshold;' but the height of the threshold varies under different circumstances: it may rise or fall. When it falls, as in states of great lucidity, we grow conscious of things of which we should be unconscious at other times; when it rises, as in drowsiness, consciousness sinks in amounts. This rising and lowering of a psycho-physical threshold exactly conforms to our notion of a permanent obstruction to the transmission of consciousness, which obstruction may, in our brains, grow alternately greater or less.

The transmission-theory also puts itself in touch with a whole class of experiences that are with difficulty explained by the production-theory. I refer to those obscure and exceptional phenomena reported at all times throughout human history, which the 'psychical-researchers,' with Mr. Frederic Myers at their head, are doing so much to rehabilitate; such phenomena, namely, as religious conversions, providential leadings in answer to prayer, instantaneous healings, premonitions, apparitions at time of death, clairvoyant visions or impressions, and the whole range of mediumistic capacities, to say nothing of still more exceptional and incomprehensible things. If all our human thought be a function of the brain, then of course, if any of these things are facts, — and to my own mind some of them are facts, — we may not suppose that they can occur without preliminary brain-action. But the ordinary production-theory of consciousness is knit up with a peculiar notion of how brain-action *can* occur, — that notion being that all brain-action, without exception, is due to a prior action, immediate or remote, of the bodily sense-organs *on* the brain. Such action makes the brain produce sensations and mental images, and out of the sensations and images the higher forms of thought and knowledge in their turn are framed. As transmissionists, we also must admit this to be the condition of all our usual thought. Sense-action is what lowers the brain-barrier. My voice and aspect, for instance, strike upon your ears and eyes; your brain thereupon becomes more pervious, and an awareness on your part of what I say and who I am slips into this world from the world behind the veil. But, in the mysterious phenomena to which I allude, it is often hard to see where the sense-organs can come in. A medium, for example, will show knowledge of his sitter's private affairs which it seems impossible he should have acquired through sight or hearing, or inference therefrom. Or you will have an apparition of some one who is now dying hundreds of miles away. On the production-theory one does not see from what sensations such odd bits of knowledge are produced. On the transmission-theory, they don't have to be 'produced,' — they exist ready-made in the transcendental world, and all that is needed is an abnormal lowering of the brain-threshold to let them through. In cases of conversion, in providential leadings, sudden mental healings, etc., it seems to the subjects themselves of the experience as if a power from without, quite different from the ordinary action of the senses or of the sense-led mind, came into their life, as if the latter suddenly opened into that greater life in which it has its source. The word 'influx,' used in ·Swedenborgian circles, well describes this impression of new insight, or new willingness, sweeping over us like a tide. All such experiences, quite paradoxical and meaningless on the production-theory, fall very naturally into place on the other theory. We need only suppose the continuity of our consciousness with a mother sea, to allow for exceptional waves occasionally pouring over the dam. Of course the causes of these odd lowerings of the brain's threshold still remain a mystery on any terms.

.   .   .

But still, you will ask, in what positive way does this theory help us to realize our immortality in imagination? What we all wish to keep is just these individual restrictions, these selfsame tendencies and peculiarities that define us to ourselves and others, and constitute our identity, so called. Our finitenesses and limitations seem to be our personal essence; and when the finiting organ drops away, and our several spirits revert to their original source and resume their unrestricted condition, will they then be anything like those sweet streams of feeling which we know, and which even now our brains are sifting out from the great reservoir for our enjoyment here below? Such questions are truly living questions, and surely they must be seriously discussed by future lecturers upon this Ingersoll foundation. . . .

But into these higher and more transcendental matters I refuse to enter upon this occasion; . . .

42

SCIENCE AND IMMORTALITY: A NEGATIVE REPORT

Bertrand Russell

(See Reading 6 for a biographical note.)

. . .

It remains to inquire what bearing modern doctrines as to physiology and psychology have upon the credibility of the orthodox belief in immortality.

That the soul survives the death of the body is a doctrine which, as we have seen, has been widely held, by Christians and non-Christians, by civilized men and by barbarians. Among the Jews of the time of Christ, the Pharisees believed in immortality, but the Sadducees, who adhered to the older tradition, did not. In Christianity, the belief in the life everlasting has always held a very prominent place. Some enjoy felicity in heaven — after a period of purifying suffering in purgatory, according to Roman Catholic belief. Others endure unending torments in hell. In modern times, liberal Christians often incline to the view that hell is not eternal; this view has come to be held by many clergymen in the Church of England since the Privy Council, in 1864, decided that it is not illegal for them to do so. But until the middle of the nineteenth century very few professing Christians doubted the reality of eternal punishment. The fear of hell was — and to a lesser extent still is — a source of the deepest anxiety, which much diminished the comfort to be derived from belief in survival. The motive of saving others from hell was urged as a justification of persecution; for if a heretic, by misleading others, could cause them to suffer damnation, no degree of earthly torture could be considered excessive if employed to prevent so terrible a result. For, whatever may now be thought, it was formerly believed, except by a small minority, that heresy was incompatible with salvation.

The decay of the belief in hell was not due to any new theological arguments, nor yet to the direct influence of science, but to the general diminution of ferocity which took place during the eighteenth and nineteenth centuries.

From Chapter V, "Soul and Body," of *Religion and Science* (1935). Reprinted by permission of the publishers, Oxford University Press, Inc.

It is part of the same movement which led, shortly before the French Revolution, to the abolition of judicial torture in many countries, and which, in the early nineteenth century, led to the reformation of the savage penal code by which England had been disgraced. In the present day, even among those who still believe in hell, the number of those who are condemned to suffer its torments is thought to be much smaller than was formerly held. Our fiercer passions, nowadays, take a political rather than a theological direction.

It is a curious fact that, as the belief in hell has grown less definite, belief in heaven has also lost vividness. Although heaven is still a recognized part of Christian orthodoxy, much less is said about it in modern discussions than about evidences of Divine purpose in evolution. Arguments in favour of religion now dwell more upon its influence in promoting a good life here on earth than on its connection with the life hereafter. The belief that this life is merely a preparation for another, which formerly influenced morals and conduct, has now ceased to have much influence even on those who have not consciously rejected it.

What science has to say on the subject of immortality is not very definite. There is, indeed, one line of argument in favour of survival after death, which is, at least in intention, completely scientific — I mean the line of argument asssociated with the phenomena investigated by psychical research. I have not myself sufficient knowledge on this subject to judge of the evidence already available, but it is clear that there could be evidence which would convince reasonable men. To this, however, certain provisos must be added. In the first place, the evidence, at the best, would only prove that we survive death, not that we survive for ever. In the second place, where strong desires are involved, it is very difficult to accept the testimony even of habitually accurate persons; of this there was much evidence during the War, and in all times of great excitement. In the third place, if, on other grounds, it seems unlikely that our personality does not die with the body, we shall require much stronger evidence of survival than we should if we thought the hypothesis antecedently probable. Not even the most ardent believer in spiritualism could pretend to have as much evidence of survival as historians can adduce to prove that witches did bodily homage to Satan, yet hardly anyone now regards the evidence of such occurrences as even worth examining.

The difficulty, for science, arises from the fact that there does not seem to be such an entity as the soul or self. As we saw, it is no longer possible to regard soul and body as two "substances," having that endurance through time which metaphysicians regarded as logically bound up with the notion of substance. Nor is there any reason, in psychology, to assume a "subject" which, in perception, is brought into contact with an "object." Until recently, it was thought that matter is immortal, but this is no longer assumed by the technique of physics. An atom is now merely a convenient way of grouping certain occurrences; it is convenient, up to a point, to think of the atom as a nucleus with attendant electrons, but the electrons at one time cannot be identified with those at another, and in any case no modern physicist thinks of them as "real." While there was still material substance which was supposed to be eternal, it was easy to argue that minds must be equally eternal; but this argument, which was never a very strong one, can now no longer be used. For sufficient reasons, physicists have reduced the atom to a series of events; for equally good reasons, psychologists find that a mind has not the identity of a single continuing "thing," but is a series of occurrences bound together by certain intimate relations. The question of immortality, therefore, has become the question whether these intimate relations exist between occurrences connected with a living body and other occurrences which take place after that body is dead.

We must first decide, before we can attempt to answer this question, what are the relations which bind certain events together in such a way as to make them the mental life of one person. Obviously the most important of these is memory: things that I can remember happened to *me*. And if I can remember a certain occasion, and on that occasion I could remember something else, then the something else also happened to me.   It might be objected that two people may remember the same event, but that would be an error: no two people ever see exactly the same thing, because of differences in their positions. No more can they have precisely the same experiences of hearing or smelling or touching or tasting. My experience may closely resemble another person's, but always differs from it in a greater or less degree. Each person's experience is private to himself, and when one experience consists in recollecting another, the two are said to belong to the same "person."

There is another, less psychological, definition of personality, which derives it from the body. The definition of what makes the identity of a living body at different times would be complicated, but for the moment we will take it for granted. We will also take it for granted that every "mental" experience known to us is connected with some living body. We can then define a "person" as the series of mental occurrences connected with a given body. This is the legal definition. If John Smith's body committed a murder, and at a later time the police arrest John Smith's body, then the person inhabiting that body at the time of arrest is a murderer.

These two ways of defining a "person" conflict in cases of what is called dual personality. In such cases, what seems to outside observation to be one person is, subjectively, split into two; sometimes neither knows anything of the other, sometimes one knows the other, but not vice versa. In cases where neither knows anything of the other, there are two persons if memory is used as the definition, but only one if the body is used. There is a regular gradation to the extreme of dual personality, through absent-mindedness, hypnosis, and sleep-walking. This makes a difficulty in using memory as the definition of personality. But it appears that lost memories can be recovered by hypnotism or in the course of psycho-analysis; thus perhaps the difficulty is not insuperable.

In addition to actual recollection, various other elements, more or less analogous to memory, enter into personality — habits, for instance, which have been formed as a result of past experience. It is because, where there is life, events can form habits, that an "experience" differs from a mere occurrence. An animal, and still more a man, is formed by experiences in a way that dead matter is not. If an event is causally related to another in that peculiar way that has to do with habit-formation, then the two events belong to the same "person." This is a wider definition than that by memory alone, including all that the memory-definition included and a good deal more.

If we are to believe in the survival of a personality after the death of the body, we must suppose that there is continuity of memories or at least of habits, since otherwise there is no reason to suppose that the same person is continuing. But at this point physiology makes difficulties. Habit and memory are both due to effects on the body, especially the brain; the formation of a habit may be thought of as analogous to the formation of a water-course. Now the effects on the body, which give rise to habits and memories, are obliterated by death and decay, and it is difficult to see how, short of miracle, they can be transferred to a new body such as we may be supposed to inhabit in the next life. If we are to be disembodied spirits, the difficulty is only increased. Indeed I doubt whether, with modern views of matter, a disembodied spirit is logically possible. Matter is only a certain way of grouping events, and therefore where there are events there is matter. The continuity of a person throughout the life of his body, if, as I contend, it depends upon habit-formation, must also depend upon the continuity of the body. It would be as easy to transfer a water-course to heaven without loss of identity as it would be to transfer a person.

Personality is essentially a matter of organization. Certain events, grouped together by means of certain relations, form a person. The grouping is effected by means of causal laws — those connected with habit-formation, which includes memory — and the causal laws concerned depend upon the body. If this is true — and there are strong scientific grounds for thinking that it is — to expect a personality to survive the disintegration of the brain is like expecting a cricket club to survive when all its members are dead.

I do not pretend that this argument is conclusive. It is impossible to foresee the future of science, particularly of psychology, which is only just beginning to be scientific. It may be that psychological causation can be freed from its present dependence on the body. But in the present state of psychology and physiology, belief in immortality can, at any rate, claim no support from science, and such arguments as are possible on the subject point to the probable extinction of personality at death. We may regret the thought that we shall not survive, but it is a comfort to think that all the persecutors and Jewbaiters and humbugs will not continue to exist for all eternity. We may be told that they would improve in time, but I doubt it.

SUGGESTED READINGS

1. Collections of Writings on the Philosophy of Mind

CHAPPELL, V. C. (ed.). *The Philosophy of Mind.* Englewood Cliffs, N. J.: Prentice-Hall, Inc., 1962.

FLEW, ANTHONY (ed.). *Body, Mind, and Death.* New York: Macmillan, 1964.

GUSTAFSON, D. F. (ed.). *Essays in Philosophical Psychology.* Garden City, N. Y.: Doubleday, 1964.

HAMPSHIRE, STUART (ed.). *Philosophy of Mind.* New York: Harper & Row, 1966.

VESEY, G. N. A. (ed.). *Body and Mind.* London: Allen & Unwin, 1964.

2. General Discussions of the Mind-Body Problem

BEARDSLEY, M. C. and E. L. *Philosophical Thinking.* New York: Harcourt, 1965. Chapter 11.

BROAD, C. D. *The Mind and Its Place in Nature.* London: Routledge & Kegan Paul, 1925. Chapters 3, 14 [partly in Edwards-Pap].

DUCASSE, C. J. *Nature, Mind and Death.* LaSalle, Ill.: Open Court, 1951 [partly in Alston, Edwards-Pap].

FEIGL, HERBERT. "The 'Mental' and the 'Physical'," in H. FEIGL et al. (eds.) *Minnesota Studies in the Philosophy of Science.* Minneapolis: University of Minnesota Press, 1958.

HOOK, SIDNEY (ed.). *Dimensions of Mind.* New York: New York Univ. Press, 1960. Part I.

KNEALE, WILLIAM. *On Having a Mind.* Cambridge: Cambridge University Press, 1962.

PAP, ARTHUR. *Elements of Analytical Philosophy.* New York: Macmillan, 1949, Chapter 12.

PRATT, J. B. *Matter and Spirit.* New York: Macmillan, 1926 [partly in Mandelbaum-Gramlich-Anderson].

TAYLOR, RICHARD. *Metaphysics.* Englewood Cliffs, N. J.: Prentice-Hall, Inc., 1963. Chapters 1, 2.

WISDOM, JOHN. *Problems of Mind and Matter.* London: Cambridge Univ. Press, 1934. Part I.

3. Dualism

PLATO. *Phaedo.*

McDOUGALL, WILLIAM. *Body and Mind.* London: Methuen, 1911.

4. Parallelism

CLIFFORD, W. K. "Body and Mind," "Things-in-Themselves," in *Lectures and Essays.* London: Macmillan, 1879. Vol. II.

FECHNER, G. T. *Religion of a Scientist,* ed. W. LOWRIE. New York: Pantheon, 1946.

HOFFDING, HAROLD. *The Problems of Philosophy.* New York: Macmillan, 1905.

LEIBNIZ, G. W. *Exposition and Defence of the New System.*

5. Physiological Materialism

BUCHNER, LUDWIG. *Force and Matter.* London: Asher, 1884.

ELLIOT, HUGH. *Modern Science and Materialism.* London: Longmans, Green, 1919.

FEYERABEND, PAUL. "Materialism and the Mind-Body Problem," *Review of Metaphysics,* Vol. 17 (1963).

HOBBES, THOMAS. *De Corpore.* [Partly in R. S. PETERS, ed., *Body, Man, and Citizen.* New York: Collier Books, 1962.]

LUCRETIUS. *On the Nature of Things,* Book III.

SMART, J. J. C. "Sensations and Brain Processes," *Philosophical Review,* Vol. 68 (1959).

6. Behaviorism

CARNAP, RUDOLF. "Psychology in Physical Language," in A. J. AYER, ed., *Logical Positivism.* Glencoe, Ill.: Free Press, 1959.

FARRELL, B. A. "Experience," *Mind,* Vol. 59 (1950).

HEMPEL, C. G. "The Logical Analysis of Psychology," in H. FEIGL and W. SELLARS, eds., *Readings in Philosophical Analysis.* New York: Appleton, 1949.

SKINNER, B. F. "Behaviorism at Fifty," in T. W. WANN, ed., *Behaviorism and Phenomenology.* Chicago: University of Chicago Press, 1964.

TOLMAN, E. C. "Operational Behaviorism and Current Trends in Psychology," in M. H. MARX, ed., *Psychological Theory.* New York: Macmillan, 1951, pp. 87-102.

WATSON, J. B. *Behaviorism.* New York: Norton, 1924.

7. Minds and Machines

ANDERSON, A. R. (ed.). *Minds and Machines.* Englewood Cliffs, N. J.: Prentice-Hall, 1964.

HOOK, SIDNEY (ed.) *Dimensions of Mind.* New York: New York University Press, 1960. Pt. II.

SLUCKIN, W. *Minds and Machines.* London: Pelican Books, 1954.

8. Criticisms of Materialism and Behaviorism

AUNE, BRUCE. "Feelings, Moods, and Introspection," *Mind,* Vol. 72 (1963).

EWING, A. C. "Professor Ryle's Attack on Dualism," *Proceedings of the Aristotelian Society,* Vol. 53 (1952).

LEWIS, C. I. "Some Logical Considerations Concerning the Mental," *Journal of Philosophy,* Vol. 38 (1941).

MALCOLM, NORMAN. "Scientific Materialism and the Identity Theory," *Dialogue,* Vol. 3 (1964).

PAP, ARTHUR. *An Introduction to the Philosophy of Science.* New York: Free Press of Glencoe, 1962. Chapter 20.

PLACE, U. T. "The Concept of Heed," *The British Journal of Psychology,* Vol. 45 (1954).

RUSSELL, BERTRAND. *Philosophy.* New York: Norton, 1927, Part III.

SCRIVEN, MICHAEL. "A Study of Radical Behaviorism," in *Minnesota Studies in the Philosophy of Science,* Vol. I. Minneapolis: University of Minnesota Press, 1956.

SHAFFER, JEROME. "Could Mental States Be Brain Processes?" *Journal of Philosophy,* Vol. 58 (1961).

WHITELEY, C. H. "Behaviorism," *Mind,* Vol. 70 (1961).

9. One's Knowledge of Other Minds

AYER, A. J. *The Problem of Knowledge.* London: Penguin Books, 1956. Chapter 5.

BROAD, C. D. *The Mind and Its Place in Nature.* London: Routledge & Kegan Paul, 1925. Chapter 7.

MALCOLM, NORMAN. "Knowledge of Other Minds," in *Knowledge and Certainty.* Englewood Cliffs, N. J.: Prentice-Hall, 1963.

———. "Wittgenstein's Philosophical Investigations," *ibid.*

MILL, J. S. *An Examination of Sir William Hamilton's Philosophy*. London: Long-
    mans, Green, 1872. Chapter 12.
PRICE, H. H. "Our Knowledge of Other Minds," *Proceedings of the Aristotelian
    Society*, Vol. 3 (1931).
STRAWSON, P. F. *Individuals*. London: Methuen, 1959. Chapter 3.
WISDOM, JOHN. *Other Minds*. Oxford: Basil Blackwell, 1952.
————. J. L. AUSTIN, and A. J. AYER. "Other Minds," *Aristotelian Society*, Sup-
    plementary Volume 20 (1946).

10. Personal Identity

AYER, A. J. *The Problem of Knowledge*. London: Penguin Books, 1956. Chapter 5.
BROAD, C. D. *The Mind and Its Place in Nature*. London: Routledge & Kegan Paul,
    1925. Chapter 13.
BUTLER, JOSEPH. "Dissertation of Personal Identity," in A. FLEW, ed., *Body, Mind,
    and Death*. New York: Macmillan, 1964.
GRICE, H. P. "Personal Identity," *Mind*, Vol. 50 (1941).
HUME, DAVID. *Treatise of Human Nature*, Bk. I, Pt. IV, Secs. 5, 6, and Appendix
    [partly in Edwards-Pap].
JAMES, WILLIAM. *Psychology*. New York: Holt, 1893. Chapter 12.
PENELHUM, TERENCE, "Hume on Personal Identity," *Philosophical Review*, Vol. 64
    (1955).
————. "Personal Identity, Memory, and Survival," *Journal of Philosophy*, Vol. 56
    (1959).
QUINTON, ANTHONY. "The Soul," *Journal of Philosophy*, Vol. 60 (1963).
SHOEMAKER, SIDNEY. "Personal Identity and Memory," *ibid*. Vol. 56 (1959).
————. *Self-Knowledge and Self-Identity*. Ithaca, N. Y.: Cornell University Press,
    1963.

11. General Treatments of Immortality

DUCASSE, C. J. *A Critical Examination of the Belief in a Life After Death*. Spring-
    field, Ill.: C. C. Thomas, 1961.
SETH, ANDREW PRINGLE-PATTISON. *The Idea of Immortality*. London: Oxford Uni-
    versity Press, 1922 [partly in Abernethy-Langford, Bronstein-Schulweis].
TSANOFF, RADOSLAV. *The Problem of Immortality*. New York: Macmillan, 1924.

12. Arguments in Support of Immortality

BUTLER, JOSEPH. *The Analogy of Religion*, 1736, Ch. 1 [partly in Smart].
MARITAIN, JACQUES. "The Immortality of the Soul," in *The Range of Reason*. New
    York: Scribner's, 1952 [in Alston].
McTAGGART, J. M. E. *Some Dogmas of Religion*. London: Arnold, 1906. Chs. 3, 4.
PLATO. *Phaedo* [partly in Bronstein-Schulweis, Hick, Smart].
ROYCE, JOSIAH. *The Conception of Immortality*. Boston: Houghton Mifflin, 1900.
ST. AUGUSTINE. "On the Immortality of the Soul," in W. J. OATES, ed., *Basic Writ-
    ings*. New York: Random House, 1948.
TAYLOR, A. E. *The Christian Hope of Immortality*. New York: Macmillan, 1947
    [partly in Bronstein-Schulweis, Abernethy-Langford].
TENNANT, F. R. *Philosophical Theology*. London: Cambridge Univ. Press, 1928. Vol.
    II, Appendix, Note E [in Abernethy-Langford, Bronstein-Krikorian-Wiener,
    3rd ed.].

13. Arguments Against Immortality

FLEW, ANTONY (ed.). *Body, Mind, and Death*. New York: Macmillan, 1964. Intro-
    duction.

Hume, David. "Of the Immortality of the Soul," 1756 [in Edwards-Pap].

Lamont, Corliss. *The Illusion of Immortality*. New York: Putnam, 1935.

Lucretius. *On the Nature of Things*, Bk. III.

Martin, C. B. *Religious Belief*. Ithaca, N. Y.: Cornell Univ. Press, 1959, Ch. 6.

Russell, Bertrand. *Why I Am Not a Christian and Other Essays*. New York: Simon and Schuster, 1957.

Sellars, R. W. *The Next Step in Religion*. New York: Macmillan, 1918. Ch. 11 [partly in Alston].

14. *The Bearing of Psychical Research on the Problem of Immortality*

Broad, C. D. *The Mind and Its Place in Nature*. London: Routledge & Kegan Paul, 1925. Ch. 12.

———. *Lectures on Psychical Research*. London: Routledge & Kegan Paul, 1962.

Ducasse, C. J. *Nature, Mind, and Death*. LaSalle, Ill.: Open Court, 1951. Chs. 20, 21.

Flew, Antony. *A New Approach to Psychical Research*. London: C. A. Watts, 1953, esp. Ch. 7 [partly in Alston].

Murphy, Gardner. "An Outline of Survival Evidence," *Journal of the American Society of Psychical Research*, 1945.

Part V

THE
FOUNDATIONS
OF
KNOWLEDGE

INTRODUCTION

The central aim of philosophy, we have seen, is to find the most reasonable answer to various fundamental questions to which science cannot provide answers. Logically, it seems the first thing we should do, if we are joining in this enterprise, is to get clear when it is correct to say that an answer to a question is reasonable, or well-supported, or well-justified. In other words, we should be clear about what kind of standard we are to use in order to appraise proposed answers to the questions that interest us.

It might seem that we should begin by posing a *definition* of words like "reasonable" or "well-supported." Such definitions have been put forward, but they are controversial and complicated and would serve, at the present stage, to confuse the issues rather than clarify them. We assume that everyone has a rough understanding of these terms from his ordinary usage of them. What we shall seek is a set of general propositions about *when* a belief is reasonable.

Some philosophers would prefer to say that the logically first question is not when we have a reasonable belief, but rather when we *know*. Obviously, for it to be reasonable for a person to believe a proposition *h* is rather similar to his knowing that it is true. It may be helpful, therefore, to digress a moment and point out two respects in which the meanings of these terms differ. First, "knowledge" implies truth; however reasonable it may be for someone to believe a proposition *h*, we do not say he knows it to be true, if it is in fact not true. Whereas, obviously, belief in a proposition may be very reasonable, even when the proposition is false. Incidentally, a proposition being true does not imply that anyone or everybody might reasonably believe it; it may be true that the Supreme Court has decided to announce a certain conclusion next Monday; but obviously I may not know that it has, and my belief that it will so announce may have no support by evidence whatsoever. Second, knowledge implies that a high standard of evidence has been attained (how much is required may vary from one context to another), whereas to say that a belief is well-supported or reasonable does not imply so much. My belief that Mrs. X is about to begin a divorce action may be well-supported, given that several persons have told me what they have "heard," since it is unusual to hear so much convergent rumor when the rumor is not substantially correct. But I shall not correctly say I *know* in these circumstances — although I should be able to do so if Mrs. X has told me, or her lawyer has communicated her intentions. It is not suggested that the foregoing remarks provide a definition of "know." Some philosophers have suggested that "I know that *p*" means (1) "*p* is true" and (2) "I believe that *p*" and (3) "I have conclusive evidence that *p*," but there are difficulties with this proposal — for one thing, "conclusive evidence" requires explanation in order to be helpful.

THE SCEPTIC'S DOUBTS

In order to get clear under what conditions it is correct to say that any belief of ours is reasonably held, well-supported, etc., we shall consider when a belief may be thought to be reasonably secure from sceptical attack. For if there are conditions under which a belief may not reasonably be doubted, the same conditions are ones in which it is reasonably held.

What does the sceptic say? In the first reading below, Descartes is playing devil's advocate and temporarily takes the part of the sceptic. The view there put forward, and the reasons offered, are rather typical. Philosophers have, however, been sceptical to different degrees. Very extreme sceptics have denied that anyone ever knows anything, or even that anyone is ever better justified in believing any proposition than in believing its contradictory. Some have held that this is true even for the sceptical thesis itself! Some philosophers not inappropriately labelled "sceptical" have gone less far. Some have thought only that there are certain types of propositions about which there is not knowledge or even well-warranted belief; for instance, propositions asserting something about the world which is not being observed by the person at the time, such as that yonder dog will continue to have a tail a minute from now (or will exist at all), or that he did have a tail a moment ago (or existed at all). Or the same for propositions affirming "laws" of nature, or more hypothetical entities such as atoms or electrons.

How may such charges be met? Scepticism is sometimes attacked by criticizing the reasons offered for being a sceptic. Take, for instance, the reasons offered by Descartes. One line of argument he uses relies on the fact of past mistakes: things sometimes look different from what they are, or we have thought we were seeing something when in fact we were asleep. To this critics sometimes reply that it is an argument inconsistent for a sceptic; for if one knows he made a mistake, at least he does know something — in particular, say, that something had a certain property different from the one it seemed to have, or that one really was asleep when one thought one wasn't. Another argument Descartes uses is appeal to logical possibility: God *could* have made us with "memories" of events that never happened; or He could have made us so that arguments which strike us as sound ones actually are not. And what reason have we for thinking that actually He didn't? The critic may reply to the last point that if it is seriously supposed that we can never tell a good piece of reasoning from a bad one, at least the sceptic should stop writing at that point, since, by hypothesis, no one could identify a good argument even if it were offered. Moreover, he may urge that it does not follow, from the fact that a state of affairs is logically possible, that we can reasonably believe it is the fact.

REASONING THAT JUSTIFIES BELIEFS

The answer that philosophers traditionally have made to the sceptical challenge has not consisted simply in an attack on the sceptic's own arguments; it has consisted in the detailed defense of a positive view — in laying out, step by step, the kind of defense that may be given for a belief. The detailed kind of defense made has been by no means uniform, but we shall be able to present here only one kind, not only in the present introductory remarks but also in the readings in this chapter. The theory here represented is not, however, just one among many that might have been chosen for representation; insofar as there is a "traditional" view in such matters, the theory here outlined is *the* traditional view of Western thought of at least the past four hundred years. Other theorists often have hard words for it, but they (some are called "coherence theorists," others "contextualists") are, after all, snipers taking pot shots at the Establishment. Of course, the Establishment may be wrong, but one could hardly understand what the snipers are shooting at if one does not know what it is. The reader can hardly make a mistake in learning it first, even if later he forsakes it in subtle and sophisticated ways.

What is this theory? First, it argues that there are certain propositions that any reasonable person must accept as well-warranted or even as absolutely certain without being supported by an argument from other propositions taken as already known. Thus, these propositions are thought to be, in some sense, *self-evident*. They may legitimately be used as premises in any argument. Second, it is argued that use of certain rules of inference is justified. Sometimes it is held that principles which in effect authorize following certain rules of inference are themselves self-evident members of the class of premises just mentioned. However this may be, it is argued that it is reasonable to draw certain types of inference from any premises we may have. The third thesis consists in the claim that any well-justified belief may be shown to be so by starting from the class of well-justified premises and making use of justified rules of inference. If a belief is well-warranted, its legitimacy can be traced in this way; one thing some philosophers do is work out the details of the logical underpinning, along this line, of some proposition in which they happen to take a special interest. But let us look at a few of the details.

First, what kinds of propositions have been claimed to be self-evident, acceptable as premises without demonstration? Traditionally, two sorts: (1) descriptions of what is observed and (2) "truths of reason." Examples of descriptions of what is observed which the present writer, according to the theory, might use as premises for any argument at the present time are (although there is controversy about what they are): "There is a pencil on the desk in front of me"; "I am writing on a typewriter"; "There is a pressure sensation at my midriff." Some philosophers would argue that such propositions as at least the first two of these can be demonstrated, and that what are more properly taken as premises are something like the following: "There is a green, elongated, pencil-like patch in my visual field"; or "There is a greenish appearance, of the sort I remember to have been present when a typewriter was in front of me. . . ." This controversy will be discussed further in the section on the theory of perception. But, for the present, it may be helpful to point out that philosophers who regard descriptions of what is observed as suitable premises will urge that it is hardly possible not to be correct in believing any proposition that merely describes what we can see or feel. Such propositions are among those Russell calls "hard data" in Reading 44 — along with "truths of reason".

As for "truths of reason," it is pointed out that there are some propositions which we can know to be true just by thinking of them. For instance: "If a plane figure is square, it is not circular"; "If an individual is mortal, he is not immortal"; "2 + 2 = 4." The reader will probably not be disposed to doubt that he does know these propositions to be true and, further, that observation is neither needed nor useful in establishing their truth. If we use the term "a priori" so as to mean that a person can know or be justified in believing a statement *a priori* if and only if he can know it, or be justified in believing it without any more reliance on observation than what is required in order to understand the statement we can say that we know these propositions *a priori*. Obviously we do need some experience or observation in order to know what words like "circular" and "square" mean; but it would be absurd to suggest that, in order to know that no squares are circular, we must make a survey of square things. In contrast, if we want to know whether any animal with a cloven hoof chews the cud, we have to make some inquiries. Of course, in order to know whether this latter statement is true, we first have to have experience enough to understand the statement, e.g., what it is to "chew the cud." But this is not enough. We need to make observations of species of animals with a cleft hoof. Such statements can only be known *a posteriori*. (A statement is said to be known "a posteriori" if and only if it is a statement that is known, but *not a priori*.) Truths of reason, then, can be known a priori, by reflection; that is why they are called "truths of reason."

We shall see later that there is a good deal of controversy about which propositions are truths of reason, but probably the reader will hardly be disposed to deny that the statements listed can indeed be known to be true just by reflection.

We have, then, some premises to which we may appeal in support of our beliefs. But how may we use these to support beliefs not included among the premises? The kind of reply to the sceptic which we are describing answers roughly as follows: given we are well-justified in accepting certain premises, we are equally well-justified in accepting any propositions to which we may move, from these premises, by a *valid deductive argument*; and we are justified in accepting any propositions to which we may move, from these premises, by a *valid inductive argument,* with a degree of conviction depending on the type of argument used.

The reader who wishes to decide whether certain of his beliefs are justified or not will not find the foregoing point of much assistance until he knows which are to count as "valid deductive arguments" and which as "valid inductive arguments." On this matter the present volume cannot, of course, hope to be complete; the purpose of an elementary course in logic is to make these conceptions clear, and to help the student become skillful in applying valid principles of reasoning. Nevertheless, there are some things it may be helpful to say here.

First, *valid deductive arguments.* It is agreed by everyone who accepts reasoning at all that a valid deductive argument is a piece of reasoning in which the conclusion is guaranteed by (in a sense, contained in) the premises. Take, for instance, the reasoning: "All men are mortal; Socrates is a man; therefore Socrates must die." Evidently, to say that Socrates is a man and that *all* men die is already to have committed one's self to the death of Socrates. (Socrates might not die, but that is to say that one of the premises could be false.) If the premises are true, so is the conclusion. A piece of reasoning is deductively *in*valid if in some way the conclusion goes beyond what is guaranteed by the premises (something is got out of the hat). Since everyone, when he is being careful, has a pretty reliable sense of when this is happening, everyone can detect an invalid argument in simple cases.

Another manner of identifying valid deductive arguments has been suggested above by our remarks about "truths of reason." For among truths of reason are some simple propositions of logic. For instance: "If all *A*-things have the property *B*, and if *x* is an *A*-thing, then *x* has the property *B*"; or "If any statement is true, then it is not false"; or "Any meaningful statement is either true or false"; or "If any property belongs to all things of a certain kind, it belongs to each particular thing of that kind"; or "If some proposition *p* is true, and if, given *p* is true, some other proposition *q* is true, then it may be asserted correctly that *q* is true." Now, if we have a set of premises of this sort which we know to be true by reflection, we can use them as principles for drawing inferences from premises that are not truths of reason. (We can also use them for drawing inferences from premises that are truths of reason; this is what demonstrations amount to, in logical theory.)

The foregoing remarks do not take us very far, but hopefully they take us far enough to give a clue about how to criticize certain arguments. Take St. Thomas' first, or third, argument for the existence of God (Reading 2). In order to appraise these arguments, we shall first identify their premises. The first argument, for instance, takes as a premise of observation that there is change, or motion, in the world — and this affirmation is obviously correct. When we have listed the premises, we can ask ourselves which are ones *reasonably* taken as premises for this argument — either not requiring proof because in the above sense self-evident or reasonably taken to have been proved already by a different argument. If some statement used as a premise is not legitimately so taken, we shall reject the argument as a whole. Once we have satisfied ourselves about the legitimacy of the premises, we shall go on to examine the argument. Do the premises really guarantee the conclusions? Is it *impossible* for the premises to be true but the conclusion false? Can we regard the movement from premises to conclusion as authorized by some logical principle which is a "truth of reason"? If the answer is negative, then the argument is unacceptable. And, if so, we need not believe the conclusion even if we accept the premises.

Now let us consider *valid inductive arguments*. There is a good deal of controversy about how many different types of inductive argument should be recognized, but it is convenient, and probably correct, to recognize at least the following two types, and to say that they are valid inductive arguments: (a) enumerative inductive inferences and (b) hypothetical inductive inferences.

An *enumerative* inductive inference is essentially an extrapolation of past observations. Consider the following rough rule: "If one has examined samples of kind F, and all examined samples have been G, then believe [bet on, take as true] that the next observed sample of F will be G more strongly than that it won't be G." (This is very vague; for instance, it doesn't say what odds it is reasonable to lay, with any given number of samples. Any precise theory must fill all this in.) If we follow this rule, then, after examining various pieces of copper and noting that all conduct heat rapidly, we shall believe that the next sample will conduct heat more strongly than we shall believe it won't. Extrapolations of past experience in accordance with this (or a better, more precise) rule are generally viewed as valid inductive inferences. Obviously, all experimental sciences make use of this rule, conducting their inferences accordingly; if one couldn't rely on this rule, there would be no point in performing experiments. We may not feel very happy with the rule, just as stated; but clearly we do not wish to reject all rules of roughly this sort, however we wish to modify in detail, and make more precise, the one suggested.

Hypothetical inductive inferences are different. Roughly, they are inferences from known facts to propositions which, if true, would constitute the best explanation of these facts. For instance, Sherlock Holmes once told a man, much to his astonishment, that he had done much manual work, probably as a carpenter. Holmes inferred this from the observation that the man's right hand was larger than his left, along with some general principles he could justify by enumerative induction. Roughly, Holmes argued that the fact that the right hand was larger was explained by supposing that the man had done labor primarily with his right hand (which would be the case were he a right-handed carpenter), and therefore asserted that the man had in fact done manual labor. More specifically, we can take Holmes to argue in the following way: Suppose we assume that the man has done manual labor, primarily with his right hand. Then it follows from the principle (known by enumerative induction) that muscles get larger when exercised, that his right hand will be larger. Thus the supposition explains the fact that his right hand is larger. But is this the *best* explanation? Well, we can look around for other possibilities. We might just suggest that the man was born that way. But we happen to know (again by enumerative induction) that people are rarely born with one hand decidedly larger than the other. So this assumption is initially implausible, as compared with the assumption that the man had done manual labor, say, as a carpenter. Holmes, on reflection, could not think of any assumption initially as plausible as the one that the man had worked with his right hand which would lead us to expect, by principles themselves supportable by inductive reasoning, that the man's right hand would be larger. So he inferred that the man must have been employed in the way suggested.

This kind of inference we incline to accept, on reflection. Inferences of this sort are very important in science. The whole of atomic physics, for instance, is based on them. (See Reading 53, by William Kneale.) The most substantial argument for the existence of God (see Reading 4, by A. E. Taylor) has this form.

All of these considerations bring us out at the following place in our reply to the sceptic: We have some premises, either from observation or truths of reason, which a reasonable person cannot possibly doubt. We are justified in believing these. Obviously we are also justified in believing propositions they guarantee — propositions to which we are led from the premises by a valid deductive argument. But we are also justified in believing propositions that are extrapolations of the evidence, of the sort authorized by the principle of enumerative inference; and in believing propositions that are necessary for an explanation of the basic evidence, of the sort authorized by the principle of hypothetical inference. (At least we are if we are justified in following these rules of inductive inference; we shall come to this.)

What we say to the sceptic we can say to ourselves; we are justified in believing those propositions to which we are led, from observation premises or truths of reason, by valid deductive or inductive arguments of the kind described, and of other kinds that might be added.

Problems About Truths of Reason and Principles of Deductive Inference

It has already been suggested that philosophers are not agreed upon the general strategy of a reply to the sceptic, as sketched in the preceding pages. We shall not go into that issue in this book. Moreover, some persons are unconvinced as to the force of any lines of reply and remain sceptical.

There is also, however, a vast amount of controversy about how in detail the strategy should be executed. What looks simple when viewed from a distance, it turns out, becomes complicated and difficult when seen from close by. What exactly are the acceptable "truths of reason" (granted there are some)? What are acceptable rules of deductive inference? *Exactly* what forms of enumerative and hypothetical inference do we wish to espouse? And, in each case, what sort of defense can be given for the choice we make? These are among the questions we shall find debated in most of the following readings. One further matter of controversy we postpone to a later chapter: what kinds of statements can be accepted, without further "proof," as being simply descriptions of what is observed. (See Part VI, on the theory of perception.)

We may begin by surveying some problems, which are discussed below, about truths of reason and the principles of deductive inference.

There are three readings in this area. They take different stands in what may be described as the controversy between "empiricism" and "rationalism." Roughly, the empiricist is a person who thinks that *no fact about the world* can be known *a priori*, viz., without reliance on observation. The rationalist is a person who thinks some such facts can be known; rationalists differ among themselves about which such facts are, and how important they are. Among our authors, Mill and Ayer are in the empiricist tradition; Ewing, with Bertrand Russell, is in the rationalist camp. (Descartes is also a rationalist, but his rationalist views do not come out in the following reading.)

In the war between these groups, we may distinguish a number of issues which constitute the main local engagements.

(1) First there is the question of the status of mathematics. We can view the principles of chemistry and psychology pretty clearly as inductive inferences based on observations: the chemist or the psychologist will reply to the sceptic by citing his observations and showing how the principles of inductive inference lead one from these to the laws of chemistry or psychology. But can we view the assertions of mathematics in this way? or those of the logician? Obviously the mathematician and the logician use no laboratory equipment and do not appeal to observations in support of what they say. Must we, then, regard all of mathematics and logic as truths of reason or deductive inferences from these?

J. S. Mill represents one form of empiricist view seldom defended today. He urges that geometry, arithmetic, and even logic are in the end, after all, dependent on observation; the principles of these subjects are generalizations of what we find in experience, just like those of physics or psychology. In a different kind of world, the principles of arithmetic, geometry, and logic would be different. In contrast, today both empiricists and rationalists deny that either arithmetic or logic is dependent on observation; observation, they say, does not tell us what is true everywhere, and necessarily so, whereas we have this kind of knowledge in logic and arithmetic. Some extreme rationalists would say the same for geometry; they suppose we can know a priori that space can have three and only three dimensions, and that Euclid's postulates are true of actual space. Euclid's geometry, they would say, is true necessarily of all space. But most philosophers at the present time would not strongly dispute Mill's general view of geometry, to the effect that what is necessarily true (and known a priori) in geometry is simply that the theorems must be true if the postulates are so, and that the truth of the postulates is a matter of observation. (There are complications here; some element of convention and simplicity is also involved.) But as for arithmetic and logic, it is generally agreed, Mill was mistaken. These are independent of observation; they are true in all possible worlds; and they are "truths of reason." (Empiricists, however, find the phrase "truths of reason" misleading, as will appear in a moment. Such is the view of Ayer.)

(2) If we grant that the propositions of mathematics and logic are not derived from observation but are, or are based on, truths of reason, the question arises as to what is the scope of "truths of reason." In our discussion above, we suggested that some "truths of reason" are legitimate premises for inference, along with descriptions of what is observed. But how to identify a truth of reason was not explained; it was stated only that there are some propositions we can know just by thinking about them, and some examples were presented, which, it was suggested, were propositions the reader would agree are known to be true without reliance on observation in any way. But then, what is to prevent a person from claiming that almost any proposition he believes, and for which he can produce no observational support, is a "truth of reason"? In fact, a great many propositions have been claimed to be truths of reason; not only the principles of logic and arithmetic, but Archimedes' principle of the lever, the impossibility of perpetual motion, the conservation of energy and of matter, some of the inverse square laws (e.g., of gravitational attraction), and the basic principles of ethics (e.g., "Any action which is right for X is also right for Y, provided the circumstances are the same in relevant respects"). If one reads philosophers like Descartes and Leibniz (and the same for the scientists of their day), one finds that a considerable number of important propositions are said to be knowable just by careful reflection, without the need of observational support.

A good many philosophers have felt that the whole concept of truths of reason is a somewhat dangerous one, and that, unless its use is severely restricted, there is an open invitation to claim as a truth of reason any proposition for which there is no evidence of observation but which one much wants to believe. These philosophers have thought, however, that there is one clear line that can be drawn, that one type of proposition can fairly be claimed to be knowable by reflection without observation, and that none other can be. Indeed, the claim that there is such a line is the defining belief of "empiricists." An empiricist philosopher holds that *analytic* propositions, and only analytic propositions, are knowable a priori (without benefit of observation) and properly counted as truths of reason. Rationalist philosophers, by definition of "rationalist," deny this in one way or another. An example of an analytic proposition is "Whatever is square is rectangular" or "All bachelors are unmarried."

What, then, is an "analytic" statement or proposition? Some writers use the term as identical in meaning with "a priori" — in which case, of course, the thesis of empiricism would hardly be open to criticism but would be of no interest.

There has been a good deal of controversy among empiricists about exactly how the term "analytic" should be defined; and it is sometimes held by critics of empiricism that no clear definition can be given of a kind that would enable us to draw a line between analytic and synthetic (nonanalytic) statements where the empiricist would like to draw one.

One type of definition that has had considerable support, and seems to have some plausibility, is the following. It is said that a statement is analytic if and only if its truth (or falsity) can be determined from *facts about the meanings* of the words of the sentence used to make it, and *from these alone.* For instance, take "All bachelors are unmarried." Obviously we do know this statement to be true without observing bachelors. And surely a crucial reason for our ability to know this is the fact that "bachelor" means something like "unmarried, never married, male." Of course, this one fact about meanings by itself does not enable us to determine the truth of the statement; the meanings of "all" and "are" are also relevant — for, obviously, if "all" meant what "no" actually means, the statement would be false. An important fact for our ability to know that the statement is true is the fact that statements of the form "All S are P" mean the same as statements of the form "No S are not-P." Hence our statement means the same as "No bachelors are married." Now, it is clear that what has to be the case in order for this statement to be false is for there to be at least one thing that is both a bachelor and married. But if we identified anything as married, we should, by our previously cited point about the meaning of "bachelor," have to classify it as *not* a bachelor. So, obviously, we cannot possibly find anything that is married and a bachelor. Hence "No bachelors are married" cannot be false, and so "All bachelors are unmarried" must be true.

The proposal is that when any statement can be determined to be true or false in this way, by considering the meaning of its terms, the statement is to be called "analytic."

It is sometimes contended that according to this definition the statement "Nothing red all over is green all over," which we seem to know to be true a priori, is a synthetic statement — contrary to the thesis of empiricism. For, it is said, one cannot show this statement to be true by reference to the definitions of "red" and "green" just because these terms, in their most important use, are so simple that they *do not have any definitions*. To this objection empiricists tend to reply that the meaning of a word is properly explained not merely by giving a verbal definition relating it to other words (as we did for "bachelor"), but also by showing samples (as we can do for "green") which make clear in what circumstances the term is to be used and when not. And, the rejoinder goes, if we allow ourselves rather broadly to take this kind of information about meanings into account, we can treat the above statement about red and green to be an analytic statement by our definition of "analytic," after all.

It may be a useful exercise for the reader to consider whether, according to the above definition, the following statements are analytic: "The sun always rises in the east"; "A person always ought to do his duty."

If the above definition is satisfactorily clear, the empiricist's thesis may be important and plausible. An advantage of formulating the thesis in this way is that light is shed on how statements of logic can be known to be true and what their status is.

At any rate, it is today a highly controversial question whether there is some clear statement of the empiricist thesis which is true. Ayer affirms below that there is such a true formulation of the empiricist thesis; Ewing denies it. Some philosophers today think that the whole analytic-synthetic distinction is fundamentally misguided, but we cannot consider this issue here; readings on that topic are suggested at the end of this section.

Should we, or should we not, impose on ourselves the restriction of refusing to affirm any proposition as known, unless it is either analytic or can be supported by observation? The empiricist answer is in the affirmative, although for further reasons for this restriction the student must look to the readings.

(3) It was mentioned above that empiricists think it somewhat misleading to talk of "truths of reason" at all. This is because the empiricist finds it mysterious to suppose that one could, just by thinking, find out anything about the world. How could one find out that there are such things as apples, or that there is a law of gravity, just by taking thought? And if we speak of "truths of reason," we at least suggest that pure thought can find out facts about the world, like the pervasiveness of gravitational attraction.

What, then, is the empiricist to say about a priori knowledge? Is mathematical knowledge not knowledge of facts about the world? Many empiricists incline to answer in the negative.

This may seem strange. But first we should notice that it seems much less strange to say that deductive reasoning tells us *no new facts*. At least, if we have said that all men are mortal and that Socrates is a man, are we stating a *further* fact by saying that Socrates is mortal? Some would say that we are, but many empiricists would say that we are not — that we are only stating part of what we had already said in different words. We would hardly say that "The sun is larger than the moon" states a fact different from that stated by "The moon is smaller than the sun." And, many empiricists would say, no conclusion of a valid deductive argument really brings out a fact different from what had already been stated by the premises. Consider, then, a principle of logic: "Any meaningful statement is either true or false"; or "If a statement is true, it is not false." Do these statements tell us anything about the world? What would the world be like in order for either of these statements to be false? Many empiricists would say that the truths of logic *put no restrictions* on the world, and, since they place no restrictions on it, they also say nothing positive. (Whenever we say anything positive, such as that the apple is green, we restrict the universe, ruling out the apple being red or yellow.) Since these statements do not restrict the world, empiricists tend to say, they do not state a *fact* about the world. We can say, if we like, that they are true; but they do not state facts at all in the way in which physics does. And the same for "2 + 2 = 4" and all the propositions of arithmetic. What they show, if anything, is something about the conventions of our symbolism, or about our conceptual schemes.

"Truths of reason," empiricists think, are (if we wish to use the phrase at all) a matter of conventions about the use of language. The truths of logic derive from conventions about the use of logical words. These "truths" set no restrictions on what the world is like; they only set restrictions on how we shall speak, because of our self-adopted conventions about what words shall mean. There is no puzzle about these "truths," for we can know by reflection what we have decided to mean by certain words and hence can know by reflection what our conventions about meaning permit us to say with sense. Thus the mystery about how thinking alone can reveal "truths" is removed.

Rationalists deny all this. The truths of logic, they think, are important, although abstract, statements about the world. They do place restrictions on what it can be — logical restrictions. Even "All bachelors are unmarried" is a truth and states a fact — true because of the relation between the property of being a bachelor and the property of being unmarried. (The property of being a bachelor *includes* the property of being unmarried.)

Ayer, of course, is defending the empiricist view here; Ewing is criticizing it.

Problems About the Principles of Inductive Inference

Although there are problems about "truths of reason," at least there is agreement about the rules of valid deductive inference, and there is no serious doubt that we know a priori the principles of deductive logic. In the case of inductive inference, however, the situation is somewhat different. In the first place, writers about inductive logic do not agree on the precise character of the rules; indeed, some writers think it misguided to attempt to formulate precise rules for inductive inference. Moreover, while most philosophers agree that it is reasonable to follow the rules of inductive inference, there is a great deal of controversy about what the reason is. It has been clear since the time of Hume that a person would not be *contradicting* himself if he conceded the premises of an inductive inference but refused to accept the conclusion. It is by no means an obvious a priori truth, a truth of reason, that if all observed samples of *A*-things have had the property *B*, the next observed sample of an *A*-thing will be *B*, or even that it *probably* will be, in at least some sense of the word "probable." Nor is it an obvious truth of reason that the supposition which best explains the known facts of observation is always, or even usually, a true supposition.

The readings on inductive logic in the present chapter do not attempt to provide any precise formulation of such rules; they are concerned either with explaining why there is a problem of justifying any such rules or with providing a justification for the general policy of inductive inference. The readings from Hume and Russell provide clear statements of the problem, Russell's differing from Hume's primarily in his introducing the concept of probability (without, however, explaining the sense in which he is using the word). Readers of Russell's paper sometimes mistakenly think he is providing a *solution* of the "problem"; in fact, what he does is simply *formulate* a principle that would, if we knew it to be true, provide a conclusive reason for using the first rule of inductive inference; he then explains why this principle cannot itself be claimed to be established or even supported by observation without circularity of reasoning.

The readings drawn from Mill, Strawson, and Reichenbach do, however, attempt to justify use of the first rule of inductive inference, and the reading from Kneale attempts to justify use of the second rule of inductive inference. More exactly, what Mill attempts to show is that we should be justified in using recognized methods of experimental inference if we could justify what he calls the Universal Law of Causation or the Uniformity of Nature; and he then argues that, for special reasons, it is justified to use the rule of enumerative inference to justify this general principle. It is usually thought today that Mill's argument is circular, taken as an argument to establish the legitimacy of inductive inferences. Strawson's paper is an interesting example of the very popular thesis that attention to the use of language will resolve many traditional philosophical problems. Strawson's view essentially is that if the "problem" about induction is to show that it is "rational" or "justified" to use the rule of enumerative inference, then the solution of the problem is to see that, as we use the terms "rational" and justified" in the context of science, it is an analytic proposition (given the definitions of these words) that it is rational to use the rule of enumerative inference. The Reichenbach paper represents a thesis often called "pragmatic" in contemporary literature. The essence of it is that if reliable predictions of unobserved events (e.g., that the *next* observed sample of copper will be a rapid conductor of heat) are possible at all, it must be because there are laws, at least statistical laws, in nature. The reason for using the rule of enumerative inference, then, is that so doing will lead to expectations about the future, or to belief in general laws, which will be correct expectations or beliefs *if* there are laws and if reliable prediction is possible. So, while we cannot prove that use of the rule will lead to correct predictions, we *can* say that *if* correct predictions can be reliably made, this rule will lead us to them. If a reliable method of prediction is possible, use of this rule will, at least in the long run, succeed in yielding reliable predictions. If success is possible, use of this rule will work, although we cannot know in advance that our world is of the sort in which successful prediction is possible in the long run. The conclusion of the proposal is that, since human beings need to make predictions, they had better use the rule of induction, although it is not an a priori truth that use of it will lead to true predictions.

Some philosophers, e.g., Reichenbach and Carnap, are of the opinion that no *second* rule of inductive inference is needed, at least none that requires a separate justification. They think that the status of theories like the atomic theory can be sufficiently accounted for by enumerative induction and the theory of probability (specifically by Bayes' Theorem or the Inverse Theorem). William Kneale, however, thinks that this view is not correct. In Reading 53 he explains the second rule and suggests the kind of justification he thinks can be given for using it. The views on this subject of philosophers like Reichenbach and Carnap are too complex for inclusion in the present volume; the selection from Kneale provides an adequate introduction to the topic, which is one of lively interest today among philosophers of science. Since the second rule, in effect, asserts that one should believe a supposition which is involved in the best "explanation" of the observed facts, it is important to get clear what an explanation is. This topic, too, is a highly controversial one today among philosophers of science. It is discussed in Reading 54, by Hospers.

43

SCEPTICAL QUERIES:
MEDITATIONS ON
FIRST PHILOSOPHY

René Descartes

René Descartes (1596-1650) was born in France, but lived mostly in Holland. He was a mathematician and a founder of modern theory of knowledge.

MEDITATION I

OF THE THINGS WHICH MAY BE BROUGHT WITHIN THE SPHERE OF THE DOUBTFUL

It is now some years since I detected how many were the false beliefs that I had from my earliest youth admitted as true, and how doubtful was everything I had since constructed on this basis; and from that time I was convinced that I must once for all seriously undertake to rid myself of all the opinions which I had formerly accepted, and commence to build anew from the foundation, if I wanted to establish any firm and permanent structure in the sciences. But as this enterprise appeared to be a very great one, I waited until I had attained an age so mature that I could not hope that at any later date I should be better fitted to execute my design. This reason caused me to delay so long that I should feel that I was doing wrong were I to occupy in deliberation the time that yet remains to me for action. To-day, then, since very opportunely for the plan I have in view I have delivered my mind from every care [and am happily agitated by no passions] and since I have procured for myself an assured leisure in a peaceable retirement, I shall at last seriously and freely address myself to the general upheaval of all my former opinions.

Now for this object it is not necessary that I should show that all of these are false — I shall perhaps never arrive at this end. But inasmuch as reason already persuades me that I ought no less carefully to withhold my assent from

From René Descartes, *Meditations on First Philosophy*, 2nd ed., 1642 (first published in 1641), in *The Philosophical Works of Descartes*, trans. by E. S. Haldane and G. R. T. Ross, published by Cambridge University Press, Cambridge, 1931, and reprinted with their permission.

matters which are not entirely certain and indubitable than from those which appear to me manifestly to be false, if I am able to find in each one some reason to doubt, this will suffice to justify my rejecting the whole. And for that end it will not be requisite that I should examine each in particular, which would be an endless undertaking; for owing to the fact that the destruction of the foundations of necessity brings with it the downfall of the rest of the edifice, I shall only in the first place attack those principles upon which all my former opinions rested.

All that up to the present time I have accepted as most true and certain I have learned either from the senses or through the senses; but it is sometimes proved to me that these senses are deceptive, and it is wiser not to trust entirely to any thing by which we have once been deceived.

But it may be that although the senses sometimes deceive us concerning things which are hardly perceptible, or very far away, there are yet many others to be met with as to which we cannot reasonably have any doubt, although we recognise them by their means. For example, there is the fact that I am here, seated by the fire, attired in a dressing gown, having this paper in my hands and other similar matters. And how could I deny that these hands and this body are mine, were it not perhaps that I compare myself to certain persons, devoid of sense, whose cerebella are so troubled and clouded by the violent vapours of black bile, that they constantly assure us that they think they are kings when they are really quite poor, or that they are clothed in purple when they are really without covering, or who imagine that they have an earthenware head or are nothing but pumpkins or are made of glass. But they are mad, and I should not be any the less insane were I to follow examples so extravagant.

At the same time I must remember that I am a man, and that consequently I am in the habit of sleeping, and in my dreams representing to myself the same things or sometimes even less probable things, than do those who are insane in their waking moments. How often has it happened to me that in the night I dreamt that I found myself in this particular place, that I was dressed and seated near the fire, whilst in reality I was lying undressed in bed! At this moment it does indeed seem to me that it is with eyes awake that I am looking at this paper; that this head which I move is not asleep, that it is deliberately and of set purpose that I extend my hand and perceive it; what happens in sleep does not appear so clear nor so distinct as does all this. But in thinking over this I remind myself that on many occasions I have in sleep been deceived by similar illusions, and in dwelling carefully on this reflection I see so manifestly that there are no certain indications by which we may clearly distinguish wakefulness from sleep that I am lost in astonishment. And my astonishment is such that it is almost capable of persuading me that I now dream.

Now let us assume that we are asleep and that all these particulars, e.g. that we open our eyes, shake our head, extend our hands, and so on, are but false delusions; and let us reflect that possibly neither our hands nor our whole body are such as they appear to us to be. At the same time we must at least confess that the things which are represented to us in sleep are like painted representations which can only have been formed as the counterparts of something real and true, and that in this way those general things at least, i.e. eyes, a head, hands, and a whole body, are not imaginary things, but things really existent. For, as a matter of fact, painters, even when they study with the greatest skill to represent sirens and satyrs by forms the most strange and extraordinary, cannot give them natures which are entirely new, but merely make a certain medley of the members of different animals; or if their imagination is extravagant enough to invent something so novel that nothing similar has ever before been seen, and that their work represents a thing purely fictitious and absolutely false, it is certain all the same that the colours of which this is composed are necessarily real. And for the same reason, although these general things, to wit, [a body], eyes, a head, hands, and such like, may be imaginary, we are bound at the same time to confess that there are at least some other objects yet more simple and more universal, which are real and true; and of these just in the same way as with certain real colours, all these images of things which dwell in our thoughts, whether true and real or false and fantastic, are formed.

To such a class of things pertains corporeal nature in general, and its extension, the figure of extended things, their quantity or magnitude and number, as also the place in which they are, the time which measures their duration, and so on.

That is possibly why our reasoning is not unjust when we conclude from this that Physics, Astronomy, Medicine and all other sciences which have as their end the consideration of composite things, are very dubious and uncertain; but that Arithmetic, Geometry and other sciences of that kind which only treat of things that are very simple and very general, without taking great trouble to ascertain whether they are actually existent or not, contain some measure of certainty and an element of the indubitable. For whether I am awake or asleep, two and three together always form five, and the square can never have more than four sides, and it does not seem possible that truths so clear and apparent can be suspected of any falsity [or uncertainty].

Nevertheless I have long had fixed in my mind the belief that an all-powerful God existed by whom I have been created such as I am. But how do I know that He has not brought it to pass that there is no earth, no heaven, no extended body, no magnitude, no place, and that nevertheless [I possess the perceptions of all these things and that] they seem to me to exist just exactly as I now see them? And, besides, as I sometimes imagine that others deceive themselves in the things which they think they know best, how do I know that I am not deceived every time that I add two and three, or count the sides of a square, or judge of things yet simpler, if anything simpler can be imagined? But possibly God has not desired that I should be thus deceived, for He is said to be supremely good. If, however, it is contrary to His goodness to have made me such that I constantly deceive myself, it would also appear to be contrary to His goodness to permit me to be sometimes deceived, and nevertheless I cannot doubt that He does permit this.

There may indeed be those who would prefer to deny the existence of a God so powerful, rather than believe that all other things are uncertain. But let us not oppose them for the present, and grant that all that is here said of a God is a fable; nevertheless in whatever way they suppose that I have arrived at the state of being that I have reached — whether they attribute it to fate or to accident, or make out that it is by a continual succession of antecedents, or by some other method — since to err and deceive oneself is a defect, it is clear that the greater will be the probability of my being so imperfect as to deceive myself ever, as is the Author to whom they assign my origin the less powerful. To these reasons I have certainly nothing to reply, but at the end I feel constrained to confess that there is nothing in all that I formerly believed to be true, of which I cannot in some measure doubt, and that not merely through want of thought or through levity, but for reasons which are very powerful and maturely considered; so that henceforth I ought not the less carefully to refrain from giving credence to these opinions than to that which is manifestly false, if I desire to arrive at any certainty [in the sciences].

But it is not sufficient to have made these remarks, we must also be careful to keep them in mind. For these ancient and commonly held opinions still revert frequently to my mind, long and familiar custom having given them the right to occupy my mind against my inclination and rendered them almost masters of my belief; nor will I ever lose the habit of deferring to them or of placing my confidence in them, so long as I consider them as they really are, i.e. opinions in some measure doubtful, as I have just shown, and at the same time highly probable, so that there is much more reason to believe in than to deny them. That is why I consider that I shall not be acting amiss, if, taking of set purpose a contrary belief, I allow myself to be deceived, and for a certain time pretend that all these opinions are entirely false and imaginary, until at last, having thus balanced my former prejudices with my latter [so that they cannot divert my opinions more to one side than to the other], my judgment will no longer be dominated by bad usage or turned away from the right knowledge of the truth. For I am assured that there can be neither peril nor error in this course, and that I cannot at present yield too much to distrust, since I am not considering the question of action, but only of knowledge.

I shall then suppose, not that God who is supremely good and the fountain of truth, but some evil genius not less powerful than deceitful, has employed his whole energies in deceiving me; I shall consider that the heavens, the earth, colours, figures, sound, and all other external things are nought but the illusions and dreams of which this genius has availed himself in order to lay traps for my credulity; I shall consider myself as having no hands, no eyes, no flesh, no blood, nor any senses, yet falsely believing myself to possess all these things; I shall remain obstinately attached to this idea, and if by this means it is not in my power to arrive at the knowledge of any truth, I may at least do what is in my power [i.e. suspend my judgment], and with firm purpose avoid giving credence to any false thing, or being imposed upon by this arch deceiver, however powerful and deceptive he may be. But this task is a laborious one, and insensibly a certain lassitude leads me into the course of my ordinary life. And just as a captive who in sleep enjoys an imaginary liberty, when he begins to suspect that his liberty is but a dream, fears to awaken, and conspires with these agreeable illusions that the deception may be prolonged, so insensibly of my own accord I fall back into my former opinions, and I dread awakening from this slumber, lest the laborious wakefulness which would follow the tranquillity of this repose should have to be spent not in daylight, but in the excessive darkness of the difficulties which have just been discussed.

44

THE PREMISES
OF KNOWLEDGE

Bertrand Russell

Bertrand Russell (1872-   ) was for many years Fellow of Trinity College, Cambridge, and Lecturer in Philosophy at Cambridge University.

In this lecture, I wish to apply the logical-analytic method to one of the oldest problems of philosophy, namely the problem of our knowledge of the external world. What I have to say on this problem does not amount to an answer of a definite and dogmatic kind; it amounts only to an analysis and statement of the questions involved, with an indication of the directions in which evidence may be sought. But although not yet a definite solution, what can be said at present seems to me to throw a completely new light on the problem, and to be indispensable, not only in seeking the answer, but also in the preliminary question as to what parts of our problem may possibly have an ascertainable answer.

In every philosophical problem, our investigation starts from what may be called "data," by which I mean matters of common knowledge, vague, complex, inexact, as common knowledge always is, but yet somehow commanding our assent as on the whole and in some interpretation pretty certainly true. In the case of our present problem, the common knowledge involved is of various kinds. There is first our acquaintance with particular objects of daily life — furniture, houses, towns, other people, and so on. Then there is the extension of such particular knowledge to particular things outside our personal experience, through history and geography, newspapers, etc. And lastly, there is the systematisation of all this knowledge of particulars by means of physical science, which derives immense persuasive force from its astonishing power of foretelling the future. We are quite willing to admit that there may be errors of detail in this knowledge, but we believe them to be discoverable and corrigible by the methods which have given rise to our

From Bertrand Russell, *Our Knowledge of the External World*, Lecture III, 1929, published by George Allen & Unwin Ltd., London. Reprinted by permission of the publisher.

beliefs, and we do not, as practical men, entertain for a moment the hypothesis that the whole edifice may be built on insecure foundations. In the main, therefore, and without absolute dogmatism as to this or that special portion, we may accept this mass of common knowledge as affording data for our philosophical analysis.

It may be said — and this is an objection which must be met at the outset — that it is the duty of the philosopher to call in question the admittedly fallible beliefs of daily life, and to replace them by something more solid and irrefragable. In a sense this is true, and in this sense it is effected in the course of analysis. But in another sense, and a very important one, it is quite impossible. While admitting that doubt is possible with regard to all our common knowledge, we must nevertheless accept that knowledge in the main if philosophy is to be possible at all. There is not any superfine brand of knowledge, obtainable by the philosopher, which can give us a standpoint from which to criticise the whole of the knowledge of daily life. The most that can be done is to examine and purify our common knowledge by an internal scrutiny, assuming the canons by which it has been obtained, and applying them with more care and with more precision. Philosophy cannot boast of having achieved such a degree of certainty that it can have authority to condemn the facts of experience and the laws of science. The philosophic scrutiny, therefore, though sceptical in regard to every detail, is not sceptical as regards the whole. That is to say, its criticism of details will only be based upon their relation to other details, not upon some external criterion which can be applied to all the details equally. The reason for this abstention from a universal criticism is not any dogmatic confidence, but its exact opposite; it is not that common knowledge *must* be true, but that we possess no radically different kind of knowledge derived from some other source. Universal scepticism, though logically irrefutable, is practically barren; it can only, therefore, give a certain flavour of hesitancy to our beliefs, and cannot be used to substitute other beliefs for them.

Although data can only be criticised by other data, not by an outside standard, yet we may distinguish different grades of certainty in the different kinds of common knowledge which we enumerated just now. What does not go beyond our own personal sensible acquaintance must be for us the most certain: the "evidence of the senses" is proverbially the least open to question. What depends on testimony, like the facts of history and geography which are learnt from books, has varying degrees of certainty according to the nature and extent of the testimony. Doubts as to the existence of Napoleon can only be maintained for a joke, whereas the historicity of Agamemnon is a legitimate subject of debate. In science, again, we find all grades of certainty short of the highest. The law of gravitation, at least as an approximate truth, has acquired by this time the same kind of certainty as the existence of Napoleon, whereas the latest speculations concerning the constitution of matter would be universally acknowledged to have as yet only a rather slight probability in their favour. These varying degrees of certainty attaching to different data may be regarded as themselves forming part of our data; they, along with the other data, lie within the vague, complex, inexact body of knowledge which it is the business of the philosopher to analyse.

The first thing that appears when we begin to analyse our common knowledge is that some of it is derivative, while some is primitive; that is to say, there is some that we only believe because of something else from which it has been inferred in some sense, though not necessarily in a strict logical sense, while other parts are believed on their own account, without the support of any outside evidence. It is obvious that the senses give knowledge of the latter kind: the immediate facts perceived by sight or touch or hearing do not need to be proved by argument, but are completely self-evident. Psychologists, however, have made us aware that what is actually given in sense is much less than most people would naturally suppose, and that much of what at first sight seems to be given is really inferred. This applies especially in regard to our space-perceptions. For instance, we instinctively infer the "real" size and shape of a visible object from its apparent size and shape, according to its distance and our point of view. When we hear a person speaking, our actual sensations usually miss a great deal of what he says, and we supply its place by unconscious inference; in a foreign language, where this process is more difficult, we find ourselves apparently grown deaf, requiring, for example, to be much nearer the stage at a theatre than would be necessary in our own country. Thus the first step in the analysis of data, namely, the discovery of what is really given in sense, is full of difficulty. We will, however, not linger on this point; so long as existence is realised, the exact outcome does not make any very great difference in our main problem.

The next step in our analysis must be the consideration of how the derivative parts of our common knowledge arise. Here we become involved in a somewhat puzzling entanglement of logic and psychology. Psychologically, a belief may be called derivative whenever it is caused by one or more other beliefs, or by some fact of sense which is not simply what the belief asserts. Derivative beliefs in this sense constantly arise without any process of logical inference, merely by association of ideas or some equally extralogical process. From the expression of a man's face we judge as to what he is feeling: we say we *see* that he is angry, when in fact we only see a frown. We do not judge as to his state of mind by any logical process: the judgment grows up, often without our being able to say what physical mark of emotion we actually saw. In such a case, the knowledge is derivative psychologically; but logically it is in a sense primitive, since it is not the result of any logical deduction. There may or may not be a possible deduction leading to the same result, but whether there is or not, we certainly do not employ it. If we call a belief "logically primitive" when it is not actually arrived at by a logical inference, then innumerable beliefs are logically primitive which psychologically are derivative. The separation of these two kinds of primitivenesses is vitally important to our present discussion.

When we reflect upon the beliefs which are logically but not psychologically primitive, we find that, unless they can on reflection be deduced by a logical process from beliefs which are also psychologically primitive, our confidence in their truth tends to diminish the more we think about them. We naturally believe, for example, that tables and chairs, trees and mountains, are still there when we turn our backs upon them. I do not wish for a moment to maintain that this is certainly not the case, but I do maintain that the question whether it is the case is not to be settled off-hand on any supposed ground of obviousness. The belief that they persist is, in all men except a few philosophers, logically primitive, but it is not psychologically primitive; psychologically, it arises only through our having seen those tables and chairs, trees and mountains. As soon as the question is seriously raised whether, because we have seen them, we have a right to suppose that they are there still, we feel that some kind of argument must be produced, and that if none is forthcoming, our belief can be no more than a pious opinion. We do not feel this as regards the immediate objects of sense: there they are, and, as far as their momentary existence is concerned, no further argument is required. There is accordingly more need of justifying our psychologically derivative beliefs than of justifying those that are primitive.

We are thus led to a somewhat vague distinction between what we may call "hard" data and "soft" data. This distinction is a matter of degree, and must not be pressed; but if not taken too seriously it may help to make the situation clear. I mean by "hard" data those which resist the solvent influence of critical reflection, and by "soft" data those which, under the operation of this process, become to our minds more or less doubtful. The hardest of hard data are of two sorts: the particular facts of sense, and the general truths of logic. The more we reflect upon these, the more we realise exactly what they are, and exactly what a doubt concerning them really means, the more luminously certain do they become. *Verbal* doubt concerning even these is possible, but verbal doubt may occur when what is nominally being doubted is not really in our thoughts, and only words are actually present to our minds. Real doubt, in these two cases, would, I think, be pathological. At any rate, to me they seem quite certain, and I shall assume that you agree with me in this. Without this assumption, we are in danger of falling into that universal scepticism which, as we saw, is as barren as it is irrefutable. If we are to continue philosophising, we must make our bow to the sceptical hypothesis, and, while admitting the elegant terseness of its philosophy, proceed to the consideration of other hypotheses which, though perhaps not certain, have at least as good a right to our respect as the hypothesis of the sceptic.

Applying our distinction of "hard" and "soft" data to psychologically derivative but logically primitive beliefs, we shall find that most, if not all, are to be classed as soft data. They may be found, on reflection, to be capable of logical proof, and they then again become believed, but no longer as data. As data, though entitled to a certain limited respect, they cannot be placed on a level with the facts of sense or the laws of logic. The kind of respect which they deserve seems to me such as to warrant us in hoping, though not too confidently, that the hard data may prove them to be at least probable. Also, if the hard data are found to throw no light whatever upon their truth or falsehood, we are justified, I think, in giving rather more weight to the hypothesis of their truth than to the hypothesis of their falsehood. For the present, however, let us confine ourselves to the hard data, with a view to discovering what sort of world can be constructed by their means alone.

Our data now are primarily the facts of sense (*i.e.* of *our own* sense-data) and the laws of logic. But even the severest scrutiny will allow some additions to this slender stock. Some facts of memory — especially of recent memory — seem to have the highest degree of certainty. Some introspective facts are as certain as any facts of sense. And facts of sense themselves must, for our present purposes, be interpreted with a certain latitude. Spatial and temporal relations must sometimes be included, for example in the case of a swift motion falling wholly within the specious present. And some facts of comparison, such as the likeness or unlikeness of two shades of colour, are certainly to be included among hard data. Also we must remember that the distinction of hard and soft data is psychological and subjective, so that, if there are other minds than our own — which at our present stage must be held doubtful — the catalogue of hard data may be different for them from what it is for us.

Certain common beliefs are undoubtedly excluded from hard data. Such is the belief which led us to introduce the distinction, namely, that sensible objects in general persist when we are not perceiving them. Such also is the belief in other people's minds: this belief is obviously derivative from our perception of their bodies, and is felt to demand logical justification as soon as we become aware of its derivativeness. Belief in what is reported by the testimony of others, including all that we learn from books, is of course involved in the doubt as to whether other people have minds at all. Thus the world from which our reconstruction is to begin is very fragmentary. The best we can say for it is that it is slightly more extensive than the world at which Descartes arrived by a similar process, since that world contained nothing except himself and his thoughts.

We are now in a position to understand and state the problem of our knowledge of the external world, and to remove various misunderstandings which have obscured the meaning of the problem. The problem really is: Can the existence of anything other than our own hard data be inferred from the existence of those data? . . .

45

LOGIC AND MATHEMATICS BASED ON OBSERVATION

John Stuart Mill

The Theorems of Geometry are Necessarily True Only in the Sense of Following from the Axioms

§ 1. If, as laid down in the two preceding chapters, the foundation of all sciences, even deductive or demonstrative sciences, is Induction; if every step in the ratiocinations even of geometry is an act of induction; and if a train of reasoning is but bringing many inductions to bear upon the same subject of inquiry, and drawing a case within one induction by means of another; wherein lies the peculiar certainty always ascribed to the sciences which are entirely, or almost entirely, deductive? Why are they called the Exact Sciences? Why are mathematical certainty, and the evidence of demonstration, common phrases to express the very highest degree of assurance attainable by reason? Why are mathematics by almost all philosophers, and (by some) even those branches of natural philosophy which, through the medium of mathematics, have been converted into deductive sciences, considered to be independent of the evidence of experience and observation, and characterized as systems of Necessary Truth?

The answer I conceive to be, that this character of necessity, ascribed to the truths of mathematics and even (with some reservations to be hereafter made) the peculiar certainty attributed to them, is an illusion; in order to sustain which, it is necessary to suppose that those truths relate to, and express the properties of purely imaginary objects. It is acknowledged that the conclusions of geometry are deduced, partly at least, from the so-called Definitions, and that those definitions are assumed to be correct representations, as far as they go, of the objects with which geometry is conversant. Now we have pointed out that, from a definition as such, no proposition, unless it be

From John Stuart Mill, *System of Logic,* Book II, Chapters 5, 6, and 7.

one concerning the meaning of a word, can ever follow; and that what apparently follows from a definition, follows in reality from an implied assumption that there exists a real thing conformable thereto. This assumption in the case of the definitions of geometry, is not strictly true: there exist no real things exactly conformable to the definitions. There exist no points without magnitude; no lines without breadth, nor perfectly straight; no circles with all their radii exactly equal, nor squares with all their angles perfectly right. It will perhaps be said that the assumption does not extend to the actual, but only to the possible, existence of such things. I answer that, according to any test we have of possibility, they are not even possible. Their existence, so far as we can form any judgment, would seem to be inconsistent with the physical constitution of our planet at least, if not of the universe. To get rid of this difficulty, and at the same time to save the credit of the supposed system of necessary truth, it is customary to say that the points, lines, circles, and squares which are the subject of geometry, exist in our conceptions merely, and are part of our minds; which minds, by working on their own materials, construct an *à priori* science, the evidence of which is purely mental, and has nothing whatever to do with outward experience. By howsoever high authorities this doctrine may have been sanctioned, it appears to me psychologically incorrect. The points, lines, circles, and squares which any one has in his mind, are (I apprehend) simply copies of the points, lines, circles, and squares which he has known in his experience. Our idea of a point, I apprehend to be simply our idea of the *minimum visible*, the smallest portion of surface which we can see. A line as defined by geometers is wholly inconceivable. We can reason about a line as if it had no breadth; because we have a power, which is the foundation of all the control we can exercise over the operations of our minds; the power, when a perception is present to our senses or a conception to our intellects, of *attending* to a part only of that perception or conception, instead of the whole. But we cannot *conceive* a line without breadth; we can form no mental picture of such a line: all the lines which we have in our minds are lines possessing breadth. If any one doubts this, we may refer him to his own experience. I much question if any one who fancies that he can conceive what is called a mathematical line, thinks so from the evidence of his consciousness: I suspect it is rather because he supposes that unless such a conception were possible, mathematics could not exist as a science: a supposition which there will be no difficulty in showing to be entirely groundless.

Since, then, neither in nature, nor in the human mind, do there exist any objects exactly corresponding to the definitions of geometry, while yet that science cannot be supposed to be conversant about non-entities; nothing remains but to consider geometry as conversant with such lines, angles, and figures, as really exist; and the definitions, as they are called, must be regarded as some of our first and most obvious generalizations concerning those natural objects. The correctness of those generalizations, *as* generalizations, is without a flaw: the equality of all the radii of a circle is true of all circles, so far as it is true of any one: but it is not exactly true of any circle; it is only nearly true; so nearly that no error of any importance in practice will be incurred by feigning it to be exactly true. When we have occasion to extend these inductions, or their consequences, to cases in which the error would be appreciable — to lines of perceptible breadth or thickness, parallels which deviate sensibly from equidistance, and the like — we correct our conclusions, by combining with them a fresh set of propositions relating to the aberration; just as we also take in propositions relating to the physical or chemical properties of the material, if those properties happen to introduce any modification into the result; which they easily may, even with respect to figure and magnitude, as in the case, for instance, of expansion by heat. So long, however, as there exists no practical necessity for attending to any of the properties of the object except its geometrical properties, or to any of the natural irregularities in those, it is convenient to neglect the consideration of the other properties and of the irregularities, and to reason as if these did not exist: accordingly, we formally announce in the definitions, that we intend to proceed on this plan. But it is an error to suppose, because we resolve to confine our attention to a certain number of the properties of an object, that we therefore conceive, or have an idea of, the object denuded of its other properties. We are thinking, all the time, of precisely such objects as we have seen and touched, and with all the properties which naturally belong to them; but for scientific convenience, we feign them to be divested of all properties, except those which are material to our purpose, and in regard to which we design to consider them.

The peculiar accuracy, supposed to be characteristic of the first principles of geometry, thus appears to be fictitious. The assertions on which the reasonings of the science are founded, do not, any more than in other sciences, exactly correspond with the fact; but we suppose that they do so, for the sake of tracing the consequences which follow from the supposition. The opinion of Dugald Stewart respecting the foundations of geometry, is, I conceive, substantially correct; that it is built on hypotheses; that it owes to this alone the peculiar certainty supposed to distinguish it; and that in any science whatever, by reasoning from a set of hypotheses, we may obtain a body of conclusions as certain as those of geometry, that is, as strictly in accordance with the hypotheses, and as irresistibly compelling assent, *on condition* that those hypotheses are true.

When, therefore, it is affirmed that the conclusions of geometry are necessary truths, the necessity consists in reality only in this, that they correctly follow from the suppositions from which they are deduced. Those suppositions are so far from being necessary, that they are not even true; they purposely depart, more or less widely, from the truth. The only sense in which necessity can be ascribed to the conclusions of any scientific investigation, is that of legitimately following from some assumption, which, by the conditions of the inquiry, is not to be questioned. In this relation, of course, the derivative truths of every deductive science must stand to the inductions, or assumptions, on which the science is founded, and which, whether true or untrue, certain or doubtful in themselves, are always supposed certain for the purposes of the particular science. And therefore the conclusions of all deductive sciences were said by the ancients to be necessary propositions. We have observed already that to be predicated necessarily was characteristic of the predictable Proprium, and that a proprium was any property of a thing which could be deduced from its essence, that is, from the properties included in its definition.

.   .   .

The Axioms of Geometry are Generalizations of Observations

§ 4.   It remains to inquire, what is the ground of our belief in axioms — what is the evidence on which they rest? I answer, they are experimental truths; generalizations from observation. The proposition, Two straight lines cannot inclose a space — or in other words, two straight lines which have once met do not meet again, but continue to diverge — is an induction from the evidence of our senses.

.   .   .

It is not necessary to show that the truths which we call axioms are originally *suggested* by observation, and that we should never have known that two straight lines cannot inclose a space if we had never seen a straight line: thus much being admitted by Dr. Whewell, and by all, in recent times, who have taken his view of the subject. But they contend, that it is not experience which *proves* the axiom; but that its truth is perceived *à priori*, by the constitution of the mind itself, from the first moment when the meaning of the proposition is apprehended; and without any necessity for verifying it by repeated trials, as is requisite in the case of truths really ascertained by observation.

They cannot, however, but allow that the truth of the axiom, Two straight lines cannot inclose a space, even if evident independently of experience, is also evident from experience. Whether the axiom needs confirmation or not, it receives confirmation in almost every instant of our lives; since we cannot look at any two straight lines which intersect one another, without seeing that from that point they continue to diverge more and more. Experimental proof crowds in upon us in such endless profusion, and without one instance in which there can be even a suspicion of an exception to the rule, that we should soon have stronger ground for believing the axiom, even as an experimental truth, than we have for almost any of the general truths which we confessedly learn from the evidence of our senses. Independently of *à priori* evidence we should certainly believe it with an intensity of conviction far greater than we accord to any ordinary physical truth: and this too at a time of life much earlier than that from which we date almost any part of our acquired knowledge, and much too early to admit of our retaining any recollection of the history of our intellectual operations at that period. Where then is the necessity for assuming that our recognition of these truths has a different origin from the rest of our knowledge, when its existence is perfectly accounted for by supposing its origin to be the same? when the causes which produce belief in all other instances, exist in this instance, and in a degree of strength as much superior to what exists in other cases, as the intensity of the belief itself is superior? The burden of proof lies on the advocates of the contrary opinion: it is for them to point out some fact inconsistent with the supposition that this part of our knowledge of nature is derived from the same sources as every other part.

This, for instance, they would be able to do, if they could prove chronologically that we had the conviction (at least practically) so early in infancy as to be anterior to those impressions on the senses, upon which, on the other theory, the conviction is founded. This, however, cannot be proved: the point being too far back to be within the reach of memory, and too obscure for external observation. The advocates of the *à priori* theory are obliged to have recourse to other arguments. These are reducible to two, which I shall endeavour to state as clearly and as forcibly as possible.

§ 5.   In the first place it is said, that if our assent to the proposition that two straight lines cannot inclose a space, were derived from the senses, we could only be convinced of its truth by actual trial, that is, by seeing or feeling the straight lines; whereas in fact it is seen to be true by merely thinking of them. That a stone thrown into water goes to the bottom, may be perceived by our senses, but mere thinking of a stone thrown into the water would never have led us to that conclusion: not so, however, with the axioms relating to straight lines: if I could be made to conceive what a straight line is, without having seen one, I should at once recognise that two such lines cannot inclose a space. Intuition is "imaginary looking;" but experience must be real looking: if we see a property of straight lines to be true by merely fancying ourselves to be looking at them, the ground of our belief cannot be the senses, or experience; it must be something mental.

To this argument it might be added in the case of this particular axiom, (for the assertion would not be true of all axioms,) that the evidence of it from actual ocular inspection is not only unnecessary but unattainable. What says the axiom? That two straight lines *cannot* inclose a space; that after having once intersected, if they are prolonged to infinity they do not meet, but continue to diverge from one another. How can this, in any single case, be proved by actual observation? We may follow the lines to any distance we please; but we cannot follow them to infinity: for aught our senses can testify, they may, immediately beyond the farthest point to which we have traced them, begin to approach, and at last meet. Unless, therefore, we had some other proof of the impossibility than observation affords us, we should have no ground for believing the axiom at all.

To these arguments, which I trust I cannot be accused of understating, a satisfactory answer will, I conceive, be found, if we advert to one of the characteristic properties of geometrical forms — their capacity of being painted in the imagination with a distinctness equal to reality: in other words, the exact resemblance of our ideas of form to the sensations which suggest them. This, in the first place, enables us to make (at least with a little practice) mental pictures of all possible combinations of lines and angles, which resemble the realities quite as well as any which we could make on paper; and in the next place, make those pictures just as fit subjects of geometrical experimentation as the realities themselves; inasmuch as pictures, if sufficiently accurate, exhibit of course all the properties which would be manifested by the realities at one given instant, and on simple inspection: and in geometry we are concerned only with such properties, and not with that which pictures could not exhibit, the mutual action of bodies one upon another. The foundations of geometry would therefore be laid in direct experience, even if the experiments (which in this case consist merely in attentive contemplation) were practised solely upon what we call our ideas, that is, upon the diagrams in our minds, and not upon outward objects. For in all systems of experimentation we take some objects to serve as representatives of all which resemble them; and in the present case the conditions which qualify a real object to be the representative of its class, are completely fulfilled by an object existing only in our fancy. Without denying, therefore, the possibility of satisfying ourselves that two straight lines cannot inclose a space, by merely thinking of straight lines without actually looking at them; I contend that we do not believe this truth on the ground of the imaginary intuition simply, but because we know that the imaginary lines exactly resemble real ones, and that we may conclude from them to real ones with quite as much certainty as we could conclude from one real line to another. The conclusion, therefore, is still an induction from observation.

.   .   .

The Truths of Arithmetic not Verbal Tautologies but, Like the Axioms of Geometry, Generalizations of Observed Facts in Nature

What we have now asserted, however, cannot be received as universally true of Deductive or Demonstrative Sciences, until verified by being applied to the most remarkable of all those sciences, that of Numbers; the theory of the Calculus; Arithmetic and Algebra. It is harder to believe of the doctrines of this science than of any other, either that they are not truths *à priori*, but experimental truths, or that their peculiar certainty is owing to their being not absolute but only conditional truths. This, therefore, is a case which merits examination apart; and the more so, because on this subject we have a double set of doctrines to contend with; that of the *à priori* philosophers on one side; and on the other, a theory the most opposite to theirs, which was at one time very generally received, and is still far from being altogether exploded, among metaphysicians.

§ 2.   This theory attempts to solve the difficulty apparently inherent in the case, by representing the propositions of the science of numbers as merely verbal, and its processes as simple transformations of language, substitutions of one expression for another. The proposition, Two and one is equal to three, according to these writers, is not a truth, is not the assertion of a really existing fact, but a definition of the word three; a statement that mankind have agreed to use the name three as a sign exactly equivalent to two and one; to call by the former name whatever is called by the other more clumsy phrase. According to this doctrine the longest process in algebra is but a succession of changes in terminology, by which equivalent expressions are substituted one for another; a series of translations of the same fact, from one into another language; though how, after such a series of translations, the fact itself comes out changed (as when we demonstrate a new geometrical theorem by algebra), they have not explained; and it is a difficulty which is fatal to their theory.

It must be acknowledged that there are peculiarities in the processes of arithmetic and algebra which render the theory in question very plausible, and have not unnaturally made those sciences the stronghold of Nominalism. The doctrine that we can discover facts, detect the hidden processes of nature, by an artful manipulation of language, is so contrary to common sense, that a person must have made some advances in philosophy to believe it; men fly to so paradoxical a belief to avoid, as they think, some even greater difficulty, which the vulgar do not see. What has led many to believe that reasoning is a mere verbal process, is, that no other theory seemed reconcileable with the nature of the Science of Numbers. For we do not carry any ideas along with us when we use the symbols of arithmetic or of algebra. In a geometrical demonstration we have a mental diagram, if not one on paper; AB, AC, are present to our imagination as lines, intersecting other lines, forming an angle with one another, and the like; but not so a and b. These may represent lines or any other magnitudes, but those magnitudes are never thought of; nothing is realized in our imagination but a and b. The ideas which, on the particular occasion, they happen to represent, are banished from the mind during every intermediate part of the process, between the beginning, when the premises are translated from things into signs, and the end, when the conclusion is translated back from signs into things. Nothing, then, being in the reasoner's mind but the symbols, what can seem more inadmissible than to contend that the reasoning process has to do with anything more? We seem to have come to one of Bacon's Prerogative Instances; an *experimentum crucis* on the nature of reasoning itself.

Nevertheless, it will appear on consideration, that this apparently so decisive instance is no instance at all; that there is in every step of an arithmetical or algebraical calculation a real induction, a real inference of facts from facts; and that what disguises the induction is simply its comprehensive nature and the consequent extreme generality of the language. All numbers must be numbers of something; there are no such things as numbers in the abstract. *Ten* must mean ten bodies, or ten sounds, or ten beatings of the pulse. But though numbers must be numbers of something, they may be numbers of anything. Propositions, therefore, concerning numbers, have the remarkable peculiarity that they are propositions concerning all things whatever; all objects, all existences of every kind, known to our experience. All things possess quantity; consist of parts which can be numbered; and in that character possess all the properties which are called properties of numbers. That half of four is two, must be true whatever the word four represents, whether four hours, four miles, or four pounds weight. We need only conceive a thing divided into four equal parts (and all things may be conceived as so divided), to be able to predicate of it every property of the number four, that is, every arithmetical proposition in which the number four stands on one side of the equation. Algebra extends the generalization still farther: every number represents that particular number of all things without distinction, but every algebraical symbol does more, it represents all numbers without distinction.

.   .   .

There is another circumstance, which, still more than that which we have now mentioned, gives plausibility to the notion that the propositions of arithmetic and algebra are merely verbal. That is, that when considered as propositions respecting Things, they all have the appearance of being identical propositions. The assertion, Two and one is equal to three, considered as an assertion respecting objects, as for instance "Two pebbles and one pebble are equal to three pebbles," does not affirm equality between two collections of pebbles, but absolute identity. It affirms that if we put one pebble to two pebbles, those very pebbles are three. The objects, therefore, being the very same, and the mere assertion that "objects are themselves" being insignificant, it seems but natural to consider the proposition Two and one is equal to three, as asserting mere identity of signification between the two names.

This, however, though it looks so plausible, will not bear examination. The expression "two pebbles and one pebble," and the expression, "three pebbles," stand indeed for the same aggregation of objects, but they by no means stand for the same physical fact. They are names of the same objects, but of those objects in two different states: though they *de*note the same things, their *con*notation is different. Three pebbles in two separate parcels, and three pebbles in one parcel, do not make the same impression on our senses; and the assertion that the very same pebbles may by an alteration of place and arrangement be made to produce either the one set of sensations or the other, though a very familiar proposition, is not an identical one. It is a truth known to us by early and constant experience: an inductive truth; and such truths are the foundation of the science of Number. The fundamental truths of that science all rest on the evidence of sense; they are proved by showing to our eyes and our fingers that any given number of objects, ten balls for example, may by separation and re-arrangement exhibit to our senses all the different sets of numbers the sum of which is equal to ten. All the improved methods of teaching arithmetic to children proceed on a knowledge of this fact. All who wish to carry the child's *mind* along with them in learning arithmetic; all who wish to teach numbers, and not mere ciphers — now teach it through the evidence of the senses, in the manner we have described.

We may, if we please, call the proposition, "Three is two and one," a definition of the number three, and assert that arithmetic, as it has been asserted that geometry, is a science founded on definitions. But they are definitions in the geometrical sense, not the logical; asserting not the meaning of a term only, but along with it an observed matter of fact. The proposition, "A circle is a figure bounded by a line which has all its points equally distant from a point within it," is called the definition of a circle; but the proposition from which so many consequences follow, and which is really a first principle in geometry, is, that figures answering to this description exist. And thus we may call "Three is two and one" a definition of three; but the calculations which depend on that proposition do not follow from the definition itself, but from an arithmetical theorem presupposed in it, namely, that collections of objects exist, which while they impress the senses thus, °°°, may be separated into two parts, thus, ∘∘ ∘. This proposition being granted, we term all such parcels Threes, after which the enunciation of the above mentioned physical fact will serve also for a definition of the word Three.

The Science of Numbers is thus no exception to the conclusion we previously arrived at, that the processes even of deductive sciences are altogether inductive, and that their first principles are generalisations from experience.

The Status of the Basic Principles of Logic

. . . Sir William Hamilton is . . . a firm believer in the *à priori* character of many axioms, and of the sciences deduced from them; and is so far from considering those axioms to rest on the evidence of experience, that he declares certain of them to be true even of Noumena — of the Unconditioned — of which it is one of the principal aims of his philosophy to prove that the nature of our faculties debars us from having any knowledge. The axioms to which he attributes this exceptional emancipation from the limits which confine all our other possibilities of knowledge; the chinks through which, as he represents, one ray of light finds its way to us from behind the curtain which veils from us the mysterious world of Things in themselves, — are the two principles, which he terms, after the schoolmen, the Principle of Contradiction, and the Principle of Excluded Middle: the first, that two contradictory propositions cannot both be true; the second, that they cannot both be false.

.   .   .

As I have hitherto said nothing of the two axioms in question, those of Contradiction and of Excluded Middle, it is not unseasonable to consider them here. The former asserts that an affirmative proposition and the corresponding negative proposition cannot both be true; which has generally been held to be intuitively evident. Sir William Hamilton and the Germans consider it to be the statement in words of a form or law of our thinking faculty. Other philosophers, not less deserving of consideration, deem it to be an identical proposition, an assertion involved in the meaning of the terms; a mode of defining Negation, and the word Not.

I am able to go one step with these last. An affirmative assertion and its negative are not two independent assertions, connected with each other only as mutually incompatible. That if the negative be true, the affirmative must be false, really is a mere identical proposition; for the negative proposition asserts nothing but the falsity of the affirmative, and has no other sense or meaning whatever. The Principium Contradictionis should therefore put off the ambitious phraseology which gives it the air of a fundamental antithesis pervading nature, and should be enunciated in the simpler form, that the same proposition cannot at the same time be false and true. But I can go no farther with the Nominalists; for I cannot look upon this last as a merely verbal proposition. I consider it to be, like other axioms, one of our first and most familiar generalizations from experience. The original foundation of it I take to be, that Belief and Disbelief are two different mental states, excluding one another. This we know by the simplest observation of our own minds. And if we carry our observation outwards, we also find that light and darkness, sound and silence, motion and quiescence, equality and inequality, preceding and following, succession and simultaneousness, any positive phenomenon whatever and its negative, are distinct phenomena, pointedly contrasted, and the one always absent where the other is present. I consider the maxim in question to be a generalization from all these facts.

In like manner as the Principle of Contradiction (that one of two contradictories must be false) means that an assertion cannot be *both* true and false, so the Principle of Excluded Middle, or that one of two contradictories must be true, means that an assertion must be *either* true or false: either the affirmative is true, or otherwise the negative is true, which means that the affirmative is false. I cannot help thinking this principle a surprising specimen of a so-called necessity of Thought, since it is not even true, unless with a large qualification. A proposition must be either true or false, *provided* that the predicate be one which can in any intelligible sense be attributed to the subject; (and as this is always assumed to be the case in treatises on logic, the axiom is always laid down there as of absolute truth). "Abracadabra is a second intention" is neither true nor false. Between the true and the false there is a third possibility, the Unmeaning: and this alternative is fatal to Sir William Hamilton's extension of the maxim to Noumena. That Matter must either have a minimum of divisibility or be infinitely divisible, is more than we can ever know. For in the first place, Matter, in any other than the phenomenal sense of the term, may not exist: and it will scarcely be said that a non-entity must be either infinitely or finitely divisible. In the second place, though matter, considered as the occult cause of our sensations, do really exist, yet what we call divisibility may be an attribute only of our sensations of sight and touch, and not of their uncognizable cause. Divisibility may not be predicable at all, in any intelligible sense, of Things in themselves, nor therefore of Matter in itself; and the assumed necessity of being either infinitely or finitely divisible, may be an inapplicable alternative.

46

ONLY ANALYTIC
STATEMENTS
ARE KNOWABLE
A PRIORI

Alfred Jules Ayer

Having admitted that we are empiricists, we must now deal with the objection that is commonly brought against all forms of empiricism; the objection, namely, that it is impossible on empiricist principles to account for our knowledge of necessary truths. For, as Hume conclusively showed, no general proposition whose validity is subject to the test of actual experience can ever be logically certain. No matter how often it is verified in practice, there still remains the possibility that it will be confuted on some future occasion. The fact that a law has been substantiated in $n - 1$ cases affords no logical guarantee that it will be substantiated in the nth case also, no matter how large we take n to be. And this means that no general proposition referring to a matter of fact can ever be shown to be necessarily and universally true. It can at best be a probable hypothesis. And this, we shall find, applies not only to general propositions, but to all propositions which have a factual content. They can none of them ever become logically certain. This conclusion, which we shall elaborate later on, is one which must be accepted by every consistent empiricist. It is often thought to involve him in complete scepticism; but this is not the case. For the fact that the validity of a proposition cannot be logically guaranteed in no way entails that it is irrational for us to believe it. On the contrary, what is irrational is to look for a guarantee where none can be forthcoming; to demand certainty where probability is all that is obtainable. We have already remarked upon this, in referring to the work of Hume. And we shall make the point clearer when we come to treat of probability, in explaining the use which we make of empirical propositions. We shall discover that there is nothing perverse or paradoxical

From A. J. Ayer, *Language, Truth, and Logic*, first published in 1936 by Dover Publications, Inc., New York, and by Victor Gollancz, Ltd., London. Reprinted by permission of the publishers.

about the view that all the "truths" of science and common sense are hypotheses; and consequently that the fact that it involves this view constitutes no objection to the empiricist thesis.

Where the empiricist does encounter difficulty is in connection with the truths of formal logic and mathematics. For whereas a scientific generalization is readily admitted to be fallible, the truths of mathematics and logic appear to everyone to be necessary and certain. But if empiricism is correct no proposition which has a factual content can be necessary or certain. Accordingly the empiricist must deal with the truths of logic and mathematics in one of the two following ways: he must say either that they are not necessary truths, in which case he must account for the universal conviction that they are; or he must say that they have no factual content, and then he must explain how a proposition which is empty of all factual content can be true and useful and surprising.

If neither of these courses proves satisfactory, we shall be obliged to give way to rationalism. We shall be obliged to admit that there are some truths about the world which we can know independently of experience; that there are some properties which we can ascribe to all objects, even though we cannot conceivably observe that all objects have them. And we shall have to accept it as a mysterious inexplicable fact that our thought has this power to reveal to us authoritatively the nature of objects which we have never observed. Or else we must accept the Kantian explanation which, apart from the epistemological difficulties which we have already touched on, only pushes the mystery a stage further back.

It is clear that any such concession to rationalism would upset the main argument of this book. For the admission that there were some facts about the world which could be known independently of experience would be incompatible with our fundamental contention that a sentence says nothing unless it is empirically verifiable. And thus the whole force of our attacks on metaphysics would be destroyed. It is vital, therefore, for us to be able to show that one or other of the empiricist accounts of the propositions of logic and mathematics is correct. If we are successful in this, we shall have destroyed the foundations of rationalism. For the fundamental tenet of rationalism is that thought is an independent source of knowledge, and is moreover a more trustworthy source of knowledge than experience; indeed some rationalists have gone so far as to say that thought is the only source of knowledge. And the ground for this view is simply that the only necessary truths about the world which are known to us are known through thought and not through experience. So that if we can show either that the truths in question are not necessary or that they are not "truths about the world," we shall be taking away the support on which rationalism rests. We shall be making good the empiricist contention that there are no "truths of reason" which refer to matters of fact.

The course of maintaining that the truths of logic and mathematics are not necessary or certain was adopted by Mill. He maintained that these propositions were inductive generalizations based on an extremely large number of instances. The fact that the number of supporting instances was so very large accounted, in his view, for our believing these generalizations to be necessarily and universally true. The evidence in their favour was so strong that it seemed incredible to us that a contrary instance should ever arise. Nevertheless it was in principle possible for such generalizations to be confuted. They were highly probable, but, being inductive generalizations, they were not certain. The difference between them and the hypotheses of natural science was a difference in degree and not in kind. Experience gave us very good reason to suppose that a "truth" of mathematics or logic was true universally; but we were not possessed of a guarantee. For these "truths" were only empirical hypotheses which had worked particularly well in the past; and, like all empirical hypotheses, they were theoretically fallible.

I do not think that this solution of the empiricist's difficulty with regard to the propositions of logic and mathematics is acceptable. In discussing it, it is necessary to make a distinction which is perhaps already enshrined in Kant's famous dictum that, although there can be no doubt that all our knowledge begins with experience, it does not follow that it all arises out of experience.[1] When we say that the truths of logic are known independently of experience, we are not of course saying that they are innate, in the sense that we are born knowing them. It is obvious that mathematics and logic have to be learned in the same way as chemistry and history have to be learned. Nor are we denying that the first person to discover a given logical or mathematical truth was led to it by an inductive procedure. It is very probable, for example, that the principle of the syllogism was formulated not before but after the validity of syllogistic reasoning had been observed in a number of particular cases. What we are discussing, however, when we say that logical and mathematical truths are known independently of experience, is not a historical question concerning the way in which these truths were originally discovered, nor a psychological question concerning the way in which each of us comes to learn them, but an epistemological question. The contention of Mill's which we reject is that the propositions of logic and mathematics have the same status as empirical hypotheses; that their validity is determined in the same way. We maintain that they are independent of experience in the sense that they do not owe their validity to empirical verification. We may come to discover them through an inductive process; but once we have apprehended them we see that they are necessarily true, that they hold good for every conceivable instance. And this serves to distinguish them from empirical generalizations. For we know that a proposition whose validity depends upon experience cannot be seen to be necessarily and universally true.

In rejecting Mill's theory, we are obliged to be somewhat dogmatic. We can do no more than state the issue clearly and then trust that his contention

---

[1] *Critique of Pure Reason*, 2nd ed., Introduction, section i.

will be seen to be discrepant with the relevant logical facts. The following considerations may serve to show that of the two ways of dealing with logic and mathematics which are open to the empiricist, the one which Mill adopted is not the one which is correct.

The best way to substantiate our assertion that the truths of formal logic and pure mathematics are necessarily true is to examine cases in which they might seem to be confuted. It might easily happen, for example, that when I came to count what I had taken to be five pairs of objects, I found that they amounted only to nine. And if I wished to mislead people I might say that on this occasion twice five was not ten. But in that case I should not be using the complex sign "$2 \times 5 = 10$" in the way in which it is ordinarily used. I should be taking it not as the expression of a purely mathematical proposition, but as the expression of an empirical generalization, to the effect that whenever I counted what appeared to me to be five pairs of objects I discovered that they were ten in number. This generalization may very well be false. But if it proved false in a given case, one would not say that the mathematical proposition "$2 \times 5 = 10$" had been confuted. One would say that I was wrong in supposing that there were five pairs of objects to start with, or that one of the objects had been taken away while I was counting, or that two of them had coalesced, or that I had counted wrongly. One would adopt as an explanation whatever empirical hypothesis fitted in best with the accredited facts. The whole explanation which would in no circumstances be adopted is that ten is not always the product of two and five.

To take another example: if what appears to be a Euclidean triangle is found by measurement not to have angles totalling 180 degrees, we do not say that we have met with an instance which invalidates the mathematical proposition that the sum of the three angles of a Euclidean triangle is 180 degrees. We say that we have measured wrongly, or, more probably, that the triangle we have been measuring is not Euclidean. And this is our procedure in every case in which a mathematical truth might appear to be confuted. We always preserve its validity by adopting some other explanation of the occurrence.

The same thing applies to the principles of formal logic. We may take an example relating to the so-called law of excluded middle, which states that a proposition must be either true or false, or, in other words, that it is impossible that a proposition and its contradictory should neither of them be true. One might suppose that a proposition of the form "x has stopped doing y" would in certain cases constitute an exception to this law. For instance, if my friend has never yet written to me, it seems fair to say that it is neither true nor false that he has stopped writing to me. But in fact one would refuse to accept such an instance as an invalidation of the law of excluded middle. One would point out that the proposition "My friend has stopped writing to me" is not a simple proposition, but the conjunction of the two propositions "My friend wrote to me in the past" and "My friend does not write to me now": and, furthermore, that the proposition "My friend has not stopped writing to me" is not, as it appears to be, contradictory to "My friend has stopped writing to me," but only contrary to it. For it means "My friend wrote to me in the past, and he still writes to me." When, therefore, we say that such a proposition as "My friend has stopped writing to me" is sometimes neither true nor false, we are speaking inaccurately. For we seem to be saying that neither it nor its contradictory is true. Whereas what we mean, or anyhow should mean, is that neither it nor its apparent contradictory is true. And its apparent contradictory is really only its contrary. Thus we preserve the law of excluded middle by showing that the negating of a sentence does not always yield the contradictory of the proposition originally expressed.

There is no need to give further examples. Whatever instance we care to take, we shall always find that the situations in which a logical or mathematical principle might appear to be confuted are accounted for in such a way as to leave the principle unassailed. And this indicates that Mill was wrong in supposing that a situation could arise which would overthrow a mathematical truth. The principles of logic and mathematics are true universally simply because we never allow them to be anything else. And the reason for this is that we cannot abandon them without contradicting ourselves, without sinning against the rules which govern the use of language, and so making our utterances self-stultifying. In other words, the truths of logic and mathematics are analytic propositions or tautologies. In saying this we are making what will be held to be an extremely controversial statement, and we must now proceed to make its implications clear.

The most familiar definition of an analytic proposition, or judgement, as he called it, is that given by Kant. He said[2] that an analytic judgement was one in which the predicate B belonged to the subject A as something which was covertly contained in the concept of A. He contrasted analytic with synthetic judgements, in which the predicate B lay outside the subject A, although it did stand in connection with it. Analytic judgements, he explains, "add nothing through the predicate to the concept of the subject, but merely break it up into those constituent concepts that have all along been thought in it, although confusedly." Synthetic judgements, on the other hand, "add to the concept of the subject a predicate which has not been in any wise thought in it, and which no analysis could possibly extract from it." Kant gives "all bodies are extended" as an example of an analytic judgement, on the ground that the required predicate can be extracted from the concept of "body," "in accordance with the principle of contradiction"; as an example of a synthetic judgement, he gives "all bodies are heavy." He refers also to "7 + 5 = 12" as a synthetic judgement, on the ground that the concept of twelve is by no means already thought in merely thinking of the union of seven and five. And he appears to regard this as tantamount to saying that the judgement does not rest on the principle of contradiction alone. He holds, also, that through analytic judgements our knowledge is not extended as it is

---

[2] *Ibid.,* Introduction, sections iv and v.

through synthetic judgements. For in analytic judgements "the concept which I already have is merely set forth and made intelligible to me."

I think that this is a fair summary of Kant's account of the distinction between analytic and synthetic propositions, but I do not think that it succeeds in making the distinction clear. For even if we pass over the difficulties which arise out of the use of the vague term "concept," and the unwarranted assumption that every judgement, as well as every German or English sentence, can be said to have a subject and a predicate, there remains still this crucial defect. Kant does not give one straightforward criterion for distinguishing between analytic and synthetic propositions; he gives two distinct criteria, which are by no means equivalent. Thus his ground for holding that the proposition "$7 + 5 = 12$" is synthetic is, as we have seen, that the subjective intension of "$7 + 5$" does not comprise the subjective intension of "12"; whereas his ground for holding that "all bodies are extended" is an analytic proposition is that it rests on the principle of contradiction alone. That is, he employs a psychological criterion in the first of these examples, and a logical criterion in the second, and takes their equivalence for granted. But, in fact, a proposition which is synthetic according to the former criterion may very well be analytic according to the latter. For, as we have already pointed out, it is possible for symbols to be synonymous without having the same intensional meaning for anyone: and accordingly from the fact that one can think of the sum of seven and five without necessarily thinking of twelve, it by no means follows that the proposition "$7 + 5 = 12$" can be denied without self-contradiction. From the rest of his argument, it is clear that it is this logical proposition, and not any psychological proposition, that Kant is really anxious to establish. His use of the psychological criterion leads him to think that he has established it, when he has not.

I think that we can preserve the logical import of Kant's distinction between analytic and synthetic propositions, while avoiding the confusions which mar his actual account of it, if we say that a proposition is analytic when its validity depends solely on the definitions of the symbols it contains, and synthetic when its validity is determined by the facts of experience. Thus, the proposition "There are ants which have established a system of slavery" is a synthetic proposition. For we cannot tell whether it is true or false merely by considering the definitions of the symbols which constitute it. We have to resort to actual observation of the behaviour of ants. On the other hand, the proposition "Either some ants are parasitic or none are" is an analytic proposition. For one need not resort to observation to discover that there either are or are not ants which are parasitic. If one knows what is the function of the words "either," "or," and "not," then one can see that any proposition of the form "Either p is true or p is not true" is valid, independently of experience. Accordingly, all such propositions are analytic.

It is to be noticed that the proposition "Either some ants are parasitic or none are" provides no information whatsoever about the behaviour of ants, or, indeed, about any matter of fact. And this applies to all analytic propositions. They none of them provide any information about any matter of fact. In other words, they are entirely devoid of factual content. And it is for this reason that no experience can confute them.

When we say that analytic propositions are devoid of factual content, and consequently that they say nothing, we are not suggesting that they are sense-less in the way that metaphysical utterances are senseless. For, although they give us no information about any empirical situation, they do enlighten us by illustrating the way in which we use certain symbols. Thus if I say, "Nothing can be coloured in different ways at the same time with respect to the same part of itself," I am not saying anything about the properties of any actual thing; but I am not talking nonsense. I am expressing an analytic proposition, which records our determination to call a colour expanse which differs in quality from a neighboring colour expanse a different part of a given thing. In other words, I am simply calling attention to the implications of a certain linguistic usage. Similarly, in saying that if all Bretons are French-men, and all Frenchmen Europeans, then all Bretons are Europeans, I am not describing any matter of fact. But I am showing that in the statement that all Bretons are Frenchmen, and all Frenchmen Europeans, the further statement that all Bretons are Europeans is implicitly contained. And I am thereby indicating the convention which governs our usage of the words "if" and "all."

We see, then, that there is a sense in which analytic propositions do give us new knowledge. They call attention to linguistic usages, of which we might otherwise not be conscious, and they reveal unsuspected implications in our assertions and beliefs. But we can see also that there is a sense in which they may be said to add nothing to our knowledge. For they tell us only what we may be said to know already. Thus, if I know that the existence of May Queens is a relic of tree-worship, and I discover that May Queens still exist in England, I can employ the tautology "If p implies q, and p is true, q is true" to show that there still exists a relic of tree-worship in England. But in saying that there are still May Queens in England, and that the existence of May Queens is a relic of tree-worship, I have already asserted the existence in England of a relic of tree-worship. The use of the tautology does, indeed, enable me to make this concealed assertion explicit. But it does not provide me with any new knowledge, in the sense in which empirical evidence that the election of May Queens had been forbidden by law would provide me with new knowledge. If one had to set forth all the information one possessed, with regard to matters of fact, one would not write down any analytic propo-sitions. But one would make use of analytic propositions in compiling one's encyclopaedia, and would thus come to include propositions which one would otherwise have overlooked. And, besides enabling one to make one's list of information complete, the formulation of analytic propositions would enable one to make sure that the synthetic propositions of which the list was com-posed formed a self-consistent system. By showing which ways of combining propositions resulted in contradictions, they would prevent one from including incompatible propositions and so making the list self-stultifying. But in so far as we had actually used such words as "all" and "or" and "not" without falling into self-contradiction, we might be said already to know what was revealed in the formulation of analytic propositions illustrating the rules which govern our usage of these logical particles. So that here again we are justified in saying that analytic propositions do not increase our knowledge.

The analytic character of the truths of formal logic was obscured in the traditional logic through its being insufficiently formalized. For in speaking always of judgements, instead of propositions, and introducing irrelevant psychological questions, the traditional logic gave the impression of being concerned in some specially intimate way with the workings of thought. What it was actually concerned with was the formal relationship of classes, as is shown by the fact that all its principles of inference are subsumed in the Boolean class-calculus, which is subsumed in its turn in the propositional calculus of Russell and Whitehead. Their system, expounded in *Principia Mathematica,* makes it clear that formal logic is not concerned with the properties of men's minds, much less with the properties of material objects, but simply with the possibility of combining propositions by means of logical particles into analytic propositions, and with studying the formal relationship of these analytic propositions, in virtue of which one is deductible from another. Their procedure is to exhibit the propositions of formal logic as a deductive system, based on five primitive propositions, subsequently reduced in number to one. Hereby the distinction between logical truths and principles of inference, which was maintained in the Aristotelian logic, very properly disappears. Every principle of inference is put forward as a logical truth and every logical truth can serve as a principle of inference. The three Aristotelian "laws of thought," the law of identity, the law of excluded middle, and the law of non contradiction, are incorporated in the system, but they are not considered more important than the other analytic propositions. They are not reckoned among the premises of the system. And the system of Russell and Whitehead itself is probably only one among many possible logics, each of which is composed of tautologies as interesting to the logician as the arbitrarily selected Aristotelian "laws of thought."

A point which is not sufficiently brought out by Russell, if indeed it is recognised by him at all, is that every logical proposition is valid in its own right. Its validity does not depend on its being incorporated in a system, and deduced from certain propositions which are taken as self-evident. The construction of systems of logic is useful as a means of discovering and certifying analytic propositions, but it is not in principle essential even for this purpose. For it is possible to conceive of a symbolism in which every analytic proposition could be seen to be analytic in virtue of its form alone.

The fact that the validity of an analytic proposition in no way depends on its being deductible from other analytic propositions is our justification for disregarding the question whether the propositions of mathematics are reducible to propositions of formal logic, in the way that Russell supposed.[3] For even if it is the case that the definition of a cardinal number as a class of classes similar to a given class is circular, and it is not possible to reduce mathematical notions to purely logical notions, it will still remain true that the propositions of mathematics are analytic propositions. They will form a special class of analytic propositions, containing special terms, but they will be none the less analytic for that. For the criterion of an analytic proposition is that its validity should follow simply from the definition of the terms contained in it, and this condition is fulfilled by the propositions of pure mathematics.

The mathematical propositions which one might most pardonably suppose to be synthetic are the propositions of geometry. For it is natural for us to think, as Kant thought, that geometry is the study of the properties of physical space, and consequently that its propositions have factual content. And if we believe this, and also recognise that the truths of geometry are necessary and certain, then we may be inclined to accept Kant's hypothesis that space is the form of intuition of our outer sense, a form imposed by us on the matter of sensation, as the only possible explanation of our *a priori* knowledge of these synthetic propositions. But while the view that pure geometry is concerned with physical space was plausible enough in Kant's day, when the geometry of Euclid was the only geometry known, the subsequent invention of non-Euclidean geometries has shown it to be mistaken. We see now that the axioms of a geometry are simply definitions, and that the theorems of a geometry are simply the logical consequences of these definitions.[4] A geometry is not in itself about physical space; in itself it cannot be said to be "about" anything. But we can use a geometry to reason about physical space. That is to say, once we have given the axioms a physical interpretation, we can proceed to apply the theorems to the objects which satisfy the axioms. Whether a geometry can be applied to the actual physical world or not, is an empirical question which falls outside the scope of the geometry itself. There is no sense, therefore, in asking which of the various geometries known to us are false and which are true. In so far as they are all free from contradiction, they are all true. What one can ask is which of them is the most useful on any given occasion, which of them can be applied most easily and most fruitfully to an actual empirical situation. But the proposition which states that a certain application of a geometry is possible is not itself a proposition of that geometry. All that the geometry itself tells us is that if anything can be brought under the definitions, it will also satisfy the theorems. It is therefore a purely logical system, and its propositions are purely analytic propositions.

It might be objected that the use made of diagrams in geometrical treatises shows that geometrical reasoning is not purely abstract and logical, but depends on our intuition of the properties of figures. In fact, however,

---

[3] Vide *Introduction to Mathematical Philosophy*, Chapter ii.
[4] cf. H. Poincaré, *La Science et l'Hypothèse*, Part II, Chapter iii.

the use of diagrams is not essential to completely rigorous geometry. The diagrams are introduced as an aid to our reason. They provide us with a particular application of the geometry, and so assist us to perceive the more general truth that the axioms of the geometry involve certain consequences. But the fact that most of us need the help of an example to make us aware of those consequences does not show that the relation between them and the axioms is not a purely logical relation. It shows merely that our intellects are unequal to the task of carrying out very abstract processes of reasoning without the assistance of intuition. In other words, it has no bearing on the nature of geometrical propositions, but is simply an empirical fact about ourselves. Moreover, the appeal to intuition, though generally of psychological value, is also a source of danger to the geometer. He is tempted to make assumptions which are accidentally true of the particular figure he is taking as an illustration, but do not follow from his axioms. It has, indeed, been shown that Euclid himself was guilty of this, and consequently that the presence of the figure is essential to some of his proofs.[5] This shows that his system is not, as he presents it, completely rigorous, although of course it can be made so. It does not show that the presence of the figure is essential to a truly rigorous geometrical proof. To suppose that it did would be to take as a necessary feature of all geometries what is really only an incidental defect in one particular geometrical system.

We conclude, then, that the propositions of pure geometry are analytic. And this leads us to reject Kant's hypothesis that geometry deals with the form of intuition of our outer sense. For the ground for this hypothesis was that it alone explained how the propositions of geometry could be both true *a priori* and synthetic: and we have seen that they are not synthetic. Similarly our view that the propositions of arithmetic are not synthetic but analytic leads us to reject the Kantian hypothesis[6] that arithmetic is concerned with our pure intuition of time, the form of our inner sense. And thus we are able to dismiss Kant's transcendental aesthetic without having to bring forward the epistemological difficulties which it is commonly said to involve. For the only argument which can be brought in favour of Kant's theory is that it alone explains certain "facts." And now we have found that the "facts" which it purports to explain are not facts at all. For while it is true that we have *a priori* knowledge of necessary propositions, it is not true, as Kant supposed, that any of these necessary propositions are synthetic. They are without exception analytic propositions, or, in other words, tautologies.

We have already explained how it is that these analytic propositions are necessary and certain. We saw that the reason why they cannot be confuted in experience is that they do not make any assertion about the empirical world. They simply record our determination to use words in a certain fashion. We cannot deny them without infringing the conventions which

---

[5] cf. M. Black, *The Nature of Mathematics*, p. 154.

[6] This hypothesis is not mentioned in the *Critique of Pure Reason*, but was maintained by Kant at an earlier date.

are presupposed by our very denial, and so falling into self-contradiction. And this is the sole ground of their necessity. As Wittgenstein puts it, our justification for holding that the world could not conceivably disobey the laws of logic is simply that we could not say of an unlogical world how it would look.[7] And just as the validity of an analytic proposition is independent of the nature of the external world, so it is independent of the nature of our minds. It is perfectly conceivable that we should have employed different linguistic conventions from those which we actually do employ. But whatever these conventions might be, the tautologies in which we recorded them would always be necessary. For any denial of them would be self-stultifying.

We see, then, that there is nothing mysterious about the apodeictic certainty of logic and mathematics. Our knowledge that no observation can ever refute the proposition "$7 + 5 = 12$" depends simply on the fact that the symbolic expression "$7 + 5$" is synonymous with "12," just as our knowledge that every oculist is an eye-doctor depends on the fact that the symbol "eye-doctor" is synonymous with "oculist." And the same explanation holds good for every other *a priori* truth.

What is mysterious at first sight is that these tautologies should on occasion be so surprising, that there should be in mathematics and logic the possibility of invention and discovery. As Poincaré says: "If all the assertions which mathematics puts forward can be derived from one another by formal logic, mathematics cannot amount to anything more than an immense tautology. Logical inference can teach us nothing essentially new, and if everything is to proceed from the principle of identity, everything must be reducible to it. But can we really allow that these theorems which fill so many books serve no other purpose than to say in a round-about fashion 'A = A'?"[8] Poincaré finds this incredible. His own theory is that the sense of invention and discovery in mathematics belongs to it in virtue of mathematical induction, the principle that what is true for the number 1, and true for $n + 1$ when it is true for n, is true for all numbers. And he claims that this is a synthetic *a priori* principle. It is, in fact, *a priori*, but it is not synthetic. It is a defining principle of the natural numbers, serving to distinguish them from such numbers as the infinite cardinal numbers, to which it cannot be applied.[9] Moreover, we must remember that discoveries can be made, not only in arithmetic, but also in geometry and formal logic, where no use is made of mathematical induction. So that even if Poincaré were right about mathematical induction, he would not have provided a satisfactory explanation of the paradox that a mere body of tautologies can be so interesting and so surprising.

The true explanation is very simple. The power of logic and mathematics to surprise us depends, like their usefulness, on the limitations of our reason. A being whose intellect was infinitely powerful would take no inter-

---

[7] *Tractatus Logico-Philosophicus,* 3.031.

[8] *La Science et l'Hypothèse,* Part I, Chapter i.

[9] cf. B. Russell's *Introduction to Mathematical Philosophy,* Chapter iii, p. 27.

est in logic and mathematics. For he would be able to see at a glance everything that his definitions implied, and, accordingly, could never learn anything from logical inference which he was not fully conscious of already. But our intellects are not of this order. It is only a minute proportion of the consequences of our definitions that we are able to detect at a glance. Even so simple a tautology as "$91 \times 79 = 7189$" is beyond the scope of our immediate apprehension. To assure ourselves that "7189" is synonymous with "91×79" we have to resort to calculation, which is simply a process of tautological transformation — that is, a process by which we change the form of expressions without altering their significance. The multiplication tables are rules for carrying out this process in arithmetic, just as the laws of logic are rules for the tautological transformation of sentences expressed in logical symbolism or in ordinary language. As the process of calculation is carried out more or less mechanically, it is easy for us to make a slip and so unwittingly contradict ourselves. And this accounts for the existence of logical and mathematical "falsehoods," which otherwise might appear paradoxical. Clearly the risk of error in logical reasoning is proportionate to the length and the complexity of the process of calculation. And in the same way, the more complex an analytic proposition is, the more chance it has of interesting and surprising us.

It is easy to see that the danger of error in logical reasoning can be minimized by the introduction of symbolic devices, which enable us to express highly complex tautologies in a conveniently simple form. And this gives us an opportunity for the exercise of invention in the pursuit of logical enquiries. For a well-chosen definition will call our attention to analytic truths, which would otherwise have escaped us. And the framing of definitions which are useful and fruitful may well be regarded as a creative act.

Having thus shown that there is no inexplicable paradox involved in the view that the truths of logic and mathematics are all of them analytic, we may safely adopt it as the only satisfactory explanation of their *a priori* necessity. And in adopting it we vindicate the empiricist claim that there can be no *a priori* knowledge of reality. For we show that the truths of pure reason, the propositions which we know to be valid independently of all experience, are so only in virtue of their lack of factual content. To say that a proposition is true *a priori* is to say that it is a tautology. And tautologies, though they may serve to guide us in our empirical search for knowledge, do not in themselves contain any information about any matter of fact.

47

CRITICISMS OF THE LINGUISTIC THEORY OF THE A PRIORI

Alfred Cyril Ewing

Meaning of the Distinction, 'A Priori' Character of Mathematics

In the theory of knowledge, the first point that confronts us is the sharp distinction between two kinds of knowledge which have been called respectively *a priori* and empirical. Most of our knowledge we obtain by observation of the external world (sense-perception) and of ourselves (introspection). This is called empirical knowledge. But some knowledge we can obtain by simply thinking. That kind of knowledge is called *a priori*. Its chief exemplifications are to be found in logic and mathematics. In order to see that $5 + 7 = 12$ we do not need to take five things and seven things, put them together, and then count the total number. We can know what the total number will be simply by thinking.

Another important difference between *a priori* and empirical knowledge is that in the case of the former we do not see merely that something, S, is in fact P, but that it must be P and why it is P. I can discover that a flower is yellow (or at least produces sensations of yellow) by looking at it, but I cannot thereby see why it is yellow or that it must be yellow. For anything I can tell it might equally well have been a red flower. But with a truth such as that $5 + 7 = 12$ I do not see merely that it is a fact but that it must be a fact. It would be quite absurd to suppose that $5 + 7$ might have been equal to 11 and just happened to be equal to 12, and I can see that the nature of 5 and 7 constitutes a fully adequate and intelligible reason why their sum should be 12 and not some other number. It is indeed conceivable that some

From Alfred Cyril Ewing, *Fundamental Questions of Philosophy*, 1951, published by Routledge & Kegan Paul Ltd., London, and by The Macmillan Company, New York. Reprinted by permission of the publishers.

of the things which make the two groups of 5 and 7 might, when they were put together, fuse like drops of water, or even vanish, so that there were no longer 12 things; but what is inconceivable is that there could *at the same time* be 5 + 7 things of a certain kind at once in a certain place and yet less than 12 things of that kind in that place. Before some of the things fused or vanished they would be 5 + 7 in number and also 12 in number, and after the fusion or disappearance they would be neither 5 + 7 nor 12. When I say in this connection that something is inconceivable, I do not mean merely or primarily that we cannot conceive it — this is not a case of a mere psychological inability like the inability to understand higher mathematics. It is a positive insight: we definitely see it to be impossible that certain things could happen. This we do not see in the case of empirical propositions which are false: they are not true but might for anything we know have been true. It is even conceivable, so far as we can see, that the fundamental laws of motion might have been quite different from what they are, but we can see that there could not have been a world which contradicted the laws of arithmetic. This is expressed by saying that empirical propositions are *contingent*, but true *a priori* propositions *necessary*. What we see to be necessary is not indeed that arithmetic should apply to the universe. It is conceivable that the universe might have been constituted entirely of a homogeneous fluid, and then, since there would have been no distinction between different things, it is difficult to see how arithmetic could have applied to it. What we do see is that arithmetic must be true of whatever can be numbered at all.

We must not be misled here by the fact that in order to come to understand arithmetic we originally required examples. Once we have learnt the beginnings of arithmetic in the kindergarten with the help of examples, we do not need examples any more to grasp it, and we can see the truth of many arithmetical propositions, e.g. that $3112 + 2467 = 5579$, of which we have never had examples. We have probably never taken 3112 things and 2467 things, put them together and counted the resulting set, but we still know that this is what the result of the counting would be. If it were empirical knowledge, we could not know it without counting. The examples are needed, not to prove anything, but only in order to enable us to come to understand in the first instance what is meant by number.

In geometry we indeed stand more in need of examples than in arithmetic, though I think this is only a psychological matter. In arithmetic we only need examples at the most elementary stage, but in geometry most people need a drawn figure, or at least an image of one in their minds, to see the validity of most proofs. But we must distinguish between an illustration and the basis of a proof. If the particular figure were not merely an illustration but the basis of the theorem, the latter would have to be proved by measuring it, but a measurement with a ruler or protractor never figures in Euclid's proofs. That the proof is not really based on the figure drawn is shown by the fact that we can still follow a proof concerning the properties of right-angled triangles even if the figure used to illustrate it is so badly drawn that it is obviously not a right-angled triangle at all. Again, if geometry were empirical, it would be a very hazardous speculation from the single example before us on the blackboard to conclude that all triangles had a property. It might be an individual idiosyncracy of some triangles and not others. These considerations should be conclusive of themselves, but we might add that recent developments in geometry have had the effect of much loosening the connection between geometrical proofs and the empirical figure. It is possible to work out non-Euclidean geometries where we cannot depend on figures.

The 'A Priori' in Logic

Another important field for *a priori* knowledge is logic. The laws of logic must be known *a priori* or not at all. They certainly are not a matter for empirical observation, and the function of logical argument is just to give us conclusions which we have not discovered by observation. The argument would be superfluous if we had observed them already. We are able to make inferences because there is sometimes a logical connection between one or more propositions (the premise or premises) and another proposition, the conclusion, such that the latter must be true if the former is. Then, if we know the former, we can assert the latter on the strength of it, thus anticipating any experience. To take an example, there is a story that Mr. X., a man of high reputation and great social standing, had been asked to preside at a big social function. He was late in coming, and so a Roman Catholic priest was asked to make a speech to pass the time till his arrival. The priest told various anecdotes, including one which recorded his embarrassment when as confessor he had to deal with his first penitent and the latter confessed to a particularly atrocious murder. Shortly afterwards Mr. X. arrived, and in his own speech he said: 'I see Father —— is here. Now, though he may not recognize me, he is an old friend of mine, in fact I was his first penitent.' It is plain that such an episode would enable one to infer that Mr. X. had committed a murder without having observed the crime. The form of inference involved: The first penitent was a murderer, Mr. X. was the first penitent, therefore Mr. X. was a murderer — is of the famous kind to which logicians have given the name of *syllogism*. The importance of syllogisms has often been exaggerated, but they are as important as any kind of inference, and we cannot deny that in many cases a syllogism has given people information of which they were not in any ordinary sense aware before they used the syllogism and which they did not acquire by observation. Inference is only possible because there are special connections between the propositions involved such that one necessarily follows from others. It is a chief function of logic to study these connections, of which that expressed in the syllogism is by no means the only one.

(A *syllogism* consists of three propositions, two forming the *premises* and the other the *conclusion*. Each proposition can be expressed by a subject and predicate connected by the verb to be, the *copula*, and if we call everything which stands as either subject or predicate a *term*, there must be three and only three terms in the syllogism. The one common to the two premises is called the *middle term*, and it is on this common element that the inference depends. The other two, having been connected by means of it, occur without it in the conclusion. Thus in the usual example of the syllogism — All men are mortal, Socrates is a man, ∴ Socrates is mortal — man is the middle term connecting Socrates with mortality so that we could, even if he had not already died, know that he was mortal.)

Other Cases of the 'A Priori'

A priori knowledge, while most prominent in mathematics and logic, is not limited to these subjects. For instance, we can see *a priori* that the same surface cannot have two different colours all over at the same time, or that a thought cannot have a shape. Philosophers have been divided into *rationalists* and *empiricists* according to whether they stressed the *a priori* or the empirical element more. The possibility of metaphysics depends on *a priori* knowledge, for our experience is quite inadequate to enable us to make on merely empirical grounds any sweeping generalizations of the kind the metaphysician desires. The term *a priori* covers both self-evident propositions, i.e. those which are seen to be true in their own right and those which are derived by inference from propositions themselves self-evident.

The Linguistic Theory of the 'A Priori' and the Denial that 'A Priori' Propositions or Inferences Can Give New Knowledge

At the present time even empiricist philosophers recognize the impossibility of explaining away *a priori* propositions as merely empirical generalizations, but they are inclined to the view that *a priori* propositions and *a priori* reasoning are merely concerned with language, and so cannot tell us anything new about the real world. Thus it is said that, when we make an inference, the conclusion is just part of the premises expressed in different language.[1] If so, inference would be of use merely for clarifying our language and would involve no real advance in knowledge. Some inferences are of this type, e.g. A is a father, therefore A is male. But are they all? That would be hard indeed to square with the *prima facie* novelty of many conclusions. Take, for instance, the proposition that the square on the hypotenuse of a right-angled triangle is equal to the sum of the squares on the other two sides. Such a

---

[1] This theory is not applied to *inductive* inference.

proposition can be inferred from the axioms and postulates of Euclid, but it certainly does not seem to be included in their meaning. Otherwise we should know it as soon as we understood the axioms and postulates. The example I gave of the murder discovered by a logical argument seems to be another case of a fact not known at all beforehand by the reasoner which is discovered by his reasoning. Extreme empiricist philosophers contend that this appearance of novelty is really illusory, and that in some sense we knew the conclusion all along; but they have never succeeded in making clear in what sense we did so. It is not enough to say that the conclusion is implicit in the premises. 'Implicit' means 'implied by', and of course a conclusion is implied by its premises, if the inference is correct at all. But this admission leaves quite open the question whether or not a proposition can follow from a different one which does not contain it as part of itself; and since we obviously can by deductive inference come to know things which we did not know before in any ordinary sense of 'know', we must treat the empiricist's claim as unjustified till he has produced a clearly defined sense of 'implicit in' or 'contained in' which leaves room for that novelty in inference which we all cannot help really admitting. In any ordinary sense of 'know' the conclusion is not in the cases I have mentioned known prior to the inference, and since the premises are and indeed must be known before we know the conclusion, it is therefore in no ordinary sense of 'part' part of the premises.

It is indeed sometimes said that the premises include the conclusion in a confused form, but it is obvious that the beginner in geometry cannot be said to be aware of Pythagoras's theorem even in a confused form though he may know all the premises from which it can be deduced. Nor does awareness of the propositions that A was B's first penitent and that B's first penitent was a murderer include even confusedly the awareness that A was a murderer as long as the premises are not combined. When they are combined therefore something new appears that was not present to consciousness before in any way; there is a new discovery.

. . .

Nevertheless, the view that inference cannot yield new conclusions dies hard, and so it will not be superfluous to bring further arguments. (1) 'This has shape' admittedly follows logically from 'this has size' and vice versa. If the view I am criticizing were true, 'this has size' would, therefore, have to include in its meaning 'this has shape', and 'this has shape' would also have to include in its meaning 'this has size'. But this would only be possible if the two sentences meant exactly the same thing, which they obviously do not. (2) Take an argument such as — Montreal is to the north of New York, New York is to the north of Washington, therefore Montreal is to the north of Washington. If the view I am discussing is true, the conclusion is part of the premises. But it is not part of either premise by itself, otherwise both premises would not be needed. So the only way in which it could be part of both together would be if it were divisible into two propositions one of which was part of the first and the other part of the second. I defy anybody to divide it in this way. (3) The proposition 'Socrates was a philosopher' certainly entails the proposition 'if Socrates had measles some philosophers have had measles', but it cannot be that the second proposition is included in the first. For the first proposition certainly does not include the notion of measles.

What is really the same view is often expressed by saying that all *a priori* propositions are 'analytic'. A distinction has commonly been drawn between *analytic* propositions, in which the predicate is in the notion of the subject already formed before the proposition is asserted, so that the proposition gives no new information, and *synthetic* propositions in which the predicate is not so contained and which are thus capable of giving new information.[2] Analytic propositions are essentially verbal, being all true by definition, e.g. all fathers are male. As an example of a synthetic proposition we could take any proposition established by experience such as 'I am cold' or 'It is snowing', but empiricists often assert that there are no synthetic *a priori* propositions. That this view cannot be justified may be shown at once. The proposition that there are no synthetic *a priori* propositions, since it cannot be established by empirical observations, would be, if justified, itself a synthetic *a priori* proposition, and we cannot affirm it as a synthetic *a priori* proposition that there are no synthetic *a priori* propositions. We may therefore dismiss off-hand any arguments for the theory. Such arguments, whatever they were, would have to involve synthetic *a priori* propositions. Further, the view must be false if it is ever true that the conclusion of an inference is not part of its premises. For, if the proposition — S is Q — ever follows validly from — S is P, the proposition — all that is SP is SQ must be true *a priori*. But, unless the concept Q is part of the concept SP, the proposition — all that is SP is SQ — cannot be analytic. Therefore our arguments against the view that in all valid inferences the conclusion is part of the premises expressed in different language are also arguments against the view that all *a priori* propositions are analytic.

The analytic view seems plausible when we are concerned with the simplest propositions of logic and arithmetic, but we must not assume that a proposition is analytic because it is obvious. Though it may be very difficult to determine precisely where analytic propositions end and synthetic propositions begin, we cannot use this as a ground for denying the latter. It is very difficult to say precisely where blue ends and green begins, since the different shades run into each other imperceptibly, but we cannot therefore argue that all blue is really green. Taking arithmetic, even if there is a good deal of plausibility in saying that $2 + 2$ is included in the meaning of '4,' there is none in saying $95 - 91$ or $\dfrac{216}{2} - \dfrac{67 + 25}{3}$ are so included. Yet, if the analytical view were true, all the infinite numerical combinations which could be seen *a priori* to be equal to 4 would have to be included in the meaning of '4'.

[2] This definition would have to be amended slightly to suit modern logicians who (I think, rightly) deny that all propositions are of the subject-predicate form, but this would not alter the principle though imparting a complication of detail with which we need not deal here.

Some empiricists, without committing themselves to the view that all *a priori* propositions are analytic, still say these are a matter of arbitrary choice or verbal convention. They are influenced here by a modern development in the view of geometry. It used to be held that the axioms of Euclid expressed a direct insight into the nature of physical space, but this is denied by modern scientists, and the view is taken that they are arbitrary postulates which geo-metricians make because they are interested in what would follow *if* they were true. Whether they are true or not is then a matter of empirical fact to be decided by science. But, even if this suggests that the premises of our *a priori* arguments may be arbitrary postulates, this does not make the subsequent steps arbitrary. From the postulates of Euclid it follows that the three angles of a triangle are equal to two right angles. If the original postulates are arbitrary, it is not certain that the conclusion is true of the real world; but it is still not an arbitrary matter that it follows from the postulates. The postulates may well be false, but there can be no doubt that *if* they were true the conclusions must be so, and it is in this hypothetical working out of the consequences of pos-tulates which may not be true that pure geometry consists. The *a priori* neces-sity of pure geometry is not therefore in the least invalidated by modern de-velopments. What is *a priori* is that the conclusions follow from the axioms and postulates, and this is not at all affected by the (empirical) discovery that not all the axioms and postulates exactly apply to the physical world. (Applied Euclidean geometry is possible in practice because it is an empirical fact that they approximately apply. The divergencies only show themselves when we consider unusually great velocities or distances.)

If not only the postulates but the successive stages in the inference were themselves arbitrary, we might just as well infer from the same premise that the angles of a triangle were equal to a million right angles or to none at all. All point in inference would be lost. Dictators may do a great deal, but they cannot alter the laws of logic and mathematics; these laws would not change even if by a system of intensive totalitarian education every human being were persuaded to fall in with a world dictator's whim in the matter and believe they were different from what they are. Nor can they change with alterations in language, though they may be expressed differently. That the truth of *a priori* propositions does not just depend on the nature of language can be easily seen when we consider that, even if we do not know any Fijian or Hottentot, we can know that also in these languages and not only in the languages we know the proposition $5 + 7 = 12$ must be true. It is of course true that by altering the meaning of the words we could make the proposition we expressed by '$5 + 7 = 12$' false, e.g. if I used '12' in a new sense to mean what other people mean by '11', but then it would be a different proposition. I could play the same trick with empirical propositions and say truly, e.g., that 'fire does not burn' or 'there is an elephant in this room' if I used 'burn' to mean 'drown' or 'elephant' to mean 'table'. This does not in the least impair the obviousness of the contrary propositions established by experience. Fin-ally, as we argued above that the proposition that there can be no synthetic *a priori* propositions would itself, if justified, have to be a synthetic *a priori* proposition, so we may argue that the proposition that all *a priori* propositions are a matter of arbitrary linguistic convention would, if true, have to be itself a matter of arbitrary linguistic convention. It therefore could not be vindicated by any argument and would be merely a matter of a new usage of words arbitrarily established by the persons who assert it, since it certainly does not express the usual meaning of '*a priori* propositions'. So we must reject any attempt to explain away the *a priori* as a genuine source of new knowledge. If the attempt had succeeded, we should have had to admit that philosophy in anything like its old sense was impossible, for philosophy clearly cannot be based merely on observation.

The views we have been criticizing contain the following elements of truth. (1) *A priori* propositions can be seen to be true and the conclusions of an inference seen to follow from their premises without any further observation, provided we understand the meaning of the words used. But to say that q follows from p once we understand the meaning of the words is not to say that q is part of the meaning of the words used to express p. 'Follow from' and 'be part of' are not synonyms. (2) If q follows from p you cannot assert p and deny q without contradicting yourself, but this is only to say that in that case the denial of q implies the denial of p. It is not to say that q is part of what you assert when you assert p, unless we already assume that what is implied is always part of what implies it, i.e. beg the question at issue. (3) An *a priori* proposition cannot be fully understood without being seen to be true. It may be impossible to understand something fully without understanding something else not included in it at all, so it may still be synthetic.

People have been inclined to deny synthetic *a priori* propositions because they could not see how one characteristic could necessarily involve another, but that this could not happen would be itself a synthetic *a priori* metaphysical proposition. People have also thought that it was necessary to give some sort of explanation of *a priori* knowledge, and could not see how this could be done except in terms of language. To this I should reply that there is no reason to suppose that *a priori* knowledge requires some special explanation any more than does our ability to attain knowledge empirically by observation. Why not take it as an ultimate fact? Human beings certainly cannot explain everything, whether there is ultimately an explanation for it or not.

.   .   .

The main argument of those who attack the notion of intuition is that apparent intuitions are liable to conflict with each other and there is then no means of deciding which is right. But this is a mistake: we can in fact test them in various ways. We can consider whether they are capable of any clear and internally consistent statement. We can ask whether they fit into a coherent system with the rest of our well-established beliefs. We can also ask whether intuitions of the same kind have been confirmed in the past. We can ask whether an intuition stands or falls by itself or is a presupposition of a whole number of other beliefs which we cannot help holding, as some (though confused) intuition of the occurrence of causation or the uniformity of nature seems a necessary presupposition of all inductive beliefs. We can consider the plausibility of giving an alternative explanation of the intuitive belief. The result may then be negative or positive. It may be that our apparent intuition will evaporate when we think of the explanation, and then the latter is probably a correct one at least as to why *we* held the belief. Or it may be that the intuition will persist unshaken, in which case the explanation is probably at least inadequate. We can again consider whether the intuition repeats itself when considered in different contexts and different moods or with different examples.

So when two people have conflicting intuitions we need not suppose that there is just an irreducible difference of intuitive faculty between them and that there is nothing more to be done about it. Arguments may well be available which without strictly proving either side to be wrong put a disputant into a position in which he can see better for himself whether he is right or wrong or at least partially confirm or cast doubt on the truth of his view. In general, the clearer we have made ourselves about a subject by inferential thought, by analysing the different factors involved and by clearing up our terminology, the more likely are we to have correct intuitions on the matter if such are available at all. Again, intellectual confusions may be revealed which were responsible for the truth of the belief in question. Thus a person who really sees that A is B may confuse B with C and will then think he sees intuitively that A is C. Some such conflicts may be caused simply or mainly by ambiguities of terminology or the attaching of different meanings to some word. And of course we need not deny that differences of intuition may sometimes be due on one side or even on both to 'wishful thinking' or to the kind of cause which it is the business of the psycho-analyst (or of a patient and tactful friend) to remove. These remarks are specially applicable to ethical disputes. We cannot of course settle all disputes in these ways, but neither can we in practice settle all disputes in science. The most we can say is that they are soluble in principle, though we may not have the ability to hit on the right way of solving a particular dispute. Similarly, there is no reason to believe that conflicts between rival intuitions would not all be capable of a solution if these methods were applied aright and with good will on both sides, though in fact we cannot so apply them.

48

SCEPTICAL DOUBTS
ABOUT INDUCTIVE
INFERENCE

David Hume

*David Hume (1711-1776) was a writer on economics and history as well as philosophy.
He is one of the leading philosophical figures of all time.*

PART I

All the objects of human reason or inquiry may naturally be divided into two
kinds, to wit, "Relations of Ideas," and "Matters of Fact." Of the first kind
are the sciences of Geometry, Algebra, and Arithmetic, and, in short, every
affirmation which is either intuitively or demonstratively certain. *That the
square of the hypotenuse is equal to the square of the two sides* is a proposition
which expresses a relation between these figures. *That three times five is
equal to the half of thirty* expresses a relation between these numbers. Propositions of this kind are discoverable by the mere operation of thought, without
dependence on what is anywhere existent in the universe. Though there
never were a circle or triangle in nature, the truths demonstrated by Euclid
would forever retain their certainty and evidence.

Matters of fact, which are the second objects of human reason, are not
ascertained in the same manner, nor is our evidence of their truth, however
great, of a like nature with the foregoing. The contrary of every matter of
fact is still possible, because it can never imply a contradiction and is conceived by the mind with the same facility and distinctness as if ever so conformable to reality. *That the sun will not rise tomorrow* is no less intelligible
a proposition and implies no more contradiction than the affirmation *that it
will rise.* We should in vain, therefore, attempt to demonstrate its falsehood.
Were it demonstratively false, it would imply a contradiction and could never
be distinctly conceived by the mind.

It may, therefore, be a subject worthy of curiosity to inquire what is the
nature of that evidence which assures us of any real existence and matter of

From David Hume, *An Inquiry Concerning Human Understanding,* first published
in 1748, Section IV.

fact beyond the present testimony of our senses or the records of our memory. This part of philosophy, it is observable, had been little cultivated either by the ancients or moderns; and, therefore, our doubts and errors in the prosecution of so important an inquiry may be the more excusable while we march through such difficult paths without any guide or direction. They may even prove useful by exciting curiosity and destroying that implicit faith and security which is the bane of all reasoning and free inquiry. The discovery of defects in the common philosophy, if any such there be, will not, I presume, be a discouragement, but rather an incitement, as is usual, to attempt something more full and satisfactory than has yet been proposed to the public.

All reasonings concerning matter of fact seem to be founded on the relation of *cause* and *effect*. By means of that relation alone we can go beyond the evidence of our memory and senses. If you were to ask a man why he believes any matter of fact which is absent, for instance, that his friend is in the country or in France, he would give you a reason, and this reason would be some other fact: as a letter received from him or the knowledge of his former resolutions and promises. A man finding a watch or any other machine in a desert island would conclude that there had once been men in that island. All our reasonings concerning fact are of the same nature. And here it is constantly supposed that there is a connection between the present fact and that which is inferred from it. Were there nothing to bind them together, the inference would be entirely precarious. The hearing of an articulate voice and rational discourse in the dark assures us of the presence of some person. Why? Because these are the effects of the human make and fabric, and closely connected with it. If we anatomize all the other reasons of this nature, we shall find that they are founded on the relation of cause and effect, and that this relation is either near or remote, direct or collateral. Heat and light are collateral effects of fire, and the one effect may justly be inferred from the other.

If we would satisfy ourselves, therefore, concerning the nature of that evidence which assures us of matters of fact, we must inquire how we arrive at the knowledge of cause and effect.

I shall venture to affirm, as a general proposition which admits of no exception, that the knowledge of this relation is not, in any instance, attained by reasonings *a priori*, but arises entirely from experience, when we find that any particular objects are constantly conjoined with each other. Let an object be presented to a man of ever so strong natural reason and abilities — if that object be entirely new to him, he will not be able, by the most accurate examination of its sensible qualities, to discover any of its causes or effects. Adam, though his rational faculties be supposed, at the very first, entirely perfect, could not have inferred from the fluidity and transparency of water that it would suffocate him, or from the light and warmth of fire that it would consume him. No object ever discovers, by the qualities which appear to the senses, either the causes which produced it or the effects which will arise from it; nor can our reason, unassisted by experience, ever draw any inference concerning real existence and matter of fact.

This proposition, *that causes and effects are discoverable, not by reason, but by experience,* will readily be admitted with regard to such objects as we remember to have once been altogether unknown to us, since we must be conscious of the utter inability which we then lay under of foretelling what would arise from them. Present two smooth pieces of marble to a man who has no tincture of natural philosophy; he will never discover that they will adhere together in such a manner as to require great force to separate them in a direct line, while they make so small a resistance to a lateral pressure. Such events as bear little analogy to the common course of nature are also readily confessed to be known only by experience, nor does any man imagine that the explosion of gunpowder or the attraction of a loadstone could ever be discovered by arguments *a priori.* In like manner, when an effect is supposed to depend upon an intricate machinery or secret structure of parts, we make no difficulty in attributing all our knowledge of it to experience. Who will assert that he can give the ultimate reason why milk or bread is proper nourishment for a man, not for a lion or tiger?

But the same truth may not appear at first sight to have the same evidence with regard to events which have become familiar to us from our first appearance in the world, which bear a close analogy to the whole course of nature, and which are supposed to depend on the simple qualities of objects without any secret structure of parts. We are apt to imagine that we could discover these effects by the mere operation of our reason without experience. We fancy that, were we brought on a sudden into this world, we could at first have inferred that one billiard ball would communicate motion to another upon impulse, and that we needed not to have waited for the event in order to pronounce with certainty concerning it. Such is the influence of custom that where it is strongest it not only covers our natural ignorance but even conceals itself, and seems not to take place, merely because it is found in the highest degree.

But to convince us that all the laws of nature and all the operations of bodies without exception are known only by experience, the following reflections may perhaps suffice. Were any object presented to us, and were we required to pronounce concerning the effect which will result from it without consulting past observation, after what manner, I beseech you, must the mind proceed in this operation? It must invent or imagine some event which it ascribes to the object as its effect; and it is plain that this invention must be entirely arbitrary. The mind can never possibly find the effect in the supposed cause by the most accurate scrutiny and examination. For the effect is totally different from the cause, and consequently can never be discovered in it. Motion in the second billiard ball is a quite distinct event from motion in the first, nor is there anything in the one to suggest the smallest hint of the other. A stone or piece of metal raised into the air and left without any support immediately falls. But to consider the matter a *priori,* is there anything we discover in this situation which can beget the idea of a downward rather than an upward or any other motion in the stone or metal?

And as the first imagination or invention of a particular effect in all natural operations is arbitrary where we consult not experience, so must we also esteem the supposed tie or connection between the cause and effect which binds them together and renders it impossible that any other effect could result from the operation of that cause. When I see, for instance, a billiard ball moving in a straight line toward another, even suppose motion in the second ball should by accident be suggested to me as the result of their contact or impulse, may I not conceive that a hundred different events might as well follow from that cause? May not both these balls remain at absolute rest? May not the first ball return in a straight line or leap off from the second in any line or direction? All these suppositions are consistent and conceivable. Why, then, should we give the preference to one which is no more consistent or conceivable than the rest? All our reasonings *a priori* will never be able to show us any foundation for this preference.

In a word, then, every effect is a distinct event from its cause. It could not, therefore, be discovered in the cause, and the first invention or conception of it, *a priori,* must be entirely arbitrary. And even after it is suggested, the conjunction of it with the cause must appear equally arbitrary, since there are always many other effects which, to reason, must seem fully as consistent and natural. In vain, therefore, should we pretend to determine any single event or infer any cause or effect without the assistance of observation and experience.

Part II

But we have not yet attained any tolerable satisfaction with regard to the question first proposed. Each solution still gives rise to a new question as difficult as the foregoing and leads us on to further inquiries. When it is asked, *What is the nature of all our reasonings concerning matter of fact?* the proper answer seems to be, That they are founded on the relation of cause and effect. When again it is asked, *What is the foundation of all our reasonings and conclusions concerning that relation?* it may be replied in one word, *experience.* But if we still carry on our sifting humor and ask, *What is the foundation of all conclusions from experience?* this implies a new question which may be of more difficult solution and explication. Philosophers that give themselves airs of superior wisdom and sufficiency have a hard task when they encounter persons of inquisitive dispositions, who push them from every corner to which they retreat, and who are sure at last to bring them to some dangerous dilemma. The best expedient to prevent this confusion is to be modest in our pretensions and even to discover the difficulty ourselves before it is objected to us. By this means we may make a kind of merit of our very ignorance.

I shall content myself in this section with an easy task and shall pretend only to give a negative answer to the question here proposed. I say, then, that even after we have experience of the operations of cause and effect, our conclusions from that experience are *not* founded on reasoning or any process of the understanding. This answer we must endeavor both to explain and to defend.

It must certainly be allowed that nature has kept us at a great distance from all her secrets and has afforded us only the knowledge of a few superficial qualities of objects, while she conceals from us those powers and principles on which the influence of these objects entirely depends. Our senses inform us of the color, weight, and consistency of bread, but neither sense nor reason can ever inform us of those qualities which fit it for the nourishment and support of the human body. Sight or feeling conveys an idea of the actual motion of bodies, but as to that wonderful force or power which would carry on a moving body forever in a continued change of place, and which bodies never lose but by communicating it to others, of this we cannot form the most distant conception. But notwithstanding this ignorance of natural powers and principles, we always presume when we see like sensible qualities that they have like secret powers, and expect that effects similar to those which we have experienced will follow from them. If body of like color and consistency with that bread which we have formerly eaten be presented to us, we make no scruple of repeating the experiment and foresee with certainty like nourishment and support. Now this is a process of the mind or thought of which I would willingly know the foundation. It is allowed on all hands that there is no known connection between the sensible qualities and the secret powers, and, consequently, that the mind is not led to form such a conclusion concerning their constant and regular conjunction by anything which it knows of their nature. As to past *experience*, it can be allowed to give *direct* and *certain* information of those precise objects only, and that precise period of time which fell under its cognizance. But why this experience should be extended to future times and to other objects which, for aught we know, may be only in appearance similar, this is the main question on which I would insist. The bread which I formerly ate nourished me; that is, a body of such sensible qualities was, at that time, endued with such secret powers. But does it follow that other bread must also nourish me at another time, and that like sensible qualities must always be attended with like secret powers? The consequence seems nowise necessary. At least, it must be acknowledged that there is here a consequence drawn by the mind that there is a certain step taken, a process of thought, and an inference which wants to be explained. These two propositions are far from being the same: *I have found that such an object has always been attended with such an effect,* and *I foresee that other objects which are in appearance similar will be attended with similar effects.* I shall allow, if you please, that the one proposition may justly be inferred from the other: I know, in fact, that it always is inferred. But if you insist that the inference is made by a chain of reasoning, I desire you to produce that reasoning. The connection between these propositions is not intuitive. There is required a medium which may enable the mind to draw such an inference, if indeed it be drawn by reasoning and argument. What that medium is I must confess passes my comprehension; and it is incumbent on those to produce it who assert that it really exists and is the original of all our conclusions concerning matter of fact.

This negative argument must certainly, in process of time, become altogether convincing if many penetrating and able philosophers shall turn their inquiries this way, and no one be ever able to discover any connecting proposition or intermediate step which supports the understanding in this conclusion. But as the question is yet new, every reader may not trust so far to his own penetration as to conclude, because an argument escapes his inquiry, that therefore it does not really exist. For this reason it may be requisite to venture upon a more difficult task, and, enumerating all the branches of human knowledge, endeavor to show that none of them can afford such an argument.

All reasonings may be divided into two kinds, namely, demonstrative reasoning, or that concerning relations of ideas, and moral reasoning, or that concerning matter of fact and existence. That there are no demonstrative arguments in the case seems evident, since it implies no contradiction that the course of nature may change and that an object, seemingly like those which we have experienced, may be attended with different or contrary effects. May I not clearly and distinctly conceive that a body, falling from the clouds and which in all other respects resembles snow, has yet the taste of salt or feeling of fire? Is there any more intelligible proposition than to affirm that all the trees will flourish in December and January, and will decay in May and June? Now, whatever is intelligible and can be distinctly conceived implies no contradiction and can never be proved false by any demonstrative argument or abstract reasoning *a priori*.

If we be, therefore, engaged by arguments to put trust in past experience and make it the standard of our future judgment, these arguments must be probable only, or such as regard matter of fact and real existence, according to the division above mentioned. But that there is no argument of this kind must appear if our explication of that species of reasoning be admitted as solid and satisfactory. We have said that all arguments concerning existence are founded on the relation of cause and effect, that our knowledge of that relation is derived entirely from experience, and that all our experimental conclusions proceed upon the supposition that the future will be conformable to the past. To endeavor, therefore, the proof of this last supposition by probable arguments, or arguments regarding existence, must be evidently going in a circle and taking that for granted which is the very point in question.

In reality, all arguments from experience are founded on the similarity which we discover among natural objects, and by which we are induced to expect effects similar to those which we have found to follow from such objects. And though none but a fool or madman will ever pretend to dispute the authority of experience or to reject that great guide of human life, it may surely be allowed a philosopher to have so much curiosity at least as to examine the principle of human nature which gives this mighty authority to experience and makes us draw advantage from that similarity which nature has placed among different objects. From causes which appear similar, we expect similar effects. This is the sum of all our experimental conclusions. Now it seems evident that, if this conclusion were formed by reason, it would be as perfect at first, and upon one instance, as after ever so long a course of experience; but the case is far otherwise. Nothing so like as eggs, yet no one, on account of this appearing similarity, expects the same taste and relish in all of them. It is only after a long course of uniform experiments in any kind that we attain a firm reliance and security with regard to a particular event. Now, where is that process of reasoning which, from one instance, draws a conclusion so different from that which it infers from a hundred instances that are nowise different from that single one? This question I propose as much for the sake of information as with an intention of raising difficulties. I cannot find, I cannot imagine any such reasoning. But I keep my mind still open to instruction if anyone will vouchsafe to bestow it on me.

Should it be said that, from a number of uniform experiments, we *infer* a connection between the sensible qualities and the secret powers, this, I must confess, seems the same difficulty, couched in different terms. The question still occurs, On what process of argument is this *inference* founded? Where is the medium, the interposing ideas which join propositions so very wide of each other? It is confessed that the color, consistency, and other sensible qualities of bread appear not of themselves to have any connection with the secret powers of nourishment and support; for otherwise we could infer these secret powers from the first appearance of these sensible qualities without the aid of experience, contrary to the sentiment of all philosophers, and contrary to plain matter of fact. Here, then, is our natural state of ignorance with regard to the powers and influence of all objects. How is this remedied by experience? It only shows us a number of uniform effects resulting from certain objects, and teaches us that those particular objects, at that particular time, were endowed with such powers and forces. When a new object endowed with similar sensible qualities is produced, we expect similar powers and forces, and look for a like effect. From a body of like color and consistency with bread, we expect like nourishment and support. But this surely is a step or progress of the mind which wants to be explained. When a man says, *I have found, in all past instances, such sensible qualities, conjoined with such secret powers,* and when he says, *similar sensible qualities will always be conjoined with similar secret powers,* he is not guilty of a tautology, nor are these propositions in any respect the same. You say that the one proposition is an inference from the other; but you must confess that the inference is not intuitive, neither is it demonstrative. Of what nature is it then? To say it is experimental is begging the question. For all inferences from experience suppose, as their foundation, that the future will resemble the past and that similar powers will be conjoined with similar sensible qualities. If there be any suspicion that the course of nature may change, and that the past may be no rule for the future, all experience becomes useless and can give rise to no inference or conclusion. It is impossible, therefore, that any arguments from experience can prove this resemblance of the past to the future, since all these arguments are founded on the supposition of that resemblance. Let the course of things be allowed hitherto ever so regular, that alone, without some new argument or inference, proves not that for the future it will continue so. In vain do you pretend to have learned the nature of bodies from your past experience. Their secret nature, and consequently all their effects and influence, may change without any change in their sensible qualities. This happens sometimes, and with regard to some objects. Why may it not happen always, and with regard to all objects? What logic, what process of argument secures you against this supposition? My practice, you say, refutes my doubts. But you mistake the purport of my question. As an agent, I am quite satisfied in the point; but as a philosopher who has some share of curiosity, I will not say skepticism, I want to learn the foundation of this inference. No reading, no inquiry has yet been able to remove my difficulty or give me satisfaction in a matter of such importance. Can I do better than propose the difficulty to the public, even though, perhaps, I have small hopes of obtaining a solution? We shall at least, by this means, be sensible of our ignorance, if we do not augment our knowledge.

I must confess that a man is guilty of unpardonable arrogance who concludes, because an argument has escaped his own investigation, that therefore it does not really exist. I must also confess that, though all the learned, for several ages, should have employed themselves in fruitless search upon any subject, it may still, perhaps, be rash to conclude positively that the subject must therefore pass all human comprehension. Even though we examine all the sources of our knowledge and conclude them unfit for such a subject, there may still remain a suspicion that the enumeration is not complete or the examination not accurate. But with regard to the present subject, there are some considerations which seem to remove all this accusation of arrogance or suspicion of mistake.

It is certain that the most ignorant and stupid peasants, nay infants, nay even brute beasts, improve by experience and learn the qualities of natural objects by observing the effects which result from them. When a child has felt the sensation of pain from touching the flame of a candle, he will be careful not to put his hand near any candle, but will expect a similar effect from a cause which is similar in its sensible qualities and appearance. If you assert, therefore, that the understanding of the child is led into this conclusion by any process of argument or ratiocination, I may justly require you to produce that argument, nor have you any pretense to refuse so equitable a demand. You cannot say that the argument is abstruse and may possibly escape your inquiry, since you confess that it is obvious to the capacity of a mere infant. If you hesitate, therefore, a moment or if, after reflection, you produce an intricate or profound argument, you, in a manner, give up the question and confess that it is not reasoning which engages us to suppose the past resembling the future, and to expect similar effects from causes which are to appearance similar. This is the proposition which I intended to enforce in the present section. If I be right, I pretend not to have made any mighty discovery. And if I be wrong, I must acknowledge myself to be indeed a very backward scholar, since I cannot now discover an argument which, it seems, was perfectly familiar to me long before I was out of my cradle.

49

THE PRINCIPLE
OF INDUCTION
NOT SUPPORTABLE
BY OBSERVATION

Bertrand Russell

In almost all our previous discussions we have been concerned in the attempt to get clear as to our data in the way of knowledge of existence. What things are there in the universe whose existence is known to us owing to our being acquainted with them? So far, our answer has been that we are acquainted with our sense-data, and, probably, with ourselves. These we know to exist. And past sense-data which are remembered are known to have existed in the past. This knowledge supplies our data.

But if we are to be able to draw inferences from these data — if we are to know of the existence of matter, of other people, of the past before our individual memory begins, or of the future, we must know general principles of some kind by means of which such inferences can be drawn. It must be known to us that the existence of some one sort of thing, A, is a sign of the existence of some other sort of thing, B, either at the same time as A or at some earlier or later time, as, for example, thunder is a sign of the earlier existence of lightning. If this were not known to us, we could never extend our knowledge beyond the sphere of our private experience; and this sphere, as we have seen, is exceedingly limited. The question we have now to consider is whether such an extension is possible, and if so, how it is effected.

Let us take as an illustration a matter about which none of us, in fact, feel the slightest doubt. We are all convinced that the sun will rise tomorrow. Why? Is this belief a mere blind outcome of past experience, or can it be justified as a reasonable belief? It is not easy to find a test by which to judge whether a belief of this kind is reasonable or not, but we can at least ascertain what sort of general beliefs would suffice, if true, to justify the judgement that the sun will rise to-morrow, and the many other similar judgements upon which our actions are based.

From Bertrand Russell, *The Problems of Philosophy,* 1912. Chapter 6. Reprinted by permission of the Oxford University Press, publisher.

It is obvious that if we are asked why we believe that the sun will rise to-morrow, we shall naturally answer, "Because it always has risen every day." We have a firm belief that it will rise in the future, because it has risen in the past. If we are challenged as to why we believe that it will continue to rise as heretofore, we may appeal to the laws of motion: the earth, we shall say, is a freely rotating body, and such bodies do not cease to rotate unless something interferes from outside, and there is nothing outside to interfere with the earth between now and to-morrow. Of course it might be doubted whether we are quite certain that there is nothing outside to interfere, but this is not the interesting doubt. The interesting doubt is as to whether the laws of motion will remain in operation until to-morrow. If this doubt is raised, we find ourselves in the same position as when the doubt about the sunrise was first raised.

The *only* reason for believing that the laws of motion will remain in operation is that they have operated hitherto, so far as our knowledge of the past enables us to judge. It is true that we have a greater body of evidence from the past in favour of the laws of motion than we have in favour of the sunrise, because the sunrise is merely a particular case of fulfilment of the laws of motion, and there are countless other particular cases. But the real question is: Do *any* number of cases of a law being fulfilled in the past afford evidence that it will be fulfilled in the future? If not, it becomes plain that we have no ground whatever for expecting the sun to rise to-morrow, or for expecting the bread we shall eat at our next meal not to poison us, or for any of the other scarcely conscious expectations that control our daily lives. It is to be observed that all such expectations are only *probable*; thus we have not to seek for a proof that they *must* be fulfilled, but only for some reason in favour of the view that they are *likely* to be fulfilled.

Now in dealing with this question we must, to begin with, make an important distinction, without which we should soon become involved in hopeless confusions. Experience has shown us that, hitherto, the frequent repetition of some uniform succession or coexistence has been a *cause* of our expecting the same succession or coexistence on the next occasion. Food that has a certain appearance generally has a certain taste, and it is a severe shock to our expectations when the familiar appearance is found to be associated with an unusual taste. Things which we see become associated, by habit, with certain tactile sensations which we expect if we touch them; one of the horrors of a ghost (in many ghost-stories) is that it fails to give us any sensations of touch. Uneducated people who go abroad for the first time are so surprised as to be incredulous when they find their native language not understood.

And this kind of association is not confined to men; in animals also it is very strong. A horse which has been often driven along a certain road resists the attempt to drive him in a different direction. Domestic animals expect food when they see the person who usually feeds them. We know that all these rather crude expectations of uniformity are liable to be misleading.

The man who has fed the chicken every day throughout its life at last wrings its neck instead, showing that more refined views as to the uniformity of nature would have been useful to the chicken.

But in spite of the misleadingness of such expectations, they nevertheless exist. The mere fact that something has happened a certain number of times causes animals and men to expect that it will happen again. Thus our instincts certainly cause us to believe that the sun will rise to-morrow, but we may be in no better a position than the chicken which unexpectedly has its neck wrung. We have therefore to distinguish the fact that past uniformities *cause* expectations as to the future, from the question whether there is any reasonable ground for giving weight to such expectations after the question of their validity had been raised.

The problem we have to discuss is whether there is any reason for believing in what is called "the uniformity of nature." The belief in the uniformity of nature is the belief that everything that has happened or will happen is an instance of some general law to which there are *no* exceptions. The crude expectations which we have been considering are all subject to exceptions, and therefore liable to disappoint those who entertain them. But science habitually assumes, at least as a working hypothesis, that general rules which have exceptions can be replaced by general rules which have no exceptions. "Unsupported bodies in air fall" is a general rule to which balloons and aeroplanes are exceptions. But the laws of motion and the law of gravitation, which account for the fact that most bodies fall, also account for the fact that balloons and aeroplanes can rise; thus the laws of motion and the law of gravitation are not subject to these exceptions.

The belief that the sun will rise to-morrow might be falsified if the earth came suddenly into contact with a large body which destroyed its rotation; but the laws of motion and the law of gravitation would not be infringed by such an event. The business of science is to find uniformities, such as the laws of motion and the law of gravitation, to which, so far as our experience extends, there are no exceptions. In this search science has been remarkably successful, and it may be conceded that such uniformities have held hitherto. This brings us back to the question: Have we any reason, assuming that they have always held in the past, to suppose that they will hold in the future?

It has been argued that we have reason to know that the future will resemble the past, because what was the future has constantly become the past, and has always been found to resemble the past, so that we really have experience of the future, namely of times which were formerly future, which we may call past futures. But such an argument really begs the very question at issue. We have experience of past futures, but not of future futures, and the question is: Will future futures resemble past futures? This question is not to be answered by an argument which starts from past futures alone. We have therefore still to seek for some principle which shall enable us to know that the future will follow the same laws as the past.

The reference to the future in this question is not essential. The same question arises when we apply the laws that work in our experience to past things of which we have no experience — as, for example, in geology, or in theories as to the origin of the Solar System. The question we really have to ask is: "When two things have been found to be often associated, and no instance is known of the one occurring without the other, does the occurrence of one of the two, in a fresh instance, give any good ground for expecting the other?" On our answer to this question must depend the validity of the whole of our expectations as to the future, the whole of the results obtained by induction, and in fact practically all the beliefs upon which our daily life is based.

It must be conceded, to begin with, that the fact that two things have been found often together and never apart does not, by itself, suffice to *prove* demonstratively that they will be found together in the next case we examine. The most we can hope is that the oftener things are found together, the more probable it becomes that they will be found together another time, and that, if they have been found together often enough, the probability will amount *almost* to certainty. It can never quite reach certainty, because we know that in spite of frequent repetitions there sometimes is a failure at the last, as in the case of the chicken whose neck is wrung. Thus probability is all we ought to seek.

It might be urged, as against the view we are advocating, that we know all natural phenomena to be subject to the reign of law, and that sometimes, on the basis of observation, we can see that only one law can possibly fit the facts of the case. Now to this view there are two answers. The first is that, even if *some* law which has no exceptions applies to our case, we can never, in practice, be sure that we have discovered that law and not one to which there are exceptions. The second is that the reign of law would seem to be itself only probable, and that our belief that it will hold in the future, or in unexamined cases in the past, is itself based upon the very principle we are examining.

The principle we are examining may be called the *principle of induction,* and its two parts may be stated as follows:

(*a*) When a thing of a certain sort A has been found to be associated with a thing of a certain other sort B, and has never been found dissociated from a thing of the sort B, the greater the number of cases in which A and B have been associated, the greater is the probability that they will be associated in a fresh case in which one of them is known to be present;

(*b*) Under the same circumstances, a sufficient number of cases of association will make the probability of a fresh association nearly a certainty, and will make it approach certainty without limit.

As just stated, the principle applies only to the verification of our expectation in a single fresh instance. But we want also to know that there is a probability in favour of the general law that things of the sort A are *always* associated with things of the sort B, provided a sufficient number of cases of association are known, and no cases of failure of association are known. The probability of the general law is obviously less than the probability of the particular case, since if the general law is true, the particular case must also be true, whereas the particular case may be true without the general law being true. Nevertheless the probability of the general law is increased by repetitions, just as the probability of the particular case is. We may therefore repeat the two parts of our principle as regards the general law, thus:

(*a*) The greater the number of cases in which a thing of the sort A has been found associated with a thing of the sort B, the more probable it is (if no cases of failure of association are known) that A is always associated with B;

(*b*) Under the same circumstances, a sufficient number of cases of the association of A with B will make it nearly certain that A is always associated with B, and will make this general law approach certainty without limit.

It should be noted that probability is always relative to certain data. In our case, the data are merely the known cases of coexistence of A and B. There may be other data, which *might* be taken into account, which would gravely alter the probability. For example, a man who had seen a great many white swans might argue, by our principle, that on the data it was *probable* that all swans were white, and this might be a perfectly sound argument. The argument is not disproved by the fact that some swans are black, because a thing may very well happen in spite of the fact that data render it improbable. In the case of the swans, a man might know that color is a very variable characteristic in many species of animals, and that, therefore, an induction as to color is peculiarly liable to error. But this knowledge would be a fresh datum, by no means proving that the probability relatively to our previous data had been wrongly estimated. The fact, therefore, that things often fail to fulfill our expectations is no evidence that our expectations will not *probably* be fulfilled in a given case or a given class of cases. Thus our inductive principle is at any rate not capable of being *disproved* by an appeal to experience.

The inductive principle, however, is equally incapable of being *proved* by an appeal to experience. Experience might conceivably confirm the inductive principle as regards the cases that have been already examined; but as regards unexamined cases, it is the inductive principle alone that can justify any inference from what has been examined to what has not been examined. All arguments which, on the basis of experience, argue as to the future or the unexperienced parts of the past or present, assume the inductive principle; hence we can never use experience to prove the inductive principle without begging the question. Thus we must either accept the inductive principle on the ground of its intrinsic evidence, or forego all justification of our expectations about the future. If the principle is unsound, we have no reason to expect the sun to rise to-morrow, to expect bread to be more nourishing than a stone, or to expect that if we throw ourselves off the roof we shall fall. When we see what looks like our best friend approaching us, we shall have no reason to suppose that his body is not inhabited by the mind of our worst enemy or of some total stranger. All our conduct is based upon associations which have worked in the past, and which we therefore regard as likely to work in the future; and this likelihood is dependent for its validity upon the inductive principle.

The general principles of science, such as the belief in the reign of law, and the belief that every event must have a cause, are as completely dependent upon the inductive principle as are the beliefs of daily life. All such general principles are believed because mankind have found innumerable instances of their truth and no instances of their falsehood. But this accords no evidence for their truth in the future, unless the inductive principle is assumed.

Thus all knowledge which, on the basis of experience tells us something about what is not experienced, is based upon a belief which experience can neither confirm nor confute, yet which, at least in its more concrete applications, appears to be as firmly rooted in us as many of the facts of experience. The existence and justification of such beliefs — for the inductive principle, as we shall see, is not the only example — raises some of the most difficult and most debated problems of philosophy.

50

AN INDUCTIVE
JUSTIFICATION OF
INDUCTIVE INFERENCE

John Stuart Mill

§ 1. Induction properly so called, as distinguished from those mental operations, sometimes though improperly designated by the name, which I have attempted in the preceding chapter to characterize, may, then, be summarily defined as Generalization from Experience. It consists in inferring from some individual instances in which a phenomenon is observed to occur, that it occurs in all instances of a certain class; namely, in all which *resemble* the former, in what are regarded as the material circumstances.

In what way the material circumstances are to be distinguished from those which are immaterial, or why some of the circumstances are material and others not so, we are not yet ready to point out. We must first observe, that there is a principle implied in the very statement of what Induction is; an assumption with regard to the course of nature and the order of the universe; namely, that there are such things in nature as parallel cases; that what happens once, will, under a sufficient degree of similarity of circumstances, happen again, and not only again, but as often as the same circumstances recur. This, I say, is an assumption, involved in every case of induction. And, if we consult the actual course of nature, we find that the assumption is warranted. The universe, so far as known to us, is so constituted, that whatever is true in any one case, is true in all cases of a certain description; the only difficulty is, to find what description.

This universal fact, which is our warrant for all inferences from experience, has been described by different philosophers in different forms of language; that the course of nature is uniform; that the universe is governed by general laws; and the like. . . .

Whatever be the most proper mode of expressing it, the proposition that the course of nature is uniform, is the fundamental principle, or general

From John Stuart Mill, *A System of Logic,* 1843, Chapters III and XXI.

axiom, of Induction. It would yet be a great error to offer this large generalization as any explanation of the inductive process. On the contrary, I hold it to be itself an instance of induction, and induction by no means of the most obvious kind. Far from being the first induction we make, it is one of the last, or at all events one of those which are latest in attaining strict philosophical accuracy. As a general maxim, indeed, it has scarcely entered into the minds of any but philosophers; nor even by them, as we shall have many opportunities of remarking, have its extent and limits been always very justly conceived. The truth is, that this great generalization is itself founded on prior generalizations. The obscurer laws of nature were discovered by means of it, but the more obvious ones must have been understood and assented to as general truths before it was ever heard of. We should never have thought of affirming that all phenomena take place according to general laws, if we had not first arrived, in the case of a great multitude of phenomena, at some knowledge of the laws themselves; which could be done no otherwise than by induction. In what sense, then, can a principle, which is so far from being our earliest induction, be regarded as our warrant for all the others? In the only sense, in which (as we have already seen) the general propositions which we place at the head of our reasonings when we throw them into syllogisms, ever really contribute to their validity. As Archbishop Whately remarks, every induction is a syllogism with the major premise suppressed; or (as I prefer expressing it) every induction may be thrown into the form of a syllogism, by supplying a major premise. If this be actually done, the principle which we are now considering, that of the uniformity of the course of nature, will appear as the ultimate major premise of all inductions, and will, therefore, stand to all inductions in the relation in which, as has been shown at so much length, the major proposition of a syllogism always stands to the conclusion; not contributing at all to prove it, but being a necessary condition of its being proved; since no conclusion is proved, for which there cannot be found a true major premise.

The statement, that the uniformity of the course of nature is the ultimate major premise in all cases of induction, may be thought to require some explanation. The immediate major premise in every inductive argument, it certainly is not. Of that, Archbishop Whately's must be held to be the correct account. The induction, "John, Peter, &c. are mortal, therefore all mankind are mortal," may, as he justly says, be thrown into a syllogism by prefixing as a major premise (what is at any rate a necessary condition of the validity of the argument) namely, that what is true of John, Peter, &c. is true of all mankind. But how came we by this major premise? It is not self-evident; nay, in all cases of unwarranted generalization, it is not true. How, then is it arrived at? Necessarily either by induction or ratiocination; and if by induction, the process, like all other inductive arguments, may be thrown into the form of a syllogism. This previous syllogism it is, therefore, necessary to construct. There is, in the long run, only one possible construction. The real proof that what is true of John, Peter, &c. is true of all mankind, can only be, that a different supposition would be inconsistent with the uniformity which we know to exist in the course of nature. Whether there would be this inconsistency or not, may be a matter of long and delicate inquiry; but unless there would, we have no sufficient ground for the major of the inductive syllogism. It hence appears, that if we throw the whole course of any inductive argument into a series of syllogisms, we shall arrive by more or fewer steps at an ultimate syllogism, which will have for its major premise the principle, or axiom, of the uniformity of the course of nature.*

It was not to be expected that in the case of this axiom, any more than of other axioms, there should be unanimity among thinkers with respect to the grounds on which it is to be received as true. I have already stated that I regard it as itself a generalization from experience. Others hold it to be a principle which, antecedently to any verification by experience, we are compelled by the constitution of our thinking faculty to assume as true. Having so recently, and at so much length, combated a similar doctrine as applied to the axioms of mathematics, by arguments which are in a great measure applicable to the present case, I shall defer the more particular discussion of this controverted point in regard to the fundamental axiom of induction, until a more advanced period of our inquiry. At present it is of more importance to understand thoroughly the import of the axiom itself. For the proposition, that the course of nature is uniform, possesses rather the brevity suitable to popular, than the precision requisite in philosophical language: its terms require to be explained, and a stricter than their ordinary signification given to them, before the truth of the assertion can be admitted.

§ 2. Every person's consciousness assures him that he does not always expect uniformity in the course of events; he does not always believe that the unknown will be similar to the known, that the future will resemble the past. Nobody believes that the succession of rain and fine weather will be the same in every future year as in the present. Nobody expects to have the same dreams repeated every night. On the contrary, everybody mentions it as something extraordinary, if the course of nature is constant, and resembles itself, in these particulars. To look for constancy where constancy is not to be expected, as for instance that a day which has once brought good fortune will always be a fortunate day, is justly accounted superstition.

The course of nature, in truth, is not only uniform, it is also infinitely various. Some phenomena are always seen to recur in the very same combina-

---

* But though it is a condition of the validity of every induction that there be uniformity in the course of nature, it is not a necessary condition that the uniformity should pervade all nature. It is enough that it pervades the particular class of phenomena to which the induction relates. An induction concerning the motions of the planets, or the properties of the magnet, would not be vitiated though we were to suppose that wind and weather are the sport of chance, provided it be assumed that astronomical and magnetic phenomena are under the dominion of general laws. Otherwise the early experience of mankind would have rested on a very weak foundation; for in the infancy of science it could not be known that *all* phenomena are regular in their course. . . .

tions in which we met with them at first; others seem altogether capricious; while some, which we had been accustomed to regard as bound down exclusively to a particular set of combinations, we unexpectedly find detached from some of the elements with which we had hitherto found them conjoined, and united to others of quite a contrary description. To an inhabitant of Central Africa, fifty years ago, no fact probably appeared to rest on more uniform experience than this, that all human beings are black. To Europeans, not many years ago, the proposition, All swans are white, appeared an equally unequivocal instance of uniformity in the course of nature. Further experience has proved to both that they were mistaken; but they had to wait fifty centuries for this experience. During that long time, mankind believed in an uniformity of the course of nature where no such uniformity really existed.

According to the notion which the ancients entertained of induction, the foregoing were cases of as legitimate inference as any inductions whatever. In these two instances, in which, the conclusion being false, the ground of inference must have been insufficient, there was, nevertheless, as much ground for it as this conception of induction admitted of. The induction of the ancients has been well described by Bacon, under the name of "Inductio per enumerationem simplicem, ubi non reperitur instantia contradictoria." It consists in ascribing the character of general truths to all propositions which are true in every instance that we happen to know of. This is the kind of induction which is natural to the mind when unaccustomed to scientific methods. The tendency, which some call an instinct, and which others account for by association, to infer the future from the past, the known from the unknown, is simply a habit of expecting that what has been found true once or several times, and never yet found false, will be found true again. Whether the instances are few or many, conclusive or inconclusive, does not much affect the matter: these are considerations which occur only on reflection; the unprompted tendency of the mind is to generalize its experience, provided this points all in one direction; provided no other experience of a conflicting character comes unsought. The notion of seeking it, of experimenting for it, of *interrogating* nature (to use Bacon's expression) is of much later growth. The observation of nature, by uncultivated intellects, is purely passive: they accept the facts which present themselves, without taking the trouble of searching for more: it is a superior mind only which asks itself what facts are needed to enable it to come to a safe conclusion, and then looks out for these.

But though we have always a propensity to generalize from unvarying experience, we are not always warranted in doing so. Before we can be at liberty to conclude that something is universally true because we have never known an instance to the contrary, we must have reason to believe that if there were in nature any instances to the contrary, we should have known of them. This assurance, in the great majority of cases, we cannot have, or can have only in a very moderate degree. The possibility of having it, is the foundation on which we shall see hereafter that induction by simple enumeration may in some remarkable cases amount practically to proof. No such assurance, however, can be had, on any of the ordinary subjects of scientific inquiry. Popular notions are usually founded on induction by simple enumeration; in science it carries us but a little way. We are forced to begin with it; we must often rely on it provisionally, in the absence of means of more searching investigation. But, for the accurate study of nature, we require a surer and a more potent instrument.

§ 3. In order to a better understanding of the problem which the logician must solve if he would establish a scientific theory of Induction, let us compare a few cases of incorrect inductions with others which are acknowledged to be legitimate. Some, we know, which were believed for centuries to be correct, were nevertheless incorrect. That all swans are white, cannot have been a good induction, since the conclusion has turned out erroneous. The experience, however, on which the conclusion rested was genuine. From the earliest records, the testimony of the inhabitants of the known world was unanimous on the point. The uniform experience, therefore, of the inhabitants of the known world, agreeing in a common result, without one known instance of deviation from that result, is not always sufficient to establish a general conclusion.

But let us now turn to an instance apparently not very dissimilar to this. Mankind were wrong, it seems, in concluding that all swans were white: are we also wrong, when we conclude that all men's heads grow above their shoulders, and never below, in spite of the conflicting testimony of the naturalist Pliny? As there were black swans, though civilised people had existed for three thousand years on the earth without meeting with them, may there not also be "men whose heads do grow beneath their shoulders," notwithstanding a rather less perfect unanimity of negative testimony from observers? Most persons would answer No; it was more credible that a bird should vary in its colour, than that men should vary in the relative position of their principal organs. And there is no doubt that in so saying they would be right: but to say why they are right, would be impossible, without entering more deeply than is usually done, into the true theory of Induction.

Again, there are cases in which we reckon with the most unfailing confidence upon uniformity, and other cases in which we do not count upon it at all. In some we feel complete assurance that the future will resemble the past, the unknown be precisely similar to the known. In others, however invariable may be the result obtained from the instances which have been observed, we draw from them no more than a very feeble presumption that the like result will hold in all other cases. That a straight line is the shortest distance between two points, we do not doubt to be true even in the region of the fixed stars. When a chemist announces the existence and properties of a newly-discovered substance, if we confide in his accuracy, we feel assured that the conclusions he has arrived at will hold universally, though the induction be founded but on a single instance. We do not withhold our assent, waiting for a repetition of the experiment; or if we do, it is from a doubt whether the one experiment was properly made, not whether if properly made it would be conclusive. Here, then, is a general law of nature, inferred without hesitation from a single instance; an universal proposition from a singular one. Now mark another case, and contrast it with this. Not all the instances which have been observed since the beginning of the world, in support of the general proposition that all crows are black, would be deemed a sufficient presumption of the truth of the proposition, to outweigh the testimony of one unexceptionable witness who should affirm that in some region of the earth not fully explored, he had caught and examined a crow, and had found it to be grey.

Why is a single instance, in some cases, sufficient for a complete induction, while in others, myriads of concurring instances, without a single exception known or presumed, go such a very little way towards establishing an universal proposition? Whoever can answer this question knows more of the philosophy of logic than the wisest of the ancients, and has solved the problem of induction.

Of the Evidence of the Law of Universal Causation

§ 1. We have now completed our review of the logical processes by which the laws, or uniformities, of the sequence of phenomena, and those uniformities in their coexistence which depend on the laws of their sequence, are ascertained or tested. As we recognised in the commencement, and have been enabled to see more clearly in the progress of the investigation, the basis of all these logical operations is the law of causation. The validity of all the Inductive Methods depends on the assumption that every event, or the beginning of every phenomenon, must have some cause; some antecedent, on the existence of which it is invariably and unconditionally consequent. In the Method of Agreement this is obvious; that method avowedly proceeding on the supposition that we have found the true cause as soon as we have negatived every other. The assertion is equally true of the Method of Difference. That method authorises us to infer a general law from two instances; one, in which A exists together with a multitude of other circumstances, and B follows; another, in which, A being removed, and all other circumstances remaining the same, B is prevented. What, however, does this prove? It proves that B, in the particular instance, cannot have had any other cause than A; but to conclude from this that A was the cause, or that A will on other occasions be followed by B, is only allowable on the assumption that B must have some cause; that among its antecedents in any single instance in which it occurs, there must be one which has the capacity of producing it at other times. This being admitted, it is seen that in the case in question that antecedent can be no other than A; but, that if it be no other than A it must be A, is not proved, by these instances at least, but taken for granted. There is no need to spend time in proving that the same thing is true of the other Inductive Methods. The universality of the law of causation is assumed in them all.

But is this assumption warranted? Doubtless (it may be said) *most* phenomena are connected as effects with some antecedent or cause, that is, are never produced unless some assignable fact has preceded them; but the very circumstance that complicated processes of induction are sometimes necessary, shows that cases exist in which this regular order of succession is not apparent to our unaided apprehension. If, then, the processes which bring these cases within the same category with the rest, require that we should assume the universality of the very law which they do not at first sight appear to exemplify, is not this a *petitio principii*? Can we prove a proposition, by an argument which takes it for granted? And if not so proved, on what evidence does it rest?

For this difficulty, which I have purposely stated in the strongest terms it will admit of, the school of metaphysicians who have long predominated in this country find a ready salvo. They affirm, that the universality of causation is a truth which we cannot help believing; that the belief in it is an instinct, one of the laws of our believing faculty. As the proof of this, they say, and they have nothing else to say, that everybody does believe it; and they number it among the propositions, rather numerous in their catalogue, which may be logically argued against, and perhaps cannot be logically proved, but which are of higher authority than logic, and so essentially inherent in the human mind, that even he who denies them in speculation, shows by his habitual practice that his arguments make no impression upon himself.

Into the merits of this question, considered as one of psychology, it would be foreign to my purpose to enter here: but I must protest against adducing, as evidence of the truth of a fact in external nature, the disposition, however strong or however general, of the human mind to believe it. Belief is not proof, and does not dispense with the necessity of proof.

.   .   .

Were we to suppose (what it is perfectly possible to imagine) that the present order of the universe were brought to an end, and that a chaos succeeded in which there was no fixed succession of events, and the past gave no assurance of the future; if a human being were miraculously kept alive to witness this change, he surely would soon cease to believe in any uniformity, the uniformity itself no longer existing. If this be admitted, the belief in uniformity either is not an instinct, or it is an instinct conquerable, like all other instincts, by acquired knowledge.

.   .   .

§ 2.   As was observed in a former place, the belief we entertain in the universality, throughout nature, of the law of cause and effect, is itself an instance of induction, and by no means one of the earliest which any of us, or which mankind in general, can have made. We arrive at this universal law, by generalization from many laws of inferior generality. We should never have had the notion of causation (in the philosophical meaning of the term) as a condition of all phenomena, unless many cases of causation, or in other words, many partial uniformities of sequence, had previously become familiar. The more obvious of the particular uniformities suggest, and give evidence of, the general uniformity, and the general uniformity, once established, enables us to prove the remainder of the particular uniformities of which it is made up. As, however, all rigorous processes of induction presuppose the general uniformity, our knowledge of the particular uniformities from which it was first inferred was not, of course, derived from rigorous induction, but from the loose and uncertain mode of induction *per enumerationem simplicem;* and the law of universal causation, being collected from results so obtained, cannot itself rest on any better foundation.

It would seem, therefore, that induction *per enumerationem simplicem* not only is not necessarily an illicit logical process, but is in reality the only kind of induction possible; since the more elaborate process depends for its validity on a law, itself obtained in that inartificial mode. Is there not then an inconsistency in contrasting the looseness of one method with the rigidity of another, when that other is indebted to the looser method for its own foundation?

The inconsistency, however, is only apparent. Assuredly, if induction by simple enumeration were an invalid process, no process grounded on it could be valid; just as no reliance could be placed on telescopes if we could not trust our eyes. But though a valid process, it is a fallible one, and fallible in very different degrees: if therefore we can substitute for the more fallible forms of the process, an operation grounded on the same process in a less fallible form, we shall have effected a very material improvement. And this is what scientific induction does.

A mode of concluding from experience must be pronounced untrustworthy, when subsequent experience refuses to confirm it. According to this criterion, induction by simple enumeration — in other words, generalization of an observed fact from the mere absence of any known instance to the contrary — affords in general a precarious and unsafe ground of assurance; for such generalizations are incessantly discovered, on further experience, to be false. Still, however, it affords some assurance, sufficient, in many cases, for the ordinary guidance of conduct. It would be absurd to say, that the generalizations arrived at by mankind in the outset of their experience, such as these, Food nourishes, Fire burns, Water drowns, were unworthy of reliance. There is a scale of truthworthiness in the results of the original unscientific Induction; and on this diversity (as observed in the fourth chapter of the present book) depend the rules for the improvement of the process. The improvement consists in correcting one of these inartificial generalizations by means of another. As has been already pointed out, this is all that art can do. To test a generalization, by showing that it either follows from, or conflicts with, some stronger induction, some generalization resting on a broader foundation of experience, is the beginning and end of the logic of Induction.

§ 3. Now the precariousness of the method of simple enumeration is in an inverse ratio to the largeness of the generalization. The process is delusive and insufficient, exactly in proportion as the subject-matter of the observation is special and limited in extent. As the sphere widens, this unscientific method becomes less and less liable to mislead; and the most universal class of truths, the law of causation for instance, and the principles of number and of geometry, are duly and satisfactorily proved by that method alone, nor are they susceptible of any other proof.

With respect to the whole class of generalizations of which we have recently treated, the uniformities which depend on causation, the truth of the remark just made follows by obvious inference from the principles laid down in the preceding chapters. When a fact has been observed a certain number of times to be true, and is not in any instance known to be false; if we at once affirm that fact as an universal truth or law of nature, without either testing it by any of the four methods of induction, or deducing it from other known laws, we shall in general err grossly: but we are perfectly justified in affirming it as an empirical law, true within certain limits of time, place, and circumstance, provided the number of coincidences be greater than can with any probability be ascribed to chance. The reason for not extending it beyond those limits is, that the fact of its holding true within them may be a consequence of collocations, which cannot be concluded to exist in one place because they exist in another; or may be dependent on the accidental absence of counteracting agencies, which any variation of time, or the smallest change of circumstances, may possibly bring into play. If we suppose, then, the subject-matter of any generalization to be so widely diffused that there is no time, no place, and no combination of circumstances, but must afford an example either of its truth or of its falsity, and if it be never found otherwise than true, its truth cannot be contingent on any collocations, unless such as exist at all times and places: nor can it be frustrated by any counteracting agencies, unless by such as never actually occur. It is, therefore, an empirical law coextensive with all human experience, at which point the distinction between empirical laws and laws of nature vanishes, and the proposition takes its place among the most firmly established as well as largest truths accessible to science.

Now, the most extensive in its subject-matter of all generalizations which experience warrants, respecting the sequences and coexistences of phenomena, is the law of causation. It stands at the head of all observed uniformities, in point of universality, and therefore (if the preceding observations are correct) in point of certainty. And if we consider, not what mankind would have been justified in believing in the infancy of their knowledge, but what may rationally be believed in its present more advanced state, we shall find ourselves warranted in considering this fundamental law, though itself obtained by induction from particular laws of causation, as not less certain, but on the contrary, more so, than any of those from which it was drawn. It adds to them as much proof as it receives from them. For there is probably no one even of the best established laws of causation which is not sometimes counteracted, and to which, therefore, apparent exceptions do not present themselves, which would have necessarily and justly shaken the confidence of mankind in the universality of those laws, if inductive processes founded on the universal law had not enabled us to refer those exceptions to the agency of counteracting causes, and thereby reconcile them with the law with which they apparently conflict. Errors, moreover, may have slipped into the statement of any one of the special laws, through inattention to some material circumstance; and instead of the true proposition, another may have been enunciated, false as an universal law, though leading, in all cases hitherto observed, to the same result. To the law of causation, on the contrary, we not only do not know of any exception, but the exceptions which limit or apparently invalidate the special laws, are so far from contradicting the universal one, that they confirm it; since in all cases which are sufficiently open to our observation, we are able to trace the difference of result, either to the absence of a cause which had been present in ordinary cases, or to the presence of one which had been absent.

The law of cause and effect, being thus certain, is capable of imparting its certainty to all other inductive propositions which can be deduced from it; and the narrower inductions may be regarded as receiving their ultimate sanction from that law, since there is no one of them which is not rendered more certain than it was before, when we are able to connect it with that larger induction, and to show that it cannot be denied, consistently with the law that everything which begins to exist has a cause. And hence we are justified in the seeming inconsistency, of holding induction by simple enumeration to be good for proving this general truth, the foundation of scientific induction, and yet refusing to rely on it for any of the narrower inductions.

51

THE JUSTIFICATION
OF INDUCTION
AND THE ANALYSIS
OF LANGUAGE

Peter Frederick Strawson

P. F. Strawson (1919-   ) is Fellow of University College, Oxford.

7. We have seen something, then, of the nature of inductive reasoning; of how one statement or set of statements may support another statement, S, which they do not entail, with varying degrees of strength, ranging from being conclusive evidence for S to being only slender evidence for it; from making S as certain as the supporting statements, to give it some slight probability. We have seen, too, how the question of degree of support is complicated by consideration of relative frequencies and numerical chances.

There is, however, a residual philosophical question which enters so largely into discussion of the subject that it must be discussed. It can be raised, roughly, in the following forms. What reason have we to place reliance on inductive procedures? Why should we suppose that the accumulation of instances of As which are Bs, however various the conditions in which they are observed, gives any good reason for expecting the next A we encounter to be a B? It is our habit to form expectations in this way; but can the habit be rationally justified? When this doubt has entered our minds it may be difficult to free ourselves from it. For the doubt has its source in a confusion; and some attempts to resolve the doubt preserve the confusion; and other attempts to show that the doubt is senseless seem altogether too facile. The root-confusion is easily described; but simply to describe it seems an inadequate remedy against it. So the doubt must be examined again and again, in the light of different attempts to remove it.

⋅ ⋅ ⋅

Suppose that a man is brought up to regard formal logic as the study of the science and art of reasoning. He observes that all inductive processes are, by deductive standards, invalid; the premises never entail the conclusions.

From P. F. Strawson, *Introduction to Logical Theory*, Chapter 9. Published by Methuen & Co., Ltd., London, 1952. Reprinted by permission of the publisher.

Now inductive processes are notoriously important in the formation of beliefs and expectations about everything which lies beyond the observation of available witnesses. But an *invalid* argument is an *unsound* argument; an *unsound* argument is one in which *no good reason* is produced for accepting the conclusion. So if inductive processes are invalid, if all the arguments we should produce, if challenged, in support of our beliefs about what lies beyond the observation of available witnesses are unsound, then we have no good reason for any of these beliefs. This conclusion is repugnant. So there arises the demand for a justification, not of this or that particular belief which goes beyond what is entailed by our evidence, but a justification of induction in general. And when the demand arises in this way it is, in effect, the demand that induction shall be shown to be really a kind of deduction; for nothing less will satisfy the doubter when this is the route to his doubts.

Tracing this, the most common route to the general doubt about the reasonableness of induction, shows how the doubt seems to escape the absurdity of a demand that induction in general shall be justified by deductive standards. The demand is that induction should be shown to be a rational process; and this turns out to be the demand that one kind of reasoning should be shown to be another and different kind. Put thus crudely, the demand seems to escape one absurdity only to fall into another. Of course, inductive arguments are not deductively valid; if they were, they would be deductive arguments. Inductive reasoning must be assessed, for soundness, by inductive standards. Nevertheless, fantastic as the wish for induction to be deduction may seem, it is only in terms of it that we can understand some of the attempts that have been made to justify induction.

8. The first kind of attempt I shall consider might be called the search for the supreme premise of inductions. In its primitive form it is quite a crude attempt; and I shall make it cruder by caricature. We have already seen that for a particular inductive step, such as 'The kettle has been on the fire for ten minutes, so it will be boiling by now', we can substitute a deductive argument by introducing a generalization (e.g., 'A kettle always boils within ten minutes of being put on the fire') as an additional premise. This manoeuvre shifted the emphasis of the problem of inductive support on to the question of how we established such generalizations as these, which rested on grounds by which they were not entailed. But suppose the manoeuvre could be repeated. Suppose we could find one supremely general proposition, which taken in conjunction with the evidence for any accepted generalization of science or daily life (or at least of science) would entail that generalization. Then, so long as the status of the supreme generalization could be satisfactorily explained, we could regard all sound inductions to unqualified general conclusions as, at bottom, valid deductions. The justification would be found, for at least these cases. The most obvious difficulty in this suggestion is that of formulating the supreme general proposition in such a way that it shall be precise enough to yield the desired entailments, and yet not obviously false or arbitrary. Consider, for example, the formula: 'For all f, g, wherever n cases

of $f \cdot g$, and no cases of $f \cdot \sim g$, are observed, then all cases of f are cases of g.' To turn it into a sentence, we have only to replace 'n' by some number. But what number? If we take the value of 'n' to be 1 or 20 or 500, the resulting statement is obviously false. Moreover, the choice of any number would seem quite arbitrary; there is no privileged number of favourable instances which we take as decisive in establishing a generalization. If, on the other hand, we phrase the proposition vaguely enough to escape these objections — if, for example, we phrase it as 'Nature is uniform' — then it becomes too vague to provide the desired entailments. It should be noticed that the impossibility of framing a general proposition of the kind required is really a special case of the impossibility of framing precise rules for the assessment of evidence. If we could frame a rule which would tell us precisely when we had *conclusive* evidence for a generalization, then it would yield just the proposition required as the supreme premise.

Even if these difficulties could be met, the question of the status of the supreme premise would remain. How, if a non-necessary proposition, could it be established? The appeal to experience, to inductive support, is clearly barred on pain of circularity. If, on the other hand, it were a necessary truth and possessed, in conjunction with the evidence for a generalization, the required logical power to entail the generalization (e.g., if the latter were the conclusion of a hypothetical syllogism, of which the hypothetical premise was the necessary truth in question), then the evidence would entail the generalization independently, and the problem would not arise: a conclusion unbearably paradoxical. In practice, the extreme vagueness with which candidates for the role of supreme premise are expressed prevents their acquiring such logical power, and at the same time renders it very difficult to classify them as analytic or synthetic: under pressure they may tend to tautology; and, when the pressure is removed, assume an expansively synthetic air.

In theories of the kind which I have here caricatured the ideal of deduction is not usually so blatantly manifest as I have made it. One finds the 'Law of the Uniformity of Nature' presented less as the suppressed premise of crypto-deductive inferences than as, say, the 'presupposition of the validity of inductive reasoning'. I shall have more to say about this in my last section.

9. I shall next consider a more sophisticated kind of attempt to justify induction: more sophisticated both in its interpretation of this aim and in the method adopted to achieve it. The aim envisaged is that of proving that the probability of a generalization, whether universal or proportional, increases with the number of instances for which it is found to hold. This clearly is a realistic aim: for the proposition to be proved does state, as we have already seen, a fundamental feature of our criteria for assessing the strength of evidence. The method of proof proposed is mathematical. Use is to be made of the arithmetical calculation of chances. This, however, seems less realistic: for we have already seen that the prospect of analysing the notion of support in these terms seems poor.

I state the argument as simply as possible; but, even so, it will be necessary to introduce and explain some new terms. Suppose we had a collection of objects of different kinds, some with some characteristics and some with others. Suppose, for example, we had a bag containing 100 balls, of which 70 were white and 30 black. Let us call such a collection of objects a *population;* and let us call the way it is made up (e.g., in this case imagined, of 70 white and 30 black balls) the *constitution* of the population. From such a population it would be possible to take *samples* of various sizes. For example, we might take from our bag a sample of 30 balls. Suppose each ball in the bag had an individual number. Then the collection of balls numbered 10 to 39 inclusive would be one sample of the given size; the collection of balls numbered 11 to 40 inclusive would be another and different sample of the same size; the collection of balls numbered 2, 4, 6, 8 . . . 58, 60 would be another such sample; and so on. Each possible collection of 30 balls is a different sample of the same size. Some different samples of the same size will have the same constitutions as one another; others will have different constitutions. Thus there will be only one sample made up of 30 black balls. There will be many different samples which share the constitution: 20 white and 10 black. It would be a simple matter of mathematics to work out the number of possible samples of the given size which had any one possible constitution. Let us say that a sample *matches* the population if, allowing for the difference between them in size, the constitution of the sample corresponds, within certain limits, to that of the population. For example, we might say that any possible sample consisting of, say, 21 white and 9 black balls matched the constitution (70 white and 30 black) of the population, whereas a sample consisting of 20 white and 10 black balls did not. Now it is a proposition of pure mathematics that, given any population, the proportion of possible samples, all of the same size, which match the population, increases with the size of the sample.

We have seen that conclusions about the ratio of a subset of equally possible chances to the whole set of those chances may be expressed by the use of the word 'probability'. Thus of the 52 possible samples of one card from a population constituted like an orthodox pack, 16 are court-cards or aces. This fact we allow ourselves to express (under the conditions, inductively established, of equipossibility of draws) by saying that the probability of drawing a court-card or an ace was $\frac{4}{13}$. If we express the proposition referred to at the end of the last paragraph by means of this use of 'probability' we shall obtain the result: The probability of a sample matching a given population increases with the size of the sample. It is tempting to try to derive from this result a general justification of the inductive procedure: which will not, indeed, show that any given inductive conclusion is entailed by the evidence for it, taken in conjunction with some universal premise, but will show that the multiplication of favourable instances of a generalization entails a proportionate increase in its probability. For, since *matching* is a symmetrical relation, it might seem a simple deductive step to move from

I. The probability of a sample matching a given population increases with the size of the sample

to

II. The probability of a population matching a given sample increases with the size of the sample.

II might seem to provide a guarantee that the greater the number of cases for which a generalization is observed to hold, the greater is its probability; since in increasing the number of cases we increase the size of the sample from whatever population forms the subject of our generalization. Thus pure mathematics might seem to provide the sought-for proof that the evidence for a generalization really does get stronger, the more favourable instances of it we find.

The argument is ingenious enough to be worthy of respect; but it fails of its purpose, and misrepresents the inductive situation. Our situation is not in the least like that of a man drawing a sample from a given, i.e., fixed and limited, population from which the drawing of any mathematically possible sample is equiprobable with that of any other. Our only datum is the sample. No limit is fixed beforehand to the diversity, and the possibilities of change, of the 'population' from which it is drawn: or, better, to the multiplicity and variousness of different populations, each with different constitutions, any one of which might replace the present one before we make the next draw. Nor is there any *a priori* guarantee that different mathematically possible samples are equally likely to be drawn. If we have or can obtain any assurance on these points, then it is assurance derived inductively from our data, and cannot therefore be assumed at the outset of an argument designed to justify induction. So II, regarded as a justification of induction founded on purely mathematical considerations, is a fraud. The important shift of 'given' from qualifying 'population' in I to qualifying 'sample' in II is illegitimate. Moreover, 'probability', which means one thing in II (interpreted as giving the required guarantee) means something quite different in I (interpreted as a proposition of pure mathematics). In I probability is simply the measure of the ratio of one set of mathematically possible chances to another; in II it is the measure of the inductive acceptability of a generalization. As a mathematical proposition, I is certainly independent of the soundness of inductive procedures; and as a statement of one of the criteria we use in assessing the strength of evidence of a generalization, II is as certainly independent of mathematics.

It has not escaped the notice of those who have advocated a mathematical justification of induction, that certain assumptions are required to make the argument even seem to fulfil its purpose. Inductive reasoning would be of little use if it did not sometimes enable us to assign at least fairly high probabilities to certain conclusions. Now suppose, in conformity with the mathematical model, we represented the fact that the evidence for a proposition was conclusive by assigning to it the probability figure of 1; and the fact that the evidence for and against a proposition was evenly balanced by assigning to it the probability figure $\frac{1}{2}$; and so on. It is a familiar mathematical truth that, between any two fractions, say $\frac{1}{5}$ and $\frac{1}{6}$, there is an infinite number of intermediate quantities; that $\frac{1}{6}$ can be indefinitely increased without reaching equality to $\frac{1}{5}$. Even if we could regard II as mathematically established, therefore, it fails to give us what we require; for it fails to provide a guarantee that the probability of an inductive conclusion ever attains a degree at which it begins to be of use. . . .

10. Let us turn from attempts to justify induction to attempts to show that the demand for a justification is mistaken. We have seen already that what lies behind such a demand is often the absurd wish that induction should be shown to be some kind of deduction — and this wish is clearly traceable in the two attempts at justification which we have examined. What other sense could we give to the demand? Sometimes it is expressed in the form of a request for proof that induction is a *reasonable* or *rational* procedure, that we have *good grounds* for placing reliance upon it. Consider the uses of the phrases 'good grounds', 'justification', 'reasonable', &c. Often we say such things as 'He has *every justification* for believing that *p*'; 'I have *very good reasons* for believing it'; 'There are *good grounds* for the view that *q*'; 'There is *good evidence* that *r*'. We often talk, in such ways as these, of justification, good grounds or reasons or evidence for certain beliefs. Suppose such a belief were one expressible in the form 'Every case of *f* is a case of *g*'. And suppose someone were asked what he meant by saying that he had good grounds or reasons for holding it. I think it would be felt to be a satisfactory answer if he replied: 'Well, in all my wide and varied experience I've come across innumerable cases of *f* and never a case of *f* which wasn't a case of *g*'. In saying this, he is clearly claiming to have *inductive* support, *inductive* evidence, of a certain kind, for his belief; and he is also giving a perfectly proper answer to the question, what he meant by saying that he had ample justification, good grounds, good reasons for his belief. It is an analytic proposition that it is reasonable to have a degree of belief in a statement which is proportional to the strength of the evidence in its favour; and it is an analytic proposition, though not a proposition of mathematics, that, other things being equal, the evidence for a generalization is strong in proportion as the number of favourable instances, and the variety of circumstances in which they have been found, is great. So to ask whether it is reasonable to place reliance on inductive procedures is like asking whether it is reasonable to proportion the degree of one's convictions to the strength of the evidence. Doing this is what 'being reasonable' *means* in such a context.

As for the other form in which the doubt may be expressed, viz., 'Is induction a justified, or justifiable, procedure?', it emerges in a still less favourable light. No sense has been given to it, though it is easy to see why it seems to have a sense. For it is generally proper to inquire *of a particular belief*, whether its adoption is justified; and, in asking this, we are asking whether there is good, bad, or any, evidence for it. In applying or withholding the epithets 'justified', 'well founded', &c., in the case of specific beliefs, we are appealing to, and applying, inductive standards. But to what standards are we appealing when we ask whether the application of inductive standards is justified or well grounded? If we cannot answer, then no sense has been given to the question. Compare it with the question: Is the law legal? It makes perfectly good sense to inquire of a particular action, of an administrative regulation, or even, in the case of some states, of a particular enactment of the legislature, whether or not it is legal. The question is answered by an appeal to a legal system, by the application of a set of legal (or constitutional) rules or standards. But it makes no sense to inquire in general whether the law of the land, the legal system as a whole, is or is not legal. For to what legal standards are we appealing?

The only way in which a sense might be given to the question, whether induction is in general a justified or justifiable procedure, is a trivial one which we have already noticed. We might interpret it to mean 'Are all conclusions, arrived at inductively, justified?', i.e., 'Do people always have adequate evidence for the conclusions they draw?' The answer to this question is easy, but uninteresting: it is that sometimes people have adequate evidence, and sometimes they do not.

11. It seems, however, that this way of showing the request for a general justification of induction to be absurd is sometimes insufficient to allay the worry that produces it. And to point out that 'forming rational opinions about the unobserved on the evidence available' and 'assessing the evidence by inductive standards' are phrases which describe the same thing, is more apt to produce irritation than relief. The point is felt to be 'merely a verbal' one; and though the point of this protest is itself hard to see, it is clear that something more is required. So the question must be pursued further. First, I want to point out that there is something a little odd about talking of 'the inductive method,' or even 'the inductive policy', as if it were just one possible method among others of arguing from the observed to the unobserved, from the available evidence to the facts in question. If one asked a meteorologist what method or methods he used to forecast the weather, one would be surprised if he answered: 'Oh, just the inductive method.' If one asked a doctor by what means he diagnosed a certain disease, the answer 'By induction' would be felt as an impatient evasion, a joke, or a rebuke. The answer one hopes for is an account of the tests made, the signs taken account of, the rules and recipes and general laws applied. When such a specific method of prediction or diagnosis is in question, one can ask whether the method is justified in practice; and here again one is asking whether its employment is inductively justified, whether it commonly gives correct results. This question would normally seem an admissible one. One might be tempted to conclude that, while there are many different specific methods of prediction, diagnosis, &c., appropriate to different subjects of inquiry, all such methods could properly be called 'inductive' in the sense that their employment rested on inductive support; and that, hence, the phrase 'non-inductive method of finding out about what lies

deductively beyond the evidence' was a description without meaning, a phrase to which no sense had been given; so that there could be no question of justifying our selection of one method, called 'the inductive', of doing this.

However, someone might object: 'Surely it is possible, though it might be foolish, to use methods utterly different from accredited scientific ones. Suppose a man, whenever he wanted to form an opinion about what lay beyond his observation or the observation of available witnesses, simply shut his eyes, asked himself the appropriate question, and accepted the first answer that came into his head. Wouldn't this be a non-inductive method?' Well, let us suppose this. The man is asked: 'Do you usually get the right answer by your method?' He might answer: 'You've mentioned one of its drawbacks; I never do get the right answer; but it's an extremely easy method.' One might then be inclined to think that it was not a method of finding things out at all. But suppose he answered: Yes, it's usually (always) the right answer. Then we might be willing to call it a method of finding out, though a strange one. But, then, by the very fact of its success, it would be an inductively supported method. For each application of the method would be an application of the general rule, 'The first answer that comes into my head is generally (always) the right one'; and for the truth of this generalization there would be the inductive evidence of a long run of favourable instances with no unfavourable ones (if it were 'always'), or of a sustained high proportion of successes to trials (if it were 'generally').

So every successful method or recipe for finding out about the unobserved must be one which has inductive support; for to say that a recipe is successful is to say that it has been repeatedly applied with success; and repeated successful application of a recipe constitutes just what we mean by inductive evidence in its favour. Pointing out this fact must not be confused with saying that 'the inductive method' is justified by its success, justified because it works. This is a mistake, and an important one. I am not seeking to 'justify the inductive method', for no meaning has been given to this phrase. *A fortiori*, I am not saying that induction is justified by its success in finding out about the unobserved. I am saying, rather, that any successful method of finding out about the unobserved is necessarily justified by induction. This is an analytic proposition. The phrase 'successful method of finding things out which has no inductive support' is self-contradictory. Having, or acquiring, inductive support is a necessary condition of the success of a method.

Why point this out at all? First, it may have a certain therapeutic force, a power to reassure. Second, it may counteract the tendency to think of 'the inductive method' as something on a par with specific methods of diagnosis or prediction and therefore, like them, standing in need of (inductive) justification.

·   ·   ·

52 🦎

A PRAGMATIC
JUSTIFICATION OF
INDUCTIVE POLICY

Hans Reichenbach

Hans Reichenbach (1891-1953) was born in Germany, taught at the University of Berlin, and was Professor of Philosophy at the University of California in Los Angeles from 1938 to 1953.

THE PROBLEM OF INDUCTION

. . . Philosophers such as Peirce have expressed the idea that a solution of the problem of induction is to be found in the theory of probability. The inverse relation, however, holds as well. Let us say, cautiously, that the solution of both problems is to be given within the same theory.

In uniting the problem of probability with that of induction, we decide unequivocally in favor of that determination of the degree of probability which mathematicians call the *determination a posteriori*. . . .

By "determination a posteriori" we understand a procedure in which the relative frequency observed statistically is assumed to hold approximately for any future prolongation of the series. Let us express this idea in an exact formulation. We assume a series of events A and $\overline{A}$ (non-A); let n be the number of events, m the number of events of the type A among them. We have then the relative frequency

$$h^n = \frac{m}{n}$$

The assumption of the determination a posteriori may now be expressed:

For any further prolongation of the series as far as s events (s > n), the relative frequency will remain within a small interval around h^n; *i.e, we assume the relation*

$$h^n - \varepsilon \leqq h^s \leqq h^n + \varepsilon$$

where ε *is a small number.*

This assumption formulates the *principle of induction*. We may add that our formulation states the principle in a form more general than that customary in traditional philosophy. The usual formulation is as follows: induction is the assumption that an event which occurred n times will occur at all following times. It is obvious that this formulation is a special case of our formulation, corresponding to the case $h^n = 1$. We cannot restrict our investigation to this special case because the general case occurs in a great many problems.

The reason for this is to be found in the fact that the theory of probability needs the definition of probability as the limit of the frequency. Our formulation is a necessary condition for the existence of a limit of the frequency near h^n; what is yet to be added is that there is an h^n of the kind postulated for every ε however small. If we include this idea in our assumption, our postulate of induction becomes the hypothesis that there is a limit to the relative frequency which does not differ greatly from the observed value.

If we enter now into a closer analysis of this assumption, one thing needs no further demonstration: the formula given is not a tautology. There is indeed no logical necessity that h^s remains within the interval $h^n \pm \varepsilon$; we may easily imagine that this does not take place.

The nontautological character of induction has been known a long time; Bacon had already emphasized that it is just this character to which the importance of induction is due. If inductive inference can teach us something new, in opposition to deductive inference, this is because it is not a tautology. This useful quality has, however, become the center of the epistemological difficulties of induction. It was David Hume who first attacked the principle from this side; he pointed out that the apparent constraint of the inductive inference, although submitted to by everybody, could not be justified. We believe in induction; we even cannot get rid of the belief when we know the impossibility of a logical demonstration of the validity of inductive inference; but as logicians we must admit that this belief is a deception — such is the result of Hume's criticism. We may summarize his objections in two statements:

1. We have no logical demonstration for the validity of inductive inference.

2. There is no demonstration a posteriori for the inductive inference; any such demonstration would presuppose the very principle which it is to demonstrate.

These two pillars of Hume's criticism of the principle of induction have stood unshaken for two centuries, and I think they will stand as long as there is a scientific philosophy.

.   .   .

Inductive inference cannot be dispensed with because we need it for the purpose of action. To deem the inductive assumption unworthy of the assent of a philosopher, to keep a distinguished reserve, and to meet with a condescending smile the attempts of other people to bridge the gap between experience and prediction is cheap self-deceit; at the very moment when the apostles of such a higher philosophy leave the field of theoretical discussion and pass to the simplest actions of daily life, they follow the inductive principle as surely as does every earth-bound mind. In any action there are various means to the realization of our aim; we have to make a choice, and we decide in accordance with the inductive principle. Although there is no means which will produce with certainty the desired effect, we do not leave the choice to chance but prefer the means indicated by the principle of induction. If we sit at the wheel of a car and want to turn the car to the right, why do we turn the wheel to the right? There is no certainty that the car will follow the wheel; there are indeed cars which do not always so behave. Such cases are fortunately exceptions. But if we should not regard the inductive prescription and consider the effect of a turn of the wheel as entirely unknown to us, we might turn it to the left as well. I do not say this to suggest such an attempt; the effects of skeptical philosophy applied in motor traffic would be rather unpleasant. But I should say a philosopher who is to put aside his principles any time he steers a motorcar is a bad philosopher.

It is no justification of inductive belief to show that it is a habit. It *is* a habit; but the question is whether it is a good habit, where "good" is to mean "useful for the purpose of actions directed to future events." If a person tells me that Socrates is a man, and that all men are mortal, I have the habit of believing that Socrates is mortal. I know, however, that this is a good habit. If anyone had the habit of believing in such a case that Socrates is not mortal, we could demonstrate to him that this was a bad habit. The analogous question must be raised for inductive inference. If we should not be able to demonstrate that it is a good habit, we should either cease using it or admit frankly that our philosophy is a failure.

Science proceeds by induction and not by tautological transformations of reports. Bacon is right about Aristotle; but the *novum organon* needs a justification as good as that of the *organon*. Hume's criticism was the heaviest blow against empiricism; if we do not want to dupe our consciousness of this by means of the narcotic drug of a prioristic rationalism, or the soporific skepticism, we must find a defense for the inductive inference which holds as well as does the formalistic justification of deductive logic.

The Justification of the Principle of Induction

We shall now begin to give the justification of induction which Hume thought impossible. In the pursuit of this inquiry, let us ask first what has been proved, strictly speaking, by Hume's objections.

Hume started with the assumption that a justification of inductive inference is only given if we can show that inductive inference must lead to success. In other words, Hume believed that any justified application of the inductive inference presupposes a demonstration that the conclusion is true. It is this assumption on which Hume's criticism is based. His two objections directly concern only the question of the truth of the conclusion; they prove that the truth of the conclusion cannot be demonstrated. The two objections, therefore, are valid only in so far as the Humean assumption is valid. It is this question to which we must turn: Is it necessary, for the justification of inductive inference, to show that its conclusion is true?

A rather simple analysis shows us that this assumption does not hold. Of course, if we were able to prove the truth of the conclusion, inductive inference would be justified; but the converse does not hold: a justification of the inductive inference does not imply a proof of the truth of the conclusion. The proof of the truth of the conclusion is only a sufficient condition for the justification of induction, not a necessary condition.

The inductive inference is a procedure which is to furnish us the best assumption concerning the future. If we do not know the truth about the future, there may be nonetheless a best assumption about it, i.e., a best assumption relative to what we know. We must ask whether such a characterization may be given for the principle of induction. If this turns out to be possible, the principle of induction will be justified.

An example will show the logical structure of our reasoning. A man may be suffering from a grave disease; the physician tells us: "I do not know whether an operation will save the man, but if there *is* any remedy, it is an operation." In such a case, the operation would be justified. Of course, it would be better to know that the operation will save the man; but, if we do not know this, the knowledge formulated in the statement of the physician is a sufficient justification. If we cannot realize the sufficient conditions of success, we shall at least realize the necessary conditions. If we were able to show that the inductive inference is a necessary condition of success, it would be justified; such a proof would satisfy any demands which may be raised about the justification of induction.

Now obviously there is a great difference between our example and induction. The reasoning of the physician presupposes inductions; his knowledge about an operation as the only possible means of saving a life is based on inductive generalizations, just as are all other statements of empirical character. But we wanted only to illustrate the logical structure of our reasoning. If we want to regard such a reasoning as a justification of the principle of induction, the character of induction as a necessary condition of success must be demonstrated in a way which does not presuppose induction. Such a proof, however, can be given.

If we want to construct this proof, we must begin with a determination of the aim of induction. It is usually said that we perform inductions with the aim of foreseeing the future. This determination is vague; let us replace it by a formulation more precise in character:

The aim of induction is to find series of events whose frequency of occurrence converges toward a limit.

We choose this formulation because we found that we need probabilities and that a probability is to be defined as the limit of frequency; thus our determination of the aim of induction is given in such a way that it enables us to apply probability methods. If we compare this determination of the aim of induction with determinations usually given, it turns out to be not a confinement to a narrower aim but an expansion. What we usually call "foreseeing the future" is included in our formulation as a special case; the case of knowing with certainty for every event A the event B following it would correspond in our formulation to a case where the limit of the frequency is of the numerical value 1. Hume thought of this case only. Thus our inquiry differs from that of Hume in so far as it conceives the aim of induction in a generalized form. But we do not omit any possible applications if we determine the principle of induction as the means of obtaining the limit of a frequency. If we have limits of frequency, we have all we want, including the case considered by Hume; we have then the laws of nature in their most general form, including both statistical and so-called causal laws — the latter being nothing but a special case of statistical laws, corresponding to the numerical value 1 of the limit of the frequency. We are entitled, therefore, to consider the determination of the limit of a frequency as the aim of the inductive inference.

Now it is obvious that we have no guaranty that this aim is at all attainable. The world may be so disorderly that it is impossible for us to construct series with a limit. Let us introduce the term "predictable" for a world which is sufficiently ordered to enable us to construct series with a limit. We must admit, then, that we do not know whether the world is predictable.

But, if the world is predictable, let us ask what the logical function of the principle of induction will be. For this purpose, we must consider the definition of limit. The frequency h^n has a limit at p, if for any given ε there is an n such that h^n is within $p \pm \varepsilon$ and remains within this interval for all the rest of the series. Comparing our formulation of the principle of induction with this, we may infer from the definition of the limit that, if there is a limit, there is an element of the series from which the principle of induction leads to the true value of the limit. In this sense the principle of induction is a necessary condition for the determination of a limit.

It is true that, if we are faced with the value h^n for the frequency furnished by our statistics, we do not know whether this n is sufficiently large to be identical with, or beyond, the n of the "place of convergence" for ε. It may be that our n is not yet large enough, that after n there will be a deviation greater than ε from p. To this we may answer: We are not bound to stay at h^n; we may continue our procedure and shall always consider the last h^n obtained as our best value. This procedure must at sometime lead to the true value p, if there is a limit at all; the applicability of this procedure, as a whole, is a necessary condition of the existence of a limit at p.

To understand this, let us imagine a principle of a contrary sort. Imagine a man who, if h^n is reached, always makes the assumption that the limit of the frequency is at $h^n + a$, where a is a fixed constant. If this man continues his procedure for increasing n, he is sure to miss the limit; this procedure must at sometime become false, if there is a limit at all.

We have found now a better formulation of the necessary condition. We must not consider the individual assumption for an individual h^n; we must take account of the procedure of continued assumptions of the inductive type. The applicability of this procedure is the necessary condition sought.

If, however, it is only the whole procedure which constitutes the necessary condition, how may we apply this idea to the individual case which stands before us? We want to know whether the individual h^n observed by us differs less than ε from the limit of the convergence; this neither can be guaranteed nor can it be called a necessary condition of the existence of a limit. So what does our idea of the necessary condition imply for the individual case? It seems that for our individual case the idea turns out to be without any application.

This difficulty corresponds in a certain sense to the difficulty we found in the application of the frequency interpretation to the single case. It is to be eliminated by the introduction of a concept already used for the other problem: the concept of posit.

If we observe a frequency h^n and assume it to be the approximate value of the limit, this assumption is not maintained in the form of a true statement; it is a posit such as we perform in a wager. We posit h^n as the value of the limit, i.e., we wager on h^n, just as we wager on the side of a die. We know that h^n is our best wager, therefore we posit it. There is, however, a difference as to the type of posit occurring here and in the throw of the die.

In the case of the die, we know the weight belonging to the posit: it is given by the degree of probability. If we posit the case "side other than that numbered 1," the weight of this posit is $5/6$. We speak in this case of a posit with appraised weight, or, in short, of an *appraised posit*.

In the case of our positing h^n, we do not know its weight. We call it, therefore, a *blind posit*. We know it is our best posit, but we do not know how good it is. Perhaps, although our best, it is a rather bad one.

The blind posit, however, may be correct. By continuing our series, we obtain new values h^n; we always choose the last h^n. Thus the blind posit is of an approximative type; we know that the method of making and correcting such posits must in time lead to success, in case there is a limit of the frequency. It is this idea which furnishes the justification of the blind posit. The procedure described may be called the *method of anticipation*; in choosing h^n as our posit, we anticipate the case where n is the "place of convergence." It may be that by this anticipation we obtain a false value; we know, however, that a continued anticipation must lead to the true value, if there is a limit at all.

An objection may arise here. It is true that the principle of induction has the quality of leading to the limit, if there is a limit. But is it the only principle with such a property? There might be other methods which also would indicate to us the value of the limit.

Indeed, there might be. There might be even better methods, i.e., methods giving us the right value p of the limit, or at least a value better than ours, at a point in the series where h^n is still rather far from p. Imagine a clairvoyant who is able to foretell the value p of the limit in such an early stage of the series; of course we should be very glad to have such a man at our disposal. We may, however, without knowing anything about the predictions of the clairvoyant, make two general statements concerning them: (1) The indications of the clairvoyant can differ, if they are true, only in the beginning of the series, from those given by the inductive principle. In the end there must be an asymptotical convergence between the indications of the clairvoyant and those of the inductive principle. This follows from the definition of the limit. (2) The clairvoyant might be an imposter; his prophecies might be false and never lead to the true value p of the limit.

The second statement contains the reason why we cannot admit clairvoyance without control. How gain such control? It is obvious that the control is to consist in an application of the inductive principle: we demand the forecast of the clairvoyant and compare it with later observations; if then there is a good correspondence between the forecasts and the observations, we shall infer, by induction, that the man's prophecies will also be true in the future. Thus it is the principle of induction which is to decide whether the man is a good clairvoyant. This distinctive position of the principle of induction is due to the fact that we know about its function of finally leading to the true value of the limit, whereas we know nothing about the clairvoyant.

. . .

These considerations lead, however, to a more precise formulation of the logical structure of the inductive inference. We must say that, if there is any method which leads to the limit of the frequency, the inductive principle will do the same; if there is a limit of the frequency, the inductive principle is a sufficient condition to find it. If we omit now the premise that there is a limit of the frequency, we cannot say that the inductive principle is the necessary condition of finding it because there are other methods using a correction c_n. There is a set of equivalent conditions such that the choice of one of the members of the set is necessary if we want to find the limit; and, if there is a limit, each of the members of the set is an appropriate method for finding it. We may say, therefore, that the *applicability* of the inductive principle is a necessary condition of the existence of a limit of the frequency.

The decision in favor of the inductive principle among the members of the set of equivalent means may be substantiated by pointing out its quality of embodying the smallest risk; after all, this decision is not of a great relevance, as all these methods must lead to the same value of the limit if they are sufficiently continued. It must not be forgotten, however, that the method of clairvoyance is not, without further ado, a member of the set because we do not know whether the correction c_n occurring here is submitted to the condition of convergence to zero. This must be proved first, and it can only be proved by using the inductive principle, viz., a method known to be a member of the set: this is why clairvoyance, in spite of all occult pretensions, is to be submitted to the control of scientific methods, i.e., by the principle of induction.

It is in the analysis expounded that we see the solution of Hume's problem. Hume demanded too much when he wanted for a justification of the inductive inference a proof that its conclusion is true. What his objections demonstrate is only that such a proof cannot be given. We do not perform, however, an inductive inference with the pretension of obtaining a true statement. What we obtain is a wager; and it is the best wager we can lay because it corresponds to a procedure the applicability of which is the necessary condition of the possibility of predictions. To fulfil the conditions sufficient for the attainment of true predictions does not lie in our power; let us be glad that we are able to fulfil at least the conditions necessary for the realization of this intrinsic aim of science.

53 🐝

THE NATURE AND JUSTIFICATION OF HYPOTHETICAL REASONING

William Kneale

William Kneale (1906-   ) *was Professor of Philosophy at Oxford University until retirement in 1966.*

THE EXPLANATION OF NATURAL LAWS

. . . The natural laws formulated by scientists are of various kinds, and it is no exaggeration to say that, if we tried to make a list of all the distinguishable laws of these various kinds which have been stated by scientists, we should soon find that we had very many thousands. It is difficult to accept all these laws as independent and ultimate. We wish to know why there are such uniformities, and it is the asking of this question, rather than the search for new uniformities, which marks the beginning of modern science. I do not wish to deny that there has been systematic study of parts of nature which amounted to little more than a search for new uniformities. What we call natural history is just the careful recording of the structures and habits of living organisms. But this example helps to prove my point. There is an obvious difference between the descriptive work of the natural historian and the explanatory work of the modern biologist, and it is customary to date the beginnings of modern biology from the first attempts to explain the generalizations made by natural historians. This aspect of science is so familiar to modern scientists that they sometimes speak of the empirical generalizations which suffice for the making of predictions about individuals as though these were the basic *facts* from which science starts, overlooking the induction by which such generalizations are themselves derived from the singular facts of experience. Thus we find the word 'phenomenon' commonly used in the writings of modern scientists not for what someone observes at a particular place and time, which was the original sense, but rather for a generalization that in certain circumstances something of a certain sort can always be ob-

From William Kneale, *Probability and Induction,* 1949. From sections 19, 21, 46, 47. Published by The Clarendon Press, Oxford, and reprinted with their permission.

served. In works on psycho-physiology, for example, there are references to the Purkinje phenomenon, which is really the *law* that in white light of gradually increasing intensity the various colours emerge in a definite order. And after a survey of the various laws of optics two eminent physicists write 'All the optical phenomena we have considered speak for the wave theory'.[1]

In order to make clear what is meant by explanation in natural science it will be convenient to begin by considering those simple cases in which empirical generalizations are explained by other laws that have been established by direct induction from experience. It has been found that the disease called pellagra does not occur among people who eat wheat as their staple cereal but does occur among people who live mainly on maize or certain other cereals. This empirical generalization is said to be explained when it is established that pellagra is due to a deficiency of vitamin B and that vitamin B is present in good quantity in wheat. Again it is established by common experience that violent effort such as running uphill leads to an involuntary increase in the rate and depth of breathing. This is explained when it is discovered that violent effort leads to an increase in the amount of carbon dioxide in the blood and that this increase in turn causes a little organ in the brain to send impulses through a nervous arc which ends with the muscles controlling respiration. Many such examples can be found in the natural sciences and particularly in biology. Whenever biologists explain generalizations about the behaviour of living organisms by reference to chemistry and physics, they are engaged in this sort of activity. In explaining such a generalization they show that, although it can rightly be called a law of biology, it need not be regarded as independent or ultimate, since it follows from other laws, namely, from laws about the constitution of organisms of certain kinds and laws about chemical substances, which are themselves to be accepted as generalizations from experience.

When we explain a given proposition we show that it follows logically from some other proposition or propositions. But this can scarcely be a complete account of the matter. For if I hear that there is a lion in my garden and demand an explanation of this curious fact, I am certainly not satisfied by a statement that there are two lions in my garden, although the first proposition follows logically from the second. An explanation must in some sense simplify what we have to accept. Now the explanation of laws by showing that they follow from other laws is a simplification of what we have to accept because it reduces the number of untransparent necessitations we need to assume, but this may not be obvious at first sight. The plain man who knows that he has to breathe harder when he climbs a hill may say that this proposition is simple enough for him and that the explanation given by physiologists, so far from removing difficulties, merely imposes a burden on his memory by requiring him to remember some propositions of which he had never thought before. If we are to understand the nature of the simplicity

---

[1] Einstein and L. Infeld, *The Evolution of Physics*, p. 120.

introduced by scientific explanation, we must not dismiss this objection as merely foolish. It is true that in our example the explanation involves a number of new generalizations and that the proposition which satisfies the plain man is simpler for his purposes than the explanation. But the plain man who makes the objection is interested only in laws which have some obvious reference to his practical affairs. The scientist, on the other hand, is interested also in laws of any kind about the subject-matter which he studies and would have considered it his duty to note the existence of the small organ in the brain even if he had not been able to establish any connexion between it and the control of respiration. For him the explanation introduces a simplification because it shows that of a number of laws which he has to assume in any case, one follows from the others and so need not be regarded as ultimate.

When a natural law is explained, we can say that it has been shown to be a necessary consequence of some other proposition or propositions, but the necessity of which we speak here is only relative to those other propositions. We are still unable to see the intrinsic necessity of the law, and it seems clear that we shall never by any advance in natural science reach a point at which we can say that natural necessities have become self-evident. What we can achieve, however, is a reduction of the number of independent laws we need to assume for a complete description of the order of nature. When only a comparatively small number of laws need be accepted as ultimate in a certain field of study, the science of that field can be presented as a system of general propositions entailed by a few postulates of high generality, that is to say, in the same fashion as a system of geometry. Such a system is often called the theory of its field. This use of the word 'theory' was originally similar to the use in mathematics by which we speak of the theory of sets and the theory of functions. But, unlike a theory in mathematics, a theory or system in natural science is to be accepted only if its postulates are confirmed directly or indirectly by experience, and so the word has come to mean a suggestion for a system or, by a further extension of usage, a suggestion for an explanation of any kind. This tendency has been encouraged, no doubt, by the attempts of physicists to make theories with the help of what may be called *transcendent hypotheses,* and to these we must now turn.

When we explain laws by showing that they are logically entailed by other laws, the propositions which serve as postulates in our system are of the same kind as those they explain, and they can be established by the same means, namely, by direct induction from experience. In physics, however, attempts have been made to explain laws by deriving them from postulates of a different kind. The oldest suggestion of this sort is the atomic theory. This was first put forward by Democritus in the fifth century B.C., but did not receive general approval from scientists until the beginning of last century, when Dalton showed that it would provide an explanation of some simple laws about the constant combining weights of chemical substances. In its modern form it explains a host of empirical generalizations, and everyone engaged in physical science assumes that with further specification it will explain still more. The novelty of the theory is that it explains laws by means of postulates which are not themselves established by direct induction from experience and cannot, indeed, be tested directly in any way. These postulates are hypotheses about the existence of objects which must, from the nature of the case, be imperceptible. Another physical theory of the same type is the undulatory theory of light, first suggested by Huyghens in the seventeenth century and later developed by Clerk-Maxwell into the general theory of electromagnetism. This is obviously not the place in which to try to expound either of these theories in detail, but it is important for our purpose to make clear the peculiar nature of the hypotheses on which they are based.

The peculiarity of the objects and processes assumed by physical scientists in the formulation of these theories is not merely that they are small in relation to the sticks and stones about which we talk in common speech. Indeed, according to later developments of the undulatory theory electro-magnetic waves may be of very large dimensions, and it is sometimes argued that in a certain sense each electron occupies the whole of space. The essential point is rather that the physical world as described in such theories cannot, from the nature of the case, be observed as sticks and stones are observed. I can see a wave passing over the surface of a pond, but it is merely senseless to speak of seeing or observing in any other way an electro-magnetic wave. It is even impossible to imagine these things, for if we try to imagine them we must attribute to them qualities such as colour or perceptible hardness which they cannot possess. I propose to call hypotheses about things of this kind *transcendent,* because I think it is necessary to indicate quite clearly that they are concerned with things which are not observable even in principle. This is a difficult doctrine, and two questions about it come to mind immediately.

In the first place, if all our ideas are derived from experience, as it seems plausible to say with Locke and the empirical school of philosophers, how can we even suppose the existence of things which are in principle unobservable? The answer is that in these hypotheses we suppose only the existence of a set of things having a certain structure which can be expressed in the language of mathematics. The sense in which the word 'structure' is used here can best be understood from an example. A tune which is heard and a musical score which is seen may be said to have the same logical structure although they are sensibly very different. That structure might conceivably be expounded to a person who had neither hearing nor sight but only touch. Structure cannot, of course, exist without content, and, when I say that in transcendent hypotheses we suppose only the existence of a set of things having a certain structure, I do not mean that we suppose the existence of a set of things having only a certain structure, for that would be absurd. What I mean is that, although we cannot even conjecture what the content is that embodies the structure, we can reasonably suppose that there is a set of things of that structure, just as a man deaf from birth can suppose that there are complex objects called tunes which embody the structures about which he reads in books on music. That transcendent hypotheses are concerned only with structure has often been overlooked in the past, because scientists and philosophers have mistakenly allowed themselves to slip some imaginative elements, such as perceptible hardness, into their conceptions of the objects mentioned in the hypotheses. Berkeley pointed out quite correctly that the hypothetical entities of the physicists were unimaginable, but he concluded wrongly that because they were unimaginable they were inconceivable.

Secondly, how can hypotheses of this kind explain laws about observable things? If the hypotheses contained no reference to the world of common sense it would, of course, be impossible to explain laws about observables by their help. The hypotheses are, however, doubly general propositions (universal and existential) of such forms as: 'Wherever light of such-and-such a colour (i.e. a perceptual object) occurs, there is a wave process of such-and-such a wave-length, and vice versa.' They are introduced for the purpose of explaining laws, and, however abstruse they may become in the course of development, they must always remain attached in this way to the world of perceptual objects if they are to achieve their purpose.

The making of transcendent hypotheses involves the introduction of a new terminology, and it is important to realize how this is related to . . . the perceptual object terminology. . . . In relation to this . . . it appears as a more comprehensive language. That is to say, the new terminology of the physicist would, if complete, provide an expression corresponding to every expression of the perceptual object terminology, e.g. 'copper', 'lightning', 'freezing', &c., but contain also expressions, e.g. 'electron', to which there is nothing corresponding in the perceptual object terminology. Natural laws which have been formulated originally in the perceptual object terminology can therefore be translated into the transcendent object terminology. When so translated they naturally appear more complex, because the new terminology is, so to say, of finer grain. Instead of a comparatively simple statement about the melting-point of a chemical substance we have a statement about the average velocity of molecules of such-and-such internal constitution at the time when the attractive forces between them no longer suffice to keep them in a rigid formation. But the greater complexity of the expressions for laws in the new terminology is intended to exhibit the necessity of the laws, and the price paid is small if the new terminology does indeed make it possible to explain the laws within a comprehensive theory.

.   .   .

When first introduced a transcendent hypothesis may be extremely vague, provided only that it entails the laws which it is intended to explain. When Huyghens tried to explain the diffraction and the interference of light by means of his undulatory theory, he had no clear idea of the nature of the waves he supposed to occur, but the wave-motion seemed to render some laws of optics intelligible and there was no rival suggestion which could do as much. The theory therefore began to win acceptance among scientists and was gradually developed by greater definition of all the necessary details. As it developed, it became capable of explaining other known laws of optics and also some laws which had not been established before by direct induction but which were verified after they had been deduced from the hypothesis. For when such a hypothesis has some degree of success, it immediately begins to dominate the interest of scientific researchers. At first they try to devise additional tests, that is, to discover more and more consequences which they can verify. Admittedly, verification of these consequences can never amount to demonstration of the hypothesis, just as the confirmation of a law of nature in many instances can never amount to demonstration of the law. But when several uniformities foretold by the theory, that is to say, deduced from the hypothesis, have been confirmed by direct induction, scientists soon cease to debate whether the hypothesis is acceptable in principle. Their interest now is to devise tests by which to decide between alternative developments of the theory in those parts or aspects that have hitherto been left indefinite.

THE RELATION BETWEEN INDUCTION AND THE HYPOTHETICAL METHOD

We must now ask whether we should apply the term 'induction' to the kind of reasoning by which transcendent hypotheses are established. This is a verbal question to be settled according to our own convenience; but it has some importance, because in trying to decide what is the most convenient usage to adopt we are led to remark similarities and dissimilarities which might otherwise be overlooked.

If we understand by 'induction' reasoning in which universal propositions are established by consideration of instances falling under them, we cannot apply the term to the reasoning which establishes transcendent hypotheses. For the essential feature of such an hypothesis is that it relates observables of certain kind to some other things which are not observable. The hypothesis is indeed a universal proposition (e.g. about all light), but it is of such a character that cases falling under it cannot be verified by observation. It can be confirmed only indirectly by the testing of its more remote consequences. If any one of these consequences is a universal proposition about observables which is falsified by experience, the hypothesis must be rejected. If, however, all the consequences we can test are universal propositions confirmed by experience, that is to say, propositions established by direct ampliative induction either before or after being deduced from the hypothesis, all the evidence in favour of the consequences is evidence in favour of the hypothesis, although the latter is still in principle capable of being falsified through the falsification of one of its consequences. The best convention is perhaps to extend the use of the word 'induction' to cover the hypothetical method but at the same time to distinguish this new application of the term by adding the adjective 'secondary'. If we refused to call such reasoning inductive, we should ignore the obvious continuity of interest between it and primary or direct induction and make it more difficult to discuss what they have in common, whereas if we omitted to add any qualification when describing the hypothetical method as a form of induction we should slur over an important distinction.

Some logicians have been so impressed by the importance of hypotheses in what we commonly call the inductive sciences that they have confused together the notions of induction and hypothetical method, supposing all induction to be an application of the hypothetical method and every use of hypotheses an instance of induction. We even find the word 'induction' applied sometimes to the use of hypotheses by historians in the tentative reconstruction of the course of past events. This seems to me an unprofitable and even dangerous widening of the meaning of the term, but I think it is interesting to see what has suggested it.

A universal proposition of natural science which is established by induction may reasonably be called an hypothesis, although, of course, not a transcendent hypothesis. The particular cases falling under it are its consequences and the verification of them can be said to confirm the hypothesis but never to prove it conclusively. It is, indeed, precisely because such a proposition can be no more than a well-confirmed hypothesis that I have called the sort of induction which establishes it ampliative. It is natural, then, that logicians should try to treat of induction together with other attempts to establish hypotheses by consideration of their consequences. But the suggestion that every use of hypotheses is a variety of induction is based on a failure to distinguish different kinds of hypotheses. Apart from laws concerning perceptual objects and postulates introduced to explain such laws, natural scientists have sometimes put forward hypotheses which are, strictly speaking, historical in character. Thus the nebular hypothesis about the origin of the solar system is not a universal proposition about the behaviour of all things of a certain kind, but rather a suggestion for the explanation of the special order found among a number of particular things. It resembles an hypothesis put forward by an archaeologist to explain the origin of Stonehenge. In each case we can do no more than look for evidence which will confirm or refute the hypothesis by verifying or falsifying some of its consequences, but in each the hypothesis is a proposition of the same kind as those we can claim to establish conclusively by observation, differing from them only in that it is about the past. We can conceive the possibility of receiving wireless messages from astronomers in some other part of the universe to the effect that records made by their predecessors over many millions of years confirmed the nebular hypothesis, just as we can conceive the possibility of finding a contemporary inscription about the building of Stonehenge. If such additional evidence were forthcoming, it would have to be treated according to the ordinary methods of historical criticism.

A specially interesting example of the making of historical hypotheses in natural science is to be found in what is usually called the theory of the evolution of species. Many empirical generalizations have been made about the organisms of various species, e.g. that lions are carnivorous, that frogs grow out of tadpoles, that wheat grains contain vitamin B. It is now assumed that these laws are to be explained by biologists in the sense of being deduced from the constitution of the organisms and the general laws of physiology. In so far as biologists are able to carry out this programme they make their study systematic or theoretical in the original sense of that word. There is, however, a further question which they may ask, namely, how there came to be organisms of these various constitutions. There are obvious similarities between species which have led natural historians long since to classify them in genera and families. But species appear to be genetically distinct, that is to say, the individuals of a species reproduced organisms of their own kind only. And so, in spite of the suggestions contained in such words as 'genus' and 'family', natural historians of earlier times felt compelled to assume that species had been established separately at some remote date in the past. The doctrine of the separate creation of species was not an invention of priests, designed to buttress a system of theology, but the best guess that could be given at the time. The theory put forward by Darwin and his successors is simply an hypothesis to the effect that what we call specific differences have come about through the accumulation of many small differences between individuals of successive generations. The laws of genetics show what can be accomplished by selective breeding. Whether, and, if so, by what stages, the organisms we know have been evolved from organisms of simpler types is a question of historical fact. It is extremely unlikely that biologists will ever be able to trace all the steps by which all the known species have been established, but they have apparently found enough to convince themselves that the general hypothesis of evolution is as probable as an historical hypothesis of that kind can be.

It seems unwise to extend the use of the word 'induction' to cover the establishment of historical hypotheses like those we have just considered and those which are put forward in social and literary studies. Historical hypotheses are quite different in logical character from the transcendent hypotheses of physics and also from the laws which are established by primary induction, for the former purport to be matters of fact, the latter to be truths of principle, and we cannot safely assume that the probability we ascribe to historical hypotheses is the same as that we ascribe to the results of induction, whether primary or secondary. I think this point worth making because it has not been realized by many otherwise estimable writers on the theory of induction, e.g. Whewell.

The Policy of Secondary Induction

Secondary induction is concerned with theories as opposed to laws or probability rules. In an earlier discussion we have seen that theories are expected to explain natural laws, and that genuine explanation always involves a simplification of what we have to accept. In order to understand the policy of secondary induction we must consider once more what we mean by our use of the word 'simplification' in this connexion. For there seem to be two notions involved, both distinct from that idea of simplicity which we have already noticed in our discussion of laws of functional relationship.

In the first place an hypothesis of secondary induction which is to explain a number of empirical generalizations established by primary induction must entail all those generalizations and have in addition some other testable consequence or consequences. It is not enough for the hypothesis to entail the generalizations which it is intended to explain, for the mere conjunction of them would satisfy this condition and we should not describe that as an explanation. Nor is it sufficient that the hypothesis should entail some new consequence which is untestable; for we can always formulate a fantastic proposition which satisfies this weak condition by merely adding to a conjunctive statement of the generalizations we wish to explain a clause such as 'All undetectable devils love hopscotch', and no one would dream of saying that a proposition so formulated was an explanation of the generalizations it covered. The history of thought shows that men have no difficulty in inventing any number of hypotheses which entail generalizations they wish to explain, and the fact that some of these which are not explanations have been accepted as such by intelligent men only proves the strength of the human craving for explanations and the deceptive power of words. For an example we may take the doctrine of vital force, once popular in biology. When philosophers of the positivist school declare that metaphysical theories are only pseudo-explanations, their objection is based on the same consideration; but they are unwise in their attempt to draw a firm line of demarcation for all time between science and metaphysics. It is not always easy to settle the question whether an hypothesis entails consequences which are both new and testable; and those who think they can give a simple rule should remember that the atomic theory of matter and all speculations about the chemical constitution of the stars were condemned as metaphysical by positivists of an earlier generation.

Let us suppose, then, that an hypothesis has been put forward in secondary induction to explain a number of generalizations established by primary induction, and that some further generalization which can be tested by observation has been derived from it. If this further generalization is confirmed by experience, are we to say that the hypothesis explains all the generalizations, both old and new? Had the new generalization been established by primary induction before the suggestion of the hypothesis, we should certainly not say that the hypothesis explained all the various generalizations merely because it entailed them all; for again the bare conjunction of the generalizations would satisfy this weak condition. But it is at least conceivable that the new generalization might have been established earlier, and the answer to the question whether the hypothesis is or is not an explanation cannot depend on an historical accident. It seems, therefore, that our hypothesis cannot be an explanation unless it entails yet another consequence which is testable by observation; and so we may continue *ad infinitum,* demanding a new testable consequence whenever a generalization derived from the hypothesis has been confirmed. In short, an hypothesis which is to be worthy of consideration in secondary induction must entail infinitely many empirical generalizations. If any of these is disproved, the hypothesis is disproved, but so long as it survives such indirect tests it may be said to explain all its consequences. Here we have one reason for speaking of the simplicity achieved in explanation. An explanatory hypothesis not only co-ordinates a number of generalizations established by primary induction, but gives promise of infinitely many others; and so long as it survives it constricts the realm of possibility more than any number of empirical generalizations entailed by it.

This conclusion seems surprising at first sight. In order to remove the appearance of paradox we must go on to consider the second kind of simplification involved in the making of theories. When we try to find an explanation of a number of empirical generalizations, we look for the hypothesis which is simplest in the sense that it employs the smallest number of independent *concepts.* It is this reduction of the number of independent concepts which makes possible a reduction of the number of independent propositions we need to accept and so gives hope of a drastic constriction of the realm of possibility. Clerk-Maxwell's general theory of electro-magnetic waves has co-ordinated empirical generalizations about heat, light, and electricity which were formerly thought to belong to separate fields of physics, and has suggested many new generalizations now confirmed by experience. But the novelty of the theory, which has made all this possible, is the provision of a single scheme within which a number of physical concepts, hitherto considered independent, can all be defined. For such reductive definition of concepts a transcendent object terminology is needed. There can therefore be no secondary induction without such terminology. But once this is recognized it can be understood how the hypotheses of secondary induction may entail infinitely testable consequences.

.   .   .

When physicists first entertained the atomic theory of matter, they did not attempt to say exactly how large the atoms were of which they spoke. They may even have thought it impossible to make any estimate of size other than the vague statement that atoms are very small in comparison with all perceptual objects. They were already committed, however, to the assertion that atoms have some size, and in the course of time their successors realized that testable consequences could be derived from more precise suggestions. Experiments were then devised for the purpose of deciding between the alternatives which had hitherto been left open, and so the work went on. At the beginning an hypothesis is valued chiefly for its co-ordination of already established generalizations, and may be little more precise than is necessary for this purpose; but if it is to retain a place in the structure of science it must be capable of development. We may, if we choose, say that the precise suggestion put forward by a later scientist is a different hypothesis from the vague suggestion put forward by his predecessor; but we may then have to declare that the earlier scientist explained nothing, because the testable consequences to be derived from his hypothesis were limited in number, and to say this is to abandon ordinary usage. There are revolutions from time to time in science, but there are also long periods of steady progress during which theories are developed by successive specifications. Newtonian physics, for example, was developed in this way for more than a century after Newton's death.

So far I have been engaged in describing the results of secondary induction, but the purpose of the description is to show the nature of the policy which leads to such results. It should now be clear what is the correct account of the matter. There is no rule of thumb for the making of valuable suggestions at this stage in scientific inquiry, because the theoretical scientist must be inventive in somewhat the same way as a novelist or a playwright. For the making of a Clerk-Maxwell a primer of scientific method is of little more use than a correspondence course in authorship would be for the making of a Shakespeare. Looking back over the history of science, we can, it is true, discuss the psychological origins of some theories. We can say, for example, that analogies have often suggested fruitful hypotheses, as when a terminology for talking of electricity was created by adaptation of that used for describing the behaviour of liquids. But analogies suggest hypotheses only to those who can see analogies, and there is no method by which we can make sure that we shall *see* in this sense of the word. No doubt persons who are familiar with what has been done already may acquire a flair for the construction of useful hypotheses, just as those versed in mathematics may acquire a facility in the construction of proofs; but it is not possible in either case to formulate rules of invention. Apart from past achievements nothing can be taught systematically. In short, secondary induction is not, like primary induction, a policy for finding good things, but rather a policy of welcoming good things when they are found.

It is this difference which accounts for a confusion to be noticed in many discussions of induction. Some writers of the Baconian tradition ignore secondary induction and try to represent all scientific effort as the application of simple rules which give even fools a good hope of success. Others ignore primary induction and deny in effect that there can be any rules of discovery. Both parties are mistaken; but the mistake of the second group is more pardonable, because the work of primary induction is taken for granted in the more advanced stages of science.

THE ACCEPTABILITY OF THEORIES

I have spoken of secondary induction as a policy. This way of approaching the problem is reasonable, because in spite of the difference between the two types of induction we speak in the same way of the probability or acceptability of their conclusions. We cannot, in the strict sense, demonstrate the truth of any theories in empirical science, nor can we say that they have probability in the sense of the theory of chances. If, then, we regard them as approvable or acceptable, this must be because they have been produced in accordance with a policy which is the only way of trying to do something we want to do. But what is it that we want to do when we welcome theories which provide simplification in the two senses mentioned above?

If the only human interest which led to the development of science were the desire to predict particular matters of fact, it would be very difficult, perhaps even impossible, to explain the importance which secondary induction has in the more advanced stages of science. Laws and probability rules of the kind we establish by primary induction are sufficient for this purpose, and secondary induction cannot help in the work except by providing theories from which further suggestions of this kind can be derived. Admittedly a great many of the generalizations we now use in making predictions were first conceived by scientists as consequences to be deduced from theories, but they are not accepted without question merely because they follow from theories. On the contrary, the continued acceptance of the theories from which they follow depends on their confirmation by primary induction. It may be argued, therefore, that, if we were more observant, all those generalizations we use for the making of predictions could have been established by primary induction alone, i.e. without the help of any suggestions from the theories with which secondary induction is concerned. In practice we can never be so observant as to notice all regularities in experience which may provide evidence for primary induction, because observation must always be directed by a selective interest of some sort. The mere determination to amass empirical information in the Baconian style would carry us a very little way on the road of scientific progress, and even false theories may be better than none at all, since, at least, they suggest lines of research. But it is true that, with good fortune in the direction of our attention, any of the empirical generalizations we use in making predictions might conceivably have been established by primary induction alone.

There is undoubtedly a strong continuity of interest between primary and secondary induction. Hypotheses of secondary induction can be confirmed or rejected only indirectly, i.e. through consideration of empirical generalizations which they entail. And conversely, the increase of acceptability which empirical generalizations get from consilience often depends on their being all subsumed under some theory of secondary induction. But it would be foolish to maintain that the sole purpose of secondary induction is to make possible more predictions. For it cannot be maintained that theories are merely devices for producing suggestions of law or probability in advance of observation and so directing our attention to aspects of experience from which we may perhaps be able to derive acceptable conclusions by primary induction. And it is not enough to say that secondary induction makes our predictions safer. The fertility of theories is due, as we have seen, to the transcendent object terminology in which they are formulated; and this is not to be treated as a shorthand system for the compendious statement of propositions about observables. In order to justify secondary induction we must therefore find some new motive or interest which it serves.

The fact that we may derive satisfaction for a time from pseudo-explanations which do not entail new testable consequences shows that we desire explanations for their own sake; and any account of scientific effort which does not give a prominent place to this desire must be seriously incomplete. Secondary induction presupposes primary induction, and is in some respects a continuation of the work of primary induction, but it begins with the attempt to find explanations for their own sake. From very early times the desire to explain has been as important in the development of science as the wish to be able to predict, and in our own time it is the dominant interest of those we call pure scientists. When the matter is considered historically, it is clear that the other benefits to be derived from secondary induction are incidental to the satisfaction of curiosity.

The intellectual satisfaction to be obtained from theories has sometimes been compared with the satisfaction derived from works of art, and there is certainly some resemblance. When we contemplate a theory which unifies a large field of science by a reduction in the number of independent concepts, we are pleased by its coherence much as we are pleased by the coherence of a good poem or a piece of good music; and we admire the skill of a great scientist much as we admire the skill of a great artist. There is, indeed, no reason why we should hesitate to speak of science as a source of aesthetic enjoyment. But it is important to recognize a difference between scientific theories and works of art in the ordinary sense. The scientist is inventive in the making of theories, but his activity is never autonomous like that of the poet or the musician. The products of his construction are hypotheses, that is to say, propositions, which must be true or false; and only those are thought worthy of consideration which may be true, i.e. are consistent with known facts. His work is more like that of a portrait-painter or that of an architect who designs a building to make the best use of a given site for a given purpose. But neither analogy is perfect. The scientist wishes for no liberty in the construction of hypotheses. He has, of course, the ordinary freedom of a prose-writer in the presentation of his theory, for there may be individual style in scientific writing just as in other branches of literature; but if he finds that recorded experience leaves him with a choice between alternatives in the development of his theory, he immediately begins to plan new observations which will strengthen the conditions he has to satisfy. His aim is to make a theory which fits *all* the facts and *has no rival*. It is true that he can never be sure he has succeeded in this; but his refusal to be content with any theory which is only one way of co-ordinating known facts shows clearly that his interest in simplification is not merely aesthetic.

When we look for an explanation we want to discover not merely *a* theory which co-ordinates some, or even all, of the empirical generalizations hitherto established by primary induction, but, if possible, *the* theory under which all possible generalizations can be subsumed. As Kant maintained, our thought is guided by the ideal of a single, all-inclusive system of natural necessity. Why we should have a craving to discover this I cannot say, but the fact seems to be beyond doubt. The rationalist metaphysician, assuming that the existence of the craving proves the possibility of satisfying it completely, tries to construct a theory of nature which shall be intrinsically necessary. He believes in effect that false theories must reveal their falsity not merely by inconsistency with observed facts, but also by internal contradictions. The empirical scientist is less confident in the power of human reason, but no less eager to find an intellectually satisfactory system. He too wants a single, inclusive theory; but he recognizes that he cannot hope to formulate it *a priori,* and adopts instead the policy of secondary induction, i.e. the policy of welcoming partial systems which accord with all known facts. In this his conduct is surely reasonable. Anyone who is not interested in understanding need not worry himself about methods of explanation; but for the rest of us the only question is how we should try to get what we want. If, as now seems obvious, we cannot get what we want in any other way, we do well to accept those partial explanations which survive all empirical tests. When we reflect on our procedure, we must admit we have no guarantee that our desire will ever be satisfied in full; but so long as a theory survives it gives us some satisfaction, and those which simplify most give most satisfaction. This is a sufficient reason for practising secondary induction.

54

THE NATURE
OF EXPLANATION

John Hospers

John Hospers (1918-   ) is Professor of Philosophy at Brooklyn College.

I

We are sometimes presented with a statement describing some observed fact, and when we ask 'Why?' we are presented with another statement which is said to constitute an explanation of the first. What is the relation between these two statements? What is it that makes the second statement an 'explanation' of the first? By virtue of what does it explain? Though everyone is constantly uttering statements which are supposed in one way or another to explain, few persons are at all clear about what it is that makes such statements explanations. . . .

The question 'What is it to explain?' admits of no general answers, for the term 'to explain' covers many activities: one may explain how, and why, and whither, and whence, and how much, and many other things. Very frequently when we ask someone to explain what he has just said we are merely asking him to restate his assertion in clearer or simpler words.

In this essay I shall treat only explaining *why*. Even within this area there are some cases with which we shall not be concerned: one may explain why the angles of a Euclidean triangle must equal 180°, and this is quite different from explaining why iron rusts. The latter is an event or a process, and I shall be concerned solely with explaining why in the special context of temporal events: roughly, why did event x happen, or why do events of class X happen? The illustration from geometry is, I should prefer to say, an

From John Hospers, "What Is Explanation?" a revised version of a paper originally published in *The Journal of Philosophy*, June 1946, in A.G.N. Flew, editor, *Essays in Conceptual Analysis*, 1956. Published by Macmillan and Company, Ltd., London; The Macmillan Company of Canada, Ltd.; and St. Martin's Press, Inc., New York. Reprinted by permission of the author, the editors of *The Journal of Philosophy*, and of the publishers.

example of giving *reasons* rather than explanations. Another example may further illustrate the point: If you ask me to explain why I hold a certain belief, I may reply by giving *reasons* for it — statements which I take to be evidence for the belief in question. Now, if I am rational, the fact that there is good evidence for *p* may explain why I believe *p* — that is, the reason for my believing *p* may also constitute an explanation of why I believe *p*. But this may not be so: the explanation of a person's believing in a benevolent Deity may be that he wants a father-substitute or that he needs a protector in a cold harsh world; but when asked to explain why he believes in a benevolent Deity he may cite reasons, *e.g.* the Argument from Design, which may have nothing to do with *why* he holds the belief. We shall be concerned here, then, with the explanation of events, not with reasons or evidences one might cite in favour of propositions.

II

What, then, is it to explain why an event occurs? (1) It has sometimes been said that we have explained it if we have stated its *purpose*. 'Why did you walk through the snow for ten miles when you could have taken the bus?' 'Because I wanted to win a wager.' 'Why does that dog scratch at the door?' 'He's cold and he wants to get in.' When such answers are given we are inclined to feel that our question has been answered and that the event has been satisfactorily explained; and it has been explained with reference to a purpose which some sentient being (s) had in attaining a certain end. This is the most primitive conception of explanation. People like to feel that there is a purposive explanation for everything: if not in terms of human or animal purposes, then of divine ones, or mysterious forces and powers. We tend to extend what holds true of some events to all events whatever; we know what conscious motivation is like from our own experience of it, and so we 'feel at home' with this kind of explanation.

We shall examine the scope and legitimacy of purposive explanation later in this paper. It is enough to remark here that if explanation must always be in terms of purpose, then the physical sciences do not explain anything. The properties of uranium, the rise of aeroplanes, the phenomena of magnetism are not explained in terms of any purposes at all; biologists even avoid talking about animal events such as the hen sitting on eggs in terms of purpose. However animistically the nature of explanation may at one time have been conceived, purposiveness is certainly no essential part of its meaning now. The stone is no longer held to fall because it wants to get to the centre of the earth.

(2) Another account of the nature of explanation is that an event has been explained when it has been shown to be an instance of some class of events which is already familiar to us. For example, when a person's behaviour seems strange to us, we are satisfied when it is 'explained' to us as being really impelled by the same sort of motives and desires as occur in us,

and are therefore familiar to us. 'Why is he introducing the man he hates to the woman he loves?' 'Because he wants them to fall in love with each other' would not generally be accepted as an explanation, for this very reason. When we observe that a balloon ascends rather than descends, unlike most objects, and it is made clear to us that air has weight and that the gas inside the balloon weighs less than would an equal volume of air, we are satisfied; the phenomenon has been 'reduced' to something already familiar to us in everyday experience, such as a dense object sinking in water while a hollow one floats. The event is no longer unusual, strange, or unique; it has been shown to illustrate a principle with which we were already acquainted. When we want to know why gases diffuse when released into a chamber from which the air has been pumped out, the explanation offered by the kinetic theory of gases is satisfactory to us because it asserts that molecules behave *like* particles with which we are already acquainted in our everyday experience.

.   .   .

Professor Bridgman holds that all explanation is of this kind: 'I believe that examination will show that the essence of an explanation consists in reducing a situation to elements with which we are so familiar that we accept them as a matter of course, so that our curiosity rests' (P. W. Bridgman, *The Logic of Modern Physics*, p. 37).

And yet I am sure that such a view as this must be mistaken. In the *first* place, we may seek explanations for the most familiar events as well as of those unfamiliar to us. We may ask why stones fall as well as why aeroplanes rise, and be curious for an answer equally in both cases. True, our motivation for asking the latter question is probably greater because the kind of phenomenon in question is (or was) less familiar; most people would not think to ask it about stones because the falling of stones is familiar and usual — but the question can as legitimately be asked in the one case as in the other. In the *second* place, the explanation may not be familiar at all: it may be far less familiar than the event to be explained. The discoloration of a painted kitchen wall when gas heat is used may be a familiar phenomenon to the housewife — surely more familiar than its explanation in terms of the chemical combination of sulphur in the gas fumes with elements in the paint, producing a compound that is dark in colour. Yet this is the true explanation. If the explanation is not familiar, one is tempted to say, it ought to be, as long as it is true. Surely its familiarity is irrelevant to its validity as an explanation. Familiarity is, in any case, a subjective matter — what is familiar to you may not be familiar to me; and yet the explanation, if true, is as true for me as for you.

The only grain of truth in the view that explaining is rendering familiar seems to be this: the law that does the explaining may not be familiar, *but* the fact that the phenomenon in question, such as the flight of an aeroplane, *can* be subsumed under a law — the fact that the behaviour *is* law-like and hence predictable — tends to make it less mysterious, less like a miracle, and thus in a sense more familiar. To show that the behaviour of something is lawlike is to show it to be a part of the order of nature, and in that sense familiar, although the particular law or laws stating the uniformity may be quite unfamiliar.

In what, then, *does* explanation consist? The answer, I think, is quite simple: (3) to explain an event is simply to bring it under a law;[1] and to explain a law is to bring it under another law. It does not matter whether the law is one about purposes or not, or whether it is familiar or not; what matters is that if the explanation is to be *true* (and we surely seek true explanations, not false ones), the law invoked must be true: indeed, this is already implied in the use of the word 'law', which refers to a true, *i.e.* a really existing, uniformity of nature; if the uniformity turned out to be only imaginary, or having exceptions, we would no longer call it a law.

In saying that explanation is in terms of laws, I use the word 'law' in a wider sense than is sometimes employed: in the sense I mean, any uniformity of nature is a law. Thus, it is a law that iron rusts, and it is a law that iron is magnetic — although both of these are usually listed in textbooks as 'properties of iron' rather than as laws. In this sense, it seems to me that explaining why something occurs always involves a law.

. . .

Sometimes, I should add, all we have available is a 'statistical law' — a law not of the form 'All A is B' or 'Whenever A, then B', but, *e.g.*, '75 per cent of A is B'. Can such a 'law' constitute an explanation? I should be inclined to say that it is, although we would still want an explanation of why 25 per cent of A's are *not* B's. If water did not always boil at 212°F. but did so only 75 per cent of the time, we might explain the boiling of this kettle of water by saying that its temperature had reached 212°, though we would still want an explanation of why the kettle of water next to it, which had also reached 212°, did not boil. In other words, our statistical law would still not answer the question, 'Why this and not that?' and in order to answer *this* question, we would need a non-statistical law of the form, 'Under such-and-such conditions, water always boils at 212°F., but under such-and-such other conditions, it does not'. It would seem, then, that a statistical law has in turn to be explained by a non-statistical one, although of course we may not, at any given stage in the progress of science, know of any non-statistical law by which to explain the statistical one.

Another example: 'Why does Johnny have a cold?' 'Because Johnny has been playing with Roger, and Roger has a cold'. It is not a law that everyone who plays with someone who has a cold also gets a cold; the best we can do here is to state a percentage of cases in which this happens. So far as it goes, this is satisfactory; some uniformity is better than none. And yet, surely, we do not rest satisfied with this; we want to go on and ask why it sometimes happens but sometimes not. And the answer to this question would be a

[1] With qualifications to be discussed later.

non-statistical law: 'People always get colds under such-and-such conditions'. Whether a statistical law can *always* be explained in terms of a non-statistical one depends not only on our powers of discovery but upon the nature of the universe. It is certainly no *a priori* truth that nature's uniformities are all of the 100 per cent variety instead of 75 per cent.

One further qualification: We have said that we explain particular events in terms of laws, and laws in terms of wider laws. But sometimes we give at least tentative explanations of them in terms not of laws but of general *hypotheses:* if a law is a well-established statement of how nature works, a statement about nature's workings that is not well established, or perhaps not even probable but only possible, cannot be a law. And yet we can use it to explain a law. But to whatever degree the hypothesis is uncertain, to that degree the explanation is jeopardized. An explanation cannot be known to be true if it involves a hypothesis which (by the definition of 'hypothesis') is *not* known to be true. Whether the explanation is a true explanation, then, depends on the fate of the hypothesis. (In the 'higher reaches' of most sciences, where the most general laws are involved, the only explanations possible are usually those in terms of very general hypotheses.)

III

So much for a general statement of what explanation consists of. I should like now to append some comments and to answer some questions to which the above account may give rise.

1. Thus far we have been content to answer the question 'Why does A do B?' by saying 'Because all A's do B'. But there are those who say that such an answer is no explanation at all. 'To say that all gases expand when heated', says Norman Campbell (*What Is Science?*, p. 80), is not to explain why hydrogen expands when heated; it merely leads us to ask immediately why all gases expand. An explanation which leads immediately to another question of the same kind is no explanation at all.'

I want to insist that the answer given *is* an explanation of the occurrence in question; to say 'Hydrogen is a gas, and all gases expand when heated' is a perfectly satisfactory answer to the question why hydrogen expands when heated. But it is *not,* of course, an answer to *another* question —Why do all gases expand when heated? — and this is probably the question which the person meant to ask in the first place. These questions must not be confused with each other; I believe Campbell's position is the result of this confusion. It is fatally easy to telescope (unconsciously) two questions into one, and then be dissatisfied with the answer. Distinguishing them, we get:

> *Question* 1. Why does this gas expand when heated?
> *Explanation.* It is hydrogen, and hydrogen expands when heated.
> *Question* 2. Why does hydrogen expand when heated?
> *Explanation.* . Hydrogen is a gas, and all gases expand when heated.
> *Question* 3. Why do all gases expand when heated?

Here we attempt to give an explanation in terms of the kinetic theory of gases. To criticize Answer 1 because it is not an answer to Question 2, or Answer 2 because it is not an answer to Question 3, is surely a confusion. I want to say that Answer 1 is a perfectly satisfactory explanation for the phenomenon referred to in Question 1, though of course not for those referred to in Questions 2 and 3. But there is a frequent tendency to telescope these questions and demand to Question 1 the answer to Question 3.

The situation may be illustrated in another way. If I ask, 'Why did the water-pipes in my basement burst last night?' someone may answer that it is because the basement got too cold, and another may answer that it is because water expands when it freezes, while yet another may say that we do not know the 'real explanation' unless we can state why water expands when it freezes. Here, again we must separate the questions:

> *Question* 1. Why did the water-pipes break?
> *Explanation.* They always do when the temperature falls to below 32°.
> *Question* 2. Why do they break when the temperature falls . . . etc.?
> *Explanation.* Because the water in them expands when it freezes, and the water on expanding breaks the pipes.
> *Question* 3. Why does water expand when it freezes?
> *Explanation.* Here we try to answer in terms of the structure of the water-molecule.

But to say that we have not explained (1) until we have explained (3) is grossly to underestimate the number of phenomena for which we do have perfectly satisfactory explanations. That is, we *do* have explanations for (1) and (2), and our having them is *not* contingent upon having an explanation for (3).

We could put our point in another away. *Logically* the answers given to each question in turn are satisfactory explanations; but *psychologically* they may not be equally satisfying, *depending on the previous knowledge of the questioner.* To the questioner who knew nothing about the relation of pipes bursting to temperature, the answer 'Because they got cold' (to the first question) would be psychologically quite satisfactory, but not to the person who already knew that it had something to do with temperature, for the question *he* meant to ask was (2) or (3). Again: If I ask why this wire conducts electricity, it is a perfectly good explanation to answer 'Because it is made of copper, and copper is a conductor of electricity'. Psychologically, however, this answer would not be equally satisfying to everyone; it *would* be to the person who knew nothing of the properties of copper (or who did not know that this wire was copper), but it would *not* be to the person who already knew the properties of copper but was really enquiring as to why copper, unlike many other substances, is a conductor of electricity.

2. Can an event have *two* explanations? Why not? Let us suppose that we want to explain an event E, and that we have a law saying that every time conditions A are fulfilled, E happens, and another law saying that every time conditions B are fulfilled, E happens. A will then be a complete explanation for the occurrence of E, and B will also be a complete explanation. Whether any such state of affairs actually occurs in the world is, of course, another question. Most of the suggested double explanations of events are in fact parts of a single explanation. Thus, for example, if we are asked to explain why the burglar committed the robbery last night, the detective may explain it in terms of his expertness at picking locks, the butler may explain it in terms of the family being out of the room, the maid may say it was because the bedroom window was open, the policeman may say it was because the night was foggy and visibility at a minimum, the sociologist may explain it in terms of the criminal's background of slum conditions, and the psychologist may explain it in terms of pseudo-aggressive impulses dating from a childhood period marked by intense family quarrels. All these explanations are probably correct enough as far as they go. It may well be that in the absence of any one of these factors the burglary would not have occurred. But these are, it would surely seem, parts and aspects of *one* complete explanation — and in explaining human actions the whole explanation may be inconceivably complex. Still, the possibility remains that in *some* cases there may be two separate and complete explanations for an occurrence; at least it cannot be ruled out *a priori*.

3. Must there be a *deductive* relation between the thing to be explained and the explanation, such that one can deduce the statement of the phenomenon to be explained from the explanation?

> All copper conducts electricity.
> This wire is made of copper.
> Therefore, This wire conducts electricity.

Here the explanation yields the desired conclusion easily, and it is quite clear that what we have here is a genuine explanation. The question is, must all explanation conform to this model? Have we failed to give an explanation if we have failed to deduce the explanandum from the explanation?

Let us first note that in many cases, if this is required, the explanation would be bewilderingly complex, and the premises in the deduction extremely numerous. Consider the burglary example just cited. From the fact that the weather was foggy and that the man had tendencies to steal and that he had a poor background . . . etc., we cannot deduce the fact that he committed the theft. We cannot deduce it, indeed, from any set of premises known to be true. What we need for deducing it is a law, to the effect that if such-and-such conditions are fulfilled an act of this kind will always occur, and then a minor premise to the effect that these conditions were in fact fulfilled. The conditions would indeed have to be extremely numerous, and the statement of the law immensely complicated. Yet such a law is required if the desired conclusion is to be deduced.

We never in fact use a deductive model in cases like this one, and it is worthy of note that we do not deny ourselves the claim that we have explained the event because of this. What, therefore, are we to say of the deductive model as a *sine qua non* for all explanation? As I see it, we have two alternatives open to us:

(*a*) We can, in the light of such examples, scrap the deductive model entirely. We can say that often one can in fact deduce the explanandum from the explanation, but that this is not essential to explanation. We might add, as some do, that to perform the deduction is one way (the best way?) to *justify* an explanation we have put forward, but that the giving of a true explanation is not dependent on this.

(*b*) We can still insist that a complete explanation does involve the deduction, but that what we often give is in fact less than a complete explanation. We list, as in the burglary example, a few salient facts and either take the remainder as too obvious to mention or do not know what they are. But such measures are concessions of failure. The fact is that the only way to be sure of our explanation is to deduce the phenomenon in question from premises which we know to be true.

I merely wish here to state these alternatives, not to decide between them. It is, surely, a matter of how liberally or how strictly we wish to use the term 'explanation'; and, though I incline toward the second alternative, I do not wish to champion without reserve a 'puristic' account of explanation which is not in fact followed by anyone — at least anyone in the psychological and social sciences — and which, it is sometimes declared, is in practice almost useless and boringly academic.

Thus far in enquiring about the need for a deductive relationship, we have considered only the explanation of particular events: we have deduced them from two premises, one stating a law and the other stating a particular condition: 'All copper conducts electricity; this is copper, therefore this conducts electricity.' 'All water freezes at 32°F., the water in the pond went below 32° last night; therefore the water in the pond froze.' And so on. But, as we saw earlier, we not only explain particular events; we also explain *laws*. And the same question could be repeated here: is the deductive requirement necessary? There is no doubt that in the 'neat, tidy' cases it is fulfilled: for example, Kepler's laws of planetary motion can be deduced from Newton's laws of motion together with the law of gravitation; and thus the latter clearly explain the former. But is this strictly a requirement for *all* explanation of laws? Again, some would say that it is — that anything short of this is not a full explanation. Others would say that it is not — that the deductive case is only the ideal one but that explanation does not require it. For example, a law can be explained in terms of a very general theory, from which the law cannot be strictly deduced, but which will nevertheless entitle the theory to be called an explanation. (The deductivist will reply that it is not *known* to be an explanation until the acid test, *i.e.* the deduction, is performed.)

4. In any case, whether deducibility is a necessary condition of explanation or not, it is not a sufficient condition. One can deduce that this watch will not work from the premises that watches will not work if gremlins get into them and that gremlins are in fact in this watch. Yet no one would accept this as an explanation for the misbehaviour of the watch. Similarly, one might deduce it from the premises that whatever God wills happens and that God has willed the misbehaviour of this watch. One can deduce anything if one selects one's premises carefully.

One might remark at this point that it is also necessary that the premises be *true*, and that this is the required addition. I would unhesitatingly agree that the premises must indeed be true — false statements cannot form parts of true explanations (indeed, if explanation is in terms of law, and a law is a true statement of a uniformity *i.e.*, one that actually occurs, when this proviso has already been implicit in our account of explanation). But suppose we make this proviso explicit — is it enough? I do not believe so . . .

What condition, then, remains to be supplied? The condition seems to be a rather simple one, yet one which it is difficult to state precisely. What we have in mind is this: we want to eliminate the indiscriminate 'explanatory' power of the gremlin-hypothesis and the God-hypothesis, even though they slip through the deductive net, because they do not enable us to explain why this happens *rather than that*. 'What explains everything explains nothing.'

This *can* be put by saying that the explanation must have *predictive* value, but this is a bit misleading. For one thing, it places undue emphasis upon the future, whereas explanation of past is just as important as explanation of future; we would have, then, to use a tenseless sense of 'predict'. For another thing, there are many explanations which seem to be true but whose predictive power is minimal or at any rate difficult to see: many biological phenomena can be explained in terms of mutations, for example, but it is not clear what these laws enable us to *predict* — certainly not where or when a mutation will occur or what kind it will be when it does arise.

Perhaps what we want to say can be best expressed by the simple proviso that the explanation must explain *other* phenomena than those it is invoked to explain, and yet, unlike the God-hypothesis, not just everything indiscriminately: in other words, it should explain other events (whether past, present, or future makes no difference), but it should all the same be *capable of disproof* by empirical observations, whether or not any actual empirical observations ever disprove it, it must be capable of testing. Without this condition it would not be considered an explanation in any science.

In fact all this is implicit in our requirement that an explanation be in terms of law or laws. A law is a universal proposition about all events or processes in a certain class, and if it holds for A, a member of the class (a present event), it also holds for members B, C, and D (future events); thus by the very nature of a law, laws explain more than a single event. The testability of explanations is also implicit in the concept of law, for a law is an empirical statement of a uniformity of nature, and, being contingent, it is always subject to disconfirmation by observation. Still, it is well to make the implicit explicit to show why the deductive requirement is not enough and what more is required of an explanation.

. . .

6. No mention has thus far been made of explanation in terms of *purpose*. And yet this is the oldest concept of explanation and still the one most frequently employed by primitive peoples. And there are contexts in which we still employ the concept of purpose in giving explanations — for example, when we say that my purpose in going to the store was to do some Christmas shopping, and that this is *why* I went.

The word 'purpose' is, of course, ambiguous. (*a*) Most frequently in ordinary usage a purpose is something of which I am conscious — a conscious intent to do something. The conscious intent is not the *whole* of the purpose: part of the criterion of whether it is my purpose to do X is whether I am disposed towards doing X, whether I take steps towards X and do X if I have the chance. (*b*) Some tendencies to act are not accompanied by any state of awareness; and here psychologists speak of *unconscious* purposes. We need not stop here over the exact interpretation of this way of speaking; let us simply say that one is said to have X as his unconscious purpose if he consistently acts, without intending it, so as to bring about X. (*c*) We speak of inanimate objects as having purposes — for example, the purpose of a hammer is to drive nails. This of course is not a purpose consciously envisaged by the hammer. All we mean here is that the mechanical object *reflects* the conscious purposes of its makers. *We* had a conscious purpose in making the hammer, and thus we speak elliptically of the hammer as having that purpose. Strictly speaking, of course, the purpose is ours and not the hammer's.

In all of these cases a purpose implies a purposer, or someone to have the purpose. We do sometimes use the word 'purpose' in another sense which carries no such implication, (*d*) when we say, 'What is the purpose of the heart?' 'To pump blood through the body.' Here purpose simply means function — *i.e.* what does it *do*? what part does it play in the bodily economy? If the word 'purpose' is used here I would view it as a 'degenerate' usage — a misleading locution in which another word, 'function', would serve much better. It is true that someone, in asking the purpose of the heart, might have in mind a theological question, 'What purpose did God have in endowing us with this organ?' but if this is meant, we are back again to purpose in sense 1, in which purpose implies a purposer and the word 'purpose' refers to conscious intent — the only difference now being that it is God's intent and not ours that is in question. But this, of course, is not what medical men generally have in mind when they ask purpose-questions about parts of organisms; else every such medical question would be a disguised theological question.

Having disentangled these senses of 'purpose', let us ask about the legitimacy of purposive explanations. Briefly I think it comes to this: explanations require laws, and if there are laws *about* purposes, there is no reason why they cannot figure in some explanations just as laws about falling bodies figure in other explanations. To the extent that laws about purposes have been established, they can be used as explanations like any other laws. Unfortunately the only laws (if any) that we are in a position to make about purposes are about human ones. Explanations in terms of divine purposes cannot be employed because no laws about divine purposes have ever been established. Even explanations of biological events in terms of animal purposes is frowned upon: we do not count it an explanation if it is said that the hen sits on her eggs *in order to* hatch chicks, because we have no indication that the hen does so with this purpose in mind; even if this is true, we do not know it, and therefore we cannot use it as a law in our explanation. In the human realm alone we know that purposes exist, and only there can we therefore employ them in explanations. We can deduce conclusions from them, thus:

> People act so as to fulfil their purposes, unless prevented by external circumstances.
> My purpose was to go shopping, and I was not prevented . . . etc.
> Therefore, I went shopping.

This way of putting it may sound rather silly, as the deductive model often does, but at any rate a deduction can be achieved from premises which are in all probability true.

The chief mistake which people are in the habit of making with regard to purposive explanation is probably that of wanting an answer to a why-question in terms of purpose when the conditions under which a purpose-answer is legitimate are not fulfilled. People extend their questioning unthinkingly from areas in which purposive explanation is in order into areas in which it is not. Thus: 'Why did he go to New York?' 'Well, in response to impulses from certain centres in his brain, some muscles in his arms and legs started moving towards the airport and . . .' 'No, that's not what I mean. I mean, why did he go? what did he go for? what purpose did he have in view?' 'He went in order to see some operas.' Contrast this with the following: 'Why did he die?' 'Well, a bullet entered his lung, puncturing some blood vessels, and the blood filled his lung so that he couldn't breathe any more, and . . .' 'No, that's not what I mean. I mean, *why* did he die?' But here we can no longer give an answer in terms of purpose — unless, that is, our talk is rooted in a theological context and we are willing to say that, just as the first person went to New York because he wanted to see operas, so the second person died because God had some purpose (intent) in seeing to it that he was murdered. If this is what is meant, one could try to answer the question in the theistic context of divine purposes; but if this context is rejected, the why-question demanding an answer in terms of purpose is meaningless, because an answer is being demanded when the only conditions under which the question is meaningful are not fulfilled. . . .

7. This leads us directly into an important question, How far can explanation go? We may explain an event in terms of a law, and this law

in terms of other laws, and so on? but must we not finally come to a stop? The bursting of the pipes is explained by the expansion of water on freezing; let us assume that water expands on freezing because the water-molecule has such-and-such a structure; now why does the water-molecule have this structure? Perhaps this can some day be explained by reference to electron-proton arrangements within the atom, and this in turn by reference to the disposition of more minute particles (if they can be called such) yet to be discovered; but sooner or later must we not say, 'That's just the way things are — this is just an ultimate law about the universe. We can explain other things in terms of it, but it we cannot explain'? Are there ultimate laws, laws which explain but cannot even in principle be explained?

In practice we come rather quickly to laws which cannot be explained further. Laws about atomic structure are typical of such laws. Laws of psychophysical correlation are another example. *Why* do I have a certain colour-sensation which I call red, indescribable but qualitatively different from all others, when light within a certain range of wave-length impinges upon my retina, and another indescribably different sensation which I call yellow when rays of another wave-length strike the retina? That this wave-length is correlated with this visual experience seems to be sheer 'brute fact' — a law[2] which cannot be explained in terms of anything more ultimate than itself.

At the same time, we should be careful in dismissing any uniformity we cannot explain as a 'brute fact' or 'basic law'. Many things, such as why this element has this melting-point and these spectral lines, were once considered basic and unexplainable properties of the element, but have since been explained in terms of the intra-molecular structure of the element. No matter how much at a loss we may be for an explanation, we can always ask and speculate. If it had been accepted as a basic law that water starts to expand when it gets below 39°F., we would never have gone on to discover anything about the structure of the water-molecule. Fruitful scientific procedure depends on assuming that no given law is basic; if scientists did not continue always to ask the question 'Why?' the process of scientific enquiry would stop dead in its tracks.

Thus, if there *are* basic laws, it seems that we cannot know of any given law that it is one. We can know that it is *not*, by explaining it in terms of other laws; but how could we know that it *is*? Discovering basic laws is epistemologically similar to discovering uncaused events: if there are uncaused events, we can never know that there are, for all we can safely say is that we have not yet found causes for them.

One further point about basic or ultimate laws: If a law is really a basic one, any request for an explanation of it is self-contradictory. To explain a law is to place it in a context or network of wider and more inclusive laws; a basic law is by definition one of which this cannot be done; therefore to ask of

---

[2] A law which would, to be sure, have to be qualified to take care of abnormal cases, *e.g.*, colour-blindness, jaundice, etc. The genesis of colour-sensations is complex and does not depend *merely* upon the kind of light-rays entering the eye.

an admittedly basic law that it be explained is implicitly to deny that it is basic and thus to deny the very premise of the argument. It is a request for explanation in a situation where by one's own admission no more explaining can be done.

Like so many others, this point may seem logically compelling but psychologically unsatisfying. Having heard the above argument, one may still feel inclined to ask, 'Why are the basic uniformities of the universe the way they are, and not some other way? Why should we have just *these* laws rather than other ones? I want an *explanation* of why they are as they are.' I must confess here, as an autobiographical remark, that I cannot help sharing this feeling: I want to ask why the laws of nature, being contingent, are as they are, even though I cannot conceive of what an explanation of this would be like, and even though by my own argument above the request for such an explanation is self-contradictory. The fact is, as we saw above, that why-questions have had answers so many times that we tend automatically to ask them here even when they can have no answers because we have ripped them out of the only context in which they have meaning — like the situation of the child who, being told what is above the table and above the ceiling of his room and above the house and above the earth, now asks what is above the universe. The question has now gone outside the context of meaningful discourse, and so has the request for the explanation of a basic law. We should remember: to explain is to explain *in terms of something,* and if *ex hypothesi* there is no longer any something for it to be explained in terms of, then the request for an explanation is self-contradictory: it demands on the one hand that you explain X in terms of a Y while insisting simultaneously that there is no Y.

SUGGESTED READINGS

Useful General Discussions

AYER, A. J. *The Problem of Knowledge.* New York: St. Martin's Press, 1956.

CHISHOLM, R. M. *Theory of Knowledge.* Englewood Cliffs, N.J.: Prentice-Hall, Inc., 1956.

Readings in the Theory of Knowledge

CANFIELD, J. V. and DONNELL, FRANKLIN H., eds. *Readings in the Theory of Knowledge.* New York: Appleton-Century-Crofts, 1964.

NAGEL, E. and BRANDT, R. *Meaning and Knowledge.* New York: Harcourt, Brace & World, 1965.

The Concept of an Analytic Statement

CARNAP, R. "Meaning and Synonymy in Natural Languages," *Philosophical Studies* VI, 1955. Excerpt in Nagel and Brandt.

GRICE, H. P. and STRAWSON, P. F. "In Defense of a Dogma," *Philosophical Review* 65 (1956). Excerpted in Nagel and Brandt.

KANT, I. *Critique of Pure Reason,* N. K. SMITH, trans. London: Macmillan, 1929. Excerpted in Canfield and Donnell, and in Pap and Edwards, *A Modern Introduction to Philosophy.* New York: The Free Press, 1965.

PAP, A. *Semantics and Necessary Truth,* New Haven: Yale University Press, 1958.

PUTNAM, H. "The Analytic and the Synthetic," Minnesota Studies in the Philosophy of Science, III, 1962.

QUINE, W. V. "Two Dogmas of Empiricism, in *From a Logical Point of View.* Cambridge, Mass.: Harvard University Press, 1953. Excerpt in Nagel and Brandt.

WHITE, M. "The Analytic and the Synthetic: An Untenable Dualism," in S. HOOK, ed., *John Dewey: Philosopher of Science and Freedom.*

Logical and Mathematical Truth

BRITTON, K., URMSON, J. O., and KNEALE, W. Symposium: "Are Necessary Truths True By Convention?" Supplementary Volume 20, Aristotelian Society, London, 1947.

CARNAP, R. *Foundations of Logic and Mathematics.* International Encyclopedia of United Science, Vol. I, No. 3. Chicago: University of Chicago Press, 1939.

CHISHOLM, R. M. "Reasons and the A Priori," in CHISHOLM, R. M., *et al. Philosophy.* Englewood Cliffs, N.J.: Prentice-Hall, Inc., 1964.

————. *Theory of Knowledge,* Chapter 5.

DEWEY, J. *The Quest for Certainty.* New York: Minton, Balch & Company, 1929.

HEMPEL, C. G. "Geometry and Empirical Science," *American Mathematical Monthly* 52 (1945) and "On the Nature of Mathematical Truth," *American Mathematical Monthly* 52 (1945), both reprinted in H. FEIGL and W. SELLARS, eds., *Readings in Philosophical Analysis.* New York: Appleton-Century-Crofts, Inc., 1949.

LEWIS, C. I. *An Analysis of Knowledge and Valuation.* LaSalle, Ill.: Open Court, 1946.

MALCOLM, N. "The Nature of Entailment," and "Are Necessary Propositions Really Verbal?" *Mind* 49 (1940).

NAGEL, E. "Logic Without Ontology," in Y. H. KRIKORIAN, ed. *Naturalism and the Human Spirit.* New York: Columbia University Press, 1944.

QUINE, W. V. "Carnap and Logical Truth," in P. A. SCHILPP, ed., *The Philosophy of Rudolf Carnap.* LaSalle, Ill.: Open Court, 1963.

REICHENBACH, H. *The Rise of Scientific Philosophy*. Berkeley: University of California Press, 1951.

RUSSELL, B. *The Problems of Philosophy*. New York: Henry Holt & Co., 1912, Chapter 7.

RYLE, G., LEWY, C., and POPPER, K. R. Symposium: "Why Are the Calculuses of Logic and Arithmetic Applicable to Reality?" Supplementary Volume 20, Aristotelian Society, London, 1946.

STRAWSON, P. F. *Introduction to Logical Theory*. New York: John Wiley & Sons, Inc., 1952, Chapter 1.

WAISSMAN, F. "Are There Alternative Logics?" *Proceedings*, The Aristotelian Society (1945-46).

Is There Synthetic A Priori Knowledge?

KANT, I. *Prolegomena to Any Future Metaphysics*. L. W. BECK, trans. New York: Liberal Arts Press, 1951. Excerpt in Nagel and Brandt.

———. *Critique of Pure Reason*. N. K. SMITH, trans. London: Macmillan & Co., Ltd., 1929. Excerpt in A. PAP and P. EDWARDS, eds., *A Modern Introduction to Philosophy*. New York: The Free Press, 1965.

LANGFORD, C. H. "A Proof that Synthetic A Priori Propositions Exist," *Journal of Philosophy*, Vol. 46 (1949).

LEIBNIZ, G. W. *Letter to Queen Sophie Charlotte*, 1702. Excerpt in Pap and Edwards, 608-611.

CHISHOLM, R. M. *Theory of Knowledge*. Englewood Cliffs, N.J.: Prentice-Hall, Inc. 87-90, and in CHISHOLM, R. M. *et al.*, *Philosophy*. Englewood Cliffs, N.J.: Prentice-Hall, Inc., 1964, 304-311.

PAP, A. "Are All Necessary Propositions Analytic?" *Philosophical Review* 58 (1949).

———. *Semantics and Necessary Truth*. New Haven: Yale University Press, 1958.

PEARS, D. F. "Incompatibilities of Color," in A. G. N. FLEW, *Logic and Language*, Second Series. Oxford: Basil Blackwell.

SCHLICK, M. "Is There a Factual A Priori?" in Feigl-Sellars, *Readings in Philosophical Analysis*, 277-294.

STOUT, G. F. "Self-Evidence," *Philosophy*, Vol. 9, 1934.

The Problem of Induction

BARKER, S. F. *Induction and Hypothesis*. Ithaca, N.Y.: Cornell University Press, 1957.

BLACK, M. *Language and Philosophy*. Ithaca, N.Y.: Cornell University Press, 1949, Chapter 3.

———. *Problems of Analysis*. Ithaca, N.Y.: Cornell University Press, 1954, 157-225.

BRAITHWAITE, R. B. *Scientific Explanation*. Cambridge: Cambridge University Press, 1953.

BURKS, A. "On the Presuppositions of Induction," *Review of Metaphysics*, VIII, 1955.

CARNAP, R. "The Aim of Inductive Logic," in E. NAGEL, P. SUPPES, and A. TARSKI, eds., *Logic, Methodology and Philosophy of Science*. Stanford, Calif.: Stanford University Press, 1962.

EDWARDS, P. "Bertrand Russell's Doubts About Induction," in A. G. N. FLEW, *Logic and Language*, First series. Oxford: Basil Blackwell, 1951.

GOODMAN, N. *Fact, Fiction, and Forecast*. Cambridge, Mass.: Harvard University Press, 1955, Chapter 3.

KNEALE, W. *Probability and Induction*. Oxford: Clarendon Press, 1949, 234-237.

SALMON, W. "Should We Attempt to Justify Induction?" *Philosophical Studies* 8 (1957). Excerpt in Nagel and Brandt.

————. "The Vindication of Induction," in H. FEIGL AND C. MAXWELL, eds., *Current Issues in the Philosophy of Science*. Holt, Rinehart and Winston, 1961.

WILLIAMS, D. *The Ground of Induction*. Cambridge, Mass.: Harvard University Press, 1947, Chapters 4 and 6.

Hypothetical Inference, Explanation, and Transcendent Theories

BARKER, S. F. *Induction and Hypothesis*. Ithaca, N.Y.: Cornell University Press, 1957, 106-200.

BECK, L. W. "Constructions and Inferred Entities," *Philosophy of Science* 17. (1950). Reprinted in H. FEIGL and M. BRODECK, eds., *Readings in the Philosophy of Science*. New York: Appleton-Century-Crofts, Inc., 1953.

HEMPEL, C. G. "A Theoretician's Dilemma," *University of Minnesota Studies in the Philosophy of Science*. Minneapolis: University of Minnesota Press, II, 1958, 37-87.

————. "The Function of General Laws in History," *Journal of Philosophy* 49 (1952).

HEMPEL, C. G. and OPPENHEIM, P. "The Logic of Explanation," *Philosophy of Science* 15 (1948). Reprinted in FEIGL and BRODBECK, eds., *Readings in the Philosophy of Science*.

MACH, E. "The Significance and Purpose of Natural Laws," trans. by F. Schick from *Erkenntnis and Irrtum*. (Leipzig: 1908), in A. DANTO and S. MORGENBESSER, eds., *Philosophy of Science*. Cleveland: The World Publishing Company, 1960.

NAGEL, E. *The Structure of Science*. New York: Harcourt, Brace & World, 1961.

POPPER, K. R. "Three Views Concerning Human Knowledge," in H. D. LEWIS, ed., *Contemporary British Philosophy*. New York: The Macmillan Company, 1956.

PUTNAM, H. "What Theories Are Not," in E. NAGEL, P. SUPPES, and A. TARSKI, eds., *Logic, Methodology and Philosophy of Science*. Stanford, Calif.: Stanford University Press, 1962.

SMART, J. J. C. *Philosophy and Scientific Realism*. New York: Humanities Press, 1963, Chapter 2.

TOULMIN, S. *Philosophy of Science*. London: Hutchinson's University Library, 1953, Chapters 2 and 4.

Part VI

PERCEIVING THE MATERIAL WORLD

INTRODUCTION

In the preceding chapter it was pointed out that most philosophers believe that there are some statements we can know to be true just by observation — statements describing what is observed. But it was pointed out that there has been controversy about which these are. Suppose, for instance, I am looking at a brick. I should then ordinarily say that I *observe* an object in front of me, that it is (say) red in color, that it has roughly rectangular surfaces, and (after feeling and lifting it) that it is relatively heavy and has smooth (but far from glassy-smooth) surfaces. May we say that these statements *do* describe what we observe, and that they can be viewed as premises of knowledge, requiring no support of evidence (and perhaps not admitting of any)? This is one question we must now discuss.

We must discuss it, however, in conjunction with two other important questions: first, the question as to what perceptual statements (e.g., "I see a red brick" or "I hear a whistle blowing") *mean* (either what we *do* mean by them, or what we *would* mean by them if we reflected carefully on the facts) or what kind of fact they assert; and, second, the question of how they may be justified if they are not self-evident. (If, in answer to the question stated in the first paragraph, we decide that they just describe what is observed, we shall presumably say they are self-evident and do not require any further justification or support, and hence this final question will not arise.)

The fact that forces us to notice complications is that we have to distinguish between what things *are* and how they *look* or *seem*. This distinction is especially obvious in the case of sound, and we may begin with this. Suppose I am standing in a station as a freight train goes through, and the engine's whistle blows as it passes. We want to say that in some sense the engineer and I, and a person a mile away, all hear the same sound, but there is obviously a sense in which we don't. For the engineer hears a sound with a

homogeneous pitch, whereas I hear first a rising and then a falling pitch
as the engine passes me. The engineer and I, again, have experiences which
differ from those of the man a mile away, since what we both hear is very
loud, while what he hears is relatively faint. We must concede that there
is some sense, then, in which the three of us do *not* hear the same sound,
since obviously one thing can't be both loud and faint, both homogeneous
in pitch and changing in pitch. Of course, the accepted explanation of the
differences is that what each of us hears is a function, at least in part, of the
state of vibration of the air in the vicinity of his ears; we distinguish this from
the source of the sound (the whistle blowing), which we think of as part
cause of the vibration going on around the ears of the various persons. In
view of all this, we could make our claims consistent if we said that we all
(the engineer and I, etc.) "hear the same sound" in the sense that each hears
something caused by the same event (the blowing of the whistle), but that
each of us hears a distinct sound different from what the others hear, in *a different sense* of "hear a sound," which we might identify by using the phrase
"hears a sound *directly*." One might then be tempted to say what is consistent
with what has been pointed out so far — that a person "hears directly" the
vibration around his ears. But a further complication makes this very inconvenient. For if my ears are stuffed with cotton, I do not hear a loud sound
even if I am standing near the tracks, so that the vibration around my ears is
very intense. There is some sense in which what I hear is then only a faint
sound, despite what is going on in the air around my ears. And, in this sense
of "hear a sound," what I hear is not even the vibration of the bones in my
ear; my ear may be in fine condition, but if the nerves connecting it with the
brain are defective, I shall hear nothing. Moreover, under certain conditions
I shall hear something (in a dream, hallucination) when there is *no* vibration
in my ears at all. In fact, if the proper portion of my brain is electrically stimulated during brain surgery, I hear a certain sort of sound, its kind depending
on the location and type of stimulus to the brain. It seems, then, that we must
recognize a sense of "hear a sound" such that hearing a sound in this sense is
logically independent of vibrations even in the eardrum.

What inferences must we draw from facts like these? First, clearly we
must distinguish between the sound we "hear" in the direct sense and the
physical source of sound in the external world; we cannot attribute to the
source all the qualities of the sound we hear directly. Second, what we hear
is a function of various things, but primarily of the auditory area of the brain;
we hear something of a certain sort if and only if our brain is in a certain typical state. As a consequence, it seems that we must say that if the observation-
premise of knowledge is a description of what we observe without inference
then in the present case the premise must be about what we *hear* "directly"
(and is a function of the state of our brain) and *not* about the qualities of a
physical process going on in something outside us (the whistle blowing). If
we hear something of a certain sort, we may have good and sufficient reasons
for saying we are hearing a diesel engine, or that we are hearing a jet plane,

but that we are is hardly a *premise,* a statement merely descriptive of observation. It further follows that, if we are to give an account of what it is to hear a whistle blowing, we must say something complicated enough to allow for all the distinctions we have been drawing.

The same distinctions must be made for vision, for the case of seeing a red brick or for seeing the sun, although at first this seems rather paradoxical. First, we have a good reason to think that if a luminous object passes us with a speed approaching the speed of light, it will look a different color from that it looks to a person travelling at the same speed; this is the reason why the spectra of distant nebulae, which are travelling away from us at high speed, are shifted toward the red end. Again, how an object looks obviously depends on things other than the object itself — in particular, on the kind of light which the object is reflecting and the kind of medium it traverses on the way to the eye. For example, the page of a telephone book will look very different to a man over fifty, when he has his glasses on, from how it will look to his naked eye. The presence of mirrors has a similar effect. How an object looks, then, depends on the kind of pattern of light rays which enters the lens of the eye; what a person sees is a function of this and not of the characteristics of the object, except as they influence this. Indeed, an object may not exist at all but will be seen if a typical pattern of light rays enters the eye; for instance, a distant star may have blown up and ceased to be luminous a hundred years ago, but we still see it up to the point when the light rays cease to arrive as a result of the occurrence of that past event. But neither is how things look a function just of the pattern of light rays which enters the eye. If the optic nerve is damaged, we see nothing at all; or if the retinal cortex is damaged, we may see only part of the object we are looking at. How things look is further influenced by cortical processes which we know little about. For instance, the moon appears much larger at the horizon than overhead; whether an object looks white or dark gray depends on the *relative* amount of light being received from it as contrasted with its environment; and so on. Moreover, we have visual experiences in dreams and hallucinations even if our eyes are shut and there is virtually no pattern of light stimulus from the external world at all. How things look is apparently a function of the kind of process going on in the visual cortex.

What, again, must we infer from this? First we must distinguish between what properties something has and how it looks (the telephone book may not be blurred, but it may look blurred); indeed it may look as if there is something of a certain sort (say, in an hallucination or dream), when there is nothing there at all. Second, what we seem to see is a function of many things, but primarily of the visual cortex; we seem to see something of a certain sort if and only if our visual cortex is in a certain typical state. Hence, if our observation-premises are to be descriptions of what we observe without inference, it seems they must be about how things *look* or how it looks as if things are (which is a function of the state of the brain), and *not* about things and their qualities. Furthermore, if we are to give an account of what it is to see a red brick, we must say something complicated enough to allow for all these distinctions.

Locke and Berkeley used the word "ideas" to refer to these brain-dependent entities which we observe, statements about which, it seems, must be the premises of our knowledge about the material world. Other philosophers have used the terms "sense data," or "the given," or "sensa" to refer to these same experiences. We do not really need any technical terminology to make the distinction, however. We can say it "looks" or "seems" or "sounds" or "feels" to me *as if* so-and-so (without implying that anything is or isn't the way it looks, or even that there is anything there at all) and this will draw the necessary contrast with what we want to say about what the world around us really is. Thus, a person who has taken mescal in a strange place may describe how things look to him without knowing how they are, and without knowing even whether he is describing things that are not there at all.

Philosophers have often used the term "naive realist" to describe the views of a person who makes no distinction between things and their properties on the one hand and how things look on the other, and who thinks no such distinction is necessary. He thinks things are just as they look when he is looking at them, and that they continue to exist just as they look when he is not looking at them. The naive realist is generally viewed as occupying a hopelessly untenable position — and he certainly is when he says that the real telephone book is both what it looks to be to the older man without his glasses and to the younger man who does not need them. Can the same page be both a blurry mass of ink and have sharply defined letters? Some philosophers have defended this position seriously, but, needless to say, it has turned out that an "object" is very different from what we ordinarily think it to be — an infinitely complex set of different "sensa," each of which is visible (audible, etc.) only to a very special kind of person. Such philosophers are sometimes called "epistemological monists," because they think that real objects and their qualities are one and the same thing as appearances or the way they look.

The first of our readings in this section, by Broad, is concerned primarily with making clear the necessity of a contrast between things and how they look (or things and sense data) and with making clear the impossibility of defending the naive realist's position.

The second reading, by John Locke, defends a view that will seem very natural to scientists at the present time. Locke regarded sense experiences ("ideas") as the *effects* of physical processes that begin (in the case of vision) with the interaction between the surface of an object and light rays and end with events, the optic nerve, the brain, or (for him) finally, in consciousness. Locke believed, however, that there is a correlation between the external world and the conscious events (sense data, ideas) produced by our bodily interaction with it sufficiently close so that for practical purposes we need not distinguish the two; we can get along very well if we identify visual sense data with the surfaces of things, for if we guide the sense data of our feet so as to go between the sense data of pieces of furniture, we shall not fall down over the furniture, etc. Our sense data "represent" the external world to us reasonably accurately. Locke distinguished, however, between some properties of things, in respect of which they *resemble* sense experiences and which he called "primary qualities," and others that he called "secondary qualities," which do not resemble sense experiences. Number, shape, size, position, and velocity, for instance, he attributed to bodies, and he argued that these features of bodies resemble our sense experiences; for visual data do have number, shape, size, state of motion, etc., although not necessarily exactly those of the body we are looking at. (A circular table viewed from an angle will look elliptical and, so far, different from the way it is; but *some* objects *are* elliptical, just as some visual sense data are.) On the other hand, color and warmth are properties that bodies have, but, he thought, the properties that color and warmth are in bodies do not resemble the warmth or color of sense experiences. For what it is for a body to be red is for its surface to be such (in virtue of the spatial disposition of its constituent small particles) as to reflect predominantly red light, so that it has the causal property of ability to produce red sense experiences in normal people; but this property is a much more complex thing than the quality red that pertains to our sensory experiences, and which the naive realist attributes to the external objects. So, Locke thought, objects that are red are not red in the same sense in which sensory experiences are red, and therefore do not *resemble* sense experiences in this respect.

According to Locke it is logically possible that a person should have the sense experiences he does, even if there were no physical objects at all, or at any rate none resembling in any respect a person's sensory experiences. This fact raised the question as to what reason he could give for claiming to know that there *are* any enduring physical things or that they have properties of certain sorts. Locke's answer is given in the concluding pages of the reading. It is not fully worked out, but the main idea is that the supposition that there are such is the best explanation of the detailed order of our sense experiences. Locke has to say, then, that we know what our sensory experiences are like directly, but that we know what the material world is like only through hypothetical inference. (Locke did not claim that people go through conscious processes of inference every time they think they see a material object of a certain sort.)

Berkeley agrees with Locke that our sense data ("ideas") must be the effects of something outside ourselves, but he comes to an entirely different conclusion about the kind of thing this something is. He thinks it cannot be something with Locke's primary qualities and these alone. He offers various reasons for this: the reasons Locke offered for thinking that secondary qualities resemble nothing in the object apply equally convincingly for the primary qualities; it is inconceivable (really, unimaginable is all he shows) that anything should have primary qualities but not qualities like color (etc.), which Locke had argued are only in the mind; an object with primary qualities could not possibly be a cause of anything; the whole idea of something having qualities like those with which we are familiar in sense experience is unintelligible; and so on. Nor did he think that Locke's view has any explanatory value; no one has ever shown how the existence of a material world explains the occurrence of sensations, and, since we do not suppose the hypothesis is necessary to explain our dreams, neither is it necessary to explain our waking experiences. (We have to see these reasons put in Berkeley's words in order to estimate with accuracy how much force, if any, they carry.) But Berkeley's main point is that Locke has misunderstood what it is to be a material object. Actually, what we mean when we assert that there exists, say, a penny in front of us is not that there is some invisible object *causing* sense experiences, as Locke thought. What it is for there to be a penny is for there to be a certain *order* in our *sense experiences*. That is, for there to be a penny is for us to see a circular copper-colored patch of a certain size in certain circumstances, see a small patch in certain other circumstances (when normally we would say we were further away), see an elliptial patch in other circumstances (when we look at it from the side), have a tactual datum of a certain kind in certain circumstances (when we touch the penny), and so on. Berkeley thus called attention to the fact that whenever there is a physical object of a certain kind, a certain regularity obtains among the sensory experiences of certain persons (in the vicinity). Locke, of course, would not have denied this; but Berkeley's novel proposal was to suggest that what it is for there to be a physical object of a certain kind is just for this kind of order to obtain among sense experiences.

One might ask how it is consistent for Berkeley to hold both that our sense experiences have to have a *cause* and that all an object is, is a certain order among sense experiences. Berkeley's answer is that our sense experiences are caused by a *mind*. We know that experiences *can* be caused, in principle, by minds, since we produce them ourselves in daydreaming and thinking. His supposition is that our sense experiences must be caused by a more powerful mind than our own, but a mind essentially like our own except for its much greater intelligence and power. This mind is God. God brings it about that there is the order in our sensory experience which makes it convenient to talk as if there were material things; he is also responsible for the order that makes natural science possible. God is both the creator and preserver of the "material universe," although there is in a sense no material universe in addition to the experience of finite minds.

Berkeley's proposal raises an interesting question: if we construe both Locke's conception of an extended material world and Berkeley's conception of an omnipotent God as alternative competing hyotheses purportedly explaining our sensory experiences, which one is the "better" or "simpler" hypothesis? Berkeley could say that his thesis is simpler because Locke believed in the existence of a God who created the material universe, with the result that Locke asserted the existence of everything Berkeley asserted, but in addition of a material world.

We saw that Berkeley argued that Locke's reasoning cannot show that qualities like shape and size really belong to external objects; a natural extension of this line of thought is to suggest that our sensory experience must have a cause but that we can have no knowledge of what this cause is like. Such a view has been held by various philosophers, including Immanuel Kant (at least according to some passages). Another possibility is one that Berkeley dismissed: the cause of sense experiences is to be found in the order of sense experiences themselves. Berkeley dismissed this suggestion on the ground that sense data ("ideas") are by definition only what is observed and therefore cannot have any causal powers they are not observed to have. Berkeley overlooked the possibility, however, that to say that a sense datum of a certain kind is caused may be merely to say that there is a lawful order in nature, such that a sense datum of this kind occurs when and only when certain other sense data could be obtained. This possibility was exploited by the *Phenomenalists* (in one sense of this term).

J. S. Mill, in the reading below, represents a phenomenalist position, which in essence is a development of Berkeley's point that what it is for there to be a physical object is for there to be a certain order in sense experiences. (Insofar, Berkeley might be called a phenomenalist.) The phenomenalist omits all the somewhat metaphysical speculations of both Locke and Berkeley about anything outside experience. The phenomenalist asserts that the only thing which we know to exist, in addition to the experiences of persons, is the fact that certain other experiences *would have occurred* under other circumstances. And this we know by induction. For instance, suppose I light a fire, go out, and return to find a heap of ashes. The phenomenalist says that we know that, had I *not* gone out but watched the fire, I would have seen the fire burn and the heap of wood slowly be reduced to ashes (that is, the order of experiences which does occur when we watch.) We know that I *would have* seen this, had I *not* gone out. And this I know on the basis of past experiences of what happens when I start a fire and do not go out. So, the phenomenalist says, what it is for there to be a material object (or process) of a certain kind, is for certain sense experiences to occur, and it to be the case that certain other experiences *would have occurred if* there had been observers of a certain kind present to have them. In this sense, an object of a certain kind (or a process) consists of *actual* and *possible* sensory experiences. Having said this, the phenomenalist can go on, if he wishes (phenomenalists do not always take this line, and there has been obscurity in their writings at this point), to say that individual sense experiences have causes, indeed, causes which are *material objects in his sense;* and to say this is to say, in part, that a certain individual sense experience would not have occurred had it not been true that certain other experiences either occurred or would have occurred in certain circumstances.

The phenomenalist claims a considerable intellectual economy over both Locke and Berkeley; he gets along with the assertion only of facts that they too assert (that certain sense experiences would have occurred in certain conditions), affirmed for reasons of simple enumerative induction from past experience; he avoids the use of hypothetical inferences to the existence of either material things or a God — things of a kind which in principle we cannot observe directly.

The phenomenalist position has attracted a great many philosophers in the last century and a half. It has been the staple view of contemporary radical empiricism and logical positivism, which have characterized the views of Locke and Berkeley as "meaningless" affirmations of a metaphysical kind. It may seem to be out of line with modern physics, which has been prolific in its assertion of the existence of different kinds of unseen small particles; but the phenomenalist takes these assertions to be, in the end, assertions of no more than that certain sensory experience (e.g., of cloud-chamber pictures, etc.) would occur in certain conditions. Phenomenalism thus looks like the hard-headed nonmetaphysical view suitable for a scientific age. And this is what its proponents have claimed for it.

Unfortunately, phenomenalism has its difficulties. The phenomenalist (and this goes for the phenomenalist part of Berkeley) says that what it is for there to be an object of a certain kind is for certain sense experiences to occur or to be obtainable. This has been challenged; the phenomenalist has been invited to specify *exactly which* sense experiences will occur or be obtainable if and only if there is a physical object of a certain sort. The phenomenalist in effect says that talk of material things can be replaced by talk of order in actual or possible sense experiences without loss. The objection is that this is just not true, that in principle no such replacement would occur. The reading by R. M. Chisholm represents one important line of objection of this sort. His proposal is that such a replacement of "There is a green pencil on my desk in front of me" will work only if one's sense experiences are a simple function of the objects in front of one. But they aren't; the sense experiences we have are a function not only of what objects are in the vicinity, but of the character of the intervening medium and the states of our own sense organs and brains. It does not follow from the fact that there is a green pencil in front of me that I shall have a sense datum of a certain kind in any specifiable circumstances (that is, ones that can be specified by referring to the order of my sense experiences); nor, indeed, does it follow from the occurrence, actual or possible, of any sequence of sense experiences, that there is a green pencil in front of me. And if this is so, phenomenalism is utterly indefensible. On account of objections of this sort, the number of supporters of phenomenalism has dwindled greatly in recent years.

What then? One view that seems to be gaining supporters is that an essentially Lockean view can be refurbished, stated more sharply and consistently, and given more support. This line is adopted by A. O. Lovejoy. He states, much more fully than Locke did, the kind of reasoning which Locke could have used to justify belief in a material world rather like our sense experience (at least in point of primary qualities), as an explanation of our experiences.

Another possibility that attracts a good many philosophers is that of attacking the conception from which the whole history of the theory of perception took its start: the conception of sense data, the given, or "ideas." If this conception were shown to be inadmissible, the various historical theories could not even be stated. At least they would be disposed of. This is the line taken by W. H. F. Barnes in Reading 61 and adverted to by C. D. Broad under the title of the Multiple Relation Theory. This line of attack has been adopted by some of the leading British "linguistic" philosophers of the past few years. Unfortunately their positive view has not received a systematic statement — partly because they tend to think no philosophical "theory" is called for here at all. We should note that the sense datum philosopher could possibly meet all the charges contained in Barnes's paper; it is very difficult indeed to show that the conception of a sense datum is inadmissible however many speculative philosophical theories one might kill off by such a showing.

We may now return briefly to a question raised in Part V: What are the ultimate premises of knowledge which we may accept without further support because they merely describe what we can observe? Most traditional philosophers would say these are statements about sense experiences, *not* statements about material things at all. "I see a green pencil in front of me" is not merely a description of what I observe; "I see a green elongated patch, which looks like a pencil" might be. The critics of the sense datum concept obviously cannot accept this view. What they do accept, and why, we cannot consider here. Some of them apparently reject the idea that knowledge has to have any premises that are reasonably believed independently of support by other knowledge.

We now know, also, the main traditional answers that have been given to the questions raised in the second paragraph of these introductory remarks. First, the question of what it means to say "I see a red brick" (or, perhaps, what a person would mean by it if he had reflected on the facts) would be answered by Locke as: "I am having a visual sense experience caused by something which has the secondary quality redness," and so on. Berkeley's answer probably would be: "I am having a visual sense experience which belongs to a brickish family of sense data and is caused by God." He would go on to say that what it is for a sense datum to belong to a brickish family is for it to be the case that under such-and-such conditions a certain further sense datum would be obtained by the observer, and so on. The phenomenalist's answer would be the same, except for the omission of reference to causation by God. Second, to the question as to how such statements can be justified (since, on the view of all these writers, they are not self-evident), Locke would reply that the statement can be justified as being the best hypothesis explaining why I am having the kind of sense experience I am having, in view of other experiences I have had in the past which must also be explained. Berkeley and the phenomenalist would justify asserting what they take "I see a red brick" to mean by appeal to past experience in which similar sense experiences were associated with certain other sense experiences, and the principle of enumerative inference; and Berkeley would go on to justify the affirmation of causation by God by appeal to some general principle about all changes requiring a cause, along with further other principles about what kinds of things can be causes. How Berkeley would defend these last principles is another matter.

55

THE CONCEPT
OF SENSE DATA

Charlie Dunbar Broad

C. D. Broad (1887-   ) was Professor of Philosophy at Cambridge University until his retirement.

The Traditional Notion of a bit of Matter. — When we ask what is meant by a bit of Matter the question is itself ambiguous. In one sense a complete answer to it would be a complete theory of Matter, and this could only be made, if at all, at the very end of our discussion. This, however, is not the sense in which I am asking the question here. All that I am asking is: "What is the irreducible minimum of properties which practically everybody would agree that an object must possess if it is to be called a bit of Matter?" I think that science and common-sense would agree that at least the following conditions must be fulfilled: (i) Its existence and properties must be independent of the minds that happen to observe it, and it must be capable of being observed by many minds. This characteristic may be summed up by saying that Matter is neutral as between various observers, or is "public" — to use a convenient word of Mr. Russell's. This distinguishes Matter sharply from any ordinary conscious state of mind. . . .

(ii) A bit of Matter is supposed to be neutral, not only between different observers, but also to be in a certain way neutral as between several senses of the same observer. We are said to see, hear, and feel a bell. This sort of neutrality is not supposed to be complete. The shape and size of the bell are indeed supposed to be in some way common to sight and touch. As regards its sensible qualities the view of common-sense is that any bit of Matter combines a number of these, and that different senses are needed to reveal different sensible qualities. Thus sight, and it alone, makes us aware of the colours of bodies; touch, and it alone, makes us aware of their temperatures; and so on. But it is part of the ordinary view of a piece of Matter that all

From C. D. Broad, *Scientific Thought*, 1923. Published by Routledge and Kegan Paul Ltd., London, and Hillary House Publishers Ltd., New York. Reprinted by permission of the publishers.

these various sensible qualities co-exist in it, whether the requisite senses be in action to reveal them all or not. If we first only look at a body, and then shut our eyes and go up to it and feel it, it is not supposed that it had no temperature on the first occasion and no colour on the second.

(iii) These two properties of publicity, as between different observers, and neutrality, as between the various senses of a single observer, are closely connected with a third feature which is held to be characteristic of Matter. Bits of Matter are supposed to persist with very little change, whether anyone happens to observe them or not, and to pursue their own affairs and interact with each other, regardless of our presence and absence.

(iv) This brings us to the fourth characteristic of Matter. It is commonly held to be part of what we mean by a bit of Matter that it shall have a more or less permanent shape and size, and that it shall have a position in Space, and be capable of moving from one position to another. It is admitted that bits of Matter are constantly changing their shapes, sizes, and positions; but it is held that they do this through their interactions with each other and not through any change in our acts of observation, and that in all their changes they continue to have *some* shape, size and position. If it could be shown that nothing in the world actually has such properties as these, it would commonly be held that the existence of Matter had been disproved, even though there were public, independent, and persistent objects. . . .

The Notion of Sensible Appearance. — I have now tried to point out what is the irreducible minimum of properties which ordinary people consider must be possessed by anything if it is to count as a piece of Matter. I have also pointed out, by anticipation, that the history of philosophy shows there to be a great difficulty in holding that there are any entities which fulfill all these conditions in a literal sense. . . . We must now consider what facts make it hard to believe that anything obeys all four conditions in at all a literal sense.

The difficulty arises because of the group of facts which we sum up by saying that it is necessary to distinguish between things as they are and things as they seem to us, or between physical reality and sensible appearance. Difficulties always arise when two sets of properties apparently belong to the same object, and yet are apparently incompatible with each other. Now the difficulty here is to reconcile the supposed neutrality, persistence, and independence of a physical object with the obvious differences between its various sensible appearances to different observers at the same moment, and to the same observer at different moments between which it is held not to have undergone any physical change. We know, *e.g.*, that when we lay a penny down on a table and view it from different positions it generally looks more or less elliptical in shape. The eccentricity of these various appearances varies as we move about, and so does the direction of their major axes. Now we hold that the penny, at which we say that we were looking all the time, has not changed; and that it is round, and not elliptical in shape. This is, of course, only one example out of millions. It would be easy to offer much wilder ones; but it is simple and obvious, and involves no complications about a transmitting medium; so we will start with it as a typical case to discuss.

Now there is nothing in the mere ellipticity or the mere variation, taken by itself, to worry us. The difficulty arises because of the incompatibility between the apparent shapes and the supposed real shape, and between the change in the appearances and the supposed constancy of the physical object. We need not at present ask *why* we believe that there is a single physical object with these characteristics, which appears to us in all these different ways. It is a fact that we do believe it. It is an equally certain fact that the penny does look different as we move about. The difficulty is to reconcile the different appearances with the supposed constancy of the penny, and the ellipticity of most of the appearances with the supposed roundness of the penny. It is probable that at first sight the reader will not see much difficulty in this. He will be inclined to say that we can explain these various visual appearances by the laws of perspective, and so on. This is not a relevant answer. It is quite true that we can *predict what particular appearance* an object will present to an observer, when we know the shape of the object and its position with respect to the observer. But this is not the question that is troubling us at present. Our question is as to the compatibility of these changing elliptical appearances, however they may be correlated with other facts in the world, with the supposed constancy and roundness of the physical object.

Now what I call *Sensible Appearance* is just a general name for such facts as I have been describing. It is important, here as always, to state the *facts* in a form to which everyone will agree, before attempting any particular *analysis* of them, with which it is certain that many people will violently disagree. The fundamental fact is that we constantly make such judgments as: "This *seems to me* elliptical, or red, or hot," as the case may be, and that about the truth of these judgments we do not feel the least doubt. We may, however, at the same time doubt or positively disbelieve that this *is* elliptical, or red, or hot. I may be perfectly certain at one and the same time that I have the peculiar experience expressed by the judgment: "This looks elliptical to me," and that in fact the object is not elliptical but is round.

I do not suppose that anyone, on reflection, will quarrel with this statement of fact. The next question is as to the right way to analyze such facts; and it is most important not to confuse the facts themselves with any particular theory as to how they ought to be analysed. We may start with a negative remark, which seems to me to be true, and is certainly of the utmost importance if it be true. Appearance is *not* merely mistaken *judgment* about physical objects. When I judge that a penny looks elliptical I am not mistakenly ascribing elliptical shape to what is in fact round. Sensible appearances *may* lead me to make a mistaken judgment about physical objects, but they *need* not, and, so far as we know, commonly do not. My certainty that the penny looks elliptical exists comfortably alongside of my conviction that it is round. But a mistaken judgment that the penny *is* elliptical would not continue to exist after I knew that the penny was really round. The plain fact is then that "looking elliptical to me" stands for a peculiar experience, which, whatever the right analysis of it may be, is not just a mistaken judgment about the shape of the penny.

Appearance then cannot be described as mistaken judgment about the properties of some physical object. How are we to describe it, and can we analyse it? Two different types of theory seem to be possible, which I will call respectively the *Multiple Relation Theory*, and the *Object Theory* of sensible appearance. The Multiple Relation Theory takes the view that "appearing to be so and so" is a unique kind of relation between an object, a mind, and a characteristic. (This is a rough statement, but it will suffice for the present.) On this type of theory to say that the penny looks elliptical to me is to say that a unique and not further analysable relation of "appearing" holds between the penny, my mind, and the general characteristic of ellipticity. The essential point for us to notice at present about theories of this kind is that they do not imply that we are aware of *anything* that *really is* elliptical when we have the experience which we express by saying that the penny looks elliptical to us. Theories of this type have been suggested lately by Professor Dawes Hicks and by Dr. G. E. Moore. So far, they have not been worked out in any great detail, but they undoubtedly deserve careful attention.

Theories of the Object type are quite different. They do not involve a unique and unanalysable multiple relation of "appear*ing*," but a peculiar kind of object — an "appear*ance*." Such objects, it is held, actually *do have* the characteristics which the physical object *seems to have*. Thus the Object Theory analyses the statement that the penny looks to me elliptical into a statement which involves the actual existence of an elliptical object, which stands in a certain cognitive relation to me on the one hand, and in another relation, yet to be determined, to the round penny. This type of theory, though it has been much mixed up with irrelevant matter, and has never been clearly stated and worked out till our own day, is of respectable antiquity. The doctrine of "representative ideas" is the traditional and highly muddled form of it. It lies at the basis of such works as Russell's *Lowell Lectures on the External World*. In this book I shall deliberately confine myself to this type of theory, and shall try to state it clearly, and work it out in detail.

The Theory of Sensa

I propose now to state more fully the theory that appearances are a peculiar kind of objects, and to consider what sort of objects they must be. The reader will bear in mind throughout the whole of the long story which follows that there is a totally different view of sensible appearance, viz., the Multiple Relation Theory, and that this may quite possibly be true. In this book I shall leave it wholly aside. On the theory that we are now going to discuss, whenever a penny looks to me elliptical, what really happens is that I am aware of an object which is, in fact elliptical. This object is connected in some specially intimate way with the round physical penny, and for this reason is called an appearance *of* the penny. It really is elliptical, and for this reason the penny is said to look *elliptical*. We may generalise this theory of sensible appearance as follows: Whenever I truly judge that *x* appears to me to have the sensible quality *q*, what happens is that I am directly aware of a certain object *y*, which (*a*) really does have the quality *q*, and (*b*) stands in some peculiarly intimate relation, yet to be determined, to *x*. (At the present stage, for all that we know, *y* might sometimes be identical with *x*, or might be literally a part of *x*.) Such objects as *y* I am going to call *Sensa*. Thus, when I look at a penny from the side, what happens, on the present theory, is at least this: I have a sensation, whose object is an elliptical, brown sensum; and this sensum is related in some specially intimate way to a certain round physical object, viz., the penny.

Now I think it must at least be admitted that the sensum theory is highly plausible. When I look at a penny from the side I am certainly aware of *something*; and it is certainly plausible to hold that this something is elliptical in the same plain sense in which a suitably bent piece of wire, looked at from straight above, is elliptical. If, in fact, nothing elliptical is before my mind, it is very hard to understand why the penny should seem *elliptical* rather than of any other shape. I do not now regard this argument as absolutely conclusive, because I am inclined to think that the Multiple Relation theory can explain these facts also. But it is at least a good enough argument to make the sensum theory well worth further consideration.

Assuming that when I look at a penny from the side I am directly aware of something which is in fact elliptical, it is clear that this something cannot be identified with the penny, if the latter really has the characteristics that it is commonly supposed to have. The penny is supposed to be round, whilst the sensum is elliptical. Again, the penny is supposed to keep the same shape and size as we move about, whilst the sensa alter in shape and size. Now one and the same thing cannot, at the same time and in the same sense, be round and elliptical. Nor can one and the same thing at once change its shape and keep its shape unaltered, if "shape" be used in the same sense in both statements. Thus it is certain that, if there be sensa, they cannot in general be identified with the physical objects of which they are the appearances, if these literally have the properties commonly assigned to them. On the other hand, all that I ever come to know about physical objects and their qualities seems to be based upon the qualities of the sensa that I become aware of in sense-perception. If the visual sensa were not elliptical and did not vary in certain ways as I move about, I should not judge that I was seeing a round penny.

The distinction between sensum and physical object can perhaps be made still clearer by taking some wilder examples. Consider, *e.g.,* the case of looking at a stick which is half in water and half in air. We say that it looks bent. And we certainly do not mean by this that we mistakenly judge it to be bent; we generally make no such mistake. We are aware of an object which is very much like what we should be aware of if we were looking at a stick with a physical kink in it, immersed wholly in air. The most obvious analysis of the facts is that, when we judge that a straight stick *looks* bent, we are aware of an object which really *is* bent, and which is related in a peculiarly intimate way to the physically straight stick. The relation cannot be that of identity; since the same thing cannot at once be bent and straight, in the same sense of these words. If there be *nothing* with a kink in it before our minds at the moment, why should we think then of kinks at all, as we do when we say that the stick looks bent? No doubt we can quite well mistakenly *believe* a property to be present which is really absent, when we are dealing with something that is only known to us indirectly, like Julius Caesar or the North Pole. But in our example we are dealing with a concrete visible object, which is bodily present to our senses; and it is very hard to understand how we could seem to ourselves to *see* the property of bentness exhibited in a concrete instance, if in fact *nothing* was present to our minds that possessed that property.

As I want to make the grounds for the sensum theory as clear as possible, I will take one more example. Scientists often assert that physical objects are not "really" red or hot. We are not at present concerned with the truth or falsehood of this strange opinion, but only with its application to our present problem. Let us suppose then, for the sake of argument, that it is true. When a scientist looks at a penny stamp or burns his mouth with a potato he has exactly the same sort of experience as men of baser clay, who know nothing of the scientific theories of light and heat. The visual experience seems to be adequately described by saying that each of them is aware of a red patch of approximately square shape. If such patches be not in fact red, and if people be not in fact aware of such patches, where could the notion of red or of any other colour have come from? The scientific theory of colour would have nothing to explain, unless people really are aware of patches under various circumstances which really do have different colours. The scientists would be in the position of Mr. Munro's duchess, who congratulated herself that unbelief had become impossible, as the Liberal Theologians had left us nothing to disbelieve in. Thus we seem forced to the view that there are at least hot and coloured sensa; and, if we accept the scientific view that physical objects are neither hot nor coloured, it will follow that sensa cannot be identified with physical objects.

The reader may be inclined to say, "After all, these sensa are not real; they are mere appearances, so why trouble about them?" The answer is that you do not get rid of anything by labelling it "appearance." Appearances are as real in their own way as anything else. If an appearance were nothing at all, nothing would appear, and if nothing appeared, there would be nothing for scientific theories to account for. To put the matter in another way: Words like *real* and *reality* are ambiguous. A round penny and an elliptical visual sensum are not real in precisely the same sense. But both are real in the most general sense that a complete inventory of the universe must mention the one as much as the other. No doubt the kind of reality which is to be ascribed to appearances will vary with the particular type of theory as to the nature of sensible appearance that we adopt. On the present theory an appearance is a sensum, and a sensum is a particular existent, though it may be a short-lived one. On the Multiple Relation theory appearances have a very different type of reality. But *all* possible theories have to admit the reality, *in some sense*, of appearances; and therefore it is no objection to any particular theory that it ascribes a sort of reality to appearances.

I hope that I have now made fairly clear the grounds on which the sensum theory of sensible appearance has been put forward. Closely connected with it is a theory about the perception of physical objects, and we may sum up the whole view under discussion as follows: Under certain conditions I have states of mind called sensations. These sensations have objects, which are always concrete particular existents, like coloured or hot patches, noises, smells, etc. Such objects are called sensa. Sensa have properties, such as shape, size, hardness, colour, loudness, coldness, and so on. The existence of such sensa, and their presence to our minds in sensation, lead us to judge that a physical object exists and is present to our senses. To this physical object we ascribe various properties. These properties are not in general identical with those of the sensum which is before our minds at the moment. For instance, the *elliptical* sensum makes us believe in the existence of a *round* physical penny. Nevertheless, all the properties that we do ascribe to physical objects are based upon and correlated with the properties that actually characterise our sensa. The sensa that are connected with a physical object *x* in a certain specially intimate way are called the appearances of that object to those observers who sense these sensa. The properties which *x* is said to *appear to* have are the properties which those sensa that are *x*'s appearances *really do* have. Of course, the two properties may happen to be the same, *e.g.*, when I look straight down on a penny, both the physical object and the visual appearance are round. Generally, however, there is only a correlation between the two.

It follows from this theory that sensa cannot appear to have properties which they do not really have, though there is no reason why they should not have more properties than we do or can notice in them. This point perhaps needs a little more elaboration, since a good deal of nonsense has been talked by opponents of the sensum theory in this connexion. We must distinguish between failing to notice what is present in an object and "noticing" what is not present in an object. The former presents no special difficulty. There may well be in any object much which is too minute and obscure for us to recognise distinctly. Again, it is obvious that we may sense an object without necessarily being aware of all its relations even to another object that we sense at the same time. Still more certain is it that we may sense an object without being aware of all its relations to some other object which we are not sensing at the time. Consequently, there is no difficulty whatever in supposing that sensa may be much more differentiated than we think them to be, and that two sensa may really differ in quality when we think that they are exactly alike. Arguments such as Stumpf's render it practically certain that the latter possibility is in fact realised.

The real difficulty is when we seem to be directly aware of some property in an object, and this property is not really present and is perhaps incompatible with others which are present. This is the kind of difficulty that the sensum theory is put forward to meet. We seem to recognise elliptical shape in the penny, when the penny really has the incompatible quality of roundness. The solution which the sensum theory offers is to "change the subject." *Something,* it admits, is elliptical, and something is round; but they are not the same something. What is round is the penny, what is elliptical is the sensum. Now, clearly, this would be no solution, if the same sort of difficulty were to break out in sensa themselves. In that case we should need to postulate appearances of appearances, and so on indefinitely.

We must hold, as regards positive sensible qualities which characterise a sensum as a whole and do not involve relations to other sensa, that a sensum is at least all that it appears to be. Now, so far as I know, there is no evidence to the contrary. Some people have thought that arguments like Stumpf's raised this difficulty; but that is simply a mistake. Stumpf's argument deals merely with the relation of qualitative likeness and difference between different sensa, and shows that we may think that two of them are exactly alike when there is really a slight qualitative or quantitative difference between them. This has no tendency to prove that we ever find a positive non-relational quality in a sensum, which is not really there.

Next, we must remember that attributes which involve a negative factor often have positive names. A man might quite well think, on inspecting one of his sensa, that it was exactly round and uniformly red. And he might well be mistaken. But then, "exactly round" means "with no variation of curvature," and "uniformly red" means "with no variation of shade from one part to another." Now universal negative judgments like these can never be guaranteed by mere inspection; and so, in such cases, the man is not "seeing properties that are not there" in the sense in which he would be doing so if a round sensum appeared to him to be elliptical. To sum up, it is no objection to the sensum theory that a sensum may seem to be *less* differentiated than it is; it would be a fatal objection if a sensum ever seemed *more* differentiated than it is; but we have no evidence that the latter ever happens.

Before going further we must remove a baseless prejudice which is sometimes felt against the sensum theory. It is often objected that we are not aware of sensa and their properties, as a rule, unless we specially look for them. It is a fact that it often needs a good deal of persuasion to make a man believe that, when he looks at a penny from the side, it seems elliptical to him. And I am afraid that very often, when he is persuaded, it is not by his own direct inspection (which is the only relevant evidence in such a matter); but by some absurd and irrelevant argument that the area of his retina affected by the light from the penny, is an oblique projection of a circle, and is therefore an ellipse. Accordingly, it is argued that we have no right to believe that such a man is directly sensing an object which is, in fact, elliptical. To this objection a partial answer has already been given, by implication. It is only when we are looking at a penny almost normally that any doubt is felt of the ellipticity of the sensum; and, in that case, the sensum is, in fact, very nearly round. Now we have seen that it is no objection to our theory that a sensum which is not quite round should be thought to be exactly round, though it would be an objection if an exactly round sensum seemed to be elliptical. The reason, of course, is that an ellipse, with its variable curvature, is a more differentiated figure than a circle, with its uniform curvature. There is no difficulty in the fact that we overlook minute differentiations that are really present in our sensa; difficulties would only arise if we seemed to notice distinctions that are not really present.

Apart, however, from this special answer, a more general reply can be made to the type of objection under discussion. The whole argument rests on a misunderstanding of the view about perception which the sensum theory holds. If the theory were that, in perceiving a penny, a man first becomes aware of a sensum, then notices that it is elliptical, and then infers from this fact and the laws of perspective that he is looking at a round physical object, the argument would be fatal to the theory. But this is quite obviously not what happens. Perceptual judgments are indeed *based upon* sensa and their properties to this extent, that if we were not aware of a sensum we should not now judge that any physical object is present to our senses, and that if this sensum had different properties we should ascribe different properties to the physical object. But the relation between the sensum and its properties, on the one hand, and the perceptual judgment about the physical object, on the other, is not that of *inference*. The best analogy that we can offer to the relation between our sensing of a sensum and our perceiving a physical object, is to be found in the case of reading a book in a familiar language. What interests us as a rule is the meaning of the printed words, and not the peculiarities of the print. We do not explicitly notice the latter, unless there be something markedly wrong with it, such as a letter upside down. Nevertheless, if there were no print we should cognise no meaning, and if the print were different in certain specific ways we should cognise a different meaning. We *can* attend to the print itself if we choose, as in proof-reading. In exactly the same way, we are not as a rule interested in sensa, as such, but only in what we think they can tell us about physical objects, which alone can help or hurt us. Sensa themselves "cut no ice." We therefore pass automatically from the sensum and its properties to judgments about the physical object and its properties. If it should happen that the sensum is queer, as when we see double, we notice the sensum, as we notice an inverted letter. And, even in normal cases, we generally can detect the properties of sensa, and contrast them with those which they are leading us to ascribe to the physical object, provided that we make a special effort of attention.

From what has just been said, it will not appear strange that, even though there be sensa, they should have been overlooked by most plain men and by many philosophers. Of course, everyone is constantly sensing them, and, in specially abnormal cases, has noted the difference between them and physical objects. But sensa have never been objects of special interest, and therefore have never been given a name in common speech. A result of this is that all words like "seeing," "hearing," etc., are ambiguous. They stand sometimes for acts of sensing, whose objects are of course sensa, and sometimes for acts of perceiving, whose objects are supposed to be bits of matter and their sensible qualities. This is especially clear about hearing. We talk of "hearing a noise" and of "hearing a bell." In the first case we mean that we are sensing an auditory sensum, with certain attributes of pitch, loudness, quality, etc. In the second case we mean that, in consequence of sensing such a sensum, we judge that a certain physical object exists and is present to our senses. Here the word "hearing" stands for an act of perceiving. Exactly the same remarks apply to sight. In one sense we see a penny; in a somewhat stricter sense we see only one side of the penny; in another sense we see only a brown elliptical sensum. The first two uses refer to acts of perceiving, the last to an act of sensing. It is best on the whole to confine words like "seeing" and "hearing" to acts of perceiving. This is, of course, their ordinary use. I shall therefore talk of seeing a penny, but not of seeing a brown elliptical sensum. I shall speak of the latter kind of cognition as "visually sensing," or merely as "sensing," when no misunderstanding is to be feared by dropping the adjective. This distinction will be found important when we come to deal with illusory perceptions.

56 ❧

SENSE EXPERIENCES
CAUSED BY OBJECTS

John Locke

John Locke (1632-1706), an English philosopher, wrote the first comprehensive treatise on the theory of knowledge.

7. *Ideas in the Mind, Qualities in Bodies.* To discover the nature of our ideas the better, and to discourse of them intelligibly, it will be convenient to distinguish them as they are ideas or perceptions in our minds, and as they are modifications of matter in the bodies that cause such perceptions in us, that so we may not think (as perhaps usually is done) that they are exactly the images and resemblances of something inherent in the subject; most of those of sensation being in the mind no more the likeness of something existing without us, than the names that stand for them are the likeness of our ideas, which yet upon hearing they are apt to excite in us.

8. Whatsoever the mind perceives in itself, or is the immediate object of perception, thought, or understanding, that I call idea; and the power to produce any idea in our mind, I call quality of the subject wherein that power is. Thus a snowball having the power to produce in us the ideas of white, cold, and round, the power to produce those ideas in us, as they are in the snowball, I call qualities; and as they are sensations or perceptions in our understandings, I call them ideas; which ideas, if I speak of sometimes as in the things themselves, I would be understood to mean those qualities in the objects which produce them in us.

9. *Primary Qualities.* Qualities thus considered in bodies are, first, such as are utterly inseparable from the body, in what state soever it be; such as in all the alterations and changes it suffers, all the force can be used upon it, it constantly keeps; and such as sense constantly finds in every particle of matter which has bulk enough to be perceived and the mind finds inseparable from every particle of matter, though less than to make itself singly be perceived by our senses, v.g., take a grain of wheat, divide it into two parts, each

From John Locke, *An Essay Concerning Human Understanding*, Book II, Chapters 8 and 9, and Book IV, Chapter 11, first published in 1690.

part has still solidity, extension, figure, and mobility; divide it again, and it retains still the same qualities; and so divide it on till the parts become insensible, they must retain still each of them all those qualities. For division (which is all that a mill, or pestle, or any other body, does upon another, in reducing it to insensible parts) can never take away either solidity, extension, figure, or mobility from any body, but only makes two or more distinct separate masses of matter, of that which was but one before; all which distinct masses, reckoned as so many distinct bodies, after division, make a certain number. These I call original or primary qualities of body, which I think we may observe to produce simple ideas in us, viz., solidity, extension, figure, motion or rest, and number.

10. *Secondary Qualities*. Secondly, such qualities which in truth are nothing in the objects themselves, but powers to produce various sensations in us by their primary qualities, i.e., by the bulk, figure, texture, and motion of their insensible parts, as colours, sounds, tastes, &c., these I call secondary qualities. To these might be added a third sort, which are allowed to be barely powers, though they are as much real qualities in the subject, as those which I, to comply with the common way of speaking, call qualities, but for distinction, secondary qualities. For the power in fire to produce a new colour or consistency in wax or clay, by its primary qualities, is as much a quality in fire as the power it has to produce in me a new idea or sensation of warmth or burning, which I felt not before, by the same primary qualities, viz., the bulk, texture, and motion of its insensible parts.

11. *How primary Qualities produce their Ideas*. The next thing to be considered is, how bodies produce ideas in us; and that is manifestly by impulse, the only way which we can conceive bodies to operate in.

12. If then external objects be not united to our minds when they produce ideas therein, and yet we perceive these original qualities in such of them as singly fall under our senses, it is evident that some motion must be thence continued by our nerves or animal spirits, by some parts of our bodies, to the brain, or the seat of sensation, there to produce in our minds the particular ideas we have of them. And since the extension, figure, number, and motion of bodies of an observable bigness, may be perceived at a distance by the sight, it is evident some singly imperceptible bodies must come from them to the eyes, and thereby convey to the brain some motion, which produces these ideas which we have of them in us.

13. *How secondary*. After the same manner that the ideas of these original qualities are produced in us, we may conceive that the ideas of secondary qualities are also produced, viz., by the operations of insensible particles on our senses. For it being manifest that there are bodies and good store of bodies, each whereof are so small, that we cannot by any of our senses discover either their bulk, figure, or motion, as is evident in the particles of the air and water, and others extremely smaller than those, perhaps as much smaller than the particles of air and water, as the particles of air and water are smaller than peas or hail-stones; let us suppose that the different motions

and figures, bulk and number, of such particles, affecting the several organs of our senses, produce in us those different sensations which we have from the colours and smells of bodies; v.g., that a violet, by the impulse of such insensible particles of matter of peculiar figures and bulks, and in different degrees and modifications of their motions, causes the ideas of the blue colour and sweet scent of that flower to be produced in our minds; it being no more impossible to conceive that God should annex such ideas to such motions, with which they have no similitude, than that he should annex the idea of pain to the motion of a piece of steel dividing our flesh, with which that idea hath no resemblance.

14. What I have said concerning colours and smells may be understood also of tastes and sounds, and other the like sensible qualities; which, whatever reality we by mistake attribute to them, are in truth nothing in the objects themselves, but powers to produce various sensations in us, and depend on those primary qualities, viz., bulk, figure, texture, and motion of parts, as I have said.

15. *Ideas of primary Qualities are Resemblances; of secondary, not.* From whence I think it easy to draw this observation, that the ideas of primary qualities of bodies are resemblances of them, and their patterns do really exist in the bodies themselves; but the ideas produced in us by these secondary qualities have no resemblance of them at all. There is nothing like our ideas existing in the bodies themselves. They are in the bodies we denominate from them, only a power to produce those sensations in us; and what is sweet, blue, or warm in idea, is but the certain bulk, figure, and motion of the insensible parts in the bodies themselves, which we call so.

16. Flame is denominated hot and light; snow, white and cold; and manna, white and sweet, from the ideas they produce in us; which qualities are commonly thought to be the same in those bodies that those ideas are in us, the one the perfect resemblance of the other, as they are in a mirror; and it would by most men be judged very extravagant if one should say otherwise. And yet he that will consider that the same fire that at one distance produces in us the sensation of warmth, does at a nearer approach produce in us the far different sensation of pain, ought to bethink himself what reason he has to say that this idea of warmth, which was produced in him by the fire, is actually in the fire; and his idea of pain, which the same fire produced in him the same way, is not in the fire. Why are whiteness and coldness in snow, and pain not, when it produces the one and the other idea in us; and can do neither, but by the bulk, figure, number, and motion of its solid parts?

17. The particular bulk, number, figure, and motion of the parts of fire or snow are really in them, whether any one's senses perceive them or not, and therefore they may be called real qualities, because they really exist in those bodies; but light, heat, whiteness, or coldness, are no more really in them than sickness or pain is in manna. Take away the sensation of them; let not the eyes see light or colours, nor the ears hear sounds; let the palate not taste, nor the nose smell; and the colours, tastes, odours, and sounds, as

they are such particular ideas, vanish and cease, and are reduced to their causes, i.e., bulk, figure, and motion of parts.

18. A piece of manna of a sensible bulk is able to produce in us the idea of a round or square figure; and by being removed from one place to another, the idea of motion. This idea of motion represents it as it really is in the manna moving: a circle or square are the same, whether in idea or existence, in the mind or in the manna; and this both motion and figure are really in the manna, whether we take notice of them or no: this everybody is ready to agree to. Besides, manna, by the bulk, figure, texture, and motion of its parts, has a power to produce the sensations of sickness, and sometimes of acute pains or gripings in us. That these ideas of sickness and pain are not in the manna, but effects of its operations on us, and are nowhere when we feel them not, this also every one readily agrees to. And yet men are hardly to be brought to think that sweetness and whiteness are not really in manna, which are but the effects of the operations of manna, by the motion, size, and figure of its particles on the eyes and palate; as the pain and sickness caused by manna are confessedly nothing but the effects of its operations on the stomach and guts, by the size, motion, and figure of its insensible parts, (for by nothing else can a body operate, as has been proved); as if it could not operate on the eyes and palate, and thereby produce in the mind particular distinct ideas, which in itself it has not, as well as we allow it can operate on the guts and stomach, and thereby produce distinct ideas, which in itself it has not. These ideas being all effects of the operations of manna on several parts of our bodies, by the size, figure, number, and motion of its parts; why those produced by the eyes and palate should rather be thought to be really in the manna, than those produced by the stomach and guts; or why the pain and sickness, ideas that are the effect of manna, should be thought to be nowhere when they are not felt; and yet the sweetness and whiteness, effects of the same manna on other parts of the body, by ways equally as unknown, should be thought to exist in the manna, when they are not seen or tasted, would need some reason to explain.

19. *Ideas of primary Qualities are Resemblances; of secondary, not.* Let us consider the red and white colours in porphyry: hinder light from striking on it, and its colours vanish, it no longer produces any such ideas in us; upon the return of light it produces these appearances on us again. Can any one think any real alterations are made in the porphyry by the presence or absence of light, and that those ideas of whiteness and redness are really in porphyry in the light, when it is plain it has no colour in the dark? It has, indeed, such a configuration of particles, both night and day, as are apt, by the rays of light rebounding from some parts of that hard stone, to produce in us the idea of redness, and from others the idea of whiteness; but whiteness or redness are not in it at any time, but such a texture that hath the power to produce such a sensation in us.

20. Pound an almond, and the clear white colour will be altered into a dirty one, and the sweet taste into an oily one. What real alteration can the

beating of the pestle make in any body, but an alteration of the texture of it?

21. Ideas being thus distinguished and understood, we may be able to give an account how the same water, at the same time, may produce the idea of cold by one hand and of heat by the other; whereas it is impossible that the same water, if those ideas were really in it, should at the same time be both hot and cold; for if we imagine warmth, as it is in our hands, to be nothing but a certain sort and degree of motion in the minute particles of our nerves or animal spirits, we may understand how it is possible that the same water may, at the same time, produce the sensations of heat in one hand and cold in the other; which yet figure never does, that never producing the idea of a square by one hand which has produced the idea of a globe by another. But if the sensation of heat and cold be nothing but the increase or diminution of the motion of the minute parts of our bodies, caused by the corpuscles of any other body, it is easy to be understood, that if that motion be greater in one hand than in the other, if a body be applied to the two hands, which has in its minute particles a greater motion than in those of one of the hands, and a less than in those of the other, it will increase the motion of the one hand and lessen it in the other, and so cause the different sensations of heat and cold that depend thereon.

22. I have in what just goes before been engaged in physical inquiries a little further than perhaps I intended; but it being necessary to make the nature of sensation a little understood, and to make the difference between the qualities in bodies, and the ideas produced by them in the mind, to be distinctly conceived, without which it were impossible to discourse intelligibly of them, I hope I shall be pardoned this little excursion into natural philosophy, it being necessary in our present inquiry to distinguish the primary and real qualities of bodies which are always in them, (viz., solidity, extension, figure, number, and motion, or rest, and are sometimes perceived by us, viz., when the bodies they are in are big enough singly to be discerned,) from those secondary and imputed qualities which are but the powers of several combinations of those primary ones, when they operate without being distinctly discerned; whereby we may also come to know what ideas are, and what are not, resemblances of something really existing in the bodies we denominate from them.

23. *Three Sorts of Qualities in Bodies.* The qualities, then, that are in bodies, rightly considered, are of three sorts.

First, the bulk, figure, number, situation, and motion or rest of their solid parts; those are in them, whether we perceive them or not; and when they are of that size that we can discover them, we have by these an idea of the thing as it is in itself, as is plain in artificial things. These I call primary qualities.

Secondly, the power that is in any body, by reason of its insensible primary qualities, to operate after a peculiar manner on any of our senses, and thereby produce in us the different ideas of several colours, sounds, smells, tastes, &c. These are usually called sensible qualities.

Thirdly, the power that is in any body, by reason of the particular constitution of its primary qualities, to make such a change in the bulk, figure, texture, and motion of another body, as to make it operate on our senses differently from what it did before. Thus the sun has a power to make wax white, and fire to make lead fluid. These are usually called powers.

The first of these, as has been said, I think may be properly called real, original, or primary qualities, because they are in the things themselves, whether they are perceived or not; and upon their different modifications it is that the secondary qualities depend.

The other two are only powers to act differently upon other things, which powers result from the different modifications of those primary qualities.

24. *The first are Resemblances; the second thought Resemblances, but are not; the third neither are, nor are thought so.* But though the two latter sorts of qualities are powers barely, and nothing but powers, relating to several other bodies, and resulting from the different modifications of the original qualities, yet they are generally otherwise thought of; for the second sort, viz., the powers to produce several ideas in us by our senses, are looked upon as real qualities in the things thus affecting us; but the third sort are called and esteemed barely powers; v.g., the idea of heat or light, which we receive by our eyes or touch from the sun, are commonly thought real qualities existing in the sun, and something more than mere powers in it. But when we consider the sun in reference to wax, which it melts or blanches, we look on the whiteness and softness produced in the wax, not as qualities in the sun, but effects produced by powers in it; whereas, if rightly considered, these qualities of light and warmth, which are perceptions in me when I am warmed or enlightened by the sun, are no otherwise in the sun, than the changes made in the wax, when it is blanched or melted, are in the sun. They are all of them equally powers in the sun, depending on its primary qualities, whereby it is able, in the one case, so to alter the bulk, figure, texture, or motion of some of the insensible parts of my eyes or hands, as thereby to produce in me the idea of light or heat; and in the other, it is able so to alter the bulk, figure, texture, or motion of the insensible parts of the wax, as to make them fit to produce in me the distinct ideas of white and fluid.

25. The reason why the one are ordinarily taken for real qualities, and the other only for bare powers, seems to be, because the ideas we have of distinct colours, sounds, &c., containing nothing at all in them of bulk, figure, or motion, we are not apt to think them the effects of these primary qualities, which appear not, to our senses, to operate in their production, and with which they have not any apparent congruity or conceivable connexion. Hence it is that we are so forward to imagine that those ideas are the resemblances of something really existing in the objects themselves; since sensation discovers nothing of bulk, figure, or motion of parts in their production; nor can reason show how bodies, by their bulk, figure, and motion, should produce in the mind the ideas of blue or yellow, &c. But in the other case, in the operations of bodies, changing the qualities one of another, we plainly discover that the quality produced hath commonly no resemblance with anything in the thing

producing it; wherefore we look on it as a bare effect of power. For though receiving the idea of heat or light from the sun, we are apt to think it is a perception and resemblance of such a quality in the sun; yet when we see wax, or a fair face, receive change of colour from the sun, we cannot imagine that to be the reception or resemblance of anything in the sun, because we find not those different colours in the sun itself. For our senses being able to observe a likeness or unlikeness of sensible qualities in two different external objects, we forwardly enough conclude the production of any sensible quality in any subject to be an effect of bare power, and not the communication of any quality, which was really in the efficient, when we find no such sensible quality in the thing that produced it; but our senses not being able to discover any unlikeness between the idea produced in us, and the quality of the object producing it, we are apt to imagine that our ideas are resemblances of something in the objects, and not the effects of certain powers placed in the modification of their primary qualities, with which primary qualities the ideas produced in us have no resemblance.

26. *Secondary Qualities twofold; first, immediately perceivable; secondly, mediately perceivable.* To conclude, beside those before-mentioned primary qualities in bodies, viz., bulk, figure, extension, number, and motion of their solid parts, all the rest whereby we take notice of bodies, and distinguish them one from another, are nothing else but several powers in them depending on those primary qualities, whereby they are fitted, either by immediately operating on our bodies, to produce several different ideas in us, or else, by operating on other bodies, so to change their primary qualities as to render them capable of producing ideas in us different from what before they did. The former of these, I think, may be called secondary qualities, immediately perceivable; the latter, secondary qualities, mediately perceivable.

Of Perception

1. *Perception the first simple Idea of Reflection.* Perception, as it is the first faculty of the mind exercised about her ideas, so it is the first and simplest idea we have from reflection, and is by some called thinking in general: though thinking, in the propriety of the English tongue, signifies that sort of operation in the mind about its ideas, wherein the mind is active; where it, with some degree of voluntary attention, considers anything. For in bare naked perception, the mind is, for the most part, only passive; and what it perceives, it cannot avoid perceiving.

2. *Is only when the Mind receives the Impression.* What perception is, every one will know better by reflecting on what he does himself, what he sees, hears, feels, &c., or thinks, than by any discourse of mine. Whoever reflects on what passes in his own mind cannot miss it; and if he does not reflect, all the words in the world cannot make him have any notion of it.

3. This is certain, that whatever alterations are made in the body, if they reach not the mind, whatever impressions are made on the outward parts, if they are not taken notice of within, there is no perception. Fire may burn our bodies with no other effect than it does a billet, unless the motion be continued to the brain, and there the sense of heat, or idea of pain, be produced in the mind, wherein consists actual perception.

4. How often may a man observe in himself, that whilst his mind is intently employed in the contemplation of some objects, and curiously surveying some ideas that are there, it takes no notice of impressions of sounding bodies made upon the organ of hearing, with the same alteration that uses to be for the producing the idea of sound! A sufficient impulse there may be on the organ; but if not reaching the observation of the mind, there follows no perception: and though the motion that uses to produce the idea of sound be made in the ear, yet no sound is heard. Want of sensation, in this case, is not through any defect in the organ, or that the man's ears are less affected than at other times when he does hear: but that which uses to produce the idea, though conveyed in by the usual organ, not being taken notice of in the understanding, and so imprinting no idea in the mind, there follows no sensation. So that wherever there is sense or perception, there some idea is actually produced, and present, in the understanding.

8. *Ideas of Sensation often changed by the Judgment.* We are further to consider concerning perception, that the ideas we receive by sensation are often in grown people altered by the judgment, without our taking notice of it. When we set before our eyes a round globe of any uniform colour, v.g., gold, alabaster, or jet, it is certain that the idea thereby imprinted on our mind is of a flat circle variously shadowed, with several degrees of light and brightness coming to our eyes. But we have by use been accustomed to perceive what kind of appearance convex bodies are wont to make in us, what alterations are made in the reflections of light by the difference on the sensible figures of bodies, the judgment presently, by an habitual custom, alters the appearances into their causes, so that from that which is truly variety of shadow or colour, collecting the figure, it makes it pass for a mark of figure, and frames to itself the perception of a convex figure and an uniform colour, when the idea we receive from thence is only a plane variously coloured, as is evident in painting. To which purpose I shall here insert a problem of that very ingenious and studious promoter of real knowledge, the learned and worthy Mr. Molineux, which he was pleased to send me in a letter some months since; and it is this: "Suppose a man born blind, and now adult, and taught by his touch to distinguish between a cube and a sphere of the same metal, and nighly of the same bigness, so as to tell, when he felt one and the other, which is the cube, which the sphere. Suppose, then, the cube and sphere placed on a table, and the blind man be made to see: quaere, whether by his sight, before he touched them, he could now distinguish and tell which is the globe, which the cube?" To which the acute and judicious proposer answers, "Not. For though

he has obtained the experience of how a globe, how a cube affects his touch, yet he has not yet obtained the experience, that what affects his touch so or so, must affect his sight so or so; or that a protuberant angle in the cube, that pressed his hand unequally, shall appear to his eye as it does in the cube." I agree with this thinking gentleman, whom I am proud to call my friend, in his answer to this problem; and am of opinion that the blind man, at first sight, would not be able with certainty to say which was the globe, which the cube, whilst he only saw them; though he could unerringly name them by his touch, and certainly distinguish them by the difference of their figures felt. This I have set down, and leave with my reader, as an occasion for him to consider how much he may be beholden to experience, improvement, and acquired notions, where he thinks he had not the least use of, or help from them; and the rather, because this observing gentleman further adds, that having, upon the occasion of my book, proposed this to divers very ingenious men, he hardly ever met with one that at first gave the answer to it which he thinks true, till by hearing his reasons they were convinced.

9. But this is not, I think, usual in any of our ideas, but those received by sight; because sight, the most comprehensive of all our senses, conveying to our minds the ideas of light and colours, which are peculiar only to that sense; and also the far different ideas of space, figure, and motion, the several varieties whereof change the appearances of its proper object, viz., light and colours; we bring ourselves by use to judge of the one by the other. This, in many cases, by a settled habit, in things whereof we have frequent experience, is performed so constantly and so quick, that we take that for the perception of our sensation, which is an idea formed by our judgment; so that one, viz., that of sensation, serves only to excite the other, and is scarce taken notice of itself; as a man who reads or hears with attention and understanding, takes little notice of the characters or sounds, but of the ideas that are excited in him by them.

10. Nor need we wonder that this is done with so little notice, if we consider how very quick the actions of the mind are performed; for as itself is thought to take up no space, to have no extension, so its actions seem to require no time, but many of them seem to be crowded into an instant. I speak this in comparison to the actions of the body. Any one may easily observe this in his own thoughts, who will take the pains to reflect on them. How, as it were in an instant do our minds with one glance see all the parts of a demonstration, which may very well be called a long one, if we consider the time it will require to put it into words, and step by step show it another? Secondly, we shall not be so much surprised that this is done in us with so little notice, if we consider how the facility which we get of doing things by a custom of doing, makes them often pass in us without our notice. Habits, especially such as are begun very early, come at last to produce actions in us, which often escape our observation. How frequently do we, in a day, cover our eyes with our eyelids, without perceiving that we are at all in the dark! Men that by custom have got the use of a by-word, do almost in every sentence

pronounce sounds which, though taken notice of by others, they themselves neither hear nor observe. And therefore it is not so strange that our mind should often change the idea of its sensation into that of its judgment, and make one serve only to excite the other, without our taking notice of it.

. . .

Of Our Knowledge of the Existence of Other Things

1. *It is to be had only by sensation.* The knowledge of our own being we have by intuition. The existence of a God reason clearly makes known to us, as has been shown.

The knowledge of the existence of any other thing we can have only by sensation: for there being no necessary connexion of real existence with any idea a man hath in his memory; nor of any other existence but that of God with the existence of any particular man: no particular man can know the existence of any other being, but only when, by actual operating upon him, it makes itself perceived by him. For the having the idea of anything in our mind no more proves the existence of that thing than the picture of a man evidences his being in the world, or the visions of a dream make thereby a true history.

2. It is therefore the actual receiving of ideas from without that gives us notice of the existence of other things, and makes us know that something doth exist at that time without us which causes that idea in us, though perhaps we neither know nor consider how it does it. For it takes not from the certainty of our senses, and the ideas we receive by them, that we know not the manner wherein they are produced: v.g., whilst I write this, I have, by the paper affecting my eyes, that idea produced in my mind, which whatever object causes, I call white; by which I know that that quality or accident (i.e., whose appearance before my eyes always causes that idea) doth really exist, and hath a being without me. And of this, the greatest assurance I can possibly have, and to which my faculties can attain, is the testimony of my eyes, which are the proper and sole judges of this thing; whose testimony I have reason to rely on as so certain, that I can no more doubt, whilst I write this, that I see white and black, and that something really exists that causes that sensation in me, than that I write or move my hand; which is a certainty as great as human nature is capable of, concerning the existence of anything but a man's self alone, and of God.

3. *This, though not so certain as demonstration, yet may be called knowledge, and proves the existence of things without us.* The notice we have by our senses of the existing of things without us, though it be not altogether so certain as our intuitive knowledge, or the deductions of our reason employed about the clear abstract ideas of our own minds; yet it is an assurance that deserves the name of *knowledge.* If we persuade ourselves that our faculties act and inform us right concerning the existence of those objects that

affect them, it cannot pass for an ill-grounded confidence: for I think nobody can, in earnest, be so sceptical as to be uncertain of the existence of those things which he sees and feels. At least, he that can doubt so far (whatever he may have with his own thoughts) will never have any controversy with me; since he can never be sure I say anything contrary to his opinion. As to myself, I think God has given me assurance enough of the existence of things without me; since by their different application I can produce in myself both pleasure and pain, which is one great concernment of my present state. This is certain, the confidence that our faculties do not herein deceive us is the greatest assurance we are capable of concerning the existence of material beings. For we cannot act anything but by our faculties, nor talk of knowledge itself, but by the help of those faculties which are fitted to apprehend even what knowledge is. But besides the assurance we have from our senses themselves, that they do not err in the information they give us of the existence of things without us, when they are affected by them, we are farther confirmed in this assurance by other concurrent reasons.

4. *Because we cannot have them but by the inlet of the senses.* First, It is plain those perceptions are produced in us by exterior causes affecting our senses, because those that want the organs of any sense never can have the ideas belonging to that sense produced in their minds. The organs themselves, it is plain, do not produce them; for then the eyes of a man in the dark would produce colours, and his nose smell roses in the winter: but we see nobody gets the relish of a pine-apple till he goes to the Indies where it is, and tastes it.

5. *Because an idea from actual sensation and another from memory are very distinct perceptions.* Secondly, Because sometimes I find that I cannot avoid the having those ideas produced in my mind. For though when my eyes are shut, or windows fast, I can at pleasure recall to my mind the ideas of light or the sun, which former sensations had lodged in my memory; so I can at pleasure lay by that idea, and take into my view that of the smell of a rose, or taste of sugar. But if I turn my eyes at noon towards the sun, I cannot avoid the ideas which the light or sun then produces in me. So that there is a manifest difference between the ideas laid up in my memory, and those which force themselves upon me, and I cannot avoid having. And therefore it must needs be some exterior cause, and the brisk acting of some objects without me, whose efficacy I cannot resist, that produces those ideas in my mind, whether I will or no. Besides, there is nobody who doth not perceive the difference in himself between contemplating the sun as he hath the idea of it in his memory, and actually looking upon it: of which two, his perception is so distinct, that few of his ideas are more distinguishable one from another. And therefore he hath certain knowledge that they are not both memory, or the actions of his mind, and fancies only within him; but that actual seeing hath a cause without.

. . .

7. *Our senses assist one another's testimony of the existence of outward things.* Fourthly, Our senses, in many cases, bear witness to the truth of each

other's report concerning the existence of sensible things without us. He that sees a fire may, if he doubt whether it be anything more than a bare fancy, feel it too, and be convinced by putting his hand in it; which certainly could never be put into such exquisite pain by a bare idea or phantom, unless that the pain be a fancy too; which yet he cannot, when the burn is well, by raising the idea of it, bring upon himself again.

Thus I see, whilst I write this, I can change the appearance of the paper; and by designing the letters, tell beforehand what new idea it shall exhibit the very next moment, barely by drawing my pen over it: which will neither appear (let me fancy as much as I will) if my hand stand still, or though I move my pen, if my eyes be shut: nor, when those characters are once made on the paper, can I choose afterwards but see them as they are; that is, have the ideas of such letters as I have made. Whence it is manifest that they are not barely the sport and play of my own imagination, when I find that the characters that were made at the pleasure of my own thoughts do not obey them; nor yet cease to be, whenever I shall fancy it, but continue to affect my senses constantly and regularly, according to the figures I made them. To which if we will add, that the sight of those shall, from another man, draw such sounds as I beforehand design they shall stand for, there will be little reason left to doubt that those words I write do really exist without me, when they cause a long series of regular sounds to affect my ears, which could not be the effect of my imagination, nor could my memory retain them in that order.

8. *This certainty is as great as our condition needs.* But yet, if after all this any one will be so sceptical as to distrust his senses, and to affirm that all we see and hear, feel and taste, think and do, during our whole being, is but the series and deluding appearances of a long dream whereof there is no reality; and therefore will question the existence of all things or our knowledge of anything: I must desire him to consider, that if all be a dream, then he doth but dream that he makes the question; and so it is not much matter that a waking man should answer him. But yet, if he pleases, he may dream that I make him this answer, that the certainty of things existing *in rerum natura* when we have the testimony of our senses for it, is not only as great as our frame can attain to, but as our condition needs. For our faculties being suited not to the full extent of being, nor to a perfect, clear, comprehensive knowledge of things free from all doubt and scruple; but to the preservation of us, in whom they are; and accommodated to the use of life: they serve to our purpose well enough, if they will but give us certain notice of those things which are convenient or inconvenient to us. For he that sees a candle burning, and hath experimented the force of its flame by putting his finger in it, will little doubt that this is something existing without him, which does him harm and puts him to great pain. And if our dreamer pleases to try whether the glowing heat of a glass furnace be barely a wandering imagination in a drowsy man's fancy, by putting his hand into it, he may perhaps be awakened into a certainty, greater than he could wish, that it is something more than

bare imagination. So that this evidence is as great as we can desire, being as certain to us as our pleasure or pain, i.e., happiness or misery; beyond which we have no concernment, either of knowing or being. Such an assurance of the existence of things without us is sufficient to direct us in the attaining the good and avoiding the evil which is caused by them, which is the important concernment we have of being made acquainted with them.

57

MATERIAL THINGS
ARE EXPERIENCES
OF MEN OR GOD

George Berkeley

George Berkeley (1685-1753), Bishop of Cloyne, wrote various important philosophical works.

1. It is evident to any one who takes a survey of the *objects of human knowledge,* that they are either *ideas* actually imprinted on the senses; or else such as are perceived by attending to the passions and operations of the mind; or lastly, *ideas* formed by help of memory and imagination — either compounding, dividing, or barely representing those originally perceived in the aforesaid ways. By sight I have the ideas of light and colours, with their several degrees and variations. By touch I perceive hard and soft, heat and cold, motion and resistance; and of all these more and less either as to quantity or degree. Smelling furnishes me with odours; the palate with tastes; and hearing conveys sounds to the mind in all their variety of tone and composition.

And as several of these are observed to accompany each other, they come to be marked by one name, and so to be reputed as one *thing.* Thus, for example, a certain colour, taste, smell, figure and consistence having been observed to go together, are accounted one distinct thing, signified by the name apple; other collections of ideas constitute a stone, a tree, a book, and the like sensible things; which as they are pleasing or disagreeable excite the passions of love, hatred, joy, grief, and so forth.

2. But, besides all that endless variety of ideas or objects of knowledge, there is likewise Something which knows or perceives them; and exercises divers operations, as willing, imagining, remembering, about them. This perceiving, active being is what I call *mind, spirit, soul,* or *myself.* By which words I do not denote any one of my ideas, but a thing entirely distinct from them, wherein they exist, or, which is the same thing, whereby they are perceived; for the existence of an idea consists in being perceived.

From George Berkeley, *A Treatise Concerning the Principles of Human Knowledge,* first published in 1710. Sentences in brackets were added by Berkeley after the first edition.

3. That neither our thoughts, nor passions, nor ideas formed by the imagination exist without the mind is what everybody will allow. And to me it seems no less evident that the various sensations or ideas imprinted on the Sense, however blended or combined together (that is, whatever objects they compose), cannot exist otherwise than in a mind perceiving them. I think an intuitive knowledge may be obtained of this, by any one that shall attend to what is meant by the term *exist* when applied to sensible things. The table I write on I say exists; that is, I see and feel it: and if I were out of my study I should say it existed; meaning thereby that if I was in my study I might perceive it, or that some other spirit actually does perceive it. There was an odour, that is, it was smelt; there was a sound, that is, it was heard; a colour or figure, and it was perceived by sight or touch. This is all that I can understand by these and the like expressions. For as to what is said of the *absolute* existence of unthinking things, without any relation to their being perceived, that is to me perfectly unintelligible. Their *esse* is *percipi;* nor is it possible they should have any existence out of the minds or thinking things which perceive them.

4. It is indeed an opinion strangely prevailing amongst men, that houses, mountains, rivers, and in a world all sensible objects, have an existence, natural or real, distinct from their being perceived by the understanding. But, with how great an assurance and acquiescence soever this Principle may be entertained in the world, yet whoever shall find in his heart to call it in question may, if I mistake not, perceive it to involve a manifest contradiction. For, what are the forementioned objects but the things we perceive by sense? and what do we perceive besides our own ideas or sensations? and is it not plainly repugnant that any one of these, or any combination of them, should exist unperceived?

5. If we thoroughly examine this tenet it will, perhaps, be found at bottom to depend on the doctrine of *abstract ideas.* For can there be a nicer strain of abstraction than to distinguish the existence of sensible objects from their being perceived, so as to conceive them existing unperceived? Light and colours, heat and cold, extension and figures — in a word the things we see and feel — what are they but so many sensations, notions, ideas, or impressions on the sense? and is it possible to separate, even in thought, any of these from perception? For my part, I might as easily divide a thing from itself. I may, indeed, divide in my thoughts, or conceive apart from each other, those things which perhaps I never perceived by sense so divided. Thus, I imagine the trunk of a human body without the limbs, or conceive the smell of a rose without thinking on the rose itself. So far, I will not deny, I can abstract; if that may properly be called *abstraction* which extends only to the conceiving separately such objects as it is possible may really exist or be actually perceived asunder. But my conceiving or imagining power does not extend beyond the possibility of real existence or perception. Hence, as it is impossible for me to see or feel anything without an actual sensation of that thing, so it is impossible for me to conceive in my thoughts any sensible thing or object distinct

from the sensation or perception of it. [In truth, the object and the sensation are the same thing, and cannot therefore be abstracted from each other.]

6. Some truths there are so near and obvious to the mind that a man need only open his eyes to see them. Such I take this important one to be, viz. that all the choir of heaven and furniture of the earth, in a word all those bodies which compose the mighty frame of the world, have not any subsistence without a mind; that their *being* is to be perceived or known; that consequently so long as they are not actually perceived by me, or do not exist in my mind, or that of any other created spirit, they must either have no existence at all, or else subsist in the mind of some Eternal Spirit: it being perfectly unintelligible, and involving all the absurdity of abstraction, to attribute to any single part of them an existence independent to a spirit. [To be convinced of which, the reader need only reflect, and try to separate in his own thoughts the *being* of a sensible thing from its *being perceived.*]

7. From what has been said it is evident there is not any other Substance than *Spirit,* or that which perceives. But, for the fuller proof of this point, let it be considered the sensible qualities are colour, figure, motion, smell, taste, and such like, that is, the ideas perceived by sense. Now, for an idea to exist in an unperceiving thing is a manifest contradiction; for to have an idea is all one as to perceive: that therefore wherein colour, figure, and the like qualities exist must perceive them. Hence it is clear there can be no unthinking substance or *substratum* of those ideas.

8. But, say you, though the ideas themselves do not exist without the mind, yet there may be things like them, whereof they are copies or resemblances; which things exist without the mind, in an unthinking substance. I answer, an idea can be like nothing but an idea; a colour or figure can be like nothing but another colour or figure. If we look but never so little into our thoughts, we shall find it impossible for us to conceive a likeness except only between our ideas. Again, I ask whether those supposed *originals,* or external things, of which our ideas are the pictures or representations, be themselves perceivable or no? If they are, then *they* are ideas, and we have gained our point: but if you say they are not, I appeal to any one whether it be sense to assert a colour is like something which is invisible; hard or soft, like something which is intangible; and so of the rest.

9. Some there are who make a distinction betwixt *primary* and *secondary* qualities. By the former they mean extension, figure, motion, rest, solidity or impenetrability, and number; by the latter they denote all other sensible qualities, as colours, sounds, tastes, and so forth. The ideas we have of these last they acknowledge not to be the resemblances of anything existing without the mind, or unperceived; but they will have our ideas of the *primary qualities* to be patterns or images of things which exist without the mind, in an unthinking substance which they call Matter. By Matter, therefore, we are to understand an inert, senseless substance, in which extension, figure, and motion do actually subsist. But it is evident, from what we have already shewn, that extension, figure, and motion are only ideas existing in the mind,

and that an idea can be like nothing but another idea; and that consequently neither they nor their archetypes can exist in an unperceiving substance. Hence, it is plain that the very notion of what is called *Matter* or *corporeal substance,* involves a contradiction in it. [Insomuch that I should not think it necessary to spend more time in exposing its absurdity. But, because the tenet of the existence of Matter seems to have taken so deep a root in the minds of philosophers, and draws after it so many ill consequences, I choose rather to be thought prolix and tedious than omit anything that might conduce to the full discovery and extirpation of that prejudice.]

10. They who assert that figure, motion, and the rest of the primary or original qualities do exist without the mind, in unthinking substances, do at the same time acknowledge that colours, sounds, heat, cold, and suchlike secondary qualities, do not; which they tell us are sensations, existing in the mind alone, that depend on and are occasioned by the different size, texture, and motion of the minute particles of matter. This they take for an undoubted truth, which they can demonstrate beyond all exception. Now, if it be certain that those *original* qualities are inseparably united with the other sensible qualities, and not, even in thought, capable of being abstracted from them, it plainly follows that *they* exist only in the mind. But I desire any one to reflect, and try whether he can, by any abstraction of thought, conceive the extension and motion of a body without all other sensible qualities. For my own part, I see evidently that it is not in my power to frame an idea of a body extended and moving, but I must withal give it some colour or other sensible quality, which is acknowledged to exist only in the mind. In short, extension, figure, and motion, abstracted from all other qualities, are inconceivable. Where therefore the other sensible qualities are, there must these be also, to wit, in the mind and nowhere else.

14. I shall farther add, that, after the same manner as modern philosophers prove certain sensible qualities to have no existence in Matter, or without the mind, the same thing may be likewise proved of all other sensible qualities whatsoever. Thus, for instance, it is said that heat and cold are affections only of the mind, and not at all patterns of real beings, existing in the corporeal substances which excite them; for that the same body which appears cold to one hand seems warm to another. Now, why may we not as well argue that figure and extension are not patterns or resemblances of qualities existing in Matter; because to the same eye at different stations, or eyes of a different texture at the same station, they appear various, and cannot therefore be the images of anything settled and determinate without the mind? Again, it is proved that sweetness is not really in the sapid thing; because the thing remaining unaltered the sweetness is changed into bitter, as in case of a fever or otherwise vitiated palate. Is it not as reasonable to say that motion is not without the mind; since if the succession of ideas in the mind become swifter, the motion, it is acknowledged, shall appear slower, without any alteration in any external object?

15. In short, let any one consider those arguments which are thought manifestly to prove that colours and tastes exist only in the mind, and he shall find they may with equal force be brought to prove the same thing of extension, figure, and motion. Though it must be confessed this method of arguing does not so much prove that there is no extension or colour in an outward object, as that we do not know by sense which is the true extension or colour of the object. But the arguments foregoing plainly shew it to be impossible that any colour or extension at all, or other sensible quality whatsoever, should exist in an unthinking subject without the mind, or in truth that there should be any such thing as an outward object.

16. But let us examine a little the received opinion. It is said extension is a *mode* or *accident* of Matter, and that Matter is the *substratum* that supports it. Now I desire that you would explain to me what is meant by Matter's *supporting* extension. Say you, I have no idea of Matter; and therefore cannot explain it. I answer, though you have no positive, yet, if you have any meaning at all, you must at least have a relative idea of Matter; though you know not what it is, yet you must be supposed to know what relation it bears to accidents, and what is meant by its supporting them. It is evident *support* cannot here be taken in its usual or literal sense, as when we say that pillars support a building. In what sense therefore must it be taken? [For my part, I am not able to discover any sense at all that can be applicable to it.]

17. If we inquire into what the most accurate philosophers declare themselves to mean by *material substance,* we shall find them acknowledge they have no other meaning annexed to those sounds but the idea of Being in general, together with the relative notion of its supporting accidents. The general idea of Being appeareth to me the most abstract and incomprehensible of all other; and as for its supporting accidents, this, as we have just now observed, cannot be understood in the common sense of those words: it must therefore be taken in some other sense, but what that is they do not explain. So that when I consider the two parts or branches which make the signification of the words *material substance,* I am convinced there is no distinct meaning annexed to them. But why should we trouble ourselves any farther, in discussing this material *substratum* or support of figure and motion and other sensible qualities? Does it not suppose they have an existence without the mind? And is not this a direct repugnancy, and altogether inconceivable?

18. But, though it were possible that solid, figured, moveable substances may exist without the mind, corresponding to the ideas we have of bodies, yet how is it possible for us to know this? Either we must know it by Sense or by Reason. As for our senses, by them we have the knowledge only of our sensations, ideas, or those things that are immediately perceived by sense, call them what you will: but they do not inform us that things exist without the mind, or unperceived, like to those which are perceived. This the materialists themselves acknowledge. — It remains therefore that if we have any knowledge at all of external things, it must be by reason inferring their existence from what is immediately perceived by sense. But (I do not see) what reason can

induce us to believe the existence of bodies without the mind, from what we perceive, since the very patrons of Matter themselves do not pretend there is any necessary connexion betwixt them and our ideas? I say it is granted on all hands (and what happens in dreams, frensies, and the like, puts it beyond dispute) that it is possible we might be affected with all the ideas we have now, though no bodies existed without resembling them. Hence it is evident the supposition of external bodies is not necessary for the producing our ideas; since it is granted they are produced sometimes, and might possibly be produced always, in the same order we see them in at present, without their concurrence.

19. But, though we might possibly have all our sensations without them, yet perhaps it may be thought easier to conceive and explain the manner of their production, by supposing external bodies in their likeness rather than otherwise; and so it might be at least probable there are such things as bodies that excite their ideas in our minds. But neither can this be said. For, though we give the materialists their external bodies, they by their own confession are never the nearer knowing how our ideas are produced; since they own themselves unable to comprehend in what manner body can act upon spirit, or how it is possible it should imprint any idea in the mind. Hence it is evident the production of ideas or sensations in our minds, can be no reason why we should suppose Matter or corporeal substances; since that is acknowledged to remain equally inexplicable with or without this supposition. If therefore it were possible for bodies to exist without the mind, yet to hold they do so must needs be a very precarious opinion; since it is to suppose, without any reason at all, that God has created innumerable beings that are entirely useless, and serve to no manner of purpose.

.   .   .   .

22. I am afraid I have given cause to think I am needlessly prolix in handling this subject. For, to what purpose is it to dilate on that which may be demonstrated with the utmost evidence in a line or two, to any one that is capable of the least reflexion? It is but looking into your own thoughts, and so trying whether you can conceive it possible for a sound, or figure, or motion, or colour to exist without the mind or unperceived. This easy trial may perhaps make you see that what you contend for is a downright contradiction. Insomuch that I am content to put the whole upon this issue: — If you can but conceive it possible for one extended moveable substance, or in general for any one idea, or anything like an idea, to exist otherwise than in a mind perceiving it, I shall readily give up the cause. And, as for all that compages of external bodies you contend for, I shall grant you its existence, though you cannot either give me any reason why you believe it exists, or assign any use to it when it is supposed to exist. I say, the bare possibility of your opinions being true shall pass for an argument that it is so.

23. But, say you, surely there is nothing easier than for me to imagine trees, for instance, in a park, or books existing in a closet, and nobody by to perceive them. I answer, you may so, there is no difficulty in it. But what is

all this, I beseech you, more than framing in your mind certain ideas which you call *books* and *trees*, and at the same time omitting to frame the idea of any one that may perceive them? But do not you yourself perceive or think of them all the while? This therefore is nothing to the purpose: it only shews you have the power of imagining, or forming ideas in your mind; but it does not shew that you can conceive it possible the objects of your thought may exist without the mind. To make out this, it is necessary that you conceive them existing unconceived or unthought of; which is a manifest repugnancy. When we do our utmost to conceive the existence of external bodies, we are all the while only contemplating our own ideas. But the mind, taking no notice of itself, is deluded to think it can and does conceive bodies existing unthought of, or without the mind, though at the same time they are apprehended by, or exist in, itself. A little attention will discover to any one the truth and evidence of what is here said, and make it unnecessary to insist on any other proofs against the existence of *material substance*.

25. All our ideas, sensations, notions, or the things which we perceive, by whatsoever names they may be distinguished, are visibly inactive: there is nothing of power or agency included in them. So that one idea or object of thought cannot produce or make any alteration in another. To be satisfied of the truth of this, there is nothing else requisite but a bare observation of our ideas. For, since they and every part of them exist only in the mind, it follows that there is nothing in them but what is perceived: but whoever shall attend to his ideas, whether of sense or reflexion, will not perceive in them any power or activity; there is, therefore, no such thing contained in them. A little attention will discover to us that the very being of an idea implies passiveness and inertness in it; insomuch that it is impossible for an idea to do anything, or, strictly speaking, to be the cause of anything: neither can it be the resemblance or pattern of any active being, as is evident from sect. 8. Whence it plainly follows that extension, figure, and motion cannot be the cause of our sensations. To say, therefore, that these are the effects of powers resulting from the configuration, number, motion, and size of corpuscles, must certainly be false.

26. We perceive a continual succession of ideas; some are anew excited, others are changed or totally disappear. There is therefore *some* cause of these ideas, whereon they depend, and which produces and changes them. That this cause cannot be any quality or idea or combination of *ideas*, is clear from the preceding section. It must therefore be a *substance*; but it has been shewn that there is no corporeal or material substance: it remains therefore that the cause of ideas is an incorporeal active substance or Spirit.

27. A Spirit is one simple, undivided, active being — as it perceives ideas it is called the *understanding*, and as it produces or otherwise operates about them is it called the *will*. Hence there can be no *idea* formed of a soul or spirit; for all ideas whatever, being passive and inert (vid. sect. 25), they cannot represent unto us, by way of image or likeness, that which acts. A

little attention will make it plain to any one, that to have an idea which shall be *like* that active Principle of motion and change of ideas is absolutely impossible. Such is the nature of Spirit, or that which acts, that it cannot be of itself perceived, but only by the effects which it produceth. If any man shall doubt of the truth of what is here delivered, let him but reflect and try if he can frame the idea of any power or active being; and whether he has ideas of two principal powers, marked by the names *will* and *understanding,* distinct from each other, as well as from a third idea of Substance or Being in general, with a relative notion of its supporting or being the subject of the aforesaid powers — which is signified by the name *soul* or *spirit.* This is what some hold; but, so far as I can see, the words *will,* [*understanding, mind,*] *soul, spirit,* do not stand for different ideas, or, in truth, for any idea at all, but for something which is very different from ideas, and which, being an agent, cannot be like unto, or represented by, any idea whatsoever. [Though it must be owned at the same time that we have some *notion* of soul, spirit, and the operations of the mind, such as willing, loving, hating — inasmuch as we know or understand the meaning of these words.]

28. I find I can excite ideas in my mind at pleasure, and vary and shift the scene as oft as I think fit. It is no more than *willing,* and straightway this or that idea arises in my fancy; and by the same power it is obliterated and makes way for another. This making and unmaking of ideas doth very properly denominate the mind active. Thus much is certain and grounded on experience: but when we talk of unthinking agents, or of exciting ideas exclusive of volition, we only amuse ourselves with words.

29. But, whatever power I may have over my thoughts, I find the ideas actually perceived by Sense have not a like dependence on *my* will. When in broad daylight I open my eyes, it is not in my power to choose whether I shall see or no, or to determine what particular objects shall present themselves to my view: and so likewise as to the hearing and other senses; the ideas imprinted on them are not creatures of *my* will. There is therefore some other Will or Spirit that produces them.

30. The ideas of Sense are more strong, lively, and distinct than those of the Imagination; they have likewise a steadiness, order, and coherence, and are not excited at random, as those which are the effects of human wills often are, but in a regular train or series — the admirable connexion whereof sufficiently testifies the wisdom and benevolence of its Author. Now the set rules, or established methods, wherein the Mind we depend on excites in us the ideas of Sense, are called *the laws of nature;* and these we learn by experience, which teaches us that such and such ideas are attended with such and such other ideas, in the ordinary course of things.

31. This gives us a sort of foresight, which enables us to regulate our actions for the benefit of life. And without this we should be eternally at a loss: we could not know how to act anything that might procure us the least pleasure, or remove the least pain of sense. That food nourishes, sleep refreshes, and fire warms us; that to sow in the seedtime is the way to reap in

the harvest; and in general that to obtain such or such ends, such or such means are conducive — all this we know, not by discovering any *necessary connexion* between our ideas, but only by the observation of the *settled laws* of nature; without which we should be all in uncertainty and confusion, and a grown man no more know how to manage himself in the affairs of life than an infant just born.

32. And yet this consistent uniform working, which so evidently displays the Goodness and Wisdom of that Governing Spirit whose Will constitutes the laws of nature, in so far from leading our thoughts to Him, that it rather sends them wandering after second causes. For, when we perceive certain ideas of Sense constantly followed by other ideas, and we know this is not of our own doing, we forthwith attribute power and agency to the ideas themselves, and make one the cause of another, than which nothing can be more absurd and unintelligible. Thus, for example, having observed that when we perceive by sight a certain round luminous figure, we at the same time perceive by touch the idea or sensation called heat, we do from thence conclude the sun to be the *cause* of heat. And in like manner perceiving the motion and collision of bodies to be attended with sound, we are inclined to think the latter the *effect* of the former.

33. The ideas imprinted on the Senses by the Author of nature are called *real things*: and those excited in the imagination, being less regular, vivid, and constant, are more properly termed *ideas* or *images* of things, which they copy and represent. But then our *sensations*, be they never so vivid and distinct, are nevertheless ideas: that is, they exist in the mind, or are perceived by it, as truly as the ideas of its own framing. The ideas of Sense are allowed to have more reality in them, that is, to be more strong, orderly, and coherent than the creatures of the mind; but this is no argument that they exist without the mind. They are also less dependent on the spirit or thinking substance which perceives them, in that they are excited by the will of another and more powerful Spirit: yet still they are *ideas*: and certainly no idea, whether faint or strong, can exist otherwise than in a mind perceiving it.

. . .

57. But why they should suppose the ideas of sense to be excited in us by things in their likeness, and not rather have recourse to *Spirit,* which alone can act, may be accounted for. First, because they were not aware of the repugnancy there is, as well in supposing things like unto our ideas existing without, as in attributing to them power or activity. Secondly, because the Supreme Spirit which excites those ideas in our minds, is not marked out and limited to our view by any particular finite collection of sensible ideas, as human agents are by their size, complexion, limbs, and motions. And thirdly, because His operations are regular and uniform. Whenever the course of nature is interrupted by a miracle, men are ready to own the presence of a Superior Agent. But, when we see things go on in the ordinary course, they do not excite in us any reflexion; their order and concatenation, though it be an argument of the greatest wisdom, power, and goodness in their Creator, is

yet so constant and familiar to us, that we do not think them the immediate effects of a *Free Spirit;* especially since inconsistency and mutability in acting, though it be an imperfection, is looked on as a mark of *freedom.*

139. But it will be objected that, if there is no *idea* signified by the terms *soul, spirit,* and *substance,* they are wholly insignificant, or have no meaning in them. I answer, those words do mean or signify a real thing; which is neither an idea, nor like an idea, but that which perceives ideas, and wills, and reasons about them. What I am *myself,* that which I denote by the term *I,* is the same with what is meant by *soul,* or *spiritual substance.* [But if I should say that *I* was nothing, or that *I* was an *idea* or *notion,* nothing could be more evidently absurd than either of these propositions.] If it be said that this is only quarrelling at a word, and that, since the immediate significations of other names are by common consent called *ideas,* no reason can be assigned why that which is signified by the name *spirit* or *soul* may not partake in the same appellation. I answer, all the unthinking objects of the mind agree in that they are entirely passive, and their existence consists only in being perceived: whereas a *soul* or *spirit* is an active being, whose existence consists, not in being perceived, but in perceiving ideas and thinking. It is therefore necessary, in order to prevent equivocation and confounding natures perfectly disagreeing and unlike, that we distinguish between *spirit* and *idea.*

145. From what hath been said, it is plain that we cannot know the existence of *other spirits* otherwise than by their operations, or the ideas by them, excited in us. I perceive several motions, changes, and combinations of ideas, that inform me there are certain particular agents, like myself, which accompany them, and concur in their production. Hence, the knowledge I have of other spirits is not immediate, as is the knowledge of my ideas; but depending on the intervention of ideas, by me referred to agents or spirits distinct from myself, as effects or concomitant signs.

146. But, though there be some things which convince us human agents are concerned in producing them, yet it is evident to everyone that those things which are called the Works of Nature, that is, the far greater part of the ideas or sensations perceived by us, are *not* produced by, or dependent on, the wills of *men.* There is therefore some other Spirit that causes them; since it is repugnant that they should subsist by themselves. . . . But, if we attentively consider the constant regularity, order, and concatenation of natural things, the surprising magnificence, beauty and perfection of the larger, and the exquisite contrivance of the smaller parts of the creation, together with the exact harmony and correspondence of the whole, but above all the never-enough-admired laws of pain and pleasure, and the instincts or natural inclinations, appetites, and passions of animals; — I say if we consider all these things, and at the same time attend to the meaning and import of the attributes One, Eternal, Infinitely Wise, Good, and Perfect, we shall clearly perceive

that they belong to the aforesaid Spirit, 'who works all in all' and 'by whom all things consist.'

147. Hence, it is evident that God is known as certainly and immediately as any other mind or spirit whatsoever, distinct from ourselves. We may even assert that the existence of God is far more evidently perceived than the existence of men; because the effects of Nature are infinitely more numerous and considerable than those ascribed to human agents. There is not any one mark that denotes a man, or affect produced by him, which does not more strongly evince the being of that Spirit who is the Author of Nature. For it is evident that, in affecting other persons, the will of man hath no other object than barely the motion of the limbs of his body; but that such a motion should be attended by, or excite any idea in the mind of another, depends wholly on the will of the Creator. He alone it is who, 'upholding all things by the word of His power,' maintains that intercourse between spirits whereby they are able to perceive the existence of each other. And yet this pure and clear Light which enlightens every one is itself invisible [to the greatest part of mankind].

58

MATERIAL THINGS
ARE ACTUAL AND
POSSIBLE EXPERIENCES

John Stuart Mill

We have seen Sir W. Hamilton at work on the question of the reality of Matter, by the introspective method, and, as it seems, with little result. Let us now approach the same subject by the psychological. I proceed, therefore, to state the case of those who hold that the belief in an external world is not intuitive, but an acquired product.

This theory postulates the following psychological truths, all of which are proved by experience, and are not contested, though their force is seldom adequately felt, by Sir W. Hamilton and the other thinkers of the introspective school.

It postulates, first, that the human mind is capable of Expectation. In other words, that after having had actual sensations, we are capable of forming the conception of Possible sensations, sensations which we are not feeling at the present moment, but which we might feel, and should feel if certain conditions were present, the nature of which conditions we have, in many cases, learned by experience.

It postulates, secondly, the laws of the Association of Ideas. So far as we are here concerned, these laws are the following: 1st. Similar phaenomena tend to be thought of together. 2d. Phaenomena which have either been experienced or conceived in close contiguity to one another, tend to be thought of together. The contiguity is of two kinds; simultaneity, and immediate succession. Facts which have been experienced or thought of simultaneously, recall the thought of one another. Of facts which have been experienced or thought of in immediate succession, the antecedent, or the thought of it, recalls the thought of the consequent, but not conversely. 3rd. Associations produced by contiguity become more certain and rapid by repetition. When

From John Stuart Mill, *An Examination of Sir William Hamilton's Philosophy*, 1865, Chapter 11.

two phaenomena have been very often experienced in conjunction, and have not, in any single instance, occurred separately either in experience or in thought, there is produced between them what has been called Inseparable, or less correctly, Indissoluble Association: by which is not meant that the association must inevitably last to the end of life — that no subsequent experience or process of thought can possibly avail to dissolve it; but only that as long as no such experience or process of thought has taken place, the association is irresistible; it is impossible for us to think the one thing disjoined from the other. 4th. When an association has acquired this character of inseparability — when the bond between the two ideas has been thus firmly riveted, not only does the idea called up by association become, in our consciousness, inseparable from the idea which suggested it, but the facts or phaenomena answering to those ideas, come at last to seem inseparable in existence: things which we are unable to conceive apart, appear incapable of existing apart; and the belief we have in their co-existence, though really a product of experience, seems intuitive. Innumerable examples might be given of this law. One of the most familiar, as well as the most striking, is that of our acquired perceptions of sight. Even those who, with Mr. Bailey, consider the perception of distance by the eye as not acquired, but intuitive, admit that there are many perceptions of sight which, though instantaneous and unhesitating, are not intuitive. What we see is a very minute fragment of what we think we see. We see artificially that one thing is hard, another soft. We see artificially that one thing is hot, another cold. We see artificially that what we see is a book, or a stone, each of these being not merely an inference, but a heap of inferences, from the signs which we see, to things not visible.

Setting out from these premises, the Psychological Theory maintains, that there are associations naturally and even necessarily generated by the order of our sensations and of our reminiscences of sensation, which, supposing no intuition of an external world to have existed in consciousness, would inevitably generate the belief, and would cause it to be regarded as an intuition.

What is it we mean when we say that the object we perceive is external to us, and not a part of our own thoughts? We mean, that there is in our perceptions something which exists when we are not thinking of it; which existed before we had ever thought of it, and would exist if we were annihilated; and further, that there exist things which we never saw, touched, or otherwise perceived, and things which never have been perceived by man. This idea of something which is distinguished from our fleeting impressions by what, in Kantian language, is called Perdurability; something which is fixed and the same, while our impressions vary; something which exists whether we are aware of it or not, and which is always square (or of some other given figure) whether it appears to us square or round, constitutes altogether our idea of external substance. Whoever can assign an origin to this complex conception, has accounted for what we mean by the belief in matter.

Now, all this, according to the Psychological Theory, is but the form impressed by the known laws of association, upon the conception or notion, obtained by experience, of Contingent Sensations; by which are meant, sensations that are not in our present consciousness, and perhaps never were in our consciousness at all, but which, in virtue of the laws to which we have learned by experience that our sensations are subject, we know that we should have felt under given supposable circumstances, and under these same circumstances, might still feel.

I see a piece of white paper on a table. I go into another room, and though I have ceased to see it, I am persuaded that the paper is still there. I no longer have the sensations which it gave me; but I believe that when I again place myself in the circumstances in which I had those sensations, that is, when I go again into the room, I shall again have them; and further, that there has been no intervening moment at which this would not have been the case. Owing to this law of my mind, my conception of the world at any given instant consists, in only a small proportion, of present sensations. Of these I may at the time have none at all, and they are in any case a most significant portion of the whole which I apprehend. The conception I form of the world existing at any moment, comprises, along with the sensations I am feeling, a countless variety of possibilities of sensation; namely, the whole of those which past observation tells me that I could, under any supposable circumstances, experience at this moment, together with an indefinite and illimitable multitude of others which though I do not know that I could, yet it is possible that I might, experience in circumstances not known to me. These various possibilities are the important thing to me in the world. My present sensations are generally of little importance, and are moreover fugitive: the possibilities, on the contrary, are permanent, which is the character that mainly distinguishes our idea of Substance or Matter from our notion of sensation. These possibilities, which are conditional certainties, need a special name to distinguish them from mere vague possibilities, which experience gives no warrant for reckoning upon. Now, as soon as a distinguishing name is given, though it be only to the same thing regarded in a different aspect, one of the most familiar experiences of our mental nature teaches us, that the different name comes to be considered as the name of a different thing.

There is another important peculiarity of these certified or guaranteed possibilities of sensation; namely, that they have reference, not to single sensations, but to sensations joined together in groups. When we think of anything as a material substance, or body, we either have had, or we think that on some given supposition we should have, not some *one* sensation, but a great and even an indefinite number and variety of sensations, generally belonging to different senses, but so linked together, that the presence of one announces the possible presence at the very same instant of any or all of the rest. In our mind, therefore, not only is this particular Possibility of sensation invested with the quality of permanence when we are not actually feeling any of the sensations at all; but when we are feeling some of them, the remaining sensations of the group are conceived by us in the form of Present Possibilities, which might be realized at the very moment. And as this happens in turn to all of them, the group as a whole presents itself to the mind as permanent, in contrast not solely with the temporariness of my bodily presence, but also with the temporary character of each of the sensations composing the group; in other words, as a kind of permanent substratum, under a set of passing experiences or manifestations: which is another leading character of our idea of substance or matter, as distinguished from sensation.

Let us now take into consideration another of the general characters of our experience, namely, that in addition to fixed groups, we also recognize a fixed Order in our sensations; an Order of succession, which, when ascertained by observation, gives rise to the ideas of Cause and Effect, according to what I hold to be the true theory of that relation, and is in any case the source of all our knowledge *what* causes produce what effects. Now, of what nature is this fixed order among our sensations? It is a constancy of antecedence and sequence. But the constant antecedence and sequence do not generally exist between one actual sensation and another. Very few such sequences are presented to us by experience. In almost all the constant sequences, which occur in Nature, the antecedence and consequence do not obtain between sensations, but between the groups we have been speaking about, of which a very small portion is actual sensation, the greater part being permanent possibilities of sensation, evidenced to us by a small and variable number of sensations actually present. Hence, our ideas of causation, power, activity, do not become connected in thought with our sensations as *actual* at all, save in the few physiological cases where these figure by themselves as the antecedents in some uniform sequence. Those ideas become connected, not with sensations, but with groups of possibilities of sensation. The sensations conceived do not, to our habitual thoughts, present themselves as sensations actually experienced, inasmuch as not only any one or any number of them may be supposed absent, but none of them need be present. We find that the modifications which are taking place more or less regularly in our possibilities of sensation, are mostly quite independent of our consciousness, and of our presence or absence. Whether we are asleep or awake, the fire goes out, and puts an end to one particular possibility of warmth and light. Whether we are present or absent, the corn ripens, and brings a new possibility of food. Hence we speedily think to learn of Nature as made up solely of these groups of possibilities, and the active force in Nature as manifested in the modification of some of these by others. The sensations, though the original foundation of the whole, come to be looked upon as a sort of accident, depending on us, and the possibilities as much more real than the actual sensations, nay, as the very realities of which these are only the representations, appearances, or effects. When this state of mind has been arrived at, then, and from that time forward, we are never conscious of a present sensation without instantaneously referring it to some one of the groups of possibilities into which a sensation of that particular description enters; and if we do not yet know to what group to refer it, we at least feel an irresistible conviction that it must belong to some group or other; *i.e.,* that its presence proves the existence, here and now, of a great number and variety of possibilities of sensation, without which it would not have been. The whole set of sensations as possible, form a permanent background to any one or more of them that are, at a given moment, actual; and the possibilities are conceived as standing to the actual sensations in the relation of a cause to its effects, or of canvas to the figures painted on it, or of a root to the trunk, leaves and flowers, or of a substratum to that which is spread over it, or, in transcendental language, of Matter to Form.

When this point has been reached, the permanent Possibilities in question have assumed such unlikeness of aspect, and such difference of position relatively to us, from any sensations, that it would be contrary to all we know of the constitution of human nature that they should not be conceived as, and believed to be, at least as different from sensations as sensations are from one another. Their groundwork in sensation is forgotten, and they are supposed to be something intrinsically distinct from it. We can withdraw ourselves from any of our (external) sensations, or we can be withdrawn from them by some other agency. But though the sensations cease, the possibilities remain in existence; they are independent of our will, our presence, and everything which belongs to us. We find, too, that they belong as much to other human or sentient beings as to ourselves. We find other people grounding their expectations and conduct upon the same permanent possibilities on which we ground ours. But we do not find them experiencing the same actual sensations. Other people do not have our sensations exactly when and as we have them: but they have our possibilities of sensation; whatever indicates a present possibility of sensations to ourselves, indicates a present possibility of similar sensations to them, except so far as their organs of sensation may vary from the type of ours. This puts the final seal to our conception of the groups of possibilities as the fundamental reality in Nature. The permanent possibilities are common to us and to our fellow-creatures; the actual sensations are not. That which other people become aware of when, and on the same grounds as I do, seems more real to me than that which they do not know of unless I tell them. The world of Possible Sensations succeeding one another according to laws, is as much in other beings as it is in me; it has therefore an existence outside me; it is an External World.

. . .

Matter, then, may be defined, a Permanent Possibility of Sensation. If I am asked whether I believe in matter, I ask whether the questioner accepts this definition of it. If he does, I believe in matter: and so do all Berkeleians. In any other sense than this, I do not. But I affirm with confidence, that this conception of Matter includes the whole meaning attached to it by the common world, apart from philosophical, and sometimes from theological, theories. The reliance of mankind on the real existence of visible and tangible objects, means reliance on the reality and permanence of Possibilities of visual and tactual sensations, when no such sensations are actually experienced. We are warranted in believing that this is the meaning of Matter in the minds of many of its most esteemed metaphysical champions, though they themselves would not admit as much: for example, of Reid, Stewart, and Brown. For these three philosophers alleged that all mankind, including Berkeley and Hume, really believed in Matter, inasmuch as unless they did, they would not have turned aside to save themselves from running against a post. Now, all which this manoeuvre really proved is, that they believed in Permanent Possibilities of Sensation. We have therefore the sanction of these three eminent defenders of the existence of matter, for affirming, that to believe in Permanent Possibilities of Sensation *is* believing in Matter. It is hardly necessary, after such authorities, to mention Dr. Johnson, or any one else who resorts to the *argumentum baculinum* of knocking a stick against the ground. Sir W. Hamilton, a far subtler thinker than any of these, never reasons in this manner. He never supposes that a disbeliever in what he means by Matter, ought in consistency to act in any different mode from those who believe in it. He knew that the belief on which all the practical consequences depend, is the belief in Permanent Possibilities of Sensation, and that if nobody believed in a material universe in any other sense, life would go on exactly as it now does. He, however, did believe in more than this, but, I think, only because it had never occurred to him that mere Possibilities of Sensation could, to our artificialized consciousness, present the character of objectivity which, as we have now shown, they not only can, but unless the known laws of the human mind were suspended, must necessarily, present.

Perhaps it may be objected, that the very possibility of framing such a notion of Matter as Sir W. Hamilton's — the capacity in the human mind of imagining an external world which is anything more than what the Psychological Theory makes it — amounts to a disproof of the theory. If (it may be said) we had no revelation in consciousness, of a world which is not in some way or other identified with sensation, we should be unable to have the notion of such a world. If the only ideas we had of external objects were ideas of our sensations, supplemented by an acquired notion of permanent possibilities of sensation, we must (it is thought) be incapable of conceiving, and therefore still more incapable of fancying that we perceive, things which are not sensations at all. It being evident, however, that some philosophers believe this, and it being maintainable that the mass of mankind do so, the existence of a perdurable basis of sensations, distinct from sensations themselves, is proved, it might be said, by the possibility of believing it.

Let me first restate what I apprehend the belief to be. We believe that we perceive a something closely related to all our sensations, but different from those which we are feeling at any particular minute; and distinguished from sensations altogether, by being permanent and always the same, while these are fugitive, variable, and alternately displace one another. But these attributes of the object of perception are properties belonging to all the possibilities of sensation which experience guarantees. The belief in such permanent possibilities seems to me to include all that is essential or characteristic in the belief in substance. I believe that Calcutta exists, though I do not perceive it, and that it would still exist if every percipient inhabitant were suddenly to leave the place, or be struck dead. But when I analyze the belief, all I find in it is, that were these events to take place, the Permanent Possibility of Sensation which I call Calcutta would still remain; that if I were suddenly transported to the banks of the Hoogly, I should still have the sensations which, if now present, would lead me to affirm that Calcutta exists here and now. We may infer, therefore, that both philosophers and the world at large, when they think of matter, conceive it really as a Permanent Possibility of Sensation. But the majority of philosophers fancy that it is something more; and the world at large, though they have really, as I conceive, nothing in their minds but a Permanent Possibility of Sensation, would, if asked the question, undoubtedly agree with the philosophers: and though this is sufficiently explained by the tendency of the human mind to infer difference of things from difference of names, I acknowledge the obligation of showing how it can be possible to believe in an existence transcending all possibilities of sensation, unless on the hypothesis that such an existence actually is, and that we actually perceive it.

The explanation, however, is not difficult. It is an admitted fact, that we are capable of all conceptions which can be formed by generalizing from the observed laws of our sensations. Whatever relation we find to exist between any one of our sensations and something different from *it,* that same relation we have no difficulty in conceiving to exist between the sum of all our sensations and something different from *them.* The differences which our consciousness recognizes between one sensation and another, give us the general notion of difference, and inseparably associate with every sensation we have, the feeling of its being different from other things; and when once this association has been formed, we can no longer conceive anything, without being able, and even being compelled, to form also the conception of something different from it. This familiarity with the idea of something different from *each* thing we know, makes it natural and easy to form the notion of something different from *all* things that we know, collectively as well as individually. It is true we can form no conception of what such a thing can be; our notion of it is merely negative; but the idea of substance, apart from the impressions it makes on our senses, *is* a merely negative one. There is thus no psychological obstacle to our forming the notion of a something which is neither a sensation nor a possibility of sensation, even if our consciousness does not testify to it; and nothing is more likely than that the Permanent Possibilities of sensation, to which our consciousness does testify, should be confounded in our minds with this imaginary conception. All experience attests the strength of the tendency to mistake mental abstractions, even negative ones, for substantive realities; and the Permanent Possibilities of sensation which experience guarantees, are so extremely unlike in many of their properties to actual sensations, that since we are capable of imagining something which transcends sensation, there is a great natural probability that we should suppose these to be it.

But this natural probability is converted into certainty, when we take into consideration that universal law of our experience which is termed the law of Causation, and which makes us unable to conceive the beginning of anything without an antecedent condition, or Cause. The case of Causation is one of the most marked of all the cases in which we extend to the sum total of our consciousness, a notion derived from its parts. It is a striking example of our power to conceive, and our tendency to believe, that a relation which subsists between every individual item of our experience and some other item, subsists also between our experience as a whole, and something not within the sphere of experience. By this extension to the sum of all our experiences, of the internal relations obtaining between its several parts, we are led to consider sensation itself — the aggregate whole of our sensations — as deriving its origin from antecedent existences transcending sensation. That we should do this, is a consequence of the particular character of the uniform sequences, which experience discloses to us among our sensations. As already remarked, the constant antecedent of a sensation is seldom another sensation, or set of sensations, actually felt. It is much oftener the existence of a group of possibilities, not necessarily including any actual sensations, except such as are required to show that the possibilities are really present. Nor are actual sensations indispensable even for this purpose; for the presence of the object (which is nothing more than the immediate presence of the possibilities) may be made known to us by the very sensation which we refer to it as its effect. Thus, the real antecedent of an effect — the only antecedent which, being invariable and unconditional, we consider to be the cause — may be, not any sensation really felt, but solely the presence, at that or the immediately preceding moment, of a group of possibilities of sensation. Hence it is not with sensations as actually experienced, but with their Permanent Possibilities, that the idea of Cause comes to be identified: and we, by one and the same process, acquire the habit of regarding Sensation in general, like all our individual sensations, as an Effect, and also that of conceiving as the causes of most of our individual sensations, not other sensations, but general possibilities of sensation. If all these considerations put together do not completely explain and account for our conceiving these Possibilities as a class of independent and substantive entities, I know not what psychological analysis can be conclusive.

It may perhaps be said, that the preceding theory gives, indeed, some account of the idea of Permanent Existence which forms part of our conception of matter, but gives no explanation of our believing these permanent objects to be external, or out of ourselves. I apprehend, on the contrary, that the very idea of anything out of ourselves is derived solely from the knowledge experience gives us of the Permanent Possibilities. Our sensations we carry with us wherever we go, and they never exist where we are not; but when we change our place we do not carry away with us the Permanent Possibilities of Sensation: they remain until we return, or arise and cease under conditions with which our presence has in general nothing to do. And more than all — they are, and will be after we have ceased to feel, Permanent Possibilities of sensation to other beings than ourselves. Thus our actual sensations and the permanent possibilities of sensation, stand out in obtrusive contrast to one another: and when the idea of Cause has been acquired, and extended by generalization from the parts of our experience to its aggregate whole, nothing can be more natural than that the Permanent Possibilities should be classed by us as existences generically distinct from our sensations, but of which our sensations are the effect.

The same theory which accounts for our ascribing to an aggregate of possibilities of sensation, a permanent existence which our sensations themselves do not possess, and consequently a greater reality than belongs to our sensations, also explains our attributing greater objectivity to the Primary Qualities of bodies than to the Secondary. For the sensations which correspond to what are called the Primary Qualities (as soon at least as we come to apprehend them by two senses, the eye as well as the touch) are always present when any part of the group is so. But colors, tastes, smell, and the like, being, in comparison, fugacious, are not, in the same degree, conceived as being always there, even when nobody is present to perceive them. The sensations answering to the Secondary Qualities are only occasional, those to the Primary, constant. The Secondary, moreover, vary with different persons, and with the temporary sensibility of our organs: the Primary, when perceived at all, are, as far as we know, the same to all persons and at all times.

59 ❧

DIFFICULTIES FOR PHENOMENALISM

Roderick Milton Chisholm

R. M. Chisholm (1916-   ) is Professor of Philosophy at Brown University.

1. Ernst Mach expressed *phenomenalism* by saying that "all bodies are but thought-symbols for complexes of sensations."[1] Where Mach uses "sensations" other phenomenalists may use "appearances" or "sense-data." And where Mach uses "thought-symbols," others may talk about language and "rules of translation."[2] But every form of phenomenalism involves the thesis that anything we know about material things may be expressed in statements referring solely to appearances. Since many of the problems I have discussed in this book would require a very different treatment if this thesis were true, I shall now state my reasons for believing it to be false.

2. I have said that whenever we perceive anything *x* to have some property *f* we have certain beliefs about the ways in which *x* appears. If a man now takes something to be a tree, he believes that, under the conditions now obtaining, he would *not* be appeared to in just the way he is appeared to unless the thing were a tree. And he believes that if he were now to act in certain ways — if he were to approach the thing he takes to be a tree, or if he were to reach out and touch it — he would be appeared to in still other ways characteristic of a tree. It is accurate to say, I think, that phenomenalism is based upon an interpretation of such facts as these.

The phenomenalist contends that, if we ask ourselves just what it is we

[1] Ernest Mach, *The Analysis of Sensations* (Chicago, 1897), p. 22.
[2] Compare A. J. Ayer, *The Foundations of Empirical Knowledge*: "What is being claimed is simply that the propositions which are ordinarily expressed by sentences which refer to material things could also be expressed by sentences which referred exclusively to sense-data" (p. 232). C. I. Lewis has noted that the label "phenomenalism" is not altogether appropriate for the view here in question; see "Realism or Phenomenalism?" *Philosophical Review*, LXIV (1955), 233-247.

are believing when we think we perceive something to have a certain characteristic, we will find that our beliefs really pertain only to the *appearances* of the thing we think we are perceiving. He then infers that our ordinary statements about physical things — such statements as "That is a tree" and "This thing is red" — logically *entail* many statements referring solely to appearances. And he concludes that, if only we were to list the appearance statements entailed by any thing statement, we would have for that thing statement the type of translation the phenomenalistic thesis requires: we would have a set of appearance statements expressing everything that the thing statement is ordinarily used to express.

But is it true that such statements as "That is a tree" and "This thing is red" *entail* any statements referring solely to appearances — to ways of sensing? The familiar facts of "perceptual relativity" suggest that our ordinary thing statements do *not* entail any statements referring solely to appearances.[3]

Whether a material thing will ever present, say, a red appearance depends partly upon the nature of the thing and partly upon the conditions under which the thing is perceived. If one knew that the thing was red and that the lighting conditions were normal, one could predict that, to a normal observer, the thing would present a red appearance; if one knew that the lights were out, or that the perceiver had a certain kind of color blindness, one could predict that the thing would present some other appearance; and so on, for any other thing and its possible appearances. To calculate the appearances, it is necessary to know both the thing perceived and the observation conditions, for it is the thing perceived and the observation conditions working jointly which determine the way the thing is to appear.

The facts of perceptual relativity thus suggest that even the simple thing statement, "This thing is red," doesn't entail *any* statement about appearances; an appearance statement is entailed only when "This thing is red" is taken in conjunction with *another* thing statement referring to observation conditions. This may be seen further if we compare first the thing statement

This is red (P)

and a categorical appearance statement

Redness will be sensed. (R)

. . . . .

May we say, then, that the statement P above entails R, as these statements would ordinarily be interpreted? Possibly it is obvious that no contradiction is involved in affirming P and denying R. The following considerations, however, may make the matter clearer.

Taken in conjunction with certain *other* thing statements Q, referring to observation conditions, P does entail R. The following is such a statement Q:

---

[3] We should say, more exactly, that such thing statements entail no *synthetic*, or *non-logical*, statements referring solely to appearances.

> This is perceived under normal conditions; and if this is red and is perceived under normal conditions, redness will be sensed. (Q)

(So far as our present point is concerned, it does not particularly matter how the expression "normal conditions" is defined.)

Taken in conjunction, not with Q, but with still *other* thing statements S, also referring to observation conditions, P entails not-R. An example of S would be:

> This is perceived under conditions which are normal except for the presence of blue lights; and if this is red and is perceived under conditions which are normal except for the presence of blue lights, redness will not be sensed. (S)

As these statements would ordinarily be interpreted, S is logically consistent with P; there is no contradiction involved in affirming one and denying the other. But the conjunction of P and S, if it is logically consistent, must entail everything that P entails and cannot entail anything logically incompatible with what P entails. If P and S entail not-R, it is impossible that P entail R. Hence "This is red" (P) does not entail "Redness will be sensed" (R). Similarly. "Redness will not be sensed" is not sufficient to *falsify* "This is red." We may draw a similar conclusion with respect to any other categorical appearance statement R'. Although there may be a statement about observation conditions, Q', such that "This is red" (P') and Q' entail R', there is also a statement about observation conditions, S', such that P and S' entail not-R'; hence P does not entail R'.

According to some phenomenalists, the appearance statements entailed by statements describing a physical thing would be considerably more complicated than "Redness will be sensed"; they would be conjunctions of conditionals of the form "If such and such should be sensed, then such and such would be sensed." The phenomenalist might hold, for example, that the thing statement

> There is really a door in front of me. (P)

entails a conditional appearance statement of this sort:

> If such-and-such visual appearances should be sensed (namely, those associated with reaching), then such-and-such tactual appearances would be sensed. (R)

Again, if P entails R, then it is logically impossible that there be a statement S, consistent with P and such that P and S entail not-R. Clearly there are many such statements S. One might be:

> Whenever I see a door, I sense such-and-such visual appearances but not such-and-such tactual appearances.[4] (S)

---

[4] Compare C. I. Lewis's example in *An Analysis of Knowledge and Valuation*, pp. 248-249, where appearance statements are said to be "probability consequences" of thing statements. Whether Lewis's view is an instance of phenomenalism depends

This statement, in conjunction with *P*, entails not-*R*. Since *S* is consistent with *P*, it is false that *P* entails *R*.

By similar reasoning it would seem possible to formulate, for any complex appearance statement *R'* that might be thought to be an analytic consequence of *P*, some statement *S'* consistent with *P* and such that *P* and *S'* entail not-*R'*.

I believe we may say, therefore, that no synthetic thing statement *P* entails any appearance statement unless *P* is taken in conjunction with some *other* thing statement referring to observation conditions. In our earlier example, "This is red" (*P*) does entail an appearance statement when *P* is conjoined with *Q*: "This is perceived under normal conditions; and if this is red and is perceived under normal conditions redness will be sensed." And we have seen that, when conjoined with statements about different observation conditions, "This is red" may entail a different statement about appearances. Thus when John Stuart Mill tried to show, with respect to his belief that Calcutta exists, that it can be expressed phenomenalistically, in terms of "permanent possibilities of sensations," he specified these possibilities by reference to himself and to the banks of the Hooghly:

> I believe that Calcutta exists, though I do not perceive it, and that it would still exist if every percipient inhabitant were suddenly to leave the place, or be struck dead. But when I analyze the belief, all I find in it is, that were these events to take place, the Permanent Possibility of Sensation which I call Calcutta would still remain; that if I were suddenly transported to the banks of the Hooghly, I should still have the sensations which, if now present, would lead me to affirm that Calcutta exists here and now.[5]

But this method of deriving appearance statements from thing statements does not suggest any way of expressing "Calcutta exists" or "This thing is red" in terms referring solely to permanent possibilities of sensation, or to appearances. For we obtain our appearance statements only by referring to still other physical things.

3. Why should one think that phenomenalism is true? If we look to the reasons phenomenalists have proposed, we will find, I think, that each is in-

---

upon how *probability* is interpreted; see George Chatalian, "Probability: Inductive versus Deductive," *Philosophical Studies*, III (1952), 49-52, and Roderick Firth, "Radical Empiricism and Perceptual Relativity," *Philosophical Review*, LIX (1950), 164-183, 319-331.

[5] John Stuart Mill, *An Examination of Sir William Hamilton's Philosophy* (New York, 1884), p. 246. Compare H. H. Price's criticism of such theories in *Hume's Theory of the External World* (Oxford, 1940), pp. 183-188. Roderick Firth has proposed a rather complex theory about the meaning of ordinary thing statements in order to deal with such problems (*op. cit.*, especially pp. 319-323). I cannot here do justice to his theory, but I believe it is fair to say: (i) the theory has some implausible consequences; (ii) it was designed with the purpose of adapting phenomenalism to considerations such as the above; and (iii) if the criticism of the ostensible *grounds* of phenomenalism, in Section 3 below, is accurate, then there is no positive reason for accepting Firth's theory.

consistent with at least one of the conclusions of the present book. The most important of these reasons are the following three.[6]

(i) Professor Lewis has said that, if phenomenalism cannot be successfully defended, "then there will be nothing left for us but skepticism."[7] In saying this, he assumed, I think, that some form of *empiricism* . . . is true. He assumed, first, with respect to those statements we would ordinarily justify by reference to perceiving, that no such statement is evident unless it is more probable than not in relation to statements about appearing. He assumed, secondly, that if we are thus confined to appearances and if phenomenalism is false then skepticism is true. And he assumed, thirdly, that if phenomenalism is true then, even though we may be so confined, skepticism is false. But according to the theory of evidence I attempted to defend . . . there is no reason to accept the first of these assumptions. The statements we would ordinarily defend by reference to perceiving may be evident even though they are not probable in relation to statements about appearing. And therefore we need not accept the thesis that if phenomenalism cannot be successfully defended "there is nothing left for us but skepticism."

(ii) I think that many philosophers have been led to accept phenomenalism because of what they believe about the genesis of our knowledge. They have assumed: first, that "before we can learn about the things that appear to us, we must learn about their appearances"; secondly, that the psychological process of perceiving developed from the more simple process of sensing appearances; and, thirdly, that this process could not have taken place unless phenomenalism is true. In . . . [an earlier chapter] I discussed the first of these assumptions and suggested an alternative. If the suggested alternative is true, then, I think, there is no reason for supposing that the *second* of these assumptions is true. Moreover, the second assumption does not seem to me to be plausible. It would be difficult to show *how* the process of perceiving might have developed from that of sensing. The difficulty would be very much like that of showing how the process of remembering might have developed from perceiving, or from sensing.

(iii) At one time Professor Ayer defended phenomenalism on the ground that "the only alternative to it, once we have agreed to the use of the sense-datum terminology, is the iron-curtain theory of perception: that physical objects are there sure enough but we can never get at them, because all

---

[6] Phenomenalism has been defended by saying that, if statements about physical things have any *meaning* at all, they are translatable into statements about appearances. Little is gained by introducing the concept of *meaning* into the discussion, however, inasmuch as the positive grounds for this view of meaning are presumably the same as those for phenomenalism. And when phenomenalism is expressed this way, the phenomenalist's problem becomes that of showing that thing statements *do* have meaning, in this sense of "meaning"; for it would be misleading to use the word "meaning" in such a way that the statement "This thing is red" could *not* be said to mean anything.

[7] C. I. Lewis, "Professor Chisholm and Empiricism," *Journal of Philosophy*, XLV (1948), 519.

we can observe is sense-data: and surely this theory at least can be shown to be untenable."[8] The doubtful step in this argument, I think, is the premise that, once we have adopted the sense-datum terminology, we must say that "all we can observe is sense data." If Ayer took "observe" to be synonymous with "perceive," then . . . the statement "All we can observe is sense-data" is false. But if he took "observe" to be synonymous with "sense" (as we have been using "sense" and as he used it in *The Foundations of Empirical Knowledge*), then, although it is now true to say that all one can observe — all one can *sense* — is sense-data, this statement no longer implies that, if phenomenalism is false, one "can never get at" physical objects. For we may now say, what might have been less appropriate at the beginning of this book, that one *can* get at them — in the only relevant sense of this expression — by *perceiving* them.

---

[8] A. J. Ayer, *Philosophical Essays* (London, 1954), p. 143.

60

OUR KNOWLEDGE OF
THE MATERIAL WORLD

Arthur Oncken Lovejoy

Arthur O. Lovejoy (1873-1962) was Professor of Philosophy at Johns Hopkins University.

. . . It seems worth while to consider afresh what reasons — other than "instincts," to which some realists seem to me to appeal too simply — can be given for believing that there is a world of existing particulars which are nobody's "ideas" — which, in other words, are independent of awareness — and to ask how much, or what sort, of knowledge of that world it is permissible to suppose that we can attain. . . .

The case for physical realism should not, I think, be made to rest primarily or wholly — as it is by Russell in his later period — upon the assumed necessity of postulating external causal objects to account for our percepts — objects about which we can infer no more than that there are differences of some kind in them, corresponding numerically, but not necessarily or probably in their qualities, to the differences between percepts. It is true that if there *are* external objects, and if they cannot be identical with our data, we must be able to infer so much, at least, about them, if we are to base any judgments whatever concerning them upon perception. And it is also true that our disposition to assume that our experiences have causes is somewhat too disparagingly described when it is called mere "animal faith." It is a faith, indeed; but . . . it is a highly critical and extremely attenuated faith. And it is a part of the general faith that reality has a greater degree of orderliness, of interconnection of parts, and therefore of intelligibility, than is manifested in the confused phantasmagoria of unsupplemented sensation. But it is not the primary form of that faith; it is derivative from something more fundamental. For there is no obvious gain in the coherency and intelligibility of the world if you merely take an isolated momentary bit of perceptual content and assert concerning it: This must have had a cause external in some sense to itself.

The more fundamental postulate to which I refer — and the better reason for accepting realism — will begin to appear if we consider what the "independence" which might be ascribed to physical reals, and would constitute the first essential of their physicality, would be. It would have to do primarily with the *time* of their existence. Consciousness in general, and the consciousness of this or that sensible object in particular, is fluctuating and intermittent. For you an object now exists and now does not exist; when you are in deep sleep or a swoon the whole world is non-existent. The primary function of "real objects," the way in which the belief in them helps us to regard the universe as more coherent than sense-experience, consists (as was implied in our definition of the notion of a "physical world") in their filling the temporal gaps between actual perceptions. The "independence" of a thing means, concretely, its continued existence, or the continuance of a connected series of events of which it is a member, at times when it is not being attended to by me, nor necessarily by any one like me. The starting-point of the argument for physical realism, I suggest, is the plain man's normal and reasonable belief that the processes of nature do not stop when he stops noticing them. It is not the "outerness" of the object perceived, *when* it is perceived, but the *persistence of something which is in some manner connected with what is perceived, during the interperceptual intervals,* that is the primary natural postulate out of which the belief in an external world, in objects which exist though they are not given in experience, arises. How irrepressible this belief is may be judged from the emphatic affirmation of it even by phenomenalists who ostensibly refuse to admit any metempirical realities. Thus Petzoldt, after declaring that "there is no scientific meaning in the assumption that there exists behind experience something-or-other as its bearer or generator," forthwith proceeds to castigate those who will not believe in "a perdurance of objects which is independent of us" — who fail to regard the fact that "things always turn up again quite independently of whether I have had my eyes open or not, at the place they previously had, or at some place wholly independent of my thought." Petzoldt, in short, apparently finds it superfluous to suppose that there are any common and independent realities behind our experiences, but impossible to conceive that there are none between our experiences.

. . .

The belief in the continuance of things or processes between perceptions is not a blank act of faith, as would be the postulation of an external causal object for a single momentary percept; it may be said to be — not, indeed, rigorously verified — but strengthened by one of the most familiar of empirical facts — namely, that the same uniform causal sequences of natural events which may be observed within experience appear to go on in the same manner when not experienced. You build a fire in your grate of a certain quantity of coal, of a certain chemical composition. Whenever you remain in the room there occurs a typical succession of sensible phenomena according to an approximately regular schedule of clock-time; in, say, a half-hour the coal is half consumed; at the end of the hour the grate contains only ashes. If you build a fire of the same quantity of the same material under the same conditions, leave the room, and return after any given time has elapsed, you get approximately the same sense-experiences as you would have had at the corresponding moment if you had remained in the room. You infer, therefore, that the fire has been burning as usual during your absence, and that being perceived is not a condition necessary for the occurrence of the process. But a consistent idealist or phenomenalist cannot say this. He is committed to the proposition either that the fire has not been or, at all events, cannot legitimately be assumed to have been, burning when no one was perceiving it; his doctrine amounts to a gratuitous assumption of the universal jumpiness or temporal discontinuity of causal sequences. The most that he can admit — and he cannot admit less — is that fires and other natural processes behave *as if* they went on when unobserved; if he desires to make this seem more intelligible, he may invoke some pre-established harmony, or resort to a species of occasionalism — assuming that when you return to the room after an hour God (as Descartes would have said) deceives you by putting into your mind a percept of a grate full of ashes, though *these* ashes are not the effects of any fire. But such "explanations" of the facts are plainly arbitrary and far-fetched; they multiply types of causal agency beyond necessity. And to be content with a mere *Philosophie des Als-Ob* in such a case — to say that, although nothing at all that was like a fire or would have caused you to perceive a fire, if you had remained in the room, was really happening while you were absent, nevertheless all goes on as though the fire had been burning during that interval — this, surely, is a singularly strained and artificial notion, wholly foreign to the normal propensities of our intelligence.

Naïve realism, however, infers more from this type of fact than is warranted; it supposes that while you were not in the room *exactly the same* phenomena were going on as you would have experienced had you been there — the play of color in the flames, the qualities experienced by you in thermal sensation, and so on. To suppose this is to assume that certain of the factors in the case — namely, your presence in the room and your psychophysical constitution — make no difference in the content of your experience. This positive assumption of the complete irrelevance of certain actual antecedents or concomitants of a given effect is not only gratuitous and improbable, but is in conflict with familiar empirical evidences of the concomitant variation of sense-data with differences in the perceptible natures or states of percipients. What is reasonably inferrible is that some process capable of causing an organism, constituted as you are, to have the perceptual experience of a burning fire, has been continuously going on while you were not in such relations to it as actually to perceive any fire. The causal theory of perception is thus derivative from, not logically prior to, the postulate of the continuance of the orderly sequences of nature during interperceptual intervals. The world of external causal entities or events is the world that you are obliged to assume when you accept the evidence for such continuance, while recognizing the probability that your own makeup, as a body or a mind or both, plays some part in determining the qualitative character of your percepts. The specific qualities characteristic of the potentially unperceived, that is, interperceptual, process, remain, so far as these considerations go, undetermined; you cannot, thus far, tell how much of what you experience is due to external events, how much to the nature of "that which is acted upon" by these events. But this does not weaken the reasons for believing that there *are* such temporally persistent and therefore independent events. Matter, or the physical order, still remains, not only as, in Mill's phrase, "a permanent possibility of sensation," but as a continuing existent capable of causing sensations under certain circumstances. . . .

Are we . . . [however] left in that state of near-agnosticism about the external world which is emplified by the utterances of certain physicists which have been quoted and by the later theory of Mr. Bertrand Russell? Is it the case that either (a) we have no reasons for believing that the background has *any* of the attributes and modes of relatedness characteristic of perceptible objects, *e.g.*, of our visual or tactual data, with the possible exception of causality and discrete multiplicity, or (b) that we have decisive reasons for believing that it has not any such attributes or modes of relatedness — so that it would be inadmissible even to accept such a belief as a provisional postulate? The usual position of the dualistic realist in the past — and until a very recent time — has, of course, been that there are some reasons for ascribing to the physical world a few of the more fundamental characteristics of the world of perception, and that, even if these reasons are not rigorously probative, the belief in question is a natural assumption which no one can prove to be false. He has held that physical things must, indeed, be denied all the characters which vary with percipients — which are manifestly functions of standpoints; and that there is no good reason for supposing that such characters as color, sensible temperature, odor, and the like, exist apart from sensation; but that there is a residuum of properties extension, shape, relative position, temporal succession, motion — which may plausibly be regarded as characterizing the components of independent physical reality. And the reason — other than "instinct" or "animal faith" — given for crediting the physical world with these characteristics has been that, by doing so, we could apparently frame a coherent, simple, unifying, scientifically serviceable set of hypotheses as to the nature of the relatively few causal processes which determine our manifold individual sense-data and explain both their diversities and their uniformities — the sort of hypotheses exemplified by the ordinary optical theory of perspective, refraction, *etc.* This position is represented, so lately as 1925, by Broad's *The Mind and its Place in Nature*. Mr. Broad in that work argues that if we "study carefully and in detail," the nature of our sensa and their correlations, we find reason to conceive the physical world "as a spatial whole on the analogy of the visual field." "The hypothesis that what appears to us as external objects and what appears to us as our own bodies are extended and stand in spatial relations . . . accounts for the correlations between . . . constituents of perceptual situations and for their variations as we move about. And it is difficult to see that any alternative hypothesis which does not logically reduce to this one will logically account for such facts" — though "about the minuter details of the physical spatio-temporal order there is room for much diversity of opinion and for much future modification and refinement, as the facts adduced by the Theory of Relativity show." Hence it is "practically certain that the nature and relations of the persistent and neutral conditions of sensa *must* be interpreted by analogy with visual sensa and their relations in the visual sense-field."

Can such a position, or any approximation to it, any longer be held? It is perhaps worth remarking — though not too much weight should be given to the fact — that men of science still seem usually to think in terms of such analogies, though with important changes in detail. They are radically agnostic about the physical world only intermittently, or when the wind is in a certain quarter. Thus physicists and astronomers are accustomed to debate, from the standpoint of the relativity theory, whether the universe is finite or infinite in extent, and, if it can be shown to be finite, of just what shape it is, and how many million years would be required for a ray of light to complete "the journey round the whole of space" and return to its starting-point. And, as Jeans tells us, "it has been quite seriously suggested that two faint nebulae," previously supposed to be extremely remote from us, "may actually be our two nearest neighbors in the sky, M 33 and M 31, seen the long way round space" — *i.e.*, that "we see the fronts of two objects when we look at M 33 and M 31 and the backs of the same two objects when we point our telescopes in exactly the opposite directions." This, Jeans remarks, is perhaps "only a conjecture"; but "many more startling conjectures in astronomy have . . . proved to be true." The raising of such questions and conjectures seems superfluous, not to say meaningless, unless it is assumed that there is a physical world which has extension and in which it is possible for light to travel, *i.e.*, to reach successively different positions. The habitual fashion of speech of our astronomers and physicists plainly betrays the fact that they conceive themselves to be concerned with the problem of ascertaining the probable nature of relatively persistent physical realities behind, and causally related to, the diversities of our transitory perceptual data.

.   .   .

We shall, . . . take three conclusions as already established: (a) there is an order of existences or events which persists when unperceived; (b) this is causally related to our sensa; (c) the particulars belonging to it cannot be identical with our sensa. Our problem, then, is whether, given these premises and the common facts of every-day experience, we can reach any further probable propositions concerning the extra-perceptual, neutral, causal order. One such proposition, manifestly, is that we have power to act upon this order. Processes which apparently go on unperceived can be initiated by percipient beings. And the unobserved interperceptual causal processes will vary (as their subsequently observed effects will show) with variations in the specific characters of our sense-data while we are initiating those processes; *e.g.*, if I build my fire of wood instead of coal, the time required for it to burn out will be shorter and the ashes which I find on returning to the room will be of a different quality. It is equally a fact of every-day experience that certain percepts or images do not initiate (or are not correlated with) processes capable of continuing during interperceptual intervals and producing observable terminable effects identical with those observable when the entire sequence of intermediate stages has been attended to. If I merely imagine or dream of a fire in the grate, I do not — after ceasing so to dream or imagine — experience the visual and tactual content called ashes. Purely visual content is not found by us to be sufficient to start fires (or to give sensible evidence of the physical equivalent of a fire having started in the extra-perceptual world), or to be correlated with the initiation by us of any physical process. The same fact is illustrated by the comparative sterility of pink rats. If I am able to initiate a physical process, my action (if experienced at all by myself) is experienced in the form of tactual and kinaesthetic as well as (in some cases) visual sense-data; it is, in short, one of the primary discoveries of experience that tactual and kinaesthetic sensations have a different and more constant relation to the physical causal order than do visual percepts or images. The former are the phases of our experience in which we as percipients appear to have causal contact with that order. And it is reasonable to suppose that this fact throws some light upon the nature of the external causal world.

Furthermore, if, like everyone else, we assume that there are many percipients, and that they can through language convey some information to one another about the characteristics of their respective sense-data, we find that each of them is able to act upon the other percipients, that is, to determine in some degree what experiences they shall have; and that this action upon them is usually, and probably always, conditioned upon initiating (in the sense and in the manner already indicated) physical processes. If I light a fire, other men as well as myself will feel the heat; they may, in consequence of my action, observe a sensible fire continuously while I do not; while if I imagine or dream of a fire, their experience remains unaffected. One of the two principal reasons why we do not regard dream-fires as indications of the occurrence of events (at least the kind of events ordinarily connected with sensible fires) in the persistent and therefore independent world is that they do not cause others to have sensations of warmth or to find perceptible ashes in their perceptible grates. Purely private percepts are called illusory, not merely because they happen to be private, but because they do not causally interact directly, or in the manner in which other qualitatively similar percepts do, with the world which is the medium of communication and interaction between us.

Now what observably happens when I thus act upon the external world and through it affect other men's experiences and my own subsequent experiences, is usually that with my perceptible body I push and pull other perceptible objects about in my perceptual space. And with the movements which I thus determine as data of my own perception there may be — under conditions empirically definable — correlated perceptions of movement in the experience of others. They report to me that they see what they call my body moving, and other objects moving in ways uniformly connected with my bodily movements. That their percepts of what they call my body are not my body itself is true — if the arguments on this matter previously set forth are correct; and it is also true that the perceptual objects which they see moving in consequence of my bodily movements are not existentially nor qualitatively identical with those which I see, nor yet with any entity in the neutral causal order. The question may nevertheless be asked: Are the causal processes in the external world which are initiated by motions (*i.e.*, by those which I perceive) and which terminate in motions (*i.e.*, those which other men perceive) also of the nature of motions? The idealist answers definitely in the negative; the phenomenalist and the all-but agnostic physicist answer that we have, at any rate, no reason whatever for thinking so. But there are, I think, certain considerations which, though not demonstrative, make an affirmative answer to the question the more plausible.

(a) In the first place, it is at least not *impossible* that the processes which cause and link together the percepts of different times and different persons are of the same general sort as the causal sequences which empirically occur within our perceptual experience. No fact of experience, obviously, can prove the contrary.

(b) It is a simpler assumption about the unperceived causal processes that they are of the same sort as those perceived, rather than of some wholly different sort. In making such an assumption we still follow the rule of continuity in our conjectures about that which we cannot directly experience. We do not postulate differences in the nature of things beyond necessity. If I suppose that, when I have the experience of moving my body and pushing and pulling something about, thereby producing effects in the neutral causal order, I *am* pushing or pulling something about, and that this *is* a way in which effects in that order are produced, I am enabled to conceive of the external world with which I am in relation in action as fundamentally homogeneous with the perceptual world; and though it may not be so, it appears to me more sensible to proceed upon the hypothesis that it is, so long as there is no good evidence to the contrary.

(c) The spaces in which our perceptible effective bodily movements take place, whether or not they are literally parts of a single Space, are at all events congruent; they fit together in a remarkable way. For example, a hundred men from as many different places are summoned to attend an international conference in Geneva. They thereupon consult maps, time-tables, Baedekers, to find the routes to take in order to reach that city. These useful works were prepared by yet other men. They do not, however, purport to be descriptions of the arrangement of things in private perceptual spaces of their authors; they profess to represent a set of spatial relations which will hold good in the perceptual experience of any inhabitant of the earth. The routes which they describe are not routes to a hundred private Genevas, but to a single

Geneva conceived to have a determinate position in some common or public spatial order. And by a series of movements of their own legs, assisted by motions of trains and steamships, which follow spatial directions symbolized in the maps and guidebooks, the delegates to the conference presently find themselves having similar (though not identical) visual and tactual percepts, for example, percepts of the Quai Mont Blanc, and in a position in which they can sit down in the same room and talk to one another. The result may be that the construction of battleships in certain other places will be discontinued. The idealistic or phenomenalistic account of this affair is that there is no common space such as is represented by the maps, and that no motion of what could strictly be called the body of any delegate took place. What happened was merely that their minds — which were throughout in no place at all — after first having private percepts of maps and then having visual and other sensations of motion, resulting, perhaps, in sensations of sea-sickness, subsequently experienced certain resemblant sense-percepts which they mistakenly called by the single name "Geneva," and others which they called the bodies and voices of their fellow delegates. In reality, therefore, the delegates never met. Their private sequences of sense-data, for no known or conjecturable reason, happened eventually to coincide in part; at approximately the time when one of them had the kinaesthetic sensations of opening his mouth and using his vocal organs, the others had correspondent visual sensations and also certain sound-sensations of (more or less) intelligible words; but they were no nearer one another when this occurred than at the beginning. Now this is, no doubt, conceivable, in the sense that is not formally self-contradictory; but it seems to me incredibly far-fetched, and I cannot avoid the suspicion that the human species (including physicists and even idealistic philosophers) is constitutionally incapable of really believing it — of thinking in this fashion of this type of experience. Men have always believed, and will, doubtless, continue to believe, that the way to arrive at a place is to go there; and they will always be recalcitrant to a view, which requires them to hold, or to regard it as probable, that (for example) the ill-fated passengers of the *Titanic* were not really in the same ship or even in the same space. So long as the experienced bodily movements of a number of separate percipients thus fit into a single spatial pattern; so long as, in consequence of motions in convergent directions in that pattern (and not otherwise), the percipients find themselves face to face; so long as (to vary the illustration) through such bodily movements (and not otherwise) they are enabled not only to destroy the bodies of other men but also to bring all *their* perceiving to an end, by firing bullets in the direction in which the other men's bodies are perceived — so long men will naturally conceive of the processes in the common world through which their respective sense-data are caused as occurring in a single common spatial or spatio-temporal order and as consisting of motions therein. That this conceived common space is literally identical with their perceived spaces they may find reason to doubt; that the bodies which effectively move in it have all the properties of the bodies sensibly perceived, or are particulars existentially identical with them, they will find good reasons for denying. But the fact that their apprehension of bodies must be recognized by them to be mediate or representational and to contain "psychic additions" and distortions need not, and pretty certainly will not, prevent them from thinking that they have bodies — unique bodies, that is, each of which belongs to one percipient, and is not merely the multitudinous aggregate of the percepts of it — bodies which are therefore assignable to the public spatial system, which have positions relative to other bodies, which can change these positions, and in doing so cause changes in other bodies and modify thereby the sense-content, or even bring to an end the existence, of other percipient beings.

In all this, it may be said, I am forgetting the theory of relativity, which shows that there is no general frame of nature, no common space or time for different percipients. But I have never observed relativistic physicists hesitating to assume that the imaginary voyagers whom they describe as roving about the heavens at enormous speeds can send light-signals to one another, whatever their relative velocities or the length of their journeys; and I find such physicists always assuming that these signals will take time in passing from one "system" to another, and that their course will be deflected if they happen to pass through the gravitational fields to be found in the neighborhood of material bodies. That relativity physics dispenses, and shows the plain man how to dispense, with the notions of a general spatial order (whatever its novel geometrical properties) or of moving entities therein, consequently still seems to me difficult to make out; and I surmise, therefore, that the plain man's prejudice in favor of the belief that he has a body which moves in a public space, and that, in general, the causal processes in the persistent neutral world consist (at least in part) of the motions of bodies, will not by this doctrine be corrected, but rather confirmed.

61 🙞

THERE ARE NO
SENSE DATA

Winston H. F. Barnes

W. H. F. Barnes (1909-   ) is Vice-Chancellor of the University of Liverpool. He was Professor of Philosophy at the University of Edinburgh.

I

Our knowledge of the physical world is subject to many doubts and uncertainties but we commonly see no reason to doubt certain facts. We all agree, when we are out of the study, that we sometimes see tables and chairs, hear bells and clocks, taste liquids, smell cheeses, and feel the woollen vests that we wear next to our skin in winter. To put the matter generally, we agree that we perceive physical objects, physical objects being such things as tables, chairs and cheeses, and perceiving being a generic word which comprehends the specific activities of seeing, hearing, tasting, smelling, and feeling. These activities are invariably directed upon an object or objects; and this fact distinguishes them from other activities of ours — if that be the right word — such as feeling pained or feeling tired, which go on entirely within ourselves. We take it for granted that by means of the former activities we become aware of the existence, and acquainted with the qualities, of physical objects, and we further regard the kind of acquaintance which we acquire in this way as a basis for the far reaching and systematic knowledge of the physical world as a whole, which is embodied in the natural sciences.

    Let us call experiences such as seeing a table, hearing a bell, etc., perceptual experiences; and the statements which assert the existence of such experiences perceptual statements. Many philosophers have cast doubt upon the claims made by such perceptual statements. They have produced arguments to show that we never perceive physical objects, and that we are in fact subject to a constant delusion on this score. As these arguments are by no means easily refuted and are such as any intelligent person interested in the

From W. H. F. Barnes, "The Myth of Sense-Data," *Proceedings of the Aristotelian Society,* Vol. 45 (1944-45). Reprinted by permission of the Aristotelian Society, A. A. Kassman, Hon. Secretary and Editor.

matter will sooner or later come to think of, they are well worth considering. Moreover, certain modern philosophers claim to show by these arguments not only that we do not perceive physical objects but that what we do perceive is a different sort of thing altogether, which they call a sense-datum. They are obliged to invent a new term for it because no one had previously noticed that there were such things. This theory is obviously important because it not only claims to settle the doubts which we cannot help feeling when we reflect on our perceptual experience, but it makes the astonishing claim that we have all failed to notice a quite peculiar kind of entity, or at least have constantly made mistakes about its nature. I hope to show that the sense-datum theory is beset by internal difficulties; that it is not necessitated by the doubts we have about our perceptual experience; and finally that the doubts which are caused in us by a little reflection are allayed by further reflection.

The arguments which philosophers such as Professors Russell, Broad and Price use to demonstrate that we perceive not physical objects but sense-data, are many and various, and no good purpose would be served by stating them all, even if that were possible. Undoubtedly, however, these arguments do cause us to doubt whether we are acquainted with physical objects when we think we are; and, these doubts demand to be resolved in one way or another. If there is such a thing as a problem of perception, it must consist in reviewing the doubts which arise in our minds in this way. I shall select for brief statement three typical arguments so as to make clear the difficulties which are thought to justify the negative conclusion that we do not perceive physical objects and the positive conclusion that we perceive sense-data. There are two *caveats* to be registered. First, in compressing the arguments into a small compass I cannot hope to do full justice to the arguments, many and various, used by the sense-datum philosophers. I must leave it to the reader to decide whether I represent their general line of argument correctly or not. More than this I cannot hope to do; nor do I think more is necessary. Secondly, I should not be in the least surprised to be told that I already have misrepresented some of these philosophers by stating as one of their contentions that we do not perceive physical objects. Some of them would maintain that in some peculiar, or Pickwickian sense, to use Professor Moore's term, we do perceive physical objects. However, as, on their view, we do not perceive physical objects in the sense in which we think we perceive them, and we do perceive sense-data in precisely this sense, the misrepresentation is purely verbal and should mislead no one.[1]

I now proceed to state the three arguments. They are all taken from

---

[1] The sense in which, on the sensum theory, we perceive [sense data], is described as *direct perception* or *direct apprehension* by the exponents of the theory to distinguish it from the perception or apprehension of physical objects which the theory as sometimes expounded allows to be possible. (*The Philosophy of G. E. Moore*, pp. 629, 640-643). This distinction is usually drawn by those philosophers who accept the position taken up by the philosophy of analysis that there are many statements such as 'I see the table,' 'I hear the bell,' which are certainly true, although the analysis of them requires careful thought; and at the same time are convinced by arguments which claim to show that we cannot in fact see the table in the ordinary sense of

visual experience, and they all pose in one way or another what we may call the "appearance-reality" problem of perception.

(1) A penny appears circular to an observer directly above it, but elliptical to an observer a few paces away. It cannot *be* both elliptical and circular at one and the same time. There is no good reason for supposing that the penny reveals its real shape to an observer in one position rather than to an observer in any other position. The elliptical appearance and the circular appearance cannot be identified with the penny or any parts of it, but they are entities of some kind. It is things of this sort which are called sense-data.

(2) The stick which looks straight in the air looks angularly bent when in water. There are good reasons for thinking that no such change of shape takes place in the stick. Yet there *is* something straight in the one case and something bent in the other, and there is no good reason for supposing either is less or more of an existent than the other. The straight-stick appearance and the bent-stick appearance are sense-data.

(3) There may seem to be things in a place when in fact there are no such things there, as illustrated by the mirages which appear in the desert and the highly coloured rodents which appear to habitual drunkards. Not unrelated to this type of experience is the one in which we see double. If an eyeball is pressed by the forefinger while one is looking at a candle flame, two flames are seen. Although it would be possible to say that one of the flames is the actual object and the other is something else, to be called a sense-datum, it seems even more evident here than in the previous instances that there is no good reason for distinguishing between the two in this way.

In all these cases there is a suggestion that what we see in certain cases cannot be a physical object or the surface of a physical object, but is some kind of non-physical entity. It is non-physical entities of this kind which are called sense-data. The argument goes even further by urging that, if in some cases we see non-material things, it is possible and indeed likely, that we do so in all cases. This plausible suggestion is accepted by certain sense-datum theorists such as Professor Broad and is extended to cover all forms of perceiving. With the acceptance of this suggestion we reach the basic position taken by one form of the sense-datum theory, viz., we perceive only sense-data, and consequently have no direct acquaintance through our senses with physical objects.

It is clear that, on this view, the term sense-datum has as part of its connotation, the not being a physical body.[2] As everything I experience is a

---

the word see. I can see no really important difference, however, between the two statements: (1) I see only sense-data in the sense in which I have been accustomed to think I see physical objects, and my relation to the physical object is not that of seeing but that of R. (2) I see only sense-data in the sense in which I have been accustomed to think I see physical objects, but I do see physical objects in the sense that I have a relation R to them.

[2] "In the common usage, some characteristic which entailed 'not a physical reality' was put into the connotation of 'sense-datum'; 'sense-datum' was so used that it would be a contradiction to say of any object that it was *both a physical reality and also* a 'sense-datum'." (*The Philosophy of G. E. Moore*, p. 634.)

sense-datum, the sense-experience of a table, for example, differs not at all, in itself, from an hallucination or an illusion. These latter again seem to differ only in degree from the images we have while we are day dreaming, or those we have while dreaming in the proper sense, or again from the after-images, or as they are more properly called, the after-sensations which sometimes follow our visual sensations. All these appearances would be regarded by certain philosophers as in principle of the same kind. This position is paradoxical to common-sense which regards perceptual experience as giving first-hand acquaintance with physical objects, and hallucinations and illusions as failing precisely in this respect. The common-sense ground for the distinction however is removed by the sense-datum theorist, and if in fact he does believe in physical objects, he has to substitute a new ground of a far more subtle and elaborate nature. In some cases he may prefer to get along altogether without physical objects, and may even urge that if we once give up the common-sense ground of distinction as untenable, there is no other ground for believing in them.[3] Such questions as these, however, are domestic problems of sense-datum theorists and need not detain us, as we are intent on coming to grips with the basis of the theory itself. It is important to note, however, that once the sense-datum theory is developed in the form stated above, it follows that, even if physical objects exist, they are never present in perceptual experience; and it becomes an open question whether they have any existence at all.

II

I shall consider later whether the arguments for the existence of sense-data in the sense indicated are valid. First, however, I want to state three considerations regarding the sense-datum itself. The first is of a very general nature and calculated to make us wonder whether a theory which departs so radically from common sense can be true; the second points out what extraordinary existents sense-data would be if there were such things; the third is directed to show that the kind of difficulty the theory was carefully framed to meet tends to break out anew within the theory.[4]

(1) The general consideration concerning the sensum theory is as follows: If the theory is true, then in all our perceptual experience sensa are interposed between us and the physical world, whereas it is one of our most strongly held beliefs that in perception we are face to face with the physical

---

[3] As Dr. Luce does, in his "Immaterialism." (Annual Philosophical Lecture, British Academy, 1944.)

[4] As the form of sense-datum theory now to be considered is that which has been clearly worked out by Prof. Broad, I propose to substitute for the word *sense-datum* in this section the word *sensum* which Prof. Broad himself uses in its place. We shall see later that what Prof. Moore and others have to say about sense-data makes it advisable to have different words for the two theories, distinguished as follows: *sense-datum*, the immediate object in perception which may or may not be identical with a part of a physical object; *sensum*, the immediate object in perception, taken to be non-physical. Prof. Price, whose views are very like those of Prof. Broad, speaks of sense-data, but would, if he had accepted this rule for the use of the two words, have spoken of sensa.

world. I do not wish to suggest that no attempt can be made to answer this obvious objection. The sensum theory can and does urge that in a Pickwickian sense of the term *perceive* we do perceive physical objects, i.e., we perceive sensa which are related in certain ways to physical objects. Nevertheless there is no doubt that, when presented with this type of explanation, we are apt to feel that we have been given a very inferior substitute in exchange for the direct acquaintance with physical objects which we have been called upon to surrender. . . .

Not only do we feel that sensa are an inadequate substitute for the physical objects which we claim to be confronted with in perception, but they seem to be embarrassingly numerous. Every appearance, however evanescent and fleeting, can claim to be an existent. As ordinary men, we contrast the intermittent character of our perceptual experience, broken as it is by sleep, lack of attention and change of place, with the permanent or relatively permanent and continuing status of physical objects. The changing facets of our perceptual experience we distribute carefully, crediting some to the physical world and disowning others as apparent only. The sensum theory credits all alike to reality, since it considers each and every one to be an individual entity. It is from this beginning that the wilder excesses of realism took their origin, in which not only reality but mind-independence was credited lavishly to almost anything that could be named, until the world began to take on the appearance of a great museum in which a few of the contents were really operative beings but the vast majority were exhibits only, ready to be produced on the appropriate occasion, but possessed of no other ground of existence.

I am not inclined to over-estimate the effect that a general consideration of this kind can be expected to have, but it is not lightly to be dismissed. There are philosophers to whom a single departure from the norms of common sense act only as a stimulus to further more exciting philosophical adventures in the realms of speculation, but I confess that, for my part, I regard such a departure rather as a danger signal, warning that it would be wise to consider whether the steps which have led to this departure are as secure as they appear to be.

It is one thing to assert of a theory, however, that it presents us with a large number of existents which seem unnecessary and which, if they existed, would make it difficult to justify our acquaintance with physical objects; it is quite another to show that the existents are not merely unnecessary but are open to grave objections. This is the second point to which we must now turn.

(2) There are two reasons for considering sensa to be very objectionable existents.

(i) In the first place, unlike physical objects they do not always obey the Law of Excluded Middle. If I contemplate an object at some distance, it often happens that I am uncertain whether it is circular or polygonal. It is necessary for me to approach closer before I can determine the matter with certainty. On the sensum theory, the mode in which the object appeared to me at first is a sensum, and every sensum *is* what it appears to be. Now this sensum appears neither circular nor non-circular. Therefore it is neither circular nor non-circular. Let us be quite clear on this point. It is not that I do not know whether it is circular or non-circular, though in fact it must be one or the other. It really is neither one nor the other. This kind of experience is more common than one is perhaps inclined to believe at first. When an optician asks you to read those minute letters inscribed at the bottom of his chart, there comes a time when you are compelled to say "I am not sure whether it is an M or an N," because the shape you see is sufficiently indeterminate for you to think it may be either. Of course, some eminent philosophers have thought that reality did not obey the Law of Excluded Middle, but it would be surprising to find Professor Broad in their company.

It is tempting to urge that we *must* know the shape of the sensum because an artist can sit down and draw something which reproduces the shape. A little reflection, however, will show that what the artist does is to draw something which, having a certain definite shape, will appear at a certain distance to be as indeterminate in shape as the object itself appeared. In other words, what the artist does is the same in principle as what a joiner might do by building another object like the first one which would give rise to the same sort of appearance as the first one. So far as I can see, all so-called sensa, i.e., colours, sounds, smells, etc., are indeterminate in this way, though under favourable conditions the range of indeterminacy is so limited that it is, for practical purposes, not of any importance.

(ii) The second reason for considering sense-data to be objectionable existents, though closely connected with the former is less formidable; but is worth mentioning because it leads up to a number of very interesting considerations. It is a necessary consequence of the fact that a sense-datum *is* what it appears to be that there is no possibility of making further discoveries about its nature. It is always possible to get to know more and more about a particular existent, such as an apple or a squirrel, and, so far as we can tell, this process need never come to an end. There is no progress to be made in our knowledge of any particular sensum. This contention may seem to go too far in view of the revelations which philosophers claim to have about sensa. It can, however, be justified. Our knowledge of things is increased either by observation or by experiment. Experiment, as a means of gaining knowledge of sensa, is clearly ruled out, since it is obvious that any movement on my part or interference with the conditions will only cause one sensum to be replaced by another. It does, however, seem as though I might increase my knowledge of a particular sensum by observing it more closely than I had done. Rather, we must say, "by observing it more closely than I am doing," for clearly, my closer observation can only yield me more knowledge if it follows uninterruptedly upon my first. It will not do for me to come back at 5 p.m. to a closer study of the sensum which my table presented at 3 p.m. Can I gain more knowledge by continuing to observe it at 3 p.m.? I think we must say that I cannot. If we were to maintain that this was possible, and that something in the sensum previously unobserved might by observation be brought to light, we should need some criterion for making certain that it was the same sensum which we were observing at a later date as at an earlier date. *But no observation or experiment can yield a criterion.* The sensum theorists offer us little help on this point. The only thing is to fall back on the principle that a sensum is what it appears to be. If we interpret this as meaning it is all that it appears to be *and nothing more*,[5] then the possibility of learning anything about a sensum is cut away at once, for the very good reason that we know all there is to know about it by simply having it. It is, I think, a very odd fact, if true, that there are existents such that their being known at all entails their being completely known.

. . .

The moral of this is that those who believe in sensa tell us so little about the laws of their existence that we are at liberty to make a variety of assumptions on quite fundamental points. For example, how do we determine the duration of a sensum? If I blink my eyes while looking at a red patch are there two sensa separated in time, or is there only one interrupted in its career? If a change occurs in my visual field has the sensum changed or been replaced by another? If the latter, is there any reason why, when no change is observed, a sensum should not be replaced by another exactly like it? It may be said that to answer these questions is not important. I am inclined to agree that it is not; but the only reason I can see for this is that, sensa being wholly fictitious entities, we can attribute to them what qualities we please.[6]

Let us consider in a more practical way the arbitrary character of the sensum theory. Prof. Broad allows that a sensum may move across one's visual field; but he would not I think, allow that it can change in size or qualities. Take the simple case where I am watching a cinema screen on which is depicted a round red patch moving across a background of different colour. Here, according to Prof. Broad, is a single sensum moving across my visual field. Supposing the round red patch remains stationary but slowly contracts in size before finally disappearing. Here, presumably, is a succession of sensa. Supposing, now, the red patch moves across the screen and as it does so it diminishes in size, have we one or a succession of sensa? The answer would have to be, I think: "A succession." There would seem, then, no reason for supposing that where the size of the moving patch is constant, there should not also be a succession of sensa. If this is so, sensa do not move, they merely rise up one after another in a certain spatial order. We could equally well allow, on the other hand, that sensa not only move but change in shape, size, colour, etc. In fact, if the essential characteristic of a sensum is that it is what it appears to be, then there is a very good case for taking this view, since there certainly *appear* to be changes in the colour and shape as well as the position of what we experience through our senses. What is worth remarking is that there is nothing which enables us to consider one alternative nearer the

[5] We shall see later that there are difficulties about other interpretations.
[6] This fact is at the bottom of Mr. Ayer's contention that the sensum theory is really only an alternative language . . .

truth than the other. As long as this kind of question can be decided only arbitrarily, it is clear that there is no way of determining the number of sensa. So we find them to have another peculiar property for existents; they are not numerable.

.   .   .

Before turning to consider the validity of the reasoning which is used to prove the existence of sensa, there is one another point which merits attention. One of the most serious arguments against the sensum theory is that, if it is true, it is extremely difficult to explain how from knowledge of our sensa we could come to knowledge of material things; and yet, according to Prof. Broad, "all that I ever come to know about physical objects and their qualities seems to be based upon the qualities of the sensa that I become aware of in sense-perception."[7] But an ever greater difficulty faces us, viz., that of being assured that material things exist at all, i.e., relatively permanent things with certain qualities and interacting with one another. Prof. Broad says: ". . . there is nothing in my sensa to force me logically to the conclusion that there must be something beyond them, having the constitutive properties of physical objects. The belief that our sensa are appearances of something more permanent and complex than themselves seems to be primitive, and to arise inevitably in us with the sensing of the sensa. It is not reached by inference, and could not logically be justified by inference. On the other hand, there is no possibility of either refuting it logically, or of getting rid of it, or — so far as I can see — of co-ordinating the facts without it."[8] Prof. Luce thinks otherwise. In rejecting the existence of physical objects over and above sensa he says: "To accept both the sense-datum *and* matter is to turn the one world into two."[9]

If I believed in sensa I should be found on the side of Dr. Luce, for the difficulties of distinguishing between a primitive belief and a primitive delusion seem to me insuperable.

III

So far we have been considering the difficulties that arise from holding that sensa form a class of existents totally different from physical objects. Though the difficulties are perhaps not sufficiently serious to destroy the theory, they seem to me quite serious enough to make it desirable to look carefully into the considerations put forward for inducing belief in such entities.

These considerations seem to me to reduce to one fundamental argument, and this argument seems to me to be false, though plausible. If I am right, then the reason for believing in sensa goes.

I quoted earlier three typical arguments for the existence of sensa. I now wish to examine carefully a single argument which embodies the principle

[7] *Scientific Thought*, p. 241.

[8] *Scientific Thought*, p. 268.

[9] "Immaterialism" (Annual Philosophical Lecture, British Academy, 1944), p. 6.

of these and other similar arguments. No one will deny, I think, that a situation may exist in which the following three propositions are true:

(i)　　　　　　　　　I see the rose.
(ii)　　　　　　　　The rose appears pink to me.
(iii)　　　　　　　The rose is red.

The belief in sensa is reached by arguing, not unplausibly, that since what I am seeing appears pink, there exists something which *is* pink; and since the rose is red, not pink, it cannot be the rose which is pink; therefore what I am seeing is something other than the rose. Whereupon the term sensum is invented and given as a name to this existent and others like it. And so we reach the conclusion:

(iv)　　　　　　　　I see a pink sensum.

The argument is fallacious. *That something appears pink to me is not a valid reason for concluding either that that thing is pink or that there is some other thing which is pink.* From the fact that a thing *looks* pink I can sometimes with the help of certain other propositions infer that it *is* pink or that it *is* red; I may also, with the help of certain other propositions, be able to infer that something in some other place is pink, e.g., the electric light bulb which is illuminating the rose. But I cannot infer, as is proposed, *merely from the three facts that I am seeing something, that it looks pink and that it is red, that there is a pink something where the thing appears pink to me.*

This, when we examine it, is the foundation stone on which the great edifice of the sensum theory has been raised. Is it surprising that the upper storeys present doubts and perplexities? But there is worse to come. Not only is the argument fallacious but the conclusion contradicts one of the premises, viz., (i) I see a rose. It does so because, in order that the conclusion should seem at all plausible, it has been assumed that, if I were to see a rose which actually possessed a red colour, I should see it as red, i.e., it would necessarily appear red to me. This again is an assumption in contradiction with propositions (ii) and (iii) taken together. As soon as this self-induced contradiction is discovered by the sensum theorists, repair work is put in hand on one or other of alternative lines: (*a*) It is accepted that I do not see the rose, and an account is given of the relation in which I *do* stand to the rose and which has been mistaken for seeing. A little reflection, of course, soon convinces those who go this way that, if this is true, it is not only roses that are born to blush unseen, but the whole world of material things. In this way sensa become an impenetrable barrier barring for ever our acquaintance through the senses with the world of material things. This is strong meat for any but really metaphysical natures, and fortunately for the sensum theory there is another way of making the necessary repairs. (*b*) The alternative procedure is something like this: It is certain that I do see the rose. I have convinced myself, however, by argument that one thing I undoubtedly see, in a plain unvarnished use of the word *see*, is a pink rose-figured sensum. Hence the sense in which I see the rose must be different, i.e., "seeing" is systematically ambiguous and what exactly is meant by seeing the rose needs to be elucidated. Seeing a rose and seeing a pink rose-figured sensum are then distinguished as quite different ways of seeing and it is convenient to refer to seeing a sensum as "directly seeing," and seeing a rose as "seeing." [10] The analysis of seeing the rose can then be made in terms of directly seeing a certain sort of sensum and at the same time having perceptual assurance that . . . etc., the complete analysis varying from one philosopher to another. [11]

There is another way in which an attempt may be made to justify the conclusion of the argument we have condemned as fallacious. I have argued that from the fact that something which is red appears pink, it does not follow that a pink sensum exists. It may be said that the existence of a pink sensum, while not following from the premises, is justified by a direct appeal to our sense experience. "I see it, therefore it is." The argument can be stated as follows: "I certainly see a pink something and to say that there is nothing pink is to say that I have no reason for believing in what I see now; and if I cannot believe in what I see now, how can I believe in what I see on any occasion, or any one else in what he sees on any occasion? If you deny the existence of this pink patch, you deny the existence altogether of the world revealed by the senses." The answer to this objection is simple, if we reflect, viz., "You never can believe in what you see on any occasion, it always may mislead you as to what the thing is. If you wish to state only that something appears to be so and so, this can safely be done. But this is not a statement about something made on the basis of a piece of evidence, it is a statement of the piece of evidence itself, which you already have before you without clothing it in words." Modes of appearance are clues to the nature of what exists, not existents. I submit that it is improper to ask whether the pink mode of appearing, which is how the rose appears to me, exists. You may ask whether the rose exists and whether it is red or pink; and in answering this question account must be taken of how it appears under different conditions and to different people. Although modes of appearance are not existents, they are the material and the only material on which thinking can operate to discover the nature of existing things; and it is an epistemological ideal that if we were to discover completely the nature of existing things, there would be nothing left in the modes of appearance which would not entirely harmonise with our system of knowledge and find its explanation there. . . .

---

[10] Prof. Moore makes this use of the two terms. It is worth pointing out that in ordinary language we should be ready to say that we were directly seeing the rose; in contrast, for example to seeing it as reflected in a mirror or seeing it through a microscope, where the indirectness would consist, no doubt, to our minds, in the interposition of a further medium between our eyes and the object in addition to the usual light and air. There is still an air of paradox, consequently, about the way in which the words seeing and directly seeing are used by sensum theorists.

[11] Philosophers tend to adopt the second alternative because it enables them to eat their cake and have it. They continue on this matter to speak with the vulgar and think with the learned, following in this respect the good Bishop of Cloyne, the inventor of philosophical analysis.

SUGGESTED READINGS

Anthologies

HIRST, R. J., ed. *Perception and the External World.* New York: The Macmillan Company, 1965.

NAGEL, E. and BRANDT, R., eds. *Meaning and Knowledge.* New York: Harcourt, Brace & World, 1965. ʹ

SWARTZ, R. J., ed. *Perceiving, Sensing, and Knowing.* Garden City, N. Y.: Doubleday & Company, Inc., 1965.

Valuable and Single-Author Books

AUSTIN, J. L. *Sense and Sensibilia.* Oxford: Clarendon Press, 1962.

AYER, A. J. *The Foundations of Empirical Knowledge.* New York: St. Martin's Press, 1956.

CHISHOLM, R. M. *Perceiving: A Philosophical Study.* Ithaca, N.Y.: Cornell University Press, 1957.

LOVEJOY, A. O. *The Revolt Against Dualism.* Wilmette, Ill.: Open Court, 1930.

MANDELBAUM, M. *Philosophy, Science, and Sense-Perception.* Baltimore: Johns Hopkins Press, 1964.

PRICE, H. H. *Perception.* London: Methuen & Co., 1933.

Is the Concept of Sensory Appearances Confused?

AUSTIN, J. L. *Sense and Sensibilia,* 1962, 20-32, 44-54.

BARNES, W. H. F. "On Seeing and Hearing," in H. D. LEWIS, ed., *Contemporary British Philosophy,* 1956.

BLACK, M. and FIRTH, R. Symposium: "Phenomenalism," American Philosophical Association, Eastern Division, I (1952). Philadelphia: University of Pennsylvania Press.

BROAD, C. D. *Scientific Thought.* New York: Harcourt, Brace & World, 1927, Chapters 7 and 8. Reprinted, in more complete form than the present text, in Swartz.

CHISHOLM, R. M. "The Theory of Appearing," in M. BLACK, ed., *Philosophical Analysis.* Ithaca, New York: Cornell University Press, 1950. Reprinted in Swartz.

FIRTH, R. "Sense Data and the Percept Theory," *Mind* 48 (1949) and 49 (1950). Reprinted in Swartz.

MOORE, G. E. *Philosophical Studies.* London: Routledge and Kegan Paul, Ltd. 1922, Chapter 5.

PAUL, G. A. "Is There a Problem About Sense Data?" London: The Aristotelian Society, Supplementary Volume 15, 1946. Reprinted in Swartz.

PRICE, H. H. "Appearing and Apperances," American Philosophical Quarterly, 1, 3-19.

———. *Perception,* 1933, Chapter 1.

QUINTON, A. M. "The Problem of Perception," *Mind* 64, (1955). Reprinted in Swartz.

RYLE, G. "Sensation," in H. D. LEWIS, ed., *Contemporary British Philosophy.* New York: Macmillan, 1956. Reprinted in Swartz.

———. *The Concept of Mind.* London: Hutchinson's University Library, 1949, 213-220. Reprinted in Hirst.

What Is Proved by the Fact of Illusion?

ARMSTRONG, D. M. "Berkeley's Puzzle About the Water That Seems both Hot and Cold," *Analysis* 15, 1955.

AUSTIN, J. L. *Sense and Sensibilia,* 1962, 20-32.

AYER, A. J. *Foundations of Empirical Knowledge,* 1956, Chapter 1. Excerpted in Hirst.

FIRTH, R. "Austin and the Argument from Illusion," *Philosophical Review* 73 (1964).

LOVEJOY, A. O. *The Revolt Against Dualism,* 1930, Chapter 1. Excerpted in Hirst.

MYERS, G. "Perception and the Time-lag Argument," *Analysis* 17 (1957)

PRICE, H. H. *Perception,* 1933, Chapter 2.

———. "The Argument from Illusion," in H. D. LEWIS, ed., *Contemporary British Philosophy.* New York: Macmillan, 1956.

TAYLOR, R. and DUGGAN, T. "On Seeing Double," *Philosophical Quarterly* 8 (1958).

Phenomenalism

ARMSTRONG, D. M. *Perception and the Physical World.* London: Routledge and Kegan Paul, 1961, 47-80.

AYER, A. J. *Foundations of Empirical Knowledge,* 1956. Chapter 5. Excerpted in Nagel and Brandt.

BERLIN, I. "Empirical Propositions and Hypothetical Statements," *Mind* 59 (1950).

CHISHOLM, R. M. The Problem of Empiricism," *Journal of Philosophy* 45 (1948). Reprinted in Swartz.

FIRTH, R. "Radical Empiricism and Perceptual Relativity, *Philosophical Review* 59, (1950).

HARDIE, W. F. R. "The Paradox of Phenomenalism," *Proceedings,* The Aristotelian Society, 46 (1945-46).

LEWIS, C. I. *An Analysis of Knowledge and Valuation.* LaSalle, Ill.: Open Court, 1946, Chapter 8. Reprinted in Swartz.

———. "Professor Chisholm and Empiricism," *Journal of Philosophy* 45 (1948). Reprinted in Swartz.

PRICE, H. H. *Hume's Theory of the External World.* Oxford: Clarendon Press, 1940, 177-192.

———. "Mill's View of the External World," *Proceedings,* The Aristotelian Society 27 (1926-27).

SELLARS, W. *Science, Perception, and Reality.* New York: Humanities Press, 1963, Chapter 3.

STACE, W. T. "The Refutation of Realism," *Mind* 43 (1934). Reprinted in A. Pap and P. Edwards, *A Modern Introduction to Philosophy.* New York: The Free Press, 1965.

The Causal Theory

BROAD, C. D. *The Mind and Its Place in Nature.* New York: Harcourt, Brace & World, 1927.

GRICE, H. P. "The Causal Theory of Perception," The Aristotelian Society, London. Supplementary Volume 35, 1961. Reprinted in Swartz, excerpted in Nagel and Brandt.

MANDELBAUM, M. *Philosophy, Science, and Sense Perception.* Baltimore: Johns Hopkins Press, 1964, Chapters 1 and 4.

Critics of the Causal Theory

ARMSTRONG, D. M. *Perception and the Physical World.* London: Routledge and Kegan Paul, Chapter 9.

AYER, A. J. *Foundations of Empirical Knowledge,* 1947, Chapter 4.

MUNDLE, C. W. "Common Sense vs. Hirst's Theory of Perception," *Proceedings,* The Aristotelian Society, 60 (1959-60).

PRICE, H. H. *Perception,* 1933. Chapter IV.

RUSSELL, B. *The Analysis of Matter.* New York: Dover Publications, Inc., 1927. Chap. 20. [Excerpt in Hirst.]

SELLARS, R. W. "A Statement of Critical Realism," *Revue Internationale de Philosophic,* I, 1938-39. [Excerpt in Hirst.]

WHITELY, C. H. "Physical Objects," *Philosophy* 34 (1959). [Reprinted in Nagel and Brandt.]

Index

705